Chancery Court Records
of
Bedford County
Tennessee

- 1830-1865 -

I0090866

Compiled By:
Helen C. & Timothy R. Marsh

Southern Historical Press, Inc.
Greenville, South Carolina

Please direct all correspondence and orders to:

www.southernhistoricalpress.com
or
SOUTHERN HISTORICAL PRESS, Inc.
PO BOX 1267
Greenville, SC   29601
southernhistoricalpress@gmail.com

ISBN #0-89308-607-X

Printed in the United States of America

This presentation of the abstracts of the earliest Chancery Court Records of Bedford County, Tennessee, contained in this book, we feel will supply a valuable missing link in the ongoing search to uncover and place before the public all available court records containing genealogical and family information surviving today. Chancery records are most valuable because of the abundance of genealogical material contained in them and not found elsewhere.

In 1822, an Equity Court was directed to be held in Columbia, Maury County, Tennessee and it would hear the causes of Bedford County along with several surrounding counties. The few cases that related to Bedford County citizens have been researched by the writers of this book and found to be few and insignificant.

In 1835, Bedford County was designated as the 6th District of the Middle Tennessee Division of the Court, to be held in Shelbyville, Tennessee. The abstracts in this book are taken from the minutes, all of which are available from microfilm now located in the Tennessee State Archives in Nashville, Tennessee. Several books of minutes were transported to the archives in Nashville by the writers last fall to be microfilmed after it was discovered by us that they had been missed in the original filming years ago. As of this date, all known early Chancery Court Minutes of the County are now on microfilm and are abstracted in this publication.

As of this date, the best source of verification and detailed examination of the original records abstracted in this book is the microfilm copies now located in the State Archives. Many of the original Minute Books have been stored and are not normally available to the general public.

Timothy R. & Helen C. Marsh
1987

CHANCERY COURT MINUTES 1830 - 1848

Page 1 - James G. Whitney]
        vs   ] Bill of Injunction
    John Sutton &] August Term 1830
    Lewis V. Greer] Judge James C. Mitchell
On 25th April 1827 and Samuel Whitworth, Bill for $120.00.
Bill made payable to Thomas P. Whitney and Orator James G.
Whitney. William O. Whitney, deceased. Signed by Lewis V.
Greer. John Sutton had a son William B. Sutton.
Thomas P. and Samuel Whitworth, final decree 9 August 1836.

Page 8 - Isaac H. Roberts, Adm of John A. Smith]
        vs   ] Orig. Bill
    Rice T. Ross & Rachel Martin]
John A. Smith, deceased, a citizen of Marion County, Tennessee,
about 28 August 1820, being in embarrassed circumstances
borrowed of Rice T. Ross, a citizen of Bedford County, for
negroes. Ross transferred negroes to Rachel Martin of Bedford
County. John A. Smith died intestate in Bedford County and
in August 1826 Isaac H. Roberts was appointed admr of John A.
Smith's estate. One negro to be sold to James Leeper of
Alabama.

Page 8 - Allen Leeper, Jason B. Shuffield,]
    John Shuffield, Andrew Patterson,]
    John P. Bruce and Joseph J. Marshall]
        vs   ] Injunction Bill
    William C. Orr, Samuel Todd,]
    Newton Cannon and others]
Samuel Anderson, one of the Judges of the Circuit Court of
Tennessee. The Bill of Allen Leeper, Jason B. Shuffield, John
Shuffield, Andrew Patterson, John P. Bruce and Joseph J.
Marshall, citizens of Bedford County. Humbly your orators
shewth to your Honor that at the last session of the Legislature of the State of Tennessee, a law passes to establish
a new county in the said State to be called Marshall and to
be composed of territory taken from the counties of Bedford,
Maury and Lincoln, but said law provided that before the territory thence designated should constitute said County of Marshall, the sheriff of the counties of Bedford, Maury and Lincoln
shall by thenselves or their deputies hold an election on the
1st Thursday of April 1836 at certain places thereby specified
in the territory therein designated and proposed to be taken
from each of the respective counties for the purpose of apper-
taining thereby whether or not a majority of the qualified
voters residing within the territory proposed to be taken from
the respective counties were willing to be attached and to
become a part of said County of Marshall and if upon the
elections so held in said counties of Bedford, Maury and Lincoln, it shall appear that a majority of the qualified voters
in the territory proposed to be taken from either of said
counties should vote against to be attached to and becoming a
part of said County of Marshall, then the law to establish
said new County of Marshall was to be void and of no effect,
but if on the other hand a majority of all the qualified voters
in the territory proposed to be taken from the said counties
of Bedford, Maury and Lincoln shall vote in favor of a proposal
to establish and become attached to said County of Marshall,
the fact of the election so resulting was to be certified to
the Governor of the State who was forthwith to issue his proclamation declaring said County of Marshall to be duly and

1

constitutionally and from therefore the territory designated
in said law was to constitute a separate and distinct of the
State of Tennessee by the name of Marshall. Said law also
appointed five commissioners whose duty it made to locate the
Seat of Justice in the territory proposed to be organized into
said new county. A majority of said commissioners proceeded
to perform the duty assigned to them previous to the first
Thursday of April 1836, the day on which the election was requested to be holden as affirmed and your orators charge but
they agreed upon its location at a point very inconvenient
to a large majority of the citizens residing in said territory
and as they believe and so charge a considerable distance from
the center of said territory. They state to your Honor that
the point agreed upon by said commissioners or a majority of
them, for the Seat of Justice is distant from the line, whereas
it is proposed, shall in future be the dividing line between
Maury County and said County of Marshall about six miles and
that it is west a few degrees north from the point as designated to said line from sald line running south a few degrees
west, it is about six miles to the dividing line between Giles
County and said Marshall County from said point running east
a few degrees north it is believed eight or nine miles to the
proposed dividing line between Bedford and Marshall Counties
running due north from said point to the nearest part of
Williamson County line, it is seventeen and onehalf miles and
the average distance to the Williamson County line which constitutes the northern boundary of the proposed County of Marshall is about nineteen miles running due south from said point
it is thirteen miles and some poles to the proposed dividing
line between Lincoln and Marshall County.

Your orators state to your Honor that they reside within
the original limits of Bedford County and within the territory
proposed to be taken from Bedford County and attached to and
made apart of Marshall County and that the greatest proportion
of territory which it is proposed to organize into said Marshall County belongs to Bedford County and within that territory
there is not a sufficient quality of territory proposed to
be taken Maury and Lincoln Counties to make three hundred and
fifty square miles the number of square miles required by the
Constitution to make a new county nor would there be required
number of square miles to constitute a new county of the
territory proposed to be taken from _____ of the then old
county should be left out the number of square miles which
is proposed to be taken from Bedford being about one hundred
and eighty five, from Lincoln eighty one, and from Maury ninety
or there abouts. Your orators present to your Honor that they
in common with many of the citizens residing in that portion
of territory which it is proposed to be taken from Bedford
County feel themselves much injured by the location of the
Seat of Justice in the proposed County of Marshall and they
believe justice to them and to the proposed County of Marshall
requiring that it shall be located near the center thereof
when they have no hesitation in stating _____ a site at
least in regard to beauty and health _____ and every other
convenience could be obtained as where it is now located.

Orators would show that many of the residences resided
near enough to one of the precincts to have attended and voted
at it but were prevented from doing so by the high stage of
water in Duck River and which could not be forded or crossed
except at a ferry and it was too far for them to go to the
precinct on the same side of the river on which they reside.

Your orators pray your Honor upon a final hearing of this
cause to rejoin said office and that the said Newton Cannon,

2

Governor, may be prevented from issuing his proclamation establishing the said Marshall County.

Signed by Allen Leeper,
Jason B. Shuffield,
Andrew Patterson,
John Bruce and
J. J. Marshall

April 9, 1836

Page 23 - Daniel McKisick]
         vs   ] Judgement
    John H. Anderson]
Sometime in 1827, to sell Lot No. 75 in Shelbyville. Defendant, Anderson, lived upon Lot No. 104, near Halls Mill, south
of river. Anderson had one tract of 50 acres sold by Mancel
Crisp, one, seventy two acre tract sold by Jabus Nowlin, fifty
acres sold by Henderson Barnam.

Page 27 - George W. Haywood]
         vs   ] Bill of Inj.   April 1827
    Dwyer Pearl]
1828 and 1829, a note $125.00 payable to Dwyer Pearl of Nash-
ville, Davidson County, Tennessee.

Page 37 - Nathaniel and James Dick & others]
         vs   ] Orig. Bill
    Ezekiel W. Brown & others   ]
Nathaniel and James Dick and Harvey R. W. Hill, William J.
McLean, Merchants and partners trading under the name of N. &
J. Dick & Co., vs Ezekiel W. Brown, George C. Searcy and Darl-
ing C. Arnold.
    N. & J. Dick and William J. McLean of city of New Orleans,
Louisiana, Harvey R. W. Hill of Davidson County, Tennessee,
stated that at August 1834 Term said a judgement against
Ezekiel W. Brown, Robert P. Harrison and Joseph C. Strong,
admrs of the Will of John A. Marrs, deceased, and Samuel
Phillips and Gordentia Waite, admrs of Robert Waite, deceased,
for $2604.36. On 19 January last they caused judgement, said
Brown try to cheat them out of money. Ezekiel W. Brown and
George C. Searcy of Fayette County, Tennessee. 25 May 1835.

Page 44 - Joseph Morton]
         vs   ] Case Dismissed
    Jonathan Mosely]

Page 44 - James Brittain]
         vs   ] Orig. Bill
    Martin C. Daniel]
Some three years ago, he entered into partnership with Martin C.
Daniel, a merchandise store at Davis' Mill, about twelve or
thirteen miles from Shelbyville, Brittain furnished the capital
and Daniel looked after store until November 1831. Martin C.
Daniel on 5 February 1833 handed Brittain over all the notes,
etc. and was to leave early next morning.

Page 58 - Henry Conway]
         vs   ] Orig. Bill   February 1836
    Robert Cannon]
Sometime in April or May 1832, Henry Conway had three slaves.
Robert Cannon bidded on slaves.

Page 59 - John W. Norvill & others   ]
         vs   ] Pet.
    Elizabeth W. Norvill & others]

Honorable Lunsford M. Bramblett, Chancelor of Middle Division, presiding in Shelbyville for Bedford and Marshall Counties.

Your petitioners, John W. Norvill, Sydney S. Norvill, David J. Novill and Edward M. Norvill, represents that David Norvill departed this life intestate in December last, that at the time of his death he was and for a long time before had been a resident of Bedford County and at the time of his death, he was seized and possessed in fee simple of five several tracts of land all situated and lying in Bedford County, to wit; the tract of land on which he resided at the time of his death, lying near the road leading from Shelbyville to McMinnville about four miles from the former containing three hundred and fifty six acres, another tract situated in the same neighborhood called "the Yell Tract" containing one hundred and seventy five acres and conveyed by Alexander C. Yell to said David Norvill, a more particular description of which may be seen by reference to said deed; another tract containing about one hundred and forty five acres called "the Kennedy Tract" and conveyed by Joseph Kennedy to said David Norvill; another tract adjoining the last mentioned and containing forty five acres called "the Swiney Tract" and conveyed by Amos Swiney to said David Norvill and another tract on the War Trace Fork of Duck River, being an undivided one half of a one hun-hundred and five acre tract called "the Cartmill Tract" and conveyed by John Cartmill to said David Norvill, the whole tract was conveyed to David but your petitioner John C. paid half of the purchase money and has the bond of said David for title, and is equally entitled to the northern half of said land. Your orator would further represent that they and five others are all of the children and heirs at law of said David Norvill, to wit, James D., Thomas, Felix B., Alexander S., and Mary Ann Norvill, the three latter of whom are minors under the age of twenty one, that John Shoffner is the regularly appointed guardian of Felix B. and John Norvill said is the regularly appointed guardian of Alexander S. and Mary Ann Norvill. They would further represent that said Thomas has transferred and conveyed by deed, regularly proved and register-ed all of his interest in said estate to William Brown. They would further represent that Elizabeth W. Norvill is the widow of said David Norvill and that the complements are desirous to have their shares in said land allotted and set apart to them and they believe it be the wish of said Elizabeth W. Nor-vill to have her dower allotted to her, and of the other de-fendants to have their shares set apart and allotted to them in tender consideration whereof they pray your Honor to make the said Elizabeth W. Norvill and the said James D. Norvill, the said William Brown, the said Felix B., the said Alexan-der S., and the said Mary Ann Norvill, defendants to the bill that a copy thereof &c issued and that your Honor decree that said lands be divided into nine equal parts and one part allotted to each heir of said David Norvill, deceased, and that said Elizabeth W. Norvill have dower layed off to have one third of said lands for her and that John W. Norvill have decreed to have the northern half of the Cartmill tract and such other and further relief grant in the premises as to your Honor may seem right and your orators as in duty bound, ever pray.   Frierson, Solicitor for Compl.

Page 61 - John Lowe   ]
              vs   ] Pet. for Partition Land
         Heirs of William Lowe]
    Your petitioner, John Lowe, a citizen of Montgomery

County, Alabama, states that Daniel Low departed this life
in the year of 1824 or 1825, that at the time of his death,
he was a citizen of Bedford County and died seized and possessed of a certain tract or parcel of land with the appurteners
situated and lying in the County of Bedford aforesaid and
bounded as follows, to wit, Beg on an ash in the Section Line,
the southwest corner of a 1200 acre tract granted to William
Brown, thence north with the west boundary of said 1200 acre
survey to a black oak the north west corner of said 1200 acre
survey, thence east with the north boundary of said 1200 acre
survey 204 poles to a black walnut on the east bank of a fork
of Rock Creek, thence south 122 poles to a red oak, thence
south 85° west 20 poles to the center of a spring, thence south
to the north east corner of a tract of 100 acres now owned
by Isaac B. Lowe, thence west to the north west corner of said
100 acre tract, thence south with the west boundary of said
100 acre survey to the south boundary of said 1200 acre tract,
thence west with the south boundary to the beginning. Your
petitioners would further state that said Daniel Low before
his death made and published his Last Will and Testament, which
after his death was duly proved and recorded in the County
Court of Bedford, that by said Will he desired the before described tract of land to his wife Martha Low for life and at
her death to his three sons, your petitioner, George E., who
is now a citizen of Tipton County, Tennessee, and William,
the latter of whom departed this life in June 1833 leaving
five children and heir at law, to wit, George E., Daniel J.,
Seymore S., Eliza Ann and Martha E., all of whom are citizens
of Bedford County. That all of said children of said William
are minors under age of 21 years, who have James Dillard for
their guardian. He would further state that Martha Low died
in 1836. Your petitioner would further state that said George
E. Low has by and conveyed his interest in said tract of land
to your petitioner and your petitioner understands that said
heirs of William Low claims the interest of said George also.
In tender consideration of the petition &c, your petitioner
prays your Honor to make the said heirs of William Low defendant to this bill that copy &c to decree that said tract of
land he divided unto three equal parts, one part, to be allot-
ed to petitioners, one part of the heirs of William Low, deceased, and one part to George Low, and such others and further
relief grant, as to your Honor may seem just and right and
your petitioner as in duty bound, will ever pray.
                                    Frierson, Solistor for Petition
Answer:
Answer of George E., Seymore S., Daniel J., Eliza Ann and
Martha E. Low, minor heirs of William Low, deceased, by their
guardian James Dillard, states they admit that Daniel Low departed this life and was a citizen of Bedford County and that
Martha Low died in 1836 and George E. Low, Sr. has no interest
at this time in said tract of land, that deed deeded 1833,
he conveyed all his interest to respondent which was proved
and recorded.   14 February 1837

Page 63 - Legget, Whitthorne, D. Bridges]
                    vs   ]   Inj. Bill
                Edwin C. Hunter   ]
     Your orator, Holden W. Leggett, Darling Bridges and
William J. Whitthorne, states that in 1834 in January, your
orator, Darling Bridges borrowed from Edwin C. Hunter the sum
of $56.25 and executed to Hunter his note for 75 hundred lbs
of cotton, payable on 25 December 1832. Sometime in January
1833, a certain Elizabeth Perry obtained judgement against

Bridges for $55.25 and was levied on a wagon and three horses
and some other articles as the property of said Bridges by
Eli Elliott and was advertised to be sold as your orator believes on 18th October 1833, some short time before the day
of sale under the Perry Judgement said Hunter whom your orators
pray may be made Deft. to this bill, came Bridges to befriend
and learned that Bridges had enough money to pay for judgement
of Perry claim.   2 June 1834

Page 78 - Jesse Boyt   ]
              vs   ]   Orig. Bill
         Anderson Smith &]
         Presley L. Cox   ]
Jesse Boyt, a citizen of Carroll County, Tennessee, sometime
in the year 1832, sold to Anderson Smith of Marshall County,
Tennessee, a tract of land about 50 acres, situated in that
part of Maury County which is now a part of Marshall County,
on waters of West Rock Creek and bounded on east by Old County
Line, dividing Bedford and Maury Counties, on north by Francis
Killingsworth on the west by Joseph Duncan and on south by
the lands of Presley L. Cox and Smith. Smith executed to
Complt. to secure the purchase money 2 notes for $56.25 each.
In November Term 1834, Maury County said injunction was
dissolved and a decree against Smith for Deft. Taken to
Shelbyville.   30 June 1837

Page 81 - Peter Graves]
              vs   ]
         John Bennett]
Peter Graves' bill of complaint against John Bennett. Graves,
your orator, states that on 19 August 1829, an execution was
issued against him in favor of Samuel King for the use &c and
placed in the hands of the Deputy Sheriff of Bedford County
who after selling your orators personal property levied on
a tract of land owned by your orator, Peter Graves, in Bedford
County, described as follows: Beg at a horn bean and two sugar
trees, thence north crossing Thompson's Creek 140 poles to
a dogwood and hickory, thence east 53(55)+ poles to white oak,
buck and black gum, thence south 44 poles to a white oak,
thence east 45+ poles to a hickory and lynn, thence south 74
poles to a chestnut and hickory, thence west 19 poles to
hickory and elm, thence north 2 poles to two ashes, thence
west to the beginning. About 100 acres or more. The land
was sold at Court House on 10 November 1829. Sheriff made
an agreement with John Bennett who resided in Bedford County
to buy said land at the sale. John Bennett stated that he
might leave the state. Adam Euless befriended your orator.
John Bennett never paid his rents on said land. After the
sale to Bennett, he settled on the south end of the tract and
cultivated said land and was to pay $60.00 per year rent on
40 acres. Your orator had as surety for Absalom Low, John
Landis and Nicholas Anthony. Peter Graves' wife's name was
Peggy, entitled to the estate of a dwelling house, smith shop,
cooper shop, spring, garden and other houses.

Page 86 - Archibald Yell & Jonathan Webster]
              vs   ]
         Jane Meadows   ]
Orators, Jonathan Webster and Archibald Yell, the former of
Bedford County and the latter of Lincoln County, Tennessee,
states that on 22 June 1818, Michael Meddows of Bedford
County made and executed his Last Will and Testament, marked
"A". In his will, he bequeathed to his wife Jane Meddows

all his estate, personal or real, during her life or widowhood and at her death the property be equally divided among
his children, to wit, my son Riley's heirs (William and Washington), Mahaly Williams, John (James), Jemima Ann, Henderson,
Rebecca, Pumphrey, Ephraim G., and Jane, making in all at the
time of the execution of the Will, and at the death of said
Michael Meddows (which was as well as now recollected in the
year 1819(been legatees besides the two heirs of Riley
(William and Washington) who was entitled to one share as the
representation of their deceased father Riley Meddows. (Michael
Meddows died in the year 1819). Since the date of said Will
and since the death of said Michael (Washington) has since
died intestate and without heirs and as James, one of the legatees and who was entitled to a full share, has since the
death of Michael, died intestate and without heirs, leaving
only eleven legatees to entrust said estate, at the death of
said Jane Meddows, your orators states that all the legatees
are of age and that said Jane Meddows is a resident citizen
of Bedford County at this time and has in her possession a
small tract of land, the quantity not given but supposed to
be worth one hundred or two hundred dollars, which land has
been paid for by her, so far as she has paid out of the property and proceeds of the balance of the personal estate consisting among other property the following negroes, to wit,
Francis about 40 years and worth $200.00, Amos about 30 years
and worth $400.00, Bal about 10 years and worth $300.00, Silvy
about 8 years and worth $300.00, Triny about 6 years and worth
$200.00, Jerry about 4 or 5 years and worth $200.00, Manerva
between 3 and 4 years and worth $150.00, Matt age 2 years and
worth $150.00, sum of $1950.00, besides the land and other
personal property not now able to describe all, is under the
control and management of said Jane Meddows.
Your orators states that they have become interested in
said estate, two shares, to wit, William and Henderson.
Michael Meddows appointed James Meddows, his son, and
Mosely Harris his executors but neither of them have taken
upon themselves the administration thereof. James having died
not very long after his father Michael and no one enjoined
(that) Mosely Harris to administer &c so that the whole amount
of said property is at the mercy and disposal of said Jane
Meddows, who, we have been informed, has been attempting to
sell or dispose of a part of said negroes and should she sell
or take the property out of the county, the heirs and legatees
may never be able to recover them from the purchaser and as
attempts have been made to sell, your orators cannot tell at
what moment the whole or part of said property may be sold
or taken out of the jurisdiction of this Court. Your orators
requiring the said Jane Meddows be compelled to give bond and
security on such an amount as will secure and compel here her
securities to deliver up said negroes and real property at
her death to those who are entitled to the same, and your
orators further pray forthwith for their delivery according
to the within foregoing and your orators further pray that
if the said Jane Meddows should fail or refuse to give security
that your Honor will order and direct that the said negroes
be taken into possession by the Sheriff of Bedford County who
shall deliver them to your orators.   4 February 1834.

Page 88 - Will of Michael Meddows.   Exhibit "A".
In the name of God Amen, I, Michael Meddows of the State
of Tennessee and County of Bedford, being sick of body but
of sound mind and memory, do make and publish and order this
my Last Will and Testament, revoking all other heretofore made

by me.
Item: I give my body to the dust and my soul to God. My desire
is after all my just debts are paid that my wife Jane Meddows
shall have all my estate, both real and personal, during her
natural life or widowhood and at her death, my deside is that
my estate be equally divided among my children, to wit, my
son Riley's heirs William and Washington, Mahaley, William,
John, James, Jemima, Ann, Henderson, Rebecca, Pomphrey G.,
Ephraim G., and Jane. In testimony whereof I have set my hand
this 22nd day of June in the year of our Lord, one thousand
eight hundred and eighteen in presence of _____.
I appoint my son James Meddows and Mosely Harris as administrators of this my last will and testament.
Mosely Harris, Jurat   Signed: Michael Meddows
John Taylor, Jurat
                        Exhibit "B"
12 October 1833, William Meddows sold to Samuel Haggard of
Bedford County for $100.00, paid for all my interest in the
estate of my deceased father Michael Meddows, according to
his Will &c.   Signed: Wm (X) Meddows
Witnesses: Hamilton Bradford
           G. G. Osborne
           R. Haggard
                        Exhibit "C"
12 October 1833, between Henderson Meddows of Bedford County
and Samuel Haggard of Bedford County, sold to Haggard for
$75.00, paid in hand, his interest in his deceased father
Michael Meddows, according to his will.
Witnesses: J. Norvill   Signed: Henderson (X) Meddows
           E. G. Meddows
           R. Haggard
                 Answer of Jane Meddows

Page 93 - Wakefield, Meaks and others]
              vs   ] Bill
           Sarah Putman   ]
Complainants William J. W. Wakefield and his wife Malissa F.,
residents of Lincoln County, Tennessee, John W. Meaks of
Bedford County, and James Cotton and Malissa Cotton, minors
who sued by their uncle and next friend the said John W. Meaks,
said James Cotton being a resident of Mississippi and the said
Malissa being a resident of Bedford County, complainants against
Samuel Putman, defendant, and resident of Bedford County.
COmpl. show to your Honor that Jesse Putman, deceased, who
resided in Bedford County, on the 6th August 1833, a short
time before his death made and executed his Last Will and Testament which on the __ day of November 1833, was duly proven
in the County Court of said Bedford County at the November
Term thereof and admitted to record and a copy of Will is herewith exhibited marked "A" and prayed to be taken as a part
of this bill. The said Jesse Putman, deceased, in his said
Will gave to his wife, the said deft. for and during her natural
life all his estate both real and personal after the payment
of his just debts. To wit, after the death of my wife and
my debts all paid, I give all the residue of my estate to John
W. Meeks, Minerva Cotton and Malissa F. Meeks and their heirs,
to be equally divided between them. Compl. was advised and
believes that said testator meant by his residue of his estate,
all his estate except his land and except what might be properly
appropriated to the payment of his debts. Compl. John W. Meeks
is the same mentioned in the said will and compl. James Cotton
and Malissa Cotton are the only children and heirs of Manerva
A. Cotton named in the will. The said Manerva A. Cotton

departed this life since November 1833. Compl. Wakefield
intermarried with the said Malissa F. Meeks mentioned in the
will. So that under the clause above quoted from said will,
Compls. are the only persons now living entitled in remainder.
They stated that no person, as they are informed ever qualified
as executor, or as administrator with the will annexed, of
said Jesse Putman, deceased. They said all just debts have
been paid and they are so informed and believe, except a debt
which was said to be due some persons in East Tennessee for
$140.00 and they are informed that the money has been sent
to pay that debt to the amount of $300.00, if that debt is
not paid, it is as complts. believe through contrivances and
paid on the part of deft. and her son Jon Wommock of the State
of Georgia. Said Jesse Putman, at the time of his death, was
the owner and had possession of the following slaves.
                      8 August 1836

Page 95 - Will of Jesse Putman. Bedford County, Tennessee.
I, Jesse Putman of the County of Bedford and State of Tennessee,
being sound in mind and memory but weak in body and knowing
that I must shortly bide adew to the affairs of time, do constitute this instrument my Last Will and Testament and first
appoint as the managers of my worldly concern, my wife Sarah
Putman and William Cotton to carry into effect this my will
in manner and form following.
    I give to my beloved wife Sarah Putman for and during
her natural life, all my estate, both real and personal, except
so much of the same as shall sufficient to give my body decent
burial, and amply pay my just debts, as also to pay to my four
brothers each one dollar as their full share of my estate,
to wit, to Joseph Putman one dollar, to Jacob ?. Putman one
dollar, ____as Putman one dollar, to Daniel one dollar and
to the heirs of William Putman one dollar, to the heirs of
James Putman one dollar, to the heirs of Nancy Lawson one
dollar, and to the heirs of Elizabeth Ray one dollar, as their
full share of my estate, and after the death of my wife, I
give to John W. Meeks one hundred acres of the land I now live
on, to be laid off so as not deprive the balance of my land
of an equal share of water, the balance of my land after the
death of my wife, I give to Manerva A. Cotton, and to Malissa
F. Meeks to be equally divided between them, and further, after
the death of my wife, and my debts all paid, I give all the
residue of my estate to John W. Meeks, Manerva A. Cotton and
Malissa F. Meeks and their heirs to be equally divided between
them, and should any of the above named persons die without
an heir, I wish their dividend to be divided between them,
the other two, having now directed and arranged my worldly
affairs according to my wish, I resign my body to the dust
from whence it came and my soul to God that gave it.
    In testimony whereof I have hereunto set my hand and sub-
scribed my name this 6th day of August 1833. In presence of
Wit: Joel Yowell   Signed: Jesse (X) Putman
     Thomas Gramer
     W. H. Gramer
                    Answer of Sarah Putman
     Her husband, Jesse Putman, departed this life.

Page 99 - Abner Vincent and others]
                vs   ] Orig. Bill
          George R. Scott and wife]
Abner Vincent and Susan Parthenia W., his wife, and Harriet J.
Wynne and William R. Wynne, the latter being a minor under
age of 21 years, who sues by his next friend Abner Vincent,

all of Weakley County, Tennessee, against George R. Scott and Polly his wife, defts. of Bedford County.

Complt. states that they are all the children of and lawful heirs and the only children and lawful heirs of William R. Wynne, deceased, of Brunswick County, Virginia, except your orator Abner Vincent, who is an heir in right of his wife, she being one of the children and heirs of said William R. Wynne, deceased. They further states that on the 15th day of December 1814 in Brunswick County, Virginia, a short time previous to the death of the said William R., he signed, sealed and published his Last Will and Testament, which was on the 26th day of December 1814, proved and recorded in Brunswick County, Virginia.

In his will, he bequeathed personal and real, to his wife Polly Wynne, for and during her natural life and after her death to be equally divided between the children of the Testator. William R. Wynne died seized and possessed of a negro man named Ben, of a negro woman named Lizzie and a negro girl named Jinny. After William R. Wynne's death, the negroes went to his widow. She continued to hold them in possession for three or four years or longer, when she intermarried of the said George R. Scott and the widow continued to hold the negroes in Virginia and then removed to Tennessee and bringing the negroes with them. Since that time, Lizzie has had three children, two boys and one girl, all of whom are in possession of George R. Scott. Negroes now six in number. Since moving to Tennessee, George R. Scott has treated his wife cruelty and has driven her from his house and would not protect and support her. Scott is threatening to sell the negroes. Wants negroes not to be sold.

Page 101 - Will of William R. Wynne.

In the name of God Amen. I, William R. Wynne of the County of Brunswick,Virginia, being sick and weak of body, but of sound mind and disposing memory, and calling to mind that it is ordained and appointed for all men once to die, do make and ordain this my Last Will and Testament, in manner and form following, that is to say,
Item: I give and bequeath to my beloved wife Polly Wynne all my estate, both real and personal after payment of my just debts to have and to hold the said property to her said Polly Wynne, for and during the time of her natural life.
Item: It is my will and desire that my beloved wife shall during her natural life as aforesaid, support, maintain and educate my two children, Susan Parthena William Wynne and Stan--tt James Wynne, also the child of my said wife is now pregnant with, provided it should live out of the property before, devised to her for term of her life, in such a manner as to my said wife may seem best, leaving her permission to exercise her discretion in the said support and educate of all my said children. It is my will and desire that at the death of my said wife, all my said estate both real and personal hence before given my wife during her natural life shall be equally divided such of my said children as shall be there living to have and to hold the said property to them and their assignees forever. It is my will and desire that if either of my said children should die before my said wife, leaving issue lawfully begotten of their bodies, then that the issue so left shall be entitled to and receive the same proportion of my estate at the death of my wife as the present of such issue would have been entitled to, had such parents been living at the time of the death of my wife.
Lastly, I nominate and appoint my beloved wife Polly Wynne

10

and my friend Rolling Horthron, executrix and executor, of
this my Last Will and Testament, hereby revoking all other
wills and codicils by me heretofore made. In witness whereof
I have hereunto set my hand and affixed my seal this fifteenth
day of December in the year of our Lord and Christ, 1814.
Wit: William Gates   Signed: William R. Wynne (Seal)
     Henry P. Mitchell
     John Tuld
     John H. Hamell
Brunswick County Court, December 26th, 1814. Proven and
Recorded.   Rutherford County, Tennessee 25 Mar 1834.
     Answer of George R. Scott in 1834. To Bill by complt.
Abner Vincent and Susan Parthena W., his wife, Hannah J. Wynne
and William R. Wynne, heirs and legatees of William R. Wynne,
deceased.
A. Vincent married Susan Parthena W.
Polly was 1st married to William R. Wynne who died in 1814
and she afterwards married George R. Scott in 1821 or 1822
in Virginia and moved to Bedford County in 1825.
Peter Wynne died in the early part of 1815 (father of Polly
Wynne).

Page 106 - M. Gilchrist   ]
             vs   ] Inj. Bill
          T. A. Peacock &]
          Bradford   ]
Malcolm Gilchrist by his agent, William Gilchrist of Bedford
County. May Term of Bedford County Court 1835. The court
ordered that John B. Jones, Anderson Sharp, William Sharp,
Robert Chambers, John W. Gollathan, John Sutton, Robert Clinkenbeard, Joseph Loyd, Thomas A. Peacock and Joel Lawrence, was
appointed jury, to lay off and mark out a road from near where
Rice Coffee lives to the Turnpike at Guy's Gap and bring in
at next term, August Term 1835.

Page 111 - Sally Wheeler   ]
             vs   ] Petition for dower
          The heirs and Admrs of]
          Lemuel Wheeler   ]
Sally Wheeler is the widow of Lemuel Wheeler, deceased, who
departed this life on 22 day of September 1835, intestate,
seized and possessed of a certain tract of land situated and
lying in Marshall County, Tennessee on the north side of Duck
River near the Fishing Ford, being the same tract on which
Wheeler resided at the time of his death. Bounded as follows:
to wit, Beginning at a hackberry and elm on the banks of Duck
River, thence north 101+ poles to an ash and spanish oak, thence
west 240 poles to a rock in Middleton Hamilton's line, thence
south 42½ poles to an ash and hickory on the banks of Duck
River, thence up said river with its meanders to the beginning,
Containing by estimation 156 acres. Your petitioners would
further state that Elizabeth Corbett wife of Needham Corbett,
Lucinda, George H., and Lemuel Wheeler are the only children
and heirs at law of said Lemuel Wheeler, that the last mentioned
are minors under age of 21 years and that James Ramsey is their
regular appointed guardian appointed by the County Court of
Marshall County. Petitioner would further state that Richard
Warner is the admr. of the estate of Lemuel Wheeler, deceased.
He wants the dower's part laid off for her.

Page 112 - James M.Riggs   ]
             Petition for sale of negroes]
Orator, James M. Riggs, Zadock Riggs and Joel D. Riggs, the

11

latter of whom is a minor under 21 years, who sues by his
guardian John H. Roberson and William C. Shepherd and his wife
Mary Shepherd, Thomas L. Douglas and his wife Nancy, Elizabeth
Riggs and Elizabeth H. Riggs and Rebecca B. Riggs, the two
latter of whom are minors under age of 21 years, who sued by
their guardian John H. Roberson, all of whom are citizens of
Marshall County, Tennessee, except William C. Shepherd and
wife Mary who are citizens of Williamson County, Tennessee,
humbly complaining would show that Joel Riggs departed this
life on the 13 day of December 1835, that at the time of his
death he was a citizen of Bedford County, that your orator
James M. Riggs was appointed admr of the estate of Joel Riggs,
deceased, at February Term, 1836 at Bedford County and that
your oratrix Elizabeth Riggs is the widow of said Joel and
your orators James M., Zadock and Joel D. Riggs, and your
oratrix Mary Shepherd, Nancy Douglas, Elizabeth H. and Rebecca
B. Riggs are the only children and distributes of said Joel
Riggs, that John H. Roberson was on the 1st Monday in February
1837, appointed guardian of your orator Joel D. Riggs and your
orators Elizabeth H. and Rebecca B. Riggs, also stated that
the personal estate of Joel Riggs consists merely the following
negroes, 10 in number. Recommended they be sold and divided
among heirs.   14 February 1837

Page 113 - Joseph H. Brittain]
              vs   ] Orig. Bill
         Joseph J. Marshall]
Orator, Joseph H. Brittain of Marshall County, early in 1835,
intered into partnership with Joseph J. Marshall also of Marshall County, Tennessee, the business of Grocery and lasted until
the year 1835, the business was to be in Bedford County, with
credit in Marshall County.   6 April 1835

Page 117 - Edmond T. Doherty, others]
            Petition of sale of land]
Edmond T. Doherty and his wife Ann, formerly Ann Nix, Elizabeth
Nix, Rebecca Nix, Francis Nix, James Nix, Lebanon Nix and Mary
Nix, the six last of whom are minors, sue by their guardian
Samuel Wilson would show that Rebecca Nix, the mother of Ann
Doherty and the above minors after the death of her husband
Lebanon Nix, and during her life time and during the year 1834
purchased a tract of land, lying and being in Marshall County
formerly Lincoln County, Preston Fork, usually known by the
name of Tory Fork of Rich Land Creek and bounded on the south
by the lands of Joseph H. Hickney, on the last by the lands
of Lemuel Elliott, on the north by W. Colman and J. Gaunt's
land and on the west by the lands of Joshua Nichols. Contains
about 275 acres from K. T. Kelly for $140.00.
     Rebecca, during the year 1834, before she obtained title
to said tract, departed this life, intestate, leaving as her
only heirs at law, Ann Nix now Ann Doherty and Jane Nix,
Elizabeth Nix, Rebecca Nix, Francis Nix, Mary Nix, Thomas Nix,
Samuel Nix, William Nix and Lebanon Nix. Your complts also
states that Edmond T(S). Dohertyand Ann his wife and Jane Nix,
Mary Nix, THomas Nix and Lemuel Nix were in the County of
Marshall, State of Tennessee, and that Elizabeth Nix, Rebecca
Nix and Francis Nix reside in Bedford County and that the
residence of William Nix and Lebanon Nix is unknown. Complts
also states that the said Rebecca at the time of her deceased,
she was possessed of a crop of cotton, which said cotton, the
said Samuel Nix, Thomas Nix and William Nix sold &c, the proceeds to the payment of the balance of $40.00 remaining due
for said land, also that William Nix proceed the deed to be

12

made himself which has been registered in the Register's
Office in Lincoln County, Tennessee and proceeded to divide
the land between him and Thomas Nix and Samuel Nix.
      Edmond S(T). Doherty stated that since the death of
Rebecca, he has intermarried with Ann Nix and he has become
interested in the tract of land.

Page 119 - Thomas Black   ]
            vs   ]
        William P. Batte & others]
Orator, Thomas Black, a citizen of Bedford County, states that
William P. Batte on 8 March 1834, executed and delivered a
note for $12.00 and also 2nd note of $50.00. Orator stated
that in the month of December 1834, William P. Batte left the
County and State and not been seen and for some time past a
citizen of McCracken County in the State of Kentucky, and did
not pay of his note. Orator states that William Allison, one
of the admrs of Henry Batte, deceased, the father of said
William P. Batte, has in his hands at this time $16.00 in cash
which is due to William P. Batte from his father. Money came
from sale of negroes belonging to the estate of Henry Batte,
deceased. Also a tract of land on Weakley Creek about 86
acres, also 260 acres of land which Henry Batte died seized
and possessed, allotted to Rebecca Batte his widow, as her
dower and on which she now resides.   14 April 1837

Page 123 - Absalem Halby and wife   ]
            vs   ] Orig. Bill
        John Deason and Joseph Rushing]
Complts. Absalem Halby and Elvy Halby his wife against John
Deason and Joseph Rushing.
      Absalem Halby and wife Elvy Halby of Anson County, North
Carolina, states that Shepherd Deason was the father of said
Elvy Halby and that the said Shepherd Deason died intestate
some years since whilst your petitioner was but a child leaving
the said Elvy and Joel R. Deason his only heirs at law. Also,
that Shepherd Deason was the son of Enoch Deason, late of
Bedford County. Enoch Deason died some five years since having
first made and published his Last Will and Testament which
was duly proven and recorded in the County Court Clerk's
Office of Bedford County. Enoch appointed John Deason and
Joseph Rushing, both of Bedford County, the executors. The
will said Enoch willed and bequeathed all his property to his
wife Rebecca Deason during her natural life and after bequeath-
ing to his own children, then living, being nine (9) in number
the portions allotted them to have and to his grandson Joel
Deason, $63.00 which he had before sent to him. Elvy Halby,
his granddaughter, $25.00 sent to her. He then bequeathed
to his son John Deason at the death of his widow all of which
he was possessed and then bequeathed as follows: "The other
property shall be divided so as to make each legatees equal
counting in what they have already had given by my will my
grandson John Deason, son of William Deason, my son, an equal
portion with my nine above named children; also that the widow
of said Enoch Deason is now dead that said executors refer
under said will to pay to your complt. their portion as legatees
and that they are advised that they are entitled under said
Will and Testament, to an equal legacy with the other legatees.
Absalem Halby(Hally) intermarried with Elvy Deason, the granddaughter of Enoch Deason before the death of him the said Enoch
Deason and by means became interested in her portion of the
estate." (Halby could be Hally, which is written both ways
in this instrument)

Page 125 - Will of Enoch Deason.

I, Enoch Deason, considering the uncertainty of this natural life and being of sound mind and memory (blessed be Almighty God for the Son) do make and publish this my Last Will and Testament in manner and form following, that is to say, First, given and bequeathed unto my beloved wife Rebecca Deason her lifetime if she should be the longest lived, all the property, perishable and unperishable, to wit, negroes, household and kitchen furniture and stocks of various kinds and that the clear profits shall be appropriated for the maintenance of my beloved wife Rebecca aforesaid entirely, no trading or trafficking of any of the above property without the _____ of my term and legal assign.

2nd Item, I give and bequeath unto my daughter Martha Rushing which I heretofore lease her.

3rd Item, I give and bequeath unto my son William Deason $577.00 which I heretofore loaned to him.

4th Item, I give and bequeath unto my daughter Nancy Rushing $36.00 which I heretofore loaned her.

5th Item, I give and bequeath to my daughter Milly Rushing $24.00 which I heretofore loaned her.

6th Item, I give and bequeath unto my son Absalom Deason $301.00 which I heretofore loaned him.

7th Item, I will and bequeath unto my son Absalom Deason $169.00 which I heretofore loaned him.

8th Item, I will and bequeath to my son Joel Deason $58.00 which I heretofore loaned him.

9th Item, I give and bequeath unto my daughter Belinda Cooper $37.00 I heretofore loaned her.

10th Item, I give and bequeath unto my daughter Rebecca Loyd $12.00 which I heretofore loaned her.

11th Item, I give and bequeath unto my grand son Joel R. Deason $63.00 I heretofore loaned him in full of his legacy.

12th Item, I give and bequeath unto my grand daughter Elicy Halby $35.00 at the distribution of the aforesaid profits after the death of my wife Rebecca.

The tract of land and premises whereon now I live, I give and bequeath unto son John Deason to be wholly his property; the other profits shall be divided so as to make each legatee equal counting in what they have already had given by my will. My grand son Joel Deason, son of William Deason my son, an equal part with my nine above named children and if any child has had more than there will be property to make the rest in proportion to that one or more, the rest shall not have received os such a legatee for anything, and I do wholly and positively appoint authorize and empower my son John Deason and my son in law Joseph Rushing both citizens of this County, to wit, Bedford, my two and lawful executors and assigns, and wish them at such times as may become necessary to divide the above property or such property as may be given by suitable _____ and give it out as will be according to my above request and they my executors shall led and direct so that there shall be no unnecessary exceptions of said properties my son John Deason and son in law Joseph Rushing. I hereby appoint sole executors of this my Last Will and Testament hereby revoke all other wills made by me. In witness whereof I have hereunto set my hand and seal this January 20th 1830.

Wit: John Sugg   Signed: Enoch Deason (Seal)
     John R (Rust)

14

Page 127 - James Edward   ]
              vs   ] Bill of Complaint
         Robert Hill, Lydia Hill]
         & Silas Crofton   ]
Complt. James Edwards against Robert W. Hill, Lydia Hill and
Silas Crofton. Your orator, James Edwards, states that Robert
Hill of Maury County, Tennessee, on 22 November 1831 sold a
certain tract of land in Bedford County to one Silas Crofton
who was then a citizen of Maury County, but now of _____
County in the Western District of this State, for which Crofton
executed to the said Robert Hill his three several notes. Land
bounded: Beg at Richard Hill corner, running north to William
Bingham's corner, thence east to Hugh Bingham's corner, thence
south to Levi Coldwell's corner, thence west to the beginning.
About 32½ acres, dated 22 November 1831.
Wit: L. B. Jones   Signed: Robert Hill
     James Thompson

Page 132 - Lemuel & Jesse G. Rainy, admrs.]
              vs   ]
         Barzellia G. & Isaac Rainey   ]
     Orators, Samuel Rainey of Giles County, Tennessee and
John G. Rainey of Maury County, Tennessee, states that sometime
in the summer of 1833 your orator Lemuel was called upon and
did make a settlement between Brazellia G. Rainey and Isaac
Rainey, who were then merchants and partners in trade of one
part and Isaac Rainey who was the other of your orators and
the said Barzellia G. and Isaac N. and that at that time the
claims and demands of the said Isaac, against the Brazellia G.
and Isaac N., were equal or nearly equal to the claims and
demands of the said Brazellia G. and Isaac N. against the said
Isaac. Isaac Rainey during the year 1833 and 1835 was the
owner of a farm of 160 or 170 acres of land in Bedford County
with 60 or 70 acres cleared. He also had 6 negroes. The said
Brazellia G. Rainey and Isaac N. Rainey were merchants and
partners in trade. Orator states that on 18 June 1836 Isaac
Rainey died having made his will. He died in Bedford County.
Your orators were appointed admrs. Will probated July 1836
Bedford County.

Page 137 - Martin Wisner   ]
              vs   ]
         Lucy Lowe & others   ]
Martin Wisner of Marshall County, Tennessee against Lucy Lowe,
widow of William Lowe, deceased, and George C. Lowe, Jr., Seymore S. Lowe, Daniel Lowe, Eliza Ann Lowe and Martha Lowe,
minor heirs of William Lowe, deceased, all of Bedford County.
     Your orator, Martin Wisner, states he is the admr. of
William Lowe, deceased, on August Term 1834, he was security
for Daniel Barksdale and William W. Barksdale, admrs of the
estate of said Lowe, they were unable to make bond and security.
Your orator was appointed admr.
     Orator states that William Lowe died before his mother,
the widow of said Daniel and that his heirs of Wa----? had
there further showed propitious to them. He would have stated
that William Lowe after his father's death at the request and
by the permission of his mother, moved on part of said tract
of land and remained until his death, that his widow the said
Lucy Lowe remained on it until the death of Daniel Lowe's
widow and that after the death of Daniel Lowe's widow which
occurred sometime in 1836. The said Lucy was endowed by order
of court of one third part of that part of land bequeathed,
which was propitiatings to the heirs of your orators, intestate.

Your orator is advised to that all the lands that ascended
to the heirs of William Lowe, deceased, made the will of Daniel
Lowe dividing his lands to his three sons and liable for the
debts of said William Lowe, deceased.
   The lands of William Lowe, deceased, lies in Bedford
County of about 110 acres. James Dillard was guardian of the
minor heirs of William Lowe, deceased.   6 February 1839

Page 144 - Jordan C. Holt   ]
                   vs   ] Inj. Bill. Judgement against
          Banks M. D. Burrow   ] Banks M. D. Burrow.
Orator states that B. M. D. Burrow owns no property. Also,
Ephraim Burrow, deceased, by his Last Will and Testament duly
proven and recorded in Bedford County devised to his wife Eve
Burrow, negroes, balance divided between his children, eleven
in number, one of whom is Banks M. D. Burrow.

Page 145 - Will of Ephraim Burrow.
   I, Ephraim Burrow, being in sound senses and memory but
knowing that men was born once to die. In the name of God
Amen. This is my Last Will and Testament.
No. 1, Jordan all my just debts to be paid.
No. 2, I will to my beloved wife the tract of land I now live
on containing 250 acres of land during her lifetime and at
her death, the land is to be equally divided between Madison
Burrow and Leathy Burrow, also I give to her the following
negroes, named here, free a negro man, and Sarah his wife,
Nathan and Jane and Mary her child, three negroes I give to
her only her lifetime, after her death these negroes is to
be sold and to be equally divided after the lowest price negro
is made even with the highest priced negros, so that each
child's negroes shall be made even, then if any money left
to be equally divided amongst all my children, the balance
that I give to my beloved wife is to be as her own property
to expose as she pleases to live or and also at her death to
give to who she pleases if anything left. Two gray mares,
four cows and calves, six choice of the other cow kind, all
the sheep, two sows and pigs and twenty cases of other hogs
for her meat and all the geese and duck and chickens, three
beds and all the furniture and steads that belonged to them,
one cupboard and all the furniture that belongs to it such
as dishes, plates, cups, knives and forks and all the bottles
and bowls and everything that to the use table and cupboard
takes to when setting meal, also and table and candlestands,
one <u>claugh</u>(?), one chest and trunk, one pair of fire dogs,
shovel and tongs, one kettle and two pets, four windsor chairs
and four split-bottom chairs, two of the best plows, two pair
of chains, all the corn and wheat and oats and potatoes that
is raised on the plantation for her own use and to expose as
she pleases at her death and the clock to stay in the house
and at her death it is to be Madison Burrow own property also
Hannah and her child Greenville, till her death, then to be
equally (divided) among all my children.
No. 3, I give to my son Solemon Burrow, one negro girl named
Madaline worth $50.00, and one hundred and fifty dollars to
be taken off his own not stand he gave for lent money.
No. 4, I give to my son Ephraim Burrow one negro girl named
Martha and $50.00 to be paid when the property is sold and
money collected out of the whole this negro is worth $150.00.
No. 5, I give to my son Jesse Burrow one negro man worth
$400.00 named Daniel and the trust of land he now lives on,
containing of 60 acres of land also my right of half that last
entry that lies between him and James Burrow and the other

16

half to James Burrow of that entry.

No. 6, I give to my son Banks M. Burrow one negro boy named George worth $100.00 to be paid when the collected of the estate also tract of land that he now lives on that is all the right that I have for it.

No. 7, I give to my son James Burrow one negro girl named Leah worth $150.00 and $50.00 to be paid when collected out of the estate also 50 acres of land beginning above Jesse Burrow's on the branch and half that near entry.

No. 8, I give to my son Doctor Alfred Burrow one negro named Joe worth $400.00, this negro Joe is to be his property till his death, then is to be taken and sold and the money to be divided among his children, at the youngest coming of age.

No. 9, I give to my son Madison Burrow one negro boy named Allen, also, the choicest colt of Remus or Words and my saddle and bridle, this is worth $200.00.

No. 10, I give to my daughter Frances Black one negro girl named Patsy during her lifetime at her death this negro girl and increase to be taken and to be hired out till the youngest child comes of age, then to be equally divided amongst all her children. This negro is worth $350.00.

No. 11, I give daughter Hetty Wilhoite one negro girl named Susan during her lifetime, at her death this negro girl is to be hired out till the youngest child comes of age, then to be equally divided among all of her children. This negro is worth $350.00.

No. 12, I give to my daughter Nancy Black one negro girl named Maria during her lifetime and at her death this negro and increase to be hired out until her youngest child comes of age, then to be equally divided among all her children. This negro is worth $300.00.

No. 13, I give to my daughter Leathy Burrow one negro girl named Harriett, this negro is worth $200.00 and also the _____ that belongs to the beds as the other girls got and <u>one</u> <u>borrowed</u>(/).

Now I do apart this to be my Last Will and Testament as is wrote down to my beloved wife and to every child is wrote down and then that has been priced is to draw at my wife's death from them negroes till the negroes ever worth then that has got the highest priced negro till the negroes is made all over or one price. Signed this 4th day of July 1833

Signed: Ephraim Burrow (Seal)

Page 147 - Richard Mitchell & others]
             vs   ]   Bill
    Hugh Houston & others]

Complt. Richard Mitchell and Cynthia H., his wife, Tabitha R., Eli C., Elvira(Eliza) M., Susan J., Jeremiah J., and Elizabeth M. Ownby, minors under age of 21 who sues by their guardian Edward Ownby, Edward Doyle and Tabitha his wife, Edmund R. Cheek, Eli Cheek, Arthur Alexander and Nancy his wife, all citizens of Marshall County, Tennessee against Hugh Houston, Benjamin R. Cheek and THomas D. Cheek, also of Marshall County, Tennessee.

Complt. states that your orators are some of the heirs at law of Jeremiah Cheek who departed this life in the year 1823; that Cynthia H. Mitchell, Tabitha R., Eli C., Eliza M., Susan J., Jeremiah J. and Elizabeth M. Ownby are the heirs at law of Polly Ownby, deceased, who was a daughter of said Jeremiah Ownby; that Tabitha Doyle, Edmund R. Cheek, Eli Cheek and Nancy Alexander are children of said Jeremiah Cheek; that deft. Benjamin R. and Thomas D. Cheek and James and Jeremiah Cheek, and Polly _____ are the balance of the children and

heirs at law of Jeremiah Cheek, deceased; that the said Jeremiah before his death made and published his Last Will and
Testament, which since his death has been regularly proven
and admitted to record in Bedford County Court; the said
Jeremiah Cheek being at the time of his death a citizen of
Bedford County; that defts. Hugh Houston and Benjamin R. Cheek
were appointed executors of said will, and duly qualified as
such at the ___ Term _____ of the County Court of Bedford
County, and took upon them the execution of said will; that
by the provision of said will (a copy attached) said executors
were directed upon the death of Tabitha Cheek, wife of Jeremiah Cheek, to sell all of the property and estate of Jeremiah
and divide the same amongst the children of said Jeremiah;
that said Jeremiah at the time of making said will and at the
time of his death was seized and possessed of a certain tract
of land with the appearances lying in that part of Bedford
County which now constitutes a part of Marshall on the waters
of West Fork of Rock Creek, being the same tract on which said
Jeremiah resided at the time of his death, containing one
hundred and eighty acres (180); that upon the death of said
Tabitha Cheek which happened in 1834, said executors on the
6th day of May 1834 proceeded to sell said tract of land, and
the same was bid off by said Thomas D. Cheek for the sum of
eight hundred and thirty dollars ($830.00). Your orators ex-
pressly charged that previous to said sale the said Thomas D.
Cheek, and the said Benjamin R. Cheek, one of the executors
of said Jeremiah entered into a contact to purchase said tract
of land in partnership, and the same was to bid off by said
Thomas D. for their joint benefit; that said Benjamin R.,
although one of the executors, ans as such bound to sell said
land for the best price did in consequence of his interest
in said contract endeavored to elemate competition by _____
devise persons from bidding that he might get the better bar-
gain, and when told that your orator Edward Ownby would perhaps
run the land upon him, answered that he should not know of
the sale, and according by your orator Edward Ownby who at
that time lived in Sumner County and who was willing to have
given fifty dollars for said land was kept in ignorance of
the sale until after it was over; that said Thomas D. also
endeavored to keep down competition by recommending that your
orator Edward Ownby should not be informed by the time of sale,
and also by representing that he and his brother Benjamin R.
wished to purchase in partnership; that said Thomas D. bid
off said land in pursuant of said contract and that in consequence of said contract and of the unlawful means complied by
said Thomas D. and Benjamin R. to keep down competition said
tract of land sold for about one-half of it's value; that said
land is now worth three or four hundred dollars.

Page 149 - Copy of Jeremiah Cheek's Last Will and Testament.
State of Tennessee, Bedford County.
    In the name of God Amen. Being sound in mind and memory,
I publish this my Last Will and Testament hereby revoking all
other wills by me made, it being the fourth day of July in
the year of our Lord one thousand eight hundred and twenty
three (4th July 1823).
First, After committing my soul to God, I will that so much
of my estate as will lay my body in the ground, will be appropriated for that use, and after all my just debts are paid
after my decease, I will that the stud horse be sold. I also
will that the children that is now single, when they marry
receive in proportion to those that are now married. The
following property, to wit, one horse, one cow and calf, one

18

bed and furniture, a piece. I also will that my beloved wife
Tabitha Cheek after the above division is made to have all
the balance of my estate during her natural life or widowhood.
I also will that after her death or marriage, that all the
estate be sold are equal divided be made amongst all my children. I will that Hugh Houston and Benjamin R. Cheek be the
executors of my estate. Signed, sealed and delivered the day
and date above written in the presence of us.
Test: John Pexton   Signed: Jeremiah (X) Cheek
      William S. Callahan
A copy Teste from the original now on file my office.
                              William D. Orr, Clerk of
                              Bedford County Court.

Page 152 - J. J. B. Crunk   ]
                vs   ] Petition
           John Craig, Admr.]
Joseph J. B. Crunk of Marshall County, Tennessee against John
Craig, admr. of William Craig, deceased, a citizen of Bedford
County.
     Crunk states that sometime in the early part of the year
1835, William Craig departed this life intestate, leaving as
his distributees and heirs at law, his widow, and several
children. That at the time of his death, said William Craig
was possessed as of his own right, of several slaves and other
personal property of considerable value; that not long after
the decease of said William Craig, his son the said John Craig
took upon himself the burden of administering upon the estate
of him the said William, and gave bond and qualified as such
in the County Court of Bedford County and that more than two
years have elapsed since he took out letters of administration
and that he has not yet had a settlement with the County Court.
     Also that sometime last summer, he became the attorney
in fact of Benjamin F. Craig and one of the heirs and distributees of the said William Craig, deceased, by a regular proven
of attorney from the said Benjamin F. to your petitioner, which
was duly acknowledged before and certified by the clerk of
the County Court of Tipton County, Tennessee and herewith filed
marked Exhibit "A".   16 June 1837

Page 156 - Lewis Shepherd   ]
                vs   ]
           J. N. Thomas & Co]
           & others   ]
Bill of Complaint of Lewis Shepherd of Bedford County against
Mary Green and Williamson R. Burdette of Bedford County and
J. N. Thomas and Co. where residence is in Alabama.
     Orator, Lewis Shepherd states that sometime in August
1837, he became the security of the said Mary Green in a note.
Payable to Willie B. Walker, admr. of T. C. Green, deceased.
That Mary Green is now possessed of some personal property
amounting over $100.00 (May 1838)

Page 159 - J. M. Yowell   ]
                vs   ]
           Brents & Meadows]
J. M. Yowell of Marshall County, Tennessee against Thomas
Brents and Soloman Meadows, both of Marshall County, Tennessee.
     Orator states that he is admr. of Thomas Meadows, deceased,
and that at last Term of Circuit Court of Marshall County,
Thomas Brents obtained a judgement against your orator.
                    12 February 1839

Page 162 - Peggy Stewart   ]
              vs   ]   Petition
         James Gambrell &   ]
         William Stuart   ]
Peggy Stewart against James Gambrelle and William Stuart, all
of Bedford County.
     She stated that her late husband William Stuart departed
this life in October 1834, leaving his Last Will and Testament
in which he appointed James Gambrell and William Stewart his
executors. He also appointed another executor, but the two
named alone served. Will was duly admitted and probated at
November of Bedford County Court 1834. A copy annexed.

Page 163 - Will of William Stewart.
     In the name of God Amen. I, William Stewart of the
County of Bedford and State of Tennessee, being of sound mind
and memory, do make and publish this my Last Will and Testament
hereby revoking and making void all former wills by me at any
time heretofore made and
First, I direct that my body be decently entered at Sugar Creek
Meeting House in said county in the manner suitable to my con=
ditions in life and as to such worldly estate as it hath pleased God to entrust me with, I dispose of the same as follows,
First, I direct that all my debts and funeral expenses be paid
as soon after my decease as possible out of any moneys that
I may die possessed of or may first come into the hands of
my executors from any portion of my estate real or personal.
Secondly, I give and bequeath to my loving wife Peggy Stewart,
one negro girl named Do--(?), one negro boy named Sikem(?),
also part of the tract of land whereon I now live, that is
to say all the land lying south of the land remaining from
east to west, also I give and bequeath to my loving wife Peggy
Stewart, one sorrel mare, saddle and bridle that she now ride,
also one cow and calf, and sow and shotes, two ewes and lambs,
one featherbed and furniture and one cupboard and furniture,
also one pot, one oven, one skillet, one bar and share plow
and gear to have and to hold during her life or widowhood.
Thirdly, I give to my son-in-law Isaac Barnett, one dollar.
Further, 4th, I give and bequeath to my grand son Burton
Barnett,
5th, to my grand daughter Lucindy Barnett one negro girl Nelly,
one sorrel filly and one saddle also one bed and furniture
to have and to hold during her natural life.
7th, I give and bequeath to my grand son Joshua Stewart, $25.00.
8th, I give and bequeath to my grand son William Stewart,
$150.00.
9th, I give and bequeath to my son John Stewart, one mare and
saddle and bridle that he now has.
10th, I will and bequeath to my son Samuel Stewart, Jemima
Guly, Malinda Hix, Patsey Gambrelle, William Stewart, Nelly
Hix, the negroes that I will here named, one named Jenny, one
named Chand, one named Hannah, one named Ben, one named Dick,
one named Jim, one named Adam, one named Lish, and one named
Phill, one named Samson, one named Jenny Ben, one named Rose,
one named Liza, to have and hold during their natural life
which is to be equally divided amongst them.
11th, I give and bequeath to my son William Stewart one certain
tract of land lying in Bedford County on the waters of Big
Flat Creek, formerly known by the name of _____ Tract which
the said William Stewart, Jr. now lives on to have and to hold
during his natural life.
12th, Also the balance of my perishable property not otherwise
disposed of to be equally divided amongst my own children,

also the balance of my land lying on the north side of the
land to rented out and the proceeds thereof to be equally
divided amongst my own children which my wife Peggy Stewart
is to have the privilege of wood and water during her natural
life or widowhood and at her death or widowhood the property
then remaining in her hand to be equally divided amongst my
own children, that is to say, Samuel Stewart, Jemima Girly,
Malinda Hix, Polly Gambrell, William Stewart and Nelly Hix.
I do hereby make ordain and appoint my esteemed neighbor and
friend, James Gambrell, Esq., my son-in-law John Hix and my
beloved son William Stewart, Executors of this my Last Will
and Testament. In witness whereof, I, William Stewart, Sen.,
the said testator have to this my Last Will written on and
sheet of paper, set my hand and seal, this twenty seventh day
of September in the year of our Lord, one thousand eight
hundred and thirty five.
Signed, Sealed   Signed: Wm. Stewart (Seal)
Wit: Samuel Morris
     John Patton
     Zachus Cheshires

Page 165 - John J. Fuqua]
              vs   ]
           E. J. Frierson]
Complt. John J. Fuqua against Erwin J. Frierson, both of Bedford County. Fuqua states that sometime in 1836 he sold a note
for $75.00 to said Erwin J. Frierson drawn by one John Blessing
and William D. Green, said note due in October 1836.
                              11 February 1839

Page 168 - John Ragsdale &   ]
           William Armstrong   ]
              vs   ]
           James L. Armstrong,]
           guardian &c   ]
Complt. John Ragsdale, Sen. and William Armstrong against
James L. Armstrong and Richard Warner of Marshall County, Tennessee, guardian of Sophia F. Sutton and Elizabeth Sutton, minor
heirs of William B. Sutton, deceased.
     Orators states that in 1831 the said John being indebted
to the said William for about $160.00, and to one William B.
Sutton for about $65.00 and being possessed of a tract of land
in Bedford County, about 100 acres, lying near Wilson Creek
bounded on the east by land of John Ragsdale, on the north
by land of Elizabeth Stammer, on the west by the land of
Martin Adams, on the south by land of Adam, William and David
Telford. Deed January 1831. William Armstrong having married
the daughter of your orator, the said John Ragsdale, Sen.
William B. Sutton died in 1833 and James L. Armstrong
was appointed his executor and Richard Warner and orator the guardian of his two children and only heirs, Sophia Sutton and
Elizabeth F. Sutton.   12 February 1839

Page 172 - Flower Swift   ]
              vs   ]
           J. W. Swift &]
           Thomas W. Swift]
Flower Swift of Bedford County stated that on the 4th day of
August 1838, he made and executed to Jacob W. Swift and Thomas
W. Swift of Bedford County, a certain deed (herewith filed
as part of this bill) for land, negroes, horses, and other
personal property, a note to be payable 4 August 1840.
     Deed: Flower Swift to Thomas W. Swift and Jacob W. Swift,

dated 4 August 1838. For $10,000 for tract of land on which
said Flower Swift now lives, lying in Bedford County and bounded as follows: Beginning at the north east corner of John
Wilhoite's land on the north side of Duck River, the same being
a scaley bark hickory, thence south to the river to an ash
and sugartree on the banks of the river, thence with the meanders of said river east to a black oak and white oak, Edward
Kimmons' line, thence east to a beach John McCustian's corner,
thence north to James Story's corner, thence west with said
Story's line, thence south with said Story's line to a gum,
thence west to the beginning. Containing about 200 acres.
And also the following slaves named, Austin, Frank, Charity,
James, John, Lucy, Richard, Harriett, Martha and Thomas, also
9 head of horses, all horned cattle of him the said Flower
Swift, being 40 in number &c.
4 December 1838   Signed: FLower Swift (Seal)

Page 174 - Daniel Barksdale]
                vs   ]
            Samuel Doak   ]
Orator, Daniel Barksdale of Lincoln County, Tennessee, stated
that in August 1834, he borrowed $250.00 from Samuel Doak of
Bedford County and agreed to give a mortgage or a certain
stallion horse.

Page 179 - Eakin & Brothers   ]
                vs   ] Orig. Bill
            Charles Lucas & others]
Complts. John, William, Spencer and THomas Eakin, the two
former, residents of Bedford County and the two latter citizens
of Davidson County, Tennessee, who are merchants and partners
under the firm and style of Eakin & Brothers, against Charles
Lucas, B. Maupin and Benjamin Kimbro, citizens of Bedford
County.
        Orators states that Charles Lucas is indebted to them
by a note due May 23, 1837 for $98.31½ and others, stated Lucas
sold to Robert B. Maupin about 120 acres.
            Inventory of Charles Lucas sold to:

John Eakin	Jacob C. Burrow	Grayson Stuart
George W. Heard	James Holt	Adam Euless
Dudley Hitt	Elijah Parker	Joel Harrison
Charles W. McLean	Elijah Parker, Jr.	(6 March 1838)
Benjamin Kimbro	Wm. P. Elkins	
Gabriel Maupin	Thomas Cribbs	
Moses Payne	Daniel Hooser	
John H. Miles	Nimrod Burrow	
Joseph W. Scott	Blan Maupin	
Jacob Coble	Lorenzo D. Walker	

Page 186 - William F. Long & others]
                vs   ]
            Lewis Shepherd &   ]
            Jos Thompson   ]
Orators, William F. Long, Wiley B. Watkins and Newcom Thompson,
Sr., all of Bedford County, states that about the 10th August
1837, one of your orators, to wit, the said Newcom THompson,
Sen., took a Deed of Trust from John J. Fuqua, upon a negro
boy named Jesse to execute two notes. 14 February 1839

Page 192 - Heirs of William Blanton]
            Exparte sale of land   ]
Orators, Wilkins Blanton, Willis Blanton, Charles Blanton and
Smith Blanton of Bedford County and Horace Blanton, Burwell

Blanton and Sanford Blanton, citizens of Alabama and Elizabeth
P. Blanton, Henderson G. Blanton, Jasper N. Blanton, minor
heirs of William Blanton, deceased, by their guardian and
mother Sarah Blanton states that they are the only heirs of
said William Blanton, deceased, except two daughters who have
intermarried, to wit, Susan wife of Leighton Ewel(Ewell) and
Mary wife of James Nichol which two latter are also parties
to this suit, but hereby relinquish their interests in the
subject matter. Also stated that father and husband of Sarah
Blanton departed this life seized and possessed of three
several small tracts of land in Bedford County, containing
in all 159+ acres, all which lies adjoining resident so and
that several tracts of land have been surveyed, follows: Beg
at an elm and iron wood, thence north 5° east 31½ poles to
an elm, thence north 30° west 50 poles to a stake, thence north
28 poles to a hornbean, thence east 4 poles to an elm and cedar
stump, B. Maupin's corner, thence north 12° west 42 poles to
a blackoak said Maupin's corner, thence north 40 poles to
middle of Duck River, thence north 36½° west 129 poles to a
whiteoak on the bank of said river, thence south 2° west 91
poles to a stake, thence south 14° west 10 poles to a beech,
thence south 10° east 114 poles to a stake, thence south 81
poles to a stake in the road, thence east 86½ poles to the
beg. Containing 109 acres. Also, one other tract beginning
at the same corner, thence east 53 poles to a dogwood, thence
south 136 poles to a stake, thence west 42 poles to a sassafras
stump school land, then north 52 poles to a black walnut,
thence west 68 poles to a stake, thence north 33 (poles) and
thence fourth degrees east one hundred and two poles to the
beginning, containing 50+ acres.
     Also states that the interest in said land beginning to
said Mary Nichol and Susan Ewel have been disposed of and that
said heirs have no interest what so ever in said land, that
the said Sarah Blanton although by love entitled to dower in
said land, has relinquished and hereby relinquished the same,
and asks to come in with the children as a tenant in common,
orator states it would be impracticable to divide said land.
                         12 August 1839

Page 195 - George P. Ruth   ]
               vs   ]
          Martin C. Groce &]
          Samuel Williams   ]
George P. Ruth, Jailor of Bedford County, against Boyd M. Groce
of Henry County, Alabama and Samuel Williams of Martin County,
North Carolina.
     Orator, George P. Ruth states that a certain negro man
who calls himself Jerry, has been lodged in the jail of Bedford
County. The said negro is claimed by two persons. Orator
unable to determine which one negro belongs to. 13 June 1839

Page 202 - Alexander Ray & others   ]
               vs   ]
          William Roberson & his wife]
Your orators, Alexander Ray, John Ray, Mary Ray, James M. Ray,
George M. Ray and James A. Trice by his guardian William Trice,
citizens of Bedford County, that they are heirs at law of James
Ray, deceased, who departed this life on the 5th day of August
A.D. 1835, from whom a certain tract of land descended to your
orators and to William Roberson and Jenny his wife as tenants
in common.
     Orators also states that the said tract of land was convey-
ed to said James Ray, and by Mary Daugherty and originally

                              23

contained 640 acres but that the same has since been altered
in shape and deminished in size by the sale of three several
small tracts off of said tract by the said James during his
life, to wit, 85 acres to Alexander Ray April 4, 1822, 115½
acres to John Ray March 27, 1822, 158+ acres to Henry Moore
June 14, 1829, making in all 359 acres which have been sold
off said tract leaving 281 acres, which last mentioned
remainder of said 640 acres tract is still subject to the dower
interest of Jane Ray, widow of said James Ray, deceased. But
said widow, Jane Ray has already applied to Circuit Court of
Bedford County to have her said dower laid off and allotted
to her out of said remaining 281 acres which was granted by
said Circuit Court at the December Term.
    Deed: Bounded: Beg on an ironwood, beech and ash, and
running west by the middle 120 poles to a buckeye, thence south
9 poles to a large beech, thence south 69° west 96 poles to
a forked lynn, thence west will the middle 82 poles to a
hickory, thence south 5½° east 279 poles to an elm and mulberry
on the north boundary line of the school land, thence east
4¼° with said line, 140 poles to a large ash, the north east
corner of the school land, thence south 5½° east 146+ poles
to a white oak, ash and ironwood, thence east 4¼° north 92
poles to the main fork of Sinking Creek, thence down said
creek with the meanders of the same, 176 poles to a beech
marked "G.B.", thence north with the middle 296 poles to the
beginning. Orator wants land sold.   18 December 1837

Page 204 - Amos McAdams   ]
              vs   ]
         Robert L. Landers, Adm]
         William Carter   ]
Amos McAdams of Bedford County against Robert L. Landers, adm.
of William Carter, deceased, also of Bedford County.
    Orator states that on 1st October 1836, he borrowed of
William Carter, deceased, late of Bedford County, for sum of
$1000.00 for which he executed his note jointly with John
Sutton. Orator states that on 2nd day January 1837 William
Carter's house was burnt and he together with his wife and
2 or 3 of his children and all his furniture, papers &c were
also consumed with the house.   13 August 1839

Page 209 - William McGrew]
              vs   ]
         B. & W. Bowers]
William McGrew of Bedford County against William Bowers of
Alabama.
    Orator, William McGrew, states that John Bowers died in
Bedford County sometime in the summer of 1836 and that before
that time he had made and published his Last Will and Testament
in which he bequeathed certain negroes to be sold and proceeds
equally divided among his children being 9 or 10 in number,
also, said John Bowers nominated as executors of his will the
said Benjamin and William Bowers who qualified. Green Bowers
sold all interest in negroes to orator.

Page 211 - Will of John Bowers.
In the name of God Amen. I, John Bowers, Sen., of Bedford
County, State of Tennessee, knowing that it appointed one for
all men to die and considering the uncertainty of natural life,
and being of sound mind and memory blessed be the Almighty
God for the same do make and publish this my Last Will and
Testament in manner and form following, that is to say,
1st, I direct all my just debts to be paid.

2nd, I give to my beloved wife Mary Bowers, all my land whereon
I now live and four negroes by the name of Miles and Isom and
C--la and Phebe and my stock of every kind, and all my household and kitchen furniture of every description and all of
my crop to her own use, during her lifetime, and at her death
to be rqually divided between the heirs of my body, on the
following conditions, my son in law to reside or live on this
plantation, and if she chooses she hereby vests the little
of all the land and negroes before named in sons, except a
equal share with my sons or childrens part which is to be her
own.
3rd, I give to my son William, two negroes by the name of
Shedrick and Harriett.
4th, I give to my son Benjamin two negroes by the name of
Anderson and Elender.
5th, I give to my son Jesse two negroes by the name of Mary
and Gilbert.
6th, I give to my son David two negroes by the name of Lewis
and Eliza.
7th, I give to my son Green two negroes by the name of Charity
and Westley and Sarah and Charles.
8th, I give to my son Henry two negroes by the name of Charity
and Charles.
9th, I give to my son Solomon two negroes by the name of
Malinda and James.
10th, I give to my son Lemuel two negroes by the name of Ila
and A---.
11th, I give to the children of Mary R. Hedrick that she now
has and may have one negro girl by the name of Millia, and
if they die without heirs of their body, the girl Millia and
increase is to return to the heirs of my body.
12th, I give to my son Giles one negro boy named Young and
also three hundred dollars in place of a negro to his share.
13th, I give to my son John three hundred dollars in place
a negro, to his share.
14th, I allow Jonathan and Easter, and Stephen and Winny to
be equally divided between all my sons, after taking out of
them the amount of three hundred dollars to Giles Bowers and
three hundred dollars to John Bowers, Mary R. Hedrick and her
children is to have one share equally with one of the sons
shares in the 14th article.
15th, I give Mary R. Hedrick ten dollars to her own use to
be paid her by my wife Mary Bowers to her own use.
16th, I desire to be buried at the discretion of my executrix,
which I here appoint William Bowers and Benjamin Bowers,
executors of this my Last Will and Testament. In witness where
of I have hereunto set my hand and seal the fifteenth day of
June, eight hundred and thirty six (15 June 1836).
Wit: Granville H. Frazier   Signed: John Bowers (Seal)
     Repts. T. Osborn

Page 214 - Elizabeth Whitaker]
              vs   ]
         Robert Powell   ]
Oratrix, Elizabeth Whitaker stated that on 16th day of February
1813, Elizabeth J. Roberson of Sussex County of Virginia, duly
executed and published her Last Will and Testament, and shortly
afterwards, died on the 1st day of April 1813, after the death
of the said testator, the said will never having been cancelled
or revoked, was duly proved in the Court of Sussex County,
aforesaid. Recorded. William Parham, the executor named and
at same court relinquished his rights and Robert Powell was
duly appointed and qualified as admr of the estate.

Your oratrix stated that she was one of Mary Powell's children, and is one of the four legatees and devises mentioned in the second clause of said will. She also stated that she intermarried with _(blank)_ Whitaker who has since died and she is now a feme sole. Also states that Semore and Martha, two of the legatees and devises under the 2nd clause of said will, died intestate and without issue, before the youngest one of the said devises arrived at lawful age and before there was any distribution of the property devised by said 2nd clause amongst the four devises, therein mentioned, and your oratrix and Thomas the only survivors amongst said devises and entitled to the sole benefit of the devise contained in the said 2nd clause. Your oratrix stated that at the time of her decease a considerable personal estate, consisting of negroes, stock, farming utensils, furniture &c which came to the hands of the admr with will annexed. Oratrix stated that the admr instead of leasing out the land, lived on and occupied it himself for many years. The rents of which were annually worth a large sum of money, and that he has since sold the property for a large sum of money. Oratrix states that she has not received any of the same except a negro girl which her husband in his life time got into his possession. She charged that she is entitled to a considerable amount from said admr.

Page 215 - Will of Elizabeth J. Roberson.
I, Elizabeth J. Roberson of the County of Sussex do hereby make my Last Will and Testament, that is to say,
1st, I give and bequeath unto my cousin Ann Collier two _(blank)_.
2nd, I give and bequeath unto my sister Mary Powell's four children, to wit, Seamore, Elizabeth, Thomas and Martha P. Powell, all the rest of my estate both real and personal of what nature or kind _(blank)_ it may be not herein before part-icularly disposed of, I desire that the land be rented or leased out until the youngest child shall arrive at the age of twenty one years, then the whole, both real and personal to be equally divided among the several children herein before named or as may be a living at that time, to them their heirs, executors, admrs and assignees forever.
Lastly, I do hereby constitute and appoint my friend merchant William Parham, executor of this my Last Will and Testament hereby sealed with my seal and dated this 16th day of February 1813.
Test: Francis Gregory   Signed: Elizabeth J. Roberson
      Isaac Colbert
      Martha McKinnon

Page 220 - Marlin Wade and others   ]
                 vs   ]
           John W. Hamblin and others]
Orators William S. Wade, Martin F. Wade, Edward B. Tuck and Ann his wife, and Marmaduke Wade, the last two minors who sue by their guardian William S. Wade, Mary Wade and Michael Wade minors also sue by Jacob Morton their guardian, all of Bedford County, Josiah C. Brassfield and Elizabeth his wife of Limes-stone County, Alabama, against the Mayor and Aldermen of the town of Shelbyville, John W. Hamblin and Thomas Knott citizens of Bedford County.
     Orators states that at April Term 1837 of Bedford County Circuit Court, they recovered a judgement against the Mayor and Aldermen of Shelbyville for $448.00 plus cost. The only property the town owns is two town lots, have been levied and will soon be sold. (Case dismissed - 4 November 1838)

Page 222 - Martha A. Cooper]
              vs   ]
         Abram B. Cooper]
Martha A. Cooper wife of Abram B. Cooper. Martha A. Cooper
of Bedford County stated that she has been a citizen of Bedford
County and that more than three years last past, that she intermarried with said Abram B. Cooper in said County and State
in the year 1834, that they continued to live together until
September 1837 when said Cooper left your oratrix and went
to the Republic of Texas, as she is informed and believes,
and has not since that time made any provisions for the sub-
sistence of your oratrix, where he still remains, and where
it is probable he intends permanently to reside.

Oratrix also states that since her said husband has been
absent, she has the utmost confidence that he had been guilty
before his departure, of the most flagrant violations of the
marriage vow, and that on many occasions and with several
women of loose and immoral characters, he did illicit cohabit,
and of and by such gross and immoral practices, did once or
twice contract disease called gonorrhea, of these humiliating
and horrid facts, your oratrix being young and inexperience,
and entertaining for her said husband the most confining and
unsuspecting affection remained in utter and happy ignorance
until since his departure from this county and until his wanton
neglect and desertion led her to inquire unto the cause thereof.
The discovery which resulted from those inquiries is so dis-
graceful and exhibits such utter moral de----ment(?) that your
oratrix cannot consent ever to live with again &c...her said
husband, and instead of her former tender confidence and
affection, she can now only feel the most _____ shame for his
character and the most _____ disgust for his _____ person.

Oratrix feeling degraded by bearing this _____ name of
her late husband, grately, humbled and injured by being his
wife, prays to divorce him.   3 September 1838
Divorce granted 12 August 1839.

Page 225 - John Tillman, Exr of]
              Samuel Escue   ]
                 vs   ]
            L. C. Temple   ]
Orator, John Tillman, Exr of Samuel Escue, against Leonard C.
Temple, James and Frances Story, all of Bedford County.

Orator states that at February Term 1836 Bedford County
Court, the said Leonard C. Temple was duly appointed admr of
Elizabeth Temple, deceased.

Orator stated that Samuel Escue departed this life in
December last (1835) having first made and published his Last
Will and Testament in which your orator was nominated his sole
executor. Orator believes Temple has mortgaged two of the
negroes to James and Frances Story. 14 February 1838

Page 228 - Francis Vannerson &]
              Sopha Pearson   ]
                 vs   ]
            Elizabeth Vannerson]
              & others   ]
Francis Vannerson of Bedford County and Sophia Pearson of
Lawrence County, Alabama against Elizabeth Vannerson and Catharine Vannerson of Bedford County, Thomas Vannerson residing
in Pittsylvania County, Virginia, William Vannerson residing
in Natchez, Mississippi and Albert Vannerson residing in Jackson County, Tennessee.

Orator, Francis Vannerson and your oratrix Sophia Pearson,

states that their father William Vannerson departed this life
intestate in Hawkins or Sullivan County, Tennessee, in the
year of 1802 or 1803. Said intestator left a widow Elizabeth
Vannerson now residing in Bedford County and seven lawful
children and heirs, all of whom are minors, to wit, your orator
and oratrix, the last of whom afterwards intermarried with
Charles Pearson who has since died and she now a sole and a
married woman, Thomas Vannerson now residing in Pittsylvania
County, Virginia, William residing in Natchez, Mississippi,
Alford since dead without issue and intestate, Albert residing
in Jackson County, Tennessee and Catharine residing in Bedford
County, all of whom are now of lawful age, all of whom your
orator and oratrix pray may be made defts to this bill.
    Orators states that their father at his death owned and
possessed of several negroe slaves for life, besides other
personal estate and shortly after his death, his widow, the
said Elizabeth Vannerson removed said slaves and all his movable
estate to Bedford County (Virginia), when she removed to Bedford
County, Tennessee, bringing her negroes with her.
                    5 February 1838

Page 234 - Jacob Forsyth & Co.]
                  vs   ] Orig. Bill
             Kelsey & Huston   ]
Orators Jacob Forsyth and John A. Forsyth, Commission Merchants
in trade under name of Jacob Forsyth & Co. of Pittsburg, Pennsylvania, states that sometime in year 1836, Henry B. Kelsey
and Abner Huston (Houston) of Marshall County, Tennessee, became indebted to your orators.   8 February 1839

Page 236 - James G. Whitney]
                  vs   ] Orig. Bill
             John W. Gardner]
Orator, James G. Whitney of Bedford County, stated that some
two years since one Joshua Holden purchased a certain horse
from said John W. Gardner called the "____ Colt" which he
executed a note. Orator states Holden has left this state
and is in Alabama.   23 July 1839

Page 239 - Benjamin and William Bowers]
                  vs   ]
             Henry Bowers   ]
Benjamin, of Bedford County, and William Bowers of Blount
County, Alabama, against Henry Bowers of Arkansas County, Arkansas.
    Orators states that Henry Bowers on the 3rd day of Oct-
ober 1836 together with one Jesse Bowers as his security, executed to complts., a note. The Complts are executors of John
Bowers, deceased.   10 February 1840

Page 240 - James Hart]
                  vs   ]
             William Guy]
Orator, James Hart states that during the year 1828, said Guy
requested your orator to build a cotton gin.
                    15 August 1838

Page 247 - Thomas Davidson]
                  vs   ]
             John M. Sharp]
Orator, Thomas Davidson of Marshall County, Tennessee, states
that in January 1833, as he thinks, took unto partnership with
him in a country store in Bedford County, John M. Sharp who

is at this time a citizen of Iredell County, North Carolina, but was then a citizen of Bedford County. Disolved 10 February 1840.

Pahe 249 - James G. Blackwell]
                vs   ]
        B. M. G. Blackwell]
Orators, James G. Blackwell against Brice M. G. Blackwell of Bedford County, George W. Record, Joel Yowell, James Osborne, James C. Record, William Williams, William S. Anderson and Hugh McCleland, all of Marshall County, Tennessee, except Hugh McCleland of Missouri.
    Orator states that at June Term 1838, he obtained a judgement against Brice M. G. Blackwell and Joel W. H. Blackwell.
    Orator states that Brice M. G. Blackwell has an equitable title to three Town Lots in Lewisburgh(Lewisburg), Marshall County, Tennessee, Lot No. 283 in Block No. 2 and Lot No. 12 in Block No. 3 in the Town of Lewisburg. 8 February 1840

Page 252 - Dicey Thomas]
               vs   ] Bill for Divorce
        D. Thomas   ]
Dicey Thomas of Bedford County, states that about 14 years before filing this bill, she was lawfully married to D. Thomas who at that time and many years before of Bedford County. They lived together in the utmost peace for about a year after their marriage when her husband desserted her and she believes has left the state. She has been informed that said D. Thomas has since been married in Kentucky or that he had been seen in that state within the last 2 or 3 years, with a woman who has passed as his wife. He is to appear in August Term 1839 for final hearing. Decree: 10 February 1840

Page 253 - Henry Meghee]
               vs   ]
        John Davis]
Henry Meghee of wake County, North Carolina, states that he is the father of one Norvill Meghee who departed this life in April or May 1836, intestate, having neither wife or children. That Norvill at the time of his death was a citizen of the county...(incomplete)
(no page 254 & 255)

Page 256 - Thomas A. Jones]
               vs   ]
        George Cathey]
Thomas A. Jones of Marshall County, Tennessee, states that sometime in the year 1837, one George Cathey of Marshall County, Tennessee, then occupied a certain tract of land in the vicinity of Farmington and that he said he had two tracts of land, containing 150 acres and bounded on north by the lands of Charity E(Evans?), on the east by William Appleby, on the south by another tract of land owned by said George Cathey, and on the west by David H. Miller and the said George Cathey being desirous to dispose of the land within the said boundary proposed to sell the same to your orator and orator agreed to purchase same. 8 October 1839

Page 263 - John Fitts]
               vs   ]
        Hiram Edy]
John Fitts of Winston County, Mississippi, stated that your orator is the owner of two negro boys, Moscow age about 10

years, and Henry age about 12 years, both of yellow complection
and worth 5 to 6 hundred dollars each, they were born in Mississippi. He also stated that some weeks before he settled
on a farm in Republic of Texas and left Mississippi with his
brother, Oliver Fitts, for Texas, with said 2 negro boys and
35 other slaves belonging to your orator. Orator states that
he was detained by business for a few days at (Lewisville?),
Mississippi and sent his brother on with the negroes. Orator
did not overtake them until they had reached Texas, and when
he arrived, he had learned that his brother whilst in a fit
of intoxication was induced by deft Hiram Edy to sell him the
two negroe boys for #1100.00 in Texas currency. Orator be-
leives Edy has taken the boys are now in Bedford County.
Oliver Fitts, the brother, had no right to sell the two boys.
Orator states that he has the mother of the two boys and three
brothers and sisters, that they are a family of negroes which
he has owned for several years.   25 January 1839

Page 265 - William and Lucy Armstrong]
                    vs   ]   Orig. Bill
          James and Catharine Baxter]
William and Lucy Armstrong of Maury County, Tennessee against
James and Catharine Baxter of Marshall County, Tennessee.
Complts states that sometime in the year 1833, Jeremiah Baxter
departed this life in that part of Maury County which has since
stricken of into the new County of Marshall, having before
that time made and published his Last Will and Testament, which
will was proven in Maury County, Tennessee in 1833. At the
time of the death of Jeremiah Baxter, he was seized and possessed of a large estate both real and personal which came into
the possession in said deft in the year 1833. Orator states
that shortly after the deft qualified as executor and executrix,
they retained an inventory of the property of said estate,
which was false and in error. Orator states in the will:
Item 5, states "I give all of the property they have taken
away from my house with all the increase they have had, and
all the balance of my property both real and personal to be
equally divided between them, namely, James Baxter, Nancy,
Lucy, Sally and Eliza". Orator states that Nancy was now
married to Edmund Woodward of Davidson County, Sally was then
married to Edmund B. Smith, late of Marshall County, Tennessee
and now a residence of _____ County, Kentucky, Lucy was then
married to your orator and Eliza to Joseph B. Hiland (Wiland)
of Marshall County.

Page 267 - Will of Jeremiah Baxter.
In the name of God Amen. I, Jeremiah Baxter of the State of
Tennessee, Marshall County being very low in body but in perfect mind and memory and calling to mind that it is appointed
for men once to die, therefore I do ordain this my Last Will
and Testament, first of all - I give my soul to Almighty God
who made it and my body I commend to the ground to be buried
in a decent manner at the discretion of my executors.
Item 1st, I give unto my beloved wife Catharine Baxter all
of my tract of land lying on the south side of Silver Creek
also I give her six negroes, to wit, Harry, Sible and her two
children, Sofrony and Mary, Easter and Charity, also, three
head of horses, Bit, Rock and Dick and all my stock of cattle
and hogs, four featherbeds and furniture, one bureau, one sugar
chest, one dressing table and all my chairs to sit on and five
hundred weight of custings, two spinning wheels and a clock
(reel), one flan wheel and one half of my crop that is now
growing to have and to hold in during her natural life and

30

after her death to be equally divided between my two children,
Fletcher and Mandy, and if either of the children before
named should marry before the death of my wife, she must
divide with them toe above named property as she can spare
it.
Item 2nd, I give unto my son Nathaniel Baxter, one negro boy
named Daniel, one horse called Bob, saddle and bridle, one
featherbed and furniture and one thousand dollars in cash.
Item 3rd, I give to my son Montgomery Baxter, one negro boy
named Jarrett, one horse named Jim and one saddle and bridle,
featherbed and furniture and one thousand dollars in cash.
Item 4th, I give unto my daughter Elizabeth Hiland, one hundred
and ten acres of land deeded to me from John Vincent, Esq.,
whereon the said Vincent now lives, also negro woman, Mariah
and her child Huston.
Item 5th, I give to my five oldest children all the property
they have taken away from my house with all the increase they
have had and all the balance of my property both real and
personal to the same five oldest children to be equally divided
between them, to wit, James Baxter, Nancy, Lucy, Sally and
Eliza and all the property I have given to my daughter Eliza
I give to her during her natural life and after her death to
be equally divided between her children and not to be sold
or hired without her consent, I also leave to my grandson
Robert Williamson, one negro by named Dick, that is now in
the hands of William Armstrong and if Armstrong should refuse
to give up the negro boy to my grandson Robert Williamson,
I give unto the said son Williamson, four hundred dollars out
of the other property I have left to my daughter Armstrong.
I appoint my beloved wife Katharine Baxter my executrix and
my son James Baxter my executor to this my Last Will and Testament, July 1st 1838.
Signed, Sealed in the presence of   Signed: Jeremiah Baxter(Seal)
Test: Peter Williams
      James Williams

Page 268 - Christian Freeman &   ]
          others Exparte Petition]
Orator Christian Freeman and oratrix Eleanor wife of said Freeman and Nimrod Higinbotham and James Higinbotham, minors who
sue by their guardian Benjamin Phillips and Jordan C. Holt
and Herod F. Holt, executors of the Last Will and Testament
of Joshua Holt, deceased, and Jacob Albright and Abner Freeman,
all state that James Higinbotham, the father and ancestor of
complts Eleanor Freeman, James Higinbotham and Nimrod Higinbotham, died many years since, seized and possessed in fee
simple of a tract of land in Bedford County on the waters of
Flat Creek, and bounded by the lands of Archibald Reives on
the east, by the lands of Lewis Wilhoite on the south by the
lands of Jacob Albright on the west, and by the lands of Elijah
Lacy on the north, about 25 acres which tract of land on the
_____ of said James Higinbotham to complts, James Higinbotham,
Jr., Nimrod Higinbotham and Eleanor Freeman formerly Eleanor
Higinbotham, as joint tenants in common. Orators states that
Joshua Holt, the late guardian of the minor heirs of James
Higinbotham _____ sold said tract of land to your orator Jacob
Albright for $500.00 which is ____ about $700.00 and $800.00
and he gave bond to Albright. Joshua Holt was grandfather
of Eleanor Freeman, Nimrod Higinbotham and James Higinbotham.
                    24 June 1840

Page 269 - Thomas Hamilton]
                    vs   ]   Inj. Bill
         E. B. Dysert   ]
Thomas Hamilton of Marshall County, Tennessee states that on
the 10th day of November 1835, he executed his note to said
Eli B. Dysert for $125.00.

Page 273 - Thomas Greer   ]
                    vs   ]   Inj. Bill
         B. B. Bradford]
Thomas Greer of Bedford County states that on __ day of ___
____, that Benjamin B. Bradford of Bedford County but whose
residence now unknown, started a suit against your orator.
Suit is to recover certain Books of Account, at which time
the suit was brought up, in the hands of your complt. The
books were the books of the firm of Bradford & Greer who were
partners in merchandise in Shelbyville. Bradford claimed the
books and account notes. Also Bradford on __ day of ___ ____,
commenced a suit against Henry C. Bradford for the same cause
of action.   4 December 1837

Page 274 - Q. T. Mayfield]
                    vs   ]   Inj. Bill
         John Sutton   ]
Quals T. Mayfield of Bedford County against John Sutton of
Bedford County. Orator states that on 27 December 1832 he
intermarried with Elizabeth F. Sutton, daughter of said John
Sutton, who is still living. He stated that whilst he was
paying his address to his said wife and before his marriage
the said John Sutton well knowing that your orator was address-
ing his said daughter, as an additional inducement to your
orator to continue his address fraudulently represented to
your orator that a certain tract of land situate in said county
together with the appurtenances thereunto belonging was the
property of his said daughter, also that he married his said
wife under a firm belief from what John had said to him and
others that said land belonged to his wife, the daughter of
said Sutton. Orator states that John Sutton even took the
trouble to take your orator upon the land and point it out
to him as the property of his intended wife. Orator also
stated that John Sutton had before that time made the same
representation to at least two other young gentlemen who address
his daughter before your orator, also before his marriage to
said daughter, he (orator) was not a citizen of Bedford County
and did not know or suspect that the facts in relation to the
title of said land were different from that John represented
them. Orator states that his said marriage he took possession
of said land and has continued to live upon it, improving it
and claiming it as his wife, until a short time ago and after
he had quarrelled with your orator about another matter, John
Sutton told him that the title was not in his wife's name.
The two tracts of land was conveyed one from William Ashbrooks
to John Sutton, 160 acres, and another from John Donalson to
John Sutton for 278 acres. John Sutton's son was William B.
Sutton.

Page 279 - Charles C. Tallafaro (Taliaferro)]
                    vs   ]
         Nathan Eavins(Evans), admr   ]
         of Francis Greer   ]
Charles C. Tallafaro of Bedford County against Nathan Eavins
of Bedford County, admr of Francis Greer, deceased.
     Your orator states that about the 30 March 1835, was

32

indebted to the deft's intestate, the said Francis Greer, for
$148.00, orator wanted to take a mortgage &c and did not know
and also wanted to save the expense of a lawyer. He executed
a bill for two negroes, Bill and Harriet, worth about ten or
eleven hundred dollars to said Francis Greer. Francis Greer
is the sister of your orator. Francis Greer died about 8th
of last April 1839 very suddenly having been well less than
24 hours before her death, with out having made conveyance.
The negroes have never been in the possession of Frances Greer
but always in possession of your orator. He applied to the
defendant Nathan Eavins who was appointed her admr to recover
said negroes.   31 March 1835

Page 282 - John and James House]
                 vs   ] Orig. Bill
         Simms & McIntoush   ]
Jack(John) House of Hot Springs, Arkansas and James House of
Logan County, Kentucky against John Simms of Bedford County
and John McIntoush and wife Susan of Roberson(Robertson) County,
Tennessee.
      Orators states that some 18 years ago, their father de-
parted this life in Bedford County, having before made and
published his Last Will and Testament in which he devised to
your orator the tract of land in Bedford County on the waters
of Sugar Creek, containing some 180 or 200 acres. This devise
was, to wit, at the death or marriage of his wife, widow, Susan
House (same Susan McIntoush) and the rents and profits were
to go to your orators from that time and the land to be absolutely theirs. The land was rented by executor until your
orators arrive at full age. Orators stated that Susan moved
some 16 years ago, your orators have not received any profits
from rented land. John Simms was executor of said Will and
Testment who with Susan House qualified as such. They sold
timber off land and some 8 years ago, sold the land without
the Court's knowledge and used the money for himself. Orators
stated that Susan has intermarried with John McIntoush which
marriage is still existing. Orators have now reached 21 years
since 18 months since and the Junior about one month. They
desire land be returned to them.   2 July 1839
      Answer of John Simms. He stated that Duke House or Green
D. House, died in Bedford County in 1821. Simms said he sold
land to pay debts of Duke House.

Page 285 - Will of Duke House.
State of Tennessee, Bedford County. In the name of God Amen.
I, Duke House of Bedford County and State of Tennessee, being
in perfect mind and memory, and calling to mind the mortality
of my body and that there is an appointed time for all men
to die, do make, ordain and constitute this my Last Will and
Testament, that is to say first and prior, I give my soul to
God who gave it, and my body to the earth to be buried at the
discretion of my executors hereafter mentioned, as to such
worldly goods wherewith it has pleased God to bless me with,
after all my jusy debts are paid.
1st, It is my wish that a part of my lands he sold to pay my
debts.
2nd, I lend to my loving wife Susan House all my land not sold
during her widowhood, but should she marry, the lands are to
be rented out and the money arising from it to be for the
benefit of my two sons Jack and James.
3rd, I give and bequeath to my wife Susan, my beds and furniture of every description with the kitchen furniture and all
my stock to have forever.

4th, I give to my two sons, Jack and James, all my lands not
sold to pay my debts to be equally divided between them when
they arrive at the age of 21.
5th, I give to my two sons, Jack and James, all the money and
property that may fall to my part of my mother-in-law's estate
to be equally divided between them when they become of age.
6th, It is my wish to buried in a decent manner.
I hereby constitute my loving wife Susan House, executrix and
John Simms, executor to this my Last Will and Testament whereof
I hereunto set my hand and office, my seal. This the twenty
eighth day of March in the year of our Lord, Christ, one
thousand eight hundred and twenty one. (28 March 1821).
Test a true copy.   23 July 1839

Page 286 - John A. Ferguson   ]
              vs   ] Bill
          Blackman C. Dobson & others]
Orator, John A. Ferguson against Blackman C. Dobson, John
McGrew and William Wilhoite, all of Bedford County.
     Orator stated that on 11 October 1838, that Blackman C.
Dobson, executed a certain note to pay John Barrett $210.00
and that your orator is now owner of said note against Dobson,
and believes Dobson has left the State and that William Wilhoite
is indebted to Dobson for $250.00 and also John McGrew is in-
debted to Dobson for $700.00 or $800.00.

Page 289 - Benjamin F. Bowers]
              vs   ]
          William P. Bowers   ]
Orator, Benjamin F. Bowers of Bedford County, states that
William P. Bowers is indebted to him for about $900.00, a
balance for a judgement rendered in the Circuit Court of Blount
County, Alabama. William P. Bowers is living in Blount County,
Alabama. Orator states that William had an interest in a tract
of land belonging to John Bowers in his life time, in Bedford
County, interest being an eleventh part of 137 acres is not
sufficient. He states that William P. Bowers had the same
interest in some slaves with the personal property, to wit,
Isham and Miles, 2 men; Celia, infant child and P-----, these
slaves are now in the possession of your orator as one of the
executors of the Last Will and Testament of John Bowers,
deceased. William Bowers did not come to Bedford County for
12 or 14 years, made conveyances but had the same done in
Franklin County, Tennessee, nor did said Jesse who also lives
in Blount County, Alabama.   1840.

Page 291 - Sarah H. Harris & others]
            Exparte Petition   ]
Oratrixes, Sarah H. Harris and Esther J. Harris, sue by their
guardian and father, D- Samuel J. Harris of Mecklenburg County,
North Carolina and Joseph R. McKinley of Bedford County.
     Oratrixes states that Joseph R. McKinley purchased of
Samuel J. Harris, the one undivided tenth part of a tract of
land of 850 acres, situated, lying and being in the County
of Bedford , on the Turnpike Road, north of Shelbyville, on
_____ as the Nathaniel Alexander(?) tract of land for $600.00
and has taken a title bond thereof from said Samuel J. Harris,
who sold the same for his daughters who _____ they would further represent to your Honor that said tenth part of said
tract of land belongs to your oratrixes, Sarah H. Harris and
Esther J. Harris who are minors and the children of Samuel J.
Harris. Samuel J. Harris was appointed guardian of Sarah H.
and Esther J. Harris in Mecklenburg County, North Carolina.

30 December 1840

Page 292 - John Wilks & others]
                    vs   ] Att. Bill
          Kelsey & Huston   ]
Orators, John Wilks, John R. B. Jones and Milton B. Holt of
Marshall County, Tennessee, states that on 21 September last
(1839(, one Henry B. Kelsey and Abner Huston (Houston) of
Marshall County, Tennessee, executed a note for $300.00.

Page 296 - John L. Neil &   ]
           Edw. A. Moseley   ]
                    vs   ] Inj. Bill
           William Eoff &   ]
           John Roberson, Jr.]
John L. Neil and Edward A. Moseley of Bedford County against
William Eoff and John Roberson, Jr., also of Bedford County.
     Complts states that William Eoff and others petitioned
Bedford County Court to have a road established as a public
highway from near Davis' Mill to the head of Puncheon Camp
Creek, which road was surveyed to go through fields of several
persons. One field belongs to the heirs of Henry C. Martin,
also Edward A. Moseley.   8 October 1839

Page 298 - Preston Frazer]
                    vs   ]
           John A. Fortune]
Orator Preston Frazer of Bedford County, states that John A.
Fortune of Green County, Alabama, in the month of February
1837, gave a note. Fortune brought said Fortune son, a lad
about 14 years of age, from Greensborough, Alabama to Lincoln
County, Tennessee, seven days travel and furnished said boy
a horse to ride, and paid all expenses of horse and boy on
the way.   3 October 1839

Page 306 - William S. Jett   ]
                    vs   ]
           Blackman C. Dobson]
William S. Jett of Bedford County, stated that sometime in
July or August last (1839), one Blackman C. Dobson of Bedford
County, executed a note.   1838

Page 307 - Jason T. Britian by his]
           guardian, James Wortham]
                    vs   ]
           Wilks Blanton & others]
Jason T. Brittain, a minor, who sues by his guardian James
Wortham against Theodrick F. Bradford, William Galbreath, John
Tillman and Wilkins Blanton, all of Bedford County, and William
F. Long of Talledega County, Alabama.
     Orator states that he is the only heir at law of James
Brittain, deceased, and that James Brittain departed this life
sometime in June or July 1833, having previously made and
published his Last Will and Testament of which he appointed
deft William F. Long executor and qualified and also orator
states that James Brittain left his business in a very deranged
condition and his estate greatly in debt. Several judgements
were brought against the estate. A tract of land was sold
to Frederick F. Bradford, about 75 acres, adjoining the Town
of Shelbyville on the east of said town, and bounded on the
west by the said town, on the south by the land of Clement
or Henry Cannon, on the southeast by Duck River and on the
northeast by the Winchester Road. 15 January 1840

Page 312 - Price C. Steele & others]
            Exparte Petition   ]
Price C. Steele and Winfield S. Brame of Bedford County, stated
that Price C. Steele was legally appointed guardian of the
minor heirs of Warren L. Brame, deceased. Winfield S. and
Hellen P. Brame, the youngest of said heirs and who is still
a minor, Winfield S. Brame has arrived at the age of 21 years
and is desirous of having a settlement with his guardian and
taking his share of his estate. There are 3 or 4 slaves, one
a man about 28 years named Ephraim, a woman named Sis aged
about 55 years, a negro girl named Prudence 8 or 9 years old
which said negroes belong to your petitioner Winfield S. and
Hellen P., minors. Hellen P. Brame by her guardian Price C.
Steele and Winfield S. Brame heirs of Samuel S. Brame, deceased.
     29 June 1841, final decree, to be divided to heirs.

Page 313 - George Davidson & others   ]
                    vs   ]
            The Bank of State of Tennessee]
George Davidson, Thomas Davis and Clement Cannon filed against
Bank of State of Tennessee. They stated that on 13th July
1829, a judgement in the County Court of Davidson County against
one Thomas Sanders and one Giles Burditt, now deceased, and
your orators by Bank of State of Tennessee for $1025.60.
                    28 September 1840

Page 315 - William Waite   ]
                    vs   ] Inj. Bill
            The Bank of Tennessee]
Orator states that his land is about to be levied by the
Sheriff of Bedford County, issued in Davidson County, Tennessee.
                    29 September 1840

Page 317 - Washington Short]
                    vs   ]
            Judah Hooper   ]
Washington F. Short of Bedford County filed against Judah
Hooper of Bedford County. Orator, W. Short states that sometime before April 1837, James Hooper departed this life and
left a will which was proven and recorded, by which he left
several negroes to his wife, the said Judah during her natural
life, remainder to his three sons, George, William and Joseph
Hooper, among the other property their request is and was a
negro girl named Sultana, worth about $350.00, also by a bill
dated 21 February 1840, duly proven and registered, William
and George Hooper conveyed to your orator three undivided remainder interest in and to said negro girl Sultana, so that
now your orator now owns two undivided third parts of the remainder interest in negro girl Sultana after the termination
of the life estate of the Judah, who is now in possession of
said girl Sultana. Orator states that Judah Hooper plans to
sell negro and plans to move to Missouri. 24 March 1841

Page 319 - Will of James Hooper.
In the name of God Amen. I, James Hooper of the County of Bedford and State of Tennessee, being of sound and giving mind
and memory, do constitute and appoint this to be my Last Will
and Testament in manner and form following, my soul, I leave
in the hands of God who gave it and as to my body, I wish it
to be decently interred at the discretion of my executors herein after named. I wish in the first place that all my just
debts shall be paid from such property as my executors shall
think most advisable. I lend to my wife Judah Hooper during

36

her natural life or widowhood, my negroes, Tom, Charles, Peter, Hannah and Sultana, my house, lands and farming utensils, my oxen and cart, wagon and gear, household and kitchen furniture, all of my stock of every description.

I will and bequeath unto my son George Hooper at the death of my wife, my cart and oxen, and the tract of land I purchased of David Keele, and one third of all my perishable property and said household and kitchen furniture. And, as to the property loaned my wife as above, I will and bequeath the heirs of my oldest son William Hooper, one half of the land whereon I now live and the third od all the perishable property loaned to my wife as above, at her death and also one third of all my household and kitchen furniture which property I wish to remain in the hands of William Hooper and his wife Elizabeth Hooper, from and after the death of my wife during their natural lives, then to be divided among the lawful heirs of the said William Hooper and his wife Elizabeth.

I also will and bequeath to my son Joseph Hooper at the death of my wife, one half of the tract of land whereon I now live, to be rqually divided between Joseph and the heirs of William Hooper, and one third of all the perishable property and also one third od all the household and kitchen furniture and farming utensils to be equally divided between my three sons, William, George and Joseph, excepting such as hereafter willed aand direct my executors that in the division of the land between the heirs of William Hooper and Joseph Hooper as named above that and regard he had to the quantity and timber so that each may have the same value as regards the soil and timber. This division not to take place until my wife's death.

I nominate and appoint Richard Bandy, executor and my wife Judah , executrix, to this my Last Will and Testament. In witness whereof I have hereunto set my hand and seal this 28th July 1836.
Test: D. McLean   Signed: James (X) Hooper
     Jos. H. Lile
          Will proven April 1837 in Bedford County

Page 320 - C. W. Black]
               vs   ] Filed 25 November 1840
          John Lanier]
Claiborne W. Black filed against John Lanier former of Bedford County and latter of Lincoln County, Tennessee. Orator states that he executed a note to one Barnett Medcalf for $444.90, due 1939.

Page 324 - William Williams &]
          Robert McCrory   ]
               vs   ]
          Alex'd E. McClure]
William Williams and Robert McCrory of Marshall County, Tennessee states that one Alexander E. McClure, formerly of Marshall County, Tennessee, on the 6 day of July 1839 executed a note for $400.00 payable to Eli B. Dysart and endorsed (note) by Dysart.

Page 325 - Bell & Horner   ]
               vs   ] Orig. Bill, filed 26 January 1839
          William Gilchrist]
Samuel Bell and James S. Horner, both of Philadelphia, Pennsylvania, and partners trading under firm of Bell & Horner, against William Gilchrist of Little Rock, Arkansas. Orators states that in 1833 placed in the hands of William Gilchrist

an attorney at law and then of Bedford County to collect a
note by Thomas Coldwell and other notes by Kenneth L. Anderson
and George Davidson, one on Robert Waite.

Page 327 - Daniel G. Stephenson]
                    vs   ] Inj. Bill, filed 15 March 1841
          Newton F. Neil   ]
Orator, Daniel G. Stephenson stated that at August Term 1840,
he obtained a judgement against Newton F. Neil of Bedford
County, for $273.00.

Page 328 - William A. Gaunt & others   ]
                    vs   ]Bill, filed 7 December
          Benjamin Broughton & others]   1840
Orator William A. Gaunt stated that he is the admr of the
estate of John Gaunt, deceased, he qualified &c in Bedford
County. He states he had paid all the debts of his intestate
except one of $27.00 or $28.00 which is in a judgement in
Circuit Court of Bedford County against your orator. Orator
stated that Benjamin Broughton of Bedford County married Mary,
a daughter of your orators intestate also that Alexander Bryant
of Tennessee married _____ another daughter of his intestate,
also Jacob Shaddy, Jr. of Bedford County, married _____ another
of intestate daughter also intestate John Gaunt left a widow
Sarah to share in the estate and also the following children,
Elizabeth, Caroline, John, William and Eliza, James who will
the daughters and widow above mentioned constitute the heirs
of John Gaunt, deceased and who are minors and have your
orator for their guardian and with the widow join with your
orator and welcome complts in this bill.

Page 333 - William Word, admr   ]
                    vs   ]filed 6 Dec
          Sophia Bryant heirs &   ]   1838
          Creditors of William Bryant, deceased]
William Word, admr of William Bryant against Sophia Bryant,
widow of William Bryant, deceased, and Mary Ann Dennis, Elizabeth and Cuthbert Bryant, minor heirs of William Bryant,
deceased, and creditors of said estate. Orator William Word
of Bedford County, states that sometime about August or September 1838, William Bryant departed this life intestate in
Bedford County, and your orator was appointed admr of his
estate in October Term 1838. Your orator sold the personal
property of the said estate which amounted to $476.28 and
found notes amounting to $171.75 and believe part of the notes
to be too much (or in wrong).
     William Bryant died seized and in possession of two tracts
of land in Bedford County, about 110½ acres held by deed, bounded, beginning a large rock, near black walnut, marked as a
corner in the south boundary line in the Schooler tract,
running south to the true meridian, one hundred and ten and
a forth poles to a stake, a dogwood and beech pointers, the
south east corner of the Harrison Word tract, thence north
to the meridian 110 poles to a stake and pointers in the south
boundary of the Schooler tract, thence east with said line
to beginning. Containing about 60 acres. Also, another tract,
beginning at a cherry tree in Jane Words west boundary line
running west 89½ poles to a sugartree, thence south with John
C. Hix's line to the south boundary line of a original school
tract, thence east to a dead mulberry, Thomas Word south east
corner of his 20 acre tract, thence north to beginning. Containing about 50½ acres.

38

Page 337 - William Scott Haynes]
                              vs   ] filed 2 January 1840
              James Russ, Jr.   ]
Orator William Scott Haynes of Bedford County states that sometime in October 1838 your orator and James Russ, Jr. entered
into partnership under the firm of Haynes & Russ, establishing
a printing business in Shelbyville and to publish a newspaper
known as "The Western Star". Your orator was to act as Editor.
                         25 October 1838

Page 343 - Hiram Holt   ]
                              vs   ] filed 13 April 1840
              Young & Wilks]
Orator Hiram Holt states that at December Term 1839 of the
Court of Bedford County, that THomas W. Young, assignee of
Jesse M. Wilks, obtained a judgement against your orator for
about $600.00. Young a citizen of _____ County, Alabama, Wilks
of Warren County, Tennessee.

Page 345 - Mansfield Whitehead   ]
                              vs   ] Bill, filed 7 Dec 1840
              Elizabeth & Lydia M. Davis]
Mansfield Whitehead against Lydia Davis, heir at law and Elizabeth Davis, widow of Jos. M. Davis, deceased, all of Bedford
County. Orator states that some years ago, William Farmer
and James Russell jointly purchased from Thomas Powell a certain tract of land in Bedford County in District No. 10, contains about 160 acres. Also, that since the purchase, said
Farmer and Russell have departed this life but that Russell
before his death sold all his interest in said tract of land
to Jos. M. Davis and the interest of Farmer, deceased, to Jane
Dement and Ann O. Bryant, his only heirs at law. Powell at
this time was a citizen of Mississippi. 160 acres, beginning
at the south east corner of a tract of land granted to Nathaniel Taylor, thence south 83½° west 140 poles to a stake on
Clem's Creek, thence down said creek with its meanders to the
north boundary line of said tract, thence north 83½° east 144
poles to beginning. 80 acres. Other tract beginning at Nathaniel Taylors south east corner, thence south 6° east 88 poles,
15 links to an elm, thence west 6° south 144½ poles to two
ash saplings, thence north 6° west 88 poles, 15 links to a
stake in said Taylor's line, thence with said Taylor's line
to beginning.

Page 347 - E. J. Frierson]
                              vs   ]filed 20 June 1839
              John J. Fuqua]
Orator states that on 5 January 1838 recovered a judgement
by warrant before William Burnett, a J.P., against John J.
Fuqua, both of Bedford County, for $82.87½. Orator states
that Fuqua owns interest in a lot in Town of Shelbyville which
he purchased from Kenneth L. Anderson and in 1837 and took
a bond. Lot located: Beginning at a stake in the north boundary
line of the old Corporation of Shelbyville 63 feet, 6 inches
west of the south east corner of a two acre tract formally
owned by G. W. Hiveley, thence west with said old corporation
line 18 poles to a stake, thence north 18 poles and 15 feet
to a stake, thence east 18 poles to a stake, thence south to
the beginning. About 1 acre. It being the place on which
John Ringstaff formally resided and which he conveyed to said
Anderson by deed dated 31 December 1836.

Page 350 - Thomas Kimmons]
                vs   ]
          Eunice Warner]
Orator states that in the spring or summer of 1835, your orator
and William D. Warner, being engaged in mercantile business
executed a note. Sometime in 1836 and after said note fell
due, Eakin & Brothers commenced suit against Eunice Warner,
the mother of William D. Warner and also against Edward Kimmons,
the father of your orator.

Page 359 - William Carlisle]
                vs   ] filed 12 August 1840
          Harbert Smith   ]
Orator, William Carlisle of Bedford County states that John
Stephens departed this life in 1831 and at August Term 1831,
Willliam and James Stephens, his sons were appointed his admrs
with the will annexed, entered into bond with Andrew Hartsfield, Martha Stephens, Charles S. Mattox, your orator, Josiah
Stephens and John Stephens, Jr., as their securities. Some
12 or 18 months afterwards Will Stephens one of the admrs also
died, and your orator and Andrew Hartsfield became and were
appointed his executors. Your orator and Hartsfield collected
and paid off the debts and settled the affairs of the estate
of Willie Stephens. They turned over $1200.00 to Harbert
Smith who had before that time intermarried with and was then
and still is the husband of Mildred, the widow of Willie
Stephens, deceased, and who was also appointed guardian of
John H. Stephens, Margaret Jane Stephens, William S. Stephens
and Leander Stephens, minors and heirs of said Willie Stephens,
deceased. Smith did not know that there was another debt of
estate of Willie Stephens. In April 1839, Jordan C. Holt
guardian of Tranquilla, H----- and Lafayette Stephens, minor
heirs of John Stephens, deceased, brought suit against admis-
tration bond given by Willie and James Stephens which suit
was determined at December Term 1839.

Page 265 - B. F. Bowers   ]
                vs   ] filed 27 January 1840
          William P. Bowers]
Benjamin F. Bowers of Bedford County stated that William Bowers
of Alabama, was indebted to him by note, 18 March 1837, and
that William P. Bowers had an eleventh interest in a tract
of land in Bedford County, about 138 acres, whereon John Bowers
lived at the time of his death, said remainder is in the possession of Mary Bowers, widow of said John Bowers and also that
said William has the same interest (1/11th) also some slaves.

Page 366 - Robert J. King]
                vs   ] Orig. Bill, filed 11 August 1840
          Mathew Mullins]
Orator Robert J. King of Bedford County, is the owner of a
tract of land in Bedford County on Duck River and bounded as
follows: Beginning at a stake in the west boundary line of
the section called No. 4 in the Deed of Partition of a 5000
acre tract granted by North Carolina to John G. and Thomas
Blount between John Overton and Jenkins Whiteside, the same
being the south west corner of a tract sold by Thomas Whiteside to William Hoozer, thence south 152 poles to a stake on
the north bank of Duck River, thence up said river with its
various meanders to a bunch of small lynn trees, the same being
the south west corner of a tract conveyed by said Thomas Whiteside to William Hoozer by deed bearing date 25th December 1832,
thence north with the line of said Hoozer's tract aforesaid

40

258 poles to a stake, the same being the north west corner
of Hoozer's tract last aforesaid, thence west 195 poles to
the beginning. He purchased this property with intention of
making it his permanent home and settled on it. He became
disappointed in it because below on Duck River lies a tract
of land belonging to Mathew Mullins on which he has erected
a mill and dam extending across Duck River which to back and
pond the water that your orators land and the comforts and
convenience of his home are greatly injured. He said the back
water has ruined a spring on your orators land situated near
the bank of the river, it has overflowed several acres of
bottom land.

Page 370 - James M. Jones & wife]
                 vs   ] Orig. Bill
         John Bruton & others]
James M. Jones and wife Polly, formerly Polly Wilhoite, of
Bedford County against Jacob Wilhoite, Jane Wilhoite, minors
who have Price Wilhoite for their guardian and Emily Burton,
formerly Emily Wilhoite, all of Bedford County and John Bruton
whose residence is unknown.
     Complts state that Polly Jones is the sister of Willey
Wilhoite, deceased, who died intestate without issue and that
she on the __ day of ___ ____ intermarried with James M. Jones
by which he became interested in the real estate belonging
to said Polly Wilhoite, deceased. Co,plt James stated that
said Willey Wilhoite was seized as of his own right a tract
of land lying on Big Flat Creek in Bedford County, adjoining
the lands of Mrs. Polly Wilhoite and others, about 120 acres
and that he left some brothers and sisters, his only heirs
at law. Jones also stakes that he purchased the interest in
said lands of them by the heirs and he obtained deeds therefore, and purchased the share and interest of John Burton
(Brunton, Brewton) and wife Emily and paid for same, $90.00
and has not yet obtained a deed but has a Title Bond.

Page 272 - George W. Haywood]
                 vs   ] filed 13 September 1839
         Simeon Marsh   ]
Orator George W. Haywood of Marshall County, Tennessee and
residing in Bedford County, states that about 1834, he recovered a decree against Simeon Marsh of Giles County and Thomas Ross
of Marshall County, Tennessee for about $750.00 or $800.00
and cost of Chancery Court at Columbia and at Supreme Court
at Nashville, they stated that Ross paid half of the judgement
to Supreme Court and your orator took out an execution for
the balance against the property of said defts directed by
Sheriff of Giles County, Tennessee and intended to be satisfied
by the said Marsh. Your orator and Marsh planned to settle
this by themselves. On 24 March 1834 or before the date, orator
purchased a piece of land (in then Bedford, now Marshall County,
Tennessee) of said Marsh & Ross for $135.75 and took their
title bond for some and executed to them three several notes
for the purchase money. Marsh became owner of said three notes
and traded one of them to "Crutcher & Marsh" (the last his
son) the note due in December 1835, your orator paid the said
note to Ephraim Patrick the subsequent holder and owner of
the same. The amount of the other two notes, Marsh agreed
should be credited and given to your orator to be cancelled.
The one first due was given up to him and promised to give
the other as soon as he could get it, he sent it was in the
hands of Thomas Ross or misplaced and later Marsh sent a
letter to your orator, Marsh promised to meet your orator and

give note to him. Marsh still holds said note and never paid the part of cost to Court at Columbia, he believes.

Page 377 - Lemuel Bowers]
           vs   ]   filed 21 January 1841
    Benjamin F. &]
    William Bowers]
Lemuel Bowers of Alabama against Benjamin F. Bowers and William Bowers of Bedford County. Orators states that he is a son and legatee of John Bowers, deceased, late of Bedford County. He stated that before his death, John Bowers made and published his Last Will and Testament in which he appointed Benjamin F. and William Bowers his executors who after the death of John Bowers, they qualified for such. Orator said the will directed that 4 negroes, Jonathan, Esther, Stephen and Winny be divided equally among his eleven children. Orator states that there were several negroes, the names he does not know. Orator states that Benjamin F. and William Bowers tried to sell the negroes and told that John Bowers died intestate.

Page 377 - Will of John Bowers (same as on page 24)

Page 380 - Rebecca & Cyntha Ann McNealy]
          vs   ]Orig. Bill, filed
  Amos McAdams & others   ]23 April 1838
Rebecca McNealy and Cyntha Ann McNealy, minors, who sue by their next friend, Hardin R. Cathey, all of Bedford County against John Tune, John B. Armstrong and wife Rebecca and Amos McAdams. Orator states that they, Rebecca and Cyntha Ann McNealy, are the only heirs at law and distributes of their father _____ McNealy, deceased, who departed this life intestate sometime in the year 1820 or 1821, at the time of his death among other property, he was the owner of a certain negro woman slave for life named Charlotte now about 30 years old, that shortly after his death, his widow Margaret McNealy took upon herself the administration of his goods and chattels rights and credits, that sometime after that and after the two years allowed for her to settle, the said Margaret sold or exchanged said negro woman Charlotte to James B. Armstrong and wife for a negro girl of inferior value.

Page 384 - Daniel Jackson]
          vs   ]Orig. Bill, filed 15 June 1841
    Green Hill   ]
Orator states that in the summer of 1839, your orator at the request of one Green Hill rented for said Hill a certain tract of school land in the 19th District of Bedford County from the Commissioners of the school lands in said district for the year 1840. Your orator had no use for said land and would not have rented it on his own account but as said Hill was a friend and requested your orator to rent it for him and that he would pay the rent to the Commissioners when due. Your orator befriended him and did bid it off at $82.50 and your orator and Hill executed a joint note to the Commissioners due 25 December 1840. Hill was to pay the rent. Your orator removed to Mississippi without any suspicion whatever that said Hill would refuse to take said land there rented as he declared and declared to others that the land was rented for him.

Page 387 - Enoch Trott & others]
          vs   ]Inj. Bill, filed 10 Feb 1841
    Robert Reed   ]

Enoch Trott and Robert Reed against Jacob Greer, admr of
Kizziah Galbreath, deceased. Orator states that in September
1838, purchased from Kizziah Galbreath, a certain tract of
land in Bedford County for which he agreed to pay $450.00 in
2 notes. Kizziah Galbreath died in the spring of 1839, intestate. Jacob Greer was appointed admr of Kizziah and that
immediately commenced suit against your orator. Since the
death of Kizza, one Levin Wood of Orange County, North Carolina who claims to be the only heirs at law of said Kizziah
and also the only distributee, has commenced a suit against
your orator, Trott, and one Clement Cannon to whom your orator
had sold a part of said land. Wood stated that at the time
that Kizziah sold the land to your orator, she was weak in
mind and wanted the sale voided.

Page 389 - George W. Carpenter   ]
                    vs   ]Orig. Bill, filed
         The heirs of Abram B. Morton, Admr]21 December 1838

George W. Carpenter of Philadelphia, Pennsylvania against
Samuel Morton, Jesse B. Morton, Jacob Morton and Alexander B.
Morton of Williamson County, Tennessee, heirs at law of A. B.
Morton, deceased, late of Bedford County and against Martha
Tignal Morton, Allen Morton and SOlomon Morton, the last two
being minors, heirs of Abram B. Morton, deceased, in right
of their father Elisha Morton, deceased, are against William
Morton, Fanny G. Morton, Samuel Morton, Thomas Morton, Abraham
Morton, Isaac Morton and Martha Morton, the five last named
being minors, all residing in Williamson County, Tennessee
and heirs of Abram B. Morton, deceased, in right of their
father Abner W. Morton, deceased, against Jacob J., Nina E.,
Abram W. and James A. Morton, who are minors, residing in
Williamson County, Tennessee and who are heirs of Abram B.
Morton, deceased, in right of their father William Morton,
deceased, and against Silas M. Morton, Bud Link and Averalla
his wife, residing in Haywood County, Tennessee, who are heirs
of the said Abram B. Morton, deceased. The said Bud Link being
an heir in right of his wife, and against Francis N. Kimbro,
Solomon M. Kimbro, Dicy Kimbro, Polly H. Kimbro and THomas
H. B. Kimbro, who resides in Davidson County, Tennessee and
who are heirs of said Abram B., deceased, in right of their
mother Elizabeth Ann Kimbro, deceased, and against John McMurray
residing in Smith County, Tennessee and Samuel, Sarah L(S).,
Mary, Washington, Amanda B., Lucy, America, William and Fanny
McMurray, the four last being minors, all residing in Davidson
County, Tennessee and all of said McMurray being heirs of
said Abram B., deceased, in right of their mother Polly R. McMurray,
deceased, and against John, Averalla H., Sarah, William, Thomas,
Charles, Silas and Mary McMurray, the six last named being
minors, children of Samuel and Dicy McMurray, residing in
Davidson County, Tennessee, and who are heirs of the said Abram
B., deceased, in right of their said mother Dicy, deceased,
and against John Morton and Solomon G. Morton, living in Davidson County, Tennessee, heirs of the said Abram B., deceased,
and against Absalom D. Morton residing in the State of Alabama,
who is a minor and is an heir of said Abram B., deceased, in
right of his father George W. Morton, deceased, together with
the other children of said George W., deceased, who also reside in Alabama, but whose christian names are unknown to your
orator, and who he prays may be made defendants, hereto when
their names are ascertained. Your orator George W. Carpenter
states that he obtained a judgement against Clement Cannon,
James McKisick and William Gilchrist, admrs of Abram B. Morton,

deceased, late of Bedford County.

Page 393 - Jacob Morton   ]
                vs   ] Inj. Bill, filed 9 Oct 1841
          D. H. Lindsley & others]
Orator of Bedford County states that William Brown obtained
a judgement against Dudley H. Lindsley of Bedford County.

Page 297 - Wiley B. Watkins   ]
                vs   ]Orig. Bill, filed
          Solomon & William Brown] 16 November 1839
Willie B. Watkins, orator, bought a race horse (mare) named
Fanny Doak, and took note.

Page 400 - Clement Cannon   ]
                vs   ]Inj. Bill, filed 17 Dec 1841
          John Tillman & others]
Orator states that on 25 January 1836, he entered into co-partnership with Theodrick F. Bradford and John Tillman for the
purpose of erecting, putting into operation and working a
cotton spinning factory on Duck River, in or adjoining the
Town of Shelbyville. On 27 March 1837, the said John Tillman
assigned, sold and transferred all his interest in said co-partnership to the said Bradford. Orator furnished a site for
the building for the factory and Bradford proceeded to build
a dam across Duck River.

Page 406 - Thomas Davis   ]
                vs   ]
          William F. Long,]
          John Tillman   ]
          Wilkins Blanton]
          Wm. Galbreath   ]
Thomas Davis of Bedford County against William F. Long of
Talladega County, Alabama, John Tillman, William Galbreath
and Wilkins Blanton, all of Bedford County.
     Orator Thomas Davis states that about the 9th of November
1835, deft William F. Long, being the executor of James Britain,
deceased, obtained a decree from the Chancery Court at Franklin,
Williamson County, Tennessee, authorizing him to expose to
public sale or private sale, a certain tract of land belonging
to said estate, about 74+ acres in Bedford County, adjoining
the Town of Shelbyville. To wit, Beginning at a _____ on the
bank of Duck River at the Scull Camp Ford running north 8°
west 31 poles to a stake in the road leading from said Ford
to Shelbyville, thence north 57½° west 70 poles to a stake,
thence north 52° west 48 poles to a stake, thence north 49½°
west 105½ poles to a stake, thence south 35½° west 27 poles
and 3 links to a sugar tree, thence north 64½° 18 poles to a
stake, thence 9½° east 36 poles to a stake, thence north 49½°
west 3+poles to a stake, thence 11½ poles to the southeast
corner of Collins' lot, thence south 40 feet to a stake, thence
west 11 poles and 2 links to the north east corner of Lot No.
3, thence south to the Town line 29 poles and 9 feet to a
stake, thence east 20 feet to a stake, thence south 40 feet
to a stake, thence west 20 feet to a stake, thence south 19
poles to 3 ironwoods, thence east ___ poles to a stake, thence
south 80° east 6 poles to a stake, thence 57° east 5 poles
to a stake, thence south 47½° east 214 poles to a white oak
on a high bluff of Duck River, thence up said river to the
beginning. By said decree said Long as a Commissioner to sell,
was ewquired to take bond &c.
     Orator states that on 18 February 1836, William F. Long

sold said tract of land to Theodrick F. Bradford (who is no
party to this suit, and is dead) and took two notes but one
of the note was paid before the death of said Bradford and
the other not has been paid. The said notes were assigned
by said Long to Samuel Escue, by whom it was assigned to
George Davidson who assigned it to William Hoover who sued
your orator.

Page 410 - John A. Ferguson   ]
                vs   ]
         William P. Sims &   ]
         Walter B. Sims   ]
William P. Sims of Davidson County Tennessee and Walter B.
Sims of Marshall County, Tennessee.
Orator stated that William P. Sims brought action of excitement
was commerced against him in court for one moiety of the mills
and a tract of land, called "Sims Mills" on Duck River about
two miles above Shelbyville. William P. Sims' mother is
Rebecca Sims.

Page 414 - Freeman Burrow   ]
                vs   ] filed 12 November 1838
         Dudley P(L). House,   ]
         Robert F. Arnold &   ]
         William Burrow   ]
All of Bedford County. Your orator Freeman Burrow states that
he is an old man about 70 years old, whose body and mental
energies are equally impaired, that being possessed of four
certain negroes as his own property, about February or March
last. Your orator made a Deed of Trust to Jacob Coble for
the same to secure said Coble in a debt of about $70.00 and
also a tract of land, one about 50 acres and other about 5
acres, which Coble had purchased from your orator, the same
which your orator purchased of Robert Cannon which had been
paid for by the Whiteside heirs. Coble has since brought
back the money and wanted back the 50 acres. Coble was still
dissatisfied and said property had a valuable distillery on
it worth $150.00 or $200.00 at least. Your orator states that
about 9 October 1838 Robert F. Arnold and William Burrow, the
latter being a son of your orator and Arnold being brither-
in-law to William came to your orator's house and having asked
for a dram and having been informed that there were no spirits
about the house, proposed to send a negro girl named Betsy,
about 11 years old, and a boy, Jackson about 7 years old after
same to a neighboring still house that Jacob Coble, your
orator consented, not knowing of their wicked design. They
carried the negroes to Huntsville, Alabama and sold them to
Stephen S. Ewing.

Page 419 - James L. Armstrong & others]
                vs   ]Orig. Bill, 4 Mar 1838
         Leonard C. Temple, John B. &   ]
         Charlotte B. Dickson   ]
Orators, James L. Armstrong and Mason O., his wife, and Robert
H. Temple, William P. Temple, James T. Temple and Hannah M.
Temple, minor heirs of Dempsey P. Temple, deceased, who sue
by their guardian Mary Temple, all of Bedford County against
Leonard C. Temple, also of Bedford County and John B. Dickson
and Charlotte B. his wife of Arkansas.
     Your orators and oratrixes states that they are the heirs
at law of Elizabeth Temple, deceased, late of Bedford County,
who departed this life in Bedford County about the month of
January 1836, James L. Armstrong being an heir at law in right

of his wife, Mason P. who is one of the children of the said
deceased and the said Robert H., William P., Jane T., Hannah
M., being heirs in right of their father Dempsey P. Temple,
deceased, who was one of the children of the said Elizabeth
Temple, deceased. The said Leonard C. Temple and Charlotte
B. Dickson being also children and heirs of said Elizabeth
Temple, deceased, and the said John B. Dickson being an heir
in right of his wife. Your orators and oratrixes also state
that Elizabeth Temple died intestate, leaving money, choices
in action and personal property to the value of several thous-
and dollars, and that at the February Term 1836 County Court,
the said Leonard C. Temple was by said court appointed and
qualified as admr and singular, the goods and chattels, rights
and credits of the said intestate, he qualified, but did not
make proper returns on estate.

Page 431 - John T. Burnett   ]
                vs   ]
          Joseph M. Burnett]
          James Clardy   ]
John T. Burnett of Bedford County filed against James Clardy
and Joseph M. Burnett of Bedford County. Orators states that
about 19 March 1838, he sold a tract of land in Bedford County,
about 200 acres, to his brother Joseph M. Burnett and made
a deed for same Joseph M. Burnett has pretended to sell said
land to his father in law James Clardy of Bedford County and
made deed for same.

Page 435 - J. & A. Owen   ]
                vs   ] Orig. Bill, filed 19 April
          Jesse Alrige(Alridge)]   1839
Orators Jesse N. and Allen C. Owen of Lawrence County, Alabama,
states that Jesse Alridge and Thomas J. Harris, partners in
trade, executed to your orators their due bill. Orator states
that alridge to void payments of his debts, ran off his negroes
from Alabama to Bedford County and where they are now.

Page 437 - John Gaunt's heirs]
                vs   ] Orig. Bill
          Lewis Gaunt's heirs]
Orators and oratorixes, Benjamin Broughton and wife Mary, Alexander Bryant and wife Ann, Jacob Shaddy and wife Patsy, Elizabeth Gaunt, Caroline Gaunt, John Gaunt, William Gaunt, Eliza
Jane Gaunt, the five last of whom are minors who sue by their
next friend Sally Gaunt, all of whom are citizens of Bedford
County and that they are the only heirs at law of John Gaunt,
deceased, who departed this life in Bedford County and some
2 years ago (18__) and previous to his death, he bought and
paid for interest in three several tracts of land of his father,
Lewis Gaunt, about 580 acres which lands are in Bedford County.
Orators states that the heirs at law of Lewis Gaunt, deceased,
and William A. Gaunt and Lewis Gaunt and James Gaunt who reside
in Bedford County and Robert J. B. Gaunt a minor who has George
W. Record and wife Mahulda for his guardian and John Aldridge
and wife Peggy and Caroline, Jane, Jesse, Nathaniel Aldridge
and others and two others whose names are not yet at present
known to orators who are minors and have James Aldridge their
father for their guardian and who reside in the State of Alabama and Jesse Gaunt who resides in _____ County, Tennessee,
and Samuel _____ and wife Nancy who also reside in _____ County
and Abraham Gaunt who lives in Wayne County and the children
of Patsy Ray, deceased, who was a daughter of Lewis Gaunt,
the names of which children are unknown and are minors and

46

have no guardian. Orators states that John Gaunt, deceased,
owned interest in 2 lots of land near Town of Richmond, Bedford
County and bounded: Beginning at a stake in the cross roads
at Richmond, running south 10 poles to a stake, thence east
8 poles to a stake, thence north 10 poles to a stake, thence
west 8 poles to the beginning, a half acre. Other lot, beginning at a stake in the west boundary line of Philip Philips
and M. ___ Campbell running west 8 poles to a stake, thence
south 20 poles to a stake, thence east 8 poles to a stake in
said Philips and Campbell's line, thence with said line 20
poles to the beginning. They stated that these two tracts
of land could not be divided between them and that it would
be to their advantage to have the land sold and the proceeds
divided between them.   29 June 1842

Page 440 - Theodocia H. Clardy]
                 vs   ] Orig. Bill
        John M. Clardy   ]
Theodocia H. Clardy against George W. Hobbs and Sarah his wife,
John M., James R., Allen, Ann, Noble L., Nancy E., Caroline
P., Theodocia and Richard S. Clardy.
        Oratrix Theodocia Clardy, widow of Richard S. Clardy who
departed this life in the year 1834, that previous to his death
he made and published his Last Will and Testament which after
his death was duly proven in County Court of Bedford County.
In said will, he authorized the oratrix to sell the tract of
land on which he the said Richard S. Clardy resided on at the
time of his death, which tract of land by said will was devised
to your oratrix until the youngest child of testator becomes
21 years of age and then he equally between her and the children
of testator. Oratrix states that the tract on which she resided
was a small tract and his motive for having it sold was that
a larger tract better suited to his growing family might be
procured. She said she did sell said land for $900.00 and
with the proceeds and $300.00 arising from the sale of the
personal property of their estate of said Richard S. Clardy,
she purchased from one Isaac James in 1835 a tract of land,
200 acres, and took from said James a deed which has been duly
proven and recorded and she agreed to give $1800.00 and execut-
ed to him her own note with her brother Robert H. Majors as
her security for $600.00 in addition to the $900.00. Oratrix
states the land now is worth $2,000.00. Now she admits that
due to hard times, she is unable to raise the $600.00 and that
her brother Robert H. Majors has been compelled to pay for
it for her. Oratrix wishes to sell part of the land to pay
off her debt. (9 children now living of Richard S. Clardy and
entitled to share of this land: John M. Clardy, James R. Clardy,
Sarah Hobbs wife of George W. Hobbs, Mary Ann, Noble L., Nancy
E., Caroline P., Theodocia and Richard S. Clardy, all of whom
are minors under 21 years and without guardian except John M.
Clardy). Court marked tracts. The said tracts does not include the mansion house or any other buildings. Theodocia
has right to mansion house.   10 October 1841

Page 443 - Craig & Dillard   ]
                 vs   ] Orig. Bill
        Flora Craig & others]
William H. Craig and James Dillard of Bedford County, the latter
for himself and admr of estate of John Craig, deceased, against
Flora Craig and Polly Craig widow of William Craig, deceased,
and _____ Craig, William Craig, John Craig and James Craig,
six last of whom are minors and the only heirs at law of John
Craig, deceased.

Orator, William H. Craig, states that William Craig departed this life sometime in March 1834, leaving his widow and ten heirs at law. He owned at the time of his death, a tract of land in Bedford County, bounded by lands of John ____ on the north, on the west by the lands of James Adams, on the south by lands of Zachariah Davis and Alfred Anderson and on the east by lands of Peter Garrin, by Solomon Durrett, about 200 acres. Orator James Dillard states that John Craig who was one of the heirs of William Craig, deceased, departed this life sometime in January last (1838) intestate and that your orator took upon himself as admr of his estate and gave bond and administered at February Term 1839. Not enough to pay debts of John Craig.   27 December 1841

Page 445 - William J. Peacock]
                    vs   ] Orig. Bill
           Notly W. Maddox   ]
Your orator states that on the 23rd December 1836, Thomas A. Peacock sold Notly W. Maddox, a negro man named Alick and executed a single bill with Notly Maddox and C. T. Maddox as his securities. Orator said the obligation has failed.
                    12 March 1838

Page 446 - Abra Parsons & wife   ]
                    vs   ] Orig. Bill
           Martin Walton & wife & others]
Orator, A. Parsons for himself and as admr of Willis H. Moore, deceased, and Eliza Ann Parsons of Rutherford County, Tennessee, John J. Williams of Hardiman County, Tennessee, and James Porter and ____ Porter, admr of Jeremiah Baxter, deceased, of Marshall County, Tennessee.
    Orator stated that Nancy Moore, the mother of your oratrix, Eliza Ann and of Willis H. Moore, deceased, departed this life sometime in the year 1822 or 1823, leaving the said Eliza Ann and Willis H., her only children and heirs at law. Orator also states that Nancy Moore was the daughter of Benjamin Cox and that she intermarried with Thomas C. Moore whose children, Eliza Ann and Willis H, also that Nancy Moore departed this life before her father Benjamin Cox died.
    Orator states that Benjamin Cox departed this life in the fall of 1824 intestate in Dickson, Tennessee and shortly after the widow Winford received her dower share, she made bond &c. Winford Cox paid part of bill.
    Thomas C. Moore died sometime in 1833 in Bedford County, also Sterling Brewer, a part of said bill, died sometime years since.
    Winford Cox has since the death of Benjamin Cox, intermarried with Martin Walton and that your orator, Abra Parsons, some three or four years since intermarried with your oratrix, Eliza Ann. Willis H. Moore departed this life intestate in Bedford County and at the ___ Term of Bedford County Court, admr of his estate, was granted to your orator Abra Parsons.
    Orator & oratrix prays that Martin Walton and wife Winford, John J., William and James Baxter, Katharine Baxter Porter, admrs &c of Jeremiah Porter, deceased.

Page 450 - William H. Duncan &]
           Guin Foster   ] Orig. Bill
                    vs   ]
           James Reeves   ]
William H. Duncan and Guin Foster of Bedford County and James Reeves of Williamson County, Tennessee.
    Orators stated that sometime in January last and James

Reeves, a total stranger to your orator, went to William H.
Duncan's house and made great complaint that a negro boy which
belonged to your orator had stolen or robbed from his pocket
$145.00 in bank notes.   9 December 1841

Page 455 - Farnick Frazer &]
           Sarah Cooper   ]
                 vs   ] Inj. Bill, filed 3 May 1841
           James Mullins, Exr]
           J. B. Pinson   ]
Orators stated that on 23 March 1835, they together with John
B. Cooper executed a note of Abraham (D.) Cooper to one Sterling Goodrum for $375.00 due December 25, 1835. Goodrum sold
said note to John B. Pinson who was a note shaver. Orators
thought the note had been paid until after Abraham left the
county. A suit has been commenced against orators and the
said Pinson who died after the commencement of the suit.
James Mullins, exr of Pinson. 21 April 1841

Page 457 - Jett & Mosely]
                 vs   ] Orig. Bill
           Holt & Cannon]
William S. Jett and William Mosely of Bedford County against
Hiram Holt and Minos Cannon of Bedford County. Orators states
that Hiram Holt failed to account for certain of your orators
which he understood to convey to the _____ and at the late
December Term of Court, they obtained a judgement against Holt
for $544.50 debt. Holt's brother is Herod F. Holt.

Page 460 - William Anderton]
                 vs   ] Orig. Bill
           Thomas E. Simpson,]
           Michael Womack &   ]
           Anthony Floyd   ]
William Anderton of Franklin County, Tennessee against Thomas
E. Simpson, Michael Womack and Anthony Floyd of Bedford County.
    Orator stated that he on about 14 September 1839 sold
two tracts of lands in Bedford County to deft Thomas E. Simpson
which was paid in part by notes on Michael Womack. Womack
made a deed of same to his son in law Anthony Floyd.
    Land situated, in two surveys: One, 48 acres, on waters
of Little Flat Creek. Other tract, borders the above tract.

Page 462 - J. J. Cooper & others]
                 vs   ] Orig. Bill
           E. F. Gibbs & others]
Orators, Johnathan J. Cooper and Edward Whitman, executors
of the Last Will and Testament of Dennis T(S). Springer,
deceased, for themselves and for Sarah, widow of said Dennis,
and for Susan, Washington, Jane, James, Catharine, Robert,
John, Sarah and Ann, children and legatees of said Dennis T.
Springer against E. F. Gibbs and others, creditors of said
Dennis T. Springer.
    Orators states that Dennis S. Springer departed this life
sometime in July last (1840-1841) having made and published
his Last Will and Testament of which he instructed and appointed
your orators, Johnathan J. and Edward (Whitman), executors
who qualified and gave bond in Bedford County Court, all of
Bedford County. Orators states that Dennis bequeathed that
certain of his property of his land and personal property should
be sold to pay his debts, and a part of the balance of the
money should be laid out for the benefit of his widow in other
lands and the remains of his money to his legatees. Also that

Dennis was indebted at the time of his death to more than the amount of his property and that his estate is insolvent. Dennis had been sued by several persons for debts.

Page 466 - Carlos D. Steel   ]
                vs   ] Inj. Bill, filed
        John Tillman, Exr & others]   8 April 1841
Orator Carlos D. Steel, states that William Escue, late of Bedford County, departed this life sometime in December 1837, that previous he made and published his Last Will and Testament in which he nominated and appointed one John Tillman of Bedford County. Said will was proven in January Term 1838. Tillman states the estate is insolvent.
     Edmond Tipton and wife Rachel, formerly Rachel Escue, widow of William Escue, and child Sarah, the only child of William and Rachel Escue. Edmond Tipton is guardian of Sarah. Edmond Tipton and his wife reside in Hickman County, Tennessee.

Page 473 - William H. Wisener,]
           Blakemore & Steele &]
           Fogleman   ]
                vs   ] Orig. Bill
           John Tillman &   ]
           S. Doak   ]
William H. Wisener, George W. Fogleman, Carlos D. Steele and John A. Blakemore, all of Bedford County, states that they became the securities of one Leonard C. Temple on an administ- ration bond jointly with Samuel Doak (Doak marked out) Escue deft Tillman testator about the __ day of February 1838. Also that John Tillman qualified as executor and that the heirs of Elizabeth Temple and all who were interested with faithful administration of her estate, instituted suits in Bedford County Circuit Court against your orators and Tillman about __ day of ___ 1839 and suit still pending. Escue's estate is insolvent, so your orators will have to pay said sum, re- covered against them by the heirs of Elizabeth Temple and on bond of said Leonard C. Temple who is insolvent for sometime. Leonard C. Temple has removed to Madison County, Mississippi sometime before the two years allotted by law for settling up the estate of his intestate.   12 October 1841

Page 479 - Leonard C. Temple]
                vs   ] Orig. Bill
           Theo. Bradford   ]
Orator of Bedford County states that sometime in May 1836, your orator being somewhat embarrassed in circumstances and in need of money, applied to Theodrick F. Bradford of Bedford County for a loan with 10 years as security.

Page 491 - John Crook & wife Elizabeth]
                vs   ] Orig. Bill
           Mary Ann Greer & others]
John Crook and Margaret his wife of Henderson County, Tennessee against Mary Ann Greer, John H. Moore and Thomas Greer, execu- tors of Joseph Greer, deceased, the two former of whom are citizens of Lincoln County, Tennessee and the latter of Bedford County.
     Orators states that Jacob Harmon, the father of your orat- rix, Margaret, died many years ago, seized and possessed in fee simple, of a tract of land in Bullitt County, Kentucky, containing 1000 acres granted to him by patent bearing date the 25th day of May 1791(1790) lying on Floyd's Fork of Salt River. They also stated that Jacob (Harmon) died intestate

leaving 10 children and heirs at law of whom your oratrix,
Margaret, is one, and she consequently is entitled by descent
to one tenth of said tract of land. Also, orators states that
Joseph Greer, deceased, the late husband of Mary Ann Greer
another of the children, and heir at law of Jacob (Harmon)
proposed to the other heirs at law of said Jacob Harmon to
convey them interests in said tract of land and to him to enable him to sell said tract of land and he the said Joseph
promised to make sale of the same and account with the other
heirs for their shares. They are informed that he made an
absolute purchase of the slaves of same of said heirs, but
your orators said that they never did sell or intended to sell
their interest in said land to said Joseph on the 9th of
August 1825 in pursuance of said proposition made by said
Joseph, they executed to him a Deed of Conveyance of their
interest in said tract but at the sametime he executed to them
an obligation in these words, "Whereas, John Crook and Margaret
his wife hath signed a Deed of Conveyance to me for their
share or one tenth part of a tract of land for one thousand
acres of land lying in Bullitt County, Kentucky, granted to
her father Jacob Harmon by patent bearing the date the 25th
day of May 1791(1790), lying on FLoyd's Fork of Salt River,
thereby to enable me to sell and convey away the same to who-
ever may purchase of me. Now, I do hereby acknowledge that
so soon as I can sell and convey away the same that I am bound
to account to them for their share as quick as received after
deducting the cost and charges that may occur on their share
in so doing. Witness my hand and seal this 9th of August 1825.
                              Signed: Jacob Greer (Seal)
     Orators stated that Jacob Greer departed this life 1831
without having made sale of land, that previous to his death,
he made and published his Last Will and Testament by which
he appointed his widow Mary Ann Greer, his son Joseph Greer
and Thomas Greer and John H. Moore, his executors. Will was
proven and probated and Mary Ann, Thomas and John H. Moore
qualified and made bond. Joseph Greer's will had the following
clause: "The lands in Kentucky belonging to the heirs of Jacob
Harmon, deceased, my beloved wife, being one of the heirs and
I being authorized as agent to dispose of the same for the
benefit of all the heirs. I wish this land to be sold and
such as has conveyed to me without consideration to have an
equal proportion of the money arising from said sale the balance
divided amongst all my heirs".

Page 493 - Moses Neely   ]
                vs   ] Inj. Bill, filed 11 September 1841
           Daniel H. Hime]
Orator states that suring the summer of 1840, he contracted
with the deft Daniel H. Hime to purchase a male ass.

Page 496 - John Tillman   ]
                vs   ] Att. Bill
           Hiram Holt & others]
John Tillman of Bedford County against Minos Cannon of Bedford
County and Hiram Holt of Alabama. Orator states that on 19
July 1839, Hiram Holt executed an obligatory which he promised
to pay Mathew Cunningham $960.00 on or before 25th December
1840. Also a note to same amount to William Word.

Page 498 - Willis Cannon   ]
                vs   ] Inj. Bill
           Abid Parsons & wife]
Orator, Abid Parsons, admr of Willis Moor(Moore), deceased,

                           51

of Bedford County. Orator states that Willis Cannon before
April Term 1840 was summoned to Circuit Court in two cases.
Orator stated that Thomas C. Moore was appointed admr of his
deceased wife Nancy Moore in February 1826, that Willis Moore,
the plaintiff's intestate and his present wife were the only
legal heirs and distributees of said Nancy Moore, that said
Willis Moore departed this life in 1833 during cholera in
Shelbyville, without issue or marriage, whereby the wife of
said Parsons became entitled to the share of her said brother
Willis, that whatever sums is recovered in either of said suits
will belong to said Abid Parsons in right of his wife, the
one half as the heir of said Nancy and the other as the heir
of said Willis, deceased, on whose estate for the purpose of
collecting the same the said Parsons was appointed admr.
Orator believes Parsons has paid off &c.
(Page 502) - Nancy Moore, wife of Thomas C. Moore and mother
of defr, Abid Parsons and Willis, deceased, was the daughter
of Benjamin King Cox who died and left either a legacy or a
distributive share of his property to his daughter Nancy then
while and the wife of said Thomas C., her husband the said
Thomas C. did not reduce said property to possession during
the lifetime of his wife Nancy, for she died shortly after
her father. When Nancy died, Thomas C. collected from the
estate of her deceased father, the legacy, a share left to
Nancy before her death, was appointed her admr. He collected
the share of Benjamin Cox, for himself and his children.
Thomas C. Moore before he died gave his wife's share to his
children. Moore was appointed guardian of his children.
A. Parsons states that he married the daughter of Thomas C.
Moore.

Page 507 - Newton F. Neil]
               vs   ]   Orig. Bill
           Preston Frazier]
Orator on 7th day of January 1839, was the owner of two(2)
cedar rafts consisting of 1600 pieces of cedar lumber, one
of which was in the mill dam of William Horseley on Duck River
near Columbia, and the other in a mill dam a few miles higher
up said river. Orator stated that Preston Frazier proposed
to him to become a partner with him in transporting said rafts
to market, that he would be at the expense of conveying said
rafts to market for one half of what they would sell for, and
that he would account with orator for the other half as soon
as convenient, after the sale of said rafts, a written contract
was produced as part of this bill. The market was in the State
of Louisiana or Mississippi or Memphis, said timber being intended mainly for railroads. Frazier took rafts into his possession and proceeded down Duck River, your orator not knowing
what Frazier had done. Orator received a letter from him dated
Memphis, July 8th 1839, saying he had sold $815.00 worth to
a railroad company, but had to sell on a Christmas Credit and
proposed your orator to shave off the notes and get money for
them, when in fact, your orator has learned by accident said
Frazier received from said company at Memphis $472.23 in ad-
vance for said lumber sold by him.

Page 512 - John Tillman, Exr of]
           Samuel Escue   ]
               vs   ] Orig. Bill, filed 10 July
           Carol D. Steele   ]   1839
John Tillman, executor of Last Will and Testament of Samuel
Escue, deceased, states that Samuel Escue and Carlos D. Steele
formed a partnership in mercantile business in 1835. Samuel

Escue departed this life in December 1837 after making his
Last Will and Testament of which your orators was appointed
sole executor. Will proven January Term 1838 in Bedford
County.

Page 527 - Baxter & Ragsdale]
                vs   ] Orig. Bill, filed 14 April 1842
           Matt Martin &   ]
           E. A. Mosely   ]
Orator Baxter H. Ragsdale of Coffee County, Tennessee files
against Matt Martin and Archibald Mosely both of Bedford County,
guardian of the minor heirs of Henry Martin, deceased. Orator
stated that Baxter H. Ragsdale of Coffee County, Tennessee,
that sometime in the month of December 1839, he contracted
with the defts for the rent of some land and the hire of a
negro, amount of $106.53+.

Page 532 - Jordan C. Holt   ]
                vs   ] Inj. Bill, filed 21 August 1840
           James M. Johnson]
Jordan C. Holt, admr of Daniel John(son), deceased, against
James M. Johnson of Bedford County. Orator states that sometime in the summer of 1838, his intestate, Daniel Johnson,
entered into partnership with James M. Johnson, business of
mercantile in Rowesville.

Page 540 - Mary Dobson   ]
                vs   ] Orig. Bill
           Robert T. Cannon et al]
Oratrix, Mary Dobson against Robert T. Cannon, Justina E. Ashburn, Mary T. Ashburn, Hazzard T. Ashburn and Clement Ashburn,
all of Bedford County. Oratrix Mary Dobson stated that on
14 June 1810 she intermarried with Minos Cannon who departed
this life on 7 April 1823 and on the 8th July 1825 she intermarried with Thomas F. Ashburn who departed this life on 8th
July 1833 of cholera and on the 16th February 1834 she intermarried with Archibald Dobson, who departed this life January
11th 1841. By the death of her husband Minos Cannon, she became entitled to dower of his lands and the same was duly set
apart to her and consists of about 130 acres lying in Bedford
County on both sides of Duck River, the boundaries will be
furnished hereafter to your Honor. On the death of Thomas F.
Ashburn she acquired a certain interest in six negroes, Sarah
aged 55, Sydney aged 30, Wilson aged 26, Sally aged 16, Caty
aged 24, Susan aged 15. Caty was conveyed to your oratrix
by her father to have and to hold for during the life of your
oratrix and at her death the same to go in remainder with her
increase to go to the Ashburn children. The boy Wilson was
conveyed to your oratrix by her father, also, to her own separate use by will which was proven, by which your oratrix was
to have one-fifth of all said Ashburn property and the balance
was to go to his children by your oratrix, to wit, Justina E.,
Mary F., Hazzard F. and Clement Ashburn. All of the property
has remained in possession of the family and is now in their
possession. The negroes were never divided. When Dobson and
your oratrix intermarried he took out letters of administration
with the will annexed upon the estate of Ashburn and took possession of the negroes and other effects as such. Your oratrix
is informed and believes that Dobson took no inventory nor
made any report or settlement of the estate whatever. For
sometime before his death, Dobson became and was subject to
constant interrogation. For at least 6 months previous to
his death, he was affected with mania a fate(?) and was in-

53

capable of attending to his business. His business affairs
became greatly confused and in debt. He made a deed in 1840
to Robert T. Cannon, son of your oratrix.

Land to Robert T. Cannon: 130 acres in Bedford County
on both sides of Duck River, adjoining lands of Clement Cannon,
Andrew Reed and Keziah Galbreath, deceased, being the dower
for life of the said Mary Dobson in a tract of land belonging
to her first husband Minos Cannon and the place on which Washington Goodwin now lives, the interest of the said Archibald
and Mary in said dower being only for the life of the said
Mary, also one negro woman, Sally about 50 years, a slave for
life, a negro man Nelson a slave for life age about 30 years,
a negro boy Sidney about 35 years of age, and a negro woman,
Kate about 24 years old, a negro girl, Sarah 16 years of age,
and a negro girl Susan about 13 years old, also one lot in
the Town of Shelbyville, Bedford County. Lot No. 23 also lot
No. 34, 4 beds and bedsteads and furniture and other articles,
and the interest of the said Archibald and Mary Dobson in and
to the above named negroes.

Page 546 - David Orr   ]
                vs   ] Inj. Bill, filed 28 June 1841
           Robert L. Landers]
David Orr against Robert L. Landers, admr of estate of William
Carter, deceased. David Orr of Bedford County, states that
William Carter departed this life intestate in January 1837,
seized and possessed of a valuable real and personal estate
and at February Term 1837 in Court Robert L. Landers was
appointed and qualified as admr of estate of William Carter,
deceased. Orator states that there are eight (8) heirs and
that Larkin B. Orr and Martha Orr his wife, who are or were
entitled to one distributive share of same estate in said right
of the said Martha Ann who is one of the children of the said
William Carter and on the 2nd day of August 1837 transferred
and conveyed by deed to your orator all their claim and interest
in and to the estate in right of Martha which said deed is
registered. Orator said it has been over 4 years since Robert
L. Landers was appointed admr of Carter's estate and he has
not as yet made settlement.

End of Chancery Court Minutes   1830 - 1837

CHANCERY COURT MINUTES,   1837 - 1845

Page 1 -   February 1837 - Dower - Elizabeth W. Norvill, widow
of David Norvill, deceased of Bedford County. To, James D.,
John W., Thomas, Sidney S., David J., Edward M. B., Alexander
S., Felix B. and Mary Ann K. Norvill, heirs at law of David
Norville, deceased. The tract of land on which the said David
Norvill resided at the time of his death, with two others,
adjoining hereto are bounded as follows: Borders M. & D.
Gilchrist, heirs of Vaughn, Elijah Bomar's corner, crossing
Butler's Creek. Out of which tract or amount of lands we proceeded to lay off and by marked boundaries set apart to Elizabeth W. Norvill, the widow of the late David Norville, deceased,
the following described tract as her dower out of his said
lands aforesaid, upon which tract of land are situated the
dwelling house in which the said David Norvill resided next
before his death and now occupied by the said Elizabeth Norvill
together with all the buildings &c for use during Elizabeth's
natural life. Bounded by Bomar's corner, crossing Butler's
Creek. Plat drawn in original instrument. Lor No. 1 goes

Elizabeth Norville. Lot No. 2 goes to Mary Ann K. Norvill,
Lot No. 3 goes to David J. Norvill, Lot No. 4 goes to James D.
Norvill, Lot No. 5 goes to Felix B. Norville, Lot No. 6 goes
to Thomas Norville, Lot No. 7 goes to Alexander S. Norville,
Lot No. 8 goes to John W. Norville, and Lot No. 9 goes to
Edward M. B. Norville.

Page 8 -   John Low   ]
                 vs   ] 2nd Monday February 1837
           George E. Low & others,]
           heirs at law of   ]
           William Low, deceased   ]
Commissioners to divide a tract of land situated in Bedford
County on waters of East Fork of Rock Creek, held in common
tenancy by John Low, George E. Low and the heirs of William
Low, deceased, to wit, George E., Junior, Seymore S., Daniel,
Eliza Ann, and Martha Lowe and make report at next term of
court. John Lowe gets land that borders near the grave of
Daniel Lowe, deceased, the Shelbyville-Pulaski Road, the house
where James Harbin once lived, J. Darnell's still house, containing about 152 acres, upon which the late dwelling house
of Martha Lowe, deceased. To George Lowe gets land that borders the spring, corn crib, Shelbyville-Pulaski Road, John
Lowe's land, containing 118 acres including the barn, stables
and corn cribs. To the remaining heirs of William Lowe,
deceased, bounded by George E. Lowe, small spring, containing
110 acres including the dwelling house of the late William
Lowe, deceased and now occupied by the widow and family.
   Seymore S. Lowe, Daniel J. Lowe, Eliza Ann Lowe and
Martha Lowe, heirs of William Lowe, deceased.
This __ day of February 1837. COmmissioners: Zachariah Davis,
Solomon Durrett, John Larue, Michael Moore and Thomas Dryden.
Plat included in original instrument.

Page 11 - Ligget, Whithorn & Bridges]
                 vs   ]
           Edwin C. Hunter   ]
     Case heard August 15, 1837. Case denied.

Page 12 - Peter Graves]
                 vs   ] Deft pay Court cost.
           John Bennett]
Page 12 - Report of Jury appointed to the widow of Lemuel
Wheeler, the said Sally Wheeler, by Sheriff of Marshall County,
Tennessee. They assigned to the widow Sally Wheeler the following, with the erection and improvement thereon a tract of land
in Marshall County, Tennessee on the waters of Duck River,
containing 55 acres and 48 poles and bordered on the banks
of Duck river.   __ June 1837

Page 13 - Jesse Boyt   ]
                 vs   ] Decree in favor of Complt.
           Presley T. Cox]

Page 13 - Court rendered a decision requiring to sell so much
of the land of the heirs of Wilson Steele, deceased, as necessary to pay debts. On 12 April 1836, sale of property, off
west end of said tract was sufficient to satisfy the said debts.
Sold to John Claxton, he being the last and highest bid and
executed a note January 1, 1838.

Page 14 -   6 March 1837, proceeded to sell negro boy. Boy
was bid off by Alfred Campbell and money handed over to Henry
B. Coffey. 10 April 1837.
        James L. Armstrong, guardian of Amanda M. Bradford,
minor heir of John Bradford, deceased.

Page 14 -   Gabriel Tucker & wife   ]
                    vs   ]
            Washington D. Medearis & others]
This day came the complts by their council and suggest the
death of John Medearis, one of the defts in this cause that
he has no executor or admr.

Page 14 -   Archibald Yell &]
            Jonathan Webster]
                    vs   ] Decree
            Jane Meadows   ]
Heard on 15 August 1837, Jane Meadows not let negroes go out
of controll of this court.

Page 15 -   John W. Meeks, William J. W. Wakefield & wife,]
            James Cotton and Madison Cotton   ]
                    vs   ]
            Sarah Putman   ]
Heard 15 August 1837, negroes be returned to this area. Sally
was carried to Georgia by John Wommack but to be brought back
to Bedford County.

Page 15 -   George E. Low & others   ]
                    vs   ] Decree in favor of
            John & George E. Lowe,   ] complts.
            Exrs of Daniel Low, deceased]

Page 16 -   Abner Vincent & his wife   ]
            Susan Parthenia W. and   ]
            Harriett J. Wynn &   ]
            William R. Wynn   ]
                    vs   ] Final decree
            George R. Scott & Polly his wife]
Heard 10 August 1837, negroes are in possession of George R.
Scott and wife Polly under will of William R. Wynn, deceased.
Court ordered that at the death of said George R. and Polly
Scott, said negroes be returned to the complts.

Page 17 -   Malcolm Gilchrist   ]
                    vs   ] Case dismissed
            Theo. F. Bradford &]
            Thos. A. Peacock   ]

Page 17 -   Parsons & wife   ]
                    vs   ] Case dismissed
            William F. Long & others]

Page 17 -   Lucy Lowe   ]
                    vs   ]
            George E. Lowe & others,   ]
            heirs of William Lowe, deceased]
Lucy to get one third part of estate of William Lowe, deceased.

Page 18 -   Sally Wheeler   ]
                    vs   ] Decree
            The heirs of Lemuel Wheeler]
Sally Wheeler gets a dower part. August 16, 1837.

Page 18 - E. T. Daughterty & others]
                vs   ]
         William Nix & others   ]
Samuel Nix and Thomas Nix, two of the defts in this case was
summoned to next court for this case.

Page 18 - E. T. Daughterty & wife & others]
                vs   ] Orig. Bill
         William Nix & others   ]
Complts states that the residence of William Nix is unknown,
subpoena issued to William Nix, at was returned "not found
in my county".

Page 19 - Benjamin B. Bradford]
                vs   ] Decree, 17 August 1837
         Thomas Greer &   ]
         H. C. Bradford   ]
Deft to bring in books &c at next term.

Page 19 - Edmund B. Smith &]
         Sally his wife   ]
                vs   ]
         James Baxter &   ]
         Catharine Baxter   ]
Heard 17 August 1837, cause of executors of Jeremiah Baxter
is defective and uncertain. Negroes not to be disturbed. Deft
charged with amount of money &c.

Page 20 - Thomas Black   ]
                vs   ]
         William P. Batt,   ]
         William Allison &]
         John T. Neill   ]
Deft William P. Batt to appear in court in May Term 1837 and
answer complts bill. August 17, 1837.

Page 21 - The Administrators   ]
                vs   ] Exparte
         Heirs of Joel Riggs, deceased]
Notice of sale of negroes at the residence of late Joel Riggs,
deceased, in County of Marshall at which time and place Elizabeth Riggs bid for two of the said negroes. She bid $1.00
for 2. Bid was "knocked off". She bid $552.00 for a negro
woman Biddy and purchased her. Nancy F. Douglas bid and bought
negro Amy. Reuben Renolds bid for a negro girl Martha and
purchased her. Johnston Jourdon bid for Harriett and Reuben
Renolds bid highest and purchased her. Johnston Jourdon bid
and bought William. James M. Riggs bid and bought Mary.
James M. Riggs bit and bought Doctor. James M. Riggs bid and
bought Grant.

Page 22 - Joseph H. Brittain]
                vs   ] August 1838.
         Joseph J. Marshall]
Case in favor of complt.

Page 22 - Joseph H. Brittain]
                vs   ] August Term 1838
         Joseph J. Marshall]
Case in favor of Joseph H. Brittain. Defts pay.

Page 22 - G. W. Fogleman]
            vs   ] Attachment. Case dismissed
         B. B. Bradford]

Page 22 - E. S. Fogleman]
            vs   ] Attachment. Case dismissed
         B. B. Bradford]

Page 23   Gilbert Deer & wife,   ]
          William Devin, John Devin]
          & others   ]
            vs   ]
          Elizabeth Devin   ]
Case to report in October 1838. Sheriff of Marshall County,
Tennessee to take negroes and hire them out till next court.

Page 23 - E. S. Daugherty & wife]
            vs   ] Decree
         Samuel Nix & others]
Case heard 13 August 1838, both complts and defts are the only
heirs of Rebecca Nix, deceased. William Nix, a deft, had procured a deed to himself of the lands mentioned when it should
be made to complt and deft.

Page 24 - Absalemn Holly & wife]
            vs   ] Suit dismissed August 1837
         John Deason &   ]
         Joseph Rushing,   ]
         Exrs of ___ Rushing]

Page 24 - Lucy Lowe   ]
            vs   ]
         George E. Lowe & others]
Lucy Lowe, widow of William Lowe, desires dower, land in Bedford County on East Fork of Rock Creek, 36½ acres. Bounded
by a spring, George E. Lowe, Thomas Davidson, which is one
third of the real estate of William Lowe, deceased.
                    1 November 1837

Page 25 - Thomas Black   ]
            vs   ] Final decree. 13 August 1838
         William P. Batte,]
         John T. Neil &   ]
         William Allison   ]
Case in favor of Thomas Black.

Page 25 - Lemuel & Jesse G. Rainey]
            vs   ] Decree, 14 August 1838.
         Barzilla G. Rainey &   ]
         Isaac N. Rainey   ]
Suit withdrawn and dismissed.

Page 26 - Thomas Kimmons]
            vs   ] Inj. Bill
         Eunice Warner]
Kimmons will have to file supplemental suit.

Page 26 - William J. W. Wakefield & wife]
            vs   ] Decree,13 Aug 1838
         Sarah Putman   ]
To be presented before court.

Page 26 -   William J. W. Wakefield & wife]
            John Meeks, James Cotton &   ]
            Malissa Cotton   ]
                    vs   ]
            Sarah Putman   ]
At death of Sarah Putman, negroes that Womack took to Georgia,
required bond, to appear in next court.

Page 26 -   John W. Meek,
            William J. W. Wakefield & wife,]
            James Cotton and   ]
            Malissa Cotton   ]
                    vs   ] Same as above
            Sarah Putman   ]

Page 27 -   Abner Vincent & others]
                    vs   ] Final decree
            George R. Scott & wife]

            Abner Vincent & wife   ]
            Susan Parthena W. &   ]
            Harriett J. Wynne   ]
                    vs   ]
            George R. Scott &   ]
            Polly his wife   ]
Required G. R. Scott and wife Polly to give bond for negroes,
after the death of Polly, the negro, agreement was executed.
                    1 November 1837

Page 28 -   Jordan C. Holt]
                    vs   ]
            Banks M. Burrow]
Deft is indebted to J. S. Holt. Burrow be enjoyed from selling
his interest of negroes, during the life estate of Eve Burrow,
August 14, 1838.

Page 29 -   Gabriel Tucker   ]
                    vs   ]
            Medearis & others]
Suggestion. August 18, 1838. Case to be continued at next
court. Washington D. Medearis has deceased.

Page 32 -   Samuel Escue   ]
                    vs   ]
            Henry Beidleman & others]
Complt, Samuel Escue, has departed this life and John Tillman
has been appointed executor of his Last Will and Testament.

Page 32 -   Moffat & Marbury, Admr]
                    vs   ] 13 August 1838
            Mary Ann Clardy & others]
Report to next court.
Report: Clardy's debts were more that his assets. Executors
to sell negro girl belonging to estate of Joseph Clardy, deas-
ed, to pay for debts.

Page 33 -   B. B. Bradford]
                    vs   ]
            Thomas Greer &]
            H. C. Bradford]
Remanded for taking depositions for 5 months.

Page 34 - Heirs & widow of   ]
          William Blanton, deceased] Exparte. 15 Aug 1838
Sarah Blanton guardian of minor heirs of William Blanton,
deceased, intestate, court appointed William D. Orr guardian
of minors, Elizabeth P., Henson G., and Jasper N. Blanton and
report to next court.

Page 34 - Thomas Smith,
          David Yancy & wife Rachel,   ]
          Benjamin W. H. Medearis & others] Bill
Bill for sale of land. Report to be made at next court.

Page 34 - Gilbert Deen & wife   ]
          William Devin, John Devin & others]
               vs   ]
          Elizabeth Devin   ]
Elizabeth to give bond in ten days, if she cannot give bond,
she can take possession of negroes.

Page 34 - James Edwards]
               vs   ]
          Robert Hill,   ]
          Lidia Hill &   ]
          Silas Crofton]
The sale of land from Robert Hill to Silas Crofton was a sham
sale.

Page 37 - Samuel Phillips] Application to resign as Trustee
A Deed of Trust executed 7 February 1837 and recorded in Book
FF, page 589 in Register's Office in Bedford County. George W.
Morris is willing to accept trustee. Court agreed to let
Phillips resign and G. W. Morris be the trustee &c.

Page 38 - Martin Wisener   ]
               vs   ] Orig. Bill. Decree
          Lucy Lowe & others]
William Lowe, deceased, had bequeathed by his father Joseph
Lowe, deceased. Clerk & Master report at next court.

Page 38 - Peter Graves]
               vs   ] Land. Plat in instrument.
          John Bennet]
Peter Graves and wife Peggy be invested with estate for their
lives, both free from control of said John Bennett and they
may cut and use so much of the timber as needed.

Page 41 - Jesse Philips   ]
               vs   ]
          James C. & John H. Gamble]
Complt plea to strike out deft's plea was overruled by court
and be set down for judgement.

Page 42 - Richard K. Mitchell & others]
               vs   ] August 1838
          Thomas D. Cheek & als   ]
To sale 180 acres in Marshall County, Tennessee, belonging
to Jeremiah Cheek, deceased. Eleazor Stilwell was highest
bidder and ourchased same. 15 October 1838

Page 44 - Edward T. Daugherty & wife & others]
               vs   ] February 12,
          Samuel Nix   ]   1839
Land in question: It lies very broken, there is three springs

being very close to each other, there is only 3 or 4 acres
of land cleared on the tract and not more than 2 acres under
fence, the tract of land could not be sold for more than
$200.00 cash. The cleared land has been in the possession
of Thomas Nix one year, the widow Bird, year, and John Hackney
and family one year, and said cleared land could have been
rented annually for about $10.00, since the death of Rebecca
Nix, deceased, and that it would be greatly to the interest
of the heirs for said land to be sold and proceeds be divided
among them.

Page 46 - Thomas Roberts & others]
                    vs   ]
           Frances Parker   ]
Jonathan Parker died intestate, seized and possessed of two
tracts of land. Frances Parker is widow of Jonathan Parker,
deceased. Commissioners were appointed to lay off widow and
heirs their shares and widow is to get mansion house for her
dower.

Page 46 - John Ragsdale &   ]
           William Armstrong   ]
                    vs   ] Final decree
           James L. Armstrong &]
           Richard Warner   ]
John Ragsdale on 6 January 1831, made to William B. Sutton
and William Armstrong a deed for a certain tract of land, 100
acres, lying near Wilsons Creek in Bedford County abd borders
lands of John Rogers, Elizabeth Stammers, Martin Adams, Adam
Miller and David Tilford.

Page 47 - Heirs & widow of   ]
           William Blanton, deceased]
Heirs wants land to be sold, also that the widow had not received her dower. Wilkins Blanton was told to sell land.

Page 48 - William Word, admr of
           William Bryant
                    vs
           Sophia Bryant & others
Mary Ann, Dennis, Elizabeth and Cuthbert Bryant, minor heirs
of William Bryant, deceased. They have no regular guardian.
Court appointed William D. Orr as guardian.

Page 48 - Alexander Ray & others]
                    vs   ]
           William Robertson & wife]
Tract of land that descended to heirs of James Ray, cannot
be divided and should be sold and divided among heirs.

Page 49 - John & Jacob Forsythe   ]
                    vs   ]
           Benjamin Williams, Trustee]
           Abner Houston & others   ]
Abner Houston has absconded and left State.

Page 50 - John Freeland & wife]
                    vs   ]
           James Dixon & others]
In this cause the death of William Dixon, one of the defts.
his heirs: Eliza Dixon, Harriet Dixon, Emily Dixon, Minos Dixon,
Polly Dixon, Elizabeth Dixon, Amanda Dixon, Richmond Dixon
and Adaline Dixon are minors and have no guardian. James Dixon

61

appointed guardian. Joel Albright and Dilly Dixon, admrs.

Page 53 - William S. Anderson   ]
                      vs   ]
              Brice M. G. Blackwell & others]
Brice M. G. Blackwell owned Lots No. 2 & 3 in Block No. 2,
in Town of Lewisburg, Tennessee. He purchased same from
George W. Record who could not pay debt.

Page 55 - Thomas Smith & Polly his wife   ]
              Benjamin W. H. Medearis & others]
To sell 2 tracts of land.

Page 59 - Elizabeth Whitaker]
                      vs   ]
              Robert Powell   ]
Elizabeth J. Robeson departed this life in Sussex County,
Virginia, after he made a Last Will and Testament, 16 February
1813. To four children of her sister, Mary Powell, Seymore,
Elizabeth, Thomas and Martha P. Powell. Will proven, April
Term 1813. Seymore and Martha has died.

Page 63 - Alex. Ray & others]
                      vs   ]
              William Robertson]
Bill for sale of land. John Ray purchased same and James M.
Ray security.

Page 64 - Rebecca Ewing by her   ]
              next friend, James L. Ewing]
                      vs   ]
              David C. Mitchell, Lila A. Ewing]
              & W. D. McLeary, Exrs &c.   ]
Transferred to Chancery Court at Columbia, Tennessee.

Page 64 - Heirs of William Blanton, Deceased]
              Exparte   ]
Land sold on 8 August 1839 and bought by Robert Puryear.

Page 64 - Thomas Smith & others]
              Exparte   ]
To sell tract of land. Sold to John Woodward.

Page 66 - Samuel Williams]
                      vs   ]
              George W. Ruth &]
              Martin H. Groce]
George W. Ruth is Bedford County Jailor, to hold negro boy.

Page 69 - E. T. Daugherty & others]
                      vs   ]
              William Nix & others]
Edward T. Daugherty & others against William (Samuel) Nix &
others. To sell land of Rebecca Nix, deceased. Purchased
by William H. Wood.

Page 71 - Enoch D. Rushing &   ]
              William Rucker, admrs of]
              Edward Brown, deceased   ]
                      vs   ]
              Alexander B. Moon & others]
Court learned that Ermine Brown, the mother of the plaintiff's
intestate, Edward Brown advanced $100.00 to Ermine during her

lifetime, that the amount that he was to get has not been
learned by court, over and beyond the $100.00 advanced by his
mother, the defendants intestate. The complts are to recover
the balance of one distributive share of estate of Ermine Brown,
deceased.

Page 71 - Flower Swift   ]
                vs   ]
           Eunice Warner &   ]
           William D. Warner]
Complt to take the deposition of Joshua Hall, Jane Swift,
Edward Greer and Samuel Doak.

Page 71 - Martha A. Cooper]
                vs   ] Decree for divorce
           Abram B. Cooper]
Abram B. Cooper intermarried with Martha A. Cooper in Bedford
County in 1834. They were married 3 years before filing for
divorce. Granted.

Page 73 - Jno. M. Patrick & others]
                vs   ] No. 101, 103 & 110
           Henry B. Kelsey &   ]
           Abner Houston & others]
Abner Houston and Henry B. Kelsey are non-residents of Tennessee, that they reside in the Republic of Texas. To be
published in newspapers.

Page 77 - James L. Armstrong & Mason P., his wife &]
           Robert H. Temple, William P. Temple,   ]
           Jane T. Temple & Hannah M. Temple, minor]
           heirs of Dempsey P. Temple, deceased,   ]
           who sues by their guardian Mary Temple   ]
                vs   ]
           Leonard C. Temple, John B. Dixon &   ]
           his wife Charlotte B.   ]
Mary Temple has resigned her guardianship of the infant complts
and that Preston Frazier was appointed guardian. Report to
next court. Leonard C. Temple stated that Elizabeth Temple
died in January 1836 in Bedford County, intestate, also, he
was appointed admr of her estate and that he should bring in
report at next court.

Page 78 - John T. Burnett]
                vs   ]
           Joseph M. Burnett]
Complt sold 200 acres to Joseph M. Burnett and Joseph M. made
several notes. Joseph M. made a deed to James Wordy(?).

Page 79 - James Frizzel   ]
                vs   ] Decree for petition &
           Keziah Hays, Elijah Hays,] dower.
           & Samuel Jones, guardian]
           & others   ]
Pater Hays died sometime in the winter of 1834-5, intestate.
He left eleven heirs, to wit, nelly, Polly, C----, Mahaly,
who are minors, and to whom Samuel Jones has been appointed
guardian, and Hiram Hays, Archibald Hays, Henry Hays, Elias
Hays, James Hays, Sarah Brookshire wife of William Brookshire,
and Christiana wife of William Frizzell, to whom a certain
tract of land descended from Peter Hays, deceased, subject
to the dower of Keziah Hays, the widow of Peter Hays, deceased.
Land in Bedford County on the waters of Wartrace Fork of Duck

River, bounded by lands of James H. Clark, Grey Lynch and
Noble L. Majors, John Eoff, John Robeson, Jr., James Sutton,
James Haile and James H. Clark. Containing about 108 acres.
The widow's dower had not been laid off and allotted to her.
James Frizzell has become the owner of deed of 6/11th part,
a undivided share of said land.

Page 80 - Thomas Roberts & others]
Commissioners appointed to survey, examine and value the lands
and tenants of Jonathan Parker, deceased, late of Bedford
County, for the purpose of assigning dower to Frances Parker,
widow of Jonathan Parker, deceased, and divide the residue
among the heirs. Land borders the Thompson Creek, Adam Euliss.
Containing 183 acres. Other tract does not join the above tract.
Containing about 7½ acres. Another tract of 32½ acres, joining
C. Parker's line. Another tract of 40 acres. Making the whole
amount of land 223 acres. Plat in instrument.

Page 83 - Complainants Thomas Roberts and Priscilla his wife,
Eps(Epps), Allen, Elijah and Martha Parker in and to the lands
and tenants in said report to complt Frances Parker for dower
be devised out of them for and during the natural life of said
Frances and vested in her for that period.

Page 84 - Elizabeth Whitaker   ]
                vs   ] Final hearing.
          Robert Powell, admr of   ]
          E. J. Robertson, deceased]
12 August 1839. The complt was on 1st August 1824 entitled
to sum of $321.33+ out of the estate of Elizabeth J. Robertson,
deceased, then in the hands of the defts and admr of said
E. J. Robertson's estate.

Page 84 - John M. Sehorn & Martha his wife]
                vs   ]Judgement in favor
          George Davidson   ] of defts.
Slave in possession of and claimed by Complts were rendered
in Rutherford County, Tennessee against Frederick E. Becton
as admr of Henry Yaudell, deceased, who was appointed admr
in th State of Mississippi and was never appointed as admr
in Tennessee. Now is void.

Page 87 - Gabriel Tucker & wife]
                vs   ]
          John Medearis & others]
The death of Gabriel Tucker, one of the complts, with his wife
Matilda Hicks Tucker. The death of Washington D. medearis,
brings into court this bill against David Yancy, admr of Washington D. Medearis, to which Yancy has filed his answer to
this court, that the death of Gabriel Tucker, his widow will
be survivor and carry on this case against Yancy.

Page 88 - James G. Blackwell   ]
                vs   ]
          Brice M. G. Blackwell & others]
Sold Town Lots in Lewisburg to pay defts debts.

Page 89 - Gilbert Deer & his wife Susan Deer & others]
                vs   ]
          Elizabeth Devin   ]
William Devin, John Devin, Susan Deer wife of Gilbert Deer
and Elizabeth Nowlin wife of David Nowlin are the legitimate
children of Elizabeth Devin. A negro woman Hannah and her

increases, by the will of Bryant W. Nowlin of Virginia, loaned
to deft Elizabeth Devin, his daughter, and after her death
were to go to her children, and at this time all are in possession of Elizabeth Devin except one negro Paul who was sold
by deft in the year. Appeal taken to Supreme Court.

Page 91 - Darling D. Arnold]
                    vs   ]
           John T. Burnett,]
           William Burnett &]
           John Robinson   ]
Darling D. Arnold, a Deputy Sheriff of Bedford County, appointed John T. Burnett to be a Deputy Sheriff of Bedford County,
William Burnett and Robinson, securities. John T. Burnett
got hold of bond and has lost or misplaced and was required
to execute another bond. Deft will have to pay for bond and
court cost.

Page 92 - Roger Snell]
                    vs   ]
           Jacob Greer]
Giving Jacob Greer permission to file suit against Roger Snell.
Roger Snell was admr of Keziah Galbreath, deceased.

Page 93 - Thomas Roberts & others]
                    vs   ]
           Frances Parker   ]
Bill for sale of land. Report 10 February 1840. Land of
Jonathan Parker, deceased, 223 acres of land whereon the widow
Frances Parker now lives, her dower during her natural life.
Sale on 21 October 1839. Frederick Anthony highest bidder.

Page 94 - Benjamin & William Bowers]
                    vs   ]
           Henry Bowers   ]
Deft is now in Alabama and filing a complaint bill. Court
decree that complt in this bill recover money from deft and
that an attachment was levied upon a negro woman and her
infant child. Said negro was to be sold at highest bidder
to recover his money.

Page 94 - Thomas Davidson]
                    vs   ]
           John M. Sharp]
Sharp owed Davidson money. Sharp has filed suit against Davidson in Marshall County Court. Our Court finds in favor of
our complt and is to recover his money.

Page 95 - James G. Blackwell   ]
                    vs   ]
           Brice M. G. Blackwell & others]
To sell Lots No. 2 & 3 in Town of Lewisburg to highest bidder,
also Lot No. 12. John R. Hill was highest bidder on Lots No.
2 & 3 and also Lot No. 12. 8 February 1840

Page 95 - Dicey Thomas]
                    vs   ] Petition for divorce. Granted.
           D. Thomas]

Page 96 - James Frizzell   ]
                    vs   ]
           Keziah Hays & others]
Dower be allotted her share, widow of Peter Hays, deceased,

and heirs receive residue of the estate. They allotted to
Elias Hays Lot No. 1, bordering William Montgomery's corner.
Containing about 41¼ acres. Lot No. 2 was allotted to Keziah
Hays, widow of Peter Hays, deceased, for her dower. Containing
about 46 acres. Lot No. 3 was allotted to James Frizzell.
Containing about 53½ acres. 30 January 1840. The Commissioners
were William Gaston, Alexander Lee, William Sharp, Nathan
Chaffin and N. L. Majors.

Page 98 - George W. Ruth   ]
                 vs   ]
           Samuel Williams &]
           Bird M. Groce   ]
Negro man Drew belongs to Samuel Williams and Groce and to
leave them alone.

Page 98 - James L. Armstrong & wife Mason P.,]
           Robert H. Temple, William P. Temple,]
           Jane T. Temple and Hannah M. Temple]
                 vs   ]
           Leonard C. Temple, John B. Dickson]
           and his wife Charlotte B.   ]
Executors of Elizabeth Temple, deceased, widow of Dempsey P.
Temple, estate be liable for said money, hire of money &c.

Page 100 - Flower Swift]
                  vs   ]
            Eunice Warner]
Joshua Hall to get negroes that were in possession of William
D. Warner who is insolvent. Eunice pay the complt.

Page 101 - Dennis Bryant & his wife Elizabeth, formerly]
            Elizabeth Hastings, widow of Willis Hastings,]
            deceased, William and Mary Jane Hastings,   ]
            children and heirs at law of said Willis   ]
            Hastings, deceased, who are heirs under the   ]
            age of 21 years, who sue by their guardian   ]
            Dennis Bryant.   ]
Bill for petition and dower, 11 February 1840. Willis Hastings
died seized and possessed of two tracts of land in Bedford
County on the waters of Big Flat Creek, one 70 acres and other
purchased by said Hastings from Enoch Kizer by deed bearing
date of August 9, 1832, containing 15 acres and 135 poles,
being the tract purchased by Willis Hastings from Jane Reynolds
by deed dated 28 January 1836.

Page 105 - Letsey Cannon   ]
                  vs   ]
            William Pratt & others]
On 22 June 1840, William Pratt as the next friend of Samuel S.,
Martha, Jason T., Letsy and _____ Cannon, minor heirs of Willis
Cannon, moved that a guardian be appointed to defend a suit
on their behalf, filed against them and others by their mother
and regular guardian. William Pratt was appointed.

Page 105 - The heirs of William Blanton, deceased]
                  Exparte   ]
Bill to sell land. Sold to Robert Puryear. Sarah Blanton,
widow and minors are paid.(Paid to Sarah Blanton as she is
their regular guardian). Wilkins Blanton, one of the Commissioners. Heirs of William Blanton, deceased, are, Wilkins
Blanton, Willis Blanton, Charles Blanton, Smith Blanton,
Horace Blanton, Elizabeth P. Blanton, Houson G. Blanton,

Jasper N. Blanton, and Susan wife of Leighton Ewell and Mary
wife of James Nichols. Land sold to Robert Puryear. Land
bordered B. Maupin, Duck River and containing 109 acres. Also,
another tract bordering a school tract and consisting of 50+
acres.

Page 106 - A. G. McElrath & others]
               vs   ]
          Larkin B. Orr & others]
In this case the death of complt A. G. McElrath being suggested
and the same admitted to be true by consent of the parties.
Robert Snoddy admr of McElrath, deceased.

Page 106 - William Craig &   ]
           James Dillard   ]
               vs   ]   23 June 1840
           Flora Craig & others]
To check the land, after the widow got her dower, to see if
it could be divided or sold. Report to next court.

Page 107 - Jordan C. Holt, admr]
               vs   ]
           James M. Johnson   ]
Daniel Johnson and deft had been partners in business of mercantile and partnership had been dissolved by the death of Daniel
Johnson, deceased. The business had not been settled and there
are debts owing to and from the firm. A portion of the partnership effects or capital have been vested in Town Lots in the
Town of Rowesville. The court ordered a report of the business
and report to next court.

Page 107 - Christian Freeman & others]
           Exparte   ]
Christian Freeman and wife Elanor, formerly Elanor Higginbotham
and nimrod Higginbotham and James Higginbotham are the only
heirs at law of James Higginbotham, deceased. Complts wants
to know if the sale of land Joshua Holt sold to Jacob Albright
was fair. Joshua Holt, formerly their guardian for sometime.
Case referred to next court.

Page 108 - William Word, admr   ]
               vs   ]   Report
           Sophia Bryant & others]
To sell the land of which William Bryant, deceased, died seized
and possessed to the highest bidder. Sophia gets one third
of land. Two thirds remainder to be applied to debts of William
Bryant, deceased. Benjamin Phillips was highest bidder.

Page 108 - William H. Craig &]
           James Dillard   ]
               vs   ] 23 June 1840. Report
           Flora Craig & others]
Land can be portioned after the widow has been endowed and
that after the widow got her dower, the land cannot be divided
and should be sold. The Court of Williamson County, Tennessee,
appointed William D. Orr and Solomon Darrett as Commissioners
to lay off and set apart for the widow of William Craig, dec'd,
one third of the land mentioned in complt's bill including
the mansion house and put his in possession of the same and
to report to next court. It was recommended to sell the remaining land.

Page 110 - John Hatchett, admr of   ]
            Rebecca Nix, deceased   ]
                   vs   ]
            William Nix, THomas S. Nix]
            and Robert P. Harrison   ]
William and Thomas S. Nix has an undivided interest in common
with eight others in 200 acres of land lying in Marshall
County, Tennessee, which has been sold to William H. Wood.
It seemed to the court that William and Thomas S. Nix received
more than their share of interest of the land. They were
ordered to pay over to John Hatchett, admr of estate of Rebecca
Hix, deceased.

Page 112 - Roger Snell   ]
                   vs   ]   25 June 1840
            Jacob Greer, admr of   ]
            Keziah Galbreath, deceased]
A question to the mental capacity of Keziah Galbreath to exe-
cute a valid deed on 3 November 1838. Complt is claiming title
to this property of whom he had bought the property. Jacob
Greer came into court and stated that Keziah Galbreath was
unsound in mind and mentally incapable of executing a valid
and binding deed. Upon the following day a jury met in Bedford
County, to wit, June 25, 1840, Thomas Smith, James Orrick,
Edward B. Tuck, Jacob Stonebraker, William A. Young, Calvin H.
Head, Leonard W. Marbury, John Shofner, John H. Anderson,
Thomas Holland, Jr., Carlos D. Steele and Andrew Presgrove.
They met the next day, June 26, 1840.

Page 113 - William S. Haynes]
                   vs   ]
            James Russ, Jr.]
They were partners in printing business "The Western Star",
a newspaper in Shelbyville. The receiver should report to
next court, accounts of the firm of Haynes & Russ.

Page 114 - Price C. Steele, guardian of   ]
            Helen P. Brame & Winfield S. Brame]
Helen P. and Winfield S. Brame minor heirs of Warner(Warren?) L.
Brame, deceased. Commissioners appointed to divide slaves
between heirs, Helen P. and Cate, guardian of Winfield S. and
commissioners to make report at next court.

Page 115 - Christian Freeman & others]
            Exparte   ] Report.
Christian Freeman and wife Eleanor and James Higginbotham and
Nimrod Higginbotham are the only heirs of James Higginbotham,
deceased. Clerk & Master examined the land to see if it could
be divided wouthout injury to land, and whether the sale made
by Joshua Holt, guardian of the said heirs, was for the value
of said land and what the land is now worth. He called Elijah
Lacy and Hiram Holt and has taken their affidavits and they
report that the land cannot be divided, 42 to 50 acres, it
would be worth $8.00 per acre if sold in whole. Court ordered
land to be sold by Joshua Holt and that Abner Freeman deliver
unto Joshua Holt bond for the title to said land and that
complts Jordan C. Holt and Herod F. Holt, executors of Last
Will and Testament of Joshua Holt be cancelled. Also, Jordan
C. and Herod F. Holt deliver over complt's note for the purchase
to Benjamin Phillips the guardian of the minor heirs of James
Higginbotham, deceased.

Page 117 - Roger Snell   ]
                vs   ]27 June 1840.
          Jacob Greer, admr of   ] Final hearing.
          Keziah Galbreath, deceased   ]
"Know all men by these present, that I, Keziah Galbreath of
the County of Bedford and State of Tennessee, for and in consideration of the friendship and esteem which I bear towards
Roger Snell of the County and State aforesaid, and also in
consideration that the said Snell will take care of me for
my lifetime, which he has this day obligated himself to do
by deed bearing even date, with this I have given, granted
and conveyed, and by these presents do give, grant and convey
unto said Snell a certain tract of land in said county on the
waters of Big Flat Creek, being the tract of land on which
I now reside, and which I purchased from William Dixon, also
all my negroes, to wit, Clarissa, Eliza, Sylvia, Jim, Jerry,
Darky, Luthesia, Bob, Maxmillian, Manda and Harriett, being
eleven in number, also all my stock, furniture and property
of every description whatever to have and to hold to him the
said Snell during his natural life, and at his death the said
property to belong to the children of said Snell by his last
wife, that is, his present wife, and their heirs forever".
Witness my hand and seal this 3rd day of November A.D. 1838.
Attest: Jacob Greer   Signed: Keziah Galbreath (Seal)
        Adam S. Riggs   10 November 1838
Case Cancelled by Court.

Page 120 - Benjamin F. Bowers]
                vs   ] December 1840.
          William Bowers   ]
Deft is indebted to complt William Bowers is not a resident
of Tennessee and that he has an undivided one eleventh part
of a tract of land, 137 acres in Bedford County, upon which
John Bowers lived at the time of his death and said land had
been levied on by attached in this case. Complt to recover
his money $1020.37. Tract of land be sold by Clerk & Master.

Page 122 - Amelia Brewton]
                vs   ] Bill for divorce.
          John Brewton   ]
Complt dismisses this suit.
NOTE: This bill was marked in error and case marked out.

Page 123 - Jack and James House]
                vs   ] 30 December 1840
          John Sims & others   ]
Susan McIntosh, executrix of Duke House was authorized by the
Last Will and Testament to sell the lands claimed by the
complts in their bill and that she and her husband, John
McIntosh whom she intermarried, after the death of her former
husband Duke House, has conveyed by deed to deft John Sims.
Case dismissed.

Page 124 - Elizabeth Harwell & others]
                vs   ]
          Thomas H. Reeves & others   ]
On Bill of Complaint, which had been regularly taken for confessed against defts, and it appearing to the court that the
negro Ephraim upon which defts had levied their execution,
is the property of complt, by virtue of a Deed of Trust, executed by Thomas Woodward to deft Chitwood and not liable for the
debts of Bowling Harwell. The negro Ephraim having been delivered to complts. The court says that defts be perpetually

enjoined from selling or otherwise interfering with said negro
Ephraim as the property of said Bowling Harwell's.

Court states that deft Chitwood has not performed the
duties and obligations of Trustee, under said Deed of Trust,
executed by said Thomas Woodward. Court ordered Chitwood to
be removed from said office of Trustee and that Jesse M.
Yowell be appointed trustee.

Page 126 - Matilda Hicks Tucker   ]
                vs   ] Report.
           Thomas Smith & wife,   ]
           Benjamin W. H. Medearis,]
           Admrs and heirs of   ]
           John Medearis, deceased]
It appearing to the court that if there ever came to the hands
of John Medearis and Sarah his wife, formerly Sarah Bell, the
ancestors of defts, any money or effects, from the estate of
Thomas Bell, deceased, the ancestor of the complt out of which
she was entitled to distribution, or if any thing over came
to the hands of the said John Medearis and wife as guardian
of the complt. She has slept upon her rights and is chargeable
with negligence and the court is of opinion that by the great
lapse of time, not sufficiently accounted for, has lost her
right to the relief sought for, by this bill. The case about
the negroes in possession of Sarah Medearis be dismissed.

Page 126 - Sarah H. Harris & others]   29 December 1840.
                Exparte   ]
Court is not satisfied, whether it is for the interest of
complts Sarah H. and Esther J. Harris, for the sale of their
undivided tenth part of the tract of land mentioned in complt's,
to be ratified or whether it would be to their interest for
the same to be sold, at all, and whether said sale is fair.
Clerk & Master make report about sale of land.
Report: Recommanded that the land be sold, to Joseph R.
McKinley. 30 December 1840.

Page 128 - _____ McDowell]
                vs   ] 31 December 1840.
           Whitney & Organ]
Deft Whitney has died since last Term of this Court and Carlos
D. Steele became his admr. The case to be continued.

Page 129 - George W. Carpenter   ]
                vs   ]
           The heirs of Abram B. Morton, deceased]
Abram B. Morton, late of Bedford County, departed this life
intestate and seized by title of a lot or parcel of ground
in the Town of Shelbyville, being the interest lot whereon
he resided at the time of his death, with the buildings and
improvements thereon, and where on his widow has resided and
that at her decease said lot descended to defts (except K. L.
Anderson) who are his heirs at law, subject however to the
dower, right of his widow, which is one third during her life
time. It also appears to the court that George W. Carpenter
on 13 day of November 1834 recovered a judgement _____ _____
in the Bedford County Court against Clement Cannon, James
McKissick and William Gilchrist, admrs of said Abram B. Morton,
deceased. Judgement still remains in full force and unpaid.
Clerk & Master is to sell at public auction lot (subject to
widow's dower), and apply money towards debts.

Page 130 - A. G. McElrath & others]
               vs   ]
          Larkin B. Orr & others]
Larkin B. Orr, admr of Joseph McElrath, deceased, at August
Term 1833 in Bedford County. Orr has not paid over to complts
their distributive shares. It is ordered by the court that
complts recover of the deft L. B. Orr and David Orr and the
deft Robert L. Landers, admr of the Goods and Chattels, rights
and credits of William Carter, the amount of their distributive
shares. Clerk & Master to give a report.

Page 131 - Clement Cannon]
              vs   ]
          John Tillman   ]
No injury by putting into operation a dam on Duck River.

Page 132 - John Tillman &   ]
           William Galbreath   ]
               vs   ]
          Clement Cannon & others]
To report as to what value of the factory house, dam and running
works erected by Theodrick F. Bradford near the Town of Shelbyville, and the cost. It was the price paid by Bradford for
the machinery and castings &c purchased for said factory. Wants
cost of repairs and including the expense of carriage traveling
expenses &c. What were the services of said Bradford in super-
intending said works and all the matters relating to the partnership is worth.

Page 134 - John Freeland & wife]
               vs   ]   June Term 1841
          James Dixon & others]
In this case, upon affidavit of James Dixon, setting forth
that Jeremiah Claunch and Matthew Cunningham and J. A. Freeland
and his securities for the prosecution of this cause are insolvent. Ordered by court that complts give other and better
security on or before the 1st day of the next Term of this
Court or the case will be dismissed.

Page 135 - James Houston]
               vs   ]
          Haynes & Ramsey]
James Houston has departed this life since the institution
of this suit and that it is ordered that this cause be renewed
in the name of Benjamin F. Houston, who has been appointed
admr of James Houston, deceased.

Page 139 - William A. Gaunt, admr of]
           John Gaunt, deceased, & al]
               vs   ]
          Benjamin Broughton & others]
The admr is holding money out of the estate of John Gaunt,
deceased, and that B. Broughton and wife have been advanced
in the life of John Gaunt the sum of $300.00 and that Alexander
Bryant and wife the sum of $300.00 and Jacob Shaddy and wife
the sum of $92.00. The court says there are nine distributees
including the widow of John Gaunt, deceased, in which $2195.12
be divided among the heirs. The widow gets $243.90. The
remainder is divided into eight shares, the number of children
of John Gaunt, deceased. Ordered that William A. Gaunt pay
over to Sarah Gaunt, the widow of John Gaunt, deceased, her
share. That he pay over to Elizabeth Gaunt, Caroline Gaunt,
John Gaunt, William and Eliza Jane Gaunt each $330.40½, to

71

Benjamin Broughton and wife $30.40¼, to Alexander Bryant and
wife $30.40¼, and to Jacob Shaddy and wife $238.40¼, and that
the admr can retain an equal amount.

Page 140 - The heirs of John Gaunt -]
                vs   ]
           The heirs of Lewis Gaunt]
William A. Gaunt appointed guardian for the heirs of Martha
Ray, deceased.

Page 140 - Benjamin F. Bowers]
                vs   ] Report
           William Bowers   ]
Land of William Bowers be sold to pay $1020.37 on 8 March 1841,
the tract of land, one eleventh part of the land, and Benjamin
F. Bowers was highest bidder.

Page 141 - Benjamin F. Bowers   ]
                vs   ]
           William P. & Jesse Bowers]
William P. Bowers and Jesse Bowers are indebted to Benjamin F.
Bowers. The sale of land of William P. Bowers to be sold to
pay complt. The land being part of the land belonging to his
father, John Bowers, deceased.

Page 142 - Mansfield Whitehead   ]
                vs   ]
           Elizabeth & Lydia M. Davis]
Jose. M. Davis, deceased, the late husband of deft Elizabeth
Davis and the father of Lydia M. Davis, at the time of his
death, held title in trust for complt of a certain tract of
land in Bedford County in District No. 10 and bounded by lands
of Nathaniel Taylor and Clem's Creek. Containing 82½ acres.
Court is to take the land from Elizabeth & lydia M. Davis and
put it in the hands of complt.

Page 143 - Carlos D. Steele, admr of]
           Wilson Steele, deceased]
To sell enough land of Wilson Steele's estate to pay debts.
Invested in John Claxton and his heirs. Land bordering lands
of Arthur Donelson and Woods line. Containing 60½ acres.

Page 144 - Theodocia Clardy   ]
                vs   ]
           John M. Clardy & als]
In the affidavit of George W. Hobbs, that defts Mary Ann,
Noble L., Nancy E., Caroline P., Theodocia and Richard S.
Clardy are minors and have no guardian. George W. Hobbs
appointed guardian.

Page 146 - Washington F. Short]
                vs   ] Report
           Judah Hooper   ]
"Know all men by these present that I, Judah Hooper, og the
one part and Washington F. Short of the other part, have this
day compromised a suit, now pending in the Chancery Court of
Bedford County. That Washington F. Short this day purchased
the lifetime estate, claim and interest that Judah Hooper hath
in and unto the negro girl Sultina named in the bill, now registered in the office of the Clerk of Chancery Court. We
further agree in our compromise that Washington F. Short is
to pay all costs. This 30 March 1841.

Page 147 - John Gaunt's heirs]
                vs   ]
          Lewis Gaunt's heirs]
Referred to take proof and report to next court. Report, the
land or lots in Richmond cannot be divided without injury to
said land. Ordered land to be sold.

Page 149 - Robertson J. King]
                vs   ]
          Matthew Mullins]
Took leave to take depositions of Henry Crosser, William Young,
William H. Cates, Joseph S. Cates, William Hooser, James M.
Johnson, Nathan Hix, William Galbreath, Thomas Nichols, Wiseman
Arnold, Jerry A. Miller and Benjamin Moseley. To report.

Page 150 - Richard Bandy   ]
                vs   ] Cause be dissolved.
          Turner, Page & Co.]
Defts in this case, John A. W. Page and James R. Bedford, sur-
viving partners of the late firm of John A. W. Page and James R.
Bedford and Wade H. Turner, partners under name of Turner,
Page & Co. Recover from complts Richard Bandy and Enoch D.
Rushing and William Rucker, his securities for the injunction.
To recover monies from Bandy.

Oage 150 - William Word, admr of   ]
           William Bryant, deceased   ]
                vs   ]   Report.
           Sophia Bryant, heirs &   ]
           creditors of Wm. Bryant, dec'd]
Benjamin Phillips purchased the following tracts of lands as
follows, (land of Sophia, widow of William Bryant, deceased).
Land borders lands of Harrison Word. Another tract borders
lands of James Words, John C. Hix, Thomas Words and containing
50½ acres.

Page 153 - Theodicia H. Clardy   ]
                vs   ]
          John M. Clardy & others]
Complt advanced one third of the purchase money of a tract
of land in Bedford County and bounded by Otter Fork of the
Wartrace Creek, Dickinson tract and Peter Daniel's corner.
Containing about 200 acres.

Page 154 - Craig & Dillard   ]
                vs   ] Report.
          Flora Craig & others]
Commissioners assigned to lay off and set apart to Polly Craig,
widow of William Craig, deceased, her dower. Land that William
Craig, deceased, seized of as follows, lands borders John
Medearis, John McAdams, Anderson's old line, E. H. Heaslett,
William Craig, Dowdy's line, Matthew Brooks, Durretts' corner
and containing about 200 acres, the same being in three tracts
or deeds of 100, 60 and 40 acres. Plat in this instrument.

Page 157 - John Tillman &   ]
           William Galbreath   ]
                vs   ]
           Clement Cannon & others]
John Tillman, William Galbreath, Clement Cannon and Theodrick
F. Bradford entered into partnership in the manufacturing of
cotton yarns. They were to build a dam across Duck River near
Shelbyville &c.

73

Page 162 - Alexander Norton et als]
                    vs   ]
             John Patton & others   ]
Andrew Patton, admr of THomas Patton, deceased, is to be a
party defts.

Page 164 - John Gaunt's heirs]
                    vs   ] Report.
             Lewis Gaunt   ]
Town lots in Richmond to be sold. William D. Orr, Esq., to
survey and lay off, making the aggregate, separate from the
widow's dower, 421 acres. Sale 11 October 1841. The tracts
or Town Lots containing half acres bid off by James H. Curtis.
William H. Craig purchased other lot in village. The tract
of land containing 165 acres was bid off by Benjamin Delk.
The tract containing 108 acres was bid off by Jacob Shaddy.
A tract containing 148 acres was bid off to Americus Gifford.

Page 165 - William Norton   ]
                    vs   ]
             Sarah Burditt, et al]
To amend bill to include the heirs of William Burditt, deceased.

Page 165 - William F. Long & Co.   ]
             & Samuel Doak   ]
                    vs   ]
             The Union Bank of Tennessee]
William F. Long has died. His name removed from bill.

Page 166 - William S. Jett &]
             Hillery Moseley   ]
                    vs   ] 29 December 1841.
             Hiram Holt &   ]
             Minos Cannon   ]
Sale of land where Holt now lives on 9 July 1840, about 200
acres.

Page 167 - Daniel Jackson]
                    vs   ]
             Green Hill   ]
In 1837, Green Hill rented a tract of school land. Hill is
to pay complt $92.55.

Page 168 - Levin Wood   ]
                    vs   ]
             Enoch Trott &]
             Clement Cannon]
The deed executed by Keziah Galbreath, late of Bedford County
in favor of Enoch Trott, a tract of land in Bedford County,
containing 182 acres. Land borders lands of Andrew Reed, Flat
Creek and John B. Cummings. (Was executed by Keziah Galbreath
when she was insane and wholly incapable of doing any act
binding in law, and that she remained of unsound mind and incapable of doing any act binding in law, up to the time of
her death.) Enoch has sold 35 acres to Clement Cannon. Levin
Wood is lawful brother of Keziah Galbreath. She has no other
brother or sister.

Page 169 - Thomas Smith & Polly his wife]
                    vs   ] Exparte.
             David Yancy & his wife & others]
Bill for the sale of land. Clerk & Master collect money and
pay debts and then pay the remainder to: To Thomas Smith and

wife Polly, one fourth. To John, Richard White, Haywood and
Benjamin Phillips and James Armisted and Martha J. his wife,
also one fourth part. To the heirs or assignees of Benjamin
W. H. Medearis, deceased, one fourth part. To David Yancy
and Rachel his wife, James Loyd and Sarah his wife, Henry S.
Blakemore and wife Margaret. To the guardian of Polly Catherine,
George W., John T., Martha F., and William Medearis, minor
orphans of Washington D. Medearis, one fourth part. To Elizabeth Medearis, widow of Washington D. Medearis, deceased.

Page 173 - Theodocia H. Clardy   ]
              vs   ]
          The heirs at law of   ]
          Richard Clardy, deceased]
Appointed in June 1841, Commissioners to lay off and allot
and set apart to Theodocia H. Clardy one third of the tract
of land (in value) at December Term 1841. The dower tract
borders the Otter Fork, Tillman Dickson's line, Robert H.
Majors, Elnathan Davis' line, and Peter Daniel's old corner.
Containing 196+ acres. Theodocia H. Clardy's dower is to taken
out of the above tract of land. Plat in instrument.

Page 175 - John Gaunt's heirs]
              vs   ] 27 December 1841.
          Lewis Gaunt's heirs]
Survey plat in this instrument.
The Eastern Tract (afterwards purchased by Benjamin Delk) of
165 acres, bordering lands of James Gaunt, Sarah Gaunt, John
Gaunt, Alexander Bryant and Jacob Shaddy's land where on they
now lives.
Middle Tract on which Jacob Shaddy lives (and since purchased
by said Jacob Shaddy). Land borders land whereon John Fields
now lives. Containing 108 acres.
The Western Lot or Tract on which John Fields now lives (since
purchased by Americus Gifford), containing 148 acres.

Page 178 - Thomas Davis   ]
              vs   ] December 1841.
          John Tillman &   ]
          William Galbreath & others]
Court believes that William F. Long, executor of James Brittain,
deceased, was appointed commissioner of Chancery Court at
Franklin to sell the tract of land described in complt bill
and on 8 February 1835, he sold said land to Fredrick F. Bradford. Thomas Davis was security for said Bradford. Portion
of money was paid by Bradford before his death and that Davis
has since paid the balance to William Hoozer to whereon the
note was assigned, that a judgement for $539.50 was obtained
by said Hoozer on said notes against Thomas Davis on 5 December
1839, and Thomas Davis has paid judgement and is entitled to
be substituted to the benefits of the lein on the lands, for
the purchase money retained by the vender, that he is entitled
to have said land sold. Clerk & Master to sell said land and
pay Thomas Davis.

Page 180 - George W. Carpenter   ]
              vs   ] Report.
          The heirs of Abraham B. Morton, deceased]
On 9 August 1841, he sold the house and lot in Shelbyville,
at auction, the house in which belonged to Abraham B. Morton
had lived before his death and is now occupied by his widow,
that George W. Carpenter by his attorney purchased for $230.00
(last bidder). Court ordered sale valid.

Page 184 - Mary Dobson   ]
                 vs   ]
           Robert T. Cannon & others]
Mary Dobson on the 14 June 1810 intermarried with Minos Cannon
who died 7 April 1823, that she again intermarried with Thomas
T. Ashburn on the 4th of July 1825 who died 8 July 1833, that
on the 16th February 1834 she intermarried with Archibald Dobson who died 11 January 1841. That by the death of her husband
Minos Cannon, she became entitled to dower of his lands, which
was laid off and set apart to her, and consists of a tract
of about 130 acres, lying in Bedford County on both sides of
Duck River, adjoining the lands of Clement Cannon, Andrew Reed
and the heirs of Keziah Galbreath, that on the death of her
husband Thomas T. Ashburn, she acquired a certain interest
in six negroes and it appearing by her husband Ashburn, she
had the following children, to wit, Austin E., Mary T., Hazzard
T., and Clement Ashburn, all of whom are minors and defend
by their guardian James Wortham, and it appearing that two
of the above negroes, Caty and Nelson, were and are the seperate
property of Mary Dobson, and that by the Last Will and Testament
of Ashburn, be directed that complt should have one fifth of
his property, and the balance equally to be divided between
the children above named, and it further appearing that after
the marriage of complt with Dobson, the latter took out letters
of administration with the will annexed upon the estate of
Ashburn, and that during the life of Dobson he did not reduce
the interest of complt in said negroes into his possession
as her husband, but took control of them only as admr of Ashburn, and it further appearing that said Dobson died seized
and possessed of two certain lots of land lying in the Town
of Shelbyville, the same being Numbers 33 & 34 in the plan
of said town, and being the lots on which complt now lives,
out of which she is entitled to dower. On 23 November 1840,
Archibald Dobson made a Deed of Conveyance in Trust to deft
Robert T. Cannon of the above property. It appearing to the
court that at the time of the execution of said deed, Archibald
Dobson was affected with insanity from drunkenness and incapable
of making a valid deed. Court set the deed aside. The commissioners laid off to complt her dower of the one third of the
two Town Lots which included the mansion house.

Page 186 - William Word, admr &c   ]
                 vs   ] 29 June 1842. Report.
           Sophia Bryant and heirs   ]
           of William Bryant, deceased]
William Word appointed to sell the lands of William Bryant
died seized and possessed, begs leave to report also that
Benjamin Phillips has paid to him all the purchase money of
said land. William Word reported that on 16 March 1840, land
was sold by him to Benjamin Phillips and he has paid in full
for said land and is entitled to legal title of said land.
Court ordered all rights vested in Sophia Bryant, widow of
William Bryant, deceased, Mary Ann, Elizabeth and Cuthbert
Bryant, minor heirs of William Bryant, deceased, be devested
in Benjamin Phillips. Land bordered school land, Harrison
Word, and containing about 60 acres. Another tract of land
bordering James Word's line, John C. Hix, school land and
Thomas Word. Containing 50½ acres.

Page 187 - William Yeates & wife & others]
                 vs   ]
           Mary Moore, admrx of   ]
           James Moore, deceased, & others]

76

Both complts and defts are heirs of James Moore, deceased, and that Mary Moore is the widow of James Moore, deceased, and she holds in her possession of a negro girl. It is necessary to sell said negro so the estate can be divided and that said widow has failed to sell negro girl. Court ordered that the negro girl Sylla be sold and report to next court.

Page 189 - William S. Jett &   ]
             Hillery Mosely   ]
                  vs   ]   29 June 1842
             Hiram Holt &   ]
             Minos Cannon   ]
That the tract of land described in bill, although conveyed by Holt & Cannon by deed absolute on its face, was in reality instituted to secure the payment of $1000.00 by Cannon to Holt. And Holt was entitled by contract to redeem said land on the payment of the $1000.00 plus interest. Court also says that Jett & Mosely received a judgement in Circuit Court of Bedford County at December Term 1840 against Holt for $544.00 debt. Holt has no property (personal) with which to satisfy the judgement. Court ordered a sale of all property of Holt's and Cannon to pay debts. The land to be sold is tract on which Holt now resided on 9 July 1840. Containing about 200 acres and lying on the waters of Flat Creek.

Page 190 - John Clark & Margaret his wife]
                  vs   ]
             Thomas & Mary Ann Greer and   ]
             John H. Moore   ]
Joseph Greer, deceased was a mere attorney to sell the tract of land described in complt's bill for the heirs at law of Joseph Harmon, deceased, of which Margaret Clark is one. Joseph in pursuance of the Last Will and Testament of Joseph Harmon, sold said land in 1837 for $3700.00. Court ordered that complts recover of defts $397.75, that being one tenth part of money.

Page 190 - David Orr   ]
                  vs   ]
             R. L. Landers, admr of]
             William Carter   ]
Court is not sure as to the distributive share of Martha Orr, wife of Larkin B. Orr, in the estate of William Carter and that amount of money Landers has had to pay for Larkin B. by reason of said William Carter, deceased, having been the surety of said Larkin B., as the admr of Joseph McElrath, deceased, and amount Larkin B. owes the estate of Carter for property purchased from his administration. Ordered refund to Clerk & Master and they will ascertain the share for Martha Orr.

Page 191 - John Tillman]
                  vs   ]
             Hiram Holt &]
             Minos Cannon]
Hiram Holt at time the complt filed this bill, was a citizen of Alabama and is indebted to complt. Court ordered the conveyance of 200 acres from Holt to Cannon. Land was purchased by William S. Jett.

Page 191 - William D. Orr   ]
                  vs   ]
             James McKisick & others]
Larkin Holt is dead (one of the defts). Case to be refiled.

Page 192 - Willis Cannon   ]
                vs   ]
         Abid Parsons & wife]
Thomas C. Moore, admr of his wife Nancy Moore. Abid Parsons
and wife claiming to be one of the distributees of Nancy.
Parson's wife being a daughter of Nancy Moore. Willis Moore
is a son of Nancy Moore. Only two children.

Page 193 - Michael Wommack & others]
                vs   ]
         Joseph Watson & others   ]
The land described in original bill descended from Charles
Jones to his heirs and that the dower of Rebecca Jones has
been allotted her dower. Report of land... The size of the
land and number of heirs, the court believes the land should
be sold and proceeds be divided among the heirs. To report
after sale of property.

Page 194 - Letsy Cannon   ]
                vs   ]
         William Pratt & wife & others]
              and   ]
         William Pratt & wife & others]
                vs   ]
         Letsy Cannon   ]
Letsy Cannon failed to satisfy the court that the mistake in
Deed of Conveyance from her and Willis Cannon to their children. Court wants this part of bill dismissed. The heirs are
to recover their share from Letsy Cannon. Letsy has kept the
shares of the said wards and has kept wards and clothed and
boarded &c all wards, except Catharine Pratt for last 4 years,
but Catharine has had two of the use of slaves. Court ordered
Cross Bill be dismissed.

Page 194 - Elizabeth Moss, Newton F. Neal &]
         John K. Lawell   ]
                vs   ]
         Abraham Mayfield   ]
On 2nd January 1827, Neal & Lawell erected a Bill of Sale to
Abraham Mayfield for a negro woman named Leanna, a negro boy
Phil, one negro boy Isaac, one negro girl Goodlow, one boy
John, one boy alfred. Mayfield has had in his possession a
negro woman Leanna and her 8 month old child, and others. Court
to make report of value of hire of negroes and report at next
court.

Page 196 - Newton F. Neil]
                vs   ]
         Preston Frazer]
On 7 January 1839, Neil and Frazer entered into a written contract, to convey to market at his (Frazer) expense, two rafts
of cedar timber belonging to Neil. Preston Frazer was to get
half profits, which he dod not give Neil the other half of
profits. Report of account and to pay complt $953.21.

Page 197 - John Freeland & Mary his wife
                vs
      James Dixon, Nancy Dixon, Joel Albright   ]
      and Delilah Dixon, admr and Eliza, Harriet,]
      Emily, Polly, Minos, Elizabeth, Amanda,   ]
      Richmond and Adeline Dixon, children and   ]
      heirs of William Dixon, deceased.   ]
              and   ]

78

Mary Freeland by her next friend &c]
                    vs   ]   Cross Bill
John Freeland   ]
John Freeland and Mary his wife has failed to give proof. Mary
said that the lands were divided among his children, the said
James, William and Nancy Dixon by Deed of Partition executed
20 March 1822(1842). Court said John and Mary Freeland had
not lived together as man and wife for upwards of 20 years
and during that time John has not provided for Mary, she had
resided on the land and supported by her children. Case to
be dismissed. Cross Bill to be dismissed. John Freeland is
not to interfere with the rents &c of lands in North Carolina.
Mary is to get all the estate. James Dixon collects for himself and as guardian of Nancy Dixon, also James Dixon for
guardian of said Mary Dixon, Delilah and Eliza Dixon and other
heirs of William Dixon, deceased, to pay Mary Freeland $50.00
annually for her natural life. (Mary was widow of William
Dixon).

Page 207 - Daniel Williams & others]
                    vs   ]
            Simeon E. Long,   ]
            Lamick W. Ezell & others]
Jacob Williams, deceased, at the time of his death which
happened in 1839 in Lauderdale County, Alabama, was seized
and possessed of a certain tract of land situated and lying
in Giles County, Tennessee on a branch of Weakley's Creek and
bounded by lands of James Robison, Thomas Hudson's land, Robert
Walker. Court states that the estate of Jacob Williams and
intestate had not been administered upon. Oratrix Rachel
Carter, wife of your orator Benjamin Carter, _____ Murrell
wife of John Merrell, Daniel Williams and John Williams, Nancy
Bartlett wife of William Bartlett, Cyrus A. Williams, Mary
Jane and Nancy Williams, and James W. Williams are the only
heirs at law of Jacob Williams. Bailey Needham filed a bill
in Giles County, Tennessee to recover a debt, he had land sold
on 2nd July 1831 and deft Lamick W. Ezell purchased land, who
sold part of land to Simeon E. Long who sold 99 acres to John
S. Crenshaw who sold same to William S. Crenshaw and Bramblett
has purchased part of said land. Report to next court.

Page 213 - William G. Cowan]
                    vs   ]   27 December 1842.
            William Dwyer &   ]
            Jane his wife   ]
William Dwyer is not a resident of Tennessee. He is indebted
to Cowan on several notes. Court says that William Dwyer owns,
in his own right, of the undivided 5/6 and in right of his
deceased wife, during her natural life, the 1/6 of a tract
of land in Bedford County on Big Flat Creek, known and designated in the division of the lands of Jacob Wilhoite, deceased,
among his heirs, as Lot No. 3, containing about 121 acres.
Also, that he owns in right of his wife, a tract of land lying
in Marshall County, Tennessee containing 106 acres and 36 poles
on waters of Wilson Creek and designated as Lot No. 8 in the
lands of Jacob Wilhoite, deceased, being the part allotted
to his daughter Jane Dwyer. Court orders Dwyer pay complt
$450.09.

Page 214 - Thomas S. Parsons]
                    vs   ]
            James Claxton &   ]
            Benjamin Brown   ]

Parsons had obtained a judgement against Claxton. Claxton,
on 5 August 1840, conveyed a tract of land in Bedford County,
District No. 8, on which Claxton now residing, containing between 300 and 400 acres is in trust to Brown. Report on
survey.

Page 216 - John & Alfred Smizer, Exrs &c]
                    vs   ]
         John Crick & Alfred Balch   ]
Alfred Balch is owner of a tract of land in Bedford County
and that Balch sold said tract to his co-deft John G. Crick
on 29 December 1839. The complts testator John Smizer, Sr.,
in his life time held a obligatory of Balch. John Smizer, Sr.
made a Last Will and Testament.

Page 217 - Mary Dobson   ]
                    vs   ] Report.
         Robert T. Cannon et al]
Court ordered that Mary Dobson's dower be laid off to her,
her dower interest in 2 Town Lots of which her late husband
Archibald Dobson, Lots No. 33 & 34. Lot No. 34 borders on
the east side of Martin Street and containing fourteen thousand,
five hundred and twenty square feet of ground, on the one third
part in quantity of said two lots (nearly one half acre lots)
including mansion house.

Page 218 - Alexander Norton & wife]
           Thomas Patton, a minor]
                    vs   ]
           Jane Patton & others   ]
689 acres laid off as the two shares of Archibald Patton and
Daniel Patton. one fourth laid off to Jane Patton on 23rd
October 1823 by John Scott and Andrew Erwin, includes the 15
acre field and small lot adjoining on the creek above the lane
including the barn, cribs &c, the grass lot, peach orchard
and a 12 acre field adjoining below the lane, and the said
Alexander Norton in right of his wife and of her ward may take
possession. Report to be made. Andrew Erwin admr of Thomas
Patton, deceased.

Page 220 - Robert Mathews   ]
                    vs   ] Report of Clerk & Master.
         William Dwyer & others]
Report as to how much money is due the complt from deft.
William Dwyer a non-resident of Tennessee, that he has no property in Tennessee, he owns $102.97. That he owns an undivided
interest of 5/7 part of a tract of land in Bedford County
described as said bill, and that deft Jacob Wilhoite and the
wife of Dwyer (whose given name is unknown) are respectively
the other 2/7 parts. Land describes, to wit, bordering _____
Burrow's line, Eve Burrow's field, William Word's line and
Lot No. 1. Court orders deft to pay complt.

Page 221 - William P. Sims & others]
                    vs   ] Report.
         John A. Ferguson &   ]
         Uriah Cross   ]
Sale of land. Walter Sims purchased the land.

Page 223 - James H. Locke, admr of   ]
           James Thompson & others   ]
                    vs   ] Report.
           Creditors of James Thompson, deceased]

James Thompson, deceased, intestate. Insolvency of estate.
Clerk & Master to make report.
Report: Heirs of James Thompson, deceased, Martha Ann Thompson
and William Thompson, minors. Their guardian is Wilson Turrentine.

Page 224 - Leonard W. Marbury]
                    vs   ]
          Jeremiah Claunch &   ]
          Frederick A. Ross   ]
Claunch is indebted to Marbury. Claunch has left the State
of Tennessee. Claunch's land in Bedford County on Beech Creek,
is to be sold. Land borders lands of Robert McFarland, Robert
Baker and William Pratt. Containing about 176 acres. The said
land being a part of a tract containing 5000 acres granted
by the State of Tennessee to David Ross also another tract
granted to David Ross containing about 834 acres.

Page 227 - John Long, admr of   ]
           William F. Long, deceased]
                    vs   ]
          Mary Long & Preston Frazer]
Preston Frazer, shortly after the death of William F. Long,
security, took from the pockets of said Long $105.75 to which
he had no right. Court ordered Frazer to pay John Long, admr.
William F. Long in his lifetime paid to James Long of Alabama
a debt of $250.00. Which was owning by said Mary to said James.
(Mary wife of William F. Long, deceased, she was sister of
Preston Frazier and was widow Temple).

Page 227 - Benjamin F. Houston   ]
                    vs   ] March Term 1839
          James S. Haynes &   ]
          John Ramsey, admrs of   ]
          Christopher Houston, deceased]
At Chancery Court in Pulaski, Tennessee, a bill was filed
against James Houston (who filed this bill and who having died,
this suit has been revivied in the name of Benjamin F. Houston,
his admr.) in favor of defts Ramsey & Haynes, admrs of Christopher Houston, deceased, for $370.80.

Page 229 - Joseph Robinson & Jane Robinson]
                    vs   ]
          John Robinson, Jr. & others   ]
Willis W. Wilhoite be appointed guardian for Lewis, Richard,
Jesse, Henry, Houston, Alexander Robinson, minor heirs of
Alexander Robinson, deceased.

Page 229 - Thomas Davis   ]
                 vs   ]
          John T. Shanks &]
          David Green   ]
John T. Shanks (is a non-resident) owns a debt to complt. Davis
filed an attachment bill on estate of John T. Shanks' Town
Lot in Shelbyville, known in the Town plan as Lot No. 74
occupied as a work shop by deft David Green. Said lot should
be sold. Report: The Report is that Shanks to pay Davis.

Page 229 - D. P. T. House & others]
                    vs   ]
          Freeman Burrow & others]
Freeman Burrow filed original bill in court against Dudley
P. T. House, William Burrow and Robert F. Arnold on 12 November

1838 and gave John Bennett and Phillip Edmondson his securities.
Original bill dismissed.

Page 231 - Joseph Robinson et al   ]
                vs   ]
            Alexander Saunders & others]
Joseph Robinson is admr of John Robinson, Sr. and is ready
to distribute the shares of estate among those entitled, both
complt and deft are all distributees of John Robinson, Sr.,
deceased. Court says that some of the distributees had received part of estate during his lifetime but does not know the
amount. Clerk & Master to make report. Alexander Saunders
and wife not be charged with the value of a negro woman Cynthia
but only with her heirs. Report at next court.

Page 231 - Richard Cunningham, Martha his wife & others]
                vs   ]
            William Woods, Smith Bolin, Alexander Eakin,]
            Robert Moffat & others   ]
Richard Cunningham and wife Martha had in their possession
a negro girl Malinda, in their own right. Negro girl was
purchased by Giles R. Brown with money which belonged separate-
ly to Martha Cunningham. They had a negro girl for 2½ when
she was taken away by the defts. Court said defts were to
pay them.

Page 234 - Court gives $2.00 per day to Benjamin Kimbro as
Sheriff.

Page 234 - Joseph Kincaid   ]
                vs   ] 29 December 1842.
            James McGill & others]
A note executed by W. D. Manning to defts, Walker & Dunnaway
for a tract of land, 133 acres sold by Walker & Dunnaway to
Manning, land, borders McGill's tract, Peter R. Proby's tract,
Little Flat Creek, Samuel Flemming, J. Hiles, Peter Kirby,
and John Gardner. Containing about 151½ poles.

Page 236 - Elizabeth Short]
                vs   ]Bill for divorce. William Short is
            William Short] now dead.

Page 236 - Coleman Nichols]
                vs   ] Bill for divorce. Case dismissed.
            Jane Nichols   ]

Page 237 - John Huffman   ]
                vs   ] 27 June 1843. Report.
            James H. Clark]
He advertised for sale to highest bidder the lands and mills.
The highest bidder was Peter R. Proby. The land belonged to
Clark. Land borders the Barren Fork of Duck River, John Hix,
Anthony _____, and containing about 30 acres. The land where
on there is now a valuable grist and saw mill.

Page 237 - William Yeates and Mary Ann his wife]
            Edmund L. Heart and wife & others   ]
                vs   ]
            Mary Moore, admr, William McClure &]
            wife, and Harriett E. Moore   ]
Mary Moore, admr of James Moore, deceased, begs to leave to
report: That she did on 4 August 1842, sell negro girl Sella
and William Yeates bid her off. There are eight distributes

of the estate of James Moore, deceased. SOme years ago he
sold his interest in estate to William yeates. Court ordered
the negro girl turned over to William Yeates and others.

Page 239 - Roger Snell   ]
                vs   ]
         Jacob Greer, admr of   ]
         Keziah Galbreath, deceased]
Jacob Greer recover from Roger Snell and James Deery $310.25.

Page 239 - John & Alfred Smizer, Exr &c]
                vs   ] Report of Clerk &
         John G. Crick & Alfred Balch]   Master.
Recommends to sell land. 26 June 1843. Land situated in
Bedford County bordering lands of Cromer, Mrs. Bayler, T. B.
Carlton, Ivy Phillips and John Ray. About 100 acres. John
and Alfred Smizer executors of estate of John Smizer, deceased.

Page 240 - Allen C. McDowell   ]
                vs   ]
         Carlos D. Steele, admr of   ]
         James G. Whitney, deceased &]
         John C. Organ.   ]
In February 1839, complt had in his own right and possession
a negro girl Harriet and that he placed said negro into hands
of John C. Organ as security for note of the Brandon Bank.
Whitney became in possession of said negro and then sold negro
and Whitney has since died.

Page 241 - William G. Cowan   ]
                vs   ] Report.
         William Dwyer and Jane his wife]
Court to sell land on waters of Flat Creek on 18 March 1843.
William and Mary Dwyer's land borders the waters of Wilsons
Creek devised to Jacob Wilhoite by his father and James
Williams.

Page 242 - James H. Locke, admr &c   ]
                vs   ] Report.
         Creditors of James H. Thompson, deceased]
Sale of land, undivided 1/5 part of a 25 acre tract lying on
the north side of Duck River near Thompson's Ford in Bedford
County, it being part of the land of Joseph Thompson, deceased,
which was allotted to William F. Thompson as one of the heirs
of Joseph Thompson, and William S. Wade being the highest
bidder became the purchaser of the land, containing 25 acres
which descended to James Thompson from his father Joseph Thompson, deceased, situated in Bedford County and adjoining the
lands of James H. Locke on the south and lands of Newton C.
Thompson on the east, on north by school land and on west by
the lands of Felix Turrentine. Wade purchased with Elizabeth
Thompson as security. Another tract of 15 acres in Bedford
County on the north side of Duck River, about one mile from
Thompson's Ford, it being the land granted by State of Tennessee
to James Thompson, by Grant No. 11,232 and Elizabeth Thompson
being the bidder and became the purchaser. Also another tract
of 10 acres granted by the State of Tennessee to James Thompson,
deceased, by Grant No. 7,206, situated in Bedford County and
on the north side of Duck River, near Thompson's Ford and
Newcom Thompson being the purchaser.

Page 243 - Nancy Bearden & heirs of] Exparte.
         Eli Bearden, deceased   ]

To lay off dower and sell lands. Eli Bearden departed this
life about 1831, leaving a widow Nancy Bearden and Willis
Bearden, minerva now wife of William B. Hix, Nimrod Bearden,
Charlotte now wife of James H. Claunch, John T. Bearden, Nathan
Bearden, Nancy now wife of George T. Walsh (adult children
and heirs of said Eli) and Winn (Wynn) Bearden, Allen Bearden,
and Elizabeth Bearden, minors and heirs of Eli who sue by their
next friend John T. Bearden and no other heirs. Eli Bearden
died seized and possessed of the 13 tracts of land, which all
lyes adjoining each other in Bedford County. That Nancy
Bearden, widow of said Eli, deceased, has not as yet had any
dower in said land laid off and allotted to her, and that the
residue of land is now owned by the children and heirs herein
before named. Report on lands says that the land cannot be
divided and must be sold. After the dower is allotted to the
widow, Kindred Pearson, commissioner, to sell residue of land.
One tract of 30 acres borders Kebble Terry's land. Another
tract of 20 acres. Another tract of 17½ acres. Another tract
of 28 acres borders lands of Samuel Pollock, another tract
of 48 acres bordering lands in the name of Malcom Gilchrist.
Another tract of 58 acres borders Wiley Snell, Samuel Pollock,
Henry Hastings and Woodly's line. Another tract of 20 acres.
Another tract of 21½ acres borders lands of William M. Evans,
Cooper's line, and Jacob Fuller's line. Another tract of 9
acres borders Daniel Gilchrist's tract. Another tract of 34½
acres borders Lewis Russell and Samuel Pollock. Another tract
of 5 acres. Another tract of 10 acres. Another tract of
12½ acres borders Samuel Pollock.

Page 247 - Joseph & Jane Robinson   ]
                  vs   ]   Report.
            John Robinson, Jr & others]
Court said that 5%on the amount collected and disbursed by
Joseph Robinson as admr of John Robinson, Sr., deceased, is
reasonable compensation for his services. Also allow Rachel
Robinson, widow of John Robinson, Sr., deceased, the sum of
$597.40. To Alexander Sanders and wife $687.65, to James
Robinson $852.40, To Mary Biggers $440.40, and to William
Robinson $277.40, and to Jane Robinson $350.40, and all the
other distributees have been advanced in his lifetime equal
to their distributive shares.

Page 249 - Jacob C. Burrow &   ]
            Adelade Marshall   ]
                  vs   ]
            William R. Burditt & others]
Deft William R. Burditt has died. Case sent to rules.

Page 250 - A. Knight   ]
                  vs   ]   28 June 1843
            Bennett Cully &]
            James S. Fowler]
James S. Fowler on 27 December 1839 sold to Cully a tract of
land in Bedford County on the waters of Barren Fork of Duck
River and Doddy's Creekand bounded by lands of Elijah Holt's
line. About 100 acres. Cully made notes and did not pay.
Court says that Cully has no property except the land. Court
ordered the land to be sold.

Page 251 - John W. Cobb   ]
                  vs   ]
            Andrew C. Wood & Wilie F. Daniel]
In 1838, complt sold to A. C. Wood a tract of land in Bedford

County, on waters of Beech Creek in District No. 23, containing
130 acres and bounded by lands of Bond and Lile, N. Cannon,
Duck River, and Wiley F. Daniel. The land where deft Wood
now lives at the filing of this bill (December 1843). Wood
executes several notes which are still due and unpaid and that
he has no other property except the land. Court ordered that
the land to be sold.

Page 252 - George W. Carpenter]
              vs   ]
         R. K. Flack & others]
Rufus K. Flack was a member of the firm of Davidson & Flack
of Mississippi and that the firm executed notes in 1836 and
due. Davidson is now dead and that Doak & Cannon are indebted
to Flack. Court orders Doak & Cannon to pay Flack and Flack
to pay complt.

Page 252 - John Wilson   ]
              vs   ]
         John W. Key &]
         David Rutledge]
Deft Rutledge owes complt $200.00 and Rutledge transferred
to Key and debt due December 1841. Deft was to sell tobacco
and applied to debt to complt.

Page 254 - Leonard W. Marbury]
              vs   ]
         Jeremiah Claunch &]
         Frederick A. Ross]
Clerk & Master sold a tract of land, 176 acres, to Jesse W.
Brown. Brown executed his note with Joseph Morton as security.
Prior to filing this bill, Jeremiah Claunch had sold about
50 acres of land out of the said tract of 176 acres, and that
he was only entitled to the balance. He said Brown was deceived
in making said purchase. Court said sale to be set aside and
note executed by Brown and his security be delivered up to
be cancelled. Clerk & Master sold the tract of 19 acres and
47 poles to Thomas M. Claunch who was highest bidder but has
failed to comply with the terms of sale. Court ordered said
sale of last tract be set aside and cancelled. Also, to sell
remaining portion of 176 acres of land on which Jeremiah
Claunch had not, before the filing of the bill in this case,
sold and disposed of said land that he also resell tract of
19 acres and 47 poles. Report at next court.

Page 254 - Joshua Averett et al]
              vs   ]
         Jacob Harrison et al]
George W. Ruth produced his account for keeping the negroes
indispute between these parties in the jail of Bedford County.
Also Dr. George W. Fogleman produced a medical account for
said negroes in jail.

Page 256 - Alexander Norton & wife & Thomas Patton]
              vs   ]
         Jane Patton, John Patton & others   ]
                 and   ]
         John & William Patton   ]
              vs   ]
         A. Norton & others   ]
In 1814, complts in cross bill. John and William Patton paid
to Patton & Erwin a part of the purchase money for the tract
of land described in complt's bill as having been purchased

by Thomas Patton from Patton & Erwin for $1262.00 and that
the children and heirs of said Thomas have ever since the death
of said THomas Patton recognized said money as a charge upon
said land and that delaying the claim of said John and William
Patton has been caused by a general understanding amongst the
heirs at law of Thomas Patton that Jane Patton, the widow of
Thomas Patton, deceased, was not to be disturbed during her
lifetime. Court said that in Thomas Patton's lifetime he sold
several portions of lands, one to Neely S. Patton, one to James
and Dobbs, one to Vanoy(Vannoy), and one to Jonathan Webster.
Court said that the widow is to get one third of the estate
and money. Archibald Patton was an ancestor of Thomas Patton,
which estate Archibald bought a share from Daniel Patton.
Andrew Erwin, admr of THomas Patton, deceased. Court ordered
that the deft pay complts Alexander and Jane C. Norton their
share.

Page 259 - (illegible), admr of   ]
           Hugh Snelling   ]
                vs   ]
           Lemuel Snelling & others]
Lemuel Snelling and others, are distributees of Hugh Snelling,
deceased. The defts, among themselves, divided the negroes
of the estate of Hugh Snelling and appointed John H. Anderson,
William Hooser, Kinchen Stokes, Percy Yell, George Cotner and
Neely Coble to make division. Anderson was taken sick and
R. T. Ashburn was selected in his place. The division, to wit,
To deft, Elizabeth Snelling, negro slaves, Tom, Kate and her
child, Phillis and Green.
To deft, R. S. McConnell and wife: Gill, clarisa, Martin and
old James.
To deft, Lemuel Snelling: Henry, Little Bill and Jane.
To deft, John Snelling: young James, Kiz and her child, Dick
and Wilis.
To deft, Susannah Searcy: Big Bill, Haley, Tempe and little Tom.
To deft, L. H. Arnold: Isham, Barbary and her child, Betsy
and Reamy.
Hugh Snelling had already given to Leonard Snelling $1321.00,
to Susannah Searcy $127.00, to L. H. Arnold $349.00, to John
Snelling $665.00, to R. S. NcConnell and wife $349.00, and
to Elizabeth Snelling $15.00.

Page 261 - John Tillman &   ]
           William Galbreath   ]
                vs   ] 25 December 1843.
           Clement Cannon & others]
John P. Steele appointed guardian of minor heirs of Theodric
Bradford, deceased.

Page 262 - Nancy Bearden & others]
           Exparte Petition   ]
Kindred Pearson who was appointed commissioner to sell said
land has been unable from bodily indisposition to perform duty,
D. D. Hix be appointed in his place and make report to next
court.

Page 263 - Allen Knight   ]
                vs   ]
           Bennet Cully &   ]
           James S. Fowler]
Clerk & Master advertised land for sale. Land in Bedford
County on waters of Barren Fork of Duck River and Doddy's Creek.

Page 267 - Plat of Thomas Patton's land.

Page 270 - Mary B. Atkins   ]
                vs   ] Bill for divorce.
          H. W. Atkins,   ]
          William N. Taylor & others]
Complt to bring in more information to next court.

Page 270 - Lewis A. Boyd]
                vs   ]
          Joshua Hall   ]
Lewis A. Boyd is dead, notified by his solicitor. Case refiled
in name of Richard H. Sims, admr of Boyd.

Page 271 - Earps, Hooper & Wolf]
                vs   ]
          William Gilchrist   ]
William Gilchrist is now dead.

Page 272 - Lemuel Rainey]
          Exparte   ]
Lemuel Rainey, admr of Isaac Rainey, deceased, whose Last Will
and Testament directs that the negroes mentioned in the petition should be sold, after the death of Sarah Rainey his wife,
and their proceeds divided, in certain proportions in said
will mentioned among his children and it also appearing to
the satisfaction of the court that the said Sarah Rainey died
in the month of April last (1843). It is therefore ordered
&c by court that Lemuel Rainey sell negroes to highest bidder
on credit of twelve months, taking bond with good security
for the payment of the purchase money, at the Court House in
the Town of Lewisburg, Marshall County, Tennessee.

Page 272 - Adaline Wilhoite & others]
          Exparte   ]
Petition for division of negroes of John B. and Jacob Wilhoite.

Page 273 - William Albright & Louisa his wife,]
          William Wood, Robert Wood & others,   ]
          heirs at law of Levin Wood, deceased.]
                vs   ]
          Enoch Trott & Clement Cannon   ]
Rented land in possession of Trott, by indication of court,
says deft Trott destroyed, cut down and consumed valuable
timber. Ordered by court, Trott is to pay complts for damage.

Page 273 - Walter H. Sims &]
          John G. Sims   ]
                vs   ]
          William T. McGrew]
Complts sold to deft a tract of land and notes were made. Deft
has not paid for said land. Land in Bedford County, about
a mile east of Shelbyville and containing 126 acres and bounded
by lands of Robert Cannon and Uriah Cross. Clerk & Master
to sell said land.

Page 275 - Harrison Austin & wife Emily]
                vs   ] 28 December 1843
          John Brewton & Pearce Wilhoite]
Wiley Wilhoite died some eight or ten years ago, that he was
the brother of Emily the wife of Harris Austin and that Pearce
Wilhoite was appointed admr of Wiley Wilhoite, deceased. Wiley
Wilhoite left a small personal estate when he died and that

out of the estate Emily Austin is entitled to $8.00 and inter-
est. Emily, wife of Harris Austin, about the time of the death
of Wiley Wilhoite, was the wife of John Brewton, that he deserted her, and fled to parts unknown, that she afterwards in the
year 1841 married Harris Austin, that she has since heard that
said John Brewton is still living and that she never obtained
any divorce from said Brewton. Court ordered Pearce Wilhoite,
admr of Wiley Wilhoite, pay over to said Emily, now wife of
Harris Austin $8.00 and interest, as distributee share of the
estate of Wiley Wilhoite, that neither said John Brewton nor
Harris Austin shall receive any part thereof.

Page 275 - Elisha G. Forrest]
                 vs   ]
           John P. Wood &   ]
           Green L. Poplin   ]
John P. Wood is not a resident of this state. At last court
process had been regularly executed on deft Green L. Poplin.
Wood is indebted to complt for several notes. John O. Wood
is a distributee of Jonathan Wood, deceased, and is due a share
from estate from Green L. Poplin, admr of said estate. The
share is not enough in value to pay said debts.

Page 276 - Andrew Reynolds   ]
                 vs   ]
           Arthur Campbell & others]
William D. Orr appointed guardian to defend for the minor heirs
of James Reynolds, deceased, who have no regular guardian.
(James Reynolds could be Jane Reynolds).

Page 276 - Alfred Campbell, admr of]
           Jane Reynolds, deceased]
                 vs   ]Report from Clerk & Master.
           Andrew Reynolds & others]
To take an account of the admr of Jane Reynolds, deceased,
estate and report to next court.

Page 277 - Russell Rollow   ]
                 vs   ]
           Samuel & Newcum Thompson]
Russell Rollow is a non resident of Tennessee. A suit is to
be filed against deft's attorney Thomas C. Whiteside.

Page 278 - Robert Mathews   ]
                 vs   ]   Report.
           William Dwyer & Jane whi wife &]
           Jacob Wilhoite   ]
Sale on land on 11 March 1843. William G. Cowan was the best,
highest and last bidder and he became the owner of said property
or land, and executed notes with Robert Moffat as his security.
William Dwyer's 5/7 parts of land. Land in Bedford County
on waters of Big Flat Creek, Lot No. 3 in the division of the
lands of Jacob Wilhoite, deceased, and assigned in said division
to Willie Wilhoite. Land borders Polly Burrow, Eva Burrow,
William Word's line, and containing about 121 acres.

Page 279 - Delilah Ray]
                 vs   ] Divorce Decree.
           James Ray   ]
Delilah Ray was legally married to James Ray in the early part
of the year 1840 and at the November Term following the Circuit
Court of Williamson County was convicted of the infamous crime
of horse stealing and was sentenced to prison in the public

jail and penitentiary house of State of Tennessee at Nashville
for three years and three months and he is there at this time.
Divorce granted.

Page 283 - James Deery   ]
              vs   ]
          Samuel Pollock &]
          John Hastings   ]
Pollock was a resident of Alabama on the day the case was filed
and is indebted to complt and also entitled to a distributee
share of the estate of Susannah Hastings, deceased, late of
Bedford County. John Hastings is admr of the estate of Susannah
Hastings and as such hold the distributive share of deft Pollock
which is in money. Ordered by the court that Hastings pay
the complt.

Page 284 - Lemuel Broadway, admr of]
           Daniel L. Mallard   ]
              vs   ]
          Minos Cannon & others   ]
L. Mallard was appointed admr of Mallard's estate at November
Term 1841 in Bedford County and qualified &c. That Mallard
died seized and possessed of the following tract of land, situated in Bedford County which Mallard purchased from William
Stewart, the land whereon Mallard lived on and the purchase
of said land is void. Clerk & Master to make a report. Ann
appeal to Supreme Court in Nashville.

Page 286 - William & Thomas Allison, Exrs of]
           Robert Allison, deceased   ]
              vs   ]
          John & Ruthy Cook and others   ]
That Robert Allison the testator complt intestate was appointed by the Chancery Court of Granville County, North Carolina
at the March Term 1839 of said court, trustee to hold certain
negroes: Wiley, Hogan, Jane and Jenn and their increase in
trust for defts, Ruthy Cook and her children which had been
bequeathed to them by Coleman R. White of said County of Granville and that said Robert executed to the Master of said
court. A bond for $5000.00 for the performances of said trust
and also that Robert has lately departed this life and that
no suitable person can be found who is willing to except the
appointment of Trustee and that it is necessary and proper.
Negroes to go to John and Ruthy Cook and their children and
negroes not to be removed from Bedford County.

Page 289 - This day, William J. Whitthorne was appointed Clerk
& Master of the Chancery Court at Shelbyville for the next 6
years to fill the vacancy by the death of Robert P. Harrison,
made bond &c. 27 December 1843.

Page 292 - William R. Looney, Exr.   ]
              vs   ] 28 February 1844
          Cyrus N. Allen & wife & others]
William A. Russell, William E. Russell, Martha E. Russell,
Samuel G. Russell, Josephus Russell and James R. Russell have
no regular guardian and Cyrus N. Allen being present in open
court and consenting to serve, was appointed guardian, to answer
and defend them.

Page 292 - Elisha G. Forest   ]
              vs   ] Report of Clerk & Master
          John P. Wood & G. L. Poplin]

The amount in the hands of Green L. Poplin as admr of Johnathan
Wood, deceased, and what part is coming to John T. Wood as
one of the legatees of Johnathan Wood, deceased. There are
seven legatees. Court ordered Green L. Poplin to pay Forest
and balance be divided among legatees.

Page 294 - Walter H. & John G. Sims]
                vs   ]Report of Clerk & Master.
            William T. McGrew   ]
August Term 1844. To sell land to highest bidder. Land in
Bedford County, District No. 3. Bordered by Robert Cannon
and Uriah Cross, containing 126 acres. Walter H. Sims was
highest bidder.

Page 294 - Benjamin Phillips]
                vs   ]
            Robert T. Cannon]
Sale of Town Lots by Robert T. Cannon as admr of Archibald
Dobson, deceased, was void. Complt was the buyer of the lots,
subject to the widow dower.

Page 296 - Nancy Bearden & others] 29 August 1844.
            Exparte   ]
D. D. Hix appointed to sell land belonging to the estate of
E. M. Bearden, deceased, Joseph E. Couch became the highest
bidder and purchaser. Land borders widow's dower, John Bearden,
widow Fuller, B. D. W. Shook, Simpson's line, and M. Cunningham.

Page 297 - Demarquis D. Hix, admr with   ]
            the will annexed of Valentine Kyser, deceased]
Exparte Petition to sell slaves. Advertised to sell slaves.

Page 298 - Alfred Campbell   ]
                vs   ]
          Andrew Reynolds &   ]
          Arthur Campbell   ]
                and   ]
          Andrew Reynolds, admr]
                vs   ]
          Arthur Campbell, Exr   ]
These xases are to be heard together, and if it appears that
the distributive share of Richard Reynolds in the estate of
Jane Reynolds is equal to the amount of a note executed to
said Andrew Reynolds, as admr of said Jane Reynolds by said
Richard Reynolds, for the price of a negro purchased by Richard at the sale of the property of Jane, that Andrew have a
credit for said note is so much of it as may amount to the
distributive share of Richard. Case is to be referred to Clerk
& Master to report at next court.

Page 300 - William W. Adams & others]
                vs   ]
            William H. Craig & others]
Defts, Sophina J., William, John, Polly Ann, James, Elisha
and Elijah Craig are minors and have no regular guardian and
Newcomb Thompson appointed guardian.

Page 300 - A. Norton & wife &]
            Thomas Patton   ]
                vs   ]
            Jane Patton   ]
Upon the affidavit of Abram Martin, court ordered Clerk & Master
hear proof and report to next term of court what amount of

90

money Jane Patton paid in a compromise of a suit with Andrew
Jackson respecting the lands in controversy and where it was
paid, and the interest on payment up to this time.

Page 300 - James H. Lock, admr of   ]
            James Thompson, deceased & others   ]
                vs   ]
            The Creditors of said James Thompson, deceased]
Report of admr. The estate of James Thompson was sold 24 March
1843, one small tract of land, 10 acres purchased by Newcomb
Thompson with Moses Marshall as security. One tract of 15
acres, purchased by Mrs. Elizabeth Thompson with James H. Locke
as security. One tract of 25 acres, purchased by William S.
Wade and Mrs. Elizabeth Thompson as his security. 90 acres.
Page 302 - Notes and Credits with named: John P. Moon, William
Ogilvie, William Little, Green L. Poplin, James Thompson,
William S. Wade, J. J. Lents, John F. Thompson, Peter Capley,
A. P. Moon, Coldwell & Moseley, Thomas S. Barnhill, Robert
Sykes, Collins & Perry, James Pascals, Benjamin Earnhart,
A. M. & D. J. Wheeler, William B. Wheeler, William B. Jones,
J. W. Swift, Jennings Moore and George Fisher. Land bounded
by Joseph Thompson, land belonging to the heirs of Joseph
Thompson, deceased, James Turrentine, Bluff of Duck River and
John McMullin. Newcomb Thompson purchased the land.

Page 307 - Richard H. Sims, Guardian &c]
            Exparte Petition for   ]
            division of slaves   ]
Commissioners to make a report. They were to divide slaves
between Mary R. Stone formerly Mary R. Davis and Charlotte S.
Davis, children and heirs of Henry Davis, deceased, and agree-
ably to the said decree presented to us by Richard H. Sims
the guardian of Mary R. and Charlotte S., whom this day at
the house of the said Richard H. Sims provided to make division
&c. Mary R. Stone was allotted boy Edmond & Sandy. Charlotte
S. was allotted Mina and child and boy Ransom. Both having
equal share of slaves.

Page 308 - Joel Whorley   ]
                vs   ]
            E. Brown & others]
John Alvin and Henry Brown are under age and has no guardian.
William J. Whitthorne appointed their guardian.

Page 309 - George Davidson, admr of   ]
            James G. Whitney, deceased   ]
                vs   ]
            William Sharp, George W. Fogleman,   ]
            William D. Norton and Martha his wife,   ]
            John Bell, William A., & Wiley Hickerson]
James G. Whitney departed this life in the month of August
1840. C. D. Steele was appointed admr of the estate. Shortly
after the death of Whitney, Joel W. R------(?) delivered to
deft Martha the widow of said Whitney amongst other things
as the property of said Whitney $440.00 in bank notes &c on
the firm of Hickerson & Co. Court ordered complt to recover
from Norton and his wife Martha, the debt &c.

Page 311 - Lemuel Broadway, admr of]
            Daniel S. Mallard   ]
                vs   ] Clert & Master to report.
            Minos Cannon & others   ]
To sell land to pay creditors &c. Land borders James Reagor,

91

Martin Friddle, Alfred Campbell, and Ann Brumfield.   Containing
115 acres.

Page 313 - John W. Mayfield   ]
              vs   ]
         George L. Rodgers & others]
Court asks that negroes billed together with other negroes
of Abram Mayfield and a value farm belonging to Abran Mayfield
which were conveyed to complt, his son.   Court sais the convey
of negroes to complt was done to hinder and delay the creditors
of Abram Mayfield.   Bill dismissed.

Page 313 - John Tillman   ]
              vs   ]
         John T. Neil & others]
         (Sarah Escue)   ]
                and   ] Bill and Cross Bill.
         C. D. Steele   ]
              vs   ]
         John Tillman & others]
Report of Clerk & Master.   Names in creditors ¢c.   Minos Cannon,
Mathew Cunningham, Robert Hurst, Joseph Greer, Jno. S. Williams,
C. D. Steele, Moneys of Blessing property, James Story, Thomas
C. Whiteside, William L. McGrew, John W. Hamlin, D. _ . Brown,
George W. Ruth, B. F. Barnes(?), F. B. Fogg, James Mullins,
L. Shapard, William F. Long and many more on report.

Page 318 - Joel Whorley   ]
              vs   ]
         Elizabeth Brown & others]
Complt has paid all purchase money due to Thomas Russell for
a tract of land originally belonged to Thomas Russell but which
he sold to Susan Brown and to whom he gave a good title.   Jesse
Brown has since died leaving Elizabeth Brown, Paschal, Jesse,
Thomas, Elizabeth, David V., John, Alvin, Henry and William
Brown and Cynthia Whorley are his only heirs at law.   Land
in Bedford County on waters of Sinking Creek bordering lands
of Benjamin Taliaferro, Robert White and containing about 140
acres.

Page 319 - William W. Adams et al   ]
              vs   ]
         William H. Craig & others]
William H. Craig and wife Talitha Craig and answer to the deft.
James Adams is the ancestor of William W. Adams and sold in
his lifetime a tract of land to John Craig, deceased, and executed to said John __?_ a bond &c.   Deft William H. Craig
had bought under a decree since the death of John Craig, dec'd,
and widow Talitha Craig is the widow and the other defts are
the heirs at law of John Craig, deceased.   There is due the
admr William W. Adams of James Adams, deceased.   Court wants
enough of the land sold, just enough to pay debts &c.   Report
to next court.

Page 319 - George W. Haywood, admr   ]
              vs   ]
         Creditors, widow and heirs of]
         William Gilchrist, deceased]
The death of Martha Ann Gilchrist, one of the defts.

Page 322 - Earps, Hooper & Wolfs   ]
                    vs   ]
            The heirs of William Gilchrist]
William J. Whitthorne was appointed guardian of Malcolm Gilchrist, Catharine M. Gilchrist, Adelade Gilchrist, and Sarah
Gilchrist, heirs at law of William Gilchrist, minor defts in
this cause.

Page 323 - David Hime   ]
                    vs   ]
            Jordan C. Holt]
David Hime is a minor under the age of 21 years. The sale
of land is void.

Page 324 - Michael Womack   ]
                    vs   ]Report by Clerk & Master.
            Joseph Watson & others]
            & Stephen Watson   ]
David Floyd purchased the land mentioned in this bill, containing about 100 acres which was sold by Robert P. Harrison and
has paid off purchase money. Land in Bedford County on waters
of Flat Creek and bounded by lands of William Boone and by
the dower lands of the widow of Charles Jones, lands of Elijah
and David Floyd, Elijah and Anthony Floyd, William Ray and
William Word.

Page 325 - George Davidson   ]
                    vs   ] 24 February 1845.
            William Drummond &]
            Leonard W. Marbury]
In 1841, William J. Peacock hired to deft Drummond two negro
slaves for the year 1841. Note was executed.

Page 326 - Demarquis D. Hix, admr with the will] Exparte.
            annexed of Valentine Kyser, deceased]
Petition to sell slaves. Thomas C. Brown purchased boy Sam.
Robert Cannon purchased "Old George". Moneys to be paid to:
Jacob Kyser, William Kyser, Valentine Kyser, Jr., Daniel Kyser,
Enoch Kyser, Jesse B. Gant and Mary Hime, each one share, the
remaining to be subdivided one eights into three parts and
pay to Mary Hasty wife of Joseph Hasty one part, ie, one third
of one eighth to William Troxler one part, ie, one third of
one eighth. They shall divide the remaining one third of one
eighth into two parts and pay to Nathaniel Hubbard one part,
ie, one half of one third of one eighth and to Nancy Dacus
wife of John Dacus one part, ie, one half of one third of one
eighth.

Page 327 - William Word, Exr of] Petition for sale of slaves.
            Cuthbert Word   ]
Cuthbert Word, testator, bequeathed to his widow Jane Word
during her natural life, three slaves, to wit, Jim, Jack and
Fanny, the last of whom has since had issue, a son aged about
12 months, and at her death to be equally divided among his
children, who are seven (7) in number and it further appearing
to the satisfaction of the court that said Jane Word has lately
departed this life, and the court being satisfied that said
slaves cannot be divided without a sale, between the legatees
and distributees, and there is no form in the rule authorizing
the executors to sell said slaves. Court ordered the sale
of the slaves.

Page 328 - J. B. Dysart &   ]
           Josiah Burcheen   ]
                vs   ]
           Samuel Winstead &]
           John T. Neil   ]
It appears to the court that complts are judgement creditors
of deft Winstead, by judgement rendered by Lile A. Ewing, a
Justice of the Peace for Marshall County, Tennessee, for
$154.75 and cost of suit on 13 August 1842. Constable found
"no property to be found". Winstead conveyed to deft Neil
a tract of land. Court ordered the land to be sold to pay
the debts. Clerk & Master to report.

Page 328 - Mary C. Brame   ]
                vs   ] 25 February 1845
           Barksdale & Mabry]
That the transaction entered into between Anderson T. Clay
and complt Mary Brame by which said property was conveyed to
complt was fraudulent and void. Bill dismissed.

Page 331 - James H. Locke, admr of   ]
           James Thompson, deceased   ]
                vs   ]24 March 1843
           The creditors of James Thompson]
Clerk & Master report. Three undivided fifth parts of a twenty
five acre tract, lying on the north side of Duck River near
Thompson's Ford in Bedford County, it being the part of the
land of Joseph Thompson, deceased, which was allotted to
William F. Thompson as one of the heirs of Joseph Thompson
and William S. Wade being the best, last and highest bidder,
became the purchaser of the same at price of $50.00, said Wade
also the best, last and highest bidder for another tract of
land, containing 25 acres, which descended to James Thompson
from his father Joseph Thompson, deceased, situated in Bedford
County adjoining lands of James H. Locke, Newton C. Thompson,
Felix Turrentine and William S. Wade executed his note to the
Clerk & Master. Another tract of land containing 15+ acres
on north side of Duck River, about one mile from Thompson's
Ford, it being granted by the State of Tennessee to James
Thompson by Grant No. 11232 and Elizabeth Thompson being the
highest bidder for $5.00. Another tract of land of 10 acres,
granted by State of Tennessee, Grant No. 7216, to James Thompson and Newcom Thompson being highest bidder and purchaser,
price $11.00. Another tract of land was sold.

Page 333 - James H. Locke, admr of]
           James Thompson &c   ]
                vs   ]
           The Creditors of   ]
           James Thompson, deceased]
John Lentz purchased a tract of land in Bedford County, of
90 acres and bordered by the bluff of Duck River, Turrentine's
corner and James Thompson's Tennessee entry. John J. Lentz
purchased said land.

Page 335 - A Power of Attorney from Eliza W. Harrison of the
County of Bedford and State of Tennessee to James S. Mayfield
of Lagrange in the Republic of Texas, dated the 22nd day of
February 1845 was acknowledged in open court by the said Eliza
W. Harrison to be her act and deed for the purpose therein
contained, which was ordered by the court to be so certified
for registration.

Page 335 - James McKisick]
           vs   ]
        James Mullins]
An execution fee $37.06¼ for cost of suit which James McKisick
recovered against William M. Orr, December Term 1842 of this
court, was placed in the hands of Benjamin Kimbro, one of the
Deputy Sherriff of Bedford County on 25 November 1843 that
said Kimbro has failed to return said execution according to
law and that James Mullins had notice on the 16th January 1845
that a motion would be made against him on this day for a
judgement against him on account of his deputy's failing to
return the execution. Ordered by the court that McKisick recover of Mullins the cost &c.

Page 336 - William W. Adams & others]
               vs   ]Report by Clerk & Master.
          William H. Craig & others]
Sale of land. On 11 November 1844, he sold land to Archibald
Adams. Land borders lands of Thomas Coffee, Pulaski Road and
containing 101 acres and 151 poles.

Page 337 - James Damron   ]
               vs   ]Report by Clerk & Master.
          Johnathan Owens & others]
To sell land. On 9 November 1844. William Guy being the purchaser and money has been paid. The land in which Johnathan
Owens, James Damron, John N. Watkins, James Knight, John Wilson
and Alexander Williams had interest in sold land to William
Guy. Land borders lands of Lot No. 2 of the Guy family shares
of the Worke land and containing 187 acres and 131 poles.

Page 338 - Widow & Heirs of   ]
           Travis C. Nash, deceased]
              Exparte   ]
Travis C. Nash, late of Bedford County, departed this life
intestate on the 7th day of April 1844, that he left as his
heirs and legal representatives, Johnana Nash his widow who
is entitled to dower in his estate, also Levi C. Johnson and
wife Elizabeth formerly Elizabeth Nash, Benjamin Garrett and
wife Emily formerly Emily Nash, William M. Harvel and wife
Louisa formerly Louisa Nash, James C. Nash and Travis C. Nash,
Francis M. Nash, Granderson Nash, Lafayette Nash, William
Nash, Thomas Nash, Augustus Nash, George W. Nash, John R. Nash
who has since died leaving a son and heir at law James R. Nash,
Mary McGimpsey wife of John W. McGimpsey formerly Mary Nash
and none others. Travis C. Nash died seized of land, to wit,
one tract inBedford County of 429 acres conveyed to intestate
by deed, dated November 1838 from Edward Cross and wife Margaret. Another tract containing 47 acres+ conveyed by C. D.
Steele on 19 October 1839. Another tract lying in Lincoln
County, Tennessee on waters of Mulberry Creek, dated 3 December
1840 conveyed by Thomas L. D. Parks. Another tract in Bedford
County of 10 acres and 86 poles, granted by Grant No. 17461
on 26 April 1843, all of which lands are fully described in
the deeds and grants. Caleb Houston, Price Steele, William
Galbreath and William Rainy, three of whom are to lay off dower
for the widow.

Page 340 - William R. Looney, Exr of   ]
           William Russell, deceased   ]
              vs   ]
           George W. Whitsell & wife & others]
Court believes the intestate intended to make all legatees

by his will but some are larger than others. Clerk & Master
to examine and bring report to next court.

Page 340 - Willis & Willis M. Hopwood]
                    vs   ]
             George W. Nash   ]
Deft is indebted to complt. George W. Nash is the owner, as
one of the heirs at law of Travis C. Nash, deceased, of one
fifteenth of the lands belonging to said Travis C. at the time
of his death which are situated lying in Bedford County in
District No. 5, upon which the attachment had been heard. Court
ordered said land of George W. Nash's interest be sold to pay
debt.

Page 341 - Alexander Norton & wife &]
             Thomas Patton   ]
                    vs   ]
             James Patton & others   ]
                   and   ] 26 February 1845
             John & William Patton   ] Bill and Cross Bill.
                    vs   ]
             A. Norton & others   ]
Clerk & Masters reports that John Patton only had possession
of the Allison tract in the years, 1837, 1840, 1841, 1842 &
1843. Jane Patton having had possession from 1831 up to 1839.
Just how long Jane Patton boarded with Jane C. W. Patton, about
4 years. Like to know whether Thomas Patton ought to be charged with board and clothing while living with John and Jane
Patton. Andrew Erwin, admr of Thomas Patton, deceased.
(Jane C. W. Patton)
Report: Jane Patton paid to John Scott, Esq., the agent of
James Jackson, to whom Andrew Jackson gave up his claim and
interest in the suit, sum of $255.00 in three equal annual
installments starting in 1825 and ending 1828. (long report).

Page 347 - Damron   ]
                    vs   ]
             Owen & others]
Joseph McKinly withdrew his agency as agent of Alexander
Williams and now money to be paid over to Richard Williams.

Page 348 - William P. Sims]
                    vs   ]
             John A. Furgason]
Clerk & Master to make report as to whether John A. Furgason
purchased the mills sold under by previous bill.

Page 349 - John McGuire, admr of   ]
             Hugh Snelling, deceased]
                    vs   ]
             Lemuel Snelling & others]
In this case, John A. Moore guardian of Elizabeth Snelling,
an idiot who is one of the defts, wants account of the administ-
ration of Peter Lee former admr of Hugh Snelling and of John
McGuire admr of all matters not already settled by decree of
Supreme Court.

Page 349 - Elizabeth Snelling who sues &c   ]
                    vs   ]
             Lemuel Snelling & Peter Lee, admr]
             of Hugh Snelling   ]
In this case, the death of Peter Lee, admr of Hugh Snelling,
is suggested and recorded to be served against John McGuire,

admr of Hugh Snelling.

Page 350 - Peter Lee, admr of   ]
          Hugh Snelling   ]
               vs   ]
          Lemuel & John Snelling & others]
Peter Lee has departed this life since last Term of the Court.
Bill revived in the name of John McGuire.

Page 350 - Joseph & Jane Robinson]
               vs   ]
          David Robinson & others]
Due Richard Robinson the sum of $595.04, to David Robinson
$740.75, to Alexander Sanders and wife $730.02, to James M.
Robinson $911.25, to Mary Biggers $466.85, to William Robinson
$278.75, to Jane Robinson $359.05, to recover from Joseph
Robinson.

Page 352 - Smith Arnold and wife   ]
               vs   ]
          Wilson A. Arnold & others]
Elizabeth Arnold wife of Smith Arnold to get negro Mariah,
Harriet and her infant child. Margaret Jane Arnold wife of
Wilson C. Arnold gets Lindsey and a tract of land of about
45 acres lying on Duck River, one mile east of Shelbyville,
being the land conveyed by William S. Jett to Elizabeth Arnold
by deed dated July 10, 1843 and recorded in Bedford County
of three tracts.

Page 357 - William S. Jett   ]
               vs   ]
          Jacob C. Burrow &]
          A. R. Marshall   ]
The property was conveyed by Wiley B. Watkins by Deed of Trust
to Jacob B. Burrow and Adelaide R. Marshall to pay debts of
Watkins. Court says that Burrow and Marshall has let the land
be wasted &c and they are to pay William S. Jett the deft.

Page 359 - George Simmons   ]
               vs   ]
          Kindred Pearson, Jr. &]
          Kindred Pearson, Sr.]
Kindred Pearson, Jr. is indebted to firm of Hudspeth and
Simmons, in all $195.47. Kindred Pearson, Jr. as a distributive
of William Pearson, deceased, received enough from Kindred
Pearson, Sr. to pay the debt.

Page 359 - William Word, Exr of   ] Exparte Bill for sale of
          Cithbert Word, deceased]   slaves.
William Word, exr of the Last Will and Testament of Cuthbert
Word, deceased. He sold slaves to Thomas S. Word.

Page 360 - Nelson Blackman   ]
               vs   ]
          John Johnson et als]
John Johnson, as admr of Joseph Johnson, deceased, money in
which complt is entitled to a distributive portion. Court
orders Clerk & Master to find out how much money is on the
hands of John Johnson and report.

Page 361 - Thomas Thompson & wife]
               vs   ]
          Jordan C. Holt   ]

Jordan C. Holt is regular guardian of Tranquilla Thompson.
Holt is to report to court.

Page 361 - James P. Dysart &]
          Josiah Burcheen]
              vs   ] Clerk & Master Report.
          Samuel Winstead &]
          John T. Neil   ]
Bill for debts. Deft Winstead ordered by Lile A. Ewing, a
Justice of the Peace of Marshall County, Tennessee. Bill filed
13 August 1842. Winstead had conveyed to Neil payment of debt
in which Winstead indorsed the tract of land. Court ordered
land to be sold to pay debts. Lands sold to Josiah Burcheen
for %150.00 on 24 June 1845. Land bounded by lands of Temple
and Chapman, and land entered in the name of William Cook.
Containing about 75 acres.

Page 363 - Lemuel Rainey]
           Exparte &c   ]
Admr of Lemuel Rainey was appointed to sell negroes. The negro
man Jacob was sold to Allen Morris, negro woman Nancy because
of her age would not sell for anything. Negro woman Seaton
and her children did not sell. Barzellai G. Rainey had taken
them to the State of Mississippi and did not bring them back
by the day of sale and has not yet brought them back. Commissioners heard that some person in DeSota County, Mississippi,
has administered upon and sold slaves. Court ordered that
all the right, titles &c in interest of the heirs of Isaac
Rainey, deceased, by his admr Lemuel Rainey, in slave Jacob
be devested out of them and into the hands of Allen Morris
the purchaser.

Page 363 - Mary Gaunt   ]
              vs   ]
           Absalom B. &]
           Lewis Gaunt]
It is agreed between the undersigned Mary Gaunt and Absalom B.
and Lewis Gaunt, the latter two are admr of William A. Gaunt,
deceased, a suit now pending between Mary Gaunt and Absalom B.
and Lewis Gaunt, admr of W. A. Gaunt, involves the title to
certain negroes. Mary Gaunt relinquished all claims to said
negroes, except Mariah and her children which she is to have
until her death. Mary Gaunt is to have negro man George who
is now in possession of Mary Gaunt and all of the household
and kitchen furniture and farm utensils &c now in her possession. Asks that this case be dismissed. March 18, 1845.

Page 364 - Richard H. Sims &]
           Thomas Lipscomb]
               vs   ]
           James Story   ]
Complts and Thomas Davis formerly executed the writing obligatory to one Mrs. Sarah Martin, where they promised to pay her
$105.00, notes dated 3 December 1838, and that Thomas Davis
furnished to John W. Ragsdale money to pay said notes and he
transferred obligatory to James Story who has brought suit.

Page 365 - William R. Brasee]
               vs   ]
           Robert H. Smith &]
           G. A. Sublett   ]
Robert H. Smith, a non-resident of Tennessee, and is indebted
for $100.00 and that G. A. Sublett is indebted to Robert H.

Smith for $55.00. Court order defts paid.

Page 365 - John McGuire, admr of   ]
             Hugh Snelling   ]
                vs   ]
             Lemuel & John Snelling & others]
John McGuire still has in his hand a large amount of money
belonging to the distributees of estate. John and Lemuel are
distributees, R. S. McConnell and Frances his wife, Susannah
Searcy, James H. Arnold and Louisa his wife are distributees
of Hugh Snelling, deceased. Court ordered Elizabeth Snelling
to refund $326.17 to admr.

Page 366 - Elizabeth Snelling by her   ]
             next friend, John A. Moore]
                vs   ]
             John McGuire, admr &   ]
             Lemuel Snelling   ]
Lemuel Snelling is indebted to Elizabeth Snelling and that
the admr of Hugh Snelling, deceased, owes Lemuel Snelling.
Ordered debts be paid.

Page 366 - David Yancey, admr]
                vs   ]
             Thomas Smith   ]
Thomas Smith is admr of John Medearis, is holding money of
estate which is to be divided among heirs of John Medearis.
John Medearis had left four children where he died. But that
Benjamin W. D. Medearis, one of the heirs, has been advanced
in the lifetime of his father, a sum greater than his distributive share and that he is not to receive any part of slaves.
The heirs of Mrs. Martha Phillips who was a daughter of John
Medearis have never been advanced anything from the estate
of her father. Court ordered one third part given to them.
David Yancey, admr of Washington D. Medearis, is entitled to
one third part of said estate. Thomas Smith by right of his
wife is entitled to one third of estate.

Page 368 - John Davis, a minor who sues   ]
             by his next friend Johnathan Carter]
                vs   ]
             William Robinson   ]
Court says in 1827, John Davis, the father of John Davis, complt
and the former husband of deft Winfred Stratton, departed this
life in Pittsylvania County, Virginia, intestate, a distribution of the slaves of the estate of John Davis, was made between
Winfred and John Davis who was the only child and heir of John
Davis, by whom the negro boy Ira was allotted to Winfred. Winfred and her present husband, deft, Thomas Stratton removed
by Ira from Virginia to Tennessee in 1828 and Stratton sold
negro boy Ira to deft Robinson who had him in possession in
January 1844. Court ordered complt to recover from Stratton &
Robinson.

Page 369 - Joshua Averitt &]
             Adam Frelick   ]
                vs   ]
             Jacob Harrison &]
             James Burton   ]
Clerk & Master to deliver over to Robert Harrison or his agent
any notes in his possession which was taken for the hire of
negroes as the property of Jacob Harrison.

Page 370 - Thomas Thompson & wife]
                    vs   ]
            Jordan C. Holt & others]
Clerk & Master to make report on hire of negroes belonging
to Tranquilla Thompson. Jordan C. Holt is guardian of Tranquilla Thompson.

Page 370 - American Board of Commissioners]
            for Foreign Missions   ]
                    vs   ]
            Samuel Doak   ]
It is the intention of the testator James McCarver to devise
to American Board of Commissioners for Foreign Missions the
sum of $15.00. Also Henry Blagg is the executor of the Last
Will and Testament of James McCarver and Samuel Doak was his
security and as such has funds in his hands belonging to
testator estate.

Page 372 - Andrew Reynolds, admr   ]
                    vs   ]
            Arthur Campbell & others]
                    and   ]
            Alfred Campbell   ]
                    vs   ]
            Andrew Reynolds &   ]
            Arthur Campbell   ]
There are eight distributees of the estate of _____ Reynolds,
deceased, that John Reynolds to have $19.24½, that Arthur
Campbell have $112.80, that James Reynolds have $643.06½, that
Benjamin Reynolds have $681.91½, that David Reynolds have
$681.90, and that Andrew Reynolds former admr has failed to
pay owner to them said estate into the hands of Alfred Campbell, admr and that Arthur Campbell is his security. Court
ordered that Alfred Campbell recover of Andrew Reynolds and
Arthur Campbell $1154.99.

Page 373 - Wildow & heirs of] 15 March 1845. Exparte.
            T. C. Nash   ]
Commissioners to lay off the dower to the widow and make partition of real estate of T. C. Nash, deceased. Report: To
Johnannah Nash her dower out of the estate of Travis C. Nash,
her deceased husband, land in Bedford County, to wit, Beg at
the north east corner of the tract of land whereon the said
Travis C. Nash lived before his death, on the waters of Falling
Creek, containing about 125 acres which was one third of the
value of the tract of land. Johnannah Nash relinquished her
right of dower in other estate, she was given the dower in
land above, it being the homeplace. To Augustus Nash, Lot
No. 1, containing 16 acres. To James R. Nash, Lot No. 2, con-
taining 19 acres. To Thomas Nash,Lot No. 3, containing 25
acres. To Francis M. Nash, Lot No. 4, containing 35 acres.
To Lafayette Nash, Lot No. 5, containing 27 acres. To Abner
Nash, Lot No. 6, containing 22 acres. To Granderson Nash,
Lot No. 7, containing 18 acres. To John McGimpsey and wife
Mary formerly Mary Nash, Lot No. 8, containing 12 & 4 acres.
To William Nash, Lot No. 9, containing 23 acres. To George W.
Nash, Lot No. 10, containing 29 acres. To T. C. Nash, Lot
No. 11, containing 20½ acres. To William H. Harvel and wife
Louisa formerly Louisa Nash, Lot No. 12, containing 40 acres.
To Benjamin Garrett and wife Emily formerly Emily Nash, Lot
No. 13, containing 36¼ acres. To Levi Johnson and wife Eliza-
beth formerly Elizabeth Nash, containing 48 acres, Lot No. 14.
To James Nash, Lot No. 15, containing 77 acres. (Plat inclosed(.

CHANCERY COURT MINUTES 1840 - 1848

Page 1 -   William Norton   ]
                    vs   ]Filed 18 December 1840
           Sarah Burditt & others]
William Norton of Bedford County against Sarah Burditt, Nathan
Ivy in his own right and as guardian of Giles P. Burditt,
Samuel S. Burditt, Elizabeth G. Burditt, William M. Burditt,
Hmapton Burditt, Kenneth L. Burditt and Sarah Burditt, minors,
Matilda Burditt and Mary Ann Ivy, William Cown and Patience
his wife, Thomas Gregory and wife Rachel, all of Bedford
County, except William Cown and wife who reside in State of
Missouri. William Norton states that 3 April 1839, all the
defts above named, filed petition in court as heirs of William
Burditt, deceased, they having sold property in Bedford County,
containing 10 acres and including a valuable saw mill and grist
mill, was sold on 27 July 1839 to your orator, Thomas B. Moseley
has rented mills &c. Case Dissolved.

Page 4 - Newton T. Neil, Elizabeth Moss & others]
                    vs   ]4 March 1841.
           Abraham Mayfield   ]
Newton T. Neil, John K. Lowell and Elizabeth Moss all of Bedford County against Abraham Mayfield of Bedford County.
Orators, Neil, John K. Lowell and E. Moss in the year 1819
and for a long time before your oratrix Elizabeth was a child
of Samuel Moss who is now dead, that Samuel owned two negroes
which they now belong to your oratrix Elizabeth Moss by her
father's will, that on 14 August 1819 Samuel by deed of conveyed to his son James J. Moss and to your oratrix's two sons,
John K. Lowell and Newton F. (the latter by the name of Newton
Foot). On 2nd January 1827 negro Loanner had five children.
(Samuel was living on 15 April 1839) These were conveyed to
Abraham Mayfield. Will of Samuel Mayfield. I, Samuel Moss
of the County of Mecklenburg County, Virginia, know ye that
I, Samuel Moss for and in consideration of the natural love
and affection which I have and bear unto my son James J. Moss
and my wife's two sons, Newton Foot and John K. Lowelland for
divers good causes and consideration we hereunto ----- had
given and granted and by these present do give and grant unto
James J. Moss, Newton Foot and James K. Lowell, to them and
their heirs forever two negroes, the same as descended to me
in right of my wife by her father's will (test) a negro woman
Leanna and a negro girl Patsy, them and their increase, to
have and hold and enjoy to them the said James J. Moss, Newton
Foot and John K. Lowell, their heirs, executors and assignees
forever and the said Samuel Moss the above named negroes and
their increase to the above named James J. Moss, Newton Foot
and John K. Lowell, their heirs &c against all persons whatso-
ever shall and will warrant and forever defend by these present
reserving never the less as follows, to wit, I have given a
Deed of Trust upon the above negroes in favor of Henry Trott
and made Charles King, Sr., Trustee for the sum of $255.00.
Which sum I am bound to pay in said ---- before mentioned and
for which the said negroes are bound in said Deed of Trust
and further I reserve to myself and to my wife Elizabeth Moss
her life to hold and enjoy the above conveyed negroes and their
increase, and after the death of myself and my wife, the above
negroes and their increase to be equally divided as a love
conveyed share and share alike. I witness whereof I have hereunto set my hand and seal this 14th day of August A.D. 1819.
Zachariah Sherrin   Signed: Samuel (X) Moss (Seal)
John Sangfore   Warren County May Court 1820

Page 14 -   Freeman Burrow   ]
                      vs   ]
            William Burrow,   ]
            Robert F. Arnold   ]
            & Dudley P. T. House]
Orator, Freeman Burrow is an old man about 70 years of age,
whose bodily and mental energies are greatly impaired that
being possessed of four negroes as his own on about February
or March last, your orator made a Deed of Trust to Jacob Coble
for the same to secure said Coble in a debt of about $70.00
and to secure Coble in the possession and title to two tracts
of land, the one of about 50 acres and other about 5 acres
which Coble had purchased from your orator, and which your
orator had purchased from Robert Cannon and which land had
been sued for by the heirs of Whiteside. Orator had refunded
the purchase money and taking back the said 50 acres so that
Coble's deed is still unsatisfied as to the $70.00 and as to
the 5 acres, which has a valuable distillery on it, it is worth
$150.00 or $200.00 at least. Orator states that on 9 October
1838, Robert F. Arnold and William Burrow (son of orator) and
Arnold being brother in law to William, came to orator's home
and asked for a dram and being informed that there were no
spirits in the house. Robert F. Arnold and William Burrow
said they would send two negroes to a neighbor's still house,
viz, Jacob Coble. Arnold and Burrow said they were going over
to Wiley Daniel's and would return by the time the negroes
returned with whiskey. But they overtook the negroes and
seized them and carried them to Huntsville, Alabama and sold
them as their own property to one Stephen S. Ewing of that
place.

Page 22 -   William G. Cowan]
                      vs   ] Filed 3 December 1842
            G. W. Fogleman,]
            Fordyce Wilson &]
            Ebenezer Wilson]
Orator states that he obtained 10 judgements against Fordyce
Wilson on 16 December 1841. A judgement was levied upon a
tract of land of Fordyce Wilson, about 40 acres, on waters
of Falling Creek and adjoining the place in which Fogleman
then resided, now to be sold in 1842 to Ebenezer Wilson.

Page 28 -   Peter Lee, admr of   ]
            Hugh Snelling, deceased   ]
                      vs   ]
            Lemuel Snelling, John Snelling,   ]
            Susannah Searcy, James H. Arnold &   ]
            wife Louisa H., Robert S. McConnell]
            & wife Fanny and Elizabeth Snelling]
            an idiot.   ]
Orator states that Hugh Snelling departed this life, intestate,
in April 1841 in Bedford County. He died seized of a large
property, both real and personal and the following persons
are his distributees and heirs at law, to wit, Lemuel Snelling,
John Snelling, Susannah Searcy, Louisa H. Arnold wife of James
H. Arnold, and Elizabeth Snelling an idiot whose guardian is
John A. Moore. The foregoing are the children of said Hugh.
In addition to them are Fanny (Frances) McConnell wife of
Robert S. McConnell who is an illegitimate daughter of Nancy
Snelling, deceased, who was a daughter of Hugh Snelling. Hugh
Snelling left a large amount of property and negroes to be
divided among his heirs. In 1811, Lemuel Snelling was about
to move to Tennessee from the State of North Carolina where

his father had lived. The old man said his negroes were an
expense to him and wanted Lemuel to take some to Tennessee
with him. Hugh Snelling came to Tennessee about 7 or 8 years
later. When Lemuel left North Carolina in 1811, he rode a
horse, which had been his father's but he left a good one of
his own with his father for him with the old gentleman's free
one sent, no boot was desiring or demanded at the time but
a simple exchange. A dwelling house for the old man on the
land purchased for him the year before he came to Tennessee,
for bringing out from North Carolina a young sister, boarding
and supporting her upwards of a year during which time she
was much afflicted and died, this daughter during the time
had a child at respondent's house which rendered the whole
affliction. The mother being a young girl died shortly after
the birth of the child, the respondent kept the illegitimate
infant upwards of two years after its mother's death. The
mother and child were entirely supported and attended to by
respondent and the medical bill and personal expense were
jointly borne by him and his brother John Snelling, one of
the defts in this bill.
     A suit was filed against William Hickman who had purchased
a negro from Thompson Gray, a son in law of the old gentleman
and to whom the negro had only been borned. John Snelling
states that Frances McConnell is stated as the illegitimate
daughter of Hugh Snelling, because as stated in the bill an
illegitimate daughter of Nancy Snelling, daughter of Hugh
Snelling. Nancy the mother of Frances (who has now married
to deft McConnell) died about 20 years before her father Hugh
and Has never received any property from her father. She had
no property at her death. Frances could only exhibit the
property of her mother, but as her mother died without any
she cannot inherit from her mother's father.

Page 41 - T. D. Connally & Brother]
                    vs   ] Filed 24 December 1841.
           Calvin Thompson et als]
Thomas D. Connally and George Anderson Connally, merchants
co-partners in trade, citizens of Madison County, Tennessee
against James Thompson, Newton Thompson and Martha Thompson,
all of Bedford County, obtained several judgements which were
rendered before David Shrofshire, Esq., J.P. of Madison County,
Tennessee.

Page 52 - Thomas Davis   ]
                  vs   ]
          John T. Shanks &]
          David Green   ]
Thomas Davis of Bedford County and John T. Shanks of Missouri
and David Shanks of Missouri. Orator states that Shanks and
Green formerly were residents of Bedford County before going
to Missouri and that they are indebted to orators by notes.
Shanks left for Missouri in 1837 or 1838. Orator states that
the only property of John T. Shanks in Bedford County, is a
home and lot in Shelbyville now occupied as a work shop by
David Green. Said Lot No. 74. Orator asks for lot to be
attached. Shanks sold lot to Letitia Green but was not registered. (Letitia is mother of David Green). Augustus H. White
obtained a judgement against Shanks on lot No. 74, sold on
12 April 1828 by sheriff and Daniel McKisick became the purchaser.

Page 56 - Samuel Doak   ]
                  vs   ]
          James Smith & others]
Samuel Doak states that in 1842 at the request on one Samuel
Winston who was an agent of a man by the name of Monday, a
citizen of Mississippi, a reward was offered for delivery of
two runaway negroes belonging to Monday. The negroes were
brought in by 14 in number, James Smith, Isham Mosely, John
Blackwell, Jr., Richard Sims, Joseph Thompson, Green Evans,
James Wiggins, John Wiggins, William McAmie, George Thompson,
Jordan Holt, William D. Warner, Michael Holt and Joshua Holt.

Page 61 - Samuel T. Cannon & others]
                  vs   ] Filed 18 October 1844
          George Pratt & others   ] (23 District)
Samuel T. Cannon, Martha M., Jason H. T. and Letsy Cannon,
minors who sues by their guardian Letsy Cannon, Sr., against
William Pratt and his wife Catherine and George Pratt, all
of Bedford County.
Orators states that they and deft Catherine are the children
of Willis and Letsy Cannon who were formerly husband and wife
but have since been divorced on February 13, 1833 and registered in the Register's office. Letsy Cannon, Sr. loaned to
William and Catherine Pratt two negroes, Sinai and Jack.
Exhibit A: Willis and Letitia Cannon &c. Made 13 February 1833.
Between Willis Cannon and Letsy Cannon of Bedford County of
one part and Catharine Cannon, Samuel T. Cannon, Martha Cannon,
Jason H. Cannon and Letsy Cannon, children and issues of Willis
and Letsy Cannon of the other part. Witnessed that the said
Willis and Letsy Cannon, for and inconsideration of the love
and affection which they have towards the said Catharine,
Samuel, Martha, Jason H., and Letsy Cannon and the further
consideration of $100.00 to them in hand paid by Clement Cannon
and James Brittain, the funds of the said children aforesaid,
receipt acknowledged by Willis and Letsy Cannon to the above
named children and any other children which Willis and Letsy
may have after the following property, to wit, One tract of
land, situated in Bedford County on the south side of Duck
River, being part of a 5000 acre tract formerly belonging to
the estate of Walter Sims. Land borders lands of Minos Cannon,
Edmond Green, John G. Sims and containing about 200 acres,
being the land conveyed by David Sims to said Willis Cannon
on 10 February 1822. Another tract of land on the south side
of Duck River and on the waters of Duck River and Flat Creek.
Land bordering lands of Jacob Whit, grant of land to James
Grant from the State of North Carolina, Edmond Green and containing about 70 acres. Also, another tract of land on south
side of Duck River, bordering lands of where Nathaniel Johnston
now lives, Sim's Mill, Robert Morgan's line and containing
about 106½ acres, except 10 acres heretofore conveyed by Willis
Cannon to Thomas Saunders and also 13 negroes, to the heirs
of Willis and Letsy Cannon forever. Made 13 July 1833.

Page 71 - Allen Knight   ]
                  vs   ]
          Bennett Cully &   ]
          James S. Fowler]
Orator states that 27 December 1839, James S. Fowler sold to
Bennett Cully, a tract of land on the waters of the Barren
Fork of Duck River and Doddy's Creek and bounded by lands of
Elijah Holt, Doddy's Creek, Barren Fork, Cully's field, and
containing about 100 acres.

Page 73 - John W. Cobb   ]
            vs   ]
         W. F. Daniel &]
         A. C. Wood   ]
John W. Cobb against Andrew C. Wood and Wiley F. Daniel, all
of Bedford County. Orator stated that on February 1838, he
sold Andrew C. Wood a tract of land in Bedford County on waters
of Beech Creek in District No. 23, containing 130 acres and
bounded by Bond and Lile, N. Cannon and Duck River, Wiley F.
Daniel, being the land on which Wood now lives and he has resided for several years. Wood still owes last payment on land.
Orator states that the legal title to said land is in Wiley F.
Daniel who contracted to sell said land to Thomas Terry from
which your orator purchased and then orator sold to said Moore.

Page 75 - Willis W. Wilhoite]
            vs   ]
         William T. McGrew,]
         William S. Jett &]
         Samuel Phillips   ]
Orator states that he recovered a judgement against William T.
McGrew, on money due orator for land and mills of Duck River
near Shelbyville. Land borders north bank of Duck River and
containing 1 acre and 8 poles. Another tract of land borders
an island in Duck River where James Sharp built a mill and
Wilson Coats's original line, Cannon's line. Another tract
of land borders an island in Duck River on which Thomas Saunders
built a mill and containing about 15 acres. Also, another
tract of land bordering Duck River, lands of the heirs of Wilson
Coats, deceased and Sterling Newsom, containing about 34¼ acres.
Making in all about 70 acres.

Page 85 - Joseph McCamy   ]
            vs   ]
         Thomas J. Purdy & others]
Alexander Eakin, John Eakin and William G. Cowan]
Orator states that he obtained a judgement against Thomas J.
Purdy. It was against the property of Purdy but shortly before
he obtained the judgement, Purdy conveyed all his property
(land and 2 negroes) to different persons but chiefly to
Alexander and John Eakin, one or both of whom purchased his
land and negro slaves. Case dismissed.

Page 87 - Thomas Newsom]
            vs   ]
         John Sutton &]
         Minos Cannon]
Orator states that John Sutton and Hiram Edde executed to him
their joint note of $182.50 in part consideration of a lot
in the Town of Shelbyville sold by your orator to Edde.
Exhibit A: John Sutton states he sold to Minos Cannon and his
heirs, a tract of land in Bedford County on the waters of Big
Flat Creek, upon which John Sutton now lives and which was
bought from Stephen Hastings for $1.00 in hand.

Page 92 - Jesse M. Yowell   ]
            vs   ]
         Alexander & William A. Allen]
Jesse M. Yowell of Marshall County, Tennessee against Alexander
Allen of Bedford County and William A. Allen of Giles County,
Tennessee. Orator states that Alexander Allen had executed
several notes to your orator. Orator learned that Alexander
Allen owned a large estate of some 20 negroes and other personal

property and real estate, but during the year 1842, he became
embarrassed financially, he conveyed away all his property
in trust.

Page 96 -   Henry Yancy & others]
                 vs   ]
            Philip Brooks &   ]
            Caswell High   ]
Orators and oratrixes Henry, James, William, Elizabeth, Francis,
Louisa, Rebecca and Jane Yancy, minors by their guardian, next
friend and brother Henry and Alexander Yancy, a citizen of
Virginia and Elizabeth Yancy against Caswell High and Philip
Brooks of Bedford County. Orators states that they are the
children of Kavenaugh Yancy who intermarried with one Elizabeth Watts of the State of Virginia, about 35 years ago, the
father of said Elizabeth, Frederick Watt, dead, and by his
will bequeathed among other property, a negro woman named
Violet about 30 years of age, to the said Elizabeth during
her natural life for her separate use, remainder to your orators
and oratrixes, the children and heirs of said Elizabeth, your
oratrix the said Elizabeth represents that her life estate,
has not yet expired. The foregoing fact will more fully appear
by reference to the Last Will and Testament of the said Fredrick Watts which will be exhibited at the hearing of this
cause. There never was any title to said negro in the husband
of your oratrix Elizabeth the said Kavenaugh Yancy nor is there
yet any title to the same in the said Kavenaugh, yet the defts
to this bill have caused said negro woman Violet to be levied
on by Lewis Shapard, a constable of Bedford County, as the
property of said Kavenaugh Yancy to satisfy certain debts,
which they pretend to have against Kavenaugh of about $50.00,
your orators and oratrixes further states that being very
ignorant of law and of their legal rights, and as their father
the said Kavenaugh has for sometime become embarrassed in his
circumstances. Your orators Henry and James paid to the said
Kavenaugh $200.00 for his interest in said negro named in said
will and took his Deed of Relinquishment to the same dated
October 13th, 1840 and duly proven and registered. Your orators
suppose that their father had no interest in the property bequeathed to the separate use of their mother during her life.
Remainder to her children, but when the last named Deed of
Purchase was made, they had not taken council in the cause.
At present they charge that Kavenaugh Yancy never had any interest in said property but that if he had the same was conveyed to your orators Henry and James for a full and valuable
consideration. Your orators will exhibit said deed from Kavenaugh to them at the hearing of this cause. Orators and Oratrixes states that said negro Violet belongs exclusively to
them and not to said Kavenaugh Yancy, and therefore that his
creditors have no right to sell her for his debts and ought
to be enjoined from so doing. Said negro is of peculiar value
to them and cannot be fully compensated for in damages.

Page 99 -   Coffman Leib   ]
                 vs   ]
            Michael Marcus]
Leib and Marcus, both of Bedford County. Coffman Leib commenced merchandising in Shelbyville in co-partnership with Michael
Marcus under the name and style of Marcus & Leib. Orator
states that they started the business with out any agreement
in partnership but a misunderstanding between them, that all
the articles of Dry Goods &c as they might purchase should
be bought and sold in the partnership of Marcus & Leib and

the partnership to last as long as it exists in that name.
Orator states that his partner went on to Philadelphia about
10 February last and returned within five weeks. He went to
purchase goods for the firm, he purchased about $2400.00 worth
of goods to be paid for out of partnership fund, orator says
the goods be brought on to Shelbyville and sold only in partnership name of Marcus & Leib. Marcus has cause part of the goods
to be stopped in Nashville, about 10 or 11 hundred dollars
worth stopped in Nashville and attempting to sell them under
his own name by auction without letting your orator know about
it.

Page 101 - Levin Wood   ]
                vs   ]
          Enoch Trott &]
          Clement Cannon]
Levin Wood of Orange County, North Carolina against Enoch Trott
and Clement Cannon of Bedford County. Orator states that he
is the brother and only heir at law of Keziah Galbreath, dec'd,
late of Bedford County, who departed this life intestate and
without any heirs of her body. Orator states that for several
months before the death of Keziah, she was insane and wholly
incapable of transacting any business which would be binding
in law, and so remained up to the time of her death. Orator
states that she was the owner by title in fee simple of a
tract of land in bedford County, about 182 acres, and which
is described and bounded by lands of Keziah Galbreath and
Andrew Reed, Flat Creek, John B. Cummings and Dixon's line.

     Orator states that after Keziah became insane she sold
and conveyed by deed on 25 September 1838, all her rights and
title to land to Enoch Trott for $450.00, which is little more
that half the value. Trott executed a note and is still unpaid.

     Bill of Review: of William Allbright and Louise his wife,
William Wood, Ann Wood, Robert Wood, Levin Allbright, Handy
Wood, John Thompson and Elizabeth his wife, Sila and Sarah
his wife, Vestal and Mary his wife, Washington Wood, Martha
Wood, Lafayette Wood, Maria Wood and Levin Wood, the last five
being minors who sue by their next friend William Allbright,
heirs of Levin Wood, deceased, late of North Carolina against
Enoch Trott and Clement Cannon, defts. Orators and oratrixes
states that Levin Wood, deceased, late of Orange County, North
Carolina, on 13 August 1839 filed his original bill in Chancery
Court against Trott and Cannon, alleging that he was the brother of and only heir of Keziah Galbreath, deceased, late of
Bedford County, who died without heirs of her body &c.

Page 110 - James Walker   ]
                vs   ]
          William Brown]
Orator states that being great need of money, be borrowed of
deft William Brown $391.00. Orator secured the payment by
a Deed of Trust on real estate, when time for payment came
due, he was unable to pay. Brown wanted land to be sold. Your
orator states to avoid the sale of the land under the Trust
for cash and sold the same to John Scott.

Page 113 - Delila Ray]
                vs   ] Bill for Divorce.
          James Ray]
Delila Ray, by her next friend William Lamb of Bedford County,
filed against James Ray formerly of Bedford County but at present confined in the Public Jail and Penitentiary house at

Nashville. Oratrix states that she was lawfully married to
James Ray in Bedford County about 14 December 1840. That at
the November Term of Circuit Court of Williamson County, Tennessee, said James Ray was convicted of the crime of horse
stealing and sentenced to imprisonment in the public jail for
three years and three months. She desires her marriage to
be dissolved. Final decree, 27 December 1843.

Page 114 - William Brown   ]
                 vs   ]
            James Sadler &   ]
            Gabriel B. Knight]
Orator states that he recovered a judgement against James
Sadler for about $223.00 plus cost. Both are of Bedford County.
Orator states that Sadler is insolvent. He also said that
Sadler sold a negro woman to Gabriel B. Knight since the suit
was filed. Case was dismissed.

Page 116 - George Rogers   ]
                 vs   ]
            John W. Mayfield &]
            Abraham Mayfield   ]
A bill of complaint of George Rogers, Sons, partner of the
T----- firm of Jacob Rogers & Sons, a citizen of Baltimore,
Maryland filed in the Chancery Court at Shelbyville against
Abraham Mayfield and John W. Mayfield, both of Bedford County.
Orator states that at the December Term 1842 Circuit Court
of Bedford County, received a judgement against Abraham Mayfield
and one Robert Mathews and Wilkins Blanton on a note by William
S. Mayfield (who was not sued), orator states that a few days
previous to rendition of his judgement conveyed by one more
conveyance all of his property real and personal, to his son
John W. Mayfield which conveyance was registered. This cause
is dismissed.

Page 117 - James Deery   ]
                 vs   ]
            Samuel Pollock &]
            John Hastings   ]
James Deery of Bedford County, Samuel Pollock of Benton County,
Arkansas and John Hastings of Bedford County. Orator states
that Pollock is indebted to him for about $118.25¼ due 1827.
At the time of the note Pollock was a citizen of Bedford County.
Pollock was insolvent. Orator states that lately Susannah
Hastings departed this life, intestate, who at the time of
her death was a citizen of Bedford County, leaving five negroes
and perhaps other property, that there are six distributees
of Susannah of which Pollock is one, that John Hastings at
the ____ Term of Bedford County was appointed admr of Susannah.

Page 119 - William F. Long & Co &   ]
            Samuel Doak   ]
                 vs   ]
            The Union Bank of Tennessee]
William F. Long, Rufus K. Flack, surviving partners of the
firm of William F. Long & Co. and Samuel Doak filed against
President, Directors & Co. of Union Bank of Tennessee. William
F. Long of Talladega County, Alabama, Rufus K. Flack of (blank)
County of Mississippi and Samuel Doak of Bedford County for
merchants of Shelbyville, sometime during 1836, said firm re-
ceived a note for $4000.00 by Benjamin Williams payable to
J. R. Walker and indorsed to J. T. H. Claiborne and by him
to D. W. Harley and by him to William F. Long & Co.

Page 130 - Samuel G. Thompson   ]
             vs   ] Att. Bill.
        Samuel Mitchell & others]
Orator Samuel G. Thompson, a minor, who sues by his guardian
Joseph R. McKinley, states that 7 or 8 years ago William R.
Guy was appointed guardian of your orator, with some three
others and intended into bond with Samuel Mitchell, Thomas N.
McLain and John B. Cooper his securities. He also states that
the effects which came into the hands of William R. Guy, as
guardian, amounted to $800.00 to go to the three wards includ-
ing your orator. Orator states that Guy never expended anything for the support of your orator and is liable to pay the
whole of said $260.00 plus interest. George has left State
of Tennessee, Guy and Mitchell both live in Arkansas and Thomas
N. McLain lives in Mississippi and John B. Cooper in the State
of Alabama. None of them owns any property in this state,
except Samuel Mitchell who owns a stallion horse in Bedford
County now in possession of Robert Denniston.

Page 132 - Carlos D. Steele, admr]
             vs   ]Att. Bill filed 20 Aug 1844.
        Peter Rowlett   ]
Orator states that James G. Whitney formerly of Bedford County,
on 1 June 1840, absconded from Bedford County where he then
resided to parts unknown and took with him all the property
or nearly so, negro slaves, also he was much embarrassed with
debt. Bill dismissed.

Page 136 - Elisha G. Forest   ]
             vs   ] Filed 26 May 1843.
        John P. Wood &   ]
        Green L. Poplin, admr   ]
        of Johnathan Wood, deceased]
Orators stated that John P. Wood is indebted to your orator.
Elisha G. Forest of Marshall County, Tennessee, John P. Wood
of Alabama, and Johnathan Wood, deceased, of Bedford County.
John P. Wood is a child and distributee of Johnathan Wood who
departed this life intestate a few months ago in Bedford County,
possessed of some valuable property, also that Green L. Poplin
was since the decease of Johnathan Wood, was appointed admr
of his estate.

Page 139 - Walter H. & John G. Sims]
             vs   ]Filed 17 May 1843.
        William T. McGrew   ]
Orators sold to William T. McGrew a tract of land in Bedford
County on the waters of Duck River in District No. 3. Land
bounded by the lands of Robert Cannon and Uriah Cross and containing about 136 acres. McGrew paid part of payment and made
notes.

Page 141 - Thomas S. Parsons]
             vs   ]
        James Claxton &   ]
        Benjamin Brown   ]
Orator is admr of John Claxton, deceased, a citizen of Giles
County, Tennessee, filed against James Claxton and Benjamin
Brown, both of Bedford County. Orator obtained a judgement
against Claxton and Brown.

Page 143 - Benjamin Philips]
             vs   ]
        Robert T. Cannon]

Orators states that in February 1842, Robert T. Cannon offered at public sale, 2 Town Lots in Shelbyville, known as Lot No. 33 and 34. Cannon was admr of Archibald Dobson, deceased, subject to the dower interest of Mary Dobson, widow of Archibald Dobson.

Page 153 - Smith Bowlin   ]
              vs   ]
         William & N. Suggs]
Smith Bowlin of Rutherford County, Tennessee and William and Nehemiah Suggs of Bedford County. Orator on 16 March 1844 obtained a judgement against William Sugg.

Page 154 - John A. Blakemore]
              vs   ]Bill of Discovery & Inj.
         James Wilson   ]
John A. Blakemore of Bedford County and James Wilson of Marshall County, Tennessee.

Page 159 - Jesse M. Yowell   ]
              vs   ]
         Alexander Allen &]
         Jesse Coleman   ]
Jesse M. Yowell of Marshall County, Tennessee and Alexander Allen and Jesse Coleman of Bedford County. Orator recovered a judgement against A. Allen. Alexander Allen sold on 20 Oct 1842 to Jesse Coleman, property. Land in Bedford COunty and land on which he now lives and bounded by lands of Mrs. Stepen's and Herbert Smith and John Brame and by school land and other property. Case dismissed.

Page 162 - Joshua Averett &]
         Adam Frelick   ]
              vs   ]
         Jacob Harrison &]
         James Burton   ]
Joshua Averett and Adam Frelick, both of Autauga County, Alabama and Jacob Harrison formerly of Alabama and now of Bedford County and also James Burton of Bedford County. Orators states that 6 February 1840, deft Jacob Harrison executed a mortgage or Deed of Trust to them to secure large debts.

Page 170 - Nancy Bearden & others   ]
         Exparte Petition to   ]
         lay of dower and sell land]
Nancy Bearden (widow of Eli Bearden), Wallis Bearden, William B. Hix and his wife Minerva, Nimrod Bearden, James G. Claunch and wife Charlotte, John T. Bearden, Nathan Bearden, George T. Walsh and his wife Nancy (adult heirs of Eli Bearden) and Wynn Bearden, Allen Bearden and Elizabeth Bearden by their next friend John T. Bearden filed Exparte in Bedford County. Orators stated that about 1831, Eli Bearden departed this life intestate in Bedford County, leaving your oratrix Nancy his widow and his other children and heirs being ten in number. All estate had been disposed of in a manner satisfactory to all. Eli Bearden died seized and described of 13 deeds and grants exhibited as such, A, B, C, D, E, F, G, H, I, J, K, L, and M, and Nancy has not yet received her dower. After she is to get her dower, the land left to be sold. Land bordered by the widow's dower, John Bearden, widow Fulton, B. D. W. Shooks, Simpson's corner, and M. Cunningham's land. J. C. Couch was purchaser. Another tract of land borders M. Cunningham, J. Couch's line, J. P. Couch's line, D. D. Hix, E. Woosley.

John T. Bearden purchaser.

Page 173 - Mary B. Atkins   ]
                 vs   ]
             Henderson W. Atkins]
Mary B. Atkins of Bedford County, states that she was lawfully
married some 12 years ago (ca 1830) to Henderson W. Atkins
of Virginia and that she lived with him in that state for about
4 years when they moved to Tennessee where your oratrix has
resided ever since. She said she was a dutiful loving and
affectionate wife. She said that for some 5 or 6 years since
the said Henderson W. Atkins changed his treatment of her and
he became turbulent quarrelsome and without any cause whatso-
ever, he would often commence difficulties with her and even
inflicted personal injuries on her, she had scars to show.
She said that some two or three weeks before the birth of her
youngest child, he whipped, beat and bruised and has left
scars that she will take to the grave. He even drove her from
her bed when her infant was only eight days old and forced
her to leave his house in the night by means of which she was
compelled to seek shelter from neighbor. After this he left
her when the infant was not a month old and has not lived with
her since but is now living in adultery in Virginia. She says
that it will be two years in April since he left. She said
that when she married said Atkins, she was possessed of a large
estate in which in settlement with her guardian, the said
Atkins removed mostly in negroes of which was 14, all of whom
he had squandered and spent leaving her destitute. She had
three children. Atkins shortly before he left, sold the last
of the negroes and made notes to William A. Taylor. She believes that he gave security Reuben Stramler who with Taylor
lives in Franklin County, Tennessee and also John Taylor and
John Motlow of Lincoln County, Tennessee. She states that
left other notes with William Tolley also of Lincoln County,
Tennessee. Deft William N. Taylor says that about 9 January
1838 he purchased slaves.

Page 179 - Alexander Brown]
                 vs   ]
             Solomon Brown]
Orator states that on 1st November 1841, he was in need of
money and applied to Solomon Brown, a money lender and shaver
for a loan of $300.00 and sold to him a note on Anderson T.
Clay for $80.00. Brown did loan him $300.00 in bank notes.

Page 186 - Martin Smith]
                 vs   ] Inj. Bill.
             Jeremiah Ellis]
Martin Smith of Bedford County and Jeremiah Ellis of Davidson
County, Tennessee. Orator states that on 27 July 1826, Jeremiah Ellis obtained a judgement against him in Davidson County,
Tennessee for $138.75 and cost. Ellis has since placed the
note in the hands of James Mullins of Bedford County and he
has levied it upon a negro named Nancy the property of your
orator.

Page 190 - Rosal Rollen   ]
                 vs   ]Att. Bill, filed 23 Jan 1842
             Samuel & Newcom Thompson]
Orator states that sometime in December 1839, Samuel Thompson
at the request of your orator loaned and advanced to him $210.00
in bank notes. He mortgaged a negro woman, Rachael, age about
25 years.

Page 203 - John Dean   ]
              vs   ] Inj. Bill.
          John Nichols]
Orator states that in early part of the year 1840, John Nichols
of Missouri, who was then a citizen of Bedford County but has
since removed to Missouri, was elected to the Office of Constable in Bedford County and your orator was one of his securities. But in latter part of the year 1841, John Nichols having
failed to pay our money which he had collected in his official
capacity to a large amount.

Page 208 - Richard H. Sims,] Exparte Petition for to sell land.
          Guardian &c.   ]
Orator, guardian of Mary R. Davis and Charlotte Davis. Orator
states that his wards, Mary R. Davis and Charlotte S. Davis,
inherited from their grandfather John Sims who died sometime
in the year 1841 certain negro property whose names are as
follows, negro man Edmond aged about 40 years, one boy Sandy
4 years old, woman Mima and her two children. Orator states
that before the next term of this court, his ward Mary E. will
have married and he desires the division of property to be
divided among his wards. Mary and Charlotte S. Davis are the
children and heirs of Henry Davis, deceased.

Page 210 - Thomas P. Powell   ]
              vs   ] Inj. Bill.
          James Mullins &   ]
          Thomas C. Whiteside]
Orator Thomas P. Powell stated that his father Robert Powell
died sometime in the summer of 1842 and orator was duly appointed admr and that T. C. Whiteside had brought suit against him.
Suit dismissed.

Page 215 - James W. Head & others   ]
              vs   ]
          Jesse P. Tucker & others]
James W. Head, Charlotte Head and Littleton Averett and wife
Sarah, the two former are of Bedford County, two latter of
Rutherford County, Tennessee files against Jesse P. Tucker
and wife Elizabeth, Isreal Harris and wife Martha, and John A.
Head, all of Bedford County, except John A. Head of Giles
County, Tennessee. Orators stated that Enoch Head departed
this life intestate in January last (18--), died seized of
two tracts of land in Bedford County in District No. 8. One
of 414 acres, the one of which he lived at the time of his
death, the other had 48 acres of which Enoch had purchased
from John Thompson. Orators stated that Charlotte is the widow
and your orators James W. Head and Sarah Averett who has intermarried with Littleton Averett, John A. Head, Elizabeth Tucker
wife of Jesse P. Tucker, Martha Harris wife of Isreal Harris
and Mary head are the only children and heirs at law of Enoch
Head. Also, that since the death of Enoch Head, Mary Head
has departed this life having first made and published her
Last Will and Testament which was proven in Bedford County,
by which she devised your orator and oratrixes Charlotte and
Sarah, all her interest in the estate of Enoch Head. The
devises desires the estate to be divided as such, to Charlotte
1/7 of land and each of the children, 1/7 part including Mary,
deceased. Case dismissed.

Page 217 - Joel Whorley   ]
              vs   ]
          Elizabeth Brown]

112

Orators files against Elizabeth Brown, Rachael, Jesse, Thomas,
Elizabeth and Daniel C. Brown, Cynthia Whorley, John, Abram(?)
and Henry Brown, the last three are minors and William Brown
who is a citizen of Washington County, Arkansas. Orator states
that some years ago intermarried with Cynthia Brown, a daughter
of Jesse Brown, Sr., that in the year ---- your orator contracted with Thomas Russell to purchase a tract of land and applied
to his fahter in law Jesse Brown to become his security for
purchase money which was $700.00 which Jesse Brown refused
and that he would execute his own note for the purchase money
and take the deed and orator was to pay debts as they came
due. Brown died intestate and the following are the widow
and heirs at law of Brown, to wit, Elizabeth Brown, widow,
and Paschall, Jesse, Thomas, Daniel P., William, John, Alvin
and Henry Brown, Elizabeth Brown, Jr., Cynthia Whorley wife
of your orator, all of Bedford County, except William who is
a citizen of Washington County, Arkansas. (All are of age except John, Alvin and Henry who are minors). The land lying
on the waters of Sinking Creek in Bedford County, bordering
lands of Benjamin Taliaferro, Robert White's grant, and containing 140 acres.

Page 220 - Thomas C. Williams   ]
                 vs   ]
           William Bennett & others]
Orator files against Blackman C. Dobson and wife Martha Jane
and others. Orator states that his father Jesse E. Williams
departed this life some 12 or 14 years since, that at the time
of his death he was the owner of slaves (9), that since the
death of his father Jesse E. Williams, Peggy (slave) has had
4 children. Also widow Martha Jane Williams has intermarried
with Blackman C. Dobson, Julia A. Williams who has since intermarried with Isreal Fonville, Airy A. Williams who has since
intermarried with Thomas White, Elizabeth M. Williams who has
since intermarried with Joseph A. Cunningham, Mary E. Williams
who is a minor and has Gabriel B. Knight for her guardian and
Elizabeth M. Williams, his widow who has intermarried with
William Burnett, in all seven (7) distributees. (Guardian
of Jesse E. Williams minors were made at May Term 1839 in Bedford County and that at November Term 1831 Burnett appointed
admr of Jesse E. Williams' estate.)

Page 228 - William Brown   ]
                 vs   ] Inj. Bill, filed 23 December 1843.
           Alexander Allen &]
           Herbert Smith   ]
All of Bedford County. Orator states that on 21 February 1843,
he recovered two judgements against Allen. Case dismissed
24 February 1845.

Page 229 - Robert Cannon   ]
                 vs   ] Inj. Bill, filed 27 Feb
           Walter H. & John G. Sims]   1844.
Orator states that Walter H. and John G. Sims obtained a judgement against your orator and that early in year 1840, he purchased from W. H. and J. G. Sims, two tracts of land, one about
82 acres and another for about 132 acres, in all 214 acres.
Orator said that he had no good title to said tracts of land
as yet. Orator states that Thomas D. Wilson a resident of
Louisiana had an interest in one share of said tracts. T. D.
Wilson is a brother in law to Walter H. and John G. Sims and
that he would relinquish all interest in said tract of land.
Amended bill, May 22, 1844.

Answer of Walter H. Sims, admr of John G. Sims, deceased -
John G. had died sometime last year (1843) in Williamson County,
Tennessee, intestate.
Exhibit A: I, Thomas D. Wilson of Caddo Parish, Louisiana,
appointed John A. Hollan of Williamson County, Tennessee, my
lawful attorney for me to sell and convey deed with all interest
is a tract of land in Bedford County the same in which I inherited as an heir of my son Walter Sims Wilson who inherited
the same as the only heir of his mother, one of the heirs of
John G. Sims, deceased, or in right of my late wife Ann H.,
formerly Ann H. Sims, 4 January 1840.
Exhibit B: 11 June 1842, between Thomas D. Wilson of Caddo
Parish, Louisiana of one part and John G. Sims, Walter H. Sims
and Boyd M. Sims of Williamson County, Tennessee of other part.
That in 1836, John G. and Walter H. and Boyd M. Sims and their
sister Ann H. Sims were heirs of their father John G. Sims,
deceased, seized of land in Bedford County on waters of Duck
River. Land bounded by lands of J. Wood's, the Duck River,
Arnold's corner, Dowdy's corner, Moores and Sutton corner,
Holland's corner, Mabry's line, Hamilton's Branch and containing 650 acres. Anothe tract of land, borders lands of Cross,
south bank of Duck River, and containing 67 acres and 61 poles.
Another tract, on south side of Duck River, containing 17 acres
and 47 poles. Another tract, on south side of Duck River,
borders Dunaway's corner, Beavers' corner, and containing 33+
acres and where the said Thomas D. Wilson intermarried with
Ann H. Sims in October 1836 and she had one child, the issue
of said marriage, born in October 1837 and said Ann H. died
in November 1837 and said child died in February 1839 by means
T. D. Wilson became entitled to a life estate in 1/4 of said
lands.

Page 237 - William Brown]
                  vs   ] Inj. Bill.
         James Sadler &]
         Samuel Doak   ]
Orators states that on 13 August 1843, he recovered a judgement
against James Sadler. No property found of the deft.

Page 239 - Daniel Gilchrist]
                  vs   ] Filed 6 February 1844.
         Jesse Watson &]
         James Hoover   ]
Daniel Gilchrist of Alabama and Jesse Watson and James Hoover
of Bedford County. Orator states that on 17 December 1842,
he recovered a judgement against Jesse Watson. "No property
found" of Jesse Watson. Also, Jesse Watson purchased of James
Hoover a tract of land of 100 acres in Bedford County and bounded by lands of William Murfree, Oliver Bingham, Joseph Loyd,
and Robert Clinkenbeard and the heirs of Joseph Loyd in District
No. 5. Case dismissed.

Page 240 - William Hime   ]
                  vs   ] Inj. Bill.
         James Christian]
Orator stated that he contracted with James Christian for the
purchase of a certain tract of land in Bedford County, containing about 20 acres, Lot No. 5 in the division of the lands
of John Himes, deceased. The land descended to the wife of
said Christian from her father John Hime, and she at the time
of the contract was a minor. Case Dismissed.

Page 242 - George Davidson]
              vs   ] Inj. Bill, filed 4 March 1844.
        Samuel Jones &]
        Neely S. Coble]
Orator states that on 23 February 1844 judgements were obtained
before William Galbreath, Esq. One in favor of Samuel Jones
and one in favor of Keller McClure, two others in favor of
your orator and one William B. M. Brame. Case dismissed.

Page 244 - William B. Gibson, admr of]
        Samuel K. Gibson, deceased]
              vs   ]
        Micajah T. Cooper   ]
Samuel K. Gibson, deceased, formerly of Coffee County, Tennessee. Orator states that Samuel K. Gibson departed this life
intestate in Bedford COunty in February 1841 and at July Term
1842, he was appointed admr of his estate. Micajah T. Cooper
of Bedford County. At the time of intestate's death, he was
engaged in the mercantile business in Bedford County in co-
partnership with Micajah T. Cooper having commenced in 1839
and continued until Gibson's death. Need to check all records
and books of the firm. Many names listed in books.

Page 255 - William R. Looney, Exr &c]
              vs   ]
        George W. Whitesell & others]
Orators states that in January 1842, William M. Russell departed this life at his residence in Bedford County having made
a Last Will and Testament and filed. In February 1842, he
was confirmed as executor of William M. Russell, deceased.
The following legatees of George W. Whitesell and wife Mary
Deltha, Cyrus N. Allen and wife Lucy Caroline Word, Joel C.
Russell, Sally Malvina Freeman and the heirs of her body whose
husband is Otheniel Freeman, William A. Russell, Margaret Ann
Louise Butler Russell, Martha Freeman Russell, the last three
who are minors and also the children of James R. Russell,
deceased, who was a son of your orator's intestator, to wit,
William E. Russell, Martha Elizabeth Russell, Samuel S. Russell,
Simpson Russell and James R. Russell, all of whom reside in
Bedford COunty. There are large debts against, probably more
than was asset to cover. William M. Russell made a Last Will
and Testament:
I, William M. Russell, do make and publish this my Last Will
and Testament, hereby resolving and making void all other wills
by me at any time made.
First, I commend my soul to God who gave it and direct that
my burial expenses and all of my debts be paid as soon after
my death as possible out of any money I may die possessed of
or may first come into the hands of executors and as to my
property I direct that it be disposed of as follows, viz...
1st, Leaving to my son James R. Russell in money and property
to amount of five hundred and ten dollars ($510.00). I with-
hold from his heirs anything further until the rest of my children be made equal with him.
2nd, Those for bequeath unto George W. Whitesell and his wife
Mary Deltha(Deetha) who is my daughter, a certain negro girl
named Clary at $250.00. Having given them other effects to
the amount of $40.00.
2nd, I give unto Cyrus N. Allen and his wife Lucy Caroline
Word (Ward) who is my daughter a certain negro girl name Lizza
at $250.00 having given them other effects to the amount of
$8,00.
3rd, I give and bequeath unto my son Joel Calaway Russell a

certain negro boy named Stephen at $800.00 and my horse Jim
at $25.00.
4th, I give and bequeath unto my daughter Sally Matilda Freeman
and the heirs of her body a certain negro girl named Huldah
at $250.00.
5th, I give and bequeath to my son William Allen Russell a
certain negro boy named Tom at $600.00 and direct that my
executor furnish him with a man's saddle worth $23.00 out of
my money belonging to my estate when the said William Allen
Russell shall arive to the age of maturity.
6th, I give and bequeath unto my daughter Margaret Ann Louisa
Bathe(Butler, name given above) Russell, a certain negro girl
named Nancy at $250.00.
7th, I give and bequeath unto my daughter Martha Freeman
Russell, a certain negro girl named Harriet at $250.00.
8th, I direct Mariah and Sterling my negro man and negro woman
be hired out to the highest bidder annually until the youngest
of children come to be of lawful age. I also direct that
Stephen be hired out for one year to the highest bidder before
his being delivered to my son Joel C. Russell and I further
direct that Tom be hired out annually to the highest bidder
until my son William A. Russell arrives at lawful age the
money receiving for the hire of said negroes to be donated
to the clothing, boarding and schooling of my three youngest
children, that is to say, William A. Russell to be schooled
one year and Margaret B. Russell one year and Louisa one year,
and Martha Freeman Russell eighteen months. I further state
that my land, horses, hogs, oxens, corn, fodder and all of
good effects in and out of doors not heretofore bequeathed
be sold to the highest bidder on twelve months credit. I also
appoint William R. Looney my true and lawful executor and
appoint Cyrus N. Allen guardian of my two youngest daughters
Margaret and Louisa Butler and Martha Freeman Russell and that
they my youngest daughters be by their guardian put in possession of their mother's saddle and bridle. In testimony whereof
I this day set my hand and affix my seal, January 7th, 1842.
Attest: William H. Craig   Signed: William M. Russell (Seal)
        Stephen Freeman

Page 262 - Nelson Blackwell & others]
              vs   ]
        John Johnson & others   ]
Orators Nelson Blackwell and Susan his wife, William Reddin,
Joseph Reddin, John Reddin, David Davenport and his wife Emaline, Matilda Reddin, William Calhoun and Martha his wife,
Elizabeth Reddin and Robert Reddin, the two last of whom are
minors and sue by their next friend Mark Reddin, all of whom
are citizens of Coffee County, Tennessee. Elisha Blackwell
and Susan his wife, Joseph B. Blackman, William J. Blackman,
Jeremiah Blackman, John E. Blackman, Caroline Blackman, Ellenor
Blackman and Mary Blackman, the last four of whom are minors
and sue by their guardian Benjamin Blackman, all of whom are
citizens of Lancaster District in State of South Carolina,
David Chase and Catherine his wife, James J. Blackman and
Burrel C. Johnson who are citizens of Harris County in State
of Georgia, file this case in Chancery Court at Shelbyville
against John Johnson, admr of Joseph Johnson, deceased, and
Susannah Johnson who are citizens of Coffee County, Tennessee.
    Orators states that sometime in the month of September
1842, Joseph Johnson who was a citizen of Coffee County, Tennessee, departed this life intestate leaving the following
persons his heirs and distributees, to wit, John Johnson son
of Joseph, Joseph Reddin, William Reddin, John Reddin, Matilda

116

Reddin, Elizabeth Reddin, Robert Reddin, Susanah Blackman formerly Susan Reddin and now the wife of Nelson Blackman, Emaline
Davenport formerly Emaline Reddin and now the wife of David
Davenport, Martha Calhoun formerly Martha Reddin and now the
wife of William Calhoun, who are the grandchildren of said
Joseph, being the children of Elizabeth Reddin who was the
daughter of said Joseph, and who departed this life previous
to the death of said Joseph. Susanah Blackman who was the
daughter of said Joseph and the wife of Elisha Blackman, Catherine Chase formerly Catherine Blackman and now the wife of
David Chase, James J. Blackman, J. B. Blackman, William J.
Blackman, Jeremiah Blackman, John E. Blackman, Caroline Black-
man, Ellenor Blackman and Mary Blackman who are the grandchildren of said Joseph, being the children of Letha Blackman who
was the daughter of Joseph and who departed this life previous
to the death of said Joseph, Burrel C. Johnson who is the
grandson of said Joseph, the only son of William Johnson who
was the son of said Joseph and who departed this life previous
to the death of Joseph, and Susanah Johnson who is the widow
and relict of said Joseph.
     Joseph died seized and possessed of a large estate, both
real and personal. Also at the time of the County Court of
Coffee , Tennessee, said John Johnson was appointed admr of
Joseph's estate and as such he had advertised portions of the
estate for sale and purchased the property himself. They also
said they had applied to him for their distributive share and
he has neglected alleging that said Joseph in his life time
had given the greater portion of his estate to him by Deed
of Gift. Commissioners was selected to review the Deed of
Gift and found it to be invalid. Orators stated that John
got the best tract of land on which Joseph died also six slaves
besides a large amount of personal property. They stated that
Joseph in his life time had purchased and paid for with his
own money, two other tracts of land in Coffee County, Tennessee,
one known as the Cole place, and the other as the Horton place
but for which deed was executed to John Johnson and the orators
charge that they are void. December 18, 1843.

Page 274 - Alexander Ray]
                   vs   ]
              William Potter]
Orator states that in the fall of 1844, he drove to the State
of Alabama a large number of fat or pork hogs for the purpose
of selling them, that on 19 December 1844 after he arrived
in Sumpter County, Alabama and placed 157 head of hogs in the
lands of William Potter also a citizen of Bedford County, as
his agent to sell. Potter sold the hogs and orator does not
know what price he was paid for same.

Page 279 - John P. Steele &   ]
           Jno. L. Cooper   ]
                   vs   ]
           Amos McAdams & others]
Orators states that sometime in the year of 1836, Amos McAdams
also of Bedford County and Charles D. Cooper and your orator
purchased of the heirs of at law of Nathaniel Alexander, deceased, their shares of a tract of land in Bedford County,
Lot No. 6 in the division of a 500 acre tract granted to Caleb
Phifer. The said Amos McAdams purchased one half or five
shares in said land,the said Charles D. Cooper and your orator,
jointly purchased the other five shares, also that after the
purchase and before deed was recorded, they decided to divide
property between them. Amos McAdams was to take all the land

Which lies on the east side of said Turnpike Road and the said
Cooper & Steele was to take jointly all on the west side so
soon as deed be obtained. Amos mislead them in the amount
of acreage in his part of property.

Page 291 - Ephraim Hunter   ]
              vs   ]
         William Sharp &   ]
         Martin & Samuel Hancock]
Ephraim Hunter of Bedford County and William Sharp of Bedford
County and Martin and Samuel Hancock of Coffee County, Tenn-
essee. Orator states that on 13 April 1843, he recovered a
joint judgement against William Sharp and William Sharp, Jr.
"No property to be found". Orator claims that Sharp pretended
to sell property to Martin Hancock. Martin and Samuel Hancock
are the brothers in law of said William Sharp, Sr. The deed
and witnessed by John Bell who is a son in law of William
Sharp, Sr. and by William Sharpe, Jr. who is the son of William
Sharp, Sr. Also, slaves were sold to James Sharp of Franklin
County, Tennessee.

Page 298 - G. W. Haywood   ]
              vs   ] Inj. Bill.
         Malcolm Gilchrist & others]
Orator states that in April Term 1844, he was appointed by
Court, admr of the estate of William Gilchrist, deceased. He
said the state of insolvency of Gilchrist's estate. At the
time of Gilchrist's death, he owned a parcel of land adjoining
the Town of Shelbyville wherein Wilkins Blanton now lives.
Containing about 30 acres, and also Lot No. 96 in the Town
of Shelbyville. He was indebted to an amount that will re-
quire part of the land to be sold. Heirs, Malcolm Gilchrist,
Catherine Mary Gilchrist, Adelaid Gilchrist and Sarah Gilchrist, all are minors and have no guardian. Gilchrist left
Martha Ann Gilchrist his widow all in Arknasas.

Page 315 - William & Thomas Allison   ]
         Exrs of Robert Allison, deceased]
              vs   ]
         John & Ruthey Crook   ]
Orators, as exrs of Robert Allison, deceased, against John
Crook and Ruthey his wife, and Coleman R., Mary Ann, Eliza H.,
Elizabeth and Celia S. and Francis C. Crook, children of said
John and Ruthey B. Crook, all citizens of Bedford County.
    Orator states that some years ago Coleman R. White of
Greenville, North Carolina depa ted this life after having
previously made and published his Last Will and Testament and
after his death was proven &c. Among other things, he bequeathed his executor in trust for his said daughter Ruthey and her
children during their lifetime, of the said Ruthey the following slaves, four, Wiley, Maryan, Jane and __?__. White's will
was proven in Greenville, September Term 1838.

Page 321 - Robert Harrison]
              vs   ]
         James Mullins &]
         J. B. Hall   ]
Orator states that sometime in last winter he purchased a family
of negroes from James Benton and took his bill of sale. Benton
had purchased said negroes from Jacob Harrison.

Page 324 - Mary L. Powell   ]
              vs   ]
         Thomas P. Powell]
Mary L. Powell against Thomas P. Powell, Robert James Powell
and Richard Henry Powell, the last two being minors and children of Thomas Powell. Oratrix states that about fifteen years
since (1827), she with her husband Robert Powell moved to Bedford County from Sussex County, Virginia, previously they resided on a valuable tract of land in Sussex County, Virginia,
the land she inherited from her father. Oratrix states that
her husband became embarrassed in his affairs before leaving
Virginia and said it was necessary to sell her property to
clear his debts. He owned and possessed several slaves and
not wishing to sell them out of the family and having no other
property to sell to pay his debts, he persuaded your oratrix
to consent to a sale of her land. In consideration thereof
that he would convey a portion of the slaves to your oratrix
to have and hold as her separate property and a deed was made
to that effect. Oratrix and her husband came to Tennessee
and in about 6 or 7 years their son Thomas P. Powell came out
from Virginia and settled in same neighborhood and soon took
from her, the conveyance, by violence and gave negroes to
Thomas P. and his two sons (grandsons), Robert James and Richard Henry, sons of Thomas P. This act was not to be done until
after the death of Robert Powell.
Exhibit A: I, Robert Powell of Bedford County, for and in consideration of the natural love and affection which I bear to
my wife Mary L. and my sons Thomas P. and Seymore R. and my
grandsons Robert James Powell and Richard Henry Powell, sons
of my son Thomas P. and also inconsideration of the sum of
one dollar to me in hand paid by my said wife, sons and grandsons. I convey to my wife the south division of my land to
be divided into two parts by measuring 120 feet due south from
my grainery and running from that point due east and west to
Jesse Stegal's line in the last and Benjamin Wade's line in
the west dividing my tract into two parts provided my wife
survives me. If my wife survive me, she is to have the aforesaid south division during her natural life and at her death,
the same is to go to my son Thomas P., his heirs and assignees.
I have also given, granted and conveyed and by these present
do give and grant and convey unto my said wife a horse worth
$40.00, a cow and calf, 10 loads of corn, 5 bushels of wheat,
500 lbs of pork or bacon and one bed, bedstead and furniture
all of which she is to have at my death if she survives me.
I have also given, granted and conveyed and by these present
doth give give and convey unto my son Thomas P. Powell, his
heirs and assignees, northern division of my land to be divided
as aforesaid and the following negroes, Ellis, Joe, R----y,
Wincey, Mary and all the rest of my estate, both real and
personal of which I may die possessed except what has heretofore or may hereafter be otherwise disposed of in the conveyance. I also give to my son Thomas P. my old slave Kate with
a particular request that he support her comfortably as long
as she lives. I have also given, granted and conveyed and
by these present, do give grant and convey unto my son Seymore
R. two hundred dollars ($200.00) to be paid to him out of my
estate at my death provided he survives me also all claims
which I have against him for money paid for him, bonds lifted
or I have also given granted and conveyed and by these present do give grant and convey unto my daughter Elizabeth H.
Whitaker one dollar. I have also given granted and conveyed
and by these present do give grant and convey unto my grand
sons, Robert James Powell and Richard Henry Powell, the

119

following negro slaves, to wit, Chaney and Maria with this
understanding that if both boys live until the oldest arrives
at the age of 21 years and both negroes are also then living,
Robert James is to have Chaney and her increase and Richard
Henry is to have Maria and her increase or if either of said
negroes dies before Robert James comes of age then an equal
division of the surviving ones that is Chaney, Maria and their
increase is to be made between said two boys or their heirs.
It is distinctly understood that no gift contained in this
conveyance is to take effect until after my death that I reserve to my self a life estate in my land and negroes. In
witness whereof I have hereunto set my hand, affixed my seal,
this 25th day of March A.D., 1836.
Signed, Sealed and delivered   Signed: Robert Powell
in presence of us this 25th day
of March 1836(Elam)Elen (his mark) Pucket
and Littleberry Turner, Jurat
Exhibit E, Robert Powell died at his residence in Bedford
County. T. P. Powell got one large Bible. Answer of Respondant Thomas P. Powell: Thomas P. Powell denies that complt owned
said land in Sussex County, Virginia as alleged in her bill
but said land belonged to Robert, says Deed of Conveyance for
slaves by Robert to complt was not in Robert's handwriting
and says Robert stated to him said Thomas Powell in his lifetime that he did not make said deed. Respondant never heard
of such paper until about 1834 when his father said Robert
came to his house and informed him that complt had shown him
such a paper and that he had never executed said paper and
desired that respondant get it from her, which he did against
her will.
Sale of personal property of Robert Powell, deceased. Exhibit E.
List of those buying. S. P. Powell, Nancy Powell, J. N.
Porter, Mary L. Powell, T. P. Powell and John Nailor, 23 Sept
1842 for 165.84.

Page 335 - Will of Seymore Robinson.
In the name of God Amen. I, Seymore Robinson of the Parish
of Albermarle and County of Sussex, being sick and weak in
bodybut of sound mind and memory, Blessed be God, for the same,
do make and ordain this my Last Will and Testament ____ _____
and form following imprimis my will and desire is that my loving wife Elizabeth Robinson have the use of my whole estate
both real and personal except what money may be due to me at
the time of my death or that may arise from the sale of such
of my personal estate as my executors may think can be reason-
ably spared during her natural life or widowhood upon her
giving to my said executors bond and approval security for
the bringing up maintaining and educating all my children and
for not embezzling or making waste of any part of my said
estate. Item, My will and desire further is that incase my
loving wife should be with child at this time of my decease
and the issue should prove a son, then I give and bequeath
to such son my land and plantation whereon I now live after
the decease or marriage of my said wife but in case it should
prove a daughter, then I desire that my whole estate both real
or personal be sold by my executors and that the money rising
from such sale together with all monies that may be due to
my estate be equally divided amongst all my daughters that
may be living at the time of such division and my loving wife.
Item, It is further my will and desire that my executors if
he or they shall think it can be conveniently done without
injuring my estate with the money now due to me and by disposing of such parts of my estate as they shall think can be best

spared purchase a negro woman which said negro so purchased,
I desire Mary (with her increase) go descend and pass as the
rest of my estate as herein before mentioned but in case such
negro be not purchased then I desire my executors may put such
money to interest until my oldest child arrives at the age
of twenty one years or marriage and that then the said money
be equally divided with the rest of my estate as herein before
directed. Lastly, I constitute and ordain my loving Friends
John Sundersant(?) and William Mason whole and sole executors
of this my Last Will and Testament hereby revoking and disa-
nulling all former wills by me heretofore made and declaring
this and no other to be my Last Will and Testament. In Testimony whereof I have set my hand and seal, this sixth day of
November 1780.
Signed, Sealed, Published and   Signed: Seymore Robinson(S.S.)
delivered in presence of
Chals. Gilliam
Jesse Smith
Dan Grant

Page 336 - Know all men by these present that I, Mary L. Powell
of Bedford County in consideration of the natural affection
and other good causes which I have to my daughter Elizabeth H.
Porter of the same county and state, I give, grant and deliver
and by these present do give grant and deliver to my daughter
Elizabeth H. Porter the following negroes, to wit, Ellis, Cama,
Chana, Mariah, Minerva, Granville, Julian, Winny and Cama
youngest child not named, to have and to hold the said negroes
forever in witness I hereunto set my hand and seal this 9th
day of August 1842.
Thomas D. Pride   Signed: Mary L. Powell (Seal)
Ann Maria L. Haskins
(Elizabeth H. may have been the wife of John N. Porter)
Court is of the opinion that the deed made of Robert Powell
to Mary L. Powell in 1826 is in full force and effect against
Robert and his legal representatives, to wit, Thomas P. Powell,
but because deed was not properly registered, property is liable
to the creditors appealed to Tennessee Supreme Court, 1846.

Page 340 - John W. Williams & wife]
            vs   ]
        Jesse R. Edwards &c   ]
John W. Williams and Keziah his wife formerly Keziah Cunning-
ham of Bedford County, William W. Cunningham a citizen of Grundy
County, Tennessee, Nancy E. Cunningham a citizen of Grundy
County, Tennessee, Benjamin B. Cunningham of Grundy County,
Tennessee, John M. Cunningham of Coffee County, Tennessee,
Langston C. Cunningham, Joseph A. Cunningham, George N. Cunning-
ham, Mary Elizabeth Cunningham and Lucy Ann Cunningham of Grundy
County, Tennessee. The said Keziah, William H., Nancy E.,
Benjamin H., John N., Landston C., Joseph A., George W., Mary
Elizabeth and Lucy Ann Cunningham being children of Benjamin B.
Cunningham, deceased, and a portion of the heirs of John Cunn-
ingham, Sr., deceased, the five last of whom being minors
and having no regular guardian. Their mother and next friend
Benjamin B. Cunningham aforesaid represents that the aforesaid
John Cunningham died intestate about the 18 day December 1842
the County of Warren, Tennessee in which and in Coffee County
he had resided in many years before his death, entitled to
a large estate of slaves, many choice action and other effects
that said intestate left your orators the following persons
his only heirs and distributees being James Cunningham and
citizen of Virginia, the heirs of William Cunningham who died

many years ago and whom names are unknown except his son
William Cunningham a citizen of Alabama, Richard Cunningham
of Bedford County, Austin Shepard and Rachael his wife formerly
Rachael Cunningham citizens of Marshall County, Tennessee,
Jesse R. Edwards and the children of said Jesse R. and Elizabeth his wife formerly Elizabeth Cunningham who is dead that
is to say Joseph Edwards citizens of Alabama, William L. B----
and Keziah his wife formerly Keziah Edwards of Coffee County,
Tennessee, John Edwards of Alabama, David Edwards, James
Edwards and Lucy C. Edwards of Warren County, Tennessee, the
last four of whom being minors and have no regular guardian
within the knowledge of your orators, William _. Kinnard a
citizen of Warren County, Tennessee and the children of himself
and wife Martha formerly Martha Cunningham who is dead, that
is to say John T. Kinnard where residence is unknown but is
believed to be beyond the limits of Tennessee, William _. Kinnard and Geirge R. Kinnard, Elizabeth E. Kinnard, Martha A.
Kinnard, and James A. Kinnard, citizens of Warren County, Tennessee of whom being minors and without regular guardian within
the knowledge of your orators, Joseph W. Cunningham a citizen
of Alabama, the heirs of Langston Cunningham, deceased, that
is to say John Cunningham, Langston Cunningham, Richard Cunningham, Samuel Hancock and wife Mary formerly Mary Cunningham
citizens of Coffee County, Tennessee, Thomas Cunningham a citizen of Mexico, William S. Cunningham of Warren County, Tennessee, Benjamin L. Douglas and wife Nancy formerly Nancy Cunningham citizens of Kentucky, Joseph R. Cunningham a citizen
of Coffee County, Tennessee being minor without guardian within
the knowledge of your orator, James Cunningham of Bedford
County and Nancy Cunningham widow of said Langston Cunningham,
deceased, a citizen of Coffee County, Tennessee, Langston,
Martha A. citizen of Coffee County, Tennessee, Archibald J.
Price and wife Elizabeth and Richard J. Price and wife Mary,
the said Langston, Martin, Elizabeth Price and Mary Price being
children of Thomas Martin and Polly his wife formerly Polly
Cunningham, this Price and minors being citizens of Coffee
County, Tennessee, Nancy Shapherd widow of Anderson Shepherd,
deceased, formerly Nancy Cunningham a citizen of Jackson County,
Alabama, Lenor(?) Cunningham whose residence is unknown but
believed to be beyond the limits of this state, John Ogden,
Benjamin C. Ogden, Mary Ann Ogden and George W. Ogden, citizens
of White County, Tennessee and children of George Ogden and
his wife Rachael formerly Rachael Cunningham being infants
and having no regular guardian, Esther Ogden and S. Berry ____
citizens of White County, Tennessee, all of whom are made defts
to the will and enjoined to answer its allegations on oath.
        Orators states that John Cunningham, Sr., deceased, was
at the time of his death and had been for many years before
his death of unsound mind and utterly incapable of transacting
business. Also, before September 1838 up to the death of said
John, his business was at that time most if not entirely
managed by the defts, Jesse R. Edwards and William Kinnard
who stated that John's mental and phyisical incapacity to trans-
act business as far back as 1838 and that Edwards & Kinnard
and perhaps others of the defts petitioned the County Court
of Warren County, Tennessee at its September Term 1838 to
appoint a jury to enquire whether or not said John was capable
of transacting his own business. On 16 October 1839, Edward
& Kinnard, James Cunningham of Virginia, Richard Cunningham
of Bedford County, Austin and Rachael Shepherd of Marshall,
the heirs of Langston Cunningham, deceased, particularly John
Cunningham and Joseph H. Cunningham of Alabama fradulently
produced fabricated writing for the said John Cunningham's,

deceased, and caused said John to sign and sent the instrument by which they made the said John unwillingly dispose of and distribute his large estate of slaves, land and money and choices in action and other effects among the said Edwards, Kinnard, Richard, James, Austin and Paul the heirs of Langston Cunningham, deceased, and Joseph H. and perhaps others of the defts to this bill. Orators stated that 16 October 1839 the slaves, land, money &c, Jesse R. Edwards took into his possession of said estate of John.

John Cunningham, Jr., admr of Langston Cunningham, dec'd, Nancy Cunningham, relict of Langston Cunningham, heirs Langston Cunningham, Jr., Richard Cunningham, Jr., William Cunningham, James Cunningham, Jr., Joseph H. Cunningham, minor all heirs of Langston Cunningham, Jr., deceased.

Page 365 - Will of John Cunningham - Exhibit 1 & 2.
To Edward's answer, October 16, 1839.
I want in the first place my Last Will which I have got, I now intend to dispose of my property. I intend that all the property I have to be divided equally amongst my children, to wit, Richard Cunningham, the heirs of Langston Cunningham, James Cunningham, and Joseph Cunningham, Austin Shepherd, William Nimrod and Jesse Edwards. I do not intend that William Cunningham shall have anything than he has already and neither do I intend that Benjamin Cunningham shall have anything more than I have already given him except a sixty six dollar note I hold on him which note I wish him to have, neither do I intend to give anything more to the heirs of Polly Martin than I have already given which is a negro boy named Bill, I give Langston Martin. I will Russell all the money on hand I have and a boy by the name of Mat. All the other property to be divided equally among the above named heirs with the exception of Nancy Shepherd, William Cunningham, Benjamin Cunningham and the heirs of Polly Martin.
Wit: David Ramsey   Signed: John Cunningham (Seal)
     John Johnsthan Woodfin
     A. B. Davis
     Geo. Strand
     Wm. Ramsey
Samuel Hancock and Mary his wife formerly Mary Cunningham.
To the Bill of Complts of John W. Williams and Keziah his wife and others. Complts are citizens of Wilson County, Tennessee for two years before and after the execution of deeds in 1839.

Page 373 - Joseph Thompson, admr of   ]
           Tarlton J. Reeves, deceased]
                  vs   ]
           Benjamin S. Reeves   ]
Joseph Thompson of Bedford County. Complt states that Tarlton J. Reeves, late of Bedford County, departed this life intestate in the month of December 1846 and at January Term 1847, your orator was appointed admr of his estate. Orator states that sometime before the death of Tarlton J. Reeves, in summer of 1845, he placed in the hands of his brother Benjamin S. Reeves in Bedford COunty, two teams horses and two new road wagons with all the gear which were loaded with bacon, feathers and other articles of trade. These wagons and teams were put into the hands of Benjamin S. as the agent of Tarlton J. being for the purpose of being taken by Benjamin S. to Alabama or other part of the south and sold for the benefit of Tarlton J. Reeves. Benjamin S. was to get only a portion of the profits as Tarlton J. furnished all. Benjamin S. did in 1845 take wagons to Alabama and sold and collected but never accounted for any

to Tarlton J. in his lifetime. Orator states that Tarlton J.
Reeves died in Alabama at the residence of Benjamin. Benjamin
S. Reeves is now in Bedford COunty, but a citizen of Alabama
(Hayneville, Lowndes County, Alabama).

Page 388 - George Bussey   ]
                vs   ]
          William A. Gant heirs]
George Bussey of Bedford County. Orator states that he purchased of William A. Gant, since deceased, a tract of land in Bedford County in District No. 18 and partly divided in the title
bond executed by said Grant to your orator herein filed under
Exhibit "A" or a part of this bill. Orator states that all
the purchase money had been paid and your orator is entitled
to said tract of land but William A. Gant has refused to give
him a title. Orator states that William A. Gant of Bedford
County departed this life intestate. William A. Gant was never
married and therefore his heirs are his brother and sisters
to wit, Absalom B. Gant of Wayne County, Jesse B. Gant and
Samuel Harlson and wife Nancy a sister of said William A. and
citizen of Hardin County, Tennessee and A. Gi_____ and wife
Sarah Caroline, Benjamin Braughton and wife Mary, A. Bryan
and wife Mary, Elizabeth Gant, Lewis G. Ray, Martha Cotner
who has guardian John Cotner, John Cotner , James Gant, Lewis
Gant, Elizabeth, John, William and Eliza Jane Gant, the four
last being minors and have for their guardian John T. Neal,
John B., Sarah and Nancy Jane Ray children of John Ray, dec'd,
nephews and nieces of William A. Gant, deceased, and John R.,
Lewis A., Bolin P. and Martha Jane Freeman children of Stephen
Freeman who is their grandson, being grand nephews and nieces
of William A. Gant, all of Bedford County and Margaret Hayzelwood and William Hayzelwood of Bedford County, John Aldridge
and wife Margret and Jacob Shaddy and wife Martha of Missouri
and Dicey L., Ba----, Keziah Aldridge and Riley Aldridge minors
and Robert J. B(?). Gant who has G. W. Redd for his guardian
&c who resides in Alabama, said Absalom in Marshall County,
Tennessee, said Absalom B. and Lewis Gant who are brothers
of said William A. Gant are also his admrs.
Exhibit "A" - I, William A. Gant, sold and delivered to George
Bussey a tract of land in Bedford COunty on both sides of Big
Sinking Creek and containing 100 acres.

Page 394 - William Word, Trustee]
                vs   ]
          Elizabeth Harrison,   ]
          George Davidson &   ]
          Thomas Davis   ]
William Word of Bedford County. Orator states that in June
1835, Robert P. Harrison, then of Bedford County and since
deceased, was elected Clerk of the Board of County Common
School Commissioners for Bedford County. Harrison kept a record book of the school funds. There was found a balance of
$163.89 and other notes in fund. Harrison died about 1 August
1843, his widow Eliza W. Harrison was executrix. Robert P.
Harrison made and published a Last Will and Testament.

Page 408 - Ellender McCullough]
                vs   ]
          Orvill Muse   ]
Oratrix Ellender McCullough states that on 31st day of December
1845, she conveyed to Orvill Muse by Bill of Sale, a negro
boy named Joseph for $525.00. Muse took negro boy into his
possession until he sold or parted with him.

Page 412 - Samuel Doak]
           vs   ]
      Edde & Dean]
Hiram Edde & Thomas Dean. In 1837, Edde Executed to Thomas
Dean a mortgage on a negro boy.

Page 416 - Jane Griggs   ]
              vs   ]
      Robert W. Griggs]
Oratrix, a citizen of Bedford County, has resided for the last
5 years, states that about 10 years ago, she intermarried with
Robert W. Griggs and shortly afterwards Robert W. Griggs or
was before addicted to the use of spiritous liquors and was
almost always in a state of intoxication during which times
he very abused and at one time about 3 years ago he beat her
very severly so that she left him immediately and went to her
father where she stayed about 18 months. During the time
Robert W. frequently told her he regretted his treatment to
her and promised her he would reform his habits of drinking
if she would return and live with him. She returned to his
house but she had only been at home a few days when Robert W.
commenced the same course and abuse of your oratrix. He has
refused to provide for herself and children (little) of which
she has four. They lived in a log hut without chimney or doors
at all seasons and very little protection against cold and
rain and very often without food or clothing. She again left
and went back to her father's house. Robert W. Griggs is now
not a citizen of Tennessee but resides in parts unknown. Bill
for Divorce - 1 March 1848. Divorce granted.

Page 418 - Andrew Reynolds   ]
              vs   ]
      Arthur Campbell & others]
Andrew Reynolds of Franklin County, Tennessee and Arthur Campbell of Bedford County. Orator states that he was appointed
admr of Jane Reynolds, deceased, of Bedford County, also that
the following are the distributees of the said James Reynolds,
to wit, Arthur Campbell and wife Elizabeth who lives in Bedford
County, Henry Reynolds and John Reynolds who lives in Lincoln
County, Tennessee, David Reynolds who lives in Illinois, Richard Reynolds who resides in Mississippi, Moses Reynolds and
the heirs of James Reynolds who reside in Arkansas and your
orator further states that all the distributees have been advanced $100.00 each. This exceptions on Moses Reynolds and
David Reynolds who has not been advanced at all and Arthur
Campbell and wife who were advanced in the lifetime of said
James by the gift of a negro girl. Orator states that James
Reynolds who was one of the distributees has departed this
life since the said Jane, in the State of Arkansas, having
a widow Sally Reynolds and some children, names are unknown.
Orator states that Moses Reynolds is a minor and has no guardian. Jane Reynolds was the wife of William Reynolds who died
many years ago, intestate.

Page 426 - Thomas Mosely, admr &c]
              vs   ]
      Matt Martin &   ·]
      Edward A. Moseley   ]
Thomas B. Moseley, admr of estate of Nancy Elizabeth Martin,
deceased, against William D. Martin and Anderson J. Martin
and Sarah A. M. Martin, all are minors and Matt Martin being
the guardian of William D. Martin and Edward A. Moseley being
the regular guardian, all of Bedford County. Orator states

that some years ago, Henry C. Martin departed this life intestate bearing a considerable personal estate to be divided among
his five children, William D., Amanda J., Sarah N. A., and
Nancy Elizabeth Martin and all of property was delivered over
to the admr of Henry C. Martin to Matt Martin and Edward A.
Moseley who were appointed regular guardian of said four (5)
children. They also to receive negroes. Orator states that
since the heirs received their part of the estate, Nancy Elizabeth Martin departed this life intestate in Bedford County,
and your orator was appointed admr upon the estate of Nancy
Elizabeth Martin. Many years ago Barkley Martin died in Bedford County, leaving a widow but no children and having a Last
Will and Testament which after his death duly proven and recorded. By said will he devised and bequeathed his negroes
to his widow Rachel Martin, during her lifetime and after her
death to his brother Matt Martin, Sr., now deceased. A number
of years after the death of Barclay Martin, his widow Rachael
sold and conveyed her life estate in all the negroes, so devised to her, to one John Tilman who took them into possession.
In 1838 or thereabouts, John Tilman agreed with Matt Martin
to relinquish and did relinquish his claim so acquired in all
of negroes to Matt Martin in consideration of the sum of $2000
without interest for two years and on condition that Matt
Martin would divide negroes equally amongst his then living
children, and the heirs of those that were dead and that John
Tilman deliver up the negroes to Matt Martin. Matt Martin
became absolute owner of the negroes. Henry C. being dead
but had four children, to wit, William D., Amanda J., Sarah
K. A. and Nancy Elizabeth Martin his only heirs at law. That
nine shares were allowed and delivered over to the nine living
children and the 10th, slave was placed in hands of Matt Martin
and Edward A. Moseley guardian.

Page 449 - Mathew Mullins]
              vs   ]
       Horatio Clagett]
Both of Bedford County. Orator states that in the early part
of the year 1835, Horatio Clagett purchased a tract of land
on the north side of Duck River. Land bordering lands formerly
owned by John Overton and Jenkins Whiteside, Duck River, Butler
Creek, John S. Claybrook's deed to M. Mullins, James Young
and containing 360+ acres and is a part of tract of 471 acres
of land purchased by your orator, M. Mullins previous to that
time, John S. Claybrook as executor of John Overton, deceased.
Orator also states that Clagett promised and agreed to give
him for said 360+ acre tract of land the sum of $3007.50.

Page 458 - Adaline Robinson]
              vs   ]Orig. Bill, filed 22 June 1848.
       Jno. W. Mayfield]
Both of Marshall County, Tennessee. Orator states that she
is the widow of William Wilhoite filed a petition to sell the
land which her husband died seized and possessed preferring
that she to receive one third part of the proceeds rising from
the sale of said lands, to the one third of the land which
would have been all allowed to her for dower in the same. Clerk
was to pay over to oratrix $482.56+ the remainder goes to the
children of William Wilhoite at her death. Oratrix has since
intermarried with James Robinson, who received the money for
his wife and held it up to the time of his death which occured
during the year. James Robinson before his death made and
executed his Last Will and Testament in which he mades no
divorce of their sum. That he appointed Richard Warner and

John W. Mayfield, executors of said will, who refused to pay
over to your oratrix said sum of money, although she has often
requested them to do so. Oratrix is without relief.

Page 459 - Seth Thomas   ]
               vs   ]
            Bluford Davidson]
This bill was filed against Bluford Davidson in his own right.
And as admr of Carlton Davidson and Andrew A. Davidson,
citizens of Bedford COunty. Orator stated that at August Term
1841 of Circuit Court of Bedford County, he received a judgement against Calton(Carlton) and Richard M. Davidson. "No
property aforesaid" and judgement still remains unpaid. Orator
stated that on 30 July 1841 (only a few days before the court
at which time your orator recovered his judgement) the said
Carlton Davidson who was the owner of a large estate conveyed
it to Bluford Davidson his brother three tracts of land in
Bedford County on waters of Sugar Creek. Containing 206 acres.
Registered in KK, page 425 and 426. On same day 30 July 1841
Carlton Davidson conveyed by Deed in Trust to his father
Andrew Davidson all his personal property. Carlton Davidson
died in the year 1846, after his death, Bluford took possession
of all his property and paid the widow of Carlton. Andrew
Davidson conveyed all property to James S. Davidson his son.

                CHANCERY COURT MINUTES 1846 - 1853

Page 2 & 32 - Pascal Brown, Jesse W. Brown] Exparte.
              Joel Whorley & wife & others] Inventory Decree.
              13 February 1846   ]
On page 32, heirs: Pascal, Jesse W. Brown, Cynthia wife of
Joel Whorley, Thomas Brown, Daniel Brown, Elizabeth Brown,
John Brown and Robert A. Brown. Will of Jesse Brown, deceased.
Estate to be divided equally between John and Robert A. Brown.

Page 22 - The American Bible Society]
                 vs   ] 20 February 1846
           Samuel Doak   ]
Mentioned will of James McCarver, deceased. Henry Blagg exr.

Page 52 - Archibald Dobson died 1841, intestate. March Term
1841 appointed admr.

Page 57 - Daniel L. Barringer who sues as the   ]
            next friend & Trustee of Mary Ann Haley]
               vs   ]26 Aug 1846
            Frederick F. Fonville, Minos Cannon &]
            E. Coleman.   ]
Henry Mooring departed this life more than 20 years ago in
Wake County, North Carolina after making his will. Daughter
Mary Ann Haley. Daniel L. Barringer, one of the executors.

Page 76 - Jack by his next friend John Dwyer]
               vs   ]23 Feb 1847
           Henry Blagg & Samuel Doak   ]
               and   ]
           Hugh P. Mooney & others   ]
               vs   ]
           Henry Blagg & others   ]
According to the terms and provisions of the Last Will and
Testament of James McCarver, deceased. Decree that Jack be

freed from Bond and Slavery.

Page 91 - Price C. Steele, admrs & others]
                      vs   ]24 Aug 1847
          Jeptha Minta & Lewis Tucker & others]
William Warren died on the 20 day of March 1845. (Exrs of Nancy
Manor).

Page 155 - John W. Cobb, admr] 26 February 1849
          Petition to sell slave]
James H. Cobb departed this life in Bedford County on -- of
-- 184-. having previously made a Last Will.

Page 158 - Plat of John Ewell and description.

Page 180 - Barkley Martin, Exr]
                vs   ] 27 February 1849
          E. A. Mosely et al]
              and   ]
       Thos. B. Moseley, admr]
                vs   ]
          E. A. Moseley et al]
Matt Martin, executor of Matt Martin, Sr., deceased will. To
pay over to Thomas B. Moseley, admr of Henry E. Martin and
Edward A. Moseley as guardian of Amanda J. and Ann Martin,
$193.00.

Page 184 - William H. Wiseman, admr]
                vs   ] 28 February 1849.
          Randolph Newsom et als]
Archibald Reeves departed this life in Bedford County in the
year 1839, having previously made his Last Will. Thomas Newsom
executor. Distributees, to wit, Tarlton J. Reeves, Archibald
Reeves, Alexander T. Reeves, Elizabeth Reeves wife of B. J.
Reeves, Mary Newsom wife of Thomas Newsom, George W. Reeves,
Sally Campbell wife of Alfred Campbell, Pleasant H. Reeves
and Moses Reeves.

Page 195 - Bushrod Webb departed this life intestate in May
1847, Bedford County.

Page 196 - A. M. Short, guardian ¢c]
          Exparte Petition &c   ]
Be it remembered that on the 27th day of August 1849, Alfred M.
Short guardian of Martha C., Nancy C., John, Henry, Felix W.,
Eliza J., and Mary E. Carroll, exhibited his petition to the
Hon. Chancellor presiding at Shelbyville in Bedford County,
and it appearing that J. S(L). Edwards, Commissioner of Pensions
for the Government of the United States of America on the 7th
day of May 1849, certified that a Land Warrant No. 57016(4)
had been issued in the name of Mary Ann Carroll widow, Martha C.
Carroll, Nancy C. Carroll, John Carroll, Henry Carroll, Felix W.
Carroll, Eliza J. Carroll and Mary E. Carroll, children and
heirs at law of Aaron Carroll, deceased, Private in Capt.
Clark's Company, 3rd Regt of Tennessee Volunteers and could
be deposited in the General Land Office at the Seat of Government, and the court being of opinion that it would be most
for the interest of said wards for said Short to sell said
Land Warrant for their use and benefits, doth order and decree,
that he sell the same for the best price became obtain therefore
in conjunction with Mary Ann Carroll, widow, and charge himself
with the one half of such price in his account of his guardianship as aforesaid.

Page 216 - W. M. Coldwell, admr &c]
            Exparte Petition   ]
Petition of William M. Coldwell, admr of James P. Craig, dec'd,
who departed this life intestate, left a widow Mary Craig.

Page 226 - Jacob Coble, deceased, and widow Mary Coble. Jacob
died intestate.

Page 232 - William R. Looney died in Bedford County. Widow
Martha who has since intermarried with James C. Russell.
William R. Looney died intestate. He left children, Robert B.
and James M. Looney as only children.

Page 241 - 26 February 1850. John Mayfield died many years
ago, intestate. Daughter Sarah who married Thomas Shearin
but who died before her father John Mayfield. Sarah left the
following children, Rebecca Fisher wife of John Fisher, James
F. Shearin, Thomas Shearin, Elizabeth Ledbetter wife of James
M. Ledbetter, Polly Gant wife of Lewis Gant, Matthew Shearin
and Sally Shearin. Sally Shearin departed this life after
the death of her mother but before the death of her father
Thomas Shearin, leaving no children.

Page 257 - William B. Cooper el als]
                vs   ] 27 August 1850
           James Mullins &   ]
           Claiborne Bowls   ]
Joseph Palmore died many years ago in Virginia after making
his Last Will and Testament. Daughter Mary Bowls. Mary Bowls
departed this life some years ago leaving amongst other heirs,
not now before the court, complt Sarah P. who has intermarried
with William B. Cooper and complt Amanda who has intermarried
with Francis M. Miller. (Mary Bowls could be the wife of
Claiborne Bowls). Claiborne Bowls as admr of Mary Bowls.

Page 263 - In Will of Peter Singleton, deceased, to sell land.

Page 265 - James H. Cobb departed this life some years ago,
having made his Last Will and Testament. Left negroes to
John W. Cobb. To widow Sarah Elkins Cobb.

Page 281 - George W. Buchanan &   ]
           Newton K. Shofner, Exrs]
                vs   ] 27 August 1850.
           Mary Evans & others   ]
Frederick Shofner departed this life some years ago, having
first made and published his Last Will and Testament. George
W. Buchanan and Newton K. Shofner, Executors.

Page 287 - John W. Cobb, admr of] 24 February 1851.
           J. H. Cobb, deceased]
James H. Cobb, deceased. Widow Sarah Cobb.

Page 294 - Robert E. & John C. Thompson]
                vs   ] 25 February 1851.
           John F. Ferguson & others   ]
Will of Robert C. Thompson, deceased. John S. Mayfield, admr.

Page 295 - Thomas Eakin, Surveying partner &c]
           William S. Eakin & others   ]
                vs   ]24 Feb 1851.
           John B. M. Bass, Exr &c & others   ]
John Eakin and William Eakin died at the date stated in the

bill, having first made and published their Last Will and Testament, proven and recorded. John Eakin, deceased, bequeathed to his two daughters Julia A. and Sarah J. Eakin, $15,000.00 each, remainder of estate to his wife and children. William Eakin, deceased, wife Felix Grundy Eakin and their two children Jane W. and Ann Grundy Eakin to receive stock &c. William S. Eakin is guardian of Julia A. and Sarah J. Eakin.

Page 303 - William M. Shofner]
                vs   ] Divorce.
         Jane Koonce Shofner]
They married 22 February 1844 in Bedford County.

Page 308 - Lewis Singleton et als]
                vs   ] August Term 1850.
         Wiley F. Daniel, Exr &c]
Sell property of Peter Singleton, deceased. 274½ acres.

Page 321 - James S. Scudder]
                vs   ] 27 February 1851.
         George Kimbro   ]
William O. Whitney died about the year 1826, having first made and published his Last Will and Testament. Proven and recorded in Bedford County. James G. Whitney and Thomas P. Whitney, executors. To Ruthy Whitney, a negro man John and a negro woman Susannah. Daughter Harriet P. Scudder who afterwards divorced her husband James S. Scudder.

Page 338 - Play of Richard H. Sims (Estate of William Wilhoite). Land on south side of Duck River. The island is not included in the play. There is 90 poles in the island.

Page 340 - 25 August 1851. John Eakin, deceased, made and published his Last Will and Testament. Lucretia Eakin, widow, lived near Town of Shelbyville. Children, George N., Albert and Charles, youngest of children.

Page 349 - Description of school land in the case Jonas Sykes against Mahala Jones et als.

Page 351 - Felix Turrentine   ]
                vs   ] 26 August 1851.
         Joseph Williams & others]
James Turrentine, deceased, made and published his will &c. Son Felix Turrentine.

Page 347 - Lewis Whitsell, an idiot by]
         his guardian Benj. F. Greer]
                vs   ] 1 April 1852.
         Daniel L. Barringer & others]
John Whitsell departed this life some years ago after having made his Last Will and Testament. Daniel L. Barringer, his executor. Lewis Whitsell is an idioy and B. F. Greer his guardian. His former guardian was William Whitsell.

Page 403 - John C. Dolby, Philip A. Dolby et als]
                vs   ] O. Bill.
         John L. Frazier, E. J. Frazier et als]
2 April 1852. Knight Dolby departed this life in Bedford County in October 1827 after making and publishing his Last Will and Testament. Robert Waite, executor. Widow Nancy Dolby. Nine children, not named, living at his death. He lived on 100 acres on Bradford's Creek. Some children have

since died. One son James B. Dolby. Nancy Dolby, widow, died in December 1848. Eight children living.

Page 407 - Hugh C. Hurst, Exr   ]
                      vs   ] 2 April 1852.
          The widow & heirs of]
          William Gabbert   ]
William Gabbert departed this life 26 day of January 1852 in Bedford County after he made and published his Last Will and Testament. Hugh C. Hurst, Nelson Gabbert and George G. Gabbert, executors. He left widow and several children. Widow is Mary Ann Gabbert.

Page 418 - Jackson C. Kilingsworth]
                      vs   ] Divorce.
          Elizabeth C. Kilingsworth]
They were married in Bedford County on 23 day August 1848.

Page 426 - Sarah H. A. Martin married John C. Coldwell, Jr.

Page 456 - 4 March 1853. Madison L. Burrow, executor of the Last Will and Testament of Ephraim Burrow, deceased. William Campbell, admr. Jordan C. Holt against Banks M. Burrow. Madison L. Burrow is dead.

Page 466 - 4 March 1853. Isaac West departed this life in Bedford County some years ago. Left a widow Sarah West. He made a will. John A. Moore, admr. Son, John S. West.

Page 489 - Francis M. Harrison,   ]
          Mahala Jane Harrison & others]
                      vs   ] 5 March 1853.
          Joseph Morton &   ]
          Jesse Brown, Exrs & others   ]
Joshua Yates, deceased, made his Last Will and Testament. The executors stated he died intestate.

Page 490 - Hugh C. Hurst, Exr of   ]
          William Gabbert, deceased]
                      vs   ] 5 March 1853.
          The heirs & widow of   ]
          William Gabbert, deceased]
Widow Mary Ann Gabbert. Children not named.

Page 491 - Prior M. Jackson & wife Martha and others]
                      vs   ]
          James L. Armstrong, Mary Gholson & others]
5 March 1853. James Slaton departed this life many years ago after having made his Last Will and Testament. Widow Martha Slaton. Heirs at law, Susanna Jackson, Sarah Short, Rachel Baker, Elizabeth Adams, Martha Jackson who was a daughter of Abel Slaton who was a son of James Slaton, deceased, and Mary Gholson. Widow Martha Slaton desires to remove to State of Missouri. Martha Slaton is now dead. She died on the __ day of March 1847.

Page 502 - Heirs of Thomas Coffee, deceased. On page 503 is the description of land.

Page 504 - Ephraim Burrow, deceased, and Eve Burrow, deceased. Banks M. D. Burrow a son. Madison L. Burrow is also dead.

Page 518 - 31 August 1853. John Whitesell, deceased, executed
a will. Daniel L. Barringer, executor. Jacob Whitesell and
William Whitesell and J. A. Blakemore, admrs.

Page 521 - Fletcher Taylor & wife & others]
                    vs   ] August 1853.
            James Allison, Exr óf   ]
            William Allison, deceased   ]
William Hanes, deceased, of Mecklenburg County, Virginia. His
Last Will and Testament was proven and admitted to record in
that State. Daughter Sarah Ann Hanes intermarried with John
McGowan in year 1811, leaving by marriage Sarah Ann Taylor
wife of Fletcher Taylor, Elizabeth wife of Henry Arnold, Mary
H. McGowan, Thomas McGowan, Martha J. McGowan, Emily F. McGowan,
James W. McGowan and George M. McGowan and Jonh. J. McGowan,
William H. McGowan and Peter McGowan. Sarah Ann McGowan died
before any of her children reached the age of 21 years.

Page 524 - J. M. H. McGrew &   ]
            Newsom & others   ]
                    vs   ] 31 August 1853.
            George W. McGrew & others]
William McGrew of Bedford County, departed this life, 1851,
having first made and published his Last Will and Testament.
J. M. H. McGrew, Randolph Newsom and George W. McGrew, exrs.

Page 540 - John A. Scott   ]
                    vs   ]
            D. D. Hix & others]
                    and   ] Bill and Cross Bill. 31 Aug 1853.
            Mary Ann Philpot   ]
                    vs   ]
            John A. Scott   ]
William Hix, deceased, made his will. Children, Nancy Word,
Betsey Ann Mallard, John C. Hix, Alsa Stewart, Judith Gambal,
Sibby Hall, Mary Hix, Rebecca Hix, William Hix and Joshua Hix.
Widow is deceased.

Page 548 - John A. Moore, admr of Isaac West]
                    vs   ] 1 Sept 1853.
            Maria Carrack & Tabitha Jones   ]
Testator Isaac West, deceased. Isaac West's wife's mother
has a life estate on the death of my wife's mother and divide
the proceeds Ellena Thornsbury, Maria Carrack and Tabitha Jones.

Page 565 - James Reagor, admr   ]
                    vs   ] 4 March 1854.
            Abram Reagor & others]
James Reagor, admr of John Lacy, deceased. Samuel Lacy is
a non-resident and has an interest in the estate of Elijah
Lacy which is in the hands of Samuel Lacy the executor of the
Last Will and Testament.

Page 574 - Dower of plat of Mrs. Catharine Hamlin, her deceased
husband John W. Hamlin.

Page 578 - William & Henrietta Miles   ]
            by their guardian   ]
            William A. Loyd   ]
                    vs   ] 14 March 1854.
            Joseph Hornady & wife Henrietta]
James H. Myers departed this life some years ago, having first
made his Last Will and Testament. Wife Henrietta W. Miles(Myers)

132

To Henrietta Hornady, at her death, property to go to Henrietta
W. and William, now minor heirs of John H. Myers.

Page 580 - Joseph P. Thompson & others]
            Exparte Petition to sell   ] 16 March 1854.
            land and slaves   ]
Robert Allison departed this life on 24 day of May 1842, having
made and published his Last Will and Testament. Willed to
Prudence Thompson and her children a child's part of the estate.
Prudence Thompson has since departed this life and that Joseph
P. Thompson was appointed admr. She left children, Harriet M.
Thompson who has intermarried with Enoch Head, Robert C. Thomp-
son, Mary E. Thompson and Sarah Ann Thompson.

Page 590 - Hugh C. Hurst, executor of William Gabbert, deceased,
who made a will &c. Widow Mary Ann Gabbert. Children, Rebecca
Ann Epperson, George G. Gabbert, Ruthy White, Nelson J. Gabbert,
Jordan Gabbert, Barton Gabbert, Martha, Amanda Gabbert and
Lucinda Gabbert. To George W. Brown and wife one share and
James Carlisle and wife one share. (Jordan & Rebecca Ann
Epperson).

Page 600 - Mary G. Kendle(Kendall)]
                vs   ] Divorce
            John Kendle   ]
Mary G. Kendle and John Kendle wer married in Bedford County
on 4 March 1821. Mary G. is daughter of Rice Coffey. Rice
Coffey died 29 July 1853 intestate. Rice Coffey's son is
John R. Coffey.

                Chancery Court Minutes 1854 - 1858

Page 17 - Martha A. Knott]
                vs   ] Divorce.
            William M. Knott]
Martha A. Knott and William M. Knott were married on 9 day
March 1851.

Page 17 - Elizabeth Smith]
                vs   ] 5 September 1854.
            Frank Smith   ]
Elizabeth Smith and Frank Smith married and they have two
children.

Page 37 - Louise H. Arnold]
                vs   ] Divorce.
            James H. Arnold]
Louisa H. Arnold and James H. Arnold married in Bedford County
in 1832. James H. Arnold left the county in 1853 and left
the state. Left children.

Page 38 - Amanda J. J. Martin(Morton?) married Philamon Gosling.

Page 44 - Catharine Dougal & others]
                vs   ] 5 September 1854.
            John H. Gambill   ]
John Dougal, deceased, made and published his Last Will and
Testament. Widow Catharine Dougal. Selina A. L. Griffith,
his only child. Selina A. L. intermarried with Eli Griffith.
After the death of John Dougal, his widow and Eli and Selina
A. L. Griffith wanted to remove to the State of Arkansas before
the completion of the sale of land and buying land in Arkansas,

Eli Griffith died intestate, he holding the money that was
received from the sale of John Dougal's land in Bedford County.
John H. Gambill was admr of Eli Griffith's estate. Selina
A. L. had children, not named.

Page 47 - J. A. Blakemore, admr of]
          John Whitesell   ]
               vs   ]
          Jacob Whitesell & others]
               and   ] 5 March 1855.
          Lewis & Jacob Whitesell]
               vs   ]
          J. A. Blakemore, admr   ]
John Whitesell departed this life in 1842. D. L. Barringer
was appointed executor of his Last Will and Testament and
Barringer failed to settle up the estate, departed this life
in 1852 and that J. A. Blakemore was appointed admr with the
will annexed, to settle the estate of John Whitesell, deceased.
Widow Milly Whitesell to get her dower and one tenth of share
of personal estate, and that Jacob, Lewis, George W. and
William Whitesell, Emily C. Bennett, Mariah Gambill and Isabel
Thomas (and the husbands of the last three) as devises. George
W. Whitesell has departed this life, also Mariah Gambill has
departed this life and left her only two children: James and
Polly Gambill. Isabel Thomas has departed this life since
the death of her father John Whitesell. Also, it appeared
to the court that John Whitesell, one of the testator's children is entitled to a share, but he died before his father.

Page 50 - Francis C. Thomas and Elizabeth were married on
21 July 1853.

Page 51 - Emily C. Lamb]
               vs   ] 6 March 1855.
          David Lamb   ]
Emily C. was a daughter of _____ Carrell.

Page 56 - Alanson Trigg   ]
               vs   ] 6 March 1855.
          William S. Jett &   ]
          Samuel K. Whitson, admrs]
Hayden Trigg died in the year of 1845, after having made and
published his Last Will and Testament and admitted to court
at November Term 1847. William H. Trigg, George N. Whitson
and Frederick Shofner, executors, only William H. Trigg qualified. A son Alanson Trigg.

Page 72 - 6 March 1855. Nancy C. Hix intermarried with John P.
Dean.

Page 84 - Mary Ann Gabbert, widow of William Gabbert, deceased,
married _____ Hastings.

Page 91 - Family of Jonathan Parker listed.

Page 106 - David R. Vance   ]
               vs   ] 30 October 1855.
          Christina Vance & others]
Samuel Vance departed this life in Bedford County in March
1849, having made his Last Will and Testament and proven and
admitted to probation in April 1849. In the will it has, "My
two sons, David R. Vance and Robert B. Vance". Wife Christina
Vance. Plat of Vance land on page 133. Robert B. Vance has

departed this life. Robert B. Vance left daughter Eliza J.
Vance and son Robert Vance.

Page 126 - John T. Neil,   ]
          George W. Ruth   ]
                vs   ] 3 November 1855.
          Airy E. Kincaid & others]
Joseph Kincaid of Bedford County, departed this life in the
spring of 1844, having made his Last Will and Testament, proven
and recorded in April Term of Court 1844. John T. Neil,
George W. Ruth and Airy Kincaid, executors. Wife Airy Kincaid
and children, not named. It stated that should Airy Kincaid
and children go to Missouri, his brother William M. Kincaid
be appointed testamentary guardian of his children here and
in Missouri. Brother William M. Kincaid did not accept the
guardianship and moved to California.

Page 134 - William Young & wife Eliza C.   ]
                vs   ] February 1856.
          Robert T. Cannon, Mary Rebecca Cannon]
          & Letsey M. Cannon   ]
William Hooser departed this life in Bedford County, having
made a Last Will and Testament. He left: Eliza J. wife of
William Young, Letsey M. later married Robert T. Cannon and
Letsey gave birth to two children and died, to wit, Mary
Rebecca Cannon and Letsey M. Cannon.

Page 151 - State of Tennessee   ]
                vs   ] 3 March 1856.
          Silas Pratt, Andrew Pratt]
          & John Wallace   ]
George Pratt departed this life in Bedford County in May of
1855 after making his Last Will and Testament. Andrew Pratt
and John Wallace, executors. One of the heirs, Silas Pratt.

Page 157 - Plat for McAdams (J. B.) and wife Catharine and
James Dixon. (Flat Creek)

Page 158 - William T. Tune, admr &c]
                vs   ] March 1856.
          Jonathan Cooper & others]
Alsa Harris' will. Wife Jane Harris. Lewis Tucker and William
Vincent, executors. Jane Harris, deceased, left brothers and
sisters, not named.

Page 190 - Ruth White   ]
                vs   ] 30 August 1856. Divorce.
          Joseph White]

Page 201 - Middleton Holland & others]
                vs   ] 1 September 1856.
          Mary Green & others   ]
James Green, late of Coffee County, Tennessee, departed this
life in 1853, leaving a will. David R. Vance and W. M. Green,
executors. Widow Mary Green, children, both married and under
21 years.

Page 208 - Plat of land for Littleberry Green. 14 July 1856.

Page 212 - Elizabeth Tune]
                vs   ] 30 August 1856. Divorce.
          John Tune   ]

Page 233 & 396 - Hiram H. Holt &   ]
                K. M. Pybus, Exrs of   ]
                Jordan C(ane) Holt, deceased]
                       vs   ] 3 September 1856.
                Isaac B. Holt & others   ]
Jordan C. Holt, deceased, died in Bedford County in 1853. His
will proven October Term 1853. Wife Margaret Wilhoite. K. M.
Pybus and Hiram C. Holt, executors. Children, Isaac B. Holt,
(Emily) wife of Hiram H. Nease, (Caladonia) Scales wife of
J. H. C. Scales, Alice Isora(Isadora) Holt, Frances J. Holt,
Jordan C. Holt, Jr. and his wife Jane and his children Susan,
Margaret C. and Jordan C. Holt, 3rd, Margaret wife of Benjamin
Moseley and Huldah H. wife of James L. Hix.

Page 287 - Alfred Ransom &   ]
            Felix Turrentine, exrs]
                   vs   ] 4 March 1857.
            David P. Orr & others]
David Orr, deceased, made his Last Will and Testament. Joseph
Anderson as executor of Frances Jane Orr, deceased. They left
granddaughters Gilly Ann Harris and Martha Ann Burton.

Page 302 - Malinda Nichols]
                   vs   ] Divorce.
            Malcom Nichols]
Malinda Nichols and Malcom Nichols married in Bedford County.
(3 Aug 1857) (now together)

Page 345 - Elizabeth H. Quimby]
                   vs   ] 4 Sept 1857. Divorce.
            H. B. Quimby   ]
Now living together.

Page 347 - Ann Shofner   ]
                 vs   ] 3 September 1857. Divorce.
            William M. Shofner]
Ann Shofner and William M. Shofner married in Bedford County
in 184_, they had two children, Elizabeth aged about 5 years
and Madison aged about 1 year and 6 months. She has one child
whom has since died. Granted.

Page 390 - Blan Maupin, deceased, widow Elizabeth intermarried
with Buford Bennett some time last winter or spring (1857).
Sarah L. Maupin, Mary A. Southern (S. F. Southern), Jane E.
Maupin, Thompson P. Maupin and Betty M. Maupin are the only
children of Blan and Elizabeth Maupin. 4 September 1857.

Page 411 - 2 March 1858. Susannah Hall and Robert P. Hall
married 20 September 1857.

Page 445 - Robert B. Davidson   ]
                   vs   ] March 1858.
            R. Newsom, T. D. Thompson,]
            exrs & others   ]
Sterling Newsom departed this life in Bedford County, having
made his Last Will and Testament. Randolph Newsom and Terry D.
Thompson, executors. He left children and grandchildren, not
named.

Page 472 - W. J. W. Wakefield, exr &c]
                   vs   ] 4 March 1858.
            William Morton,   ]
            John Morton & others   ]

Plat of John Sutton's land, District No. 4 of Bedford County, on page 476.

Page 488 - Plat of William Gabbert's widow Mary Ann (now Hastings) land.

Page 501 - Mary J. Christopher]
                    vs   ] 31 August 1858. Divorce.
             D. J. Christopher]
Mary J. Christopher is to be known as Mary J. Wells.

Page 502 - Mary E. Wynn]
                    vs   ] 31 August 1838. Divorce.
             F. J. F. Wynn]
Mary E. Wynn's maiden name was Mary E. Haskins. They were married several years ago. They had one child John Thompson Wynn now of 12 years. Changed her name back to Mary E. Haskins.

Page 523 - Benjamin F. Whitworth, Trustee &c]
             Anna F. Smalling & others   ] 3 September 1858.
             Exparte Petition   ]
Anna F. Smalling and her children, heirs of her father Jacob Morton, deceased, who made a will.

Page 533 - John W. Wiggins   ]
                    vs   ] 3 September 1858.
             D. F. Jackson & wife & others]
William O. Forbes made a will. Widow Nancy Forbes. Left children, not named and under age of 21 years.

Page 533 - Joel & Loton Shofner, exrs]
                    vs   ] 3 September 1858.
             M. Shofner & others   ]
John Shofner, deceased, leaving a will. Joel and Loton Shofner, executors. The legatees of John Shofner, deceased, are, Joel, Mike, D. M. Shofner, Mary Boyers wife of Thomas Boyers, E. Jane Wardlaw wife of James M. Wardlaw, Julia B. Morton wife of G. W. C. Morton, and Martha Motlow wife of F. Motlow.

Page 551 - William Murphree &]
             Emaline Jacobs, exrs]
                    vs   ] 4 September 1858.
             John Lipscomb Jacobs]
John Jacobs departed this life having made his Last Will and Testament, proven and recorded. Witnesses to will are: William Heron, Sherwood Lisenby and James Claxton. Son Briant Jacobs, daughter Nancy Masters, wife Emaline Jacobs, son John Lipscomb Jacobs. Wife Emaline Jacobs and William Murphree, executors. Will dated 6 July 1854.

Page 574 - Plat of John B. Wynn's, deceased, estate. Waters of Wilson Creek, 10th District of Bedford County. 26 October 1857.

Page 576 - Mary Boyers, by her next friend]
             G. W. C. Martin   ] 22 November 1858.
             Exparte Petition   ]
John Shofner, deceased, made a will. Mary Boyers is a daughter of said John Shofner. Eight children in all. (not named)

Page 586 - Andrew Pratt &   ]
            John Wallace, exrs   ]
                 vs   ] 23 November 1858.
            James M. Burnett &   ]
            wife Parthenia & others]
Andrew Pratt has died since last Term of Court. Peter E. Clardy
was appointed admr with the will annexed of said Andrew Pratt.
Nancy Kizer, one of the devisees, under the will of the testator
to get one fourth of the 1/10 of said estate (her third child).

Page 593 - Benjamin Moseley & others]
                 vs   ] 23 November 1858.
            J. H. C. Scales & others]
Jordan C. Holt, deceased, made a will. He willed his entire
estate to his children. His wife died before the testator.
Caledonia Scales wife of J. H. C. Scales was living, one of
his children.

        Chancery Court Settlement Book "B"   1848 - Feb 1851

Page 1 -   Seth Thomas   ]
                 vs   ]
            Bluford & Andrew Davidson]

Page 8 -   Peter Singleton came from Virginia, 35 years ago
to Bedford County, ca 1813. Wife Sally Brooks Singleton. His
will executed 11 September 1835. Peter Singleton died in the
year 1839. Sally Singleton died last February 1848. Many
slaves. No issue. Wiley F. Daniel, executor. Mrs. Sally
Brooks Singleton had brothers and sisters. (see 1850 Census
for list of slaves).   Chancery Court, 26th day of Feb 1851.
7th October 1850, sale of 274½ acres.

Page 20 - John Tillman   ]
                 vs   ] Bill filed 14 May 1849.
            Matt Martin, Jr & others]
John Tillman and wife Rachel P(K)., formerly Rachel Martin.
John L. Tillman and wife Sarah, formerly Sarah Martin. Edmund
A. Mosely, admr of Betty Mosely, formerly Betty M. Martin.
Thomas D. Mosely, admr of Rebecca Mosely, formerly Rebecca
Martin. Matt Martin, Sr. died __ day of October 1846 (made
will, in which he appointed his two sons. Barclay and Matt
Martin, Jr., as executors, appeared in Court,1846).
Matt Martin, Sr. Last Will and Testament (abstract)
Rachel P., daughter of Matt Martin, Jr. married John Tillman;
Sarah, daughter of Matt Martin, Jr. married John L. Neil;
Betty M., daughter of Matt Martin, Jr. married Thomas B. Mosely,
died since Matt Martin, Sr. (intestate), executor Edmund A.
Mosely; Rebecca, daughter of Matt Martin, Jr. married Thomas B.
Mosely, died since Matt Martin, Sr., executor Thomas B. Mosely.

Page 21 -   The said Matt Martin left the following children
in addition to his four daughters, named to wit, Barclay Martin,
Matt Martin, Jr., Hattie B. _____ is still living, Lucy Bradford and Polly Marshall and also the following grandchildren
to whom he bequeathed ___ certain portions of his property
(to wit), Barclay M. Bradford, Theoderick F. Bradford, William
Bradford, Caroline M. Bradford, and Elizabeth Bradford, children of said Luct Bradford. The said Lucy Bradford had one
other daughter _____ who intermarried with one _____ Jones

138

and she has departed this life leaving one child, Lucy G. Jones
but whether before or after the testate, your orators do not
know said Lucy Bradford has also lately departed this life
and also William D. Martin, son of H. A. Martin and Amanda J.
Martin, who was a son of Matt Martin, Sr. but died several
years before his father said William D. had departed this life
since the testator and said Matt Martin, Jr. in his admr and
the said James Mullins for their regular guardian. Matt M.
Marshall son of said Polly Marshall, grandson of the testator
is also a legatee under said will for the bequest and devisees
of the different legatees reference is made to the caps of
said will hereto annexed. Your orator further states that
by the said will of said Matt Martin, Jr., is bequeathed a
larger portion of personal property more than the other children and also $18,000.00 worth of real estate. Negroes (many
in number and named in will) were sold in May 1847. The executors were qualified in November 1846. Will of Matt Martin, Jr.
dated 1845.

Page 23 - Edward A. Mosely took up slave (purchased by another
person). Edward A. Mosely's wife is Betty M. Mosely.
    In tender consideration of the promises and for as much
as your orator, are deliverable in the Honorable Court, your
orators pray that said Barclay Martin, Matt Martin, Jr.,
George Davidson and Thomas C. Whiteside. The first of whom
lives in Maury County, Tennessee and the three last in Bedford
County. He made defendants...

Page 27 - Matt Martin, Jr. married 1835 and settled on his
father's land and homeplace.

Page 28 - E. W. Tipton who is son in law of John Tillman.

Page 29 - Barclay Martin living in Maury County, Tennessee.

Page 34 - Paid Willis Cannon for one fine coffin for Mrs.
Rachel P. Tillman. $16.00.
Paid Dr. J. G. Searcy for medical bills, attention and visit.
$25.00.
Paid W. R. McFadden for shrouding. $10.05.
Paid Dr. Thomas Lipscomb for medical account and visits, &c.
$13,62.
Paid William Elmore receipt for tombstone and lettering on
said stone. $184.90.

Page 39 - In bill (sale of slaves), of James H. Locke against
others (page 36). All of whom reside in bedford County, except
John Watkins who reside in Rutherford County and Thomas C. H.
Miller and Adolphus S. Adams who reside in Marshall County,
Tennessee.

Page 51 - Richard Bandy had a son George W. Bandy.

Page 62 - James L. Scudder]
              vs   ] August 1849.
          George Kimbro   ]
Both of Bedford County. James L. Scudder's matural grandfather
was William O. Whitney, late a citizen of Bedford County, died
about the year 1826. Made will and published. Appointed sons:
Thomas P. and James G. Whitney executors, also widow Ruthy
Whitney as executrix. Named daughter Harriet P. Scudder, mother
of James L. Scudder. Harriet P. Scudder's husband was Philip
J. Scudder. (between whom family difficulties existed).

Harriet P. Scudder was lawfully divorced from her husband, Philip J. Scudder and never lived with him after execution of said will and on or about the year 1830 the said Philip J. Scudder died, and the said Harriet P. survived him, and who still survives after the divorce, the said Thomas P. and James G. Whitney acting as Executors of will. Later, Harriet P. Scudder contracted and entered into marriage with one Henry Harrell. Later, Henry Harrell left the country, greatly in debt, leaving (1849) Harriet P. Harriet P. now wife of William J. Wisener, Esq.

Page 70 - James L. Scudder]
            vs   ] 27 Feb 1851. Decree.
      George Kimbro]
William O. Whitney died about the year 1826, having made and published his Last Will and Testament and proven. James G. Whitney and Thomas P. Whitney were appointed executors and gave bond and qualified. Gave among other property to Ruthy Whitney, a negro man John and a negro woman Susannah. To his daughter Harriet P. Scudder and son James L. Scudder. Said Harriet P. Scudder was divorced from Philip J. Scudder. Harriet P. Wisener.

Page 72 - James L. Scudder]
            vs   ] 29 Aug 1849.
      George Kimbro]
Ruthy Whitney of Bedford County, a material witness, is aged and infirm to give her deposition.

Page 72 - A. A. Robinson (Mrs. Adaline A. Warner (Wilhoite)]
            vs   ]
      Jordan C. Holt   ]
A. A. Robinson of Marshall County, Tennessee against Jordan C. Holt of Bedford County. William Wilhoite and John Wilhoite (many years ago) were partners in a set of mills, situated in Bedford County on Duck River, grist and saw mills, then in June 1839, William Wilhoite, who was at the time husband of A. A. Robinson, departed this life intestate in District No. 7. John Wilhoite was appointed admr upon the estate of William Wilhoite, deceased, at July Term 1839. Also, John Wilhoite was guardian of her children (2), John R. and Jacob B. Wilhoite. Shortly after the death of William Wilhoite, Samuel Thompson was appointed guardian of the two children, then after estate was sold, John Wilhoite was guardian of said children. 30 September 1851.

Page 80 - (Mrs) A. A. Robinson]
            vs   ] 31 August 1853. Final Decree.
      Jordan C. Holt   ]
"It appearing to the court that there came into the hands of John Wilhoite as the admr of William Wilhoite, deceased, after deducting his vouchers and his allowance, on 1st day of July 1841, sum of $3,416.78. John Wilhoite, deceased, Jordan C. Holt, admr.

Page 82 - (Mrs) A. A. Robinson   ]
            vs   ] 1 April 1852.
      Jordan C. Holt, admr of]
      John Wilhoite, deceased]
John and William Wilhoite were engaged for a series of years as partners in a set of grist and saw mills in Bedford County, continued up to the time of the death of William Wilhoite in the month of June 1839 and that John Wilhoite would up, settled

and collected all the debts and accounts due said firm and
sold and transferred all the property belonging to the firm
of every kind and description. And that John Wilhoite was
also appointed admr of the estate of William Wilhoite, deceased,
John Wilhoite is now dead and that Jordan C. Holt appointed
admr for children, two, only heirs of William Wilhoite.

Page 83 - Orators: John C. Dolby, Philip A. Dolby, Thomas D.
Dolvy, Warren L. Dolby, Benjamin H. Y. Dolby and George W.
Dolby, the last being a minor who files this bill by his next
friend Warren K(L). Dolby, citizens of State of Texas. Woodson
K. Dolby, Francis Ann Dolby, Rhoda Jane Dolby, William G. Dolby
and Minerva E. Dolby, the last two being minors who file this
bill by their next friend Woodson K. Dolby, Charlotte T. Waite,
John S. Morrison and Francis P. his wife formerly Francis P.
Waite, citizens of Bedford County, would represent that Knight
Dolby departed this life in Bedford County of which he was
a citizen in the month of October A.D. 1827, having made and
published his Last Will and Testament, proven and admitted
to record, November Term 1827, and Robert Waite approved as
executor.

Page 84 - Will of Knight Dolby (often recorded as Dalby):
The said Knight Dolby gave and devised all his real and personal
property to his wife Nancy Dolby during her natural life and
at her death to be equally divided among all his children,
and that he died seized and possessed of tract of land on which
he then resided and which is embraced in said bequest of said
will and situated in Bedford County, adjoining the lands of
Charles F. Sutton and others, and on the south side of Bradfords
Creek and bounded by Spradlin's line, Frazier's line, William
Waite, Chamber's line, and containing 100 acres. Which tract
was surveyed by John Bradford to said Knight Dolby, deceased,
by deed dated 31 July 1818. Knight Dolby left nine children
living at the time of his death, to whom he divided said land
at the death of his wife, to wit, Your orators: John C. Warren,
Phillip A. and Thomas D. Dolby, Martha C. Gun wife of Francis
B. Gun, Polly H. Waite wife of William Waite, Edward B. Dolby,
Agnes B. Wood wife of _____ Wood and James B. Dolby. Your
orator states that Nancy or Ann Dolby, the widow of said Knight
Dolby, deceased, departed this life in the month of December
1848 and after his youngest son had become of age, that since
decease of said Knight Dolby, his son Edward B. Dolby, his
daughter Polly H. Waite and her husband and his daughter Agnes
B. Wood and her husband has also died, that the said Edward B.,
your orators Benjamin H. Y., George W., Woodson K., Francis
Ann, Rhoda Jane, William G., and Minerva E. Dolby, together
with Emily Jeffers wife of Elijah Jeffers, his only children
and heirs and entitled to an undivided ninth part of said tract
of land, that George W., Peter H. and William Waite, Mary A.
Buckaloo wife of William Buckaloo together with your orators
Francis P. Morrison and Charlotte T. Waite are the only children of the said Polly H. Waite, deceased, and are also entitled
to an undivided one ninth part of said tract of land and that
William M. Wood, Sarah Ann Thompson, Rachael W. Waite wife
of Peter H. Waite, Jane Womble wife of John W. Womble and
Knight D. Wood, are the only children and heirs of said Agnes
B. Wood, deceased, and as such also entitled to an undivided
ninth part of said land. All of the above heirs become entitled
to the possession of the above described land upon the death
of said Nancy Dolby, the widow of said Knight Dolby, deceased.
    It is said that John Sutton executed a judgement against
said deceased at June Term 1827. Deputy Sheriff K. L. Anderson

sold tract of land to James Deery, 19 February 1828, for
$100.00. Sheriff James Wortham made sale void. The said
Knight Dolby, deceased, had enough personal property to settle
judgement with Sutton.

Robert Waite, executor of the Last Will and Testament
of Knight Dolby, deceased, soon and within two years of said
sale, redeemed the said tract of land from James Deery for
benefit of widow and heirs by paying him $180.33+, 11 February
1830. It was learned about 16 January 1839, Deery relinquished
for said tract of land to James B. Dolby, one of the children
of Knight Dolby, deceased. James B. Dolby on about 31 December
1840 made a pretended sale and conveyance of said tract of
land for $800.00 to John S. Frazer, which James B. Dolby manag-
ed to obtain possession of land from the tenant of the said
Nancy Dolby who was then in the Republic of Texas where she
remained until her death. Frazer took possession of tract
of land which he held until his death which occured ten days
ago (December 21, 1840).

The orators said the true and rightful owners are: John C.,
Warren K., Phillip A. and Thomas D. Dolby, Martha C. Gun wife
of Francis B. Gun, children of Edward B. Dolby, deceased, Polly
H. Waite, deceased, Agnes B. Wood, deceased, James B. Dolby
or the heirs of his bargainer, John S. Frazer. Nancy Dolby,
widow died December 1848.

John S. Frazer, deceased, left a widow Eliza Jane Frazer
and only one child, John S. Frazer who is a minor and has no
guardian and that Samuel H. Whitthorne had been appointed admr.

Your orators pray that your Honor, that James Deery,
Eliza Jane Frazer, John S. Frazer and Samuel H. Whitthorne,
admr &c citizens of Bedford County, James B. Dolby, William
Buckaloo and his wife Mary A. Buckaloo, are citizens of Coffee
County, Tennessee, Francis B. Gun and Martha C. his wife,
Elijah Jeffers and Emily his wife, George W. Waite, Peter H.
Waite and Rachel W. Waite his wife, William Waite a minor,
whose guardian is G. G. Osborne, William M. Wood, Gabriel
Thompson and Sarah Ann his wife, John W. Womble and Jane his
wife, Knight D. Wood a minor with no guardian, all non-residents
of Tennessee, but citizens of Texas and other parts beyond
the State of Tennessee.

Page 100 - Edward B. Dolby, deceased, has eight living children,
three in Illinois and five in Tennessee. Warren K. Dolby,
F. B. Green and Martha C. his wife, Thomas D. and Philip A.
Dolby, all of the State of Texas.

Page 101 - Mathew Mullins and Jane his wife,]
           Amos Sweeney and wife & others   ]Original Bill
                     vs   ]Feb 27, 1851.
           Elias H. Brandon, Lewis Weatherford,]
           Margaret Brandon & others   ]
Charles Brandon died April 1838, intestate, upwards to 80 years
of age. (stated he became insane before death). Amos Sweeney
and wife Hester. Lemuel Snelling and Sarah his wife. Matthew
Mullins and Jane his wife. John Norvill and America his wife.
Robert J. King and Charles B. King. Robert Brandon, a minor
by his next friend Charles B. King. Thomas Pannell and Polly
his wife.

Elias H. and Hester (Hetty) Sweeney, Elizabeth Hensley,
John King who went to Williamson County, Tennessee, Caroline,
Nancy, Robert, Sarah and Elizabeth Lee are minors. James
Chambers and Mary his wife. Aaron Shannon and Elizabeth his
wife. Robert Turner and Elizabeth his wife (Hetty said "Nancy"
not Elizabeth). Rachel Falkner. Elias H. McFadden. Willis

McFadden and Nancy his wife. Jonathan Smith and Mary his wife
went to Lincoln County, Tennessee. Andrew Mise and Sally his
wife. John W. Brandon, son. Andrew J. Brandon, son. _____
Buchanan and Caroline his wife. Mary Brandon, daughter. Elias
Brandon. _____ Smith and Catherine his wife. Elias H. Brandon, son, went to Missouri. Margaret Brandon, daughter.
In Deed Book "HH": Charles Brandon to Margaret.
Hetty Sweeney, daughter of Charles Brandon and 2nd wife, and
Amos Sweeney married 25-30 years ago. Elias H., youngest son
of Charles and his 2nd wife. Elias H. Brandon moved to Illinois
and returned to Tennessee and lived with and took care of his
father. After his father's death, he moved to Missouri.

Page 117 - Gwynn Foster   ]
                  vs   ] Orig & Inj Bill
            William D. Hill &]
            John Shuffield   ]
William D. Hill preparing to remove to Arkansas from Tennessee,
"trying to settle partnership in business".
Names: Enoch P. Rushing and others.

Page 140 - Nelson Blakemore]
                  vs   ]
            John Johnson   ]
Nelson Blakemore and Susan his wife.
William Reddin, Joseph Reddin and John Reddin.
David Davenport and wife Emeline.
Matilda Reddin.
William Cothorn and Martha his wife.
Elizabeth Reddin, Robert Reddin and both minors.
(All of the above are of Coffee County, Tennessee)
Silas Corean and Ann his wife of Livingston County, Kentucky.
Elisha Blakemore and Susan his wife.
Joseph B. Blackman.
William J. Blackman.
Jeremiah Blackman.
John E. Blackman.
Caroline Blackman.
Eleanor Blackman.
Mary Blackman.
(last four are minors and citizens of Lancaster District, South
Carolina)
David Chase and Catherine his wife.
James J. Blackman.
Burrell C. Johnson.
(all above are citizens of Harris County, Georgia)
James McLean and his three children reside in Texas.
All above names are against John Johnson, admr of Joseph John-
son, deceased, and Susannah Johnson who are citizens of Coffee
County, Tennessee.
Joseph Johnson of Coffee County, Tennessee, died September 1842.
Susannah, widow of Joseph Johnson.
Heirs: John, son of Joseph Johnson; Elizabeth, daughter of
Joseph Johnson and who died before her father, married _____
Reddin and had the following children, Joseph, William, John,
Matilda, Robert, Elizabeth, Susan who married Nelson Blackman,
Emaline who married David Davenport, Martha who married William
Calhoun, Polly who married James McLean; Susannah, daughter
of Joseph Johnson, who married Elisha Blackman; Letha, daughter
of Joseph Johnson, who died before her father, married _____
Blackman and had the following children, Catherine who married
David Chase, James J., Jeremiah, John E., Caroline, Eleanor
and Mary Blackman; William, son of Joseph Johnson, who died

before his father and had a son Burrell.

Page 151 - William Gosling,   ] Bill. Jan 25, 1836.
              John W. Cowan & Co. & others]
Organized Cotton Mill on Duck River in Shelbyville. Partnership and built mill: Theoderick F. Bradford, John Tillman and
Clement Cannon. Clement Cannon owned land the Cotton Mill
was built on. Dam was constructed. $9000 cost of Mill and
Dam. Tillman sold out in 1837 to Bradford. Bradford sold
his part in 1839 to John Tillman and William Galbreath.
1841, John Tillman sold all his interest to William Gosling.
1843, Clement Cannon sold his one fourth interest to John Eakin,
William Eakin and Thomas Eakin.
1843, Co-partnership was formed, William Gosling, Thomas C.
Whiteside, Thomas Eakin, John Eakin, William Eakin and E. J.
Frierson. Cotton Mill operated until August 1, 1850, it having
been dissolved by the death of the partners John Eakin, William
Eakin and E. J. Frierson. Reorganized same year, 1850, under
the name Gosling, Whiteside & Co.

Page 171 - James C. Tribble, admr of   ]
              William Bearden, deceased &]
              Nancy his wife & Josephine]
              the only child   ]
                    vs   ] Bill of Complaint
              Daniel Dean and   ]
              James Keelin(g)   ]
Daniel Dean and James Keelin are non-residents of Tennessee.
James C. Tribble named admr of William Bearden's estate in
November Term 1849. William Bearden died August 1849.

Page 173 - Middleton Holland   ]
                    vs   ] Bill of Complaint
              Julia Ann Holland,   ] 19 September 1850.
              Mary Jane Holland,   ]
              Martha Ann Holland,   ]
              Moses Ayers Holland,   ]
              Matilda Holland,   ]
              Mitchell Brittain Holland,]
              & William Montgomery Holland]
Middleton Holland had brother Franklin Holland. On 19 September
1850, Isaac Barnett, by deed, convey to your orator and his
brother Franklin and their heirs forever, two tracts of land,
adjoining each other in Bedford County, 25th District, on Gages
and Normans Creek. One tract borders John G. and Thomas Blount
5000 acre grant, on Barren Fork of Duck River. Other tract
borders the above tract and joins R. F. Calahan's land and
Matthew Moss field. Franklin Holland died 8th January 1850.
Widow Julia Ann and six children (named above), all residents
of Bedford County.

Page 179 - James M. Jones   ]
                    vs   ] Bill of Complaint
              Winston W. Gill & others]   22 August 1849
James M. Jones, citizen of Bedford County, that he purchased
from Thomas S. Brown, then a citizen of Bedford County, a tract
of land on waters of Flat Creek, 110 acres for $1000.00. Tract
did not have clear or valid title. It was titled to one
Joseph Clark of Mississippi.

Page 190 - Walter Sims & wife Mary E.]
                    vs   ]Bill of Complaint
              James L. Scudder   ]

Walter Sims and Mary E. Sims his wife, citizens of Davidson
County, Tennessee. On or about the 9th June 1820, one John S.
Green purchased from Philip J. Scudder an undivided fourth
part of a tract of land, 1000 acres or the fourth part of a
100 acre land Warrant No. 3549, which was within the present
limits of Haywood County. It was executed, which Green had
never registered but a copy thereof herewithin filed. In
Autumn of 1823, John S. Green and Walter Sims who were partners
in trade mortgage various tracts of land to John G. Sims, admr
of Walter Sims, deceased.
        Court ordered land to be sold, May Term 1834. One fourth
part (undivided) of said 1000 acre tract was bought by Mrs.
Rebecca Sims and soon after she conveyed same to Mary E. Sims
for her sole and separate use.
        Philip J. Scudder had undivided one fourth part of tract
of land and after the death of Scudder, departed this life
in the year 1830, leaving two heirs, namely a daughter who
was married sometime previous to the year 1838, and a son
James L. Scudder, who only attained his majority a year or
two ago.
        Jos. G. Whitney was guardian of James L. Scudder until
his death of said Whitney in the year 1840, and that from the
year 1842, William H. Wisner acted as his guardian until he
attained his majority.
        Sometime previous to the year 1838, the 1000 acre tract
of land was taken possession of by Richard C. Taylor and other
persons who pretended to claim title. Philip J. Scudder failed
to give title to John S. Green and was never registered, but
the title of Mary E. Sims was recognized by Thomas C. Ryall,
husband of one of the heirs and by Jos. G. Whitney, who then
the guardian of James L. Scudder, the only heir.
        Walter Sims acted in behalf of his wife and of the heirs
of Scudder, to recover 250 acres purchased by Taylor and two
others, Green and Carter, the 4th day of October 1838.
James L. Scudder a citizen of Bedford County.
        Exhibit "A": Land warrant for 1000 acres under the certi-
ficate of D. McGavock, Register of West Tennessee, No. 3549,
in lieu of so much of a Military Warrant issued to Nathaniel
Lowrance, a Lieutenant, No. 2020 for 2,560 acres to be placed
in hands of Richard Wighton to locate. When located, 1000
acres to be vested in John S. Green, his part of locating expenses. 9 June 1820.
        John G. Sims, admr of Walter Sims, Sr., deceased. James L.
Scudder and his sister who married Thomas C. Ryall.
        Walter Sims and Mary E. Sims his wife of Marshall County,
Tennessee.
        James Mullins, Sheriff of Bedford County from 1st Monday
in April 1840 to 1st Monday in April 1846. William D. Orr
was Deputy.
        From 1836 to May 1842, Robert P. Harrison hept a Tavern
in Shelbyville. Made a will. Widow was executrix. Names:
Eliza W. Harrison. Robert P. was Clerk and Master of Chancery
Court.

Page 212 - Ab L. Landers, admr upon the
          estate of Leighton Ewell, deceased
                        vs
                Mary Ewell, William P. Chamberlain and wife Martha,
                Lewis W. Hall and wife Lucy, George W. Heard and
                wife Katherine, John H. Scott and wife Virginia,
                Alexander Kimbro and wife Sarah, John Ewell, Philip
                L. Ewell, Joseph Ewell, David R. Vance and wife
                Ann E., William M. Ewell, Asa M. Elkins and wife

Ann of Texas, and Dabney Ewell. John Ewell departed this life
in Bedford County in the year 1826.
Will of John Ewell: (died 1826)
To my wife Mary Ewell, slaves, hosehold and kitchen furniture,
&c and horses. Appointed his brother Leighton Ewell who lives
out side State of Tennessee, as one of the executors, if he
would remove to Tennessee, but if he failed to move, he wished
him replaced by Dabney Ewell (brother) and Jonathan Webster
appointed as executors.
Jonathan Webster is now dead and Dabney Ewell now resides in
Coffee County, Tennessee.
Widow Mary Ewell died in 1861.
Daughter Martha who married William P. Chamberlain is living
in Arkansas. Daughter Anna who married Asa M. Elkins, living
in Texas and Anna died in Texas ca 1851. Son John lives in
Louisiana. Daughter Lucy who married S. W. Hall. Daughter
Catherine who married George W. Heard. Daughter Virginia who
married John H. Scott. Daughter Sarah who married Alexander
Kimbro. Son Philip K. Ewell. Son Joseph Ewell. Son Leighton
Ewell departed this life after his father in 1831, out of
state, and left two children Ann E. who married David R. Vance
and William Ewell a minor. Widow and mother Mary Ewell on
24th day of August 1848, divided all personal and real property.
Son Thomas Ewell died unmarried years ago. Son Maxey Ewell
who died years ago unmarried. Named slaves, August 1848:

Slaves	Age	Sold to
Silvia	55	A. Kimbro
Sam	36	John Ewell. Sold to Frank Keller,dec'd.
Lewis	23	P. K. Ewell. Sold to John Ewell, to LA.
Richard	21	George W. Heard. Sold to Brandon King
Susan	20	George W. Heard.
Evaline	11	Mary Ewell.
Squire	10	Asa M. Elkins, went to Texas.
Henry	8	Jos. Ewell. Sold to P. K. Ewell, to Mary Ewell.
Jenny	32	
Mary	11	
Eveline	8	Wm. P. Chamberlain, went to Arkansas.
Silvia	5	
Harriet	3	
Judy	15	J. H. Scott, Sold to Jeptha Shofner.
Harriet	30	
Little Sam	11	L. W. Hall.
Isaac	9	Sold to Zach Cully.
Reuben	2	

Page 223 - Anna Elkins died in Texas. Recorded 19 August 1852.

Page 227 - William S. Eakin, John R. Eakin and Argyle P. Eakin,
citizens of Davidson County, Tennessee.
    Lucretia Eakin, Julia A. Eakin, Sarah J. Eakin and Alex-
ander E. Eakin, Thomas L. Eakin, James H. Eakin, last five
names are minors. Guardian of above is William S. Eakin.
    George W. Eakin, Charles Eakin and Albert Eakin, minors,
guardian is widow Lucretia Eakin, all citizens of Bedford
County. All descendants of John Eakin, deceased.
    Stated: John Eakin departed this life on 19th day of
September 1849, after making his Last Will and Testament, leaving widow Lucretia and eleven children. Will proven and recorded October Term 1849 in Bedford County.
    John Eakin, deceased, before he died, had Lot # 30 and
sold said lot to John C. Cowan. John Eakin also had Lot # 10,
sold to Alexander Eakin. Other lots &c sold and divided among

146

heirs.

Page 230 - Petition of Jeptha Mintor as Trustee of Martha Ann
Key and John W. Key and wife Martha, filed in Chancery Court
at Shelbyville. Bought a negro girl Rose, wishes to exchange
Rose for a negro man William age 20 years, and obtaining title
to same. Difference in price of $300.00, he being a blacksmith.
August 27, 1852. Jeptha Mintor is brother of Martha Ann Key.

Page 232 - Jordan C. Holt, Benjamin Mosely and Jordan C. Holt,
Jr., all of Bedford County, 27 June 1849.
     John Fisher, admr of Rebecca Fisher, James F. Shearin,
Thomas S. Shearin, Jesse M. Ledbetter and Elizabeth his wife
filed against Lewis Gant and Matthew Shearin, admrs of Thomas
Shearin, deceased, and Polly Gaunt wife of Lewis Gaunt. Slaves
(to be sold). A negro woman was sold to Jordan C. Holt and
he found that she was not a sound person and soon died and
he wants a bill against sellers of slave.

Page 235 - A joint and separate answer of Lewis Gaunt and wife
Mary, Jesse M. Ledbetter and wife Elizabeth, James F. Shearin,
Thomas Shearin, Matthew Shearin, H. H. Stephens and wife Sarah,
and Michael Fisher (a minor by his guardian H. H. Stephens)
                    vs
Jordan C. Holt and others
The said bill, that J. M. Ledbetter and wife Elizabeth, James
F. Shearin, Thomas Shearin and John Fisher as the admrs of
Rebecca Fisher, deceased, filed in Chancery Court in Bedford
County against Matthew Shearin and Lewis Gaunt as admrs of
Thomas Shearin, deceased. Charging that among other things,
five slaves, before named, were really the property of complts,
and deft and not the property as the admrs of Thomas Shearin,
deceased, which has already been heard by Chancery Court, wherein it was decreed by Court that the slaves, including slave
Francis, were decreed to be the property of Respondants in
their own right, as the heirs at law of Thomas Shearin's first
wife and not the property of Thomas Shearin, deceased, estate.
Court also said it was impracticable to divide the slaves.
It was decreed that the slaves be sold by Court at public sale,
and they were sold by said court. Jordan C. Holt bought the
girl Francis. They said they knew nothing about the slave
girl Francis being sick with a disease before the date of sale.
They knew her for a long time and did not know she was sick
of any disease, especially sick enough to die. In 1849, she
was hired to R. L. Dwiggins who resides within short distance
of Jordan C. Holt.

Page 239 - William W. Coldwell   ]
                    vs   ] Bill of complaint
          Mary A. Craig, Martha A. Craig,]
          Henry Clay Craig, Robert M. Craig,]
          and Rebecca N. Craig   ]
All defts are of Bedford County. William W. Coldwell said
that James B. Craig departed this life intestate on the __
day of ___ 184_, leaving widow Mary H. Craig and following
children: Martha, Henry Clay, Robert M., and Rebecca N. Craig,
all of whom are minors under the age of 21. William W. Coldwell
admr of Craig's estate, February 1848, the widow and heirs
wanted to sell a tract of land of 20 acres, upon which there
was a Tannery. They wanted to sell so that they could buy
another tract of land from Charles Philpot, 107 acres for
$1,025.00, the widow paid $100.00 on account and that Philpot
bought the 20 acres, $620.00. Balance $350.00. February 1848.

Page 242 - G. L. & F. Sloan   ]
              vs   ]Bill of Complaint.
         John W. Key, Jeptha Minter &]
         Margaret C. Key   ]
George L. Sloan and Frederick Sloan and John W. Key, Jeptha
Minter and Margaret C. Key, all of Davidson County, Tennessee,
December 12, 1843. Recovered a judgement against John W. Key
for $759.50. In 1844, it was placed in hands of James Mullins,
then Sheriff of Bedford County and returned April Term 1844.
There was no property of John W. Key to be found in Bedford
County. Another judgement was placed in hands of James R.
Terry, a Deputy Sheriff, also said no property could be found
of John W. Key. They said that on or about the 17th day of
October 1843, so they believe, he made a pretended sale to
Jeptha Minter, his brother in law, for pretended consideration
of $1,200.00 of a tract of land, being in Bedford County in
Civil District No. 9, containing about 148½ acres, being at
the road leading from Shelbyville to Middleton.
     Martha C. Key living with her son John W. Key.
     Jeptha Minter a citizen of Rutherford County, Tennessee.
Margaret C. Key of Virginia.

Page 248 - John J. Shriver]
              vs   ] Bill of Complaint, 13 December 1845.
         Thomas Eakin   ]
John J. Shriver a citizen of Bedford County. Thomas Eakin,
surviving partner of the late firm of William & Thomas Eakin
and all, composed of John Eakin, William Eakin and Thomas Eakin,
the two former of whom are now dead, the later resides in
Davidson County, Tennessee.
     Thomas J. Shriver purchased from the late firm of W. & T.
Eakin & Co., a tract of land in Bedford County, 552 acres and
18 poles and took from John Eakin, William Eakin, and Thomas
Eakin, deed filed. John Eakin and William Eakin is now dead,
leaving said Thomas Eakin sole surviving partner.
     Orator states that he has never had entire 552 acres,
only 501 acres and 32 poles, the remaining 51 acres and 14
poles, he never possessed. On the eastern part of said tract,
Mrs. Elizabeth Snelling is in actual possession and has been
every since the purchase aforesaid of about 34 acres, holding
permanent title. On the northern part, William Hoover was
and is in possession holding and claiming in like manner, about
5 acres. On west there and from 12 to 15 acres which are in
possession of Joseph Freeman, Daniel Nichols and _____ Price,
all holding part of which was part of James Smalling and
Benjamin Whitworth and bought some land.

Page 251 - Answer of Thomas Eakin, surviving partner of the
former W. & T. Eakin & Co. to the bill filed against him by
John J. Shriver in Chancery Court.

Page 254 - Robert E. Thompson &]
           John C. Thompson   ]
                vs   ] Bill of Complaint.
           William S. Mayfield,]
           Erwin J. Frierson,]
           David Jones &   ]
           John F. Thompson   ]
Robert E. Thompson and John C. Thompson are citizens of Wilson
County, Tennessee. Their father Robert C. Thompson departed
this life in Williamson County, Tennessee of which he was a
citizen in the early part of the year 1832, leaving a widow
Martha A. R. Thompson and Robert E. and a daughter Mary Bell

148

Thompson, only children and heirs or legatees of Robert C.
Thompson. A short time before his death Robert C. Thompson
made and published his Last Will and Testament which at the
July Term 1832 of County Court of Williamson County, Tennessee,
was duly proven and recorded. Martha A. R. Thompson, the widow
and mother, was executrix and declined and renounced the execution thereof. William S. Mayfield, then a citizen of Bedford
County was appointed admr of said deceased will. 3rd Day of
July 1832. William S. Mayfield never made a return of the
estate. On October Term 1832 in Williamson County, Tennessee,
Mayfield made a partial return, did not include slaves or book
debts and accounts. Mayfield in the year 1833 sold 800 acres
in Gibson County, Tennessee on Rutherford's Fork of Obion,
to a man by the name of Mosely for $680.00. Sister Mary Bell
Catherine died many years ago when but an infant and they as
their only brothers and heirs are entitled to the whole of
the land. After Robert C. Thompson deceased for two or three
years, widow Martha R. Thompson remarried with Herbert Owens
and she died in 1844. Said Mayfield was holding deed to a
Town Lot No. 26(36) in Town of Jackson. William S. Mayfield
and E. J.Frierson are citizens of Bedford COunty and John F.
Ferguson a citizen of Marshall County, Tennessee. David Jones
a citizen of the State of Mississippi.

Page 259 - Will of Robert C. Thompson   July Term 1832.
          State of Tennessee
          Williamson County   March 2, 1831.
I, Robert C. Thompson of the State and County aforesaid, revoking all former wills made by me.
First and Last, it is my will that my will, that my beloved
wife, Martha A. R. Thompson have and I do by this bequeath
unto her during her widowhood all that I possess, both real
and personal, with the express qualification, that my three
children, Robert E. and John C. and Mary Bell Catherine Thompson
are to receive from my said wife as they may marry or come
of age, their respective proportions, share and share alike,
that every profit increase or the like of the original stock
is to be applied by my executors to the use and benefit of
my three children as well as the original stock, save as much
as may be necessary for the support of the family and upon
the intermarriage of my wife, I will and bequeath to my two
sons R. E. Thompson and John C. Thompson, the tract of land
on which I now live, with all its rights &c as far as my said
deed holds, and to my daughter Mary Bell Catherine Thompson,
I bequeath a negro woman named Lucy about 17 years old with
her child increase with two thousand dollars in cash, to be
put out on interest by the County Court until she becomes of
age. The two thousand dollars are to be raised from sale of
eight or fourteen hundred acre tract of land lying in Gibson
County, Tennessee, Western District on Rutherford's Fork of
Obion, as well as from a Town Lot No. 26 in Jackson, Madison
County, Tennessee which I now do in my Last Will and Testament
direct my executors or some one empowered by her to sell as
specifily as possible the above land and town, upon one, two,
three or four years, one fourth in hand to pay debts. It is
understood that bond and approved security is to be required.
My executrix may have the land laid off in lots and sell them
and after all the debts are paid and my daughter Mary Bell
Catherine Thompson gets her two thousand dollars, the balance
is to be equally divided between my two sons, above named,
and all other notes, bonds for land or money. I will to my
two sons and by this constitute my beloved wife Martha A.
Thompson, sole executrix, to this Last Will and Testament for

the purpose of carrying it into full effect and in so doing
it is not my will should give security for Letters Testamentary.
In witness hereof, I have set my hand and seal this 22nd March
1831.   Signed: R. C. Thompson (Seal)

Page 264 - Burrell G. White, citizen of Davidson County, Tennessee, John T. Neil of Bedford County and Augustus H. White
of Rutherford County, Tennessee. Bill of Complaint, 11 Nov
1848. Augustus H. White filed in Chancery Court of Bedford
County, Shelbyville, against William Blakely, a non-resident
of State of Tennessee, and against Willis Burk and William R.
Blakely, admr of William Blakely, Sr., deceased, John T. Neil
and others residing in Bedford County and against all the heirs
and distributors of William Blakely, Sr., deceased, to attach
a fund in the hands of John T. Neil or to come unto his bonds
as Clerk of Circuit Court of Bedford County and Commissioners
under said Circuit Court to sell and to receive the proceeds
of certain land belonging to the estate of William Blakely,
Sr., deceased, and subject the portion thereof to which William
Blakely, the non-resident was entitled as one of the heirs
&c of William Blakely, Sr., deceased, to the payments of certain debts specified in said bill, which the said Augustus H.
White held against William Blakely, the non-resident, all said
debts to about $174.37.
    On 10th day February 1849, after he (orator) purchased
claims from Augustus H. White, John Kirkman of Davidson County,
files his bill against Augustus H. White and John T. Neil,
alleging that he was in a judgement creditor of said Augustus
H. White by judgement recovered before a Justice of the Peace
of Rutherford County, Tennessee on 5th August 1848 for $143.60
plus cost of suit.

Page 272 - Flora L. Ewing   ]
              vs   ]Bill of Complaint.
         Joseph Thompson,]
         Nicholas P. Cheatham]
         Edmond B. Cheatham &]
         William Little   ]
Oratrix Flora L. Ewing (who being both an infant and female,
sued by her guardian and next friend, Milton P. Wheat) shows
that Flora L. Ewing's father, James Ewing departed this life
many years ago in the County of Adair in State of Kentucky,
where he resided and where Flora L. Ewing resided and now resides, leaving a considerable real and personal estate, which
by laws of Kentucky, descended to Flora L. Ewing and James
Ewing. Estate consisted of five slaves, Jack, Margaret, Porter,
Resin and George. A. Coldwell and said Milton P. Wheat, being
the regular guardian in Kentucky of the estate of Flora L.
Ewing and her brothers.
    10th November 1849, Flora L. Ewing intermarried with
Nicholas P. Cheatham, with whom she lived but a month or two,
his language being to her so bad she separated herself from
him. Flora L. states that she is still under age of 21 years,
that she never did join or attempt to join her husband in sale
of slave Porter.
    In 1844 until 1850, when Nicholas P. Cheatham and his
father Edmund B. Cheatham.......
    Complainant being a minor or a married woman, or that
she has any brothers or sisters.......

Page 280 - Orator William H. Wisener a citizen of Bedford
County, on April 14, 1847, he recorded a judgement against
one Lewis Wilhoite for $1500.47 and $1.75 cost of suit. No

property to be found by Sheriff of Bedford COunty. He also
stated that one Robert Moffat recovered a judgement against
Wilhoite before William Galbreath, Esq., a J.P. of Bedford
County on 4th November 1846 for $24.15 and 87½ cents cost of
suit. No property to be found, and that on 11th November 1844,
said Moffat recovered a judgement before Thomas Davis, Esq.,
a J.P. of Bedford County, for $5.01 and 87½ cents for cost
of suit, no property to be found.

Lewis Wilhoite, some five years ago, was owner of a valuable tract of land in bedford County, ___ acres, upon which
he lived in Civil District No. 22, which was levied upon and
sold by Sheriff of Bedford County. Samuel Doak became purchaser and before the purchased he agreed with Wilhoite that
whenever he got able, he might redeem said land. Doak had
purchased all or nearly all of Wilhoite's personal property.
It was agreed by said Wilhoite and Doak and John Wilhoite and
William Wilhoite, the two later being sons of Lewis, that said
Doak should sell or convey all of the said property both real
and personal to said John and William upon the same conditions
upon which said Doak held it. John and William finally got
the property.

Page 294 - Bill of Complaint of Allen Chandler, a citizen of
Coffee County, Tennessee against Richard Muse of Bedford County.
Allen Chandler in the year 1841, he contracted to purchase
from Richard Muse, 280 acres of land, in three separate tracts,
but they were to adjoin each other, and were to be situated
in Coffee County, Tennessee. Allen Chandler was to pay
$1000.00. He paid part in hand and other on two notes on 2nd
November 1841, one of which was $145.00 or 6 dollars due 1st
January thereafter. The other one, for $333.33 to fall on
1st January 1843.

Page 296 - Answer of Richard Muse to the bill of Allen Chandler.
He admits that he sold to complt three tracts of land containing
280 acres as set forth in bill.

Page 299 - Bill of Complaint of Pleasant Smith, Thomas W. Evans
and W. H. Evans, partners in trade under the name "Fun and
Style by Evans and Smith", citizens of Davidson County, Tenn-
essee, filed in Chancery Court in Shelbyville against George
Foster, William D. Hill, Augustus Wilson, David J. Wheeler,
Samuel P. Phillips, R. C. Ogilvie, William Foster and David G.
Deason, all citizens of Bedford County.

They recovered two judgements before Wilie Perry, a J.P.
of Bedford County, against George Foster and William D. Hill,
partners trading under the firm, name and style of W. D. Hill
and Co. on __ day of ___ 1849, amounting to $380.95, plus cost
of suit. They would now state as they are informed and believe,
that deft George Foster on the 7th day of December 1848 transferred by deed of that date to one Augustine Wilson, a negro
man Ben age about 14 years, for about $500.00, which is alleged
he received at the time of the transfer, but complt charge
that said sale was not entered to by them...

Page 308 - Thomas Lane, Exr of will]
           of Robert Lane, deceased]
                      vs   ]Bill of Complaint.
           America (Lane) Purdy and]
           Wiley Purdy   ]
America (Lane) Purdy of Bedford County and Wiley Purdy of
Marshall County, Tennessee. Robert Lane departed this life
on the 29th day of April 1849, during a temporary trip from

his residence in Marshall County, Tennessee, where he then
resided. That he made a nun-cupative will, which was proven
and recorded in Marshall County, appointed Thomas Lane and
James G. Barksdale as executors. Barksdale refused to qualify.
(June Term 1849, Marshall County, Tennessee)
     All of the property of which Robert Lane died seized and
possessed of, after payment of debts &c.... was to be divided
between his wife and his five children, one of whom had departed this life, an infant, since the death of Robert Lane.
     Slaves: Sarah, Winston, Job, Missouri and John who he
has had control and management of since his appointment.
     Martin W. Oakley guardian of the children. They all agreed
to sell all land and slaves of Robert Lane. Thomas has continued to hire out the slaves until 15th September 1850. Thomas
Lane said the negroes were taken out of the possession of the
persons to whom they were hired and removed by some persons
to Thomas Lane unknown up to the County of Bedford and placed
in possession of America Purdy, who now has them, claiming
them as her own. The negroes are now in possession of America
(Lane) Purdy, who is now living in Bedford County, separate
and apart from her husband, Miles Purdy, and if said property
was further removed the estate might be seriously injured,
as she is without any or much other visible means by which
said property may be finally secured and if it should now be
secretly removed that he has demanded said slaves which refuses
to give up....

Page 309 - Answer of America (Lane) Purdy, alias Lane, to bill
by Thomas Lane, executor, against her and Miles Purdy in
Chancery Court, Shelbyville. She admits the death of her husband, Robert Lane and his making a non-cupative will and its
probate and the appointment and qualification of Thomas Lane
as executor, as stated in bill. She admits that her late husband left a considerable estate, both real and personal property, all of which, is legal comtemplation for the two years
allowed by law for settling estates and in the legal custody
of complt though in fact it was in respt's actual possession
until about July or August 1850.

Page 312 - Bill of Complainant of William C. McMurry and
William H. Saffaraus, partners, who reside in Davidson County,
Tennessee, filed against Flower Swift and Jacob W. Swift of
Bedford COunty. They recovered a judgement against Jacob W.
Swift, December Term 1849, December 5th, the sum of $9.00 and
court cost.

Page 314 - Your Petitioners: Giles P. Burditt, Samuel S. Burditt, William M. Burditt, Keneth L. Burditt, Sarah J. Burditt,
the three latter being minors of their mother Sarah Burditt,
Nathan Ivy and his wife Mary Ann, Abram Castell and wife Mahala
and Patience, Samuel and Elizabeth Casteel, the latter three
being minors of William Casteel, William and James Gregory
also minors of Thomas Gregory, William J. Whitthorne and Thomas
B. Moseley represent to your Honor that they are except Giles
P. Burditt, who claim the right of redemption in the interest
claimed owners of tract of land, lying and being in Bedford
County on Noah's Fork of Duck River, being 134 or 135 acres,
joining lands of John S. Davis, Matt Finch and Thomas B. Moseley, being the tract on which Patience Burditt, deceased, resided at time of her death, being a greater part of land conveyed
by Lewis McKnight to William Burditt, Sr. by deed, dated 5th
September 1834, also tract of 17 acres conveyed to Patience
Burditt by William Norton by deed dated 23rd July 1839, in

exchange of 18 acres of said McKnight tract. William Burditt,
Sr., deceased, by the Last Will and Testament devised all his
estate, real and personal (which include said land) to his
wife Patience Burditt during her life and in event of her
death or marriage the estate was to descend to the widow Sarah
(widow of son William Burditt, Jr., deceased) during her life
or widowhood, and after her death to be equally divided among
the children of his son William Burditt, deceased. Your petitioners, Giles P., William M., Samuel S., Ambros H., Sarah J.,
and Keneth L. Burditt, Mary Ann Ivy, Mahala Casteel, together
with PatienceCavin wife of William Cavin, Elizabeth Casteel
about ___ years ago, and Rachel Gregory who died several years
ago and since the death of William Burditt, Sr., are as were
the only children of William Burditt, Jr., deceased, and the
grandchildren of William Burditt, Sr.
     William and James Gregory are minors and have no guardian
and the only children and heirs of Rachel Gregory, deceased,
and as such entitled to one undivided 11th part of the above
tract of land, and that Samuel and Elizabeth Casteel are the
only children and heirs at law of Elizabeth Casteel, deceased,
and are entitled to one 11th part of said land. Also William
Cavin and Patience his wife sold and conveyed their interest
in said land to petitioner Thomas B. Moseley by deed, dated
___ 1839.
     Sarah Burditt has be deed executed the 24th day of June
1851, given and relinquished all her interest in the said land
to her children and grandchildren, which said deed will be
produced. The land is so small that it cannot be divided fair-
ly into eleven parts and some be subdivided. It was suggested
it to be sold.

Page 316 - Petition of David Bledsoe, Lewis Gant and his wife
Mary, James M. Ledbetter and wife Betsey, Mathew Shearin,
Thomas Shearin, Andrew J. Shearin, John Wesley Shearin,
Hu L. W. Shearin, Newton C. Shearin, Edward Shearin and Willie
Francis Shearin, the last five being minors who partition by
their guardians Thomas Shearin and Sarah Shearin, filed in
Chancery Court in Shelbyville, complaining your petitioner
David Bledsoe, would state that he procured Thomas Shearin
to purchase in his life time for him a small tract of land,
being about 39 acres of James Pickle, for $100.00. Title of
land was in the name of Thomas Shearin, although David Bledsoe
paid most of the purchase money. The amount of the purchase
money yet due to Thomas Shearin's estate, he being dead, is
about $27.00. Thomas Shearin died before this arrangement
could be made (Thomas to pay and receive title) and the title
to said land descended to his children. Land sold to Franklin
Capley.

Page 317 - John P. Dromgoole & others]
                    vs   ] Bill of Complaint.
          C. & L. Schaffer   ]
The bill of complaint of John P. Dromgoole, E. D. Dromgoole,
and James Daniel, filed in Chancery Court at Shelbyville against
Charles Schaffer and J. L. Schaffer, residents of State of
Pennsylvania. John P. Dromgoole and E. D. Dromgoole and James
Daniel are citizens of State of Tennessee. That, Charles
Schaffer and John L. Schaffer are partners in trade under the
name, firm and style of C. & J. L. Schaffer, received a judgement against the orators, J. P. Dromgoole and E. D. Dromgoole
and James Daniel in Circuit Court of Bedford County on 27th
day of August 1851 for sum of $721.80, balance of debt and
further sum of $12.24 for cost of suit.

Page 321 - John M. Stokes   ]
              vs   ] A Bill, filed 15 Sept
         John F. W. Bowles & others]   1850
John M. Stokes recovered a judgement against John F. W. Bowles,
and William B. Cooper for $40.37½ plus $12.81¼ cost of suit.
No property of William B. Cooper to be found, except said
Cooper's estate, during the joint lives of himself and his
wife, in a small tract of land of 50 acres, being about a
ninth or tenth of said tract of land which was levied on for
said debt and cost of suit.
        John F. W. Bowles executed a Trust Deed to Edmond Cooper,
Esq., in which he conveyed one four horse wagon and one bay
horse, one sorrel horse, one sorrel mare and one black horse,
one bed and furniture and one bureau to secure certain debts
and liabilities, to wit, a debt to said Cooper of $25.00,
William B. Cooper and William Whitesell security.

Page 328 - Daniel McLaughlin & others]
              vs   ] Bill of Complaint.
         Jordan C. Holt, admr   ]
Daniel McLaughlin and wife Nancy A. citizens of Bedford County,
filed against Jordan C. Holt, also of Bedford County. Orators
stated that Jordan C. Holt was appointed admr of William Burgess, deceased, by court at the ___ Term 183_ and that the
William Burgess left six (6) distributees, Mary Jane Burgess,
Elizabeth E. Burgess, John Burgess, Richard Burgess, Joseph L.
Burgess and your oratrix Nancy A. McLaughlin formerly Nancy A.
Burgess, and that the estate of William Burgess at the time
of his death was worth two thousand dollars. Jordan C. Holt
was appointed guardian of said distributees of William Burgess
at May Term 1836, afterwards he received monies &c belonging
to them from their father's estate, sum of $267.16, amount
due them, after paying debts.
        Daniel McLaughlin and Nancy A. Burgess intermarried on
or about the 7th day of September 1848, and they had called
on said Holt at frequent times for a settlement and ask him
to turn their monies over to them, amount of $300.00 and that
he refused.
Answer of Jordan C. Holt: Jordan C. Holt stated in November
1834, he was appointed admr of William Burgess' estate. He
stated that William Burgess left seven heirs instead of six
named in the bill. He also stated that William Burgess,
deceased, left estate worth $2000.00. He also stated in May
Term 1836, he was appointed guardian of six children. Holt
said that Richard Burgess died several years ago, but since
he collected as guardian aforesaid the ourchase money of the
aforesaid tract of land.
        Respondant states about 4th September 1848, he paid Vilsey
(Wilsey?) Burgess for board and clothing said Mary A. some
14 years, a sum of $65.00.

Page 333 - James Mullins   ]
              vs   ] Inj. Bill, filed 10 Dec 1849.
         Godfrey M. Fogg,]
         Isaac B. Holt &]
         Hugh L. Davidson]
Orator James Mullins of Bedford County, states that Godfrey M.
Fogg of Davidson County, Tennessee, started injunction ___
Term 1849 against Absalom L. Landis, the tenant in possession
of a house and lot in the Town of Rowesville in Bedford County.
The lot belonging to James Mullins and said Landis a tenant.

Page 337 - David Elliott, a citizen of Jackson County Alabama, claims that sometime since a portion of the heirs and distri- butees of Joseph Elliott, filed in Chancery Court in Jackson County against your orator, David Elliott and Richard N. Elliott who were a portion also of the heirs and distibutees of Joseph Elliott, and against others, alleging among other things, that a negro man named Jeff and aged about 21 years, and a negro girl about 2 years of age and named Sophronia, belonging to the estate of Joseph Elliott. Said negroes and another who has since died were claimed by Richard N. Elliott, uder a deed from his father, the said Joseph Elliott, and the bill seeks to have said deed set aside and the negroes deliver- ed up as a part of the estate of Joseph Elliott.

David Elliott also stated that Richard N. Elliott departed this life sometime in the fall of 1852 in Bedford County, in- testate and that William Lowe of Bedford County was appointed admr by Bedford County Court and has obtained a decree to sell the negro slaves.David Elliott states that Richard N. Elliott left a wife surviving him and no children and that she has intermarried with William Lowe and has departed this life late- ly in Bedford County. William Lowe of Bedford County could not sell the slaves until case was settled in Jackson County, Alabama, as being a part of Joseph Elliott's estate. 17 August 1853.

Page 339 - Jonas Sykes   ]
              vs   ] Bill, filed 6 Feb 1851.
         Mahala H. Jones & others]
Jonas Sykes filed a Bill of Complaint against Mahala H. Jones, Ann E. Jones, James B. Jones, Jonas S. Jones, Robert A. Jones, Martha T. Jones, and Felix Turrentine, all of Bedford County.

Jonas Sykes stated that William B. Jones purchased on 1st day of December 1846, Lot No. 9, of school land, situated in Bedford County, Range 3, Section 6, 77 acres and 21 poles for $538.90. Sykes also stated that William B. Jones was in strait- ened circumstances, being poor and not able to meet payment, in order to help pay his debts, he sold to Felix Turrentine a portion of said lands, 20 acres for about $100.00, he then paid on his debt for two installments. Sykes stated that on the __ day of July 1848, William B. Jones died intestate and Jackson Nicholds, admr of his estate. William B. Jones was son in law of Jonas Sykes. William B. Jones left a widow, Mahala H. Jones and the following heirs and children, Ann E. Jones, James B. Jones, Jonas S. Jones, Robert A. Jones and Martha T. Jones, all of whom are minors and no guardian. Answer of Felix Turrentine. He admits that William B. Jones purchased the tract of school land.

Page 342 - William Little & others]
              vs   ] Filed 13 September 1850.
         John W. Maxwell & others]
Bill of Complaint of William Little, William Taylor and Robert Allison filed against John W. Maxwell, John D. Cooper and Christopher S. Dudley, all citizens of Bedford County. William Little states that "The General Assembly of the State of Tenn- essee, enacted during its Session of 1849-1850, a law by which the Common School System of Bedford County was intended to be made more uniform in its blessings and more practicable in its administration of the good of the people of the county than it had ever been before under the working for the system of "School Land", devised &c by the "wisdom of the State", assembled in the Legislature of 1839-1840, by the operation of the Act of 1849-1850, passed February 8, Chapter 198,

entitled "An Act to amend the laws in relation to Common Schools in Bedford County. It was intended to give force and effect to the School System by causing the two funds, provided for the education of the children, to pass through the same channel and be received, accounted for and expended by one and the same Commissioners, instead of being controlled by separate Commissioners, without co-operation, or arrageement between them".

William Little stated that the County Court of Bedford County at its July Term 1850, adopted the said system. The Sheriff of Bedford County was ordered to hold elections at different places in the several Townships and Fractional Townships in the county for the purpose of electing three Commissioners, who should manage and control the Common School System in their respective districts. The elections were to be held on the 27th day of July 1850 at the places designated by the County Court ...

Page 346 - John L. Cooper &   ]
           J. Culverhouse, Admrs]
           Exparte   ]
Your petitioners, John L. Cooper and Jeremiah Culverhouse would respectively represent that Moses Jones, late of Bedford County, departed this life some few months since having made and published his Last Will and Testament which was proven at the last Term of the County Court of said county, that the persons named as executors therein, renounced the execution thereof, at said court, that the court appointed your petitioners as admrs with the will annexed and gave bond &c. It is necessary to sell slaves belonging to the estate of Moses Jones and consultation of the widow, it is thought best for all to sell the slaves, Sam and Major, the latter of whom was hired out in the lifetime of the deceased until the 25th of December next.

Page 347 - Tempy Bledsoe]
              vs   ] Bill of Complaint.
           J. J. Russell &]
           Benjamin Delk]
Tempy Bledsoe a resident of Bedford County, that on 22nd day of September 1851, she bought of J. J. Russell, a tract of land lying and being in Bedford County and borders lands of Benjamin Delk, Andy Morrison, John Redd and Sarah King, about 60 acres. J. J. Russell has left the State of Tennessee, whereabouts is unknown.

Page 349 - Nancy A. Cobb   ]
              vs   ] Divorce, filed 18 August 1848.
           Charles Cobb &]
           John J. Shriver]
Nancy A. Daniels married in 1843 in Bedford County to Charles Cobb. Nancy said after a few years Charles Cobb became indifferent towards her, staying away from home and spending much of his time with women and houses of ill fame. In 1847, he left her with one Mary Smith, of bad character, moved to Coffee County, Tennessee. She said Charles Cobb had spent all her money and property left to her. Recently, er mother, Frances W. Daniel departed this life intestate and leaving her five negroes, Rochester, Henry, Ellen, Minerva and William, worth $2500.00 or #3000.00 and other property. She believes that her husband is trying to sell some. She requested a restraint by injunction. She asked for her marriage be dissolved. Sworn by Nancy A. Cobb on 18th August 1848.

Page 351 - W. W. Coldwell, Admr] To sell slave, filed 29 August
            Exparte Petition   ]   1849.
William W. Coldwell of Bedford COunty represents that James P.
Craig who was a citizen of Bedford County, departed this life
intestate on the __ day of ___ 184_, and at the Term of County
Court 184_, your petitioner was appointed admr of all singular
goods and chattels of said deceased's estate and gave bond.
Also, your petitioner has sold the perishable property and
that the estate is still in debt to about $350.00. $323.20
besides interests and cost is due and owing from said estate
to one Charles T. Philpot, for purchase money of a tract of
land which was ordered to be made at last court term. The
note of which was executed by Mary A. Craig, the widow of said
deceased and which is a debt of said estate.

Page 352 - Robert Matthews   ]
                vs   ] Bill of Complaint.
            Foster W. Dunaway]
Robert Matthews of Bedford County filed against Foster W. Dunaway of Mississippi and Williamson S. Haggard of Bedford County.
Robert Matthews stated that Foster W. Dunaway is justly indebted to him for about $91.00 for goods, wares, and merchandise,
purchased of him in the year 1850. Dunaway purchased sometime
in 1849, purchased a tract of land in the Village of Fairfield.
Money is still due on this land. Dunaway is a non-resident
of the State of Tennessee and has no personal property to which
debt could be paid.

Page 353 - Samuel Doak   ]
                vs   ] Bill, filed December 29, 1848.
            William Wilhoite]
Orator Samuel Doak states that on the 27th day of January 1847,
sold and deeded to John Wilhoite and William Wilhoite, both
of Bedford County, a tract of land, containing 230 acres lying
in Bedford COunty, on the waters of Flat Creek, bounded by
lands of Eve Burrow, the widow Reaves and others, being the
land on which Lewis Wilhoite then lived, 230 acres, which land
he purchased at a sale by Bedford COunty Sheriff on 4th Nov
1843, and a slae and transfer of said land to John Wilhoite,
they executed their notes under seal jointly to your orator
for $1221.60, dated 27th January 1847, payable 12 months after
date with interest.

Page 355 - Eakin & Co.]
                vs   ] Bill of Complaint, 18 August 1852.
            C. C. Carter]
Thomas Eakin, William s. Eakin, Adam G. Adams and William D.
McLanahan (McClanahan), partners, trading under the name of
Eakin & Co., filed against C. C. Carter of Bedford County.
Charles C. Carter was partner in trade with orators in the
Village of Rowesville, Bedford COunty. Part of the goods are
still at Rowesville in the Store House of C. C. Carter.

Page 357 - Marmaduke Williams]
                vs   ] Bill.
            Richard S. Williams]
Marmaduke Williams states that on the 7th October 1845, he
and Charles Lonis Williams became securities for Richard S.
Williams for payment of $350.00, on 1st February 1846, to one
John T. Brown. Suit issued to Sheriff of Tuscaloosa County,
Alabama where orator and Company Security resided 5 June 1847.
Total amount $382.01. (Williamson was son in law of Alexander
Greer and resides in Tuscaloosa, Alabama.

Richard S. Williamson had a son named Thomas G. Williamson.

Page 361 - Edde & Reeves   ]
                    vs   ] Orig. Bill.
          Benjamin & William Brown]
Orators Hiram Edde, Tarleotn J. Rives and _____ Rives, all
citizens of Bedford County states that sometime in early part
of 1841, he borrowed from Benjamin Brown $400.00, and gave
Brown a bond for payment thereof. He also gave security for
a negro boy named John. Negro boy is still with him.
     William Brown was a son of Benjamin Brown.
     December 25, 1842, at this time, Hiram Edde was engaged
in rebuilding the bridge at Shelbyville, wanted $100.00 to
help pay for bridge repair. Full amount $450.00 plus $35.00
for bridge.

Page 368 - James C. Word   ]
                    vs   ] Bill, filed 11 April 1850.
          David S. Evans & others]
James C. Word filed against James F. Cummings, David S. Evans
and Samuel Doak, all of Bedford County. James L. Armstrong
recovered a judgement on December Term 1849 for $875.50 plus
cost against James F. Cummings. Cummings has since resold
a negro to A. J. Greer. No money paid him for original debt.
Orator believes Cummings advanced portion of money paid by
Evans to A. J. Greer for purchase of the Tavern House and Lot
in Town of Shelbyville, known as "Shelbyville Inn" from Seborn
and Kenney.

Page 372 - Francis M. Harrison & others]
                    vs   ] Orig. Bill, filed
          Joseph Moreton, Jesse Brown]   8 December 1851.
          & others   ]
Francis M. Harrison, Mahala Jane Harrison, Joshua Harrison,
Malinda A. Harrison, William Harrison, Elijah P. Harrison,
Pollu Ann Harrison and Sarah Elizabeth Harrison, seven of the
last named are minors of Tyre Harrison and of Joseph R. Bledsoe,
Martha Jane Bledsoe, minors of John U. Bledsoe, all of Bedford
County, against Joseph Moreton(Morton) and wife Anna, Jesse
Brown and wife Patsey of Bedford County, Elijah Vickers and
wife Ibby of Lincoln County, Tennessee, Joseph Bartley and
wife Nancy of Missouri, John Patton and wife Sarah of Miss-
issippi, William Yates, Elizabeth Patton, and Samuel Balch
and wife Hannah of Mississippi, and Joseph Moreton and Jesse
Brown as executors of the Last Will and Testament of Joshua
Yates, deceased. Joshua Yates died in 1849, a citizen of Bed-
ford County, leaving a will, proven and recorded in October
Term 1849. He left eight children, to wit, Anna wife of Jos.
Morton, Patsey wife of Jesse Brown, Nancy wife of Joseph Bartley, Sarah wife of John Patton, Ibby wife of Elijah Vickers,
Hannah wife of Samuel Balch.
     William Yates and Elizabeth Yates, a feme sole.
     Rebecca wife of Tyre Harrison died before her father and
left, Francis M., Mahala Jane, Joshua, Malinda A., William,
Elijah P., Polly Ann and Sarah Elizabeth Harrison (heirs).
Malinda wife of John U. Bledsoe, died before her father and
left, Joshua and Martha Jane, only children.

Page 377 - George Davidson]
                    vs   ] Orig. Bill, filed Feb 8, 1847.
          Hiram Edde   ]
Orator George Davidson of Bedford County states that on 8 December 1842, William S. Jett sold to Hiram Edde, a tract of

land in Bedford County, about 200 acres, on which Hiram Edde
now resides and bounded by land formerly owned by Joshua Holt
and Kizer's land and land devised by Joshua Holt to his son
Hiram Holt.

Page 378 - A. Rice & Co.   ]
                vs   ] Filed 2 March 1846.
          Andrew & Isaac S. Davidson]
Albert G. and Orville Rice and John D. McFarland of Hawkins
County, Tennessee against Andrew and Isaac S. Davidson of Bedford County. At last August Term, they being partners in trade,
recovered a judgement against Andrew and R. M. Davidson for
$1524.44 and cost and interest. On 26 December 1843, conveyed
to his son Isaac S. Davidson for negroes, $4000.00 and also
on same day he conveyed to his son Isaac, the tract of land
upon which Andrew resided for $1600.00, that on the 20th Jan-
uary 1844, Andrew also conveyed to his son Isaac another tract
of land on 70 acres for $600.00.
Answer of Isaac S. Davidson: He admits he bought the negroes
and lands of Andrew Davidson, the deed to land was registered
much later because it had been mislaid or lost, but was found
later and registered. Andrew Davidson sold because of his
old age, upwards of 80 years, and very firm.

Page 383 - Benjamin Barnhill   ]
                vs   ] Filed 19 July 1852.
          Solomon Rheaves (Reaves)]
Benjamin Barnhill said that sometime in last winter, perhaps
in February, he made a trade with one Solomon Rheaves (Reaves)
of a stallion known as "The Black Legged Solomon Horse".

Page 388 - George Davidson   ] Attachment & Orig. Bill.
                vs   ] Filed 23 January 1855.
          M. L. Burrow & others]
George Davidson filed against Madison L. Burrow, Banks M. D.
Burrow, Doctor Alfred Burrow and Jordan C. Holt. Orator
George Davidson of Bedford County on 8th April 1852, he removed a judgement before William Galbreath, Esq., a J.P. against
Banks M. D. Burrow for $99.00 plus cost. Banks M. D. Burrow
had no property to be found.
     In 1833, Ephraim Burrow, father of Banks M. D. Burrow,
departed this life in Bedford County. His wil was proven and
admitted to record shortly. Ephraim Burrow bequeathed a number
of slaves to his widow Eve Burrow for life and at her death
to be sold and divided among his children. He had 16 slaves.
Eve Burrow having recently died, slaves were to be sold on
3 February next. He had a brother named Doctor Alfred Burrow
who lives in Alabama.

Page 393 - George Davidson]
                vs   ] Orig. Bill, filed 15 November 1850.
          John Tillman &]
          B. M. Tillman]
George Davidson filed against John Tillman and Barclay M.
Tillman. George Davidson of Bedford County, shows that on
27th September 1850, he and his sons John and William Davidson,
in their firm George Davidson & Sons, recovered before John W.
Hamlin, Esq., a J.P. of Bedford County, a judgement against
John Tillman of Bedford County and on same day he and William
B. M. Brame, in the name of Davidson & Brame, recovered a judge-
ment.
John Tillman's answer: He admits he executed a deed for 4 acres
19 November 1849, near Shelbyville, to his son Barclay M.

Tillman for $100.00. The true consideration was a negro man
Ambrose, which was given by Barclay M. Tillman, for land.
Barclay M. Tillman, a few months before that time, married
and was about settling in Shelbyville and wanted said land.
So the swap of negro Ambrose for said land. A deed was made.
In spring of 1846 and while Barclay M. was a minor, John Till-
man gave him negro Ambrose, then about 16 years of age, and
Barclay M. at the time said he had no use for said negro as
he was then boarding out from home and John Tillman kept
Ambrose in his possession for his son, paying $75.00 for 12
months hire.
Barclay M. Tillman's answer: Said John Tillman's answer is
true. Gift from father to son, one Ambrose.

Page 399 - James F. Cummings] Inj. & Att. Bill, filed
                vs   ]   3 February 1849.
            William Word   ]
Orator James F. Cummings of Bedford County said that in January
1847, he formed a mercantile partnership with William M. Word
in Town of Shelbyville, $2700.00, and Word at no time put money
or stock into business ($1300.00).

Page 403 - Samuel Doak   ]
                vs   ]Inj. Bill, 2 March 1850.
            James F. Cummings]
Samuel Doak of Bedford County filed against James F. Cummings
and Ed. J. Graham, states that on 2nd December 1848, Thomas
Lipscomb recovered a judgement against William M. Word for
$179.50 plus cost. Orator states that on 9 May 1849, Lipscomb
transferred the judgement to James F. Cummings of Bedford
County, at request of William M. Word, stating that Cummings
owed him that amount, etc. Word and Cummings had been partners
in business. Cummings moved to Mississippi.

Page 410 - C. P. Houston, Guardian. Filed 31 August 1853.
Elizabeth Houston and Caleb P. Houston of Bedford County, stated that on 28 day of March, last (1853) William Houston departed this life at his residence in Bedford County, having made
a non-cupative (verbal) will, which was later written and
proved. Widow Elizabeth and only child, William Houston, Jr.,
of very tender years. C. P. Houston, executor and guardian
of child. Estate worth $20,000.00. At death of William
Houston, he had no suitable dwelling house, having just a short
time prior to his death purchased land and planned to build,
only 2 log cabins.

Page 412 - John W. Walker and Edwards   ]
                vs   ]Jan 19, 1847.
            Caleb C. Cummings, James W. Foster,]
            James F. Cummings, John Cummings,]
            and William Word, Jr.   ]
John W. Walker and Joseph Edwards of Davidson County, Tennessee,
filed against Caleb C. Cummings, James W. Foster, John Cummings,
Jr., James F. Cummings and William Word, Jr., the former three
of Wilson County, Tennessee and the two later of Bedford County.
Walker and Edwards, partners, recovered a judgement on 28 September 1846 for $370.05 against C. C. Cummings, failed in busin-
ess in Lebanon in 1845, in Dry Good Business. C. C. Cummings
came to Bedford County in fall of 1845, Shelbyville, rented
a house and wanted to open a business with Foster (James W.).
Cummings retired from business and sold to William Word, Jr.

Page 426 - William B. Cooper & wife Sarah P.]
            and F. M. Miller & wife Amanda B.] Bill, filed
                vs   ] 14 August 1849.
            James Mullins & Claiborne Bowles]
All of Bedford County. William B. Cooper and wife Sarah P.
formerly Sarah P. Bowles and Francis M. Miller and wife Amanda
formerly Amanda B. Bowles, states that Joseph Palmer died many
years ago in Virginia, after making and publishing a Will and
Testment. Among other bequeaths, one was in which he loaned
his daughter Mary, certain negro slaves during her natural
life and at her death to belong to her children. The negroes
went into possession of Mary Bowles who was the wife of _____
Bowles. When they and their increase continued until Mary
Bowles departed this life intestate some two or three years
ago, ahen negroes became the property of the children of Mary
Bowles. Mary Bowles left as her children, Sarah P. and Amanda
B., J. F. Bowles, Claiborne Bowles, _____ Lee wife of James
Lee, and _____ Tolbert wife of T. Tolbert. Claiborne Bowles
was admr of estate of Mary Bowles. He hired out some of the
negroes for a number of years and failed to accounty with
Sarah P. or Amanda B. for their share of said hire. Orator
states on about 1st April or May 1849, the slaves disappeared
from Bedford County, where he knew not where, probably Alabama.
James Mullins on 31st day of May 1849 executed a new bill of
sale from Sarah P. and Amanda B. Mullins stated the slaves
to be found in Jackson County, Alabama.
Answer of Claiborne W. Bowles: Mary Bowles died in 1846.

Page 446 - John Shelby   ]
                vs   ]Orig. Bill, filed Nov 25, 1848.
            Hugh A. Hall &]
            Thomas Davidson]
John SHelby of Davidson County, Tennessee filed against Thomas
Davidson and Hugh A. Hall of Marshall County, Tennessee. John
Shelby said that during the year 1843, he placed under the
control of Hugh A. Hall, a number of Jacks and Jennets to be
carried or driven to North Carolina, to sell and benefit John
Shelby. When Hall returned to Tennessee, Hall refused to
Settle with John Shelby, the money. He found out that Hall
took in land lying in Bedford County, District No. 19, on
waters of Rock Creek, 841 acres, land granted to James Hurt
by State of Tennessee, Grant No. 3281 and the north east corner
of a tract of 640 acres entered in the name of William Martin,
and south west corner of another 640 acre tract in the name
of Jno. Baker on Rock Creek. Land borders land of Hart's claim
and Baker's line, Larue's line and Simmons line. Land conveyed
to Hugh A. Hall by James H. McGaughlin by deed. Hall's father
lived in North Carolina and wealthy.

Page 456 - Benjamin C. Ransom,appointed as Trustee of Rhoda
Wilson, is dead. Court appointed Jeptha Minter as Trustee.
August 25, 1846.

Page 456 - Petition of James M. Johnson.
James M. Johnson stated that Jordan C. Holt recovered a judgement against him at December 1842 Term for $84.34 and cost
and placed in hands of Benjamin Kimbro, Sheriff of Bedford
County. Johnson said he had proof of payment of debt.

Page 457 - William B. Norville   ]
                vs   ]Orig. Bill, Oct 27,
            James K. Norton & D. J. Norville]   1848.
William B. Norville of Bedford County said that on 23 October

1848, he recovered a judgement on James K. Norton for $173.43.
Orator said that Elizabeth Norville was indebted to Norton
for $169.00 and that she had departed this life some twelve
months ago, 1847, and David J. Norville was appointed admr
of her estate.

Page 459 - Petition of W. A. Young and others. Filed 28 February 1852. Petition of Claiborn McCuistion, William A. Young
and wife Susan Young, John McCuistion, Mary Jane Evans and
her husband A. J. Evans, Margaret E., William A., Ann Eliza,
Susan Victoria, John S. M., George W., Tennessee and Claiborn
Young. The said Mary Jane Evans and the last seven named,
being children of William A. and Susan Young and under age
of 21 years. Petition by their grandfather John McCuistion,
that on 23 day of October 1844, John McCuistion and William A.
Young, for love and affection to Susan Young who is daughter
of one and wife of other, conveyed a negro woman, Matilda aged
34 and her two children Narcissa and Lucinda, to said Claiborn
McCuistion in trust for use for Susan during her natural life
and at her death to be divided among children she may then
have. William A. Young purchased land in Giles County, Tennessee, 100 acres for $25.00 per acre, on waters of Richland
Creek adjoining Dolly Chapman and others.

Page 460 - John P. Steele   ]
                 vs   ]Orig. Bill, filed 17 Feb 1853.
         Catherine Summerhill]
         & Thomas Summerhill]
Orator John P. Steele of Bedford County stated that on the
12 November 1851, he sold 6 acres to A. H. Summerhill, near
Shelbyville, east of land on which R. N. Wallace lives in
General Robert Cannon's north boundary, east by Newman and
north by railroad. A. H. Summerhill purchased the land from
John P. Steele for $660.00 on January 28, 1852. Summerhill
departed this life intestate in City of Memphis on his way
to State of Arkansas, surviving him his widow Catherine Summerhill and child Thomas Summerhill, only heir and who is a minor
and has no regular guardian. No administrator was appointed,
as he may not have estate sufficient to appoint one.

Page 462 - Dent Lamar   ]
                 vs   ] Att. & Inj. Bill.
         Robert Harrison &]
         Jacob Harrison   ]
Dent Lamar of Autauga County, Alabama, against Robert Harrison
and Jacob Harrison both of Bedford County. Orator states that
he recovered a judgement December 1848 in the name of Nicholas
Langford who sues for the use of Dent Lamar against Jacob
Harrison. Robert Harrison sometime bought a large number of
negroes from one James Burton to whom he executed his note.
Registered in Register's Office, Shelbyville in book "MM",
page 238.

Page 464 - Thomas S. Word]
                 vs   ]Orig. Bill, filed May 2, 1848.
         John W. Dacus]
Thomas S. Word of Bedford County filed against John W. Dacus
of Tipton County, Tennessee. Orator said that on the 20th
day of September 1842, he purchased from John W. Dacus, a tract
of land in Civil District No. 23 in Bedford County. Dacus
lived in Bedford County at the time of sale of land and has
since moved to Tipton County where he resided when last heard
from. Orator tried to contact Dacus but failed. Said land

borders lands of Joseph Hasty, Sally Hix, Thomas S. Word, Jane
Hastings and William S. Jett. 2nd September 1842.

Page 446 - Joseph H. Sheppard]
           vs   ] O. Bill, filed 10 February 1851.
      Spencer Brown &]
      Epps Parker   ]
Joseph H. Sheppard of Davidson County, Tennessee filed against
Spencer Brown and Epps Parker of Bedford County. Epps Parker
on 8th February 1847 conveyed to Spencer Brown three negroes
for $1000.00.

Page 468 - John Williams, Sr.]
           vs   ]Att. Bill, filed 14 Oct 1851.
     R. J. Greer & others]
John Williams filed against Robert J. Greer, Benjamin F. Greer
and George W. Greer. John Williams said that two years ago
he loaned to Robert J. Greer who was a son in law of John
Williams, a negro girl slave for life, Creasy, to stay with
wife of R. J. Greer during her life. Sometime between 15th
June and 1st July last, orator's daughter, the wife of R. J.
Greer, departed this life and John Williams ordered the negro
girl returned, but R. J. Greer refused. Orator said that in
the night, R. J. Greer fled from the country, taking the said
negro girl who was worth $600.00. On 16th day of July, last,
R. J. Greer executed to his brothers Benjamin F. and George W.
Greer of Bedford County, a deed for a tract of land for
$4500.00.

Page 470 - Margaret C. Morrow et al]
           vs   ]Orig. Bill, Dec 18, 1845.
     Samuel Morrow et al   ]
George D. Stephenson and wife Mary, George Jakes and wife
Catherine, Sarah Parthenia Morrow and Margaret C. Morrow, filed
against William Gaston and wife Elizabeth, Harrison Gaston
and wife Nancy, John Sutton and wife Jane, and Samuel Morrow.
    Orators stated that James Morrow, late of Bedford County,
departed this life intestate in June 1839, leaving only children, Mary, Catherine, Sarah Parthena and Margaret C. and the
defts Elizabeth, Nancy, Jane and Samuel. James Morrow, at
the time of his death was owner of a tract of land on Scott's
Branch in Bedford County. Subsequently to the death of said
James Morrow his widow, Margaret Morrow might be endowed by
said property or land. Land bordered by lands of John Jakes.
    Recently the widow of James Morrow, departed this life.
Samuel Morrow has purchased the shares of three of his sisters,
in said dower land. Catherine Jakes and Sarah Parthena Morrow
are minors under the age of 21 years, and sues by their regular
guardian John Jakes and Margaret C. Morrow is also a minor
and sues by her regular guardian George S. Stephenson. Complts
and all of said defts except John Sutton and his wife Jane
resides in Bedford County and John Sutton and wife live in
Coffee County, Tennessee.

Page 472 - Andrew Venable & wife   ]
           vs   ]Att. & Inj. Bill,
     Henry Moore & Benjamin F. Greer] 7 June 1852.
Andrew Venable and wife Susan formerly Susan Moore, citizens
of Gibson County, Tennessee, filed against Henry Moore and
Benjamin F. Greer of Bedford County. Andrew Venable and wife
Susan said that in September 1848, Charles R. Moore, then a
citizen of Bedford County, died intestate, leaving your oratrix
Susan as his only heir, he leaving no children, he leaving

large amount of property. Susan stated as soon as the death
of Charles R. Moore, she started to procuring letters of admr
on his estate. Sometime in 18__, she intermarried with Andrew
Venable and in about two years removed from Bedford County
to Gibson County, Tennessee and taking along with her, certain
negro man named Jor, worth about $900.00 and who is now under
the control of Henry Moore, who resides in Bedford County,
negro Jor, ray away and was found at Henry Moore's. Benjamin
F. Greer was appointed adnr of Charles R. Moore, deceased.
Henry Moore is brother of Charles R. Moore, deceased, and lived
in same neighborhood.

Page 478 - Moses Reynolds, Exparte Petition, filed 25 Feb 1851.
Moses Reynolds a citizen of State of Arkansas, stated that
about year 1839, his grandmother, Jane Reynolds, departed this
life intestate in Bedford County and shortly after, Andrew
Reynolds was duly appointed admr on her estate and filed
against the heirs, admr charged to Alfred Campbell. Moses
Reynolds' father, Benjamin Reynolds, was made a party who was
represented as a child of Jane Reynolds and proceeded against
as a non-resident of the State. Benjamin Reynolds departed
this life many years ago before the death of Jane Reynolds,
his mother, having died in 1831. Moses Reynolds states that
he is the only child of Benjamin Reynolds, deceased, and as
such is a distributees of the said Jane Reynolds in the right
of his father Benjamin Reynolds, and should receive share of
estate.

Page 479 - Moses Reynolds]
               vs   ]A. Bill, filed 1st September 1851.
          John T. Neil]
Moses Reynolds, a citizen of Arkansas, says that about the
year 1839, his grandmother Jane Reynolds departed this life
intestate in Bedford County. She had a tract of land in Bedford County and shortly after her death, Andrew Reynolds and
other heirs filed to sell the lands against your petitioner's
father Benjamin Reynolds and others. Benjamin Reynolds a non-
resident. Benjamin Reynolds was a son of Jane Reynolds and
long before Jane Reynolds departed this life, Benjamin Reynolds
died, leaving a widow and your petitioner, only heir.

Page 482 - Graham, only heir]
               vs   ] Att. Bill, 7th September 1850.
          Albert G. Perkins &]
          Nicholas T. Perkins]
Richard A. Graham, Samuel L. Graham and Robert H. Bradley,
merchants and partners, residing in Franklin, Williamson County,
Tennessee, stated that Albert G. Perkins who now resides in
California is indebted to them for $462.28 plus interest, on
several notes. When note was executed, Albert G. Perkins was
in Haywood County, Tennessee and said that the deed was registered in Madison County, Tennessee, at same time the deed
was registered in Bedford County, under the control of Mrs.
Emily Perkins, wife of Albert G. Perkins.

Page 486 - James H. & N. Graham]
               vs   ] Att. & Inj. Bill, filed
          James F. Cummings &]   14 October 1850.
          D. S. Evans   ]
James N. and Nicholas Graham filed against James F. Cummings
and David S. Evans, all of Bedford County. James H. and Nicholas Graham stated that they recovered a judgement against
William B. Williams, Francis H. Ragsdale, George N. Arrington,

Charles Hickerson and James F. Cummings for $614.36 plus cost
and interest, on lot of land in Town of Manchester, Coffee
County, Tennessee, it being the lot formerly owned by John L.
Sloan and on which William B. Williams now lives. Also,
Cummings sold to David S. Evans and Archibald J. Greer the
one half of the Tavern House and fixtures in Shelbyville, and
known as the Shelbyville Inn.

Page 489 - John Pope   ]
                vs   ] Bill, filed 28 February 1852.
            Jane Pope & others]
John Pope of Rutherford County, Tennessee, filed against Jane
Pope, Mary Pope, Martha Pope, Ezzell Pope, Frances M. Pope,
Jackson S. Pope, Calloway Pope and John Pope, the last seven
are minors and have no regular guardian and all of Bedford
County. John Pope stated that John Gambell departed this life
in Rutherford County, Tennessee some years ago, he made a will.
He devised his daughter Jane Pope who was then wife of Hardy
Pope, certain part of estate to have and when she dies, it
is to go to her children and appointed John Hall as trustee.
Mrs. Jane Pope directed on 25th August, purchased of Spions
Ward for $900.00, two tracts of land in Bedford County in
District No. 10, about 120 acres. Jane and children now lives
on one of the said tracts and she desires the other, which
is distant from her, sold. Hardy Pope, husband of Jane Pope,
is now dead.

Page 495 - Doak & Reaves]
                vs   ] Orig. Bill, filed Feb 5, 1845.
            Edde & Dean]
Tarlton J. Rives filed against Hiram Edde and Thomas Dean,
all of Bedford County. Orators Doak & Rives states that he
obtained two judgements against Edde on 13th January, last,
each $116.50 plus cost. The return was by Eli Moss, a con-
stable of Bedford County. No property of deft to be found
to satisfy the same. Orator also states that Edde, sometime
in 1837, mortgaged a negro man named Dick and slave for life
to said Thomas Dean to secure the payment of the sum of
$425.00. The said negro man at the time was worth about
$700.00. The negro was placed in possession of Doak at time
of mortgage was executed and remained there ever since.
Answer of Thomas Dean: Dean denies any transactions with Edde.
He said Edde has been in embarrassed positions for the last
two or three years is true. Dean, also said he bought negro
man Dick, not mortgage. He said at the time Edde was about
to start to Texas, he wanted some money and sold negro slave,
Dick, to him for money. Edde owned other persons, also. Dick
was about 17 years old.

Page 492 - James M. Parks & wife]
                vs   ] Orig. Bill, filed
            James C. Russell &] January 23, 1849.
            wife & others   ]
James M. Parks and Cinna his wife filed against James C.
Russell and Martha E. his wife, and Robert B. and James K.
Looney. Orator and oratrix James M. Parks and wife Cinna Parks
of Jackson County, Alabama, stated that William Craig, the
grandfather of Cinna Parks, departed this life in Bedford
County in the year 1834, leaving a widow and ten children,
Nancy wife of Thomas Justice and mother of Cinna Parks, being
one of the heirs and a child of said deceased. William Craig
died, seized and possession of a tract of land in Bedford
County, 200 acres. Land bounded by land granted to John

Medearis, Solomon Durrett, McAdams' corner, Anderson's line,
and William Craig, containing 100 acres, 60 acres and 40 acres.
Orator and oratrix state that by a decree in June Term 1841,
the dower of Polly Craig widow of William Craig, deceased,
was allotted and set apart tract of land of 63 acres and 92
poles. They further state that the tract was never divided
between the children and heirs of William Craig, deceased.
They also stated that Nancy Justice formerly Nancy Craig,
mother of Cinna Parks, departed this life some eight or ten
years ago, about 1839, leaving Cinna, then a minor, her only
child and heir, never having parted with undivided interest
in the land. They also stated that after the death of Nancy
Justice, one William R. Looney, who is now dead, purchased
or pretended to buy from William H. Craig, the described tract,
with the exception of the interest of your oratrix also as
subject to the dower of said Polly Craig, and soon after his
said purchase, took possession of all of the tract except the
dower tract. They also state that Thomas Justice, father of
Cinna Parks and who was tenant by courtesy of her mother's
interest in tract of land, died some two or three years ago
(1846-1847), they also stated that the mother of Cinna died
seized and possessed of one tenth part of tract of land, which
descended to Cinna, as his only child and heir, she is to receive interest, rents &c.Since the death of Thomas Justice,
fahter of Cinna, also they stated that William R. Looney departed this life some eighteen months or two years ago (ca
1847) in Bedford County, leaving a widow Martha E. Looney,
who has since intermarried with one James K. Russell and two
children, Robert B. and James K. Looney, his only heirs and
both minors. They also stated that James C. Russell and
Martha E., his wife and Robert B. and James L. Looney of which
James C. Russell was guardian.

Page 502 - John W. Cobb, admr's   ]
              cum Testaments annexed]
              of James H. cobb   ]   Filed 26 February 1849.
              Exparte Petition to   ]
              sell slaves   ]
John W. Cobb of Bedford County states that James H. Cobb departed this life in Bedford County on the __ day of ___ after
making and publishing his Last Will and Testament, established
by Circuit Court. And that the petitioners was regularly
appointed the admr of Will and Testament. Will annexed.
Orator John W. Cobb examined the estate and states that there
is not enough estate to pay the debts, states that they should
sell one of the slaves. Negro man Edmund to be sold. James H.
Cobb died in 184_. He left a widow Sarah (Elkins) Cobb who
is to get all and when she dies to be divided amongst his
brothers and sisters. James H. Cobb owned twelve slaves.

Page 505 - Alexander S. Reeves   ]
              vs   ] Filed December 31, 1847.
         Joseph Thompson, admr of]
         T. J. Reeves, deceased   ]
Alexander S. Reeves filed against Joseph Thompson, admr of
estate of Tarlton J. Reaves. Orator Alexander S. Reeves of
Bedford County states that in 1845, he formed a partnership
in the purchase of bacon in Tennessee and reselling in Alabama,
with one Tarlton J. Reeves. They bought two wagon loads of
Tennessee 500 lbs, were to be paid 5½ cents per lb, which bacon
was placed in hands of Tarlton J. Reeves to sell at 12½ cents
per lb. Tarlton J. Reeves departed this life intestate during
the year, fall of 1846 and that Joseph Thompson was appointed

admr.

Page 508 - George N. Whitson]
                vs   ] Bill, filed August 31, 1849.
        Samuel L. Davidson]
Orator George N. Whitson of Marshall County, Tennessee stated
that on 20th May 1841, Samuel L. Davidson sold two tracts of
land situated in Texas, one known as Section No. 66 on Trinity
River of 640 acres and other 1740 acres to be divided into
two tracts in Section of 3 Forks of Trinity River. Whitson
paid at time of sale $1000.00. He claimed the land was worth
$1.00 per acre. Davidson would not give a good title to land.
Claims fraud.

Page 515 - Samuel L. Davidson]
               vs   ]Cross Bill, filed 11 Oct 1851.
        George N. Whitson]

Page 520 - Arthur Brooks & wife]
           and J. Nelson McAdams] Filed August 28, 1848.
           Exparte Petition   ]
Petition of Arthur Brooks and wife Alsey Sylvania Brooks, and
John Nelson McAdams, a minor who petitions by his guardian
James Wortham. They are the joint owners of Land Warrant
No. 13,835 for 160 acres, which was issued to Alsey Sylvania
as widow and heir at law and John Nelson McAdams as the only
child of Isaac D. McAdams, deceased, who was a Private in
Captain Edmund Frierson's Company, 1st Regiment of Tennessee
Volunteers by the Government of U. S. for his services in the
Mexican War. Arthur Brooks and wife wish to sell said land.

Page 521 - D. D. Hix, admr   ]
          Petition to sell Rail Road Stock]
D. D. Hix of Bedford County stated that William Heszlet departed this life intestate in Bedford County, ____, and he was
appointed admr of Haszlet's estate. Haszlett had $500.00 in
stock in Nashville-Chattanooga Rail Road Company.

Page 522 - John M. Keck   ] Filed 27 August 1852.
          Petition for sale of land]
John M. Keck, an infant of John Keck, owner in fee by Deed
of Gift from his grandfather John Keck, bearing date 11th January 1850, a tract of land, 49½ acres in District No. 25, on
the Barren Fork of Duck River.

Page 523 - James Mullins & William Young]Filed 30 August 1853.
          Petition to sell slave   ]
Mullins and Young stated that John Chandler departed this life
in Bedford County in 1852, after having made his Will and Testament, naming Mullins and Young as executors. Chandler gave
his whole estate to his wife for life or widowhood. They wish
to sell a slave man Jeff, age 35-40 years, and of bad and
vicious habits and cannot be controlled. Sarah Chandler and
John F. Chandler, Sarah Chandler, Newton Chandler, William
Chandler and Susan Chandler, all minors, and Louisa Chandler
who is wife of Joshua Holt.

Page 524 - Thomas J. Roane, Lydia Roane & others]
          Petition to divide land and slaves   ]
Lydia Roane, Thomas J. Roane, William H. Roane, Spencer Marshall Roane and James Henry Roane, the last two of whom are minors
and petition by their mother and guardian, all of Bedford
County, states that William Roane departed this life in the

year 1842 in Bedford County, having previously (and while
living in North Carolina) made his Last Will and Testament
which was proven and recorded in Bedford County. William Roane
died owner of two tracts of land in Bedford County. One tract
lying about three miles north east of Shelbyville and on the
waters of Hurricane Creek, adjoining the lands of the heirs
of Amos McAdams, deceased, Morgan Smith and others, and on
land which family now lives, being conveyed by John Davis to
William Roane. Registered in Bedford County, Book "66", pages
416, 417, and 418. Other tract lying on Turnpike Road leading
from Shelbyville to Murfreesboro and adjoining lands of Preston
Frazier, Joseph P. Miller and others, conveyed to William Roane
by Matthew Locke, dated 28 April 1832, for 344 acres. William
Roane died owning four slaves. Thomas J. and William H. Roane
are now over age of 21 years.

Page 526 - William R. Blakely &]
    Willis Burke, admrs]
      vs   ]Bill, filed 9 April 1851.
    William Blakely,]
    Nancy Adams & others]
William R. Blakely and Willis Burke of Texas states that
William Blakely, Sr., departed this life in Bedford County,
in year of ____, leaving as his children and distributees,
William Blakely and Nancy Adams of Arkansas, Frances Adcock
of Rutherford County, Tennessee, all are children of William
Blakely, Sr., and James Taylor of Wilson County, Tennessee,
who is also admr of William Taylor, deceased, who died since
the death of William Blakely, Sr., and who were the only distributees of Elizabeth Taylor, deceased, who was a child of
intestate Burrell P. Johnson and wife Elizabeth, Abner H.
Martin and wife Nancy and William R. Blakely (orator) and
Willis Burke's wife Lucinda, all of Rutherford County, Tennessee, except Lucinda and children of James H. Blakely, deceased, who was a son of William Blakely, Sr.
  Some thirty years since, there were three other grandchildren of William Blakely, Sr., to wit, Nancy, William and
Thomas Marshall, children of Polly Mitchell, deceased, who
was a child of William Blakely, Sr. The said children left
this country some thirty years since and removed with their
father to some north western state and have not been heard
of since by their relations. All children received their share,
except the children of Polly Mitchell, the whereabouts unknown.

Page 529 - William Brown and James G. Barksdale] 28 Aug 1852.
     Trustees &c, Petition to sell slaves]
William Brown and James G. Barksdale, trustees of Thomas and
Sarah Holland, filed that Thomas Holland on 22 January 1849
by deed, in consideration of his age and infirmities and love
and affection for his wife Sarah Holland, convey amongst other
property, a negro man Dick unto Nathan Ivy and William Galbreath as trustees.

Page 530 - William Kingre   ]
      vs   ]Orig. Bill, 17 August 1848.
    Winston Gill & others]
William Kingre stated that William Burgess, late of Bedford
County, departed this life, intestate, in 1835. At the time
of his death he was owner of a tract of land, 153 acres and
undivided variety of two other smaller tracts (one 67 acres
and other 32 acres), all in Bedford County. The homestead
on which William Burgess resided at the time of his death,
153 acres is near George Waite, McKissack and Bennett's land.

The thirty two acres, owned by William and Richard Burgess,
lying on headwaters of Sugar Creek in the Daily Hollow, borders
Andrew Evans. The 67 acre tract owned by William and Richard
Burgess, lying on Flat Creek about 1½ miles from Shelbyville,
borders John B. Cummings, Newton Cannon, Flat Creek, James
Younger and Grant of 1000 acres granted to Galbreath and
Chamberlain. William Burgess left as his only heir at law,
six children, to wit, Elizabeth Balch wife of William Balch,
Jane Rosier wife of Holiday Rosier, John Burgess, Nancy Burgess,
Joseph L. Burgess, and a son who died some years ago since
at age of 10-15 years. He also left a widow Wilsey Baker who
has intermarried with John Baker. These heirs of William
Burgess, in the year 1836, exhibited their petition to sell
the land of 67 acre tract. Sold by December 1836. William
Balch and wife in 1844, conveyed their interest in home tract
to Holiday Rosier.

Page 535 - John W. Gardner]
                    vs   ] Filed 15 October 1849.
             Jacob Harrison]
John W. Gardner of Bedford County stated that he owned a
sorrel stallion called "Boneparte" and states that Jacob Harrison, dated 21st March 1843, to purchase part of horse (kind
of a partnership). Harrison took said horse to Marshall County,
Alabama and did heavy business with not less that 100 acres.
Harrison did not pay Gardner his part of profits.

Page 541 - Pascal Brown & others]
             Bill for sale of land]
Orator Pascal Brown, Jesse W. Brown, Joel Whorley and Cynthia
his wife, Elizabeth Brown, Thomas Brown, John Brown (a minor,
who petitioned by his guardian Joseph Adams) and Robert A.
Brown also a minor (guardian Pascal Brown), all of Bedford
County. Daniel Brown, William Brown and Henry Brown all of
Alabama states that Jesse Brown departed this life in Bedford
County in 1843. He owned a tract of land in Bedford County
on Sugar Creek, a south branch of Duck River. Said land borders
lands of Greer, Johnson, Knight's lines. This tract being
the tract of land on which Jesse Brown resided at time of his
death. The widow, Elizabeth Brown is now dead (near Knight's
Campground).
Will of Jesse Brown is as follows:
Last Will and Testament of Jesse Brown. Made 13th day of November 1838. I, Jesse Brown, in a low state of health, but
sound in mind do make this my Last Will and Testament. I give
and bequeath to my beloved wife Elizabeth Brown my plantation,
whereon I now reside, also my household and kitchen furniture
and seven negroes, namely, Buck, Easter, Gust, George, Jane,
Louisa and Martha, also my wagon and horses and stock of
cattle and hogs, also my crop of corn, also my farming tools
of every kind. The above named property willed, is to be for
the use and benefit of my children that is living with me,
which my beloved wife is to have and to hold during her lifetime or widowhood. If my wife should marry, it is my desire
that my two youngest sons shall have my plantation between
them, namely, John P. Brown and Robert A. Brown, and the rest
of my property be equally divided among my ten children, namely,
Pascal Brown, Cynthia Whorley, Thomas Brown, Jesse Brown, Elizabeth Brown, Daniel Brown, William Brown, Henry Brown, including
my two youngest sons above named. But if my wife should not
marry, it is my desire for her to stay on my plantation and
remain in peacefully possession of all the property herein
willed during the time above named. After paying all my just

debts, at the death of my above named wife, that a fair division be made among my ten children, with the exception of my
plantation, that is to go to my two youngest sons as before
stated. This is my Last Will and Testament, revoking all other
wills. In witness hereof I have fixed my seal and subscribed
my name.
Test: William Carlisle   Signed: Jesse Brown (Seal)
NOTE: Not in Book, but additional information by Marsh):
Jesse Brown born about 1780 Virginia, died 1843 Bedford County,
buried in Word Cemetery. Wife Elizabeth Brown, born ____,
died 1849 and buried in Word Cemetery. Children:
1 - Pascal Brown born 1802 Virginia, died 1887 and buried in
    Pisgah Cemetery, Bedford County, wife Catharine born 1804,
    died ____.
2 - Cynthia Brown born 1805 Virginia, died 1852, married Joel
    Whorley born 1805 Virginia, died ____. Cynthia is buried
    in Sandifer Cemetery, Marshall County, Tennessee and Joel
    Whorley is buried in New Hope Cemetery, Marshall County,
    Tennessee.
3 - Jesse W. Brown born 1814 Virginia, married Martha ____,
    Jesse maybe buried in Brown Cemetery, Bedford County.
4 - Thomas Brown born about 1800 Virginia, married Mary ____,
    both buried in Dyer Cemetery, Bedford County. She has
    a marker, he does not.
5 - John F. Brown born 1828 Virginia, married Lucy A. E. ____,
    In 1850, they were in Liberty Valley, Marshall County,
    Tennessee.
6 - Robert A. Brown, born about 1830. 1853 near Shelbyville,
    Bedford County.
7 - Daniel Brown, to Alabama.
8 - William Brown, to Alabama.
9 - Henry Brown, to Alabama.
10 - Elizabeth Brown

Page 544 - John F. Brown]
                vs   ] Att. & Inj. Bill, 12 Jan 1853.
          Robert A. Brown]
John F. Brown of Marshall County, Tennessee, stated that Robert
A. Brown is indebted to him for $275.00 for various articles
furnished by the orator as well as board of himself and the
heirs and board of hands for the last two years, which debts
are due and unsettled. Orator stated that Robert A. Brown
has intended to dispose of his property and leave the country
and thereby defeat your orator. Robert A. Brown is said to
be the owner of a bay horse and also one acre of land, lying
and being in the vicinity of Town of Shelbyville and fronting
on the "Skull Camp Road", joining the lands of John Dalton
and others and which he bought from Robert Cannon.

Page 545 - Richard Bandy & others]
                vs   ] Orig. Bill, filed
          James H. Locke   ] 1st October 1849.
Orators, Richard Bandy, Enoch D. Rushing, George W. Bandy,
and William D. Hill, all of Bedford County, states that they
in order herein named endorsed for the accommodation of Washington F. Short, a Bill of Exchange for $4500.00, which was
subsequently endorsed by James H. Locke, also of Bedford
County, at the request of said Short. The bill was dated 13
April 1848 and due six months after date. It was protested
for non-acceptance and for non-payment.

Page 558 - James H. Locke   ]
                vs   ] Att. & Inj. Bill, filed
              Enoch D. Rushing,   ]   August 13, 1850.
              Richard Bandy & others]
James H. Locke filed against Richard Bandy, Enoch D. Rushing,
Wiley Perry, John M. Mayfield, William G. Height, Thomas B.
Jeffreys, Daniel G. Deason, R. W. Fain of Bedford County and
Adolphus L. Adams and Thomas C. H. Miller of Marshall County,
Tennessee, John Watkins and William Jackson of Rutherford
County, Tennessee, for $5128.67 plus cost of suit.

Page 568 - David S. Evans & others]
                vs   ] Orig. Bill, 1847.
              Swift & Barksdale   ]
Orators, David S. Evans, John C. Holt, William B. M. Brame,
Thomas C. Whiteside and David Ruth, states that they with one
James G. Barksdale and then Trustees of the "Baptist Church
of Shelbyville", and that as such, they took a deed for Lot
No. 3, in the plan of the Town of Shelbyville, in fee, from
one Alfred Balch. It was made in trust for the use of the
church, and lot and is now included in the church yard and
is necessary for the convenience of the church. The lot contains about one half acre. The lot was paid for by the voluntary contributions of the members of the church and persons
friendly to the church. Sum of $200.00 being $100.00 less
than said Balch would have sold said lot for, except for the
purpose to which it was to be applied. When the trade was
first made, it was agreed that James G. Barksdale and Jacob W.
Swift, should execute their joint notes for the same, due in
one and two years in two equal payments. Swift, who was a
member of the church and also a merchant or grocer, should
take the notes to Balch who lived in Nashville. Swift, however, in violations of the agreement and understanding, when
he carried the notes to Balch, took a deed for the same, in
fee, with general warranty to himself and James G. Barksdale.
Deed executed in October 1844 and registered in Bedford County
shortly thereafter. Swift never told any of the members of
the church of the fact that he had obtained the deed. He did
not even tell James G. Barksdale. Swift refused to make conveyance and your orators are therefore compelled to come into
this Court for to give title. The deed was executed in July,
last, and registered in October. The first deed nothing was
done. The second was executed by Balch after purchase money
was paid.
Answer of Jacob W. Swift:
He says that sometime in the year 1847, he was elected by the
members of the Baptist Church at Shelbyville of said church
but he has no knowledge of their taking a deed from Alfred
Balch for Lot No. 3 in town, in trust for the use of the church,
he believes they have procured such a deed as alleged in the
bill, but he cannot admit that they had any right to such a
deed or that it is of any validity. Swift says the lot is
including within the Church Yard, but the church is not erected
on said lot, and he cannot admit that it is necessary for the
convenience of the same. He said that he did not know the
said lot has been paid for by the voluntary contributions of
the members of said church and other persons. He said that
in the summer or fall of 1844, he made a contract with Alfred
Balch of Davidson County, Tennessee for the purchase of said
Lot No. 3, at the price of $200.00 to be paid. At the time
of the trade, the lot was intended for the use and benefit
of a Baptist Church, the building of which was then in contemp-
lation and to be erected on said lot. Deed 29th December 1844,

171

He stated that at the time the deed was made to him and Barksdale and from that time up until sometime in 1847, the complts were not elected Trustees of the Church, nor were there any other Trustees in existence to whom a deed could have been made or executed.

Page 574 - James Carter & wife & others]
               vs   ] Orig. Bill.
      Benjamin Cobb(Coble) & others]
Orators James Carter and Frances his wife, William C. Gordon and Sarah his wife, William Cobb (Coble) a lunatic files by guardian Absolom Arnold, Absolom Arnold and his wife Mary, all of Bedford County, Thomas Whiteside of Grainger County, Tennessee stated that on 20th December 1830, Jacob Cobb(Coble), deceased, late of Bedford County, purchased of Whiteside a tract of land in Bedford County on Duck River, being a part of a 5000 acre tract granted to John G. and Thomas Blount by Grant No. 235, bordered by Cobb's(Coble's) corner, road leading from Shelbyville to Rowesville, Cave Hollow, Duck River and containing about 83 acres. Jacob Cobb (Coble) departed this life intestate some 8 to 10 years after the purchase of said land, leaving your oratrixes Frances Carter, Sarah Gordon, Mary Arnold and your orator William Cobb(Coble), together with Benjamin, Samuel, Martha Ann, Catherine, Allen and Neely Cobb (Coble) and Eliza Wilhoite wife of William M. Wilhoite, his only children and heirs at law and leaving widow Mary Cobb (Coble) who has since married Richard J. Williams. Jacob Cobb (Coble) had not paid his part before his death. Benjamin Cobb (Coble), William M. Wilhoite and Eliza his wife, Samuel Cobb (Coble) a minor whose guardian is George Kimbro, Marhta Ann, Catherine and Allen Cobb (Coble) minors whose guardian is Leander Hickerson, and Neely Cobb (Coble) minor whose guardian is Richard J. Wilhoite and the said Richard and Mary his wife are all of Bedford County, defts in said bill.
Answer of Richard J. Williams and wife Mary and of Neely Cobb (Coble), a minor whose guardian is Richard J. Williams.
Widow Mary is entitled to one view to 1/11th if Gordon and wife comes in and 1/10 is he does not, and the other view to 1/3 during her natural life. The land only had 18 acres of timber on the widow's part of land.

Page 579 - Newton Shoftner &   ]
      George W. Buchanan, exrs &c]
             vs   ]Orig. Bill, filed
      Mary Evans & Ambrose Evans &] 16 August 1850.
      others   ]
$300.00 to Albert J. Shofner. Orators Newton Shoftner and George W. Buchanan, exrs of the Last Will and Testament of Frederick Shoftner, deceased, filed against Mary Evans formerly Mary widow of Frederick Shoftner who has since married with Ambrose (Abraham) Evans, Abram Evans, William M. Shofner, Martin M. Shofner, Albert J. Shofner, Lydia Shofner wife of Gabriel Shofner, Newton Shofner, Rowena Webster, Wilson Shofner, Jane Shofner, Mary Shofner, Sarah Shofner, Katherine Shofner, Caroline Shofner, the last six are infants under the age of 21 years, all of Bedford County. Frederick Shoftner departed this life on the __ day of ___ 1848, leaving his Last Will and Testament. He appointed your orators Newton Shoftner (who is also a legatee and devisee under will) together with George W. Buchanan, his executors. Will was proven at November Term 1848.

    Frederick Shoftner was twice married, by first marriage he had six children, to wit, your orator, Newton Shoftner,

172

William M., Martin N., Albert J., Lydia who married Gabriel
Shoftner and Rowena Webster formerly Rowena Shoftner. By his
last marriage he also had six children who are all under the
age of 21 years, to wit, Wilson, Jane, Mary, Sarah, Katherine
and Caroline Shoftner. Mary the widow has since married Abram
Evans.
      In will, Item, Since the death of testator, Mariah, a
slave has had a child. Item, in which Hale and Caroline are
willed to remain with widow until there is born enough children
from them to give to the last six youngest children (which
are by the last marriage), all equal to the ones to those gives
six older children.

Page 589 - William B. M. Brame & Sarah Brame] Orig Bill, filed
                    vs   ] February 1848.
            Washington B. Fonville & others]
William B. M. Brame and Sarah Brame of Bedford County filed
against Washington B. Fonville, Willis G. Reaves and wife
Virginia, Jefferson M. Stone and wife Ann O., and William B.
Fonville a minor by guardian Willis G. Reaves.Orator stated
that Melchesdic Brame departed this life intestate in the year
184_(1845), a citizen of Bedford County, leaving your oratrix
Sarah Brame as his widow, and your orator William B. M. Brame,
Washington B. Fonville, Willis G. Reaves and wife Virginia,
Jefferson M. Stone and wife Anna O., and William B. Fonville,
his only heirs at law. When Melchesdic Brame died, he had
large personal property and a tract of land, 310 acres, bounded
by William Collier, William B. M. Brame, Asa Fonville, John T.
Muse, Richard SIms and John Dongal. Melchesdic Brame advanced
in his lifetime to the mother of defts who was his daughter
and William B. M. Brame his only child. Widow Sarah Brame
stated that she was entitled to dower but had not received
or laid off to her.
Answer of Willis G. Reaves in his own right and his wife's
right, and as guardian of William B. Fonville. Willis G.
Reaves married Virginia Fonville, a granddaughter of said
Melchesdic Brame and that he is the guardian of William B.
Fonville and that his wife and ward as such grandson of Melchesdic Brame. Melchesdic Brame advanced in his life time
to their mother property amounting to $1600.00 to complt
William B. M. Brame about $600.00.

Page 592 - Martin Smith   ]
                    vs   ]Inj. Bill, 16 March 1843.
            Jeremiah Ellis]
Martin Smith of Bedford County filed against Jeremiah Ellis
of Davidson County, Tennessee. Orator said that on 27 July
1826, one Jeremiah Ellis obtained a judgement against him in
Davidson County, Tennessee for $138.75 and cost.

Page 597 - Joel Harrison   ]
                    vs   ] O. Bill.
            Robert L. Landers]
Joel Harrison said that on 27th February 1843, he executed
a Bill of Sale to Robert L. Landers for a negro man Tom at
$199.4½.

Page 602 - John Kirkman]
                    vs   ] Att. & Inj. Bill, filed 10 Feb 1849.
            A. H. White &]
            John L. Neil]
John Kirkman of Davidson County, Tennessee filed against
Augustus H. White of Rutherford County, Tennessee and John L.

Neil of Bedford County. John Kirkman said that on 5th August 1848, he recovered a judgement for about $143.60 and cost.

Page 608 - W. W. Coldwell]
            vs   ] O. Bill, filed 14 August 1852.
      Elijah Neely]
William W. Coldwell of Lawrence County, Tennessee, stated that sometime in March 1851, he transferred as indemnity to Elijah Neely of Bedford County, two negro slaves, Joshua and Mary Ann, he made note with Charles Williams security, for $1040.00. Your orator at the time of sale was a resident of Bedford County and lived near Neely. Neely is selling his land and about to move to Arkansas or Missouri and are taking negroes with him. He sold to J. J. Crunk and Matthew Cunningham a tract of land, which was mortgaged. Coldwell planned to go to Georgia to get money. The slaves came by Coldwell's wife and did not wish to part with them.

Page 620 - Daniel McLaughlin]
            vs   ]Orig. Bill, filed 21 August 1854.
      William Kingre]
Daniel McLaughlin stated that he made a "verbal contract" for a tract of land, with William Kingre some years ago. Land has about one acre in Bedford County, adjoining the road from Shelbyville to Fayetteville and on top of Elk Ridge in which your orator enacted improvements. Your orator is a poor man, his expenses of over one hundred dollars, two cabins built out of poplar timber and covered with boards nailed on and floored and hoped that William Kingre would deed said lot to your orator. Kingre helped your orator build the improvements. That his wagon hauled his timber himself for which your orator paid him. The acre is worth more now. Kingre refused to deed said lot over to your orator and has taken possession of it and boasted "Land improved for nothing".

Page 623 - B. G. White &c   ]
            vs   ]Att. & Inj. Bill, filed
      William Sharp & others] 3 April 1850.
Burrell G. White, A. H. White and Stokley White, partners under the name and style of B. G. White & Co., citizens of Bedford County filed against William Sharp, James Mullins and John T. Neil, all of Bedford County. Orators stated that William Sharp is indebted to them for about $180.00 due 31 December 1846.

Page 626 - George W. Fogleman   ]
            vs   ]O. Bill, filed
    William Sharp, Martin Hancock]13 August 1846.
    and Samuel Hancock   ]
George W. Fogleman a citizen of Bedford County stated that on 10 December 1845, he recovered a judgement against William Sharp, also of Bedford County, for $810.37 and cost. They could find no property of William Sharp. Orator also stated that William Sharp conveyed by deed on 16 August 1842, 317 acres of land for $5400.00 to Martin and Samuel Hancock and that on the same or next day he conveyed to Samuel Hancock another tract of land for $600.00, about 62 acres. He also about the same time conveyed all his slaves either to said Hancock or to one _____ Hancock. Martin and Samuel Hancock, being brothers in law of said Sharp and _____ Hancock, being his sister in law. The land mentioned is in Bedford County, in Civil District No. 1 and on which said Sharp then and still lives. Martin Hancock of Bedford County and Samuel Hancock of Coffee County, Tennessee.

Page 630 - James Burrow   ]
              vs   ]Inj. Bill, filed 24 October 1853.
         James A. Gaunt &]
         John H. Gambrell]
Orator stated that sometime in January 1853, James A. Gaunt
recovered a judgement against him for about $210.00 and cost.
Madison Burrow security.

Page 632 - William P. Campbell, admr &c]
              vs   ]Att. & Inj. Bill,
         George J. Black & wife Frances] 13 April 1847.
William Campbell, admr of Andrew J. Eaton, deceased, filed
against George J. Black and wife Frances, all of Bedford
County. Andrew J. Eaton departed this life intestate on 22
or 23 day of October 1846, being at the time of his death a
citizen of Lincoln County, Tennessee and your orator was
appointed admr of his estate. Frances Black, the mother of
your orator's intestate, was the guardian of said intestate.
George J. Black has married the said Frances since her appointment as guardian. Frances is entitled to a remainder in trust
in the estate of one Ephraim Burrow. Ephraim Burrow was the
father of Frances, by his Last Will and Testament duly proven
and recorded in Bedford County devised to his wife Eve Burrow,
seven slaves. Ephraim and Eve Burrow had eleven children.

Page 635 - A. A. Robinson & others]Filed 25 February 1851.
              Petition to sell land &c.]
Petition of John S. Wilhite and Jacob Wilhite, minors, who
petition by their guardian and mother Adeline A. Robinson and
Adeline A. Robinson in her own right, all of Marshall County,
Tennessee. They state that William Wilhite departed this life
many years ago, being at the time of his death a citizen of
Bedford County and leaving your petitioner Adeline A., his
widow, and your other petitioners his only heirs at law, and
dying possessed of a tract of land lying and being in District
No. 21 and District No. 7 in Bedford County and on both sides
of Duck River. Land bounded by Alexander Sanders, Jacob Wilhite's heirs, John Wilhite's heirs, Tillman, Sims and about
219 acres. It being the place whereon William Wilhite resided
at time of his death. After his death, his widow Adeline A.
received as dower, 73 acres including the mansion and improvements. The remainder 146 acres to other petitioners as heirs
of William Wilhite, deceased. Your petitioners state that
they are all residing in Marshall County, Tennessee, some distance from the tract of land. Adeline A., a petitioner, who
is the mother of your petitioners, and who has no other children has contracted for the purchase in Marshall County of about
800 acres of land where she now lives and which she cultivates.
The mansion house has gone to ruin by it being rented, more
and more each year, they wish to sell the land in Bedford
County and buy near where they reside now. (Land is located
at Fishing Ford at Henry Horton Park)

Page 1 -   James Blackwell]
                    vs   ] Orig. Bill, filed 27 Sept 1851
            G. W. Cunningham]
James Blackwell of Marshall County, Tennessee states that John
Blackwell, Sr., late of Marshall County, departed this life
in Marshall County sometime in the spring of 1849, having previously, to wit, on the 5th day of January 1849, made and published his Last Will and Testament. He appointed Shadrick
Mustein and William Carlisle and proved in Marshall County
at May Term 1849. Mustein alone qualified. Carlisle renounc-
ing. Your orator states that the said Mustein being desirous
of leaving this State and moving to Missouri and the Marshall
County Court appointed George W. Cunningham as admr of John
Blackwell's estate and he gave bond and qualified. There was
found in the hands of Mustein after allowing him his vouches
for payment and cost, the sum of $3624.16+, which settlement
was made on 10th April 1850 and the sum came to hands of George
W. Cunningham. In the will of John Blackwell, executed a Deed
of Gift to five of his children, several negroes. Said George
W. Cunningham in right of his wife Sarah, who was a daughter
of said John Blackwell and also a devisee and legatee under
said will, but was not included in the Deed of Gift. Some
short time after the death of John Blackwell, Sr., the said
George W. Cunningham and wife and John Blackwell, Jr., who
were dissatisfied and wanted the deed set aside. Your orator
wished that all negroes would be divided equally among the
five children. Mary Cunningham executed her notes for about
$195.00. On __ day of September 1849, your orator sold all
his interest in the estate of John Blackwell, Sr., under
Cunningham, except the land and negroes, and received $195.00
for his part of the estate. The amount of value of estate
was $3624.16+. There were no debts owning by the testator.
The devises under said will are: Gabriel Blackwell, Shrewsbury
Blackwell, Jonah Blackwell, John Blackwell, Jr., G. W. Cunningham and wife Sarah, G. M. Cunningham and wife Mary and your
orator James Blackwell. George W. Cunningham resides in Bedford County.

Page 10 - Pleasant H. Reaves]
                    vs   ] Inj. Bill, 27th March 1849.
            Joseph Thompson   ]
Pleasant H. Reaves of Bedford County states that Tarlton J.
Reaves was his guardian and that he has departed this life
two years or more since and the guardian has $550.00 and your
orator came of age and brought suit against Joseph Thompson
who is his admr and said Reaves security in his guardian bond,
which case is returnable to the April Term 1849 of Circuit
Court of Bedford County. Your orator states that at the last
Term of Chancery Court, he recovered a decree against the admr
de bonis non with the will annexed of Archibald Reaves, dec'd,
for distribution of said estate for upwards of $200.00 and
said admr recovered some $200.00 or upwards against Joseph
Thompson as admr of Tarlton J. Reaves for over payments and
interest on certain payment. Tarleton J. Reaves died in
September 1846.

Page 15 - Elizabeth Moss]
                    vs   ]Bill, filed 28 July 1852.
            Newton F. Neal]
Elizabeth Moss of Bedford County filed against Newton F. Neal

of Bedford County. Elizabeth Moss states that she is now and
has been for some years the owner of named slaves, Leana,
Martha, Philip, Alfred, Henderson, Hartwell, Grandison, Jim,
Winney, Betsey, Franklin, Polly, Ellen, Alfred, Paramelia,
Lucinda, and a child of martha's, name not now recollected,
that she is quite old and infirm and owing to her bodily infirmities, she has been unable to attend to the hiring out
and collecting the hire of said slaves, she appointed her son
Newton F. Neal as her agent. Elizabeth Moss states that Newton
F. Neal has failed to account with her, and has paid very
little of the hire.

Page 17 - Mary Jane Hopkins] August 1850.
           Widow et als   ]
The petition of Mary Jane Hopkins, widow of Eli H. Hopkins,
of William W. Hopkins as admr of Eli H. Hopkins, deceased,
and of William H., Margaret J., Alexander D., Mary W., Martha
V., and Eli J. Hopkins, minors and heirs of Eli H. Hopkins,
deceased. Their guardian was Allen Morris. Mary Jane Hopkins
stated that her husband Eli H. Hopkins departed this life intestate in Bedford County on the __ day of ___ 184_, seized
and possessed of the one half of a tract of land, willed to
him by Hugh Woods, deceased and bounded by Duck River on the
south, on west by R. Warner and containing 136 acres and entitled in remainder to the other half thereof, upon the termination of a life estate vested by the will of Hugh Woods in
his wife Minna Woods, who is yet living.

Page 19 - Nathan Ivy   ]
              vs   ]Inj. & Att. Bill, filed
          Giles P. Burdett]   31st December 1849.
Nathan Ivy states that Giles P. Burdett, late of Bedford
County and now of the State of Texas, is indebted to him. Many
years ago, William Burdett departed this life, having first
made his will in which he devised to Sarah Burdett (mother
of Giles P.) during life, and after her death to her children,
a tract of land in Bedford County on the waters of Noahs Fork
of Duck River, adjoining lands of Matt Finch, James Singleton,
Thomas B. Moseley and John Davis, about 136 acres. Sarah
Burdett is still living and has eleven children. Giles P.
Burdett is entitled to the one eleventh part of said land under
the will. Giles P. Burdett bought two of the other share by
deed, to wit, William Castell and wife Elizabeth G. formerly
Elizabeth Burdett and your orator and his wife Mary Ann formerly Mary A. Burdett.

Page 21 - Jack, by next friend,   ]
           John Dwyer   ] Inj. Bill, filed
              vs   ] 13 January 1844.
        Henry Blagg & Samuel Doak]
Jack, a slave, by John Dwyer filed against Henry Blagg and
Samuel Doak. Your orator John Dwyer for Jack said that sometime in the month of May 1841, James McCarver departed this
life in Bedford County, having made and published his Last
Will and Testament, which Henry Blagg was named executor.
James N. McCarner, a minor, is the only child and heir at law
of James McCarver and that Samuel Doak was appointed guardian.
Jack, the slave, was sold to Raleigh Morgan, but had paid
$500.00 at $100.00 annually and had his receipts of his paid
freedom.

Page 24 -   Hugh P. Mooney,   ]
            James B. Maloney & wife Eleanor C]
                 vs   ] Orig. Bill,
            Henry Blagg, Samuel Doak &   ] 4 August 1855.
          . John P. Steele   ]
Orators Hugh P. Mooney and James B. Moseley and your oratrix
Eleanor C. Maloney, states that James McCarver departed this
life sometime in May 1841, his Will and Testament was proven
in June Term 1841 in Bedford County. Blagg appointed executor.
James McCarver at the time of his death had a large personal
and real estate, consisting of slaves, stock, monies, bonds
and lands. Blagg sold said property. McCarver's only son
was to receive all his property except two small legacies,
to James Newton McCarver. James McCarver, Sr. said if his
son James N. McCarver should not be raised, he wanted his portion of the estate to be divided among my step-children, except
one hundred dollars, $50.00 to American Bible Society and
$50.00 to the Foreign Missionary Society. Since the publicat-
ion of the will of James McCarver, James Newton McCarver has
departed this life, leaving no issue, and before he reached
the age of 21 years. Your oratrix Eleanor C. Maloney formerly
Eleanor C. Thompson, John S. Thompson and Henry C. Thompson
are the only step-children of the said James McCarver. James
B. Maloney is the husband of said Eleanor C., your orators
Hugh P. Mooney is the owner of the interest of John S. Thompson
and Henry C. Thompson in said estate, having purchased their
entire interest of them. Orators states that Blagg had not
made any distribution of the effects of said estate. Henry
Blagg is a citizen now of Mississippi.

Page 28 - Will of James McCarver.
I, James McCarver of the State of Tennessee and County of Bedford, possessing presence of mind, do make and ordain this
my Last Will and Testament in manner and form, viz, I give
and bequeath unto my stepson Henry Thompson, the yellow filly
heretofore claimed by him. I give and bequeath unto my step-
daughter Eleanor Thompson, sixty dollars, or a beast worth
sixty dollars. To my only son James N. McCarver, I give the
rest of my estate after paying my just debts and funeral expenses, viz, my land and stock of all kinds, household and
kitchen furniture &c including my negro man Jack, who shall
be a slave for five years, or otherwise pay one hundred dollars
annually for five years, after which time and above specified
amount paid over to the estate, he shall be free according
to law. Furthermore, if my son, James Newton McCarver should
not be raised, I will that his portion of the estate be divided
amongst my stepchildren, excepting one hundred dollars, fifty
dollars to the American Bible Society and fifty dollars to
the Foreign Missionary Society to be used for benevolent purposes, such as Missionary and Bible Societies. I will that
my property be sold and the money when collected put to interest until my son comes of age. I will, nominate and appoint
Henry Blagg to be one of the administrators or executors of
this my Last Will and Testament. Hereby revoking and making
void all other and former wills by me at any time heretofore
made. In witness whereof I have hereunto set my hand and seal
the 22nd of May 1841.
                             Signed: James (X) McCarver.

Page 35 -   Petition of R. B. Davidson] Filed 1 April 1852.
            Guardian &c.   ]
Ro. B. Davidson, guardian of William, Albert, Robert, and John,
minor children of E. J. Frierson, deceased, also a sister of

the above, Mary A. Frierson. They have a joint estate of about
$7000.00, about $450.00 to each of them. E. J. Frierson had
been prior to his death for many years, a member of the Presby-
terian Church in Shelbyville. His children were all members
of said church. William 13, Albert 11, Robert 9, and John
4 years of age. The petitioner further states that the mother
of the children desires your petitioner to subscribe for the
three oldest of them $15.00 annually towards the support of
the Pastor of said church.

Page 36 - James Sloan]
                    vs   ] Att. Bill, filed June 8, 1849.
           Mary Worke]
James Sloan of Iredell County, North Carolina, stated that
at the February Term 1843, of the Court of Pleas and Quarter
Sessions for the County of Iredell, State of North Carolina,
he, as the admr of Alexander Worke, deceased, removed a judgement against John M--shat and Mary Work. Mary Work left Iredell County, North Carolina and came to Bedford County.

Page 39 - Daniel Dean   ]
                    vs   ]Bill, filed 3 January 1853.
           T. J. Cully & others]
Orator Daniel Dean recovered a judgement against Thomas J.
Cully before one Dudley P. S. House on the 3rd day of January
1853 for $178.86 plus cost. Land in District No. 25 of Bedford
County.

Page 41 - Edmund W. Tipton]
                    vs   ]Inj. Bill, 27 February 1849.
           Joseph A. &   ]
           William R. Reeves]
Edmund W. Tipton of Bedford County filed against Joseph A. &
William R. Reeves, both of Maury County, Tennessee. Orator
stated that in January 1845, he purchased from Joseph A. and
William R. Reeves of Maury County, a jack, named "Sam Houston"
for $400.00.

Page 46 - Robert B. & James K. Looney]
                    vs   ]
           James M. Russell & others]
Robert B. and James K. Looney, minors, under the age of 21
years, who sue by their guardian, Joseph J. Looney filed
against James C. Russell and wife Martha Russell and John
Blackwell, all of Bedford County. Orators states that their
father William R. Looney departed this life intestate a few
years ago in Bedford County, of which he was a citizen at the
time of his death. Newcom Thompson was his admr, after paying
off the debts, estate had left two negroes, Bob 15 or 16 years
and worth $600.00, and a negro woman Jinny aged about 45 or
50 years and worth $250.00, also large sum of money, all of
which was delivered to James C. Russell who had made a false
statement to County Court that he was guardian. Orators states
that they and their mother Martha wife of James C. Russell
are the only distributees of William R. Looney. They wanted
all properties sold and equally divided, three shares. Martha
was the widow of William R. Looney and remarried James C.
Russell.

Page 50 - G. W. Fogleman   ]
                    vs   ]O. Bill, 5th November 1849.
           Norville & Blakemore]
G. W. Fogleman states that Isaiah C. Brasfield in 1840 executed

a Trust Deed to Alexander S. Norville. Isaiah C. Brasfield
at this time, 1840, lived in Lincoln County, Tennessee. The
deed was registered in Lincoln County on 5 December 1840.
Shortly after it was registered, he moved to Bedford County.
Alexander S. Norville, 1840, lived in Bedford County. Brasfield is dead by 1849. He owed your orator and Dr. J. A.
Blakemore of Bedford County. Brasfield's widow lives, 1849.

Page 54 - Thomas Eakin & others]
                    vs   ]Orig. Bill, 10 August 1850.
            John M. Bass & others]
Thomas Eakin, William S. Eakin, John R. Eakin and Argyle P.
Eakin of Davidson County, Tennessee. Alexander E. Eakin,
Thomas L. Eakin, Sarah J. Eakin and Julia A. Eakin and James H.
Eakin, the five last being minors filed by their guardian
William S. Eakin and your orators George N. Eakin, Albert Eakin
and Charles Eakin who filed by their guardian Lucretia Eakin
and your oratrix Lucretia Eakin, all of Bedford County stated
that John Eakin, late of Bedford County, departed this life
on the 19th day of September 1849 in Bedford County, having
previously made his Last Will and Testament, proven November
Term 1849 in Bedford County Court. Also, that William Eakin,
late of Davidson County, Tennessee, departed this life in the
month of August 1849, having also made and published his Last
Will and Testament, proven in ___ Term 1849 in Davidson County,
Tennessee. Also, Thomas Eakin together with John and William
Eakin, deceased, had for a number of years, previous to their
deaths, been partners in business in city of Nashville and
in Shelbyville, Bedford County. John and William owned Town
Lots in Shelbyville, Lot # 37, on which a three story brick
store house and frame buildings and five brick offices, which
was conveyed to John and Spencer Eakin by James L. Armstrong,
Minos Cannon and Joseph Wardlow. Also Lot # 37, northern part,
which was bought by John Eakin & Co. and William G. Gowan(Cowan)
in ___ 1846 when sold at the instance of the heirs of Thomas
Newsom, deceased, also, ___ feet fronting on the Public Square
and running back ___ feet, bounded on north by Lot # 38 on
which his stor house, now occupied by T. M. Coldwell & Co.
as part of Lot # 38, another lot, at corner of Old Bark House,
south with Martin Street, also another Lot # 129 and 5 acres
of land on west side of Shelbyville, bounded by lands of John
T. Neil, Robert Cannon, widow Morgan, 5 acres formerly owned
by Willis Reaves, also another tract of land in Civil District
No. 8, which was conveyed to Jesse P. Tucker, one of which
tracts, about 40 acres, conveyed to him by Elizabeth Greer.
Another 160 acres by Dudley S. Crutchfield, which both were
sold to John Eakin & Co. by Price C. Steele as trustee of said
Tucker by deed dated 4 August 1848, borders Epps Taylor. Also,
two tracts of land in Coffee County, Tennessee in Civil District
No. 6, about 900 acres, borders Joseph Reddins, William Cowan,
other tract about 700 acres borders John Johnson, Vance Davidson, John Bowdains, Hugh Davidson, William Cowan. Another
tract of land in Davidson County, Tennessee, in Nashville and
distinguished in the original place of Nashville by Lot # 23,
on Public Square, bordered Calvin & Gideon Morgan, River,
Thomas Crutcher, deceased. Also, one third interest of Lots
No. 98 & 105 in Shelbyville. Lucretia Eakin is widow of John
Eakin, deceased, and the children of Lucretia and John Eakin,
William S., John R., Julia A., Argyle P., and Sarah J., Alexander E., Thomas L., James H., George W., Albert and Charles
Eakin, only children. And that Felicia Eakin is the widow
of William Eakin, deceased, and Jane W. and Ann or Nannie Eakin
are his only children, both are minors and no guardian.

Executor John M. Bass of William Eakin and John Eakin's execut-
or Thomas Eakin. John Eakin's daughters, Julia A. and Sarah
J. Eakin.

Page 69 -   Thomas H. Coldwell]
                     vs   ] Att. & Inj. Bill, filed
             William Rainey &]   4 September 1849
             James E. Wray   ]
Thomas H. Coldwell stated that James E. Wray is indebted to
him for $250.00. Wray is at this time in jail at Nashville,
for high crime, term of 8 years. James E. Wray's father John
Wray, has lately departed this life intestate in August 1849,
at the time of death, possessed about $4000.00 of property
(personal). William Rainey of Bedford County was admr.

Page 72 -   Thomas H. Coldwell]
                     vs   ]Amended & Att. Bill, filed
             John M. Wray   ]   August 29, 1850.
Continued from previous bill. James E. Wray has a brother
John M. Wray.

Page 75 -   Thomas H. Coldwell]
                     vs   ] O. & Inj. Bill, filed
             John M. Wray &   ]   19 July 1850.
             James E. Wray et als]
(Which should have been recorded before the foregoing amended
bill). Bill against John M. Wray of Bedford County, William
Rainey as admr of estate of John Wray, deceased, who resided
in Williamson County, Tennessee, William McIntosh and James E.
Wray residing in Davidson County, Tennessee. John Wray died
in Bedford County in the month of August 1849. He had four
children.

Page 85 -   Mary Jane Stammers,]
             Exparte Petition to]
             sell slaves.   ]
Mary Jane Stammers, a minor, by her guardian and father, John
Stammers to sell negro slave to William Little for $1200.00.
William Little was a dealer of slaves.

Page 86 -   Dabney Ewell, exr.] Filed August 29, 1848.
             Petition to sell land]
Petitioners, Dabney Ewell of Coffee COunty, Tennessee, Nancy
Ewell of Bedford County, William P. Chamberlain and wife
Martha of Lincoln County, Tennessee, Asa M. Elkins and wife
Anna of Texas, S. W. Hall and wife Lucy, George W. Heard and
wife Catharine, John H. Scott and wife Virginia W., Alexander
Kimbro and wife Sarah, David R. Vance and wife Ann E., William
Ewell, Philip K. Ewell and Joseph Ewell of Bedford County and
John Ewell of Louisiana. John Ewell, late of Bedford County,
departed this life in the year 1826 or 1827, having made and
published his Last Will and Testament. Jonathan Webster named
executor and Dabney Ewell. Jonathan Webster has departed this
life several years since, leaving Dabney Ewell, sole surviving
executor. Mary Ewell is widow and relict of said John Ewell,
and your petitioners, Martha Chamberlain, Anna Elkins, Lucy
Hall, Catharine Heard, Virginia W. Scott, Sarah Kimbro, John
Ewell, Philip K. Ewell and Joseph Ewell are the children of
John and Mary and said Ann E. Vance and William Ewell, the
latter of whom is a minor and no guardian, who sues by David
R. Vance, as his next friend are the grandchildren of John
and Mary, being the offspring of one Leighton Ewell, a son
of John and Mary, who departed this life since the death of

John Ewell. John Ewell, deceased, was a large holder of both
real and personal estate in Bedford County, and at the majority
or marriage of his youngest child, he desires his land to be
sold and divided. Sarah Kimbro being the youngest and that
she has married Alexander Kimbro. Mary Ewell, widow, to get
estate for life, being advanced in years. She divided slaves
between her and her children and grandchildren. All land is
in Bedford County, District No. 25, 950 acres and 11 acres.
Land bounded by lands of Isaac Troxler, David Hickerson, Loder-
ick Holt and Jesse Holt, George Cortner, Blackman Koonce, Levi
Turner, Thomas Foster, David Weaver's old tract, James Gober
and John S. Hite. The 11 acres are bounded by Levi Turner
and John Landers.

Page 89 - Louise H. Arnold]
            Petition to have]
            Trustee appointed]
Louise H. Arnold, who sues by John B. Snelling, states that
sometime in 1840 or about, her grandfather Hugh Snelling departed this life intestate, leaving a large estate of slaves
and land. That her interest therein was settled upon her by
her husband before it was reduced to his possession and the
legal title vested in one Peter Lee of Bedford County, in which
the property was and in which she and her husband resided and
still live, that since that time Peter Lee has departed this
life and there is no person to manage her estate and take care
of it. Her husband's habit of intemperance is the whole purpose, although since Lee's death, he has managed said property
and managed as to squander its proceeds while she and her
children receive nothing. She desires a Trustee appointed
to protect her and her children.

Page 89 - Louise H. Arnold & others] Filed 16 March 1854.
            Petition to sell slaves.]
Louise H. Arnold stated that she had received slaves and other
property, descended to her by Hugh Snelling, deceased. She
desires a Trustee appointed also to sell some property to pay
debts. Louise H. Arnold has three children, Robert Arnold,
Haden Arnold and Lucy H. Arnold, all minors. She was the wife
of James H. Arnold.

Page 92 - Louisa H. Arnold]
                  vs   ]Bill for Divorce, 18 July 1854.
            James H. Arnold]
James H. Arnold and Louisa H. Arnold married on __ day of February 1832 in Bedford County. James H. Arnold now a resident
of the State of Mississippi. They lived together for some
four or five years, when he commenced habits of intemperance
and soon wasted all his property and at times used violence
by striking blows upon her person and also threatening her
life. At one time she found a bowie knife hidden under the
bed where they slept. About the last of July or first of August 1853, Arnold was guilty of adultery with one Mrs. _____
Markum, a woman of bad character, near and in sight of your
oratrix home. James H. Arnold, on 1st day of November last,
left for State of Mississippi. He left owing many debts.
Louisa H. Arnold's youngest daughter is about 11 years. She
wants complete control of her daughter.

Page 94 - Louisa H. Arnold   ]
            by her next friend   ]Orig. Bill, 28 March 1853.
                  vs   ]
            John A. Moore & others]

Louisa H. Arnold stated that she received property from her
grandfather Hugh Snelling of Bedford County, who departed this
life 1840 or 1841, that she in right of her mother, received
her part of estate by deed of 4th day of May 1841. She wanted
to pay her debts but not those made by James H. Arnold.

Page 96 -   Louisa H. Arnold   ]
            by her next friend]
            John B. Snelling   ]
                 vs   ]Inj. Bill, 28 March 1853.
            Mullins & Holt   ]
She was the child of her mother, who was a daughter of Hugh
Snelling, who was married to Peter Lee. James H. Arnold had
a brother Haden Arnold. In 1835, James H. Arnold and Louisa H.
Arnold were in Franklin (now Coffee) County, Tennessee, but
soon after moved to Bedford County. Jesse Jenkins departed
this life (Coffee County), Benjamin F. Jenkins was admr of
Jesse Jenkin's estate. This all happened after the death of
Hugh Snelling. Andrew E. Mullins and D. D. Holt are of Bedford
County.

Page 102 - Newcomb Thompson, 2nd]
                 vs   ] Filed 1 April 1852.
            John McPhail & others]
            The heirs at law of]
            John T. Muse, deceased]
Newcomb Thompson, 2nd, of Bedford County filed against Jordan
C. Holt, admr., Rachel Muse, widow, and James H. Muse and
Joseph C. Muse and wife Mary, Jacob C. Muse and Marilda Muse,
all reside in Bedford County, and William H. Muse and Isaac A.
Givens and wife Hepsey C. who reside in Mississippi and Samuel
Brame and wife Rachel Abigail who reside in Louisiana, seven
in number, are the only children and heirs at law of John T.
Muse, deceased, and John McPhail, Daniel McPhail and Daniel
McPhail, Jr. who all reside in Lincoln County, Tennessee.
John T. Muse purchased his land from Thomas Davis, who purchased of Simms Maddux, who purchased of John B. Pinson, who bought
of John Blackwell, now deceased, and he learned that John Blackwell purchased of Daniel McPhail the father of John McPhail
and Daniel McPhail, Jr. Angus, John A. and Daniel McPhail
answered bill against them. Angus McPhail intermarried Ann
Sharp, daughter of Antony (Anthony) Sharp, deceased, and they
had John A. and Daniel McPhail, are the only issue of said
marriage. Anthony Sharp of Williamson County, Tennessee. Ann
McPhail now deceased. Anthony Sharp had a 1000 acre tract,
granted by North Carolina, also to Thomas Dugan.

Page 108 - W. Wallace White & wife] Exparte, filed
            Panthea, et als   ] August Term 1849.
            Petition to sell land]
W. Wallace White and Panthea his wife formerly Panthea Boyd,
Cornelia Boyd and Charlotte S. Boyd who is a minor and petition
by her guardian and grandfather Richard Boyd. W. Wallace White
and wife Panthea, Cornelia A---- Boyd and Charlotte S. Boyd
all of Warren County, North Carolina, stated that their father
Simms Boyd departed this life intestate in Bedford County and
left your petitioners, his only heirs at law. Simms Boyd had
land on waters of Sugar Creek in Bedford County and bounded
by lands of Samuel Thompson, Newcomb Thompson, Jr., William
Hughes, Blount Green and John T. Muse, about 150 acres. Your
petitioners reside in North Carolina also state that they never
expect again to reside in Bedford County.

Page 110 - Richard C. Ogilvie]
               vs   ]O. Bill, filed Feb 2, 1852.
          George T. Landers]
          & Rowland Landers]
Richard C. Ogilvie of Bedford County filed against George T.
Landers of Izzard County, Arkansas and Rowland Landers of Bed-
ford County.

Page 113 - Joseph P. Thompson, admr]
               vs   ]O. Bill, 29 Jan 1852.
          Thomas C. Allison   ]
Joseph P. Thompson admr of estate of Elizabeth Allison, dec'd,
filed against Thomas C. Allison, all of Bedford County. Orator
stated that Elizabeth Allison departed this life on the 21st
day of June 1851, intestate, and that she had some personal
property. He also stated that Elizabeth Allison was an old
woman and that one of her children Thomas C. Allison has resided with her for a number of years. Elizabeth was the wife
of Robert Allison, deceased. Robert Allison left a will.
Thomas C. Allison was about 15 years of age when his father
Robert Allison died.

Page 120 - Fletcher Taylor & others]
               vs   ]O. Bill, 11 August 1851.
          William Allison & others]
Fletcher Taylor and his wife Sarah Ann of Rutherford County,
Tennessee, of Henry Arnold and his wife Elizabeth, of Mary H.
McGowan, Thomas M. McGowan, Martha J. McGowan and George W.
McGowan, all of Bedford County. George W. McGowan being a
minor and suing by his next friend Fletcher Taylor against
William Allison, John J. McGowan, William H. McGowan and
Peter E. McGowan, all of Bedford County. Orators stated that
William Holmes of Mecklenburg County, Virginia, by his Last
Will and Testament, proven and recorded in Virginia, made a
bequeath in the words and figures following, to wit, "I lend
unto my daughter Sarah Ann Holmes during her natural life,
two negroes." Sarah Ann Holmes intermarried with John McGowan
and had lawful issues, to wit, John James, William H., Peter E.
McGowan and complainants, Sarah Ann Taylor wife of your orator
Fletcher Taylor and Elizabeth who married with your orator,
Henry Arnold and Mary H., Thomas M., Martha J., Emily F.,
Isaac W. and George W. McGowan are issues of Sarah Ann Holmes.

Page 128 - Prior M. Jackson ¢ wife Martha E.]O. Bill, filed
               vs   ]29 October 1851.
          John V. Biddle & others   ]
Prior M. Jackson and wife Martha E. filed against John V.
Biddle, Mary Campbell and Lucy Campbell, minors who have their
guardian John Q. Davidson and B. J. and C. D. Ingram and Eliza
J. Howe, all of Bedford County. Your orator and wife reside
in Missouri states that Edmund Horde, the grandfather of your
oratrix Martha E. Jackson, departed this life many years ago
in Bedford County, having made and published his Last Will
and Testament which was proven and recorded in ___ Term 1838.
He devised to his daughter Permelia M. Campbell and at her
death to her children then living, who was the mother of
Martha E. Jackson, to get a certain tract of land in District
No. 2, sold land on 18 February 1845 to John V. Biddle. Permelia
M. Campbell departed this life on the __ day of ___ 18__, leaving daughters Martha E. and Lucy Campbell, her only children.
Benjamin J. Ingram and wife Cynthia B. Ingram.

Page 134 - George W. Buchanan]Att. & Inj. Bill, filed
              vs   ]   29 December 1851.
         Banks M. D. Burrow]
George W. Buchanan of Bedford County stated that William W.
Coldwell recovered a judgement against Banks M. D. Burrow of
Bedford County. Banks M. D. Burrow is the child of Ephraim
Burrow, deceased, who departed this life leaving a will.
Ephraim Burrow's wife was Eve Burrow. Ephraim Burrow departed
this life on the __ day of ___ 183_ and Eve Burrow departed
this life on the __ day of December 1851. Madison L. Burrow
was admr of Ephraim Burrow, deceased, and as admr of Eve Burrow
deceased.

Page 139 - William Elmore]
              vs   ]O. Bill, filed 17 February 1853.
         Drury Gault   ]
William Elmore filed against Drury Gault, Martha A, Gault and
J. C. Gault. William Elmore of Rutherford County, Tennessee,
states that about 16 day of September 1852, he sold a brown
horse for $100.00 to Drury Gault, still owes for same. Drury
Gault went to Alabama, Talladega, then to Montgomery, Alabama,
and had joined a circus company and gone to parts unknown.
Hugh M. Gault departed this life intestate sometime ago and
the Court of Bedford County at September Term 1852, appointed
his widow Martha A, Gault as admrix and J. C. Gault as admr
of estate. Martha A. Gault moved to Arkansas. Drury was a
son of Hugh M. Gault. Hugh M. Gault had eight children and
his widow to survive him.

Page 143 - George Usselton]
              vs   ]Bill for Divorce, 15 August 1853.
         Susan Usselton]
George Usselton filed against Susan Usselton of Bedford County.
That on 14th day of November 1852, he married Susan E. Anglin
in Bedford County. He stated she frequently treating your
orator and his family of young daughters with the greatest
indignities. She would leave home and stay away for a week
and finally on 28 June 1853, she left. She had been with other
men.

Page 144 - James Hastings]
              vs   ]Filed 13 September 1853.
         Josiah Hastings]
James Hastings of Bedford County filed against Josiah Hastings.
Orator stated that his father Robert Hastings departed this
life many years ago in Bedford County and Josiah Hastings who
is now a citizen of Arkansas was appointed admr of his estate
and settlement on estate in December 1836. Orator's mother
Jane Hastings, widow of Robert Hastings, deceased. Had land
on waters of Flat Creek bounded by M. Dunaway, Josiah Hastings,
Thomas Word and others, on which Jane Hastings still lives.
Josiah Hastings was entitled to one eighth part of remainder.
James Hastings arrived of age of 21 in 1847.

Page 147 - Thomas Eakin   ]
              vs   ]O. Bill, filed
         William Sharp &   ]5 February 1852.
         Martin & Samuel Hancock]
Thomas Eakin of Bedford County stated that on 1st day of April
1850, a certain tract of land was sold at public sale. Land
in District No. 1, adjoining lands of John Jakes, William
Stevens and others. The property sold was property of William
Sharp of Bedford County. Thomas Eakin only surviving partner

185

of the late firm of John Eakin & Co. William Sharp by deed
dated 15 August 1842, conveyed to his brother in laws Martin
and Samuel Hancock and his sister in law Hannah Hancock.
Martin Hancock and William Sharp of Bedford County and Samuel
Hancock of Coffee COunty, Tennessee. Land situated on waters
of Scott's Branch and borders Harrison Gaston, John Jakes,
William Stevens, George Stephenson and William Robinson.

Page 156 - G. W. Heard   ]Att. & Inj. Bill, filed
              vs   ] 9 September 1853.
         A. L. Landis & others]
George W. Heard of Bedford County stated that John Ewell, late
of Bedford County, departed this life in Bedford County, having
made a Will and Testament. Absalom L. Landis, admr of estate
of Leighton Ewell, a son of John, also Anna Elkins, daughter
of John Ewell, deceased, and wife of Asa M. Elkins. Anna
Elkins departed this life intestate, your orator was appointed
guardian of her minor children. Asa M. Elkins and Anna Elkins
left the following children, James K., Lucy E., Mary M.,
Martha M., Richard S., Susan C., Maacha A. and Philip Elkins,
the first two are of age and all reside in Texas.

Page 164 - McDowell & Russell]
              vs   ]O. Bill, 10 January 1852.
         Mullins & Young   ]
Daniel D. Russell and Samuel McDowell states that Samuel
McDowell purchased of John Chandler, late of Bedford County,
his lands and mills on Duck River, about 90 acres on 4 August
1851. John Chandler departed this life in Bedford County,
after having made his Last Will and Testament which he appointed James Mullins and William Young, both of Bedford County,
as executors. Will proven December Term 1852 in Bedford County.

Page 167 - Sarah Coble]
              vs   ]Inj. Bill, 15 May 1852.
         James Carter]
Sallie Coble filed against James Carter, Benjamin K. Coble
and Thomas C. Whiteside. Sarah Coble stated that in Autumn
of 1850, she appointed James Carter her agent, to sell negro.
James Carter left this State, Benjamin K. Coble, a brother
in law of Carter.

Page 177 - George W. Buchanan &] Petition, February Term 1849.
         Newton Shofner   ]
George W. Buchanan and Newton Shofner of Bedford County stated
that Frederick Shofner departed this life on the __ day of
September 1848, having made his Last Will and Testament and
proven. That your petitioners were appointed executors at
November Term 1848.

Page 178 - James M. Culverson]
              vs   ]Bill for Divorce, 20 Jan 1851.
         Rebecca J. Culverson]
James M. Culverson of Bedford County stated that on the 26th
day of August last (1850) he married Rebecca Jane Tucker. At
that time, he was duly 18 years of age. His wife was going
with other men. James M. Culverson stated he was an orphan,
poor and friendless. Rebecca Jane Culverson was at the time
of marriage only 16 years of age.

Page 181 - R. L. Landers & A. L. Landers] O. & Inj. Bill,
              vs   ] 6 May 1852.
         J. K. Ewell & R. P. Settliff]

186

Robert L. Landers and A. L. Landers of Bedford County filed
against Joseph K. Ewell and R. P. Settliff of Bedford County.
Orators states that they were merchants in Rowesville, on 22
March 1852, they sold the business to Joseph K. Ewell and
R. P. Settliff.

Page 186 - David Jayne & sons   ]
                    vs   ]Filed July 26, 1853.
          J. P. Drumgoole, Ruth,]
          Robinson & others   ]
David Jayne & Sons, Merchants & Traders of the City of Phila-
delphia, Pennsylvania filed against John P. Drumgoole, Charles
Robinson, Rufus Ruth and James Elliott all of Bedford County.

Page 189 - S. W. Dollar & D. W. Dollar   ]
          Exparte Petition for sale of land]
Petition of Susannah M. Dollar and Daniel W. Dollar, who are
minors, by next friend Thomas Holland, Senr. to sale land.
Thomas Holland was their grandfather. The land in District
No. 3. Bordered by Michael Holt, deceased, and John McGuire.

Page 191 - Thomas Lamb   ] Att. & Inj. Bill, filed
                   vs   ]   4 March 1852.
          David Wagster]
Thomas Lamb of Bedford County filed against David Wagster of
parts unknown. Thomas Lamb sold to David Wagster on 5 September 1851, a tract of land in District No. 10 of Bedford County,
bounded by lands of Word & Simms, Arnold & Black, heirs of
Jacob Morton, deceased, about 68 acres. Never paid for land.

Page 193 - Jane C. Adams by her next friend]Inj Bill, filed
                   vs   ]28 August 1851.
          William H. Adams & others   ]
Jane C. Adams by her next friend Addison Adams states that
she is the daughter of James Bigger, late of Bedford County
who departed this life in April last, intestate, leaving a
tract of land about 396 acres and about 18 slaves and that
James R. Bigger and his wife Mariah Bigger, his widow, administered on his estate. Orator stated that she married William
H. Adams eight years ago (1843) in January last. She also
states that William H. is in habits of intoxication and perhaps
considered a drunkard. She had asked the Court to not let
William H. Adams get his hands on any more of her property.
He had already squandered some of her property. She and her
children reside in Perry County, Tennessee.

Page 195 - Widow & Heirs of   ]
          Travis C. Nash   ]Petition for dower,
                   vs   ]August 22, 1844.
          G. W. Nash & others]
Joanna Nash, widow and relict of Travis C. Nash, late of Bed-
ford County, Levi C. Johnson and wife Elizabeth formerly
Elizabeth Nash, Benjamin Garrett and wife Emily formerly Emily
Nash, William N. Harwell and wife Louisa formerly Louisa Nash,
James C. Nash and Travis C. Nash, all of Bedford County.
William N. Harwell and wife Louisa reside in Giles County,
Tennessee stated that her father Travis C. Nash departed this
life in Bedford County on April 7, 1844, intestate, leaving,
Francis M., Granderson, Abner, Lafayette, William, Thomas,
Augustus, and infants, George W. and John R. Nash and Mary
McGimpsy wife of John W. McGimpsy formerly Mary Nash. John R.
Nash has since departed this life intestate, leaving one son
and heir at law, James R. Nash. Travis C. Nash owned lands

in Bedford County and one tract in Lincoln County, Tennessee
of about 70 acres deeded to Thomas L. D. Parks and dated 3
December 1840. James R. Nash son of John Nash, deceased, who
is a resident of Rutherford County, Tennessee, are infants
and no regular guardian, and all of Bedford County, except
George W. Nash, John W. McGimpsey and wife Mary formerly Mary
Nash, who are non-residents of Tennessee.

Page 198 - William Wood & Matt Martin]
                    vs   ]Filed 19 August 1850.
          Nashville, Chattanooga Rail]
          Road Co. & John Scott   ]
Orators states that on the __ day of ___ 184_, they entered
into a contract with N. C. & R. R. Company to grade Section
57 of said railroad, of which is in Bedford County and was
to be completed in 1849. Debt due on extra materials.

Page 210 - Lewis Newsom   ]
                    vs   ]O. Bill, filed July 29, 1851.
          Letitia Cannon &]
          William Drummond]
Lewis Newsom of Lincoln County, Tennessee files against Letitia
Cannon and William Drummond of Bedford County. Lewis Newsom
states that he recovered a judgement of $179.36 on 11 day of
June 1851 against William Drummond. Orator states that
William Drummond conveyed by Deed of Trust to Letitia Cannon,
dated 1 February 1842, all rights &c on 98 acres of land in
Bedford County, on south side of Duck River and borders Isham
Reaves, Duck River, Thomas C. Ryals and John Dunnaway. She
also bought personal property.

Page 219 - Leonard Marbury   ]Inj Bill, filed
                    vs   ]26 January 1846.
          Jeremiah Claunch & others]
Leonard W. Marbury of Coffee County, Tennessee filed against
Jeremiah Claunch, James H. Claunch and William H. Wisener,
all of Bedford County and Frederick N. Ross of Hawkins County,
Tennessee. Orator states that he recovered a judgement against
Jeremiah Claunch and James H. Claunch in August 1842 for $91.34.
Claunch was owner of land in Bedford County in District No.
23, on which he now resides.

Page 224 - Rebecca C. Townsend]
                    vs   ]O. Bill, filed 14 October 1853.
          J. M. Townsend &   ]
          J. C. Word   ]
Rebecca C. Townsend states that she married John M. Townsend
some weeks ago in Bedford County and resided for some weeks
peacefully until the last Sunday 9th day of October 1853, when
he carried her to the house of her father and since that time
has refused to live with her. He, on 10th day of this month
(October) wrote to her that he did not intend to live with
her any longer and to consider herself any longer his wife,
or his house her home. She desires a divorce and support.
John M. Townsend owns land, bordering Mrs. Lee, James H. Arnold
and wife, Mrs. Smith and Kinchen Stokes in District No. 3 of
Bedford County.

Page 231 - Lucretia Eakin & others]Filed 25 August 1851.
          Petition   ]
Lucretia Eakin, George N., Albert and Charles Eakin, the three
last being minors of Bedford County by their guardian Lucretia
Eakin, that John Eakin departed this life in Bedford County

on 19th day of September 1849 having made and published his
Last Will and Testament and proven October 1849, that he devised to his wife Lucretia "The Plantation on which she resided
and his negroes during her life time, at her death said plantation and negroes thereon to his three youngest children,
George Newton, Albert and Charles", who are other petitioners.
In 1850, February Term, Lucretia was appointed their guardian.
Lucretia Eakin stated that her husband John Eakin of about
16 years ago (1835) erected on said plantation, on tract of
land, a brick dwelling house with necessary out-houses in which
he and his family resided up to the time of his death. She
states that in a few years, the house began to crack and give
way, the walls, year by year, gradually cracked more and more
and the house became a more unsafe and dangerous place to live.
The cracks in the walls became so large that when it rained
with any wind, the rain was blown in through the cracks. She
was advised to, this spring 1851, to pull it down and build
another and she has accordingly done so. The next house,
another brick on same site as old one. New house, a two story
and use some of the material out of the old one. Total cost
$5000.00 to $6000.00.

Page 237 - Thomas Lipscomb &]
             R. H. Sims   ] Inj. Bill, filed
                 vs   ] April 12, 1844.
             James Story   ]
Richard H. Sims and Thomas Lipscomb filed against Sarah Martin
and James Story, all of Bedford County. Orators state that
in the year of 1838, they together with Thomas Davis were
partners in a purchase of a drove of hogs for the Southern
Market, that they purchased from Sarah Martin a lot of hogs
and on 3rd December 1838 executed notes to her to be paid in
60 days in Tennessee or Alabama Bank notes. Thomas Davis paid
John W. Ragsdale and Ragsdale took up the note, which orators
thought the debt was settled. A suit was brought against your
orators and said Davis in the name of Sarah Martin, who sues
for the use of James Story who claims to have obtained it from
Ragsdale. Orators knew nothing of it and had not endorsed
the notes. Thomas Davis has obtained a Bankruptcy also James
Story took out Bankruptcy.

Page 243 - Henry Crowell]
                 vs   ]O. Bill, 22 November 1849.
             James B. Jones]
Henry Crowell of Polk County, Missouri, states that in February
1848, he sold all his interest in his father, Peter Crowell's
estate to James B. Jones of Bedford County. The lands are
recorded and are in Bedford County. When he sold his father's
land, Peter Crowell was still living but died some four months
later, Fall of 1848, wife still living. Peter Crowell had
executed his will in 1841 or 1842 by which he devised the lands
to his children by his then wife, of whom your orator was one,
he devised 60 acres which was devised to his wife during her
natural life, remainder to his children. Orator said at time
of sale of land to Jones, his father could not live long and
was not mentally capable of altering his will. Orator was
at the time living on a part of the land, on which he thought
would fall to him, by which he sold to James B. Jones and who
was not to take possession until after the death of his father,
but Jones took possession immediately. When your orator made
the deal, he was desirous of moving to Missouri and did move
in a few days and remained until his return on business of
which he was to receive the balance due him by James B. Jones.

Page 252 - Thomas Roberts &   ]
            Priscilla Roberts & others]
                    vs   ]O. & Inj. Bill, filed
            Nicholas Anthony &   ]   15 May 1854.
            Frederick Anthony   ]

Thomas Roberts and Priscilla formerly Priscilla Parker, Epp
Parker, Allen Parker, Elijah Parker and A. J. Pitman and wife
Martha formerly Martha Parker filed against Nicholas Anthony
and Frederick Anthony of Bedford County. Orators states that
their father Jonathan Parker departed this life intestate in
the year 1837 in Bedford County, at the time of his death,
he owned two tracts of land, adjoining each other in Bedford
County and bounded by Thompsons Creek and of about 170 acres.
Other tract bounded by Andrew Whittenburgh of about 32½ acres,
of which land descended to your orator and oratrix as his only
children and heirs at law of Jonathan Parker and who is still
living and his wife Frances Parker to get dower. Children
are, Priscilla Roberts, Epps, Allen and Elijah Parker and
Martha Pitman his only children and heirs at law. On 12th
day of February 1839, when Priscilla, still a minor but was
a married woman and orator and rest were minors with guardian,
their mother, Jonathan Parker, deceased. Dower land 101½ acres
of land. Frederick Anthony purchased the land. Nicholas
Anthony got the dower's land. Martha arrived at age of 21
about 2 years ago, in July 1852, to be 24 years July 1855.
Nicholas Anthony gave possession of his land to a son, Thompson
Anthony.

Page 260 - Charlotte Shockley]
                    vs   ] O. Bill
            Jesse Shockley   ]

Charlotte Shockley stated that she married Jesse Shockley on
the 8th day of February 1838 and lived with him and he supported her and her family several years. She now states that her
husband has turned evil and turned away from her by the smiles,
etc of women of ill-fame and lately gone to live with them,
having rented a house and farm in the country and placed said
women there, and lived in sin. Women named were, Eliza Crutchfield, Polly Crutchfield, Susan Crutchfield, Pelina Cox,
Hedessa Hall and Polly Parker. At this time he is supporting
Eliza Crutchfield. Lately he has treated your oratrix so bad
that she is now afraid and was unsafe for her to be under his
control. She states that she is the mother of the following
children, Eliza J., John W., and M. A. Chockley. Oratrix
desires alimony and support for herself and her children. Her
husband Jesse owned a negro woman and two Town Lots in the
Town of Shelbyville, upon which they lived. He also owned
several items of cattle, household furniture, etc. She desires
a divorce and wants custody of her children.

Page 264 - Charles L. Capps]
                    vs   ]Bill for Divorce, 6 August 1852.
            R. E. Capps   ]

Charles L. Capps states that he married his present wife
Rushamy E. Capps some years ago in Bedford County and lived
with her until the last few days when he learned his wife had
committed adultery. Orator has been a resident of Tennessee
for more than 12 months prior to filing this bill. Rushamy E.
Capps resided in Bedford County. Orator desires a divorce
from her.

Page 265 - James Wortham]
          vs   ]O. Bill, filed 25 January 1849.
      Minos Cannon]
James Wortham states that on 14th day of August 1845, he purchased of Minos Cannon all claims and interest which Cannon
had in the following tract of land in Bedford County, dower
land, allotted to his mother by his father Minos Cannon,
deceased, on both sides of Duck River about one and one-half
miles above Shelbyville, about 136 acres, it being one third
part of estate. Also lots allotted to his brother John M.
Cannon and James Wortham and wife in the division of said land
belonging to said heirs of Minos Cannon, deceased, 110½ acres
in both lots, a lot in Town of Shelbyville, which has a shoe
shop and owned by Robert Cannon, Robert L. Cannon, James Wortham and wife and Minos Cannon and Robert Cannon owned half of
lot and rest by others. Lot borders Willis Wilhoite on Martin
Street, Mrs. L. Morton and Minos Cannon.

Page 267 - Sarah Terry]
          vs   ]O. Bill, filed 12 February 1850 or 1851.
      Henry Brown]
Sarah Terry of Bedford County states that she is a aged and
infirmed person, age 89 years and having been a widow since
1837, at which since her husband Keble Terry departed this
life. They never had any children. That since she was widowed,
she has lived alone. At the time of her husband's death, he
had several negroes of which she has never sold any. One of
her negroes named Russell had a wife and children who was owned
by Henry Brown of Bedford County and it was her desire that
negro man Russell be with them.

Page 277 - John A. Webb & others]
          vs   ]O. Bill, 26 December 1848.
      John & William Beaty   ]
John A. Webb, Ralph Stegal and wife Nancy G., John Hart and
Elizabeth his wife, Thomas McCurdy and Susan his wife, Nathaniel Lane and Eliza his wife, Joseph Carpenter and his wife
Sallie, William, John B., Thomas, Robert, Jesse R., and W.
Stegal, minors who petitioned by their father Jesse Stegall
against John and William Beaty. Petitioners stated that Bushrod Webb departed this life intestate sometime in the month
of May 1847 in Bedford County. He died having land in District
No. 9 of Bedford County, about 215 acres, being the tract of
land on which Bushrod Webb lived, also owned a small lot of
land in the Town of Middleton in the County of Rutherford,
Tennessee, upon which was a cotton gin. Bushrod Webb bought
it from _____ McGriffin. The heirs at law of Bushrod Webb are,
John A. Webb, Ralph Stegall and wife Nancy G. who was a daughter
of Bushrod Webb, John Hart and wife Elizabeth Hart formerly
Elizabeth Beaty, John Beaty and William Beaty, all of whom
are the only children of Sally Beaty formerly Sallie Webb who
was a daughter of Bushrod Webb, James McCurdy and wife Susan
who reside in Williamson County, Tennessee, Nathaniel Lane
and wife Eliza, William Stegall, Joseph Carpenter and wife
Nancy J. Carpenter, John B. Stegall, Sallie Dysart wife of
Robert Dysart, Thomas, Robert, Jesse R. and Douglas Stegall,
all reside in Marshall County, Tennessee and are children of
Elizabeth Stegall formerly Elizabeth Webb who was a daughter
of Bushrod Webb. They desire the lands to be sold. John Beaty
and William Beaty are residents of the State of Georgia.

Page 279 - Daniel G. Stephenson]
               vs   ]O. Bill, 5 June 1844.
          Mary Temple & others]
Daniel G. Stephenson filed against Mary Temple, John S. Frazier, Robert H. Temple, William P. Temple, Jane T. Temple, and
Hannah A. Temple of Bedford County. Orator stated that in
1842, Mary Temple and Preston Frazier executed a note, promising to pay his on or before 25 December 1842, $250.00, that
he received a judgement on same in 12 August 1843 for $216.15.
Mary Temple had no land in this county. Mary Temple's children
are, Robert H., William P., Jane T. and Hannah M. Temple, all
minors. Mary Temple's brother is John S. Frazier.

Page 289 - William Shofner]
               vs   ]O. Bill, August 17, 1850.
          Jane Shofner   ]
William M. Shofner of Bedford County files against Jane Shofner
of Bedford County. He states that on 22 day of February 1844
he married Jane Koonce. They had a child about 2 years after
they married. He states that she would not let him be a husband to her after the birth of the child, saving she would
never have another baby. After 18 months, on 8th day of August 1848, she deserted and left him. He asks for a divorce.

Page 291 - Amanda Martin, who petitions]
          by her next friend and   ] Exparte, &c.
          mother Sarah Martin   ]
Amanda Martin, a minor under the age of 21 years, that she
is at this time in a very delicate state of health, asthma.
She stated that the physicians here advised her to go to a
southern country for relief. They told her if she stayed here
during this coming winter, she would probably die. Dr. Thomas
Lipscomb and Dr. James G. Barksdale. She states she has considerable amounts of property, which is in the hands of Archey
Moseley, her guardian. Her guardian states that there was
not enough to pay her to go south and live and return next
summer.

Page 293 - Mariah Bigger & others] Filed 25 August 1851.
          Petition for sale of land]
James ?. Bigger (husband) of Mrs. Biggers, John Stammers and
wife Letitia Stammers formerly Letitia Bigger, William H. Adams
and wife Jane Adams formerly Jane Bigger, Joseph Bigger, Davis
Bigger, Mary Bigger, Robertson Bigger, Mary Jabe Stammers,
the last six of whom are minors, guardian was John Stammers
and Mariah Bigger, widow of James Bigger, deceased. James
Bigger departed this life in Bedford County in April 1851,
seized and possessed of land in Bedford County on waters of
Wilson Creek in District No. 10, 396 acres. Mary Jane Stammers
mother was Margaret N. Stammers, deceased, formerly Margaret N.
Bigger. Her father John Stammers, who married with two daughters of James Bigger. Mariah Bigger, widow of James Bigger,
deceased, wants land sold.

Page 295 - D. D. Hix   ]
          Exparte, for sale of slaves]
Demarquis D. Hix states that on 24 July 1826, Valentine Kyser
made his Last Will and Testament and shortly thereafter departed this life in bedford County. The will was proven and recorded in Bedford County. In said will, Valentine Kyser conveyed
to his widow, Nancy Kyser, four negroes. Nancy Kyser departed
this life in 1844 on 1st July. They had 8 children living,
two of whom have since died, Jacob, William Valentine Jr.,

Daniel, Enoch Kyser and Mary Himes. living sons and daughters
of Valentine Kyser.

Page 298 - James R. Terry   ]
                 vs   ]O. Bill, filed 20 August 1852.
            Thomas M. Arnold,]
            O. H. Bigham &]
            William Hoover   ]
James R. Terry filed against O. H. Bigham and Samuel B. Bigham
all residents of Texas and William Hoover and Thomas M. Arnold
of Bedford County. Orator states that Thomas M. Arnold ownes
him a debt. He said he had land in Bedford County in District
No. 5, adjoining John Rushing, Webb's land, Duncan's land,
about 127 acres, the place known as the Stellard Place.

Page 301 - G. B. Sharp   ]
                 vs   ] Orig. Bill, August 17, 1850.
            John Tillman &]
            B. M. Tillman]
G. B. Sharp of Bedford County filed against John Tillman and
Barclay M. Tillman of Bedford County. Orator states that on
27th day of July 1850, he recovered a judgement against John
and Barclay M. Tillman. Orator states that Anderson Sharp,
admr of William Sharp, deceased. Orator states that John Tillman, on 19 November 1849, was owner of a lot of land, 4 acres,
adjacent to Town of SHelbyville and adjoining the resident
of Gen. Robert Cannon, deeded as gift to his son Barclay M.
Tillman.

Page 313 - Benjamin F. Greer]
                 vs   ] Att. Bill, 22 November 1848.
            C. R. Greer,   ]
            A. J. Greer &   ]
            Joseph Greer   ]
Benjamin F. Greer of Bedford County filed against Catharine R.
Greer and Archibald J. Greer of Bedford County, and Joseph
Greer of Texas. Your orator states that on 20 day of October
1838 at Columbus in the State of Mississippi, he loaned to
Joseph Greer $300.00 in money, also sold to him a horse for
$100.00. Joseph Greer soon removed from Mississippi and went
to Texas. Joseph Greer was a son of Thomas Greer. Thomas
Greer departed this life leaving a Last Will and Testament.
In will, he left Joseph $200.00 in money. Catharine R. Greer
and Archibald J. Greer were appointed executors.

Page 316 - Charles Ready &]
            William H. Sneed]
                 vs   ] O. & Inj. Bill, filed
            Jacob Harrison &]   15 October 1849.
            Joel Harrison   ]
Charles ready of Rutherford County, Tennessee and William H.
Sneed of Knox County, Tennessee filed against Jacob Harrison
of Bedford County and Joel Harrison of Alabama. Orators states
that on 2 December 1845, they recovered a judgement against
Jacob Harrison for $216.00 plus cost. Also, a mortgage on
3 September 1848 on a negro man.

Page 319 - William P. Sims & others]
                 vs   ]O. Bill, 28 April 1842.
            John A. Ferguson   ]
William P. Sims and Walter Sims and Mary E. Sims wife of Walter
SIms and Rebecca Sims states that they are the devises of one
half of a tract of land of 5 acres, lying in Bedford County

above the Town of Shelbyville on the south side of Duck River,
including the mills, known as Sim's Mills, bounded by Duck
River, mills and mill dams. Orators states that Walter Sims
and Rebecca Sims have no claim on the land and mills. Uriah
Cross is owner of the other one-half of the property.

Page 322 - John Fisher & others]
              vs   ]O. Bill, June 27, 1849.
          Lewis Gaunt & others]
Orators John Fisher admr of Rebecca Fisher, James F. Shearin,
Thomas Shearin, Jesse M. Ledbetter and Elizabeth his wife,
filed against Lewis Gaunt and Matthew Shearin admrs of Thomas
Shearin, deceased. Orators states that John Mayfield of North
Carolina many years ago, departed this life intestate in North
Carolina, that he had a daughter named Sarah who married Thomas
Shearin and who died before John, that your orators, to wit,
Rebecca Fisher, James F. Shearin, Thomas Shearin, Elizabeth
Ledbetter and Polly Gant wife of Lewis Gant, Matthew Shearin
and Sally Shearin, the latter of whom died intestate and child-
less, after the death of John Mayfield, are the only children
of Sarah Shearin. The admr of John Mayfield's estate forwarded
to Thomas Shearin, the father of your orators, for them four
negroes and several hundred dollars, in right of their mother,
the first wife of Thomas Shearin of Bedford County, in right
of their mother, the first wife of Thomas Shearin of Bedford
County, who died intestate a few months ago and that Lewis
Gaunt and Martha Shearin have been appointed admr of estate.
Orators stated that your orator, John Fisher at the ___ Term
1849 of Bedford County was appointed admr of his wife, Rebecca,
who died before the negroes and money came into hands of Thomas
Shearin. Also, stated that the children and not the husband
of Sarah Shearin are the persons entitled to their share of
the estate of John Mayfield, deceased, as she died before John.
Thomas Shearin was entitled to the share of his deceased daughter Sallie. James Shearin married Sarah Mayfield daughter
of John Mayfield, deceased, and respondent, Matthew Shearin,
know the family, which he had learned from John Mayfield in
his life time. Matthew Shearin and Polly Gaunt wife of Lewis
Gaunt who were children of his first wife, Sarah.

Page 327 - Asa M. Elkins   ]
              vs   ]Inj. Bill, May 3, 1850.
          Isaac Barnett &   ]
          William S. Wallace]
Asa M. Elkins of Texas filed against Isaac Barnett and William
S. Wallace of Bedford County, states that in the year of 1844,
he and Isaac Barnett entered into a partnership in business
of "Blacksmith Shop" and Manufacturing Wagons for sale. Equal
partners. They wanted to take their new made wagon (1844)
to Mississippi for sale and in Fall of 1844 left for Mississippi. When he returned, he explained all sales to his partner Barnett. In 1847, your orator removed to Texas.

Page 339 - Thomas Thompson & wife]
              vs   ]Bill of Complaint.
          J. C. Hall & others   ]
Thomas Thompson and Tranquilla Ann his wife, minors under age
of 21 years, who sue by John F. Thompson their guardian and
next friend, filed against Jordan C. Holt, Herrod F. Holt and
Benjamin Phillips, all of Bedford County. Orator stated that
Jordan C. Holt was appointed guardian of Tranquilla Ann some
years ago, who was then and still a minor under the age of
21 years. Orator stated that he and Tranquilla Ann married

in February last (1850). Thomas not yet 21 years and John F.
Thompson his guardian.

Page 341 - Jane Austin, et als]
                vs   ]Orig. Bill
        J. W. Wallace &   ]
        James Ragsdale   ]
Jane Austin and Catharine Nichol and Jacob Nichol of Coffee
County, Tennessee, states that on about 13th day of May last,
Jane executed a note to John W. Ragsdale for $73.00, one day
later, Catharine and Jacob Nichols her securities to the said
Ragsdale of Bedford County and sometime later assigned the
note to James Davidson, then of Franklin County, Tennessee
and since has run away to parts unknown.

Page 34_ - Joseph Anderson]
                vs   ]Inj. & Att. Bill, filed
        Henry Crowell &]   27 August 1850.
        James B. Jones]
Joseph Anderson of Bedford County against Henry Crowell of
Missouri and James B. Jones of Bedford County. Orator states
that at the July Term 1848 of Bedford County Court, he qualified and gave bond as executor of the Last Will and Testament
of Peter Crowell, deceased. Also, that John T. Neil, James
Harris and Thomas Shearon(Shearin) were also named as executors
of which all refused to qualify. Orator stated that Henry
Crowell was indebted to Peter Crowell at his death on several
bonds. Henry Crowell was a non-resident of Tennessee at the
death of his father Peter Crowell and has ever since. Henry
Crowell was a legatee of Peter Crowell, deceased, and will
be entitled to one fifth part of the estate.

Page 347 - John M. Haskins]
                vs   ]Att. Bill, filed 9 August 1851.
        Benjamin Wade   ]
John M. Haskins of Bedford County, states that Banjamin Wade
is justly indebted to him for about $550.00 for services rend-
ered and work and labor done on Wade Plantation several years
ago, about 1832. The work was done by your orator when still
a minor under age of 21 years. Soon after the services rendered, Benjamin Wade left Bedford County, about 1843, without
paying his debt. Wade has no property within Tennessee except
a tract of land in bedford County, about 95 acres in District
No. 9, bordered by John C. _____, Dennis Wheelhouse, John E.
Haskins and the heirs of John Taylor, deceased.

Page 355 - Hiram Edde & el]
                vs   ]Inj. Bill, 1 October 1849.
        Herod F. Holt &]
        Herod G. Holt]
Hiram Holt, Matthew Cunningham of Bedford County stated that
Hiram Holt departed this life some two and three years since,
intestate, no admr has been done and now more than 6 months
have elapsed since the death of Holt. He died 5 May 1845 in
Alabama. Hiram Holt, deceased, left Herod G. Holt, Rachel
Holt, Mary Jane Holt, Eleanor Holt and Henry Clay Holt, his
children and _____ Holt his widow whose christian name is unknown. Hiram Holt before his death sent his son Herod G. Holt
to Bedford County to buy bacon and stock for him and furnished
him with money to pay for the articles. He received a deed
from his father for a tract of land, and he also purchased
of Herod F. Holt, 1847, age 24 years, situated in the District
No. 22, 104 acres. Hiram at one time went to Arkansas. All

children reside in Bedford County except Henry Clay Holt and
the widow of Hiram Holt who reside in Alabama.

Page 364 - Gamble & Trice, Exrs   ]
                  vs   ]O. Bill, 5 June 1848.
         George W. Gamble,   ]
         John S. Gamble & others]
Alfred H. Gamble and Joseph Trice, Jr. of Bedford County, stated that Benjamin Gamble, late of Bedford County, departed this
life in Bedford County in April 1846, having made and published
his Last Will and Testament, dated 14th of said month. Will
and Codicil was proven and recorded in Bedford County. Orators
appointed executors of will. Rachel, widow survives Benjamin
Gamble. Children are, Alfred H. Gamble, Amzi Anderson and
wife Permelia, John S. Gamble, George W. Gamble, Harriet Johnson, Eliza Jane Gamble, Sally Bradshaw who married a man in
the State of Arkansas whose name is Yarbrough and Catharine,
Mary, and Nancy Ann Johnson children of Harriet Johnson who
are minors and have no regular guardian in this State, and
James Phillips and Benjamin Phillips, William Phillips, Joseph
Phillips and John W. Phillips all children of Susannah Phillips,
a daughter of Benjamin Gamble. Orator stated that no settlement as yet been made for the reason that as yet they have
not had Benjamin Gamble's grave covered as he had directed
in his will, which is to be done in a few days. There are
eight shares of the estate, nine counting the widow. Alfred
H. Gamble is the owner of three shares of the estate, to wit,
his own, George W. Gamble and Harriet Johnson's. Harriett
Johnson's share was bought because she was going to Arkansas
and wanted to dispose of it. No conveyance was made for the
reason that she had been previously married to a man by the
name of Johnson, who had left her and had not been heard of
for some 6 years. Harriet has since, she removed to Arkansas,
married a man by the name of Cox. Orators were advised that
the marriage is void for the reason 7 years had not lapsed
since her husband was last heard from. Those who reside in
Arkansas are Harriet Johnson and her children and also George
W. Gamble, John S. Gamble, and Sally Yarborough and her husband.
Rachel Gamble, Eliza Jane Gamble and Also Benjamin Phillips,
James Phillips and William Phillips reside in Bedford County
and Amzi Anderson and wife Permelia, and Joseph Phillips and
John W. Phillips reside in Marshall County, Tennessee. Said
Phillips are all minors and no guardian. John S. Gamble is
now temporarily in Bedford County.

Page 368 - Elizabeth Reaves   ]
                  vs   ]O. Bill, April 26, 1847.
         Joseph Thompson, admr &c]
Elizabeth Reaves of Bedford County states that sometime in
1842 she purchased a negro woman and child at her deceased
husband's sale for $685.00, which she gave her note with her
son Tarleton J. Reeves as her security to Thomas Newsom the
executor of her husband's will. Since, Thomas Newsom had died
and before settlement was made Tarleton J. Reeves has since
died intestate and that Joseph Thompson was appointed admr
of said Tarleton J. Reeves. Benjamin S. Reaves also her
security. A note on Abner Freeman for $100.00 was paid by
oratrix to Tarleton J. Reeves. Elizabeth Reeves' husband died
in Bedford County. Tarleton J. Reeves left a widow.

Page 376 - Joshua Hall, admr   ]
                  vs   ]O. Bill.
         Daniel L. Barringer]

Joshua Hall of Bedford County states that he is admr of George
Whitsell, deceased, late of Bedford County, filed against
Daniel L. Barringer. Orator states that in 1843, his intestate
took up some orders of said Barringer, as he did not owe
Barringer at that time. Orator also states that John Whitsell,
the father of intestate, departed this life sometime early
in 1842 and that at May Term 1842 Bedford County Court said
Barringer who had with John Wilhoite who had declined to quali-
fy, been appointed executor of John Whitsell's Last Will and
Testament, proved. Orator states that 2 years since appointment, Barringer has not settled the estate. George Whitsell
was a legatee of John Whitsell. Two grandchildren of George
Whitsell represented their deceased mother, February Term 1848.
John Whitsell, Jr. departed this life __ ___ ____intestate.

Page 387 - Samuel Doak   ]
                vs   ]Inj. Bill, 16 January 1849.
         John Tillman &]
         James R. Terry]
Samuel Doak of Bedford County filed against James R. Terry
and John Tillman. Orator states that the last of December
last, and Carlos D. Steele, entered into a partnership by verbal agreement to purchase a negro boy or negroes and stock
such as horses and mules for a profit, on first of January
they had a written agreement of partnership and executed a
note with Henry Cannon for negro girl for $580.00. On 9th
January, James R. Terry levied on execution on said negro girl
and took her into his possession as Deputy Sheriff of Bedford
County, in favor of John Tillman, executor of Samuel Escue,
deceased, of Bedford County, and against Carlos D. Steele.
Steele is largely in debt beyond his means.
Answer of Tillman: Steele was to have attended the sale of
Bushrod Webb's negroes and bid off the negro girl, Maria, for
$580.00 on credit of 12 months. He asked Doak and Cannon to
be his securities.

Page 391 - John Tillman, exr]
                vs   ]Inj. & Att. Bill, 8 May 1849.
         Carlos D. Steele &]
         Thomas B. Cannon]
John Tillman filed against Carlos D. Steele and Thomas B.
Cannon, all of Bedford County. Orator states that Samuel Escue
departed this life in Bedford County many years ago leaving
his Last Will and Testament and your orator was appointed exr
of his estate, he became involved in a law suit with Carlos D.
Steele who was Escue's former partner in ourchase and sales
of goods. The suit was ended in your orator's favor at June
Term Court 1842. Orator recovered a decree against Steele
for $1139.00 plus $12.82½ cost. The sale of negro girl was
enjoined by Samuel Doak who claimed negro girl as partnership
property.

Page 398 - Samuel Doak   ]
                vs   ]O. Bill, 14 August 1849.
         John Tillman &   ]
         Thomas B. Cannon]
Samuel Doak states that on __ day of May 1849, he became the
first indorser on a Bill of Exchange for $4,000.00 drown on
one Carlos D. Steele, who was largely indebted and that orator
had been bond with him for large amounts of money.

Page 404 - William H. Wisener]
                vs   ]Inj. Bill, 27 June 1848.
          Jacob C. Burrow &   ]
          James M. Johnson   ]
William H. Wisener of Bedford County states that in 1st May
1848, he recovered a judgement against Jacob C. Burrow for
$40.20 plus 87½ cents cost, and on 10th November 1845 your
orator and John P. Steele recovered a judgement against Burrow
for $23.19 plus $1.00 cost of suit. "No property to be found."
Orator states that some 3 years ago or more, John Eakin & Co.
or J. A. A. Eakin & Co. had some property sold under execution
in their favor against Jacob C. Burrow and bought the same
at the sale. Also at the sale were stocks, etc. Orator wants
some of the extra stock and or machinery sold to pay his debts.

Page 409 - Thomas P. Powell   ]
                vs   ]Inj. Bill, 20 November 1843.
          James Mullins &   ]
          Thomas C. Whiteside]
Thomas P. Powell of Bedford County states that his father
Robert Powell died sometime in summer of 1842 and that he was
appointed his executor. Robert Powell owed Thomas C. Whiteside
which dated 22 June 1840. Before death of Robert Powell, on
25 March 1842, he executed a Deed of Gift to your orator,
slaves.

Page 420 - Rebecca Ann Murfree]
                vs   ]Petition for divorce.
          William Doke Murfree]
Rebecca Ann Murfree of Bedford County states that some years
ago she married William Doke Murfree at that time of Bedford
County, with whom she had lived many years peacefully and by
whom she had issue. That about 2 years ago, a change came
over him, before that time he was affectionate and kind to
her and her children, since then he has been abusing and mal-
treating her and failing to provide for her and her two children. Sometime in November last, he left the country and has
gone to parts unknown. He stated that he had no intentions
of living with her and left. He threatened her life. He had
whipped his son William who was only 2 years old. Before he
left, he sold all her property left to her by her family and
left her destitute.

Page 423 - George Davidson   ]
                vs   ]O. Bill, filed 13 August 1844.
          William Drummond &]
          Leonard W. Marberry]
George Davidson states that on 1 January 1841, William J. Peacock hired to William Drummond, two slaves for 1841 for $164.00
to be paid December 25, 1841. Drummond refused to pay.

Page 425 - James M. McCrory]
                vs   ]O. Bill, filed 12 July 1851.
          Isham Lane   ]
James M. McCrory of Bedford County filed against Isham Lane
formerly of Bedford County, now in Texas. Orator states that
John H. Lane executed his certain bill single for $323.60 due
25 December 1847 in which he promised to pay to Rankin &
Frizzle that sum of money for value received. By due time,
Rankin & Frizzle had transferred bill to your orator. Orator
states that shortly after bill was due, that John H. Lane departed this life intestate, and Isham Lane his father was
appointed admr of his estate. His father Isham Lane, misre-

presented the estate of his son, saying he had no valued property, in fact he had more than $1000.00.

Page 427 - Daniel W. & Susannah M. Dollar   ]Exparte Petition
          who petition by their guardians,]to sell land.
          Thomas Holland, Sr. & John McGuire]26 February 1849.
Daniel W. and Susannah M. Dollar, minors, petition by their
guardians, that they are the owners in common of the one sixth
part of a tract of land in District No. 3 in Bedford County.
Land bounded by John McGuire, James G. Barksdale and Thomas
Holland, Sr., about 63 acres, it being the dower interest of
their grandmother, out of the lands of their grandfather
Michael Holt, by the death of their grandmother came down to
them. They were told that John McGuire had become the owner
in fee, as purchased from the heirs of Michael Holt, deceased,
of the other five undivided shares. They wanted to sell their
share. There was a comfortable house on the 63 acres they
wanted to sell.

Page 429 - Thomas Black]
              vs   ]O. Bill.
          Herod Burk &]
          Mark Crick]
Thomas Black of Bedford County filed against Herod Burks of
Rutherford County, Tennessee and Mark Crick of Bedford County.
Orator states that on 4 March 1846, he sold to Herod Burks,
a tract of land in District No. 10 of Bedford County and bound-
ed by Frances P. Arnold, Daniel Dwiggins, Thomas Lamb, and
Samuel Morton, about 93 acres, it being a part of the tract
of land bought by your orator and _____ Walls of the Union
Bank of Tennessee. Several notes executed. Mark Crick is
now in possession of said land.

Page 431 - John M. Lane & others   [Filed 24 February
          Petition for division of slaves[1851.
John M. Lane, Samuel L. Davidson, Hugh L. Davidson, Mary
Rebecca Moseley Davidson and Jane Vance Coleman Davidson, by
their guardian Samuel L. Davidson, being infants, Rebecca
Moseley Hughes and Sarah Hughes, infants, by their guardian
and father A. M. Hughes. Thomas B. Moseley, Jr., Sally Ann
Edins, who being minor petitioners by her next friend Thomas B.
Moseley, Jr., Lewis James Searcy, infant, petitioned by his
father Robert Searcy and Lettie Martin Moseley. They are owners
in partnership with slaves. One share was owned by Mary Edins
and Sally Ann Edins and Rebecca Edins but the Mary Edins
married with Zollicoffer, he conveyed all his interest from
Hilary Moseley to Samuel L. Davidson. The present wife of
Davidson was owner of one share, by his marriage he is now
owner of two shares and one third share of a slave, and his
three children (above named) are owners of one share in right
of their deceased mother and Rebecca Moseley Hughes and Sarah
Hughes in right of their deceased mother, are owners of one
share, and Thomas B. Moseley, Jr. and Lettie Martin Moseley
are each owner of one share, and Sally Ann Edins and Lewis
James Searcy are joint owners of two thirds of one share, the
former in right of her mother and the latter in right of his
grandmother Nancy Edins, and John M. Lane in right of his wife
one share. Slaves are now in Bedford County. Petitioned to
divide slaves.

Page 433 - John Kirkman   ]
              vs   ] Att & Inj. Bill.
          Jacob W. & Flower Swift]

John Kirkman of Davidson County, Tennessee filed against Jacob
W. and Flower Swift. Orator recovered a judgement on 8 December 1848 in Bedford County against Jacob W. Swift for $118.57
and cost and also owner of a regular transfer of a judgement
in favor of William A. Young for $97.12 plus cost. Orator
stated that on 13 November 1848, J. W. Swift sold to his father
Flower Swift a negro boy Richardson, aged 16 years, for $700.00
paid in cash and cash notes. Orator said such sale was made
to keep J. W. Swift from paying his debts.

Page 436 - George Davidson]
               vs   ]Inj. Bill, 23 April 1846.
          Robert H. Terry]
          & John R. Proby]
George Davidson of Bedford County filed against Robert H. Terry,
admr of estate of Peter R. Proby, deceased, and John R. Proby.
Orator stated that John R. Proby is indebted to him by two
notes $110.50, dated 29 December 1842. One note still due
and owing by the said John R. Proby who resides in Arkansas.
Orator stated that Peter R. Proby recently departed this life
intestate in Bedford County leaving a large amount of personal
properties. John R. Proby as one of the heirs and distributees
of Peter R. Proby, deceased. Robert H. Terry appointed admr
of Peter R. Proby, deceased, at March Term 1846.

Page 442 - W. & W. M. Hopwood]
               vs   ]Inj. Bill, 4 June 1844.
          G. W. Nash   ]
Willis Hopwood and Willis M. Hopwood of Marshall County, Tennessee, shows that George W. Nash executed to Bronson D. Caple,
since deceased, his obligations. Orator said Caple departed
this life after having made and published his Last Will and
Testament and nominated Daniel Whitaker and Pleasant Halbert,
executors, both of Lincoln County, Tennessee. After settling
the estate and handing over to Willis and Willis M. as guardians
of same of the minor children of said Caple. Orator states
that Nash resides in Mississippi. Travis C. Nash, late of
Bedford County, departed this life intestate some two months
ago, leaving said George W. Nash as heir at law. Travis C.
Nash, at time of his death, owned a tract of land of several
hundred acres upon which he resided at time of death. The
tract of land in District No. 5 of Bedford County. This tract
of land descended on the death of Travis C. Nash to his heirs
at law of whom George W. Nash was one. The number of heirs
of said Travis C. Nash are not known but supposed to be fifteen.

Page 444 - William Brame   ]Bill of Discovery and
               vs   ]Relief, filed
          William B. M. Brame, admr of] February 10, 1846.
          Melchesdek Brame   ]
William Brame of Bedford County filed against William B. M.
Brame, admr of Melchesdek Brame, deceased, who was also of
Bedford County, states that about the year 1835, your orator
became entitled to a legacy or share of about $500.00 from
his late father William Brame of Caroline County, Virginia,
that his brother Melchesdek Brame, late of Bedford County,
received the legacy of share for your orator about the same
year 1835. Orator states that his brother Melchesdek never
oaid of gave him his legacy. Melchesdek Brame died in April
1845. Orator stated that he lived with Melchesdek Brame for
about 30 years, attending to business and laboring on farm
and received no more than his board and clothing. Orator states
that _____ Term 1845, William B. M. Brame as admr of Melchesdek

Brame who died intestate. William B. M. Brame is son of Melchesdek Brame, in May 1840 he helped his father execute a will
which was never proven by Melchesdek Brame. He was never paid
from estate. William B. M. Brame said that in the will of
Melchesdek Brame, "I will my brother, William Brame to live
with my wife, or son as long as she or they may live and be
supported comfortably if he chooses for his services to me
and my family, together with his part of our father's estate
in my hands, should be refuse this provision, I wish my executors to pay him $500.00 with interest from this date as his
part of my father's estate in my hands."

Page 448 - R. G. Ellis   ]
                   vs   ]Inj. Bill, 22 September 1845.
          John McGuire & others]
R. G. Ellis of Rutherford County, Tennessee filed against John
McGuire, John Snelling and Lemuel Snelling, all of Bedford
County. Orator states that about 10th or 11th September, he
obtained a judgement to be above defendants.

Page 451 - Francis Jackson &   ]
          Mead J. Hail, Exrs &c]Att. & Inj. Bill, filed
                   vs   ]   9 December 1850.
          Robert L. Singleton   ]
Francis Jackson of Rutherford County, Tennessee and Mead J.
Hail of Bedford County, executors of Last Will and Testament
of Mead Hail, deceased, late of Bedford County, filed against
Robert L. Singleton of Bedford County. Mead Hail departed
this life in September 1850, owning several negroes. They
were ordered sold on 29 November 1850. At sale, Robert L.
Singleton bid off the slaves, four in number, for a total sum
of $2717.00. The negroes were not delivered ever to Singleton.
Singleton never paid said money.

Page 456 - Minos Cannon   ]
                   vs   ]Orig. Bill, 14 June 1843.
          Thomas G. Holland   ]
          & William Norton   ]
Minos Cannon of Bedford County states that sometime in 1842
he bought in the due course of trade, a note on one Thomas G.
Holland of Coffee County, Tennessee for $125.00 or about that
sum of William Norton of Bedford County. Orator says the note
was given for purchases of land in Coffee County, Tennessee,
135 acres in District No. 4, bounded by Elyry Keeling or Jacob
Nichols, Willis Blanton, Thomas G. Holland and John G. Walker
or Robert Wilson.
Amended: Cannon states that the land title was in the name
of Thomas Keeling, deceased, and not Norton. Thomas Keeling
departed this life intestate leaving as his heirs at law, Calvin
G. Gribles and wife Hilcy of Carroll County, Tennessee, E. B.
Keeling, Elyry Keeling, Larken Keeling, James L. Keeling,
Alfred Burrow and wife Katharine A. and Thomas A. Keeling,
all citizens of Coffee County and Harrison Keeling of Pope
County, Arkansas and Mary Keeling, the widow of Thomas Keeling,
who also lives in Coffee County, Tennessee. E. B. Keeling,
admr.

Page 465 - Minos Cannon   ]
                   vs   ]Orig. Bill, 12 December 1843.
          Jeremiah Claunch,   ]
          Robert B. Davidson]
          & John Hastings   ]
Minos Cannon of Bedford County filed against Jeremiah Claunch,

C. G. Claunch, Robert B. Davidson and John Hastings, all of
Bedford County. Orator states that on 21st October last, he
recovered a judgement against Jeremiah Claunch for $13.06 plus
cost. Orator states that in 1840, he endorsed a note on Jeremiah Claunch and James H. Claunch for $26.00 and was sued by
Elisha Garrison, the holder of the note and orator paid said
note. Orator states that Edward Green recovered a judgement
against Jeremiah Claunch and James H. Claunch for $34.50 plus
cost. Orator states that in 1843, the Clerk and Master of
Chancery Court at Shelbyville, sold lands as the property of
Jeremiah Claunch by a decree in case of Leonard W. Mayberry
against J. Claunch and F. A. Ross.

Page 473 - Minos Cannon   ]
                    vs   ]Amended Bill, February 20, 1847.
          Jeremiah Claunch &]
          James H. Claunch]
          & others.   ]
Answer of Respondant: James H. Claunch is the admr of Christopher G. Claunch and not Charles G. Claunch, alleged in the
bill. Christopher G. is or was a son of Jeremiah Claunch,
and that he died intestate, unmarried and childless and that
James was appointed admr of his estate at February Term 1846
in Bedford County.

Page 477 - Lemuel Broadaway, Admr &c]
          of Daniel L. Mallard   ]
                    vs   ] Filed 17 November 1842.
          Minos Cannon & others   ]
Lemuel Broadaway, admr of Daniel L. Mallard, widow of Daniel L.
and Nancy, Sarah Ann and Alcey R. Mallard, children and heirs
at law of Daniel L. Mallard, all of Bedford County. Daniel L.
Mallard, at the time of his death, a resident of Bedford County,
departed this life intestate in October 1841, in November 1841
Term, orator was appointed admr of said estate. Daniel L.
Mallard left a widow, Elizabeth Mallard and Nancy, Sarah Ann,
and Alsey R. Mallard, the only children and heirs of Daniel L.
Mallard. Daniel L. Mallard died seized of tract of land in
Bedford County on waters of Big Flat Creek and bounded by James
Reagor, Martin Friddle, Alfred Campbell, Mill Pond and State
Road, Ann Bumfield, and about 150 acres. The land was conveyed
to Daniel L. Mallard by William Stewart by deed dated July 17,
1841 and recorded in Shelbyville, Book "KK", page 427. Orator
states that Mallard's estate would not be enough to pay his
debts, if sold.

Page 484 - John Claxton   ]
                    vs   ]O. Bill, February 12, 1845.
          Benjamin F. Whitworth]
John Claxton of Bedford County filed against Benjamin F. Whitworth also of Bedford County. Orator states he recovered a
judgement against James Claxton for sum of $111.27 and cost.
Orator states that James Claxton had been in the habit of
borrowing large sums of money and paying large amounts of
interests to Benjamin F. Whitworth. James Claxton in the last
5 or 6 years paid Whitworth large amounts of interest.

Page 492 - Minos C. Hodges & others   ]
                    vs   ]O. Bill, 11 March 1850.
          William W. Coldwell & others]
Orator Minos C. Hodges of Bedford County stated that on __
day of February 1849, Samuel B. McCuistion of Bedford County
executed a Deed of Trust on real and personal property. By

Deed of Trust, authorized Coldwell to sell said property, &c.
Sale $1600.00.

Page 496 - John T. Neil   ]
                    vs   ]Inj. Bill, filed
            Thomas C. Whiteside,   ] 11 January 1849.
            Flower Swift, Jacob W. Swift]
            & Richard Bandy   ]
John T. Neil filed against Flower Swift, Thomas C. Whiteside,
Richard Bandy, Jacob W. Swift, Andrew Vannoy, Robert A. Jones
and Henry Halbert, all of Bedford County. Orator states that
he recovered a judgement against Jacob W. Swift on 4 January
1849 for $182.50 plus cost. Orator stated that on 10 November
1848, Jacob W. Swift was in failing circumstances, he executed
a Deed of Trust upon the following property, viz, The Town
Lot or Lots upon which he then and now resides being known
as Lot No. 65, and part of Lot No. 69 in the plan of Shelbyville, one negro woman named Agnes about 22 years and an
infant child named Tom, one negro girl Margaret 10 years, set
of blacksmith tools, 3 featherbeds, bedstead and furniture
to Thomas C. Whiteside. (This was continued on page 501, Injunction Bill, filed 28 February 1849.)

Page 518 - Jane Robinson   ]
                    vs   ]Bill for divorce, January 21, 1846.
            Joseph Robinson]
Jane Robinson stated that on February 18, 1836, she married
Joseph Robinson in Bedford County, lived with him in Bedford
County until about 4 years ago, Joseph started to abuse her
and continued for 2 years, he also ordered her to leave his
house and told her he had no use for her and that she was an
expense to him. Once she said, when she was confined to bed
with an infant only a few days, with a gun threatened to "blow
eight holes through her". She was forced to leave her husband
about 2 years ago and to seek support and protection under
her father's roof. She stayed with her father 3 months and
her husband persuaded her to return to his house and live with
him again, promising not to abuse her again. She said she
returned only in a short time her husband started again to
abuse her. In August 1844, he threw some cider upon the children and directed them to get some switches to whip her with,
which he told her she long needed but before he could carry
out the threat, company came in. He has since tryed to choke
her, beat her with his fist and threatened to cut her throat.
The last was in October 1845. She went back to her father's
house, where she has been ever since. Oratrix stated that
shortly after she married, her father let her and her husband
have a negro boy Jacob about 12 or 13 years, also a horse and
saddle ($60.00), 2 milk cows and calves, two featherbeds and
clothing and other articles at different times. The negro
boy was sold or traded by her husband. She said her husband
owned about 250 acres of land upon which he now resides and
80 acres adjoining the same, situated about three miles west
of Shelbyville, bounded by School Land, Alexander Saunders
and J. Green, John Wilhoite Phifer, and James Story. He also
owns several slaves and also stock. She asks for a divorce.
She stated she was the mother of four children, Robert J. aged
about 9 years, Rufus Alexander nearly 8 years old, Margaret
Frances about 6 years old and Thomas David about 3 years old,
who are with their father who refuses to permit them to live
with your oratrix.

Page 524 - William Albright & Louisa]
           his wife & others   ]O. Bill.
                 vs   ]
           Jordan C. Holt & others   ]
William Albright and wife Louisa, John Thompson and wife Elizabeth, Samuel Siler and wife Sarah, Sampson F. Vestal and wife
Mary, Levin Albright, Mary Wood, Washington Wood, Martha Wood,
Lafayette Wood, Mariah Wood, Levin Wood, the last four being
minors who sue by their guardian Seymour Puryear filed against
Jordan C. Holt, Handy Wood, William Wood, Ann Wood and Robert
Wood. Orators stated that their ancestor Levin Wood departed
this life intestate in North Carolina sometime in the year
____, seized and possessed of large real and personal estate
in Tennessee. Jacob Albright was appointed admr of the estate
that Levin Wood, deceased, estate in Tennessee at June Term
1843. Orators stated that before Jacob Albright could complete
the estate of Levin Wood, Jacob Albright departed this life
in Bedford County and Jordan C. Holt was appointed admr at
March Term 1845. He had (Albright) $666.24 found in estate
of Wood's estate. Jordan C. Holt never settled the estate
or turned it over to orators. Albright wrote them in North
Carolina that he was ready to turn over monies if and when
they came for it. William Albright and Seymour Puryear stated
that they did visit Tennessee in August 1845 last, and wrote
a demanding note to Jordan C. Holt. Orators stated that defendant "Handy Wood" of North Carolina who is a son of Levin Wood,
was advanced by his father an amount of property more than
enough to counter-balance any portion that may come to your
orators from funds now in the hand of Jordan C. Holt. Same
facts are true in regard to William Wood, Ann Wood and Robert
Wood of _____, who are grandchildren of Levin Wood, their
father Salret(?) Wood, having advanced by Levin Wood in his
life time.
Answer of Jordan C. Holt: He stated that Albright had the
Power of Attorney to collect from Jacob Nease, as executor
of George Nease in North Carolina the distributive share of
Sampson Nease in said estate which Holt by purchase from said
Sampson, which the said Albright agreed to collect and receive
as well as the $400.00 in further part payment of the estate
in Holt's hands are admr coming to complainants. Holt also
stated that Sally Albright, widow of Jacob Albright, deceased,
filed to collect her share in estate of her father George Nease,
sum $400.00. Holt said that Levin Wood had a decree rendered
against Enoch Trot for $160.00. Holt is trying to collect
this decree and forward a transcript sometime ago to Arkansas
where Trot resides.

Page 536 - Green L. Poplin & others]
                 vs   ]Inj. Bill, 11 July 1850.
           Thomas Eakin & others   ]
Green L. Poplin, Alfred Poplin, William Poplin and John A.
Moore, all of Bedford County, states that John Eakin and Thomas
Eakin surviving partners of John Eakin & Co. or W. & T. Eakin
& Co. (both firms are the same persons), recovered a judgement
against them on 18 August 1849 for $236.69 plus cost. Orators
said the debt is debt of Green L. and A. Poplin and other
orators. Eakin had two other debts against Green L. and A.
Poplin, all total between $1200.00 and $1300.00. Eakin sent
their notes to New Orleans and attached as the property of
Green L. and A. Poplin, two cedar rafts. After Green L. Poplin
sold said rafts on 6th October 1849 to Thomas Eakin (who had
them by the death of John Eakin became sole surviving partner
of both firms) to pay said three several debts and took from

him (he still using name of W. & T. Eakin & Co.). An instrument of writing binding himself to sell at best prices etc.
Green L. Poplin went to New Orleans in December or January
and took with him a letter from Thomas Eakin to his agents
in New Orleans. He urged the agents of said Eakin to sell
rafts but they refused saying the timber was not his but would
sell it as they pleased. The rafts were then in bad condition,
but were in good shape when delivered to them (a agent of Eakin
in New Orleans). One raft was owned by Green L. Poplin and
William S. Wade. Poplin had paid Wade for the raft and owned
it himself. William S. Wade departed this life in New Orleans
in spring of 1849 although he was a citizen of Bedford County.
Thomas Eakin lives in Davidson County, Tennessee and Newsome C.
Thompson of Bedford County be defendants to bill and pay for
rafts.

Page 548 - Nehemiah Sugg   ]
                vs   ]O. & Att. Bill, filed
          John Tilman, Lewis Tillman,]   March 22, 1850.
          William M. Brame & others]
Nehemiah Sugg of Bedford County filed against John Tillman,
Lewis Tillman, William M. Brame, Barkley M. Tillman, the presi-
dent and directors of the Branch of the Bank of Tennessee at
Shelbyville and Edmond Cooper and Robert Matthews, executors
of the Last Will and Testament of Erwin J. Frierson, deceased.
Thomas Lipscomb, James Mullins, Orville _____, admrs of Isaac
Muse, deceased. Price W. Steele, Thomas Greer, William Allison,
William Gosling, N. B. Cummings, Benjamin Brown, Thomas C.
Whiteside and William Galbreath, Trustees of Theo. F. Bradford,
Richard Warner, George Davidson, John S. Davis, John S. Frazier,
admr with the will annexed of William Guy, deceased. Drury
Brown, Butcher Sharpe, James L. Armstrong and Alex Eakin, John
Cowan and William Cowan, executors of John Eakin, deceased,
all of Bedford County and against Matt Martin executor of Matt
Martin, deceased of Davidson County, Tennessee and the President and Directors and Company of the Union Bank of Nashville,
Davidson County, Tennessee, against George Waite of Coffee
County, Tennessee and Minos Cannon who resides in the State
of Alabama. Orator states that on 13 March 1850, recovered
a judgement against the said John Tillman for several notes
on hogs. The hogs were drove south to market. John Tillman
is the father of Lewis Tillman and Barkley M. Tillman. They
had been in business of buying and selling hogs. The hogs
were from Bedford County and Rutherford County, Tennessee.

Page --- - William Pratt & wife   ]
                vs   ]O. Bill, 15 Aug 1851.
          G. W. Thompson & wife & others]
William Pratt and wife Catharine filed against George W. Thompson and wife, J. H. McGrew and wife Letitia, Samuel T. Cannon
and Jason T. Cannon, all of Bedford County. Orators stated
that Willis Cannon and wife Letitia Cannon who were the father
and mother of your complainants and defendants, executed in
the year _____, a Deed of Gift, in which they conveyed for love
and affection a tract of land on Duck River, on road leading
from Shelbyville to Winchester and Lynchburg and bounded by
lands of Robert Cannon, John Johnson, M. E. W. Dunaway, Morgan,
Reed, James Wortham and others. Also, negroes to be divided,
all children are now of age. Orators are desirous to obtain
their part of the land, they had already received their share
of the slaves. The land had two springs, the best tillable
land is on the northern part and is cleaned of the timber.
There is 75 acres in one tract and on this part there is no

water and not good land.

Page 599 - Samuel Doak &   ]
            Frederick Zollicoffer] Inj. Bill, filed
                  vs   ] 12 November 1853.
            Edmund W. Jennings   ]
Frederick Zollicoffer and Samuel Doak filed against Edmund
Jennings of Bedford County. Orators state that some years
ago they purchased of Edmund W. Jennings a negro boy Abram
for $500.00. He was bought to be sound in health but found
out he was unsound and weakness in the back as having a "large
boil" on his back. The boy continued to get worse and finally
he died.

Page 603 - Jordan C. Holt   ]
                  vs   ] Orig. Bill.
            Young Wilhoite &]
            Foster Dunaway   ]
Orator Jordan C. Holt of Bedford County stated that on the
3rd March 1845, he obtained a judgement in the name of Isaac B.
Holt for $79.89 and cost. Your orator and Drury M. Smith also
on the same day recovered a judgement in their partnership's
name of Holt & Smith, against Wilhoite for $9.50 and cost.
Orator stated that sometime ago Young Wilhoite purchased from
Grayson H. Stewart a lot or piece of land in Bedford County
and Village of Rowesville, with a house thereon, know as Lot
No. 15 in Rowesville. Situated on Main Street and bordered
by R. P. Sutliff and Main Street.

Page 607 - Joshua Woosley]
                  vs   ]Filed 7 March 1846.
            Saloma Cross]
Joshua Woosley of Bedford County stated that Asashel Cross
died some 14 years since, leaving a widow Saloma Cross, and
Elizabeth Snell, Levina, Julia, Robert, Caroline, Elizabeth,
Sarah, James, Stephen and Celia Rogers, Gincy Young, Nancy
Jamison, Spicy Robinson, Amy, James, Cynthia and Wiley Johnson,
Eliza Jane and William Cross, Cynthia Ann and James M. Cross,
his widow and heirs at law. Orator states that the widow and
heirs petitioned the court for the sale of a tract of land,
viz, in Bedford County on waters of Beech Creek, being about
100 acres, it being the lands of Asahel Cross bought of A.
Donaldson. Court ordered the land to be sold jubject to the
dower interest of the widow. Dower got her land and orator
states that she is wasting the use of the land. Timber is
cut, would injury the land. Widow sold some poplar trees or
logs to be split into rails and sold them to a man in the
neighborhood. Orator also states that Saloma Cross has in
her employ Paschal Brown who is cutting white oak and making
rails and hauling them to Brown's farm. Orator believes the
widow sold timber to Paschal Brown.
Answer of Saloma Cross: She stated that the land was sold to
Jesse Rogers. She said she sold timber to Brown because she
was old and infirm and had no other means of support for herself but by her own labor. She sold timber to buy corn to
make bread.

Page 612 - Jackson Nichols, admr of]
            Ambrose B. Covington   ] O. Bill, filed
                  vs   ] August 7, 1847.
            Eldridge Covington & others]
Jackson Nichols, admr of Ambrose B. Covington, filed against
Pinkney H. Thompson and wife Minerva, Solomon G. Reaves and

Catharine, Eldridge Covington, Christopher Covington, Jesse
Covington, and Luvice Covington, all of whom are of Bedford
County, the three latter are minors and whose guardian is
Luvicy Covington, Senr. Orator stated that Ambrose B. Covington of Bedford County, departed this life intestate a few
months since, leaving neither wife or children. The following
are the brothers and sisters of Ambrose B. Covington, Minerva
Thompson wife of Pinkney H. Thompson, Catharine Reaves wife
of Solomon G. Reeves, Eldridge Covington, Christopher Covington, Jesse Covington, and Luvicey Covington, the last three
were minors, whose guardian is their mother Luvicey Covington,
Senr. Orator was appointed admr of estate in Bedford County
on July Term 1847 and stated that there is insufficient property to pay the debts. At Ambrose B. Covington's death, he
owned 2 small tracts of land on waters of Weakley Creek in
District No. 11. Two shares allotted to Ambrose Covington
and to Solomon G. Reaves and wife, of the land of his father,
Jesse Covington, deceased, made by court in Bedford County
on December Term 1846, being Lots No. 5 and No. 7.

Page 614 - Daniel L. Barringer, Exr &c]
                    vs   ]Inj. Bill, filed
            F. F. Fonville, Minos Cannon] 9 December 1844.
            & E. Coleman   ]
Daniel L. Barringer who sues as next friend and Trustee of
Mary Ann Haley filed against Frederick F. Fonville, Minos
Cannon and E. Coleman. Orator stated that Henry Mooring, formerly of Wake County, North Carolina, departed this life more
than 20 years ago in Wake County, North Carolina, that before
his death he made and published his Last Will and Testament
and proven after his death and recorded in Wake County. Henry
Mooring loaned to his daughter Mary Ann Haley who is wife of
James H. Haley, for her natural life, certain negro slaves
and their increase, one girl named Carolina. Orator stated
that he and John Ligon were appointed executors shortly after
the death of Henry Mooring. John Ligon declined. The slaves
should not be sold by Mary Ann Haley's husband to pay his
debts. F. F. Fonville levied two executions, one in favor
of Minos Cannon for about $60.00 against James H. Haley and
Gabriel Knight and the other in favor of E. Coleman for $8.00
against Haley on a negro boy Rufus about 10 years old, a child
of Carolina. E. Coleman is a Rutherford County resident and
Minos Cannon is of Alabama.

Page 617 - Samuel Woodfin   ]
                    vs   ]Orig. Bill, filed
            Thomas Hale & others] March 8, 1844.
Samuel Woodfin filed against James McKine and Elizabeth his
wife, John Nailor and Sarah his wife, Andrew S. Edwards and
Mary his wife, Thomas Swan and Phoebe his wife, Thomas Hale
and Hannah his wife, Moses Woodfin and Rebecca Woodfin.
Orator states that sometime in 1831, he conveyed to his father
Nicholas Woodfin, a tract of land in Bedford County on head-
waters of North Fork of Duck River, bordered by Joel Dyer,
Stratam, Campbell, Nicholas Woodfin, Gilchrist's line. Orator
stated that at the time of conveyance, his father Nicholas
Woodfin was old and firm and a short time after departed this
life leaving your orator, Sarah Nailor wife of John Nailor
and Hannah Hail wife of Thomas Hail of Bedford County, Mary
Edwards wife of Andrew S. Edwards of Rutherford County, Tennessee, Phoebe Swann wife of Thomas Swann of Mississippi,
Elizabeth McKime wife of James McKime of Hickman County, Tennessee, Moses Woodfin of Gibson County, Tennessee, John Woodfin

of Fayette County, Tennessee and Rebecca Woodfin of Kentucky,
only heirs at law. Nicholas Woodfin made a Will and Testament,
he left his lands and other property to his widow (mother of
orator), for her life time. The estate cannot be placed until
after the death of his mother which has not happened as yet
(1844).

Page 623 - Jacob Wilhoite]
                   vs   ]O. Bill, filed 9 September 1845.
           Jordan C. Holt]
Orator Jacob Wilhoite stated that in 1842 he was owner of a
negro man Ned aged about 24 years and being in great need of
money, he sold Ned. Jordan C. Holt said he would take Ned
south and sell him. He executed agreement for Holt to sell
Ned and Holt took him to Alabama and sold for $700.00 or
$800.00. Since Holt returned, orator has tried to collect
his money from Holt.
Answer by Holt: Deed of Trust which Holt had executed to Mary
Wilhoite to secure her as his security on a note for $225.00
due in December 1842 to Polly Wilhoite. Holt sold Ned to
James M. Spencer of Green County, Alabama for $650.00.

Page 627 - James C. & Wiley B. Wallace]
                   vs   ]O. Bill, filed
          Thomas Wallace &   ]4 March 1848
          Thomas B. Moseley & others]
James C. Wallace and Wiley B. Wallace of Missouri stated that
about 1824, their grandfather Robert Wallace departed this
life intestate, leaving your orator's father Samuel Wallace,
John Thomas, Henry, James, Sallie, Margaret, Elizabeth, Nancy
and William Wallace, his children and only heirs at law and
also leaving a widow Elizabeth Wallace. At the time of his
death, he was owner of a tract of land in Bedford County, about
200 acres. Orators stated that the widow Elizabeth Wallace
had dower assigned to her out of said land and some 4 or 5
years since departed this life. Orators stated that after
the death of Robert Wallace, your orator's father Samuel Wallace, for a fair and valuable price, purchased the individed
interests of Thomas, Henry, James and Sallie Wallace, in said
tract of land and took bond, but which have not come to the
possession of your orators and after having fully paid the
consideration for said interests, and before Deed of Conveyance
was executed by the vendors, the said Samuel Wallace departed
this life intestate in Bedford County, leaving your orators,
his children and only heirs at law. At the time of Samuel
Wallace's death, was legal and equitable owner of five-tenth
or one-half of said tract, which descended to your orators
(they being very young). Orators said that after the death
of Samuel Wallace, the said Henry Wallace departed this life
intestate, leaving William and James Wallace, his only heirs
at law, who are minors and reside in Missouri and have no
regular guardian in this state. Also, after the death of
Samuel Wallace, Margaret Wallace departed this life intestate
and without issue and leaving your orators and the aforesaid
living children and heirs of Robert Wallace, her only heirs
at law. And at the time of her death she was the owner of
said tract of land, which descended to her from Robert Wallace
and orators states that Thomas B. Moseley is now in possession
of said land. He claimed to have had the land since 1829.
The land is one-half of a 380 acre tract conveyed by William
Peacock to Robert Wallace and other conveyed to John Cartmill,
being land on which said Moseley now resides and lies on the
waters of Wartrace Fork of Duck River. All persons previously

named and William Renwick who is now husband of Sallie Wallace,
and James Lambert who has married Elizabeth Wallace, all of
Missouri except the said Moseley, Nancy Wallace and James
Lambert who and his wife Elizabeth reside in Bedford County,
be made parties of bill.
Answer of Thomas B. Moseley: At this time, Thomas B. Moseley,
Jr. is living in Bedford County on the Wartrace Fork of Duck
River, bounded by William Waite's line, John W. Norville,
Wartrace Fork of Duck River, and top of ridge, E. A. Moseley
and Mrs. Merit's line. He purchased the land in 1846.
Answer of William J. Whitthorne, guardian of James and William
Wallace, to the Bill of Complaint of James C. and Wiley B.
Wallace.

Page 635 - Price C. Steele, admr & others]
                     vs   ]O. Bill, filed
            Lewis Tucker, William Tucker]22 January 1847.
Price C. Steele, admr and Sarah Warren, widow, and John H.
Williams and Joseph C. Warren, heirs of William Warren, deceased,
the three latter are minors who have no regular guardian, and
by their next friend Price C. Steele filed against William
Walker and David Searce(Searcy) of Bedford County and Lewis
Tucker and Jeptha Minter, executors of Nancy Maynard, deceased,
citizens of Rutherford County, Tennessee. Orator states that
April last, William Warren of Bedford County, departed this
life intestate, leaving your oratrix Sarah his widow, and your
orators John H. Williams and Joseph C. Warren, his only children and heirs at law. April 1846, Price C. Steele was appointed admr of estate. Warren's land was bought from ____ Tilford
and before Warren's death, sold 50 acres to David Searce(Searcy)
also about 70 acres to William Walker. Nancy Maynard is now
dead, she made her Last Will and Testament and was proven and
she appointed Lewis Tucker and Jeptha Minter her executors.
Answer of David Searce(Searcy); William Warren died in Bedford
County in April 1846, intestate.

Page 645 - Robert Harrison]
                  vs   ]Inj. Bill, filed 18 November 1843.
            James Mullins &]
            Isaac B. Holt]
Robert Harrison of Bedford County states that sometime last
winter he purchased a family of negroes from James Burton and
took his Bill of Sale. Burton purchased them from Jacob
Harrison. The sale took place in Alabama.

Page 651 - Alexander Allen]
                  vs   ]O. Bill, filed 22 February 1843.
            Solomon Brown]
Alexander Allen filed against Solomon Brown. Orator states
that about 1 November 1841, being in want of money, applied
to Solomon Brown, a money lender and shaver, for a loan of
$300.00 directly and indirectly for loan of $64.00 by selling
him a note on Anderson T. Clay for $80.00 which was made for
the purpose of raising money. Brown did loan him the money
in Bank Notes which then at a discount. Orator could not meet
all payments (monthly) and Brown required him to execute
another note in which the interest was up and due on demand.
In October 1842, Brown sued your orator for $144.00. Brown
wanted a Trust of Deed on negroes. All debts amounted to
$364.00.

Page 663 - Thomas Kimmons, admr.   ] O. Bill, filed
                    vs   ] May 25, 1847.
          Solomon Brown and wife & others]
Thomas Kimmons stated that his father Edward Kimmons departed
this life intestate in Bedford County in June 1845, he was
a citizen of Bedford County for several years. At July Term
1845, your orator was appointed admr of the estate. Edward
Kimmons left six children who are all his distributees, to
wit, Ellen Powell, Joshua Kimmons, Evaline Brown, Bartley
Kimmons, and William P. Kimmons, the last two are minors.
Eliza Powell was a daughter of Edward Kimmons and married
Milton Powell some years ago. Evaline Brown was also a daughter and married Solomon Brown. Milton Powell departed this
life some 18 months after Edward Kimmons, but before he recovered his wife's share of her father's estate to his possession except a negro girl and some household furniture, horse
and saddle and perhaps other articles ($600.00 value). Solomon
and wife were also advanced the same amount, the intestate
intending to make them equal. Orator said Edward Kimmons
advanced him money in 1836 ($1031.00) and executed bill to
said Kimmons for same on 11 January 1837. Orator stated that
$600.00 of that was intended by Kimmons as a gift to your
orator. Your orator had paid his debts off and had over paid
them and there is a credit on note of $380.09 for June 1837.
The credit was entered only a few days before his death and
in fact while he was on his death bed. Solomon Brown and wife
recently moved from this county for parts unknown. Eliza
Powell lives in Williamson County, Tennessee and other heirs
are all in Bedford County.

Page 668 - Peter R. Proby]
                    vs   ]Inj. Bill, filed September 3, 1844.
          John Huffman]
Peter R. Proby of Bedford County filed against John Huffman
of Coffee County, Tennessee. Orator stated that in October
or November 1842, he sold to John Huffman a tract of land in
Bedford County and executed a note for the land. Orator asked
$25.00 for the land, Huffman agreed to pay in cash notes. The
land to be turned over to Huffman when Huffman paid for the
land.

Page 677 - John Woodward]
                    vs   ]Inj. Bill, filed February 2, 1847.
          Zadock Motlow]
John Woodward of Bedford County states that about month of
April 1838, he stood in such need of money he called upon
Zadock Motlow of Lincoln County, Tennessee and borrowed $15.00.

Page 691 - Littleberry Green & others]
                    vs   ]O. Bill, 31 January 1852.
          Jesse Chockley   ]
Littleberry Green of Bedford County and a minor, who sues by
his next friend Isaac Green and Charles Lewis and his wife
Louisa formerly Louisa Burton citizens of Arkansas filed against
Jesse Chockley of Bedford County. Orator stated that Tabitha
Green departed this life intestate in Bedford County many years
ago being the owner in her own right of a tract of land located
in Shelbyville, known as Lot No. 74 and upon her death, descended to your orators and oratrixes, her only heirs at law.
David Green, who was the husband of Tabitha C. Green, was in
the possession of said lot after the death of Tabitha Green,
and while your orators were of tender age. By some means unknown to your orators, Jesse Chockley has obtained possession

of the Lot No. 74 and now claims to hold it as his own. Orator wish to sell said lot.

Page 693 - Amended Bill of Littleberry Green and others]
             vs   ]
        Jesse Chockley   ]
Filed 14 February 1853.

Page 699 - Sophia A. M. Snales(Scales)] O. Bill, filed
             vs   ] 16 October 1847.
        John Snales (Scales)   ]
Sophia A. M. Snales (Scales) of Bedford County files against John Snales (Scales). Sophia A. M. Snales of Bedford County for 5 years, she many years ago, she married John Snales and lived together a number of years. About 7 years ago she stated that her husband, John Snales, without cause, left her, that for some two or three years he wrote to her informing her of his position and prospects but for the last 5 years she has not heard from him at all. She does not now know where he resides. She had to support herself and children. Sophia states that she has two children from her marriage with John Scales, and who have been with her all the time. Children are, John A. Scales about 11 years, and Martha E. Scales about 7 years. Sophia states that she has in her possession as property of John Scales, three negroes, woman Mary Ann and two boys Archy and Lewis which negroes she received from her parents and they did not come from her husband, or any of his relations. She asks for a divorce.

Page 701 - John T. Neil   ]
        Petition for sale of land]Filed 28 August 1848.
        Warrant No. 14659   ]
John T. Neil states that J. L. Edwards, Commissioner of Pension for the Government of the United States of America, on 2nd day of May 1848, certified that a land warrant for 160 acres No. 14659, had been issued in the name of Maria Catharine Collins and Phillip Doss Collins, only surviving children and heirs at law of Henry H. Collins, deceased, late a Private in Captain Frierson's Company, 1st Regt. of Tennessee Vols, and would be deposited in the General Land Office at the Seat of Government. Petitioner states that previous to the issuance of said land warrant, to wit, on the 1st day of November 1847, he was duly appointed by the Bedford County Court, guardian of the estate of said Maria Catharine Collins and Phillip Doss Collins, that since the reception of said land warrant he had been offered the sum of $115.00, but not considering himself authorized to make a legal transfer of the warrant, he declined accepting the offer of the price, but he thinks, taking into consideration the great distance to any of the public lands upon which said warrant could be located and the expense and trouble in procuring the same to be done, it would be most for the interest of said wards to accept the price offered for said warrant. They desire that the land to be sold.

Page 703 - Malinda Goodwin   ]
             vs   ]Bill for Divorce, filed
        Washington P. Goodwin]   3 February 1849.
Malinda Goodwin of Bedford County states that on 26 February 1846, she married Washington P. Goodwin at the house of James Mason in the County of Coffee, Tennessee. Malinda and Washington P. Goodwin then being of Bedford County. The license was procured in Bedford County. Her husband took her to his home in Bedford County and then he soon began to mistreat her. She

said her husband has a violent temper and soon drove her away
from home and said he would never live with her again. This
all happened in a few months after the marriage. She had to
live about 12 to 15 miles from him but has never been to see
her.

Page 705 - Martha Allen & others]
            Petition for dower   ]
Martha Allen, Joseph Allen, Benjamin F. Allen, Martha J. Allen,
James T. Allen, and Andrew J. Allen and James Foster, states
that Hugh Allen departed this life intestate in Bedford County
some eighteen months ago, leaving Martha Allen his widow and
your other petitioners except James Foster as his heirs at
law. James Foster is admr of estate, qualified in ___ Term
1846. All of the heirs are minors and sue by their mother
and guardian Martha Allen. Hugh Allen died seized of tract
of land in Bedford County on which he lived at the time of
his death, on headwaters of Alexanders Creek, 93½ acres and
bounded by Thomas P. Wells, John Wood and Hight's line. Martha
has not yet been endowed of said tract of land, which is the
only land owned by Hugh Allen, deceased.

Page 707 - James L. Scudder   ]
               vs   ]Att. Bill, filed 4 November 1848.
          Joseph Greer,   ]
          Archibald J. Greer]
          & Carlos D. Steele]
James L. Scudder states that in the month of April 1838, he
was owner of a pony worth $30.00 or $40.00, and that he sold
the pony to Joseph C. Strong, but being a minor, the sale was
in the name of his then guardian James G. Whitney for $35.00.
Whitney got a note endorsed by Strong a bill single for $48.12½
on one Joseph Greer and due 1838 and endorsed by Strong on
4 April 1838. A few days later, Joseph Greer left this state
and went to Texas. Bill still due. Whitney departed this
life in 1840 and Carlos D. Steele of Bedford County is his
admr. Orator states that Thomas Greer a few days since departed this life in Bedford County having made his Last Will and
Testament in which he appointed executors, Archibald J. Greer,
Catharine Greer, both of Bedford County. By will of Joseph
Greer is entitled to a legacy of $300.00 or more.

Page 710 - William Vinson, admr]
               vs   ]O. Bill, filed August 13, 1847.
          Robinson & McCuistion]
William Vinson, admr of Travis C. Nash, deceased, that he recovered a judgement on 10 day April 1845 filed against Roger
Snell and John Robinson for $164.78 plus cost. "No property
found" by Sheriff. Orator stated that on 25 February 1845,
John Robinson executed a deed for $2500.00 as in deed, convey-
ing all his lands, negroes, and stock to one Claiborne McCuistion. McCuistion is the brother in law of said Robinson, a
young man and unmarried and has but little property except
that purchased of Robinson, some 8 or 10 miles from John
Robinson. Orator believes is a poor man and unable to purchase
much property and pay for it. Orator states that John Robinson
is in possession of all the property conveyed in deed which
has, sheep, stock, hogs, horses, negroes and 96 acres of land.
Robinson and McCuistion are citizens of Bedford County.

Page 714 - Washington Nash, & els]
                Exparte Petition for]Filed 28 February 1848.
                Sale of Land   ]
Washington, James C., Travis C., and Thomas Nash, Elizabeth
Johnson wife of Levi Johnson, Emily Garret wife of B. F. Garret,
Mary McGimpsey wife of John McGimpsey, Louiza Harville wife
of William M. Harville, Augustus Franklin, Grandison, Abner,
and Lafayette B. Nash, the last 5 are minors and petitioners
by their guardian L. B. Knott and James R. Nash son of John
Nash, deceased, who petition by his guardian James Venable.
Petitioners stated that William Nash departed this life intestate on 10 day of December 1847 at San Juan, Mexico, leaving
the petitioners, his brothers and sisters with the exception
of James R. Nash who is his nephew, his heir at law, he never
having been married and no children. He died seized of 2 small
tracts of land, one 23 acres and other 29½ acres in Bedford
County.

Page 714 - Charles D. Cooper]
                vs   ]Att. Bill, February 20, 1845.
            T. C. Nash & others]
Charles D. Cooper of Bedford County states that Travis C. Nash
and Benjamin Garrett executed to your orator for a valuable
consideration their joint note for $67.50 and is now due and
on 18 February 1845 your orator recovered a judgement against
Garrett for $67.66 plus cost. Orator states that just the
note was due, Travis C. Nash left the county with a drove of
horses and has not returned. Nash was to have been in Kentucky
where he intends to remain. Travis C. Nash is one of the heirs
of his father, T. C. Nash, deceased, who died in Bedford County
in 1844 leaving a large personal estate and William Vinson
of Rutherford County, Tennessee is admr of said estate, lands
in Bedford County on waters of Falling Creek and Murfreesboro
Road. One tract of land is in Lincoln County, Tennessee, about
70 acres, which land bought from Thomas L. Parks. Travis C.
Nash left his mother Joanna Nash.

Page 718 - John Chandler   ]
                vs   ]Orig. Bill, 21 January 1846.
            Samuel Watson & others]
John Chandler of Bedford County states that he is the owner
in fee of one-half a tract of land of 5 acres and a mill and
mill dam on Duck River, above Shelbyville formerly known as
Sim's Mills. The mills are very much our of repair and almost
worthless. The mills and land were sold about 2 years ago
as the property of John A. Ferguson and Uriah Cross as owners
of one part and William P. Sims and Walter Sims and wife Mary
E. as owners of the other part. Mills and land to be sold.
John A. Ferguson bid on same and became owner. He failed to
pay for it. It was bought by Samuel Watson. Proven August
Term 1845.

Page 721 - William Robinson]
                vs   ]Inj. Bill, filed March 3, 1846.
            Jo. Thompson &]
            Henry S. Frazier]
William Robinson of Madison County, Alabama filed against
Joseph Thompson of Bedford County and Henry S. Frazier of
Wilson County, Tennessee. Orator stated that on 22 October,
last (1845), he bought from James F. Snell and John S. Frazier
a negro man Nelson about 28 years for $600.00 of $550.00 which
he paid in hand and other $50.00 of which he paid in a few
days and took negro. He had to give the negro a pass to visit

Tennessee and see his wife owned by Hundley Wiggins of Bedford
County, when he was levied upon by Joseph Thompson, Deputy
Sheriff of Bedford County under an execution which purports
to have been issued from the last December Term of Circuit
Court of Bedford County in favor of Adam G. M----head and wife
Hannah who sue for the use of Henry S. Frazier against Roger
Snell. Orator stated that on 24 February 1845, Roger Snell
executed a Deed of Trust to James F. Snell and John S. Frazier
for a tract of land in Bedford County and negroes.

Page 724 - John Robinson   ]
                    vs   ]Inj. Bill, filed 6 April 1847.
              F. F. Fonville &]
              William McClure]
John Robinson of Bedford County states that at ___ Term 184_,
on petition of the heirs of James Moore, deceased, the Circuit
Court of said County decreed a certain tract of land to be
sold, which belonged to said heirs and that William McClure
became the purchaser of land and your orator became one of
his securities for the purchase money. He paid $175.50 or
more. Before bill was due, orator bought the said tract of
land.

Page 729 - Mary E. M. Bradford & others]
                    vs   ]O. Bill, 26 March 1850.
              William Gosling & others]
Barkley M. Bradford, Robert McCart and wife Caroline formerly
Caroline Bradford, Charles B. James, Lucy G. James (a minor
who having no regular guardian sues by her next friend William
F. Bradford), Theodrick F. Bradford, Jr., William F. Bradford,
and Mary E. M. Bradford, all citizens of Missouri states that
Theodrick F. Bradford, Sr., late of Bedford County, departed
this life intestate in Bedford County, leaving as his children
and heirs at law, Barkley M., Theodrick F., William F., and
Mary E. M. and Caroline who has since married Robert McCart,
and Rowena who has married Charles B. James and died in December 1846, her husband surviving and one child and heir at
law Lucy G. Frederick F. departed this life about 1st April
1840. Fredrick F. Bradford, Sr. in the month of April 1839
executed a pretended deed of all his property, real and personal to John Tillman of Bedford County.

Page 763 - Enoch D. Rushing]
                    vs   ] Filed 7 November 1845.
              Joseph H. Vannoy &]
              William Lyttle]
Enoch D. Rushing of Bedford County filed against Joseph H.
Vannoy and William Lyttle, the former of Mississippi and the
latter of Bedford County. Orator states that on 1st January
1840 he executed his note to the defendant Joseph Vannoy who
was then a citizen of Mississippi for $791.00. Vannoy had
owed your orator previously. Your orator wanted to take 2
negroes of Vannoy's which were worth much more that his bill.
Vannoy wanted to buy the negroes with a credit of 9 months
and let orator have them.

Page 776 - P. M. Jackson & wife Martha E.] O. Bill, filed
                    vs   ] July 16, 1846.
              Edwin B. Horde, Admr.   ]
P. M. Jackson and Martha E. his wife of Mississippi filed
against Edwin B. Horde, admr of estate of Permelia Campbell,
deceased. Orators stated that Abel W. Slayton departed this
life intestate in the year 1828 of Bedford County, he being

possessed of a large real and personal estate, leaving a widow
Permelia Slayton who has since died and your oratrix Martha R.,
his only heir and distributee. Also, stated that Edwin Horde
was appointed admr of estate of Abel W. Slayton in Bedford
County in 1828. He took into possession negroes Edmund Horde
afterwards on 5 December 1833 illegally transferred by deed
to Mrs. Permelia Slayton. She (Permelia) retained some of
the negroes. Permelia Slayton married William P. Campbell
who together with Permelia has since died and Edwin B. Horde
appointed admr of estate of Permelia and some of the negroes
are now with Edwin B. Horde. Martha E. stated that as only
heir, she is entitled to half of the negroes that Edwin B.
Horde has in his possession, which at this time Permelia is
a minor and that she has married P. M. Jackson.

Page 781 - Prior M. Jackson & wife]
                    vs   ]O. Bill, February 4, 1847.
          John G. Walker & others]
Prior M. Jackson and wife Martha E., citizens of Missouri filed
against John G. Walker of Coffee County, Tennessee, John Manning, Joseph Manning, Cloah Jane Manning, Martha A. P. Manning,
the last 4 are minors and have for their guardian John E.
Sharber all of whom are citizens of Rutherford County, Tennessee. Orators stated that Abel W. Slayton departed this life
intestate 7 August 1828, a citizen of Bedford County, leaving
a widow Permelia who has since died and one child, your oratrix
Martha E., his only distributee at and even now a minor and
having since married with your orator Prior M. Jackson who
sues in right of his wife. Abel W. Slayton owned a tract of
land in Bedford County, upon Noah's Fork of Duck River, bordering Noahs Fork, Dr. Norton, Samuel Bird and being about 50
acres also being the place where Abel W. Slayton resided.   A
short time after the death of Abel W. Slayton, a alias execution was issued from the Office of Pleas and Quarter Sessions
of Bedford County against James and Abel W. Slayton, which
execution was placed in the hands of one Kenneth L. Anderson,
Deputy Sheriff of Bedford County, on 24th day of September
1828, and which was levied upon tract of land above described
on the 26th September 1828 and by virtue of which alias execution said tract of land was sold to Andrew Erwin, Jr. on 8
November 1828 by Kenneth L. Anderson. Erwin later, 1828, sold
said land to Edmund Horde who sold land to Mark Manning on
6 February 1828. Mark Manning departed this life intestate
having owned land claiming it by deed from Edmund Horde, leaving above said heirs. Sometime in 1844, the heirs at law of
Mark Manning, being at the time minors, petitioned by their
guardian John E. Sharber of Bedford County. John G. Walker
bought said land 7 day February 1845.

Page 796 - William H. Wisener]
                    vs   ]Att. Bill, filed
          Joseph Greer,   ] 6 November 1848.
          Leonard C. Temple,   ]
          Archibald J. Greer &]
          Catharine Greer   ]
William H. Wisener of Bedford County stated that sometime about
the last of December 1837 or 1st January 1838, he and Joseph
Greer jointly stayed a judgement of Leonard C. Temple in favor
of Samuel Escue as his executor.

Page 1 -   James C. Gambill & others] O. & Inj. Bill, filed
                        vs   ]   2 October 1858.
            John C. Hix & others   ]
James C. Gambill and wife Patty, D. D. Hix and wife Malinda,
William Hix, Joshua Hix, John E. Frost and wife Ailsey, William
J. Gordon and wife Louisa, M. E. W. Dunnaway and wife Martha,
William Reager and wife Frances, John Hix, Elizabeth Hix, <u>blank</u>
Stanfield a minor, only child of Lucinda Stanfield, deceased,
who sues by her next friend and father Thomas J. Stanfield,
and Jemima Gurley filed against Moore Smiley and wife Lucinda,
John C. Hix, James L. Hix, J. H. M. Holt and wife Malinda and
Martha Hix a minor having no guardian, all of Bedford County,
John Stewart of Texas and William Stewart of Missouri. Orators
states that Margaret Stewart departed this life in Bedford
County in March 1858, leaving her are, Patty wife of your
orator, James C. Gambill, Malinda wife of D. D. Hix, Lucinda
wife of Moore Smiley, Jemima Gurley, John Stewart, William
Stewart, and Ellender Hix wife of John C. Hix who has departed
this life since her mother Margaret Stewart leaving her as
her children. Her husband wife of H. J. M. Holt and Martha
Hix, and that at the time of her death she was a very old lady,
feeble in body and mentally incapable of attending to her
business. Orators states several years before her death when
Margaret Stewart was of sound mind, that on __ day of May 1853,
she made and published her Last Will and Testament and was
admitted to probate in ___ Term 1858, when Moore Smiley appeared in behalf of his Luc<u>inda</u> and contested said will. It was
found in favor of your orator as executor. Margaret Stewart
owned a tract of land in District No. 18 of Bedford County.
Land bounded by James C. Gambill and James Stallings, about
67 acres and slaves. Margaret Stewart had lived with your
orator James C. Gambill about 3 years before her death. Orator
stated that she was induced by her son in law John C. Hix and
Moore Smiley to go stay with them for a while. They wanted
her to stay with them. She expressed a desire to return to
James C. Gambill and wife, because they were so kind and took
care of her. She was induced on 9 June 1857 to convey by Deed
of Gift to Lucinda Smiley, a negro girl and on 10 September
1857 to sell a tract of land which she was owner in District
No. 18, adjoining lands of James C. Gambill and James Stalling
and others to Goodrum Davis on 17 February 1858 by Deed of
Gift she conveyed to James L. Hix in trust for the benefit
of his mother Ellender Hix, during her life and at her death
to her children. Ellender Hix wife of John C. Hix, the girl
Hannah. Ellender His is dead, negro girl Hannah to be sold.
The sale of land to Goodrum Davis was voided and charged rent.

Page 8 -   James C. Gambill]
                        vs   ]Inj. Bill, filed 26 November 1856.
            James E. Newton]
James C. Gambill stated that James E. Newton held on your orat-
or for about $600.00.

Page 11 -   Mary J. Norville]
                        vs   ]Bill for divorce, August 18, 1858.
            James Norville]
Mary J. Norville states that on 10 November 1854, she married
James Norville, both of Bedford County. They lived together
for nearly 3 years. For the last 12 months, he had mistreated
her. She desires to have her maiden name restored. James

Norville has a child by his first wife and four dead children.
Her father and mother lived in the neighborhood of Wartrace
Depot. They visited them by "cars". She had a brother.

Page 15 - Joel E. Criscoe   ]
               vs   ]O. Bill, 14 February 1857.
          Presley Prince et als]
Joel E. Criscoe of Bedford County filed against Presley Prince
and wife Mary in their right and Presley Prince as admr of
Daniel Criscoe, deceased, John Pecks and wife Sophia of Bedford
County, Moses Prince and wife Sallie of Wayne County, Tennessee,
John Criscoe a non-resident of Tennessee and unknown, William
Criscoe of Mississippi, James Massey and wife Betsy of Missouri, Washington Criscoe, Sophia, Martha and William Criscoe,
widow and heirs at law of Jordan Criscoe, deceased, citizens
of Mississippi. Orator states that his father Daniel Criscoe
departed this life in August 1852, intestate, seized with both
real and personal property. Presley Prince in ___ Term 1852
made admr of his estate. He sold all property of Daniel
Criscoe and settled all debts &c 9 February 1855 and had
$2991.46 left. Orator stated that all the children, except
your orator, received personal property before their father's
death. Your orator left home at an early age, unmarried and
did not return until after the death of his father. Daniel
Criscoe died leaving his widow Sophia, who has since married
John Pecks and the following heirs at law, Mary Prince formerly
Mary Criscoe, John, William, Washington, David, and Joseph E.
Criscoe, Betsy Massey formerly Betsy Criscoe, Sallie Prince
formerly Sallie Criscoe, and Mary Criscoe and her three children, Sophia, Martha and William Criscoe, widow and jeir at
law of Jordan Criscoe, deceased, and who died since his father.
Presley Prince admr of estate.

Page 20 - Margaret A. Criscoe   ]
               vs   ]Att. Bill, 25 May 1859.
          Joel E. Criscoe & others]
Margaret Criscoe of Bedford County filed against Joel E.
Criscoe and Middleton Holland and Sam H. Whitthorne, Trustee &c,
the first of whom resides in Davidson County, Tennessee and
other two of Bedford County. Margaret Ann Criscoe states that
in the year 1848 or 9, she married Joel E. Criscoe and lived
with him until in the year 1857. She stated that her husband
was convicted of Grand Larceny and sentenced to 5 years in
prison in State Penitentiary and is now serving his time there.
She said her husband left her with one child, a daughter about
8 or 9 years and no support. She said her husband got rid
of their property but he also held interest in the dower lands
of his mother.

Page 23 - Willis W. Wilhoite   ]
               vs   ]Bill filed 21 August 1858.
          R. F. Arnold & others]
Willis W. Wilhoite filed against Robert F. Arnold and Joseph K.
Ewell. Orator states that in January 1856, Joseph K. Ewell
was owner of a tract of land in Civil District No. 25 of Bedford County, on the Barren Fork of Duck River. Bounded by
Duck River, I. L. Ayers, Three Forks Camp Ground and lands
of Sarah Cobb(Coble), and Daniel Hooser, about 122 acres. On
22 January 1856, Joseph K. Ewell sold tract of land to Robert
F. Arnold.

Page 24 - John W. Mayfield   ]
               vs   ]Inj. Bill, 19 August 1857.
          John L. Rainey & others]
John W. Mayfield filed against John L. Rainey and Martha F.
Rainey, non-residents of Tennessee and reside in Missouri.
J. W. Mayfield states that ____ Term of Court, he was appointed
guardian of Martha F. Smith who has since married with John L.
Rainey.

Page 28 - L. H. Turner   ]
               vs   ]O. Bill, filed 8 February 1859.
          Eliza R. Turner]
L. H. Turner of Bedford County states that he has been a resid-
ent of this state more than 2 years prior to filing this bill.
On 4 July 1847, he married Eliza R. Smith in Bedford County.
He lived with her until sometime in 1852 until he left her.
She gave birth to a girl child 2 years after said marriage,
which is now 10 years old and with her mother. He says the
child is his and desires custody of her. Daughter named Mary
Jane Turner. They had another daughter which was born dead.

Page 31 - John W. Mayfield]
               vs   ]Inj. Bill, 12 December 1855.
          John M. Warner &]
          Samuel J. Warner]
Orator states that he recovered a judgement against Samuel J.
Warner on 18 January 1855 for $301.16 plus cost.

Page 33 - Eunice M. Rutledge   ]
               vs   ]O. Bill, 12 August 1858.
          John W. Rutledge & others]
Eunice M. Rutledge wife of John W. Rutledge, William Brown,
Thomas Thompson, Lee Williams and Thomas Lipscomb, all of Bedford County, by Jacob R. Wilhoite, her next friend, states
that her father John Warner of Bedford County departed this
life on 17 May 1834 in Bedford County, leaving his Last Will
and Testament and 8 children. Will was made 25 April 1834.
Will: 6th Item - "It is my will after each legatees receiving
the portion heretofore devised to them in this will and at
the death of my beloved wife or impure age that all the balance
of my property be equally divided both real and personal between my 8 children, to wit, Huldah Brinson Wilhoite, Anna
Adaline Wilhoite, William Dickson Warner, Richard Jackson
Warner, Samuel Josiah Warner, John M. Warner, Van Buren Warner,
and Eunice M. Warner." Richard and Eunice Warner, executors.
Some of the legatees were minors. 250 acres of 557 acres were
sold. John M. Warner one of the legatees became purchaser
for $5000.00. On 31 August 1845, Van Buren Warner, a legatee,
departed this life, leaving no lineal descendants or issue.

Page 46 - James M. Johnson   ]
               vs   ]Inj. Bill, August 24, 1859.
          Eli H. Stephens & others]
James M. Johnson filed against Eli H. Stephens, S. M. L.
Stevens and Martha A. Stevens, all of Bedford County. Orator
states that on 23 December 1857 he recovered a judgement against Eli H. Stephens for $824.37 plus cost and others. Judge-
ment referred to in the former part of this bill paid by S. K.
Bates as security. Eli H. Stephens sold his land (371 acres)
in Bedford County on waters of Powell Creek, adjoining lands
of R. H. Sims. Eli H. Stephens nad a brother J. M. L. Stephens
and mother Martha A. Stephens. 27th October 1855, J. M. L.
Stephens bought his brother's interest in his co-partners land

Page 55 -   J. A. Blakemore]
                    vs   ]Filed 28 November 1856.
             S. Doak & others]
John A. Blakemore of Bedford County filed against Sampson
Liggett and Joshua Hudson of Marshall County, Tennessee and
William H. Wisener, John P. Steele, Carlos D. Steele and
Samuel Doak a tract of land in Civil District No. 7 of Bedford
County, bounded by Robert Cannon, Robert Cowan, J. L. Burt
and T. W. Jordan. About 13 acres. (Bought about 1 year ago,
1855).

Page 65 -   John M. Keller & others   ]
                    vs   ]Filed 4 December 1858.
             Robert H. Stephens & others]
John M. Keller, J. W. C. Keller, Malinda Thomas wife of _____
Thomas, B. C. T. Keller, Benjamin H. Keller, Sarah L. Ayers
wife of Calvin Ayers, Eliza J. Roberts wife of ____ Roberts,
Sophia A. Parker wife of _____ Parker, N. I. C. Keller and
James M. Keller filed against Robert H. Stephens, Thomas A.
Stephens, Benjamin Stephens, Joseph K. Keller, Nancy K. Keller,
Martha Ann Keller, Jane Keller and Sarah E. Keller, (only
children). Orator stated that in August 1840, Joseph Keller
made his Last Will and Testament and shortly thereafter de-
parted this life in Bedford County, and at ___ Term 1840, he
left his widow Ann Keller and Francis Keller appointed executor.
Joseph Keller at time of his death was owner of a tract of
land in Bedford County, _____ acres. Bounded by Joseph Couch,
James Finch and John Cothran, William Pepper and Asa Thomas,
Francis Keller's heirs. Tract in Civil District No. 2, on
waters of Garrison Fork of Duck River. The land was devised
to his widow Ann Keller for life, and at her death to be sold.
T.(Thomas) A. Keller who is now dead and left debts. Children
of Joseph Keller, to wit, John M. Keller, J. W. C. Keller,
Malinda Thomas, B. C. T. Keller, Benjamin H. Keller, Sarah L.
Ayers, Eliza J. Roberts, Sophia A. Parker, N. J. C. Keller,
James M. Keller, T. A. Keller who is now dead and left debts,
Joseph K. Keller, Nancy K. Keller, Martha Ann Keller, Jane
Keller, and Sarah Keller, his only children who are all minors
and reside in Missouri, and Elizabeth E. Stephens who is also
dead and left as her children, to wit, Robert H., Thomas A.,
Benjamin, Reuben and Prewett Stephens, all are minors and re-
side in Bedford County. Orator states that the executors Ann
Keller and Francis Keller are both dead.

Page 67 -   B. F. Wiggins]
                    vs   ]Inj. Bill, filed 28 March 1857.
             James A. Gant]
Benjamin F. Wiggins of Bedford County states that on 20 May
1854 James A. Gant recovered two judgements against Herod F.
Holt. Herod F. Holt and your orator for sum $409.39 plus cost,
executed by two holts on 14 February 1853.

Page 71 -   Edmund Cooper]
                    vs   ]O. Bill, filed February 28, 1859.
             Eli G. Fleming]
Edmund Cooper of Bedford County states that sometime ago, he
sold to Eli G. Fleming a tract of land on south side of the
Garrison Fork of Duck River, being a part of the Martin farm
known as "Maxwell Place". Adjoining lands of Thomas Moseley
and others. About 220 acres. First note due 1st January 1859.

Page 72 - Lyons & Co.   ]
                vs   ]Inj. Bill, filed 17 February 1858.
           Russ & House]
Benjamin and Jacob Lyons, partners, filed against James Russ,
Jr. and T. B. A. J. House, partners, all of Bedford County.
Orators stated that James Russ, Jr. and T. B. A. J. House,
partners in retail grocery business in Shelbyville and indebt-
ed to your orator for $293.30. Russ made a Deed of Trust to
G. W. Davidson of all their stock of groceries consisting of
Brandy, Whiskey, Wine Glassware &c.

Page 77 - H. S. Blakemore   ]
                vs   ]Inj. Bill, 30 November 1858.
           J. A. Blakemore & others]
Henry S. Blakemore states that a judgement rendered in favor
of Robert Mathews for about $764.46 and cost filed against
George F. Blakemore , your orator, J. A. Blakemore and R. P. S.
Kimbro in last August Term of Court. Henry S. Blakemore re-
sides in Lincoln County, Tennessee, was temporarily in Bedford
County when the process was served on him.

Page 81 - James J. Tolbert]
                vs   ] Divorce Bill, 17 August 1858.
           Susan Tolbert   ]
James J. Tolbert of Bedford County filed against Susan Tolbert
of Bedford County states that on __ day of ___ 1856, he married
Susan Weaver in Bedford County where he has lived all her life
and James J. Tolbert has resided for 1 year. They lived together for about 5 weeks and Susan deserted him. She had been
gone for 2 years.

Page 82 - Susan Weaver Tolbert]
                vs   ] Filed August 20, 1858.
           James Jordan Tolbert]
Susan Weaver Tolbert filed against James J. Tolbert, a citizen
of Cannon County, Tennessee. Susan states that on 16 April
1856 she married James Jordan Tolbert, both of Bedford County.
About 3 weeks after marriage, she was attacked with typhoid
fever and her husband deserted her, leaving her on what she
thought her death bed and she had to go to her father's house.

Page 83 - Coldwell & Cummings   ]
                vs   ]Filed 9 August 1857.
           Samuel A. Slaughter & others]
Thomas M. Coldwell and James F. Cummings states that they came
before Thomas R. Wynn, a J.P. of Lincoln County, Tennessee
filed against Samuel A. Slaughter and Company for $450.82.

Page 85 - Rose C. Powell]
                vs   ]O. Bill, filed 4 July 1859.
           Henry Powell]
Rose C. Powell of Bedford County states that on 7th December
1854, she married Henry Powell in Bedford County. After about
6 weeks, her husband left her and has gone to parts unknown.

Page 86 - John F. Neil & others]
                vs   ]Bill filed 13 December 1858.
           Jas. A. Gant   ]
John F. Neil, John T. Neil and James H. Neil filed against
James A. Gant. Orator states that on 15 March 1858 James A.
Gant recovered a judgement against your orator John F. Neil
and John T. Neil for two (1) for sum of $482.62, (2) $134.97
and cost.

Page 87 -   Ebenezer Wilson   ]
                    vs   ] Filed December 28, 1858.
            James Saunders & others]
Ebenezer Wilson of Bedford County filed against James Saunders
and Robert Terry. Orator states that on 25 December 1855,
he recovered two judgements against James Saunders of Bedford
County. James Saunders owned about 10 acres in Bedford County
on Fall Creek and adjoining your orator. Samuel Bomar and
Isreal Harris on which said Saunders still lives, land sold
and bid off in August 1856.

Page 92 - Mary E. Rutledge & others]
                    vs   ]O. Bill, 24 March 1858.
            Mailton Johnson & others]
Mary E. Rutledge who sues by her next friend Anna A. Robinson
and Richard B. Wilhoite, Narcissa E. Wilhoite and Huldah B.
Wilhoite, the two last being minors and sues by their next
friend Richard B. Wilhoite. Thomas Warner a minor sues by
his guardian Richard Warner. States that John Warner of Bedford County made and published his Last Will and Testament
and shortly died thereafter, to wit, April 1834. By his will
he devised and bequeathed his whole estate to his widow for
and during her natural life or widowhood and at her death or
marriage, his property was to be equally divided among his
eight children naming them each one of them, taking into consideration what he had given them and what, they were to receive of his estate at their majority. That among other real
estate, he was the owner of a tract of land or Town Lot in
the Town of Shelbyville, known in the plan of said town as
No. 72 and bounded by Watson Street, Lane Street, Lot No. 65
and by an alley. By the provision of said will, his widow
Eunice Warner had an estate in said lot during her life or
widowhood. That upon an exparte applications of the persons
in remainder and said Eunice Warner a decree of the Circuit
Court of Bedford County at its August (Term) 1852. A decree
was pronounced ordering and decreeing the same to be sold for
partition the said Eunice having relinquished her interest
in the same to her children and grandchildren, representing
their deceased parents. Your oratrix Mary E. Rutledge was
then not only a feme covert, but a minor. That she and her
husband joined in said petition, on it face, that she in fact
however knew nothing of it until after it was done.
     John H. Warner owned the interest of your oratrix (who
was a daughter of said John Warner, deceased) by deed. Richard
B. Wilhoite, Narcissa E. Wilhoite and Huldah B. Wilhoite are
children of Huldah B. Wilhoite, deceased, who was a daughter
of said John Warner, deceased. At the death of their mother,
she left another child died before the pretended sale of said
lot. Richard B., Narcissa E., and Hulda B., as heirs of their
mother and said minor represent their mother's share in said
lot. John Warner left eight children, two of whom ded in their
majority, unmarried and childless.

Page 97 - J. N. Blanton   ] O. & Inj. Bill, filed
                    vs   ]   October 2, 1858.
            Thos. H. Hutson & others]
J. N. Blanton of Bedford County filed against Thomas H. Hutson
and wife Mary who reside in Marshall County, Tennessee, James
A. Heazlitt of Fayette County, Tennessee, James T. Snoddy and
wife Julia Ann, John R. Heazlitt a minor who has Thomas H.
Hutson for his guardian, Emily Heazlitt a minor who has Louisa
(?) Heazlitt for her guardian, and M. V. Heazlitt who has for
his guardian James T. Snoddy, all of Bedford County and William

Heazlitt of Lincoln County, Tennessee. Orator states that some years ago, the lands belonging to the heirs at law of William Heazlitt, deceased, was sold on 25 February 1852. Heirs are William Heazlitt, John Heazlitt, Emily Heazlitt and M. V. Heazlitt and his widow Levina Heazlitt. Samuel Bobo purchased the said land or Lot No. 2, bounded by East Fork of Flat Creek, widow Heazlitt's dower, school land, and the Lynchburg Road. Later Samuel Bobo sold to M. E. W. Dunnaway who sold to Thomas Hutson.

Page 104 - Johnathan E. Prosser   ]
              vs   ]Inj, Bill, filed
          Moore Smiley & Ledbetter]   8 December 1857.
          & Brewer   ]
Johnathan E. Prosser filed against Moore Smiley, J. M. Led-better and J. R. Brewer, the last of whom reside in Lincoln County, Tennessee and the others in Bedford County. Orator states he has now pending an action of Ejection against Moore Smiley, to recover a small tract of land upon which Moore Smiley is now residing in Bedford County, adjoining lands of your orator and Hillsman Bledsoe, Nathan Evans and R. D. Williams, about 2 acres.

Page 108 - W. Morton   ]
              vs   ]O. Bill, 31 July 1858.
          W. J. W. Wakefield]
William Morton filed against W. J. W. Wakefield and John Morton, all of Bedford County. Orator states that he jointly with John Morton purchased from Griffith Randal a tract of land in Bedford County, District No. 19, about 114 acres, now in possession of Winston J. W. Wakefield as the executor of Griffith Randal, deceased.

Page 112 - Jesse Phillips]
              vs   ]Inj. Bill, filed 28 September 1857.
          Sam & F. Morris]
Jesse Phillips filed against Samuel Morris, Franklin M. Morris, all of Bedford County. Jesse Phillips states that he was the owner in February last of a small tract of land in Bedford County, in District No. 22, about 50 acres and bounded by Francis Wells, William Phillips, Samuel and Frank Morris, also he is now upwards of 83 years old, very feeble in body and mind and has been for several years, his wife is still living.

Page 117 - Mary E. Hutson]
              vs   ]Divorce, filed February 1859.
          Gabriel Hutson]
Mary E. Hutson states that in the year 185_, she married Gabriel Hutson. She said that the last 12 or 18 months has been terrible. In August 1858, she said her husband took her to her father and left her.

Page 118 - John W. White et al]
              vs   ]O. Bill, filed 13 February 1858.
          F. B. Norville   ]
John W. White and wife Margaret E. White, David L. Norville, Mary Norville, John D. Norville, William Norville, James G. Norville, Louisa Norville and Samuel Norville, the last seven are minors and their guardian is Jno. W. White, filed against Felix B. Norville, residence unknown. John Robinson, long of Bedford County died in Bedford County in the month of August 1850, having made his Last Will and Testament and your orator was appointed executor. John Robinson left his widow Mary

Robinson, who is now about 3 years deceased, and his children, to wit, an "idiot" son named Mathew Franklin, Margaret E. White and Martha C. Norville. These are the sole heirs. Martha C. Norvill died in April 1855 intestate, leaving the 7 minors (previously named in caption), her children and her Felix B. Norville who has absconded her husband her only distributees. John Robinson's will directed that the place on which he resided at the time of his death, should be sold and purchase another tract of land after paying all debts. The place to be bought was devised to your oratrix Margaret E. White wife of Jno. W. White and her sister Martha C. Norvill the other daughter of the testator and mother of the infant and of the support of the idiot Mathew Franklin.

Page 121 - Jno. W. White et als   ]
                vs   ]Amended bill, Aug 18, 1858.
             David L. Norvill et als]
Amended Bill of Jno. W. White and wife Margaret E. of Bedford County filed against Joseph H. Thompson guardian Mathew Franklin Robinson, an idiot, and against David L. Norvill, Mary Norvill, John D. Norvill, William Norvill, James G. Norvill, Louisa Norvill, and Samuel Norvill, these 7 minors under Joseph H. Thompson as guardian. Orator states that 13 February 1858, that they under the will of John Robinson, deceased, tenants of a tract of land in Bedford County together with the minors.

Page 123 - The Shelbyville and   ]
             Fayetteville Turnpike Co.]
                vs   ]Inj. Bill, filed
             The County Court of   ] 2 November 1857.
             Bedford County &   ]
             W. C. Reed   ]
Orators were given the privilege to build a Turnpike Road, leading from Shelbyville, Bedford County to Fayetteville, Lincoln County, Tennessee, to erect Toll Gates and collect rates. One erected about 2 miles of Shelbyville, one Turnpike Gate located near Robert Cannon and the lands of the devices of the late Erwin J. Frierson. At time gate was erected, there were no public road. Other gates were at Shelbyville-Farmington and Lewisburg Turnpike Road.

Page 127 - Robert F. Arnold   ]
                vs   ]Inj. Bill, 30 November 1857.
             J. K. Ewell & others]
Orator states that on 22 January 1856, he purchased from Joseph K. Ewell, a tract of land. About 104 acres.

Page 135 - Thomas J. Williams]
                vs   ]O. Bill, 16 June 1856.
             Martin Thompson]
Orator Thomas J. Williams of Bedford County filed against Martin Thompson in his own right and as the admr of Phillip J. Thompson, deceased, also of Bedford County. Orator states that about March 1854, he formed a partnership in the Grocery business with Phillip J. Thompson and Martin Thompson, forming a Grocery business in the Town of Richmond. On about 1 January 1855, the firm was dissolved. Martin Thompson continued the business.

Page 140 - John P. Steele of Bedford County said that on 11 March 1855 he sold 3½ acres of land to C. A. Robinson of Lincoln County, Tennessee.

Page 141 - White & Jordan   ]
                vs   ]Filed 24 August 1859.
           H. N. Hutton et als]
R. C. White and T. W. Jordan, partners &c under firm and style
of "White & Hordan & Allison", Anderson & Co., merchants of
Nashville and others against H. A. Hutton, George D. Hutton,
Priscilla Hutton, and infant child of H. N. and Priscilla
Hutton, whose name is nellie Hutton, all of Bedford County.
Orators states that they are judgement Creditors of H. N.
Hutton.

Page 146 - Henry Arnold   ]
                vs   ] O. Bill, filed 15 March 1858.
           L. A. Wynn &   ]
           wife Martha A. Wynn]
Orator sold last fall, a tract of land about 72 acres, bounded
by Burrel Ward (District No. 10), and Joseph Haynes.

Page 148 - Willis Cannon & others   ]
                vs   ]O. Bill, 25 July 1859.
           W. J. Whitthorne & others]
Orators and oratrixes, Willis Cannon and Euphany Wolfe, Joshua
Holding, Cynthia Holding, William Wolfe, John Addison, Eliza-
beth Addison, William Morris, J. M. Wolfe, Mary Morris,
William Handy, David S. McGaukey, Augustus C. Handy, James T.
Reid, William Blevin and Elizabeth Blevin filed against
William J. Whittorne of Bedford County, Augustus Cannon of
Lincoln County, Tennessee, Henry Miller, John D. Miller, Ann
Miller, James Davis, Anna Davis, David Miller, Minos Miller,
Samuel A. King, Nancy King, Scott Miller, Mary J. Miller, Minos
H. Miller, John Morris, Mary Morris, William Morris, and Mary
Morris. Orators states that Minos Cannon departed this life
testate in Madison County, Alabama, having made and published
his Last Will and Testament, proven and recorded in Bedford
County, and William J. Whitthorne appointed admr. One of the
chief devises Henrietta Handy died, other legatees of Minos
Cannon, to wit, William Handy, David S. McGaukey, Amelia C.
McGaukey, Augustus C. Handy, James T. Reid, William Blevins
and Elizabeth Blevins, the only children and heirs at law of
Henrietta Handy. Orators, the children of Euphany Wolfe
desires to do same. Minos Cannon, Sr. estate lying in Bedford
County.

Page 150 - S. N. White   ]
                vs   ]Filed 28 November 1857.
           J. A. Blakemore & others]
Stephen N. White said that Randolph Newsom filed against J. A.
Blakemore, W. W. Gill, Samuel Doak, C. G. Mitchell, John H.
Oneal, R. M. Whitman, and W. M. McKinney. Orator stating that
among other things that a company was formed under an Act of
Assembly, composed of all of said parties except your orator
for the purpose of slaughtering hogs and packing pork. The
business name "The Shelbyville Pork Packing Company". And
that Oneal sold out and that your orator had become a member
of the company by purchase of the interest of Jacob F. Thompson
who had purchased from said Oneal. Newsom was president of
said company.

Page 158 - B. F. Duggan, Exr &c]
                vs   ]Bill, filed July 5, 1858.
           Mary Cheatham   ]
B. F. Duggan of Bedford County states that Thomas Cheatham
lately departed this life, having made and published his Last

Will and Testament of which he appointed your orator as executor. By the will, he devised the tract of land on which
he resides and afterwards and before his death he sold said
tract of land. He also purchased other real estate, to wit,
a house and lot in Town of Shelbyville, of John H. Oneal and
also a tract of land in Bedford County on which he resided
at the time of his death the execution of his will and before
his death. By will, neither said tract of land or house and
lot was disposed of, no clause in will of disposing of his
real estate he might own at his death. He gave the Gentry's
heirs, slaves. Thomas Cheatham left no children and his heirs
and distributees are his brothers and sisters and his representatives of such as are dead and the Gentry heirs are devises
as well as others, to wit, Letitia Perry, Samuel Gentry, James
Garrett, Thomas C. Garrett, Nancy L. Garrett, William Garrett,
and Robert Garrett, the last six being minors and have for
their guardian Presley Jones, all of Bedford County, William
McCurdy and wife Elizabeth of Grand County, Missouri, Gibson
Dawdy and wife Nancy of Calaway County, Kentucky, Mary Stanfield of Maury County, Tennessee, James Gillespie and wife
Sarah of Benton County, Tennessee, Robert Taylor and wife
Phoeby of Weakley County, Tennessee, John Gillespie and wife
Permelia, and Phoeby Matilda Taylor, a minor and her guardian
is Vincent Taylor of Rutherford County, Tennessee, John Crawford and wife Diadama, and Tina Long of Pontotoc County, Miss-
issippi, William C. Cople, _____ Cople, _____ Cople, and _____
Cople, only children of Cynthia Cople, deceased, of parts
unknown to your orator, and Fanny E. Duty, Martin A. Gentry,
Letitia Smith, Nancy Gentry, Samuel J. Gentry, Wiley P. Gentry
and Mary Gentry, only children of John R. Gentry, deceased,
who resides in Randolph County, Arkansas, and Mary Cheatham,
the last being the widow of said Thomas Cheatham.
Answer of Thomas S. Steele, guardian, filed March 12, 1859:
The answer of Thomas C. Garrett, Nancy L. Garrett, William
Garrett and Robert Garrett, minor children of Dorrington
Garrett and wife Nancy Garrett, deceased.

Page 162 - Mary Cheatham   ]
               vs   ]Filed 15 February 1858.
          B. F. Duggan, Exr & others]
Mary Cheatham of Bedford County filed against B. F. Duggan,
Letitia Perry, Samuel Gentry, James Garrett, Phanny C. Garrett,
Thomas C. Garrett, Nancy L. Garrett, William Garrett, and
Robert Garrett, the last six being minors and as their guardian
Presley Jones, Jno. H. Oneal and J. H. McGrew and all of Bed-
ford County. William McCurdy and wife Elizabeth of Grand
County, Missouri, Gibson Dawdy and wife Nancy of Calaway County,
Kentucky, Mary Stanfield of Maury County, Tennessee, James
Gillespie and wife Sarah of Benton County, Tennessee, Robert
Taylor and wife Phoebe of Weakley County, Tennessee, John
Gillespie and wife Permelia, and Phoebe Matilda Taylor a minor,
having as guardian Vincent Taylor of Rutherford County, Tenn-
essee, John Crawford and wife Didame, and Sinai Long of Pontotoc
County, Mississippi, William C. Cople, _____ Cople, _____ Cople,
and _____ Cople, only children of Cynthia Cople, deceased,
of parts unknown to your oratrix and Fanny E. Duty, Martin A.
Gentry, Letitia Smith, Nancy Gentry, Samuel J. Gentry, Wiley
P. Gentry, and Mary G., only children of John R. Gentry,
deceased, of Randolph County, Arkansas. Mary Cheatham stated
that her husband Thomas Cheatham departed this life __ day
of October 1857, leaving no children. She stated that he owned
one house and lot in Town of Shelbyville, near the Big Spring
in town, adjoining the lot of James Story and which house and

lot he purchased of John H. Oneal, one tract of land on which
he resided at the time of his death in District No. 6 of Bedford County, adjoining lands of G. H. Stewart, about 200 acres,
being the place purchased by Thomas Cheatham of J. H. McGrew.
Thomas Cheatham was twice married, that his first wife was
a widow at the time of their marriage and was the mother of
five children, to wit, Sinai, Letitia, John R., Samuel and
Nancy C. who were living at the time of the death of his first
wife or if either of them had died, they had left children.
Sometime before that time your oratrix had resided in the
family of Thomas Cheatham and was kindly and affectionately
treated by Thomas Cheatham and wife. At the time of the death
of his first wife, Thomas Cheatham had the following sisters,
to wit, Elizabeth, Nancy, Didame, Mary, Permelia, Sarah, Phoeby,
Cynthia and Margaret. Thomas Cheatham had land in District
No. 10. B. F. Duggan, executor of estate. Sisters and half
sisters of Thomas Cheatham, Elizabeth McCurdy wife of William
McCurdy, Nancy wife of Gibson Dawdy, Didame wife of John Crawford, Nancy Stanfield, Permelia Gillespie wife of John Gillespie, Sarah Gillespie wife of James Gillespie, Phoebe Taylor
wife of Robert Taylor, Phoebe Malinda Taylor, only children
of Margaret Taylor, deceased, who was a sister of Thomas
Cheatham, a minoe, and children of Cynthia Cople, deceased,
who was a sister, one only of her children has your oratrix
that has learned name of and is William C. Cople and the other
three, your oratrix does not know their names.

Page 183 - B. M. Tillman   ]
                    vs   ]Filed 28 February 1859.
              William M. Robinson & others]
Barclay M. Tillman filed against John E. Bennett, G. H. Frazer,
B. Featherston and W. M. Robinson, all of Bedford County.
Orator states that as Trustee of R. N. Jones, he sold to John E.
Bennett the tract of land lying and being on the Nashville
and Chattanooga Railroad, running from Shelbyville to Wartrace,
and on which John E. Bennett is now residing. Land bounded
by R. S. Thomas in Bell Buckle Creek, Railroad to Featherston
where William M. Robinson lives, about 2 acres and 69 poles.
Buford Bennett and wife and others - Exparte - Bill to sell
slaves. Filed September 7, 1857.
Orator and oratrixes, Buford Bennett and wife Elizabeth, Sarah
L. Maupin, S. F. Southern and wife Mary A. formerly Mary A.
Maupin, Jane E. Maupin, Thompson P. Maupin and Betty M. Maupin.
Sarah L., Jane E., Thompson P., and Betty M being minors. Land
in Bedford County in District No. 2 and bounded by Doctor Harris
tract on which Moses Payne resided, Kinchen Stokes, John B.
Bates, Robert B. Maupin, about 296 acres, to John Kimbro Spring
Branch.

Page 186 - Buford Burnett & wife & others] O. Bill, filed
                    vs   ] February 28, 1859.
              Sarah L. Maupin & others   ]
Robert B. Maupin, Buford Burnett and wife Elizabeth, S. F.
Southern and wife Mary, and James T. Maupin states that on
7 September 1857 filed their bill with Sarah L. Maupin, Jane E.
Maupin, Thompson P. Maupin, and Betty Maupin who are minors,
for sale of a tract of land. Robert B. Maupin was owner of
said land. Parts of the land was sold to raise money support
of Elizabeth Maupin now Elizabeth Burnett and her children.
NOTE: Buford Burnett is same as Buford Bennett in previous
      instrument. hcm

Page 188 - Fordyce Wilson & others]
                    vs   ] Filed 22 May 1856.
            Mary V. Fogleman & others]
Fordyce Wilson of Bedford County, James M. Elliott and wife
Dorkis of Marshall County, Tennessee, and G. N. Morrison and
wife Eleanor of Arkansas filed against Mary V. Fogleman, Catharine Fogleman and Vance Fogleman, the last 2 are minors and
Mary V. Fogleman as their guardian. Orators states that
George W. Fogleman departed this life in Bedford County in
the year 1853, leaving Mary V. Fogleman his widow and Catharine
Fogleman and Vance Fogleman his only surviving children. Orator
states that on 7 April 1842, a judgement was rendered against
your orator in favor of George W. Fogleman. Your orator had
to sell a tract of land in District No. 8, bounded by James
Claxton, now owned by A. J. Goodrum, Ebenezer Wilson, Dorkas J.
Elliott and Eleanor Morrison, about 40 acres. Ebenezer Wilson
bought the said tract in 1847. Bedford County Deed Book "PP",
page 174 & 175.

Page 192 - John P. Phillips &   ]
            Wilburn Hiles   ]
                    vs   ]O. Bill, 24 February 1859.
            Saluda B. Haley & others]
John P. Phillips and Wilburn Hiles of Bedford County filed
against Saluda B. Haley widow and Amanda, James, Nancy, Louisa
and Sarah Haley, minors of John Haley, deceased, all of Williamson County, Tennessee. Orators stated that John Haley, the
husband and father of the defendants was at the time of his
death indebted by three several notes on December 25, 1857
and due 1, 2, & 3 years for $160.00 and cost of interest. The
said notes were given for the purchase of lot in the Village
of Normandy, Bedford County, sold by your orator to John Haley
in his lifetime. Bordered by Nashville & Chattanooga Railroad.
The said lot's original owner was Middleton Holland and sold
to James Crenshaw, Crenshaw sold to your orator, John P.
Phillips. Orator wants to sell said lot to Hiles.

Page 195 - Garrett Phillips, Admr &c]
                    vs   ]Filed November 16, 1859.
            Frances McCuistian   ]
Garrett Phillips, admr of Claiborne McCuistian, deceased, filed
against Frances McCuistian, Tennessee McCuistian and Claiborne
McCuistian, all of whom are of Bedford County and the last
three are minors with no guardian. Orator states that Claiborne McCuistian departed this life in May last (1859) in
Bedford County. Orator was appointed admr of estate at June
Term of Court. Claiborne McCuistian left a widow, Frances
and a daughter Tennessee and a son named John McCuistian and
in two months after the death of said Claiborne, his widow
gave birth to a son whose name is Claiborne McCuistian, all
of his children are minors, the oldest not being more than
5 years old. All lived on the place where Claiborne died.
Claiborne McCuistian was at the time of his death, the owner
of one Town Lot in the Town of Shelbyville, Lot No. __ on
which there was a frame house and a smoke house, about 2½ acres
and lies near the Town Spring, North or Dodias(Dawdy) Street,
adjoining the lots of Silas Wood on the west. He also owned
a cedar tract of land of about 35 acres on or near Duck River,
6 miles west of Town of Shelbyville, lands of Ben Earnhart,
Daniel Earnhart and the place on which Hiram Harrison lives
and is in the District No. 18, it being the place said McCuistian purchased of Ben Earnhart and holds deed for same. Also,
he owned the tract of land on which he lived and died, about

105 acres, bounded by lands of William Word, Mrs. Brown and Thomas H. Coldwell, Jason T. Cowan and Jas. M. McCuistian, land is about one and one-fourth miles west of Shelbyville and on Unionville Pike. On March 11, 1859, Court appointed John H. Baskette as guardian of McCuistian minors.

Page 198 - Cornelius Womble]
              vs   ] Filed 20 December 1858.
      John Bennett   ]
Cornelius Womble of Bedford County filed against John Bennett of parts unknown. Orator states that John Bennett is indebted to him for about $200.00. John Bennett left State of Tennessee. Bennett owned 3 horses, 1 sorrel, 1 bay, and 1 iron gray horse, which are now at his mothers. Also, he owned one fifth part in remainder of the tract of land upon which his mother now resides, located in Civil District No. 22 of Bedford County, bounded by Jacob Castleman and W. W. Gill, Sarah Chandler, John Wilson and the land upon which Isaac Bennett resided at the time of his death. Bennett is also owner of a small tract of land of about 100 acres in Bedford County and partly in Lincoln County, Tennessee and bordered by John Bledsoe, William G. Cowan, John Warren, William W. Gant and William Nelson. Bennett is also owner of two yoke of oxen, 5 or 6 pork hogs and 16 stock hogs, all of this is at his mothers. All the aforesaid property was conveyed by John Bennett to J. J. Burrow by Deed of Trust.

Page 200 - John M. Stokes   ]
             vs   ]Filed 22 June 1858.
    William & A. E. Mullins]
John M. Stokes stated that Mathew Mullins, late a citizen of Bedford County died intestate. That his sons William Mullins and A. E. Mullins were appointed admr of estate. That as such, they sold a negro boy named George (among other property) and your orator became the owner. The sale became void. Orator said that William Mullins who now resides in Marshall County, Tennessee and A. E. Mullins of Bedford County be made defts to said bill.

Page 202 - John Cotter   ]
           vs   ]Bill for Divorce, February 26, 1859.
    Martha E. Cotter]
John Cotter of Bedford County stated that he married Martha Watkins of Bedford County in June 1854 and they lived together until February 1857 and she deserted your orator. He said she had been gone about two years.
Answer of Martha E. Cotter: She stated that they lived to-gether until August 1856. She said that while she was confined to bed, by sickness and also death of the infant to which she gave birth, he would abuse her and threatened to turn her out of doors, and actually did turn her mother, who was her only constant attendant, out of doors. She said her husband owned several slaves and had threatened to go off and sell them. She said she had (by Court Rule) the slaves removed from his care. Her mother came and took her from her bed and placed her in a carriage and took her to her house. She remained there several weeks. He came by to see her and told her he had treated her badly and wanted her to go live with him again. She went with him. They lived together for 2 or 3 months and he started treating her badly again.

Page 205 - Martha Cotter]
            vs   ]Cross Bill, filed March 8, 1859.
        John Cotter   ]
Martha Cotter stated that after the second separation in June
1857, she has given birth to a son, with which she was pregnant
at the time of the separation, which is now about 16 or 18
months of age.

Page 207 - James Yancy   ] Inj. & Att. Bill, filed
            vs   ]   February 16, 1857.
        Hallyburton & others]
James Yancy of Bedford County filed against Ruben P. Hallyburton and John T. Neil and others of Bedford County. Orator
stated that in February 1857, he recovered a judgement against
Ruben P. Hallyburton and others for about $110.00 and cost.

Page 210 - Robert S. McConnell]
            vs   ]Filed 19 July 1856.
        Joseph Taylor &   ]
        F. D. Haggard   ]
Robert S. McConnell filed against Joseph Taylor and French D.
Haggard. Orator of Bedford COunty stated that in 1852 that
Joseph Taylor, French D. Haggard and your orator formed a
partnership in the purchase of horses, mules and bacon and
perhaps some tobacco to carry south and sell. They bought
one from A. Mullins, two from William C. Hoot, one from Martin
Jones, one from James Finch, one from Martin Uless and one
from James Johnson and three mules from _____ M. Gill, they
also purchased bacon from Mrs. Phillips, J. J. Phillips, C. L.
Cannon, T. M. Stokes, J. M. Smith and C. S. George and from
Robert Matthews some produce he thinks tobacco and from Bery
& Green some cooking vessels &c and borrowed money from William
C. Holt.

Page 219 - Jacob Harrison   ]
            vs   ]Inj. Bill, filed
        The Bank of Tennessee]   5 April 1858.
        & J. Wortham   ]
Jacob Harrison states that the President and Directors of the
Bank of Tennessee recovered against your orator and his en-
dorsers, A. J. Greer, Jo. H. Thompson and J. M. Elliott in
August Term 1857.

Page 225 - Thomas G. & A. L. Moss]
            vs   ]Att. Bill, filed 23 Feb 1857.
        Eli Moss   ]
Thomas G. Moss and Amzi L. Moss, minors, who by their next
friend Wiley Riggins, states that they are owners of a negro
woman Lucy and her infant child. She had been in possession
of their father Eli Moss who now lives in Bedford County who
run her off into Alabama, but she is now in Franklin County,
Tennessee and may be in a short time in Bedford County. Orator
states the negro woman was given to them by their grandfather
William Smith. Eli Moss stated that said negro woman was not
a possession of William Smith but belonged to Caswell High.
William Smith had moved to Texas.

Page 227 - Robert J. B. Gant]
            vs   ]Inj. Bill, 13 March 1858.
        Lewis Gant &   ]
        N. Thompson, 3rd.]
Robert J. B. Gant of Marshall County, Tennessee filed against
N. Thompson, 3rd and Lewis Gant of Bedford County. Orator

229

states that in April 1854, he sold to N. Thompson, 3rd three
tracts of land in Bedford County in District No. __.

Page 231 - R. S. Hollins & Co.] Att. & Inj. Bill, filed
                    vs   ]   May 21, 1858.
          G. W. Jernigan et als]
R. S. Hollins, P. T. Hollins, S. P. Carrick, partners in business filed against George W. Jernigan and C. C. Grizzard both
of Bedford County. Orator states that on 23 December 1857,
they received a judgement against George W. Jernigan for
$82.00 plus cost. On 4 May 1858 they obtained a judgement
against him for $142.78 and cost.

Page 235 - Wisener & Scudder   ]
                    vs   ]Att. Bill, 24 March 1858.
          F. L. P. Wynn & others]
William H. Wisener and James L. Scudder, attorneys, states
that they are the holders of two notes on F. L. P. Wynn but
only to be collected and applied to a judgement they have
against Elizabeth Wynn. F. L. P. Wynn has absconded and left
the state, that Edmund Cooper is indebted to said F. L. P.
Wynn in sum of about $500.00 by note left in his hands by
E. P. Wynn and also said E. P. Wynn is indebted to F. L. P.
Wynn. Mary Wynn wife of F. L. P. Wynn has filed a bill against
him for divorce, for support for herself and child. (Desertion)
Mary Wynn states that the funds in the hands of E. P. Wynn,
belonging to her former husband F. L. P. Wynn.

Page 236 - A. Wilson   ]
                  vs   ] Filed August 19, 1857.
          Clark & Keener]
Augustus Wilson of Bedford County filed against William Clark
of Bedford County. Orator states that John Ozment, a constable
of Bedford County has an execution, for collection, in favor
of William Clark for $300.00 of which $100.00 was paid by your
orator. Debt was for cedar timber. William H(?). Clark is
a young man. Clark sold to D. M(Martin) Kenner(Keener) a lot
of cedar timber and waiting some 2 years for his money. Wilson
bought cedar sticks, 6 x 8 inches, 9 feet long.

Page 242 - Freeman & Trice   ]
                    vs   ]Filed September 8, 1857.
          P. U. Doss & others]
Alsey Freeman and Joseph Trice, merchants, states that Phillip
U. Doss of Bedford County is indebted to them for $254.45,
in their own right. (Phillip's middle name inital could be
a V or U). James P. Doss of Lincoln County, Tennessee indebted
to Benjamin Mosely of Bedford County. Phillip U(V). Doss is
about to move to Alabama as his family already started and
gone and most of his possession in with his family.

Page 245 - Gwynn Foster]
                vs   ] Att. Bill, filed 22 February 1858.
          J. H. Reaves]
Gwynn Foster states that J. H. Reaves is indebted to your
orator for $290.00 with interest, being the amount of money
received from F. M. McCowan in Texas. John H. Reaves is about
to remove from Tennessee.

Page 247 - Thomas B. Mosely   ]
                    vs   ]Inj. Bill, August 11, 1857.
          Silas E. Tucker & others]
Thomas B. Mosely, Sr. of Bedford County filed against Sampson

Liggett of Marshall County, Tennessee and Silas E. Tucker of
Rutherford County, Tennessee and James M. Johnson of Bedford
County. Orator states that on 23 February 1855, he purchased
of Samuel Doak a negro girl Patsy for $500.00 cash paid to
Doak.

Page 255 - S. W. Morgan   ]
              vs   ]Inj. Bill, October 7, 1857.
          E. D. Dromgoole &]
          J. G. Evans   ]
Samuel W. Morgan of Rutherford County, Tennessee filed against
E. D. Dromgoole and J. G. Evans both of Bedford COunty. Orator
states that he recovered two judgements against E. D. Dromgoole
on 16 February 1857 for $312.63 and cost. Also that he is
jointly interested with J. E. Evans in a Livery Stable in
Shelbyville. Evans purchased all interest in said business.

Page 258 - T. B. Ivie   ]
              vs   ]O. Bill, 17 August 1858.
          David L. Evans,]
          his guardian   ]
T. B. Ivie filed against David Elkins, an idiot, David S. Evans
as his guardian, all of Bedford County. Orator stated that
he purchased of the widow and heirs of David S. Elkins, dec'd,
the dower tract of land laid off to the widow in the division
of lands of David Elkins, deceased, and on which the widow
resides, with the exception of one share belonging to the
children of Benjamin Bowers, who are minors. A contract was
made with guardian of David Elkins for his share, about 120
acres. Orator states that said tract in which Mrs. Elkins,
who is a stout hearty old lady, of some __ years is entitled
to a life estate, and that there are five shares in said land,
sold land to T. B. Ivie.

Page 259 - John H. O'Neal   ]Inj. & Att. Bill, filed
              vs   ]4 o'clock 18 September 1857.
          R. N. Jones & others]
John H. O'Neal filed against R. N. Jones, W. B. M. Brame and
W. S. Jett, all of bedford County. Orator received a judge-
ment against N. Thompson, 3rd on 11 March 1857 for $375.00.

Page 261 - F. P. McElraith & others] Inj. Bill, filed
              vs   ] 19 March 1857.
          Randolph Newsom   ]
F. P. McRaith, William Burns and John P. Steele, Trustees of
Samuel Doak & Co., all of Bedford County filed against Randolph
Newsom. Orator states that on 1st day February 1854, the firm
of F. P. McRaith & Co. and above named, purchased from Shelbyville Pork Packing Company, an engine and apparatus and all
the pumps and other fixtures.

Page 265 - Aley Dunston   ]
              vs   ] Filed 5 April 1858.
          William A. Griffis]
          & P. Nelligan   ]
Aley Dunston of Illinois filed against William A. Griffis of
Davidson County, Tennessee and Patrick Nelligan of Bedford
County. Oratrix Aley Dunston states that she was the owner
of a tract of land in Shelbyville and on 12 January 1857 she
deeded to William A. Griffis a part of the tract. Bounded
by lot oratrix sold to A. L. Stamps, William Little and others,
about 1 acre. Said lot is now in hands of Patrick Nelligan
which Griffis sold to him.

Page 268 - John H. Gambill   ]
                 vs   ]Inj. Bill, 21 February 1857.
          James Carlisle & others]
John H. Gambill of Bedford County filed against George W. Brown
and James Carlisle both reside in Bedford County. Orator
states that he recovered a judgement against George W. Brown
and John Damron in 1857 for $137.33 and cost. He is also owner
of one other judgement by transfer in favor of Wilhoite &
Brothers against G. W. Brown.

Page 269 - Amos Hurley   ]
                 vs   ] Filed October 29, 1857.
          Thomas W. Buchanan & others]
Amos Hurley, Thomas J. Gaddy, Jasper M. Gaddy, Martha Gaddy,
Mary Gaddy, Mariam Gaddy, the last two are minors with no
guardian, and present their petition by their brother and next
friend Thomas J. Gaddy, Robert Davis and Matilda J. Davis,
states that many years ago Mary Hurley was the wife of Elijah
Hurley and by whom she had four children, to wit, Amos Hurley,
Sally who married with May Buchanan, Elizabeth who married
with Archibald McElroy, Martha who married Leonard Smith. Many
years ago Elijah Hurley died in Lincoln County, Tennessee and
that Mary Hurley had slaves and after she (Mary Hurley) married
Absalom Davis and afterwards and about 16 March 1826, said
Absalom Davis and his wife Mary sold said slaves &c over to
Amos Hurley, Sally Buchanan, Elizabeth McElroy and Martha
Smith, the children of Mary Davis by her first husband, and
Polly Davis, Letty, Sally, Henry Davis, Constant M. Davis,
William Davis and Robert Davis, children of Absalom Davis by
a wife he had before Mary Davis. Mary Davis departed this
life in 1852 and Absalom Davis departed this life in 1854.
Polly Davis married Alexander Hughey and had seven children,
to wit, Parthenia who married John C. Euniss who lives in
Alabama, Mary, Franklin and Robert of full age, Sarah, Martha
and William in Lincoln County, Tennessee and that John C.
Euniss is guardian of minors of Alexander Hughey. Alexander
Hughey died many years ago and his widow Polly remarried with
Washington Wilson and then died without having any children
by Wilson, leaving Wilson surviving her and who now lives in
Lincoln County, Tennessee. Letty Davis married John Keith
of Mississippi. Sally married Thomas W. Buchanan. Henry Davis
died, leaving Robert C. Davis and Matilda J. Davis his only
children. Constant W. Davis lives in Williamson County, Tennessee. William Davis died leaving three children, John D.,
Robert and Letitia, minors and lives with Constant W. Davis
and is their guardian. Robert Davis died many years ago leaving no children and never married. May Buchanan and wife Sally
about year 1849, transferred interest in slaves to Amos Hurley
and Davis S. Buchanan (Registered in Lincoln County, Tennessee).
Martha married Smith and had children, to wit, Sarah and
William B., of full age, transferred their interest of said
slaves to Amos Hurley and David S. Buchanan. Leonard Smith
died and his widow Martha remarried Samuel Gaddy, by whom she
had, to wit, Jasper, Thomas J., Martha, Mary and Mariam Gaddy
and then she and her last husband have both died. Elizabeth
had by her first husband Archibald McElroy, children, Mary
who married John M. Commons and lives in Obion County, Tennessee, Sarah who married Davis S. Buchanan and she then died
leaving her husband and one child and said child died and then
said David S. _____, Jackson Perry and William McElroy who
lives in Mississippi. Benton McElroy of Lincoln County, Tennessee, Martha married Salomon B. Smith and lives in Obion
County. Elizabeth who married Theodore G. Smith and died

leaving her husband and one child and live in Lincoln County, Tennessee, Archibald McElroy died and Elizabeth remarried Lewis Ship and had one child Orlena, a minor. Then Elizabeth died leaving her husband Lewis Ship and her child, living in Lincoln County, Tennessee. David S. Buchanan died in Lincoln County, Tennessee, Robert Farquarson was appointed admr of said David. Answer of Thomas W. Buchanan, 1858: Buchanan said in 1844 purchased from Samuel S. Buchanan a negro woman Tennessee for sum of $380.00. S. S. Buchanan purchased from Absalom Davis the said negro woman September 24, 1840 for $320.00. Tennessee was a descendant of Violant.

NOTE: Lincoln County, Tennessee Records are:
      Elijah Hurley died before 1820 (Census), left widow Mary Hurley (Davis), over 45 years of age.
Absalom Davis, born ca 1787 North Carolina, died ca 1854 Lincoln County, Tennessee.
Mary (Hurley) Davis, born ca 1776 North Carolina, died ca 1852 Lincoln County, Tennessee.
Lincoln County, Tennessee Census:
Absalom Davis living with T. W. Buchanan, a son in law.
Mary Davis living with W. D. Sawyers, and others.
Mary Hurley Davis' children:
1 - Amos Hurley, born ca 1793 North Carolina, wife Mary born February 24, 1797, died August 17, 1853, buried Wright Cemetery, Lincoln County, Tennessee. Children: Marion born ca 1819, age 21 in 1850 Census, Amos H. born ca 1828, age 12 in 1850 Census, Washington born 1842 (8 years) 1850 Lincoln County Tennessee Census.
    (Next house is Zachariah Hurley born ca 1817 (23 years) 1850 Lincoln County, Tennessee Census)
2 - May Buchanan and wife Sally (1850 Census of Lincoln County Tennessee Census), May Buchanan born 1788 North Carolina, Sarah (Sally) Hurley born ca 1798 North Carolina, children, Sarah 19 years in 1850 Census of Lincoln County Census.
3 - Archibald McElroy already dead by 1840 Lincoln County Census. He made his will December 13, 1839 in Lincoln County. His wife was Elizabeth Hurley McElroy.
End of Note.

Page 274 - John P. Steele, Trustee &c]
            vs   ]Inj. Bill, July 4, 1857.
      Samuel S. Arnold   ]
John P. Steele of Bedford County stated that on 14 April 1857, acting as Trustee of Samuel Doak and C. D. Steele, he recovered a judgement against Samuel S. Arnold of Bedford County for $127.50 and cost. On 29 June 1857, he recovered another judgement against said Arnold for $126.63 and cost. A short time or months before the rendition of the first judgement, Arnold was the owner of several slaves and other valuable property and all at once he sold or pretended to sell them to his brother W. W. Arnold or to his brother in law E. M. B. Norville, one or both of them and W. W. Arnold later sold a portion or all of slaves. Several notes calling for money have been transferred by Samuel S. Arnold to Elijah Arnold who was the father of Samuel Arnold.

Page 281 - Epps Parker   ]
             vs   ]Inj. Bill, 17 March 1857.
      G. E. Bowden &]
      Carter Blanton]
Epps Parker states that some years ago, he executed to Carter Blanton his two notes, one for $300.00 and other for $100.00, due 25 December 1853. Execution was for "Dower Tract" of his

wife Nancy Blanton formerly Nancy Parker. The tract of land
formerly owned by Charles Parker, deceased. Nancy Blanton
departed this life and the entire title became vested in the
heirs at law of Charles Parker, deceased.

Page 283 - George W. Cunningham]
             vs   ]
      R. B. Blackwell &]
      J. Campbell   ]
Orator states that on 1 January 1857, he agreed to cultivate
a tract of land in Bedford County, which he was owner jointly
with R. B. Blackwell.

Page 288 - George M. Cunningham]
     &wife Mary   ]
        vs   ]Filed February 23, 1855.
     George W. Cunningham]
George M. Cunningham and wife Mary formerly Mary Blackwell,
states that John Blackwell, Sr., the father of your oratrix
Mary, departed this life in Marshall County, Tennessee sometime
in the Spring of 1849 and having made and published his Last
Will and Testament which was proven and recorded in Marshall
County, Tennessee at its May Term 18__. Shadrick Martin and
William Carlisle were the executors. Before the death of John
Blackwell, he executed a Deed of Gift for a portion of the
same property devised and bequeathed by the will to five of
the legatees under the will, to the exclusion of two others
who were Legatees under the will. The legatees under the will
who were not included in the Deed of Gift, to wit, John Blackwell, Jr., George W. Cunningham in right of his wife Sarah
who was a daughter of said John Blackwell, Sr. Shadrick
Martin, executor desired to remove to Missouri.

Page 295 - Mary Cunningham by   ]
     next friend   ]
        vs   ]O. Bill, March 2, 1857.
     George W. Cunningham &]
     George M. Cunningham]
Oratrix Mary Cunningham of Lawrence County, Tennessee who sues
by her next friend Elige Howard, states that George W. Cunningham relies to defeat said action. Mary Cunningham's husband
was George W. Cunningham. George W. Cunningham resides in
Bedford County and George M. Cunningham resides in Lawrence
County, Tennessee.

Page 296 - James Hallyburton   ]
        vs   ] Filed March 26, 1857.
     R. P. Hallyburton & others]
James Hallyburton filed against R. P. Hallyburton who has gone
to parts unknown and Joseph H. Thompson of Shelbyville. Orator
states that R. P. Hallyburton and your orator were engaged
for year 1856 in the business of Blacksmithing in Town of
Shelbyville ans as equal partners. Your orator was a Blacksmith by trade and as such carried on a shop. R(Reuben) P.
Hallyburton left the state.
Names from record kept by Hallyburton and recorded 1856:
1 - E. D. Dromgoole   8 - Jacob F. Thompson
2 - Dromgoole & Hallyburton 9 - Newcom Thompson
3 - John Robertson   10 - Newcom Thompson, Sen.
4 - John T. Neil   (Old Newsom)
5 - Thomas Pettis   11 - John E. Carrels
6 - James Cummings   12 - Reuben P. Hallyburton
7 - Charles A. Warren   13 - Hiram Stephens

13 - Hiram Stephens
14 - John Barrett
15 - Elick Young
16 - Nathaniel Evans
17 - Robert Blackwell
18 - Lewis Tillman
19 - John Lacy
20 - B. P. Clark
21 - Surdwith by
        R. P. Hallyburton
22 - Hiram Edde
23 - William White
24 - William Moore
25 - Jason Cannon
26 - John Acan (Eakin)
27 - Zack Harrison
28 - Benjamin Adams
29 - Jason Cannon
30 - William Ruth
31 - Silas Bivins
32 - James Harris Graham
33 - Reuben P. Hallyburton
34 - Fe Barrett
35 - Hiram Nease
36 - George Cunningham
37 - John Smith
38 - James Dixon
39 - Washington P. Goodwin
40 - William Ransom
41 - John Holt
42 - Thomas Rone
43 - Judge H. L. Davidson
44 - Newton Dunnaway
45 - William Dismukes
46 - Alex Smith
47 - Thomas Coldwell
48 - William Peach
49 - John Clark
50 - Edm'd Sims
51 - D. Crutcher
52 - Hance Hutton
53 - Clem Wade
54 - Thomas Montgomery
55 - John Bolen
56 - Elick Cotter
57 - John Goodwin
58 - J. B. Smith
59 - James M. Johnson
60 - James Grant
61 - Joseph White
62 - Joseph Green
63 - William Kingree
64 - Benjamin Ragsdale
65 - Robert Mathes
66 - Rich. Wilhoite
67 - Dick Allen
68 - Joseph Muse
69 - George Hutson
70 - George Greer
71 - J. P. Bell
72 - William Greer
73 - Shapard & Mitchell
74 - Lewis Newsom

75 - Card Scales
76 - Benjamin Moseley
77 - Allen Cannon
78 - John Drumgoole
79 - Robert Cannon
80 - Elizabeth McKamy
81 - John Thompson
82 - James Wortham
83 - Edw'd Gregory
84 - W. K. Burns
85 - J. F. Davis
86 - Samuel Hayes
87 - E. D. Drumgoole
88 - Dr. Norton
89 - James Smith
90 - Robert S. Dwiggins
91 - J. H. Nobles
92 - Giles Smith
93 - S. T. Cannon
94 - Charles Hide
95 - John M. Stokes
96 - William Peach
97 - Robert Evans
98 - Buck Thomas
99 - Samuel Moody
100 - Isaac B. Holt
101 - Edm'd Green
102 - William Holt
103 - Joshua Kimmons
104 - William Reddick
105 - E. D. Drumgoole
106 - John Blankenship
107 - Newcom Thompson, Sr.
108 - John Gambill
109 - John Nobley
110 - James Story
111 - Robert Work
112 - Robert Patterson
113 - William H. Wisener
114 - Peter English
115 - Alexander Smith
116 - Charley Robinson
117 - John Dameron
118 - Reuben P. Hallyburton
119 - Dick Allen
120 - William Armstrong
121 - John P. Dean
122 - Andrew Batt
123 - Robert M. Whitman
124 - J. M. Ruth
125 - Jack Powell
126 - Edw'd D. Drumgoole
127 - H. S. Lane
128 - William G. Laughrey
129 - Samuel Hays
130 - Willis Burke

Page 305 - George W. Stephenson   ]
              vs   ]Inj. Bill, November 21, 1857
          N. Thompson, 3rd et als]
George W. Stephenson filed against N. Thompson, 3rd, W(Willis).
W. Wilhoite and N. Thompson, Sr., all of Bedford County. Orator
states that on or about 15 August 1855, he bought from N.
Thompson, 3rd, a parcel of land lying in Bedford County in
District No. 18, about 50 acres.

Page 308 - James M. Johnson   ]
              vs   ]Inj. Bill, April 18, 1857.
          D. C. & Hayden Trigg]
          & others   ]
James M. Johnson of Bedford County filed against Daniel C.
Trigg and Hayden Trigg of Bedford County. Orator states that
Daniel C. and Hayden Trigg were tenants of a parcel of land
in Bedford County on Duck River, about 253 acres which had
been conveyed to them by R. B. & A. H. McLean as admr of C. G.
McLean, deceased. Daniel C. and Hayden Trigg sold said land
to your orator dated 12 January 1855. Your orator begin to
question the soundness of the mind of Haiden Trigg and since
the purchase of land. The Courts are to have Haiden Trigg
declared unsound of mind, these proceedings were started by
John L. Keith, Jr., the son in law of Haiden Trigg. Haiden
Trigg has died, June 1857. Daniel C. Trigg is the son of
Haiden Trigg and believes he had four other children and
several grandchildren, children of a deceased son William Trigg.
Heirs of Haiden Trigg, to wit, John W. Trigg of Bedford County,
Joseph W. Trigg, John L. Keith, Jr. and his wife Elizabeth
of Franklin County, Tennessee, W. H. Hitch and wife Esther
of Texas, children of Haiden Trigg and their husbands. And
his grandchildren, heirs of his son William, deceased, to wit,
Susan Trigg, Judith Ann Trigg, Margaret Trigg, Priscilla Trigg,
James Trigg, Daniel Trigg, and William Trigg infant, all of
Marshall County, Tennessee and John E. Hall and wife Eliza
Jane of Bedford County. Haiden Trigg had lived in Franklin
County, Tennessee.

Page 313 - John Hood   ]
              vs   ]Divorce, filed October 14, 1858.
          Elizabeth Hood]
John Hood of Bedford County states that for more than 2 years,
that he married Elizabeth Devon about 28 years ago in Williamson County, Tennessee and lived together about 17 years. He
moved to Bedford County about 12 years ago. Elizabeth left
and has not been heard from since.

Page 314 - W. G. Miller   ]
              vs   ]Att. & Inj. Bill, filed
          Thomas & Jas. G. Stevens]   September 17, 1858.
          & others   ]
W. G. Miller filed against Thomas Stevens of parts unknown
and James G. Stevens, Alexander Kimbro and A. R. Wood, all
of Bedford County and W. R. McFadden of Rutherford County,
Tennessee. Orator states that he is owner by purchase from
Alexander Kimbro, one bill executed by Thomas Stevens dated
3 September 1857, a tract of land, said Kimbro is now residing
in District No. 25 of Bedford County, adjoining John H. Scott
and others. Thomas Stevens has left the state. Orator states
that James G. Stevens is a son of Thomas Stevens and resides
in Bedford County.

Page 316 - J. J. Blackwell   ]
                      vs   ]Inj. Bill, 17 December 1857.
             Fall & Cunningham]
             & others   ]
J. J. Blackwell of Bedford County filed against Fall & Cunningham, partners of Davidson County, Tennessee and against William
H. Wisener, Asa L. Stamps, Gideon P. Baskette, Jacob F. Thompson and John H. O'Neal, all of Bedford County. Orator states
that John H. O'Neal being owner of a tract of land near Town
of Shelbyville, sold the same to Jacob F. Thompson and took
his note. Thompson sold to Asa L. Stamps. Stamps sold to
William H. Wisener. Wisener sold to your orator, a portion
of the land formerly belonging to John T. Neil, on west side
of Shelbyville and Lot No. 18 in Shelbyville and bordered by
Robert Denniston and W. A. Griffis.

Page 323 - Randall W. McGavock & others   ]
                      vs   ] Filed
             W. J. Whitthorne, Thomas Lipscomb,] August 5, 1857.
             G. W. Buchanan & James L. Scudder]
Randall W. McGavock and Serphine his wife of Davidson County,
Tennessee and William M. Churchwell and Martha E. his wife
of Knox County, Tennessee, that on 2 February 1857 sold in
Town of Shelbyville, land on south side of the Public Square,
known as the "Deery Property" and divided off into lots as
per plan, Lot No. 1, 2, & 3 to William J. Whitthorne. Lot
No. 4 & 5 to Buchanan & Lipscomb. Lot No. 6 to James L.
Scudder. Lot No. 7 to James A. Blakemore. Lot No. 10 & 11
to J. F. Cummings. Lot No. 12 & 13 to George W. Thompson.
Lot No. 14, 15, & 16 to Samuel H. Titcomb

Page 331 - Jacob F. Thompson & others] Inj. & Att. Bill,
                      vs   ] February 15, 1858.
             Pyland, Pickle & others]
Jacob F. Thompson, Newcomb Thompson, 3rd, and William Brown
filed against Hardy Pyland and Newton Pickle, both of Bedford
County. Orators states that your orator, Newcomb Thompson,
3rd, sold by deed to Hardy Pyland two tracts of land dating
5 April 1856. One of 85 acres and another of 100 acres. Your
orator has been informed that Pyland has made a pretended conveyance of part said land to James M. O'Neal, also Pyland has
pretended to sell said 85 acres to Newton Pickle but no record
can be found of same. Orators claim that Newton Pickle, J. M.
O'Neal and Hardy Pyland are committing great waste on said
land by cutting and hauling off the valuable cedar timber,
selling and pocketing the proceeds.

Page 334 - William Brown   ] Filed 30 September 1857
                      vs   ] at 10½ o'clock P.M.
             N. Thompson, 3rd & others]
William Brown, a creditor of Newcomb Thompson, 3rd, to the
Bill of Complaint of William C. Hart filed against Newcomb
Thompson, 3rd, Newcomb Thompson, Sr., George W. Thompson,
Jacob F. Thompson, John W. Thompson, James Dixon, C. S. Dudley,
all of Bedford County. Orator states that he is a creditor
of Newcomb Thompson, 3rd, and as such has obtained against
him beside other judgements the following, to wit, 1 judgement
in January 27, 1857 for $301.50 and cost, also, 1 judgement
in January 5, 1857 for $4.00, another for $400.00, also one
other for $300.00 and cost, also one against Jo Thompson and
Newcomb Thompson, 3rd for $384.23 and other against Samuel
Doak and N. Thompson, 3rd for $58.00 and all parties are in-
solvent. Orator stated that Newcomb Thompson, 3rd left

Shelbyville on the 10 o'clock train for Nashville on the 14th
or 15th inst., taking with him to Nashville, some 6 or 7
slaves, the property of said Newcomb Thompson, 3rd, for the
purpose of selling them for the purpose of paying debts owning
by him. On the next morning, Jacob F. Thompson, the brother
of Newcomb left Shelbyville on the 4 o'clock train and went
to Nashville to meet Newcomb and inform him that there was
a great excitement in Shelbyville about or on account of his
abs--es(?) that his creditors were attaching his property and
probably some of his creditors would be coming on the next
train and would attach his property there and that he must
make him (Jacob F.) a Trust Deed and secure him and that if
he did not, that he would attach the negroes himself. So the
Deed of Trust was made to said Jacob F. Thompson on tract of
land on Fall Creek, about 431 acres on which is a stream, saw
mill and also slaves, and farm animals and all household
furnishings. The story Jacob F. told about the excitement
and attaching of Newcomb's property was untrue and that there
was no excitement until after the Trust of Deed was made. Newcomb and Jacob returned to Shelbyville, leaving the negroes
in Nashville and said deed was registered late at night. The
case is voided. Orator states that Newcomb Thompson, 3rd,
has conveyed to C.(Christopher) S. Dudley a tract or lot in
the west end of town and adjoining Town of Shelbyville, about
___ acres and deed recorded in Bedford County. Orator said
sale was fraudulent and void.

Page 339 - William C. Holt   ] Inj. & Att. Bill, filed
                vs   ] September 30, 1857, at
          N. Thompson, 3rd & others]   11 A.M.
William C. Holt of Bedford County filed against Newcom Thompson, 3rd, Jacob F. Thompson, Newcom Thompson, Sr., George W.
Thompson, John W. Thompson and James Dixon, all of Bedford
County and Lewis Newsom of Lincoln County, Tennessee. Orator
filed for all creditors of Newcom Thompson, 3rd. James Dixon
was Newcom Thompson's father in law. The land that was in
Deed of Trust to Jacob F. Thompson, located about 3 miles south
of Town of Shelbyville on the Shelbyville-Fayetteville Turnpike
Road, the place on which Newcom now resides. Orator states
that Lewis Newsom of Lincoln County, Tennessee is indebted
to N. Thompson, 3rd for about $3000.00.

Page 342 - George W. Thompson]
                vs   ] Filed 12 February 1858.
          L. B. Knott &   ]
          Thomas J. Warren   ]
George W. Thompson of Bedford County filed against L. B. Knott
and Thomas J. Warren of Bedford County. Orator states that
on 5 April 1856 he sold to L. B. Knott a tract of land within
limits of Town of Shelbyville on what is now known as Depot
Street. Your orator had bought same from J. F. Cummings.
Knott, in 1856, sold said land to Thomas J. Warren.

Page 344 - W. W. Stanfield   ]
                vs   ]O. Bill, September 24, 1857.
          Jas. B. Reager &   ]
          Chas. Kirby & others]
William W. Stanfield filed against James B. Reager, Charles
Kirby (a minor under age 21 years), James R., Lucy A., Martha
E., Susan, Mary, Caroline, Clementine, Thomas and Alvis K.
Evans, all of whom are minors (under 21 years), and Nancy Evans
and Thomas J. Stanfield and Wesley Evans, all of Bedford County.
William W. Stanfield stated that he purchased a tract of land

in Bedford County in District No. 23, bounded by Mary Kirby,
John W. Gardner, James McGill, and Joseph Hyles, about 50
acres. Orator stated that at the November 1852, James B.
Kirby, deceased, and your orator as the guardian of Charles W.
Kirby who was a minor, they sold estate to John Evans. Sept-
ember Term 1853, Court appointed Wesley Evans and Thomas J.
Stanfield as admrs of John Evans, deceased. Thomas J. Stanfield was appointed to sell estate or land. Charles W. Kirby
(minor) was only child of Henry Kirby, deceased. John Evans
bought Henry Kirby's land. John Evans left surviving him
Nancy Evans his widow, James R., Lucy A., Martha Elizabeth,
Susan T., Mary Caroline, Clementine, Thomas and Alvis K. Evans,
his only children, and heirs at law, that Thomas J. Stanfield,
J. Stanfield and Wesley Evans appointed admrs of John Evans'
estate.

Page 347 - Absalom Mosely   ]
                    vs   ]Filed April 2, 1858.
          Thomas J. Williams & others]
Absalom Mosely states that Thomas J. Williams is indebted to
him by various judgements. Thomas J. Williams resides in
Missouri.

Pahe 349 - Benjamin Mosely et als]
                    vs   ]Inj. Bill, 15 January 1858.
          J. H. C. Scales et als]
Benjamin Mosely and wife Margaret formerly Margaret Holt, and
Benjamin Mosely as admr of Jordan C. Holt, Jr. and Isom Holt,
a minor, and Hiram H. Holt filed against K. M. Pybas and wife
Elenor C. formerly Elenor C. Holt, Isaac B. Holt, Hiram H.
Nease and wife Emily J. formerly Emily J. Holt, J. H. C. Scales
admr of Caledonia A. Scales formerly Caledonia A. Holt, James
L. Hix and wife Hulda H. formerly Hulda H. Holt and Isadora
Alice Holt, a minor whose guardian is Hiram H. Nease and
W. J. Whitthorne, C & M of Bedford County, and John W. Wiggins
and wife Mary K. formerly Mary K. Holt of Texas, Jane Holt
widow of J. C. Holt, Jr., Susan, Margaret and Jordan C. Holt
minors who has as guardian Ezekiel Phelps and are of Lincoln
County, Tennessee. They are the heirs or legatees of Jordan
C. Holt, Sr. The said Jordan C. Holt, Sr. died in the year
(September 11) 1853 and made a will which was proven in October
Term Bedford County. Hiram H. Holt and K. M. Pybas executors.
(Jordan Cane Holt's wife was Margaret Wilhoite. She died in
July 1853 and is buried at Center Church Cemetery, south of
Shelbyville, hcm). That since the death of Jordan C. Holt,
Sr., his son Jordan C. Holt, Jr. has died leaving his widow
Jane Holt and three minors, to wit, Susan Holt, Margaret C.
Holt and Jordan C. Holt and for their guardian they have
Exekiel Phelps pf Lincoln County, Tennessee and Benjamin Mosely
admr of Jordan C. Holt, Jr. in Marshall County, Tennessee.
Caledonia A. Scales the daughter of the said Jordan C. Holt,
Sr. has died intestate since the death of her father Jordan C.
Holt, Sr. and defendant. Caledonia was unmarried at time the
will of J. C. Holt, Sr. was made. Caledonia was a minor at
the time of her marriage to J. H. C. Scales. J. H. C. Scales
is admr of her estate. She had no children. The admr proceeded to sell all real estate and personal estate of Jordan C.
died possessed of. Hiram H. Holt became the purchaser of most
of the valuable property also Pybas bought lots of the most
valuable property, both are executors of the estate.

Page 355 - Absalom Mosely]
                vs   ]Inj. Bill, April 17, 1858.
        Nath. Porter   ]
Absalom Mosely states that Nathaniel Porter who was at the
time of Bedford COunty sold about 3 years ago(1855), a tract
of land, 50 acres, to I. N. Jones and a short time after, your
orator took the land that Porter had sold to Jones. Land in
Bedford County and joins lands of David Yancy, James Woodard,
Ben Mosely, W. Coffee and others. The title was not a clear
deed. They said the title was in the children of Berry Blackwell who resides with his children in Texas. The land was
willed to the children by Berry Blackwell by the Last Will
of their grandfather, John Blackwell, who died some years since
in Marshall County, Tennessee. All the children of Berry
Blackwell are still minors and too young too to give title
to Porter. Nathaniel Porter some 3 years since moved to Dyer
County, Tennessee.

Page 358 - Absalom Mosely   ]
                vs   ]Inj. Bill, September 10, 1857.
        Nathaniel Porter &]
        W. L. Brown   ]
Absalom Mosely of Marshall County, Tennessee filed against
Nathaniel Porter of Dyer County, Tennessee, and W. L. Brown
of Bedford County. Orator states that Nathaniel Porter formerly of Bedford County now of Dyer County, some 3 years since
sold land to Isaac N. Jones and your orator took said land.

Page 361 - Baskette & Stamps] Inj. & Att. Bill, filed
                vs   ] February 18, 1858, about
        J. W. Hamlin, et als]   4 o'clock.
Orators states that John W. Hamlin of Bedford County is indebted to your orators for $174.13 for which your orator obtained
judgement, 10 November 1857. Robert Cannon was indebted to
him. J. W. Hamlin's mother Mrs. Catharine Hamlin who is old
and in very reduced circumstances, and Robert Cannon owes her.
J. H. Hamlin states that he is 28 years of age, and has been
boarding and living with his widowed mother for the last 6
or 7 years.

Page 363 - Fay & Wisener]
                vs   ] Filed 12 August 1858.
        Joseph Ramsey]
William H. Wisener and Patrick Fay states that Wisener sold
by deed to Joseph Ramsey, Town Lot in Shelbyville. Lot No.
96, Lot No. 103, Lot No. 110, all of Lot No. 83 which lies
west of Spring Branch and that portion of the Alley or Street
which lies between Lots No. 83 and 96.

Page 364 - Ransom & Drumgoole   ]
                vs   ] Filed 11 November 1857.
        Robert M. Smith & others]
William A. Ransom and John E. Drumgoole, partners and of
Rutherford County, Tennessee filed against S. T. Crittenden,
W. J. Barrett, Robert M. Smith, Mary Jane Smith and Mary
Eveline Crittenden formerly Smith, all of Bedford County.
Mary E. Smith Crittenden is daughter of R. M. and Mary Smith.
Orators states that on 28 October 1856, Robert M. Smith with
said S. J. Crittenden executed promissory notes for $1150.00.
Orators states that R. M. Smith was owner of two slabe boys
George and Bryant. A few days before note was due, he conveyed
said negro George to his wife Mary Jane Smith and other slave
Bryant to Eveline Crittenden who is wife of S. J. Crittenden

240

of the said Robert M. Robert M. Smith has interest in land
in District No. 18 of Bedford County that he bought of William
J. Barrett and _____ Rankin. Mary Jane Smith was daughter
of H. D. Jameson who had lived in Marshall County, Tennessee.
Children of R. M. and Mary J. Smith, to wit, Elizabeth, Leonidas, Penelope, Julia and Henry Jameson Smith, last five are
minors and the Harriet W. (Smith) having died, her interest
descended to the others, or to her full sister Mary Emeline
Crittenden. Said deed of Jameson conferred the Power of
Respondent to sell the land, during her life, if she thought
best and to divide proceeds among those entitled in remainder,
and on the __ day of ___ ___, she deeming it best to sell,
she did sell 83 acres of the land for $3500.00 but she did
not then divide the proceeds according to her father's will,
but let her husband, Robert M. Smith have the money. He became insolvent.   R. M. Smith had a wife prior to Mary Jane
(Jameson) Smith. He had two daughters by first wife, to wit,
Harriet W. Smith and Mary Eveline Crittenden. Land sold in
Marshall County, Tennessee belonging to H. D. Jameson, was
sold to Allen Morris (Morris' Mills).

Page 374 - Elizabeth Smith et als] Amended Bill, filed
                      vs   ] August Term 1858.
            Ransom & Drumgoole   ]
Elizabeth, Leonidas, Penelope, Julia and Henry J. Smith, who
are all minors with no guardian and sues by their father Robert
M. Smith, all of Marshall County, Tennessee, states that on
7 November 1857, they with their mother Mary Jane Smith filed
against Adophus Adams and others and many other things made
known to your Honor that in 1850 their grandfather Henry D.
Jameson conveyed to their mother a tract of land and mills
in Marshall County, Tennessee on Duck River, about 103 acres
for life and at her death, remainder to Mary E. and Harriet W.
Smith and your orators and oratrixes the said Mary E. and
Harriet W. being half sisters, and that said deed of their
grandfather conferred the power on their mother to sell and
land and divide proceeds among those in remainder and that
their mother did sell land (83 acres) but had not divided but
their father Robert M. Smith had received said money and used
it and had become embarassed and could not pay.

Page 378 - Mary E. Wynn]
                      vs   ]Divorce, filed 5 January 1858.
            F. L. P. Wynn]
Mary E. Wynn filed against F. L. P. Wynn who has gone to parts
unknown, E. P. Wynn and Edmund Cooper who resides in Bedford
County and William Wynn of Maury County, Tennessee. Mary E.
Wynn states that on the 16th day of June 1855, she married
with F. L. P. Wynn. They lived together until he deserted
her for parts unknown, her husband became infatuated with his
sister in law, the widow of his deceased brother John B. Wynn.
F. L. P. Wynn and Mary E. Wynn had one child, a little boy,
John Thompson Wynn about 2 years old. F. L. P. Wynn went to
Illinois, 14 December 1857, to visit his brother James Wynn.
He had a brother William Wynn.

Page 381 - Thomas Nash & others   ]
                      vs   ]Petition, August 2, 1858.
            William W. Nash & others]
Thomas Nash, Grandison M. Nash, Lafayette Nash, all of Texas
and John P. Steele, James G. Neeley, James Nash, the last of
whom is a son of John R. Nash, deceased, and claims in right
of his father and _____ Parsons and wife Louisa Parsons one

of the heirs of George W. Nash, deceased, all of Bedford
County states that Francis C. Nash departed this life in
Bedford County on _____, leaving his widow Joanna Nash
who had her dower allotted to her by the Court in 1857. The
widow departed this life leaving your petitioners and William
W. Nash a son and heir of George W. Nash, deceased, who is
a minor and citizen of Bedford County, and Joanna Harville,
Coleman Harville, Thomas Harville, Frank Harville and Willis
Harville, who are all minors and children of Louisa Harville,
deceased, formerly Nash, one of the original heirs of Francis
C. Nash, deceased, and resides in the State of Alabama, all
of which last six are made defendants. Lands of T. C. Nash,
deceased, bounded by the heirs of John Hutton, William Houston,
Thomas B. Marks and wife, and Thomas Ogilvie and wife. About
125 acres, lying six miles north of Shelbyville near the
Shelbyville-Murfreesboro Turnpike Road. Francis C. Nash,
deceased, left fifteen children and your petitioner James G.
Nash has purchased the interests of George W. Nash which at
the time was one-fifteenth, also the interests of James Nash
and F. M. Nash which at the time one-fourteenth, ____ Nash
having died intestate and without issue, also the interests
of Augustus Nash, Levi C. Johnson and wife Elizabeth, John
McGimpsey and wife Polly and T. C. Nash, Jr., which purchases
by the term of deeds passes the title to one-thirteenth each
of the whole, ____ Nash having also died intestate and without
issue, all of which deeds will be produced and the Court asked
to determine the interests of the parties.
     Emily Garrett wife of ____ Garrett who has sold her in-
terest to your petitioner Lafayette Nash, owner of two shares.

Page 383 - W. W. McGill & others]
              vs   ] Filed August 11, 1858.
          W. C. Holt & others   ]
W. W. McGill and Daniel B. Shriver filed against W. C. Holt
and William S. Jett. Orators states that sometime about the
month of November 1857, your orator W. W. McGill recovered
a judgement against William C. Holt as principal and your
orator D. B. Shriver as endorsers for $216.00 and interest.
William C. Holt purchased a negro woman named Cinda and her
child Perry and the title of said negroes is still in William
S. Jett.

Page 386 - Mullins & Stokes   ] Inj. Bill, filed
              vs   ] October 4, 1858.
          William W. McGill & others]
James Mullins and John M. Stokes of Bedford County states that
on 7 August 1858, they recovered a judgement against William C.
Holt of Bedford County for $1007.00 and cost.

Page 390 - James C. Gambill   ] Att. & Inj. Bill, filed
              vs   ] January 12, 1856.
          L. C. Reid & others]
James C. Gambill filed against L. C. Reid formerly of Bedford
County, now betond the State of Tennessee, and James Stallings
and Benjamin Mosely and Jno. H. Gambill residing in Tennessee.
Orator states that L. C. Reid is indebted to him for $600.00
and cost. It being a note executed by L. C. Reid to James S.
Newton, your orator as security. Orator states that L. C.
Reid left Tennessee on a trading expedition to the south during
November 1855, he said he would be back by 1st of January but
he has not returned. L. C. Reid has interest in a tract of
land on which he lives, in Bedford County, on the Farmington-

Shelbyville Turnpike Road and adjoining the lands of William
B. M. Brame, Richard Sims and your orator James C. Gambill.
Money is still due, and is going to John H. Gambill as admr
of Eli Griffith. Benjamin Mosely is also indebted to L. C.
Reid. L. C. Reid is married, wife not named.

Page 395 - W. A. Trice   ]
                  vs   ]Petition, March 20, 1856.
            J. C. Gambill &]
            Stallings   ]
James H. Gambill a brother of J. C. Gambill. James Stallings
is son in law of James C. Gambill.

Page 399 - J. C. Gambill   ]
                  vs   ]Answer of Trice, February 4, 1857.
            L. C. Reid et als]
Two bills, 2nd filed February 16, 1848. Answer of William A.
Trice. Joseph Trice is a brother of William A. Trice.

Page 409 - Thomas Lipscomb   ]Inj. & Att. Bill, filed
                  vs   ]   24 March 1857.
            E. D. Dromgoole & others]
Thomas Lipscomb of Bedford County filed against E. D. Dromgoole,
Greer Evans, David S. Evans, M. E. W. Dunnaway and William
Griffis and P. Fay and John P. Dromgoole, all of Bedford
County. Orator states that 18th of this month, he recovered
a judgement of $166.-- against E. D. Dromgoole and also become
owner by transfer of a judgement rendered against Dromgoole
in favor of Robert Mathews for $244.65. Orator says that
Dromgoole has interest in a lot in Town of Shelbyville, known
as Lot No. __, that was purchased of P. Fay about Christmas
on 1st January 1857. On said lot there is a Livery Stable.

Page 416 - Isaac Green   ] Att. & Inj. Bill, filed
                  vs   ]   March 20, 1857.
            O. A. Mobley & others]
Isaac Green of Bedford County filed against Orvill A. Mobley,
a non-resident of Tennessee and who resides in Alabama, A. S.
Lawrence, Robert Denniston, Robert N. Jones, and J. E. Bennett,
Garrett Phillips of Bedford County and A. J. Powell and Charles
Powell of Rutherford County, Tennessee. Orator states that
endorsed a note executed by O. A. Mobley who has recently moved
to Alabama, for $400.00. Check is voided by bank. Mobley
owned several notes.

Page 421 - J. H. Burdett]
                  vs   ]Inj. Bill, April 24, 1857.
            McGrew & Kent]
Joel H. Burdett filed against J. H. McGrew of Bedford County.
Orator states that he stayed the following judgements on 16
August 1856 in favor of J. H. McGrew and against George B.
Kent for $46.29 and cost, and another for $6.76 and cost and
another for $151.74 and cost.

Page 423 - A. Crooker   ]
                  vs   ] Att. Bill, filed January 1858.
            W. W. Summers]
A. Crooker of Davidson County, Tennessee filed against W. W.
Summers. Orator states that W. W. Summers is indebted to him
for goods sold and delivered, sum of $114.83 and interest
since July 1857. Orator said at the time W. W. Summers was
a resident of Bedford County and on 8 July 1857 he conveyed
all his property, subject to execution, consisting of a lot

of fancy dry goods and millinery and a safe and chair, to L. B.
Knott in Trust by Deed. Summers has a wife and she continued
the business of selling the goods in Shelbyville. Summer left
Bedford County some two or three months ago to parts unknown.

Page 425 - James M. Warner &]
            Jno. W. Rutledge]All of Bedford County, filed
                  vs   ]   August 7, 1857.
            Thomas Baxter   ]
James M. Warner states that on or about 17th of November 1855,
he purchased from Thomas Baxter a negro boy named Anderson
for about $1550.00. Orator wanted a good carpenter and the
negro boy did not know much about carpentry.

Page 429 - W. W. Pennington]
                  vs   ]Inj. & Att. Bill, Dec. 18, 1857.
            E. P. Wynn et als]
William W. Pennington of Bedford County filed against E. P.
Wynn, F. L. P. Wynn and Edmund Cooper, all of Bedford County,
and William Wynn of Maury County, Tennessee. Orator states
that F. L. P. Wynn is indebted to him by note dated 25 December 1857 for $110.00, and F. L. P. Wynn has absconded, left
the state.

Page 432 - William A. Allen]
                  vs   ] Filed July 22, 1857.
            Martha E. Swailes]
All of Bedford County. Orator states that about 2 years ago,
he was appointed guardian of Martha E. Swailes, a minor, about
17 years old.

Page 434 - Elizabeth Huffman]
                  vs   ] Filed 29 November 1854.
            John Huffman et als]
Elizabeth Huffman of Bedford County states that she is the
widow of Peter Huffman who departed this life intestate in
Bedford County in 1821. She has never been endowed of his
real estate of which he died seized and possessed, all of which
then lay in Bedford County and consisting of about 475 acres,
lying on south side of Barren Fork of Duck River. Bounded
by Hugh Davidson, River and John Drake. Peter Huffman left
the following children, John Huffman, George Huffman, Alfred S.
Huffman, Mary wife of Thomas G. Cribbs, and Sarah wife of
James B. Dalby, the last of whom now reside in Texas. Part
of Peter Huffman's land was in Bedford County and part in
Coffee County, Tennessee. Widow lived for many years with
her son John who finally bought all the interest in the dower
land.

Page 439 - John L. Curtiss & wife]
                  vs   ] Filed 15 December 1856.
            Isaac S. Davidson   ]
John L. Curtiss and wife Nancy R. Curtiss of the State of Iowa,
states that Dr. Isaac S. Davidson of Bedford County was formerly guardian of Nancy R. Curtiss and that she is now about
20 years old, that she has lately married John L. Curtiss in
the State of Iowa, states that Isaac S. Davidson has in his
possession three slaves, Bill, a girl _____, and another girl
named Mary, and some 16 or 17 hundred dollars in money. Nancy
R. is a niece of John L. Curtiss. Iowa says that a man must
be 16 and the lady 14 years of age.

Page 441 - John F. Brown   ]
                     vs   ] Filed 30 May 1855.
            Robert W. Brown &]
            W. W. Stanfield   ]
Orator states that he recovered a judgement against Robert W.
Brown in Bedford County on 18 December 1854 for $205.62 and
cost. Robert W. Brown has interest in land in Civil District
No. 23 of Bedford County, the place where Brown now resides
and of which he purchased of W. W. Stanfield who purchased
of the heirs of John Evans, deceased. Adjoining lands of
John W. Gardner and heirs of _____ Miles, deceased, it being
the place that was once owned by John Evans and on his death,
again sold, and bought by W. W. Stanfield.

Page 444 - W. K. Rayburn & Co.   ]
                     vs   ] Filed February 23, 1857.
            Leonard Shanklin & others]
Leander Hickerson, W. K. Rayburn, David Hickerson and John
Hickerson, partners, filed against Leonard C. Shanklin, George
N. Anderson and R. W. McClure, Thomas Burnett and W. T. Myers.
Orators states that they are partners transacting business
in Bedford County under firm of W. K. Rayburn & Co. and that
they recovered two judgements against Leonard C. Shanklin on
12 February 1857 for about $150.00 and cost.

Page 445 - C. A. Fowler   ]
                     vs   ] Filed 4 July 1857.
            W. B. Parker & others]
C. A. Fowler of Bedford County filed against Walter B. Parker,
A. L. Stamps and George W. Buchanan. Orator states that on
3 June 1857, he purchased from Walter B. Parker, a lot near
the Town of Shelbyville, about one acre and forty poles,
adjoining land of George W. Buchanan and others and on which
your orator now lives.

Page 448 - J. C. Word   ]
                     vs   ] Inj. Bill, filed March 17, 1857.
            William Brown]
James C. Word said that on 7 August 1855 or about that day,
C. D. Steele and Samuel Doak executed their bill to pay your
orator $500.00.

Page 452 - H. J. M. Holt   ]
                     vs   ] Filed 18 June 1856.
            J. G. Harrison et als]
Orator of Bedford County states that Brittain Felps of Missouri
is indebted to him for $280.00 for money paid by him as stayor
of Joshua Holt, Jr., Joshua Holt, Sr., and Brittain Felps on
a joint judgement rendered in favor of Robert Hastings and
that there is a fund of about $290.00 in the hands of James G.
Harrison usually known by name of Granville Harrison, going
to Brittain Felps on two notes. Joshua Holt, Jr. secured a
Trust Deed.

Page 455 - Anne Shofner   ] Att. & Inj. Bill, filed
                     vs   ]   9 October 1856.
            William M. Shofner]
Anne Shofner of Bedford County states that she married on ___
day of ___ 185_ to William M. Shofner and she has had two
children, one is 5 years old named Elizabeth, other also a
girl aged 1 year old and 1 month named Melissa, that William
who had a former (marriage). William M. Shofner had by a
former wife a child named Sarah aged about 11 years, all of

which are living with your oratrix. Oratrix states that when
she married William Shofner, she had in her own right a slave
woman with her, three children. William had two slaves and
other property. She also states that her husband William has
abandoned her almost entirely, and has gone to another woman
named Sarah Martin. William stated that he was leaving the
state and going to Texas.
Amended Bill, filed March 1857 A.D.
Anne Shofner stated that her husband William Shofner has left
the state and was followed by a woman named Sarah Martin.

Page 460 - William J. Peacock]
                    vs   ] Filed 13 December 1855.
          William Campbell   ]
Orator states that Claiborn W. Black was appointed guardian
of the minor children of George J. Black at ___ Term 185_.
Some months ago, C. W. Black was removed as guardian and
William Campbell appointed in his stead. In 1855, a suit was
brought up against your orator on said bond, in the name of
the State of Tennessee for use of William Campbell. C. W.
Black left the country. All of Bedford County.

Page 463 - Elizabeth Tune]
                    vs   ] Filed March 6, 1857.
          John Tune   ]
Oratrix of Bedford County filed against John Tune of Bedford
County. She stated that on 12 June 1853, she married John
Tune. He began to mistreat her and she asks for a divorce.
Elizabeth Tune being now in her 60 year. She owned at time
she married two slaves, Bob and Missouri, which are in possess-
ion of her husband, and a tract of land in Tipton County, Tenn-
essee, about 200 acres. John Tune had a daughter Eveline.

Page 470 - Yowell & Medearis, Exrs &]
          George W. Buchanan   ]
                    vs   ] Filed September 29, 1856.
          Trice, Mosely, Curtiss   ]
          & others   ]
William Yowell and John T. Medearis, executors of Joel Yowell,
deceased, and George W. Buchanan filed against James W. Wallace,
Joseph Trice, Benjamin Mosely, James H. Curtiss and Morgan &
Co., and John L. Curtiss. Orators are holders of a note
executed to W. P. S. Majors as Trustee of Robert Moffat,
deceased, and assigned to their ancestor for $550.00 and note
was executed by James W. Wallace for the purchase money of
a tract of land in the suburbs of Town of Shelbyville.

Page 472 - Hugh C. Hurst & others]
                    vs   ]Inj. Bill, June 2, 1856.
          C. D. & J. P. Steele   ]
Samuel Doak, Samuel G. Hays, James Mullins and Hugh C. Hurst,
all of Bedford County filed against John P. Steele and C. D.
Steele of Bedford County. Orators stated that on 10 April
1852, C. D. Steele executed a Conveyance in Trust, on cartain
lot of machinery for the manufacture of buckets, to secure
your orator Samuel Doak against certain liabilities of Doak
for C. D. Steele. Hugh C. Hurst lives on a tract of land which
is the property of Samuel Doak.

Page 487 - John C. Hix   ]
                    vs   ] Filed January 7, 1857.
          Herod F. Holt & others]
John C. Hix of Bedford County stated that in April 1856, he

246

recovered a judgement against Herod F. Holt and Herod G. Holt
for $835.33 and cost.

Page 490 - Hugh C. Hurst   ]
                   vs   ] Filed December 25, 1856.
            George W. Brown]
Orator states that George W. Brown is indebted to him for
$300.00, that he has sued Brown on claim which is now pending.
Orator states that Brown has land in Bedford County in Civil
District No. __, bounded by R. S. Dwiggins, Joseph Morton and
L. W. Barrett.

Page 491 - James Smith & others   ]
                   vs   ] Filed April 6, 1855.
            T. M. Coldwell & others]
Orator states that Joshua Holt, Sr. departed this life, having
made his will, which has been proven and he devised certain
slaves to his wife during life and after her death, remainder
to his children and appointed Herod F. and Jordan C. Holt as
executors, thereafter the said tenant for life departed this
life and afterwards at the January Term 1853. Order to sell
slaves for distribution among remainder. Slaves were sold.

Page 494 - Wisener & Scudder   ] Att. Bill, filed
                   vs   ] March 12, 1855.
            Thomas G. Williamson & others]
William H. Wisener and James L. Scudder, partners in business,
stated that Thomas G. Williamson, Joseph M. Williamson and
Caroline Williamson are indebted to them for professional
services in the case of Williamson against Samuel and Moses
Neely and others. Bill was for a tract of land, about 240
or 250 acres in Bedford County and a decree at August Term
1854 dismissing case. The Williamsons live in Arkansas has
sold all interest in their property. Thomas G. Williamson
is a resident of Bedford County. Their land was sold.
Williamsons are entitled to fund at the death of their father
if they should not recover the land and interests during his
life by gift from him. Land is in District No. 20 of Bedford
County. Moses and Samuel Neely now reside and also a portion
of it is now in the possession of William Gabbert's heirs and
is the same purchased by Roger Snell.

Page 495 - Joseph Trice   ]
                   vs   ]Att. Bill, 20 June 1856.
            John L. Curtiss]
Joseph Trice stated that he is the endorser of John L. Curtiss
for about $250.00. Curtiss left Tennessee on the 19th inst.,
about 9 o'clock P.M. in a private buggy and is going to parts
unknown. He is the owner of a tract of land in District No.
20 which he bought of John Williams, Jr. and one that he
purchased of Thomas J. Williams, about 110 acres and about
50 acres adjoining John Williams, and about 6 or 7 acres near
Town of Shelbyville, on the Rail Road which he purchased of
Amos Hays and also 8 or 10 acres near Shelbyville which he
purchased of James W. Wallace.

Page 496 - James H. Curtiss] Inj. & Att. Bill, filed
                   vs   ]   June 21, 1856.
            John L. Curtiss]
James H. Curtiss of Bedford County filed against John L.
Curtiss who has gone to parts unknown. Orator states that
John L. Curtiss is indebted to him by note past due for $140.00
and that he is the security of the said John L. Curtiss on

a note for $150.00 past due to John McAdams, one to Morgan & Co. and one to _____ Berry. John L. Curtiss lately resided in Bedford County but during your orators absence from home because of health and being your orator's brother, has taken advantage of your orators hospitality and absconded in the right, and taking with him the child of your orator, a young girl just ripened into womanhood, all of property of John L. Curtiss that was left in Bedford County was attached. One tract was one he, John L. Curtiss bought of John Williams, Jr. in District No. 20, also a tract of land he bought of Thomas J. Williams, first containing about 100 acres and the latter about 110 acres and about 50 acres he purchased of J. McWilliams in District No. 20 and adjoining lands of John Williams. He also is owner of 6 acres near Town of Shelbyville he purchased of Amos Hays, and 8 or 10 acres he purchased of James W. Wallace and he is owner of the land your orator by title.

Page 498 - Morgan & Co.   ]Att. & Inj. Bill, filed
                vs   ]   July 12, 1856.
         Jno. L. Curtiss &]
         W. L. Brown   ]
S. D. Morgan, R. H. Gardner, C. J. Cherry and R. C. Gardner, partners, filed against John L. Curtiss who has gone to parts unknown and William L. Brown of Bedford County. Orators stated that John L. Curtiss is indebted to them for $377.80 by note dated October 21, 1854, due.

Page 500 - Benjamin Mosely]
                vs   ]Att. Bill, 20 June 1856.
         John L. Curtiss]
Benjamin Mosely of Bedford County is the security of John L. Curtiss in two notes to James A. Gant each $500.00.

Page 501 - Joseph Hastings & Elliott]
                vs   ]Bill filed August 19, 1856.
         Cannon, Reed & others   ]
James M. Elliott and Joseph Hastings of Bedford County filed against Clement Cannon, Jo Harriet Woosley, Joseph M. Woosley, Martin Reed and wife Nancy Jane formerly Nancy Jane Woosley, John H. Woosley, Ary Adaline Woosley, Thomas A. Woosley, William C. Woosley, Nathan C. Woosley, Erastus F. Woosley, Mariam T. Woosley, Virgil Cicero Woosley, and Asa L. Stamps Woosley, the last ten of whom are minors and have no guardian. Orators states that in June 1854, deft Clement Cannon sold William Woosley a tract of land in Bedford County in District No. 7 for $280.00 on one and two years credit. Orator stated that Woosley on or about 13 April 1856, departed this life intestate, leaving Jo Harriet Woosley and eleven children, to wit, Joseph M., Nancy Jane who married Martin Reed, John H., Ary Adaline, Thomas A., William C., Nathan C., Erastus F., Mariam T., Virgil C., and Asa L. Stamps Woosley, the last ten of whom including N. J. Reed are minors with no guardian, as his only heirs at law and distributees. In May Term 1856, Joseph Hastings was appointed admr of estate of William Woosley, deceased, who was his son in law. William Woosley died possessed of land of about 75 acres and on which he resided.

Page 504 - Friar Trail & wife]
                vs   ] Filed December 23, 1852, A.D.
         S. H. Whitthorne &]
         Jno. S. Frazier, Jr.]

Friar Trail and his wife Eliza Jane Trail filed against Samuel
H. Whitthorne and John S. Frazier, Jr. Orators states that
Eliza Jane formerly the wife of John S. Frazier, deceased,
who departed this life in Bedford County in the Spring of 1850,
June 20. A Last Will and Testament was produced and proven
in court. Samuel H. Whitthorne appointed admr. Oratrix being
dissatisfied with the provisions made for her in said will
filed this bill. The said John S. Frazier left only one child
John S. Frazier, Jr. of whom Preston Frazier has been appointed
guardian by court. At the death of John S. Frazier, he owned
11 negroes, Terry 50 years, Tom 32 years, Rich about 23 years,
Mathew about 20 years, Mary Ann about 28 years, Milly about
32 years, William about 12 years, Sarah about 10 years, Barbara
about 7 years old, and two boys Isam and Lewis. Eliza Jane
stated that she married Friar Trail some 12 or 18 months ago,
nut before their marriage they made a marriage contract or
agreement that she would have and hold all property both real
and personal which she then held in her possession and would
be exempt from all the liabilities of Friar Trail. She also
stated that her desire to have interest in slaves separated
from that of her son John S. Frazier, Jr.
Supplemental Bill of Friar Trail and wife:
Whitthorne has resifned as admr and January 1853 Court appointed Robert H. Temple of Bedford County in his stead.

Page 509 - True, Hendricks & others]
                vs   ]Filed February 21, 1855.
          John P. Dromgoole   ]
Lorenzo W. True, Levi N. Hendricks and H. B. Quinby filed
against John P. Dromgoole. Orators states that they together
with Quinby prior to the time of making the Deed of Trust,
were partners in manufacturing of Carriages, Barouches and
Buggies &c. Quinby sold his interest in firm.

Page 514 - Daniel A. McRea]
                vs   ] Filed 13 January 1853.
          John Bradford   ]
Daniel A. McRea, a resident of Talladega County, Alabama,
states that some fifteen years ago (about 1838) when he was
a boy, his Aunt Christian McRea gave him a negro girl by the
name of Fanny, then about 12 or 14 years old, by verbal gift
in State of Alabama and at the same time delivered the girl
to your orator who was then living with his father and she
remained there with them until 10 or 12 years ago when she
was levied on and sold by the Sheriff of Talladega County,
Alabama, as the property of your orator's father for a debt
against Malcom McRea, your orator's father and Joseph H. Bradford became the purchaser of said negro girl "Fanny". Your
orator was at that time still a mere boy and never heard of
"Fanny" until a short time since, when he learned she was in
the possession of John Bradford of Bedford County. At this
time Fanny had several children (maybe six), Fanny is now about
27 or 30 years of age. Your orator is now 22 years old.
Answer of John Bradford, filed 5 April 1853.
Bradford said he obtained Fanny from his son Joseph H. Bradford
of Coosa County, Alabama.

Page 520 - James M. Elliott   ]
                vs   ]Filed March 31, 1856.
          S. Doak, Holman & Flack]
Orator states that he recovered two judgements against Samuel
Doak for $6095.02 and cost.

Page 525 - William G. Turner]
                    vs   ]Filed 25 February 1856.
             M. A. Cummings   ]
William G. Turner of Bedford County states that on November
or December 1853, he and his brother Robert H. Turner, made
a verbal contract of partnership to carry on a Wood & Timber
Shop for the year, 1857. In 1853, he started putting his shop
together. In 1854, he loaned his brother $24.00 to purchase
some tools as he was going to Nashville. Robert H. returned
without tools and returned $15.00. Your orator took the $15.00
and went to Nashville and purchased of James Erwin $37.65 worth
of tools. Robert H. fell into debt, before contract was entered for $20.85. Your orator became sick and lay sick at his
father's for many months and at the same time Robert H. became
sick and died. Before Robert H. died, he gathered the crops
for himself even tho the hired hands were paid for by your
orator. Since the death of Robert H., N. A.(Newton A.)Cummings
the father in law of Robert H. , and a citizen of Bedford
County, admr of the estate of Robert H. and sold the partnership property including tools &c.

Page 529 - Ransom & Turrentine, Exrs]
                    vs   ]Filed February 4, 1857.
             David P. Orr & others   ]
Alfred Ransom and Felix Turrentine, executors of David Orr,
deceased, and Felix Turrentine and Martha Ann Turrentine in
their own right filed against Larkin B. Orr, William N. Orr,
Joseph Anderson, executor of Frances Jane Orr, Gilly Ann Harris,
Martha Elizabeth Burton, David P. Orr, W. J. Orr in his own
right and as admr with the will annexed of his sister Elizabeth
Orr, G. L. Orr, William C. Orr, Susan R. Orr, Martha F. Orr,
and John A. and Mary A. Orr, children of Mary A. Hall, dec'd,
formerly Mary A. Orr, who has David P. Orr as guardian, all
of Bedford COunty. Orators stated that David Orr departed
this life __ day of ___, 18__, having first made and published
his Last Will and Testament which was proven at July Term 1854
Court in Bedford County. Alfred Ransom and Felix Turrentine
appointed as executors.
Will - Item No. 6 - It is my will and I so direct that in my
case of my death before my daughter Frances Jane Orr should
marry that she shall have her choice of any of the negroes
that may be living, which negro or negroes is to be valued
to her by executors and the price charged to her in her part
or share of my estate. And further, I give to my said daughter
Frances Jane, a good horse, saddle and bridle. The balance
of my estate both real and personal it is my will that it shall
all be sold on a 12 months credit, and the money when collected
to be divided in the following manner, viz, after all my debts
are paid, giving to John Orr's children one-sixteenth part,
and the children of my sons Larkin B. and William N. each of
them one-sixth part and to be managed by the Trustees named
in the 2nd and 3rd Items in this will for the sole use and
benefit of the children of the said Larkin B. and William N.
in that way and manner as the said Trustees shall think best,
and one-sixth part to my daughter Martha Ann Turrentine, one-
sixth part to my daughter Frances Jane, and to my two grand
daughters, Gilly Ann Harris and Martha Elizabeth Burton one-
sixth part to be divided between them, so as to give to
Gilly Ann Harris $40.00 more than Martha Elizabeth, and should
either of them die before they marry, their portion is to return to my estate and be equally divided amongst the rest of
my heirs as above direction. Frances Ann Orr did not marry
before the death of the testator and that she selected a negro

named Jim which orators handed over to her and valued him at
$950.00, also a horse, saddle and bridle, that since the
death of David Orr, Frances Jane has died, having first made
and published her Last Will and Testament, in which she appointed Joseph Anderson, her executor.
Answer of David P. Orr, guardian, filed 2 March 1857.
David P. Orr, guardian of David A. Hall, W. J. Hall, and Mary
A. Hall, who was formerly Mary A. Orr a child of John Orr,
deceased, Jane Orr, Gilly Hall and John A. Hall the husband
of Gilly Hall and William C. Orr for himself and as admr for
Elizabeth Orr, deceased, Susan R. Orr, Francew Orr, all are
children and grand children of John Orr, deceased. Said will
of John Orr was made in October 1847 and he died in June 1854.

Page 533 - Stephen Galleghy   ]
                vs   ] Filed 16 February 1857.
          William Cully &   ]
          William J. Whitthorne]
Stephen Galleghy of Coffee County, Tennessee states that on
__ day of August 1855, William Cully filed a bill against your
orator and Joseph Galleghy and Daniel Stephens.

Page 535 - Middleton Holland & others]
                vs   ] Filed December 17, 1855.
          William M. Green & others   ]
Middleton Holland, Thomas Holland and James M. Elkins filed
against W. M. Green, David R. Vance and Mary Green and Robert
Arnold. Middleton Holland states that James Green, late of
Coffee COunty, Tennessee, died in Coffee County in 1853 and
at December Term 1853, his will was proven and recorded.
W. M. Green and David R. Vance were appointed executors. In
his will, he bequeathed all his property to his wife Mary Green
to make his youngest children equal with those who had married
and left him. When the youngest children reached 21 years
of age, his wife should sell a part of his land by his description, and to dispose of all personal property that she does
not need. At the death of his wife, W. M. Green and David R.
Vance should dispose of the remainder of his property, real
and personal. James Green died possessed of slaves.

Page 539 - James H. Curtiss & wife]
                vs   ]
          Benjamin Mosely   ]
James H. Curtiss and Theresa Curtiss filed against Benjamin
Mosely,   of Bedford County. Orators states that Johnathan
Mosely, the father of Theresa, departed this life in texas,
having made and published his Last Will and Testament. He
devised in his will unto oratrix part of his estate equally
divided among other children and his estate ready to divide
and being unable to go to State of Texas to receive it. Johnathan Mosely's estate on November 1854, appoint Benjamin Mosely
attorney.
Answer: Filed May 1st, 1856.
Benjamin Mosely was to go to Texas and get their share, he
was also to receive the shares of Lucy Mosely, Robert Mosely,
Absalom Mosely and his own share. Benjamin Mosely purchased
Absalom Mosely but never received it, because it was in litigat-
ion there.   Johnathan Mosely's wife named Lucy. After his
death in Texas, his widow returned to Bedford County. She
appointed Isom Mosely to sell property in Texas, as all children or legatees are in Tennessee.

251

Page 544 - James F. Cummings]
     vs   ]Filed August 10, 1854.
   Jas. T. Carter &]
   William Goodrich]
James F. Cummings of Bedford County filed against James T.
Carter who resides in Philadelphia and William Goodrich of
parts unknown. Orator states that during the year 184_, he
was in the Mercantile Business at Shelbyville in partnership
with (William) Word. The firm purchased of Jamse T. Carter
on 10 September 1847, a bill of goods for which they executed
a note due in 6 months for $451.20. After the note was ex-
ecuted the firm dissolved and your orator engaged in his own
name. He bought in 1848, goods in Philadelphia. His goods,
which was on its way to Bedford County, was attached because
of note of said Carter.

Page 548 - James F. Cummings]
     vs   ]Inj. Bill, filed 21 August 1854.
   Hart, Cummings &]
   Cushman   ]
James F. Cummings of Bedford County filed against John V. Hart,
James A. Cummings and Robert W. Cushman of Pennsylvania. Orator
states that he was engaged in business with William M. Word,
retailing of goods, wares &c in Shelbyville, Bedford County
and bought from Philadelphia for $624.44 and gave note in
September 8, 1847.

Page 553 - Alexander Downing, Admr]
     vs   ] Filed August 23, 1854.
   William Eoff, Jr. &]
   others   ]
Alexander Downing, admr of William Eoff, deceased, and of
William R. Downing and also Andrew L., John C., and Catharine
E. Downing, the last three being infants without a guardian
and suing by their father Alexander Downing, all of Coffee
County, Tennessee, and of John Robinson and wife Delila of
Cannon County, Tennessee filed against William Eoff, John Jakes
and wife Nancy and George Jakes, all of Bedford County. Orators
stated that William Eoff, Sr. departed this life intestate
in Bedford County in month of January or February last (1854).
Alexander Downing was appointed admr of the estate. William R.,
Andrew L., and John C. Downing and your oratrix Catharine E.
Downing are the grandchildren, being the children of William
Eoff's daughter Elizabeth Downing who died in the lifetime
of said intestate. Also Delila Robinson wife of John Robinson
is the daughter of William Eoff, deceased, and William Eoff
is a son of William Eoff, deceased, and that Nancy Jakes is
a daughter of William Jakes, deceased, and George Jakes is
the only child of Jane Jakes, deceased, who was a daughter
of William Eoff, deceased. William Eoff, Sr. owned a tract
of land, about 414 acres in District No. 1 of Bedford County,
where on he resided in year 1845 and afterwards. He also
owned slaves. 25 September 1845, William Eoff, Sr. executed
a deed to William Eoff, Jr. a tract of land for love and
affection. In October 1853, William Eoff, Jr. sold said land
and purchased another tract of land, William Eoff, Sr. removed
to new tract and remained there until his death. The land
was purchased from Martin Hancock and is located in Bedford
County, bounded by George Shaw, C. C. P. Shaw, William Keels
and Sharp. William Eoff, Jr. kept possession of estate of
William Eoff, Sr's estate. William Eoff, Sr's wife died some
6 months before her husband at the age about 65.

Page 566 - B. F. Wiggins   ] Inj. & Att. Bill, filed
              vs   ]   January 31, 1856.
         James Smith & others]
B. F. Wiggins of Bedford County filed against James Smith,
J. W. Crunk and William C. Crunk, all of Bedford County. Orator
stated that he is the owner of several judgements on James
Smith.

Page 568 - Hugh C. Hurst, Exr &c]
              vs   ] Filed November 10, 1854.
         Nelson Gabbert & others]
Hugh C. Hurst of Bedford County filed against Nelson Gabbert
of Arkansas and Miles Phillips, John Brown and Edmund Cooper,
the three last of Bedford County. Orator states that Nelson
Gabbert is indebted to him as executor of William Gabbert,
deceased, also as security of George G. Gabbert, citizen of
another state. Nelson Gabbert was at one time a resident of
Bedford County.

Page 573 - J. A. Blakemore, Admr &c]
              vs   ]Filed August 30, 1853.
         Jacob Whitsell & others]
J. A. Blakemore, admr of John Whitsell, deceased. Orator
stated that John Whitsell departed this life in 1842 and Daniel
L. Barringer appointed executor of his Last Will and Testament.
By will, his widow is to have the dower in his land and one-
tenth of his personal estate and balance to be divided equally
between eight of his children, except for $5.00 for his other
child, Jeremiah, one of his children, John died before his
father and his eighth part lapsed, and on the __ day of ___,
James and Polly C. Gambill in right of their mother who was
a daughter of testator filed their bill for their share of
the estate and an account was taken and the executor charged
with the whole estate and one-eighth decreed to the complainants without allowing the widow her one-tenth of the personal
estate and in no way disposing of the one-eighth devised to
John Whitsell, which has lapsed. Orator states afterwards,
Lewis Whitsell, a lunatic, by his guardian B. F. Greer filed
for his share of estate. Orator stated that the executor has
departed this life intestate and said cause revived against
your orator as admr. Jacob Whitsell another son of testator
has filed for his share of estate. Jerry Whitsell, son, gets
$5.00 (Jeremiah). George W. Whitsell, deceased, one of the
sons. Children of John Whitsell, deceased, to wit, Jacob,
Lewis a lunatic with B. F. Greer as his guardian, George W.,
William, Emily C., Jeremiah, Mariah, John and Isabel and Milly
his widow. John died intestate before his mother. George W.
has since died and his admr has received his share as ascertained in the Gambill suit and has since died. The estate of
George W. being insolvent and settled, it is now too late for
the correction of the error as to his share. Mariah has since
died leaving her husband H. Gambill and two children, to wit,
James and Mary. Isabel has died leaving her husband Mark
Thomas and three children, to wit, Nancy, John and William,
minors and no guardian. Jeremiah has since died intestate
leaving a widow Matilda J. and one child, to wit, John, a minor
and no guardian. And Emily C. has since intermarried with
one William F. Barrett, all of whom still reside in Bedford
County except James Gambill who resides in Kentucky. Milly
widow of John Whitsell. Jeremiah had a son John H. Whitsell.

Page 583 - Jacob Whitsell   ]
                  vs   ]O. Bill, February 17, 1853.
          John A. Blakemore et als]
Jacob Whitsell of Bedford County filed against John C. Coldwell
and John A. Blakemore of Bedford County and Minos Cannon of
Alabama. Orator stated that John Whitsell departed this life
in 1842 in Bedford County. Daniel L. Barringer, his admr,
now deceased, and John Wilhoite his executor who refused to
qualify. John Whitsell left the following heirs, to wit,
Lewis Whitsell, William F. Barrett and wife Emily Caroline
Barrett formerly Emily Caroline Whitsell, William Whitsell
who has since the death of his father departed this life leaving William, Mary S. Whitsell, Jerry (Jeremiah) Whitesell who
has since died leaving one child John, Mark Thomas and wife
Isabell Thomas who has since died leaving three children Nancy,
John and William (Isabell formerly Isabell Whitesell), and
Alfred H. Gambill and wife Mariah Gambill formerly Mariah
Whitesell who has also died leaving James and Mary.

Page 587 - Lewis Whitesell by his   ]
          guardian Benjamin F. Greer]   O. Bill, filed
                  vs   ]   17 July 1851.
          Daniel L. Barringer,   ]
          W. W. Whitesell & others]
Lewis Whitesell, an idiot, filed by guardian Benjamin F. Greer
against Daniel L. Barringer and John C. Coldwell, W. W. Whitesell, John S. Brown and Eli Moss, all of Bedford County and
Minos Cannon of Alabama.

Page 590 - Francis Black   ]   O. Bill, filed
                  vs   ]   20 September 1855.
          Claiborne W. Black et als]
Francis Black (female) sues by her next friend William W. Winstead filed against George I. Black and Claiborne W. Black.
Oratrix stated that she is the wife of George I. Black of Bedford County. She also stated that some years ago she obtained
a land warrant for the services of her deceased husband (by
a former husband) A. J. Eaton for services rendered in the
Mexican War, which warrant she sold and with $80.00, part of
the proceeds of said warrant she purchased from James Burrow,
a small tract of land in Bedford County in District No. 22
and adjoining lands of Thomas Connell, James R. Reese and the
heirs of William Whinsey. About 39+ acres. Her husband had
a brother Claiborne W. Black who agreed to help pay for said
land, provided a deed should be made to him for the land. This
she did. At the time C. W. Black was guardian of her children.
He failed to pay out of his money and he also took $10.00 out
of the children's money due them and paid it to James Burrow.
Oratrix said some 8 or 10 months since the said C. W. Black
(who had up to that time resided in Marshall County, Tennessee)
got into a difficulty and left this state and went to parts
unknown. He was to make the deed for the land over to her.
He left without making the deed.

Page 592 - Johnson & Smith   ]
                  vs   ]   Filed 19 February 1856.
          Gwynn Foster & others]
Anthony W. Johnson and G. P. Smith, merchants and partners
and citizens of Davidson County, Tennessee stated that on 16
February they recovered a judgement against Gwynn Foster for
$164.00 for debts and damages and cost. Orators states that
Gwynn Foster and Richard C. Ogilvie, his son in law who is
now dead (died August 1852), purchased in 1850 from George T.

Landers, 84½ acres in Bedford County. After death of R. C.
Ogilvie, at November Term 1852, the said Gwynn Foster and widow
and children of R. C. Ogilvie, deceased, petitioned for sale
of said land and court agreed to the sale. Land sold and his
daughter Eliza Jane Ogilvie, widow of R. C. Ogilvie, deceased,
became purchaser of sale.

Page 601 - John H. Watkins] Att. & Inj. Bill, filed
                  vs   ]   4 August 1856.
             John Cotter   ]
John H. Watkins as Trustee of Martha E. Cotter filed against
John Cotter, all of Bedford County. Orator states that John
Cotter married Martha E. Watkins, a sister of John H. Watkins,
in Summer of 1855. They had made a marriage contract before
the marriage to protect the slaves of Martha E. Cotter. John
Cotter and Martha E. lived together until John Cotter changed
his conduct, and threatened to run off the slaves and sell
them, for the reason that Martha E. Cotter's children, which
she gave birth before their marriage, never should have any
share of said slaves. John Cotter has now the slaves in his
possession, secretly to run them off and dispose of them.
Orator wants slaves attached so they will not be run off and
sold.

Page 602 - Barrett & Newsom]
                  vs   ] O. Bill, 22 February 1855.
             Alex. Smith,   ]
             S. Doak & others]
William J. Barrett and Randolph Newsom, partners, stated that
in September last (1854) they recovered a judgement against
Alexander Smith for $452.00. There was a tract of land convey-
ed by Trust Deed to Samuel Doak, land in Bedford County in
District No. 21, about 256 acres, known as the Snell Tract,
also owned slaves and other properties.

Page 608 - J. H. McGrew   ] Att. & Inj. Bill, filed
                  vs   ]   April 14, 1854.
             J. S. Owens & others]
J. H. McGrew of Bedford County filed against Joseph S. Owens
and Charles A. Warren and Robert Williams, all of Bedford
County. Orator said that he recovered a judgement against
Joseph S. Owens on 3 March 1854 for $110.75 and cost.

Page 610 - S. Phillips   ] Att. & Inj. Bill, filed
                  vs   ]   August 11, 1855.
             Willis Cannon & others]
Samuel Phillips of Bedford COunty filed against Willis Cannon
and wife Elizabeth Cannon of Bedford County and A. W. Majors
of Rutherford County, Tennessee. Samuel Phillips stated he
recovered a judgement against A. W. Majors and Willis Cannon
on 14 April 1855 for $249.14 and cost. Orator stated that
Elizabeth Cannon filed for a divorce from Willis Cannon.

Page 612 - S. Doak   ] O. & Inj. Bill, filed
                  vs   ]   May 11, 1855.
             William J. Barrett]
             & R. Newsom   ]
Samuel Doak filed against William J. Barrett and Randolph Newsom. Orator states that defts recovered several judgements
against your orator for $2400.00 which your orator caused to
be stayed and stay runs out on 19 May 1855.

Page 618 - Barrett & Newsom]
                    vs   ]Petition, 27 June 1855.
         Doak & Hays   ]
Petitioners stated that on or about 14 May 1855, Samuel Doak
filed his bill enjoining your orators from collecting judgements against Samuel G. Hays.

Page 621 - Thomas Shearin & others]
                    vs   ]O. Bill, 14 January 1854.
         James P. Allison &   ]
         N. F. Neil   ]
Thomas Shearin in his own right and admr of John K. Lawell,
deceased, and of Henry, Ethan, Elizabeth, William and Mary
Lawell, minors and only children of John K. Lawell, deceased,
who files this their bill by their mother and guardian Mary
Lawell filed against James P. Allison and Newton F. Neal.
Thomas Shearin stated that John K. Lawell departed this life
intestate in Bedford County in month of July last (1853) and
your orator was appointed admr of his estate. Before the
death, John K. Lawell executed two notes due in 1854 and 1855
and interest, notes dated November 1852, payable to James P.
Allison as executor of William Allison, deceased. Lawell owned
land formerly owned by William Allison and which by his Last
Will and Testament, William Allison had authorized James P.
Allison to sell. The lands adjoining lands of Robert Allison
and Newton F. Neal. Neal purchased the whole tract of land.
No writing executed deed. Newton F. Neal and John K. Lawell
were half brothers.

Page 626 - Amos Hays   ]
                    vs   ]O. Bill, February 20, 1858.
         A. C. Leming & others]
Amos Hays of Bedford County filed against A. C. Leming, John S.
Jones, Sherwood Lisenby, H. N. Hutton and Alex. G. Murphy.
Orator states that in May 1857, he and A. C. Leming formed
a partnership in the Brick Making Business and carried on the
business near Shelbyville until about 12 November 1857 when
they quit the business. John S. Jones layed the brick.

Page 633 - Rebecca Murlett   ]
                    vs   ]O. Bill, September 1, 1853.
         Mary Smotherman & other]
Rebecca Murlett of Henderson County, Tennessee stated that
in November 1842, Samuel Hawkins now a citizen of Obion County,
Tennessee, purchased from John G. Smotherman a tract of land
in Bedford County on waters of Sugar Creek. Bounded by John
White. After 1843, your oratrix purchased said land from Hawkins and executed her note payable to Hawkins and M. M. Bedwell
and John Bedwell. Oratrix stated that John G. Smotherman departed this life in 1847 intestate, leaving a widow Mary
Smotherman (who has since died intestate, no admr of estate)
and the following children, her heirs at law, to wit, Louisa
Smotherman who married W. P. Maxwell, Margaret Ann Smotherman
who married Thomas W. Sanders, Phebe and John T. Smotherman,
all of Bedford County, Calvin C. Smotherman who lives in Alabama, Thomas T. and James H. Smotherman who lives in Rutherford
County, Tennessee. Mary Smotherman appointed admr of estate.
Rebecca Bedwell which was your oratrix's name during the life
of her first husband (until her second marriage) is named in
the bill as non-resident of the state. She said that she has
all the time been a citizen of Tennessee and resided in Henderson County, Tennessee where she now lives and her name for
many years before her purchase of the land, and has been ever

since Rebecca Murlett. She held possession until recently
and now Joel Smith is owner. When your oratrix lived in
Bedford County (so says W. P. Maxwell) that she was known as
Rebecca Bedwell.

Page 638 - William Cully   ]
                      vs   ]O. Bill, August 6, 1855.
            Daniel Stephens,]
            Stephen Galleghy]
            & Jos. Galleghy]
William Cully filed against Stephen Galleghy and Jos. Galleghy
and Daniel Stephens. Orator states that he recovered a judgement against Daniel Stephens on 9 May 1854 for $150.00 and
cost. Orator states that on 6 January 1855, Stephen Galleghy
conveyed by deed a tract of land, about 333 acres, land lying
on Straight Creek, one of the waters of the Garrison Fork of
Duck River, bordered by Montgomery, James L. Armstrong, Widow
Anderson and Old Wagster Grant. Stephen Galleghy still lives
on same farm. Daniel Stephens of Bedford County and Stephen
and Joseph Galleghy of Coffee County, Tennessee.

                CHANCERY COURT RULE DOCKET   1855 - 1866

Page 1 -   James J. Smith & others] Inj. & Att. Bill, filed
                      vs   ]   7 November 1857.
            Adolphus Adams & others]
Mary J. Smith and Elizabeth, Leonidas, Penelope, Julia and
Henry Janison Smith who are all minors with no regular guardian
and who sues by their father Robert M. Smith, the husband of
Mary J. Smith filed against Adolphus Adams and Allen Morris.
They stated that sometime in the year 1830, H. D. Jamison con-
vayed to your oratrix Mary J. Smith for life and at her death
to your orators and oratrixes, who are the children of Mary J.,
in a tract of land in Marshall County, Tennessee on Duck River
on which are some mills and about 103 acres. The deed gave
to your oratrix Mary J. power to sell the land during her lifetime, if she thought it necessary and directed the proceeds
to be divided amongst those of the remainder being the other
complainants in this bill, and one Mary E. Crittenden. Mary J.
Smith decided to sell the land to Allen Morris of Marshall
County, Tennessee. Her husband received money from it and
used it for himself and it should have gone to your oratrix,
as it came from Jamison.
Answer by Mary E. Crittenden, daughter of Robert M. Smith,
both of Bedford County. Mary J. Smith is step-mother of Mary
E. Crittenden. Mary E. Crittenden has a sister Harriet W.
Smith and the children of Mary J. Smith, who departed this
life intestate and without issue leaving Mary E. Crittenden,
her only heir. 83 acres of 103 acre tract was sold to Allen
Morris for $3500.00. Mary E. is wife of S. T. Crittenden.

Page 7 -   Thompson & Jones]
                      vs   ]Bill, filed 12 September 1857.
            J. B. McAdams   ]
Robert N. Jones and Joseph Thompson of Bedford County stated
that they were securities for William Thompson for a purchase
of a tract of land purchased of J(Jesse). B. McAdams. He paid
all but $450.00 plus cost. Orators stated McAdams did not
have title to the land. The land, his wife Catherine and her
sister Eleanor McAmy and others have not joined in the bond.
Joseph Thompson has died since sale of land and James Dixon
has become the purchaser of the land. His wife now is ready

and willing to give title to James Dixon.

Page 10 - Benjamin Mosely]
                  vs   ]Inj. Bill, 17 August 1857.
           Phillip V. Doss]
Benjamin Mosely of Bedford County stated that on 19th November
1856, he and Phillip V. Doss entered into a partnership. Your
orator to furnish $5000.00 to carry on business but he was
only to furnish $2500.00 and Doss the same. Doss has only
furnished $1500.00.

Page 11 - James M. Elliott   ] Inj. & Att. Bill, filed
                  vs   ]   23 February 1856.
           William Brown & others]
James M. Elliott stated that he recovered a judgement against
Samuel Doak for $6095.02 and cost.

Page 25 - Minerva J. Bartlette]
                  vs   ]Divorce Bill, 24 April 1856.
           William L. Bartlette]
Minerva J. Bartlette of Bedford County stated that on 5th day
of March last (1854), she married William L. Bartlette of Bedford County. Minerva J. stated that she had no intention of
marrying anyone but a neighbor woman wanted her to go over
to her house and when she got there, was met by "news" that
she must marry Bartlette that evening. The arrangement had-
all been made even the license bought. Your oratrix had refused and wanted to return to her father's house, but several
persons in on the arrangement refused to let her go home and
told her it was too late, that Old Katy Leathers (who claims
to be a fortune teller) said she must marry him or she would
go to the pen (jail) or runaway from the country. They
frightened her so bad that she finally gave in. We were to
go to a J. P. and when they got to his house, he was not at
home and they started to John Wagster's, a Minister of the
Gospel in Lincoln County, Tennessee. At first she refused
to go but was finally agreed_ed. She was such a state of con-
fusion that she does not remember. She told before the minister that if she married him, that she would not live with
him. From the minister's house, she was taken to the house
of Daniel Bartlette about midnight and there she refused to
go to bed with him and others that followed them insisted she
do so. Finally she did against her will. Bartlette came in
and layed down on the bed and remained there about an hour
and then got up and left the next morning. She went to her
father's house where she has remained ever since.

Page 28 - Samuel Doak, Samuel G. Hays]
           & A. G. Woods   ]Inj. Bill, filed
                  vs   ]20 August 1855.
           Jesse Stegall & R. C. Dysart]
Samuel Doak, Samuel G. Hays and A. G. Wood of Bedford County
filed against Jesse Stegall of Marshall County, Tennessee and
R. C. Dysart. Orators states that Jesse Stegall is prosecuting,
in Bedford County a suit against your orators.

Page 35 - Sally Ann Brantley   ]
                  vs   ]Orig, Bill, April 18, 1856.
           Joe Thompson & others]
Sally Ann Brantley formerly Sally Ann Crunk, a minor, who sues
by J. J. B. Crunk filed against Jos. H. Thompson, Jr., T. W.
Crunk who resides in Bedford County and her husband William C.
Brantley who resides in Lincoln County, Tennessee, and R. H.

Mumford of Tipton County, Tennessee. Sally Ann Brantley states
that in the ____ year that George E. Low, her maternal grandfather gave to her mother Martha Crunk, now deceased, certain
slaves (5), to have the use during her lifetime and at her
death to be divided equally between Martha's children. Martha
Crunk died leaving ten children as survivors, one of whom has
since died since their mother, leaving nine. Sally Ann Brantley stated that on ___ day of November 1852 she married William
C. Brantley. In April Term 1855, an Exparte Petition was filed
in the County Court of Bedford County by Sally Ann's brother.
William C. Crunk of full age and her brothers and sisters who
petitioned by their guardian T. W. Crunk and Sally Ann only
being over 19 years old, the petition was to sell slaves which
has increased. Sally Ann is afraid that her husband will get
the proceeds from sale of slaves, she is of delicate health
and able to do but little labor and needs the assistance in
raising her children (2). She states that she and her brothers
and sisters are the owners of another portion of George E.
Low's estate, which is now under the care of the County Court
of Tipton County, Tennessee, which is in the hands of R. H.
Mumford. She also ask that her husband William S. Brantley
be enjoined from selling or transferring her interests in said
funds.
Answer of Mumford: 1854, he was executor of George E. Low,
deceased, estate. George E. Low's daughter is Martha Crunk.
Her children are Edmund Jefferson, Maria, Jim, John and David.

Page 38 - William Gosling & others]
                  vs   ]Bill, filed 20 August 1855.
           S. E. Gilliland & others]
William Gosling, Thomas C. Whiteside, Thomas Lipscomb, Thomas
Eakin, Alex. Eakin, John W. Cowan, William G. Cowan, Willis W.
Wilhoite and E. Cooper and Robert Mathews as executors of
E. J. Frierson, deceased. They are overseers of a cotton fact-
ory in Shelbyville, Bedford County, on east bank of Duck River
and of a dam across Duck River from their factory to Clement
Cannon's Mill on the west bank of the river and have such own-
ers and all to have full benefit of all water power of Duck
River at Shelbyville. They are already in process of making
cotton yarns. They were in good shape until Samuel Doak and
others built a dam some distance below your orator's dam.
They built their dam higher and water backed upon your orator's
dam. The water wheels diminished their head of water from
six to twenty inches. Doak and others conveyed dam to Samuel
E. Gilliland, Henry Cooper, Josiah Webb, Charles Mosely and
John McPhail.

Page 40 - John Armstrong & others] Att. Bill, filed
                  vs   ] 21 January 1856.
           James Morgan   ]
William Davidson a resident of Ireland and Robert Armstrong
and John Armstrong of Bedford County stated that about 1st
of September 1853, they entered into partnership with John
Morgan. Firm known as "Armstrong & Co.", to carry and sell
of Irish Linen in Shelbyville. They were to furnish capital.
William Davidson had $3020.92 in stock, Robert Armstrong the
sum of $856.53, James Morgan $1832.98, and John Armstrong
$2189.00.

Page 45 - John P. Steele   ]
                  vs   ] O. Bill, 24 August 1855.
           Mary Lowrance &   ]
           Joseph M. Burnett]

John P. Steele said that on 13 day of August 1855, he recovered a judgement for $97.00 and cost. "No property to be found". Mary Lowrance at this time was an old woman, executed a Deed of Conveyance, a negro "John Solomon". Mary was a weak minded woman.

Page 49 - Ruthy White   ]
              vs   ]I. Bill, August 18, 1855.
         Joseph White]
Ruthy White of Bedford COunty states that she married with Joseph White on 2nd April 1851, who was then and is now re- siding in Bedford County, that her name before her marriage was Ruth Luellen, being a widow at that time and having four children by her first husband Levi Luellen, three of whom re- side with your oratrix in Bedford County, to wit, Malicia A., John W., and Sarah Jane Luellen, the first of whom is about 18 years old, the second about 15 years old, and the latter about 11 years old. Oratrix states she lived in peace and harmony with her said husband until the beginning of this year when he began to abuse her and her children, threatening to drive them away from her home. She stated that Joseph White is a drunkard and has been so for part two years. At the time that she married Joseph White, she had lots of property and on 1st April 1851 they entered into the marriage contract that after her marriage, that all the property would remain to her and her children. Since marriage, she has obtained a negro boy Alfred and a negro boy George from the estate of her father William Gabbert who departed this life since her said marriage, and also a negro girl Martha who she bought at the sale of her father. Your oratrix stated that her husband has executed a Bill of Sale or Settlement of the two negroes Alfred and George.

Page 52 - John W. Rawlings   ]
              vs   ]Inj. Bill, December 7, 1854.
         John P. & Martin Hoover]
John W. Rawlings of Rutherford County, Tennessee filed against Martin and John P. Hoover, all of Bedford COunty. Orator John W. Rawlings stated that there is now pending in Circuit Court of Rutherford County, Tennesse by transfer from Circuit Court of Bedford County, an action of ejectment by your orator filed against John P. Hoover for a tract of land in Bedford County, of which John P. Hoover has possession, the said land has lots of timber. Orator states that John P. Hoover and hands of Martin Hoover are now cutting down and destroying most of the timber on said land.

Page 56 - John P. Dromgoole   ]
              vs   ]Inj. Bill, November 20, 1852.
         J. H. McGrew & others]
John P. Dromgoole filed against J. H. McGrew, John H. O'Neal and Samuel H. Whitthorne. Orator states that on 6 August 1852, he loaned to him for the purpose of being discounted in Bank, his note for $575.00 due 25 December 185_. Bank refused dis- count note.

Page 62 - James McCallum   ] Att. & Inj. Bill, filed
              vs   ]   April 24, 1854.
         Mary L. & J. W. Nowlin]
James McCallum, executor of Last Will and Testament of Samuel Mosely, deceased, and a resident of Giles County, Tennessee filed against James W. Nowlin, a non-resident of Tennessee, and a citizen of State of Texas and Mary L. Nowlin of Bedford

County. Orator states that on 1st March 1855, he recovered
a judgement in the capacity of executor of estate of Samuel
Mosely, deceased, against James W. Nowlin in the Circuit Court
of Giles County, Tennessee for $621.87 and cost. James W.
Nowlin has no property in State of Tennessee. Orator states
Jabez Nowlin, the father of James W. Nowlin, died several years
ago in Bedford County, after making his Last Will and Testament
and was proven and recorded. Jabez Nowlin's wife was Mary L.
Nowlin and they had five children. He had land on Rock Creek
near Hopewell Campground, bounded by Thomas Montgomery,
Darnell, John Larue and Meusadora B. Hamilton. They also had
eleven slaves. The Last Will and Testament left by Jebaz
Nowlin left Mary L. Nowlin and children, to wit, William J.,
B. W., James W., Light W., and Jabus S. Nowlin.

Page 66 - Mary E. M. Bradford & others] O. Bill, filed
                    vs   ] (no date).
           George Davidson & others   ]
Barclay M. Bradford, Robert McCort and wife Caroline formerly
Caroline Bradford, Charles B. Jones, Leroy G. Jones (a minor,
who having no regular guardian sues by next friend William F.
Bradford. NOTE: Leroy could be Lucy G. Jones), Theodoric F.
Bradford, Jr., William F. Bradford, and Mary E. M. Bradford,
the last three being residents of Bedford County and others
of the State of Missouri. Orators states that Theoderick F.
Bradford, Sr., departed this life intestate on Saturday the
4th day of April 1840 in Bedford County, leaving as his child-
ren and heirs at law, to wit, Barclay M. Bradford, William F.
Bradford, Theoderick F. Bradford, Mary E. M. Bradford, Caroline
Bradford who has married Robert McCort, and Roena Bradford
who married Charles B. Jones and departed this life intestate
in the State of Missouri in December 1846, leaving as her only
child and heir at law Leroy G. Jones and her husband Charles B.
Jones, surviving. At the time this bill was filed, William F.
Bradford is now in his 24th year since October last, and Mary
E. M. Bradford is not yet 22 years old. Several deeds were
made to several people who bought land of the estate.
1 - Erwin J. Frierson, lately departed this life after first
    having made his Last Will and Testament, Edmund Cooper
    as executor and Robert Mathews executor qualified in Feb-
    ruary Term 1850. He left, to wit, Mary Frierson, William
    Frierson, Robert Frierson, Albert Frierson, John Frierson,
    and Erwin J. Frierson, Jr. and his widow Mrs. Ann P.
    Frierson. All children are minors and Robert B. Davidson
    is guardian.
2 - Archibald Caruthers departed this life some years ago,
    intestate, leaving a widow Juliet Caruthers and children,
    to wit, John F., James, Sarah Elizabeth, Eliza and William
    C. Caruthers, all minors. Their mother is their guardian.
3 - John Eakin, now deceased.

Page 73 - Mary E. M. Bradford & others]
                    vs   ]Filed October 2, 1851.
           G. W. Bell & others   ]
Barclay M. Bradford, Robert McCort and wife Caroline formerly
Caroline Bradford, Charles B. Jones, Leroy G. Jones (a minor
who sues by her friend William F. Bradford as she has no guard-
ian), Theodorick F. Bradford, Jr., William F. Bradford and
Mary E. M. Bradford, the last three are citizens of Tennessee
and others are residents of Missouri, filed against George W.
Bell, Thomas C. Whiteside, William Galbraith, Mrs. Arey E.
Kincaid, James Kincaid, Mary Kincaid, and Sarah Kincaid and
also Nashville, Murfreesboro and Shelbyville Turnpike Company.

Orators states that Theodorick F. Bradford, Sr. in his lifetime
was the owner of lands described in (pretended) deeds made
by Joseph Kincaid, registered in Bedford County, Book "JJ".
Then Theo. F. Bradford , Sr. made a pretended Deed August 1839,
pages 10, 11, 12, & 13, to Whiteside & Galbreath. Orators
stated that Theo'd F. Bradford was incapable in mind of making
any binding control whatever. Joseph Kincaid on 22 April 1842
sold 100 acres of saod land by deed to George W. Bell. Theo. F.
Bradford, Sr. departed this life about the last of March 1840
intestate in bedford COunty, leaving as his heirs, to wit,
Barclay M. Bradford, Theodorick F. Bradford, Jr., William F.
Bradford, Mary E. M. Bradford, Caroline Bradford who has since
married Robert McCort, and Roena Bradford who has since married
Charles B. Jones, and departed this life intestate in December
1846, leaving as her only child Leroy G. Jones and her husband.
Joseph Kincaid departed this life in Spring of 1844, after
making and publishing his Last Will and Testament devising
to the said Arey E. Kincaid, James Kincaid, William Kincaid,
Mary Kincaid and Sarah Kincaid, his whole estate, real and
personal, the first being his wife and the four last, his
children and are also minors, guardian John T. Neil, of Bedford
County. William F. and Mary E. are not yet twenty four years
old.

Page 75 - Mary E. M. Bradford et al]
                vs   ]O. Bill, 11 October 1851.
          Jno. McGuire & others   ]
Orator & oratrix same as previous bill. Theodorick F. Bradford,
Sr. executed a pretended Deed of Trust on date 11th of said
month to John Tillman all his estate. They state the deed
that their father drew up and did not have the words "heirs"
in the deed. Someone tried to put the word "heirs". Deed
is void. After the death of said Bradford, Sr., Tillman
and Galbraith sold under said deed, 11 April 1839, a tract
of land of 133 acres in Bedford County, some three or four
miles from Town of Shelbyville, to Gabriel Blackwell by deed
dated 1st March 1841. Blackwell sold land to Michael Holt
and John McGuire, 53 acres to said Holt and 80 acres to McGuire
14 May 1841. Michael Holt held his land until his death and
was then divided among his heirs in 1842, and said 53 acres
fell to the lot Terrill Greggs and wife Malissa formerly
Malissa Holt and then they sold to Wilkins Blanton by deed
19th December 1842. Wilkins Blanton sold to George Davidson
20th March 1844, Davidson sold to Redding George, George to
John McGuire, 83 acres. Gabriel Blackwell of Marshall County,
Tennessee.

Page 80 - Mary E. M. Bradford et al]
                vs   ]O. Bill, 20 October 1851.
          William K. Ransom & others]
Barclay M. Bradford and others states that Charles B. Jones'
wife Roena Bradford, died December 1846 in Missouri. In Will
Book of Rutherford County, Tennessee, the date of will is the
15th of April 1844 in which Benjamin C. Ransom willed and bequeathed all land to his four sons, to wit, William K., Dedrick
J., Gideon M., and Benjamin F. Ransom. Benjamin F. Ransom
and William J. had in his possession 1814 acres of land.

Page 85 - Collins & Nance   ]
                vs   ]O. Bill, 11 January 1855.
          Foster & Phillips]
William Collins of Bedford COunty and Richard Nance of Rutherford County, Tennessee filed against Gwynn Foster and Samuel P.

262

Phillips, both of Bedford COunty. Orators stated that Collins
on the 13th day of December 1848 recovered a judgement against
Gwynn Foster, William D. Hill, and Enoch D. Rushing for $491.34
and cost, levied upon a one-half acre lot or tract of land
in possession of Gwynn Foster in Bedford County in District
No. 11 in the Town of Unionville, joining lands of Meredith
Blanton. Bounded by Meredith Blanton, Campground, William
Collins bought said land. Richard Nance was one of the last
endorsers on note and Nance paid part of note.

Page 94 - John Wood   ] Att. & Inj. Bill, filed
                vs   ]   10 June 1854.
           Benjamin Barnhill, Sr.]
           & others   ]
John Wood of Bedford COunty filed against Benjamin Barnhill,
Sr., Benjamin Barnhill, Jr., and David Young, all of Bedford
County. John Wood recovered a judgement on 2nd day of December
1840 against Benjamin Barnhill for $147.90 and cost. Barnhill
was purchaser of some school land in Bedford County, District
No. 11, in the division as Lot No. 2, in Range No. 3 and Sect-
ion 6. In 1854, Barnhill, Sr. and Jr. conveyed said land to
David Young for $1000.00, a part of which Young has been paid.

Page 98 - Samuel Woodfin]
                vs   ]Att. Bill, October 11, 1854.
           Young & others]
Samuel Woodfin of Bedford County stated that William VanCleave
of Bedford County is indebted to him for $118.58. VanCleave
removed from Tennessee, he probably went to Illinois.

Page 99 - Stokes & Mullins   ]
               vs   ]Inj. Bill, April 4, 1854.
          Green, Coffey & others]
John M. Stokes and James Mullins filed against Henry B. Coffey,
R. E. Coffey and W. P. Green, all of Bedford County. John M.
Stokes states that hepurchased of Henry B. Coffey on 19 April
1852, a negro man Abner age 44 or 45 years.

Page 104 - Thomas & Green Holland] Att. & Inj. Bill, filed
               vs   ]   March 7, 1854.
          William Brown & others]
Thomas Holland of Bedford County and Green Holland of Mississippi, state that they the sons and two of the heirs of
Thomas Holland, Sr. who departed this life in August 1853,
that on or about 22nd day of January 1849, he made a deed to
Nathan Ivy and William Galbraith, covering his whole estate
(except perhaps one negro girl) about 85 acres in Bedford
County on which he then resided and two negroes Dick and Fanny,
other stocks, &c. At time of deed, he was of old age and un-
soundness of mind incapable of making a binding contract. Ivy
and Galbraith resigned as Trustees by deeds, and William Brown
and James G. Barksdale were appointed in their place. Brown
now has the negro Fanny and in the process of taking her and
going to Texas, that there are still land not sold for payments of debts and is now in the possession of Sarah T. Holland
widow of Thomas Holland, Sr. Thomas Holland left children
and grandchildren, your orators, Green and Thomas and Nelson
Holland now living in Texas. Sarah Corbett wife of James
Corbett both living in _____ County, Lavinia Nelson wife of
Robert Nelson now living in Alabama, Mary Hooser living in
Rutherford COunty, Tennessee and the following grandchildren,
children of James Holland, deceased, to wit, Lavinia Patterson
wife of Eliza M. Patterson living in Kentucky, Sarah Lane wife

of _____ Lane of Bedford County, William Holland of Bedford
County, Presley Holland of Bedford County, Elizabeth Holland
of Bedford County.
NOTE: Thomas Holland, Sr. had an infant boy Thomas born some
two or three months after his death.
        Thomas Holland, Sr. married Sarah T., when he was of
advanced age. She was his third wife.
        Negro Dick and Fanny were sold to John McGuire and McGuire
is about to leave for Texas to live and take said negroes with
him.

Page 111 - Jacob Sively   ]
                 vs   ]Inj. Bill, December 10, 1853.
          V. H. Steele & others]
Jacob Sively of Texas filed against Volney H. Steele, John P.
Steele, James H. Neil and Joshua P. Miller, all of Bedford
County. Jacob Sively recovered a judgement on 18 December
1852 for $530.00 debt into continous bearings for railroad
purposes, at his mill and then delivered to the Nashville &
Chattanooga Railroad in which Volney H. Steele had made a
contract for same.
A Cross Bill, filed.

Page 128 - H. P. Furgerson, Admr]   O. Bill, filed
                 vs   ]   August 9, 1853.
          W. A. Hickerson & others]
Henry P. Furgerson in his own right and as admr of America
Furgerson, deceased, filed against William A. Hickerson, Wiley
Hickerson, Leander Hickerson, Lytle Hickerson, David Hickerson,
Joseph Hickerson, John Hickerson and Washington Hickerson,
Nancy Hickerson, all of whom reside in Coffee County, Tennessee
and Gabriel Maupin and wife Sally, and William Hord and wife
Adalaide of Bedford County. Henry P. Furgerson states that
Joseph Hickerson departed this life intestate in Coffey County
during the year 1849 or 1850, he died seized a large real and
personal estate and leaving surviving him as his only heirs
at law, W. A. Hickerson, Wiley Hickerson, Leander Hickerson,
Lytle Hickerson, David Hickerson, Joseph Hickerson, John
Hickerson, Washington Hickerson, and Sally who married Gabriel
Maupin, and Adalaide who married William Hord, and America
who married your orator Henry P. Furgerson, and his widow Nancy
who are entitled to his estate. William A. Hickerson was
appointed admr. Henry P. Furgerson married America Hickerson,
who was the youngest child of Joseph Hickerson, and as such
entitled to a distributive share in the estate of the said
Joseph Hickerson, deceased, that he married with the said
America since the death of her father, and that since his
marriage the said America has departed this life intestate,
leaving no children, and your orator, her husband surviving
her, and that your orator has been regularly appointed admr
upon her estate. Orator states that after the death of her
father Leander Hickerson was appointed guardian of said America.
Orator stated that in the lifetime of Joseph Hickerson, had
advanced his children in real and personal estate.

Page 134 - Leander Hickerson]
                 vs   ]Cross Bill, April 5, 1854.
          Henry P. Furgerson]
Leander Hickerson of Coffee County, Tennessee.

Page 138 - W. A. Hickerson   ]
                 vs   ]Cross Bill, March 7, 1855.
          Henry Furgerson et al]

W. A. Hickerson stated that Joseph Hickerson died in Coffee
County, Tennessee in 1849 or 1850. Deed: From W. A. Hickerson to Leander Hickerson. 256 acres in Coffee County for
$1025.00 in District No. 6.

Page 144 - State of Tennessee   ]   Inj. Bill, filed
                 vs   ]   26 July 1855.
            Silas Pratt & others]
State of Tennessee filed against Silas Pratt, Andrew Pratt
and John Wallace, all of Bedford County. The State states
that she recovered two judgements against Solas Pratt, April
Term 1853 for $28.41 and cost. George Pratt departed this
life in Bedford County in May 1855 after having made and
published his Last Will and Testament and proved and recorded
in which he appointed his son Andrew Pratt and his son in law
John Wallace his executors. George Pratt was the father of
Silas Pratt. In said will, George Pratt desired his two tracts
of land sold and divided among heirs.

Page 146 - William Young and wife]
                 vs   ]O. Bill, February 22, 1855.
            Robert T. Cannon et al]
William Young and his wife Eliza C. stated that William Hooser,
the father of Eliza C. Young, departed this life after having
made and published his Last Will and Testament. In said will,
he gave to your oratrix Eliza C. Young, a negro girl Emaline.
There was a mistake in the draftsman and "Esther" was the one
intended to be given her. The testator lived some years after
the execution of the will. That in like manner gave the girl
Esther to his daughter Letitia M., but this was by mistake
he intended to give her the girl Emaline. These were verbal
gifts prior to his death. Letsy M. married Robert T. Cannon
and had two children who are now living, to wit, Mary Rebecca
Cannon and Letsy M. Cannon, departed this life, her husband
and said children survive her, the children are minors with
no regular guardian. Their father Robert T. Cannon resides
in Bedford County.

Page 148 - Patrick Fay   ]   Att. Bill, filed
                 vs   ]   June 2, 1855.
            Brown & Stanfield]
Patrick Fay of Bedford COunty states that Asa L Stamps obtained
a judgement against Robert W. Brown and your orators, Robert
W. Brown being indebted to your orator.

Page 150 - David R. Vance   ]   O. Bill, filed
                 vs   ]   February 5, 1855.
            Christina Vance & others]
David R. Vance filed against Christina Vance, Eliza J. Vance
and Robert Vance and Elizabeth Vance. David R. Vance states
that his father Samuel Vance made his will in 1845, to wit,
"To my two sons, David R. Vance and Robert B. Vance, I give
and bequeath my tract of land I noe live on containing 547
acres, which I desire to be equally divided between them, or
as near as can be on account of water and timber, which one
draws the least share, the other to pay over to him until they
become equal". And in March 1849, he added a codicil in these
words, "I do further desire and direct that my wife Christina
Vance have full possession of my residence, and be supported
from and upon the proceeds of my farm and during her natural
life." A few days after making this codicil, the testator,
who resided in Bedford County and in which the lands referred
to are situated, died, and at April Term 1849 of Bedford

County Court said will and codicil were proven and admitted
to record in said County Court and your orator David R. Vance
and Willis Blanton executors. Robert B. Vance was in possession of the homestead until his death in 1852. Robert B. left
a widow Elizabeth Vance and a daughter Eliza J. Vance and said
Elizabeth Vance in about 6 or 8 months after the death of her
husband, gave birth to a son, who she named after his deceased
father Robert Vance, all of which now live in Arkansas. Samuel
and Christina Vance lived in their homestead about 30 years
in Bedford County. Robert B. Vance built a house on said land,
dwelling made of good frame house with brick chimneys, worth
$300.00.

Page 153 - Robinson & Carey   ]   O. Bill, filed
                vs   ]   22 February 1855.
           John P. Dromgoole & others]
Richard A. Robinson and George H. Carey stated that they recovered a judgement at the August Term 1853 for $214.76 and
cost, filed against John P. Dromgoole.

Page 158 - B. M. Tillman]   O. Bill, filed
                vs   ]   12 November 1855.
           John W. Campion]
B. M. Tillman stated that some few months ago, about 26 July
1855, John W. Campion called upon your orator to endorse a
note for him for $175.00.

Page 160 - Elisha Reid   ]
                vs   ]Inj. Bill, 26 December 1854.
           James Smith & others]
Elisha Reid of Bedford County filed against James Smith, Ben-
jamin F. Wiggins, John W. Crunk and J. J. Crunk, all of Bedford
County. Orator says he recovered a judgement against James
Smith and Benjamin F. Wiggins.

Page 167 - Samuel P. Allison]
                vs   ]Att. & Inj. Bill, filed
           S. J. Warner &   ] July 24, 1854.
           J. M. Warner   ]
Samuel P. Allison of Nashville, in his own name, and for the
use of the heirs at law of William Allison, deceased, filed
against Samuel J. and John M. Warner of Bedford County. Orator
stated that he sold to Samuel J. Warner a tract of land in
Bedford County, about 240 acres. Land bounded by Graves, A.
Wilson, Robert Ray and John Adams.

Page 171 - Elizabeth Chadwell]
                vs   ] Att. Bill, 27 November 1854.
           Alexr. Smith &   ]
           Samuel Doak   ]
Elizabeth Chadwell of Rutherford County, Tennessee states that
her husband Valentine Chadwell departed this life in Williamson
County, Tennessee, of which he was a citizen, some four years
ago, leaving a large estate, among other property 16 or 17
slaves, filed against John C. Sword and others, that your
oratrix to have three slaves, Jasper, Anny and Nancy, in trust
for Adaline Smith who was a daughter of Calentine Chadwell
and your oratrix. Jasper was swapped off by your oratrix with
the consent of Adaline, for negro boy John now 19 years old.
The reason for the exchange is that Jasper had a wife in
Williamson County, Tennessee and did not want to be separated
from her. The negro boy was swapped for negro woman Octavia,
this was done by Mrs. Smith. Adaline Smith who was living

266

in Bedford County with her husband Alexander Smith and so remained. Alexr. Smith sometime in June or July last executed
a Trust Deed to Samuel Doak of Bedford County for said negroes.
Case disposed of at March Term 1865.

Page 180 - No. 1 - Hugh C. Hurst]
                        vs   ]O. Bill, filed 30 Dec. 1856.
                 Edmond Cooper]
Hugh C. Hurst stated that latter part of last year (1855),
he purchased from Samuel G. Hays and James Mullins a valuable
tract of land which had been assigned to them in Trust by
Samuel Doak. Samuel G. Hays is the son in law of Samuel Doak.

Page 181 - No. 2 - Basket & Sharp   ] O. Bill,
                        vs   ] 12 March 1858.
                 Morgan, Madigan & others]
G. P. Basket and A. L. Stamps, merchants, filed against John
Morgan, L. H. Titcomb and Thomas Madigan. Orators recovered
a judgement on 28 March 1857 against L. H. Titcomb for $252.47
and cost.

Page 183 - No. 3 - Jason T. Cannon]
                        vs   ]Att. Bill, 3 October 1857.
                 Jesse Chockley]
Jason T. Cannon of Bedford County and Jesse Chockley of parts
unknown. Orator stated he is security for Jesse Chockley,
on a note by him to William Griffis for $60.00 and cost.

Page 184 - No. 4 - Henry Helbert   ]
                        vs   ]O. Bill, 19 June 1857.
                 Thomas H. Coldwell]
                 & others   ]
Henry Helbert of Bedford County filed against Thomas H. Cold-
well, W. Wilhoite, William J. Whitthorne, Samuel Haily, William
Brown, Butcher Sharp, Thomas C. Whiteside, James Story, Hugh
Jones and Charles A. Warren of Bedford County and John R. Jones
of Marshall County, Tennessee.

Page 194 - No. 4 - A. D. Fugett, Admr of   ]
                 R. S. Clardy, deceased]   O. Bill, filed
                        vs   ]   August 6, 1860.
                 James R. Clardy & others]
A. D. Fugett, admr of estate of R. S. Clardy, deceased, of
Bedford County filed against Mrs. T. H. Clardy, James R. Clardy
and N. L. Clardy, Miss Theodocia H. Clardy - Hampton Hobbs
and Thomas Hobbs, two last are minors (guardian N. L. Clardy),
and Nat Hendricks also a minor (no guardian) and A. W. Sively
and wife C. W. Sively who are non-residents of Tennessee and
reside in Mississippi. A. D. Fugett states that R. S. Clardy
departed this life in Bedford County intestate. August Term,
your orator was appointed admr of the estate. At the death
of R. S. Clardy, he was the owner of a negro girl about 6 years
old. R. S. Clardy never married. He left his mother Mrs.
T. H. Clardy and his brothers, James R. Clardy and N. L.
Clardy and his sisters, Mrs. C. W. Sively wife of A. W. Sively
and Miss T. H. Clardy and his nephews Hampton Hobbs and
Thomas Hobbs, minor heirs of his deceased sister Sarah Hobbs
who died before the intestate R. S. Clardy, and that Nat.
Hendricks, infant son of his deceased sister Mary Ann Hendricks
who are his only distributee.

Page 197 - No. 6 - Emeline Daniel & others] Inj. Bill, filed
                              vs   ] July 23, 1860.
                    Jo. Taylor & others   ]
Emeline Daniel bu next friend J. J. Shriver, and J. J. Shriver
in his own right filed against Joseph Taylor and Rufus T.
Daniel, all of Bedford County. Emeline Daniel stated that
on the 18__, she married Rufus T. Daniel and before her
marriage, they entered into a marriage contract, that all the
property of your oratrix was the owner should be separate
property of your oratrix, free from debts. Before she married,
she sold off a negro man Carrol to Joseph H. Thompson.

Page 199 - No. 7 - Edmund Cooper] Att. Bill, filed
                          vs   ] January 18, 1861.
                  E. Morris   ]
Sale of slave girl.

Page 200 - No. 8 - William H. Wiseman & others] Inj. Bill,
                          vs   ] 24 Nov 1860.
                  Patrick Fay   ]
William H. Wiseman, James Mullins and Barcley M. Tillman states
that William H. Wisener on or about __ day of ___ 185_ purchased of Patrick Fay about 90 acres of land in Bedford County,
on the Branch Rail Road, about 2 miles from Shelbyville for
sum of $5,9--.00. Fay paid for part of the note. A defect
was found in the title of the said land. Thereis about 30
of the 90 acres to which Fay has no valid title if any at all.
He purchased of P. P. and M. J. Gilchrist (if christian names
are correct). sons of Daniel Gilchrist, who set up claim on
it as devisees of their father who resided and died in Alabama,
where they still reside. Wisener desires the whole contract
resended and his purchase money returned. Land in Civil District No. 3 of Bedford County. Land on north side of Railroad
and on west side of Gilchrist tract, also corner of Blessing
tract, Benjamin A. Nelson now owned by Edmund Green.

Page 204 - No. 9 - John Wilhoite   ] Bill filed
                          vs   ] 16 April 1864.
                  Madison Jones & others]
John Wilhoite of Bedford County states that Madison Jones,
a citizen of Arkansas is indebted to your orator for sum of
$150.00, the value of a horse which Jones took from your
orator's stable in Spring of 1863 without your orators knowledge or consent. Jones left the State and took the horse.
Orator states that Jones had an undivided interest in a tract
of land in Bedford County in District No. 22, on waters of
Flat Creek, known as the Polly Wilhoite Dower or tract, who
was the grandmother of said Jones, and inherited the same
through his mother Polly Jones. Both mother and grandmother
now being dead. After their death, the land has been sold
by Bedford County Court. The land was bid off by Jacob Wilhoite
but has since transferred his bid to Isaiah Parker.

Page 206 - No. 10 - Henry Brown   ]
                          vs   ] Bill, August 22, 1864.
                  J. A. Blakemore]
Henry Brown of Bedford County states that John A. Blakemore
of Bedford County is indebted to Benjamin Brown for $200.00
money. Benjamin Brown departed this life after having made
and published his Last Will and Testament, proven and recorded
in Bedford County, June Term 1857. On the 7th day of January
1863, whilst the Confederate Army was in possession of Shelbyville and Bedford County, said Blakemore, having previously

been there on the same business, came to the house of your
orator who lived about three miles from town on the north.
Blakemore lived in town and had the confidence of the Rebels.
Your orator was for the Union and so was his wife and family,
they were kind to Union men who were in danger of being con-
scripted. Blakemore tried to pay his note with Confederate
Notes and your orator refused to take them.

Page 211 - No. 11 - John R. Jones   ] Att. & Inj. Bill,
                          vs   ] February 4, 1861.
                    Steele & Gilliland]
John R. Jones of Bedford County filed against John P. Steele
of Bedford County and Robert E. Gilliland of Lincoln County,
Tennessee. Orator states that the November Term, 6th November
1860 of Lincoln County Circuit Court, he recovered a judgement
against Robert E. Gilliland upon a note for $500.00, dated
30 November 1853. Robert E. Gilliland is a son and heir at
law of Samuel E. Gilliland now deceased. He departed this
life __ of ___ ____, after having made his Last Will and Testament and was proven and recorded at October Term 1860 of Bedford County. John P. Steele appointed executor.

Page 213 - No. 12 - James F. Calhoun]
                          vs   ]O. Bill, 28 January 1865.
                    Thomas G. Holland]
James F. Calhoun states that on 1 September 1864, he recovered
a judgement for $364.90 and cost against Thomas G. Holland.

Page 215 - No. 13 - Thomas E. Davis &]
                    Nancy H. Davis   ]
                          vs   ]O. Bill, 22 March 1864.
                    Sally Sprouse &   ]
                    Jennings Moore   ]
Thomas E. Davis and Nancy H. Davis his wife filed against
Sally Sprouse and Dr. Jennings Moore, all of Bedford County.
They stated that Mickey F. Atkinson departed this life in Bed-
ford County in January 1861 after making the Last Will and
Testament in which she devised to Nancy H. Marshall, now your
oratrix Nancy H. Davis, a tract of land in bedford County on
which she lived at her death, on Clems Creek, Civil District
No. 11, adjoining John F. Battle, James Finney and Silas
Sprouse, about 63 acres. Dr. Jennings Moore was executor.
They stated that March 1863, the Court House of Bedford County
was destroyed by fire and many of the public records. Will
Book was burned. Sally Sprouse is the only surviving sister
of the testatrix.

Page 218 - No. 14 - John H. O'Neal & others]
                          vs   ]Inj. Bill, filed
                    George Langford &   ]December 26, 1859.
                    Wood & Hurlburt   ]
Orators states that there is a suit now pending on a promisory
note, brought by George Langford. Note was on a portable
Steam Engine bought by your orator from Wood & Hurlburt through
their agent Michael Shofner, for the purpose of running the
Machinery of a Bucket Factory and Circular Saw. Wood & Hurlburt and George Langford of New York, City of Utica, County
of Oneida.

Page 224 - No. 15 - Martha A. McDougall]
                          vs   ]O. Bill, June 7, 1864.
                    W. R. McDougall   ]
Martha A. McDougall states that she is the mother of three

children, to wit, Johnny about 10 years old, Alex. about 8
years old, and Netty 6 years, and are with her at her home
in Shelbyville, that their father W. R. McDougall was her
husband, that he claims to have procured from her by decree
of accounty in State of Indiana, a divorce and that he is entitled to their possession. W. R. McDougall has deserted them
for months.

Page 226 - No. 16 - B. G. Green   ] In. & Att. Bill,
                       vs   ] 24 August 1864.
                  Margaret Watson & others]
Blount G. Green states that he is the owner of a judgement
in his own name against Mrs. Margaret Watson and Miss Sarah
Watson for sum of $45.00 and cost. Your orator also owns by
purchase for a valuable consideration of another judgement
for sum of $54.30 and cost in name of B. M. Tillman.

Page 228 - No. 17 - W. A. Trice, Trustee &c] Inj. Bill, filed
                       vs   ] December 7, 1857.
                  Salina A. Griffith   ]
William A. Trice states that L. C. Reid sometime since executed
a Trust Deed to your orator, a debt being to one Eli Griffith,
deceased, of some $800.00 (balance unpaid). C. A. Warren and
John H. Gambelle are the admrs of Eli Griffith. Eli Griffith
left a widow Salina A. Griffith who is also the guardian of
his children.

Page 233 - No. 18 - William S. Jett   ] Att. Bill,
                       vs   ] 3 February 1864.
                  John K. Phillips & others]
William S. Jett of Bedford County states that he is the legal
owner of transfer from the other members of the firm Baskette
& Jett & Co. of the assets of said firm, a note executed by
John K. Phillips dated January 1, 1859. John K. Phillips'
father Samuel Phillips has lately departed this life leaving
a Last Will and Testament. Ed'd Cooper and William Young as
executors.

Page 236 - No. 19 - Jacob Harrison &]
                  R. F. Arnold   ]O. Bill, 28 August 1858.
                       vs   ]
                  Wilhoite & Arnold]
Willis W. Wilhoite and Robert F. Arnold, son of Smith Arnold.
Orators Jacob Harrison and Absalom Arnold said that Robert F.
Arnold purchased a tract of land from Joseph K. Ewell and took
Ewell's bond for title.

Page 239 - No. 20 - W. W. Gill   ] Inj. Bill,
                       vs   ] August 22, 1864.
                  Joel H. Burditt & others]
W. W. Gill of Bedford County filed against Joel H. Burditt,
William McKinney, Elizabeth Thompson and S. P. Vest of Bedford
County. Orator states that he is the equal owner of a tract
of land lying and being in Bedford County in District No. 3.
Borders Redding Jones, J. E. Bennett, Nelson's line, Railroad,
Bell, Johnson, and Bennetts. Joel H. Burditt and William
McKinney are committing great waste on said land by cutting
down, destroying and hauling off, the most valuable timber
on the land.

Page 242 - No. 21 - W. F. Pearson]
                       vs   ] Bill, 7 February 1864.
                  R. W. Pearson]

W. F. Pearson formerly of Bedford County, now of Coffee County, states that sometime in 1862 he purchased of R. W. Pearson a certain tract of land in Civil District No. 4. Bounded by Harrison Elkins, A. Fugitt and John Ganaway and Dr. Cone (Cannon?), about 30 acres. Richard W. Pearson executed a deed to him for $1520.00. Orator said R. W. Pearson was his brother and partner in sale of goods and having no family he left the title papers in the firm papers. Their business being in the Village of Bell Buckle, Bedford County and he said that when R. W. Pearson left, he took the papers with him.

Page 243 - No. 23 - E. Cooper   ] Inj. Bill,
                        vs   ] 24 April 1857.
                Robinson & Carey & others]
Edmund Cooper filed against Jno. P. Dromgoole, Edward D. Dromgoole who resided in Shelbyville and Richard A. Robinson and George H. Carey who resides in Pennsylvania. Orator states that John P. Dromgoole came to your orator about 12 day of July 1856 and stated he had interest in a house and lot in Shelbyville which is to be sold to pay a claim to Dr. Jayne.

Page 248 - No. 24 - W. A. McGuire] Inj. & Att. Bill, filed
                        vs   ]   3 September 1858.
                J. T. McBride]
William A. McGuire of Bedford County states that by verbal agreement or contract, he purchased of John T. McBride a small tract of land in Bedford County, District No. 9. Bounded by Jordan Holder, James Foster, Jarrett now claimed William G. Hight, about 60½ acres.

Page 250 - No. 25 - John Bell   ]
                        vs   ]Bill, January 16, 1861.
                Lewis Gant & others]
John Bell filed against Sherron (Mathew Shearin) and Gant (Thomas), admrs of Lewis Gant, deceased, and William Gant and Charles Warner. John Bell of Marshall County, Tennessee states that has paid for Mosely on his security $101.35 as a balance of judgement and cost that F. B. Woods obtained against B. F. Mosely and your orator, on 2nd November 1859.

Page 252 - No. 26 - L. M. Rankin &   ] Inj. Bill
                   B. F. Whitworth   ]27 January 1858.
                        vs   ]
                Jno. W. Rutledge & others]
L. M. Rankin and B. F. Whitworth filed against John W. Rutledge, John M. Warner and J. D. Wilhoite. Your orators states that your oratrix L. M. Rankin recovered a judgement on the __ day of January 1858 against John M. Warner, Principal, John W. Rutledge security and Benjamin Whitworth as endorsers for sum $230.37 and cost. Slaves were sold.

Page 253 - No. 27 - T. A. Usselton] Att. & Inj. Bill,
                        vs   ] September 23, 1861.
                George Usselton]
Thersa Ann Frances Usselton states that in the month of February 1860, she married George Usselton and lived with him until a few days ago, when George deserted her, threatening to hurt her seriously. Oratrix stated that they had lived this year on farm rented from Dr. Lipscomb, that your oratrix and her children have made the crop. Oratrix's children are by her previous husband. She is asking for a divorce and support and also wants a restraint put on her husband to keep him from selling all her possessions. Final decree Mar 18, 1865.

Page 256 - No. 28 - F(T). K. Brown   ] O. Bill
                        vs   ] 15 April 1854.
                 V. H. Steele & others]
F(T). K. Brown states that he recovered a judgement against
Volney H. Steele on 21st January 1854 for $129.00 and cost.

Page 258 - No. 29 - William J. Cochran   ] Att. & Inj.
                        vs   ]   Bill,
                 Samuel P. Phillips & others]8 December 1860.
W. J. Cochran of Bedford County filed against William P.
Phillips, James B. Phillips, Samuel P. Phillips, and Thomas H.
Coldwell, all of Bedford County. W. J. Cochran said that on
24 February 1860, he recovered a judgement against James B.
Phillips for $228.69 and cost. Also, against William B.
Phillips on 25 February 1860 for $121.00 and cost, also, on
25 February 1860 against W. B. and J. B. Phillips for $403.85
and another for $319.43 and cost.

Page 262 - No. 31 - Scott & Whitson, Exrs]   O. Bill,
                        vs   ] 6 January 1865.
                 Sallie Vance & others]
John H. Scott temporarily residing in the State of North
Carolina and Samuel R(K). Whitson of Bedford County, executors
of the Last Will and Testament of David R. Vance, deceased,
filed against Sallie Vance, Susan C. Vance, and Virginia C.
Vance, all minors and children of David R. Vance. John I(Q).
Davidson as regular guardian who resides in Bedford County,
except Virginia C. Vance who is temporarily residing in South
Carolina. Your orators beg leave to state that David R. Vance,
late of Bedford County died at his residence in Bedford County
in July 1861 after making his Last Will and Testament. Your
orators are his executors, appointed and will proven ___ Term
1861. David R. Vance was the owner of a large real and personal estate in Bedford County, he bequeathed to his three daughters, above named. 1st - In his will that his remains be decently buried by the side of his deceased wife. 2nd - He willed that his mother be apply provided for out of the personal
property on the place. 3rd - He willed and bequeathed that
all his just debts should be paid by his executors as soon
as possible. 4th - He willed and bequeathed that all his
personal property, including his slaves be sold at public sale
by his executors on 12 months credit bond and good security
to be taken from purchases. 5th - After the death of his
mother, he willed and bequeathed that his executors should
sell his land to the highest bidder at public sale on a credit
of one, two and three years, bond and good security to be taken
and a lein retained till purchase money should be paid, and
the money when collected should be loaned on good security
for the benefit of his daughters, Sally, Susan C. and Virginia
C. Vance. 6th - He appointed Scott & Whitson as executors.
Samuel K(R). Whitson wrote said will, and thinks the terms
of the same are substantially set forth. At ___ Term 186_
of Bedford County Court, said John I. Davidson was appointed
guardian for said minor heirs, who are the only legatees and
devises of their deceased father. The mother of the deceased,
Mrs. Christina Vance, is still living, but is quite an old
lady. Her son David R. Vance lived with her and they carried
on the farm in partnership, and the provision in the will that
she should be provided for, was intended, so understood and
acted in by the family, to allow her to divide the stock and
provisions on hand until she should be satisfied and to remain
upon the Old Homestead during the remnant of her days, where
she still resides.

Page 265 - No. 32 - G. W. Thompson ¢ Co.] Att. & Inj. Bill
                    vs   ] January 29, 1861.
              J. A. Norman & others]
G. W. Thompson and J. W. Thompson, partners, filed against
J. T. Hubbard and J. A. Norman, both of Marshall County, Tennessee, and John C. Hix, executors of the Last Will and Testament of Mary Norman of Bedford County. Orators states that
on 30 day August 1860, they recovered a judgement against
J. T. Hubbard and J. A. Norman for $409.38. J. A. Norman has
an interest in the estate of his grandmother in the hands of
John C. Hix as executor. Mary Norman left a son Alex. and
in her will, willed him $600.00 and the balance to the children
of John F. Norman, deceased son, there being five in number,
J. A. Norman being one of the grandchildren.

Page 269 - No. 33 - Warren & Co.   ] Att. & Inj. Bill,
                    vs   ] February 1, 1861.
              J. A. Norman & others]
Charles A. Warren and Thomas J. Warren, partners, filed against
J. A. Norman, J. T. Hubbard, both of Marshall County, Tennessee,
and John C. Hix, executor of the Last Will and Testament of
Mary Norman, deceased, of Bedford County. Orators states that
on 19 October 1860, they recovered a judgement against J. A.
Norman and J. T. Norman and J. T. Hubbard for $450.99 and cost.
Mary Norman's estate sold to Alfred Campbell.

Page 273 - No. 34 - Michael Shofner, Admr & others] O. Bill,
                    vs   ] Jan 21,
              Jas. D. Reger(Reagor) &   ] 1862.
              Lucinda C. Stanfield   ]
Michael Shofner, admr of estate of Joshua G. Hix, deceased,
and of Ann Eliza Hix widow of Joshua G. Hix, deceased, and
of William S. Hix, Jos. B. Hix, John E. Frost and wife A(Alsy).
D. Frost, D. D. Hix, William J. Gordon and wife Louisa B.
Gordon, M. E. W. Dunaway and wife M. G. Dunaway and Elizabeth
Hix by her next friend D. D. Hix, all of Bedford County and
John D. Hix of Missouri filed against James D. Reager and
Lucinda C. Stanfield, both are minors of Bedford County. Your
orators stated that Joshua G. Hix died intestate in Bedford
County in the early part of the year 1861, leaving him, his
widow, your oratrix, Ann Eliza Hix, and no children. Michael
Shofner, admr of said estate. Surviving brothers, to wit,
William S., James B., D. D., and John D. Hix. Oratrixes, to
wit, A. D. Frost, Louisa B. Gordon, and M. G. Dunaway and
Elizabeth Hix, are his sisters and as such brothers and sisters
of Joshua G. Hix, deceased, and as such they are jointly with
the defendants James D. Reagor and Lucinda C. Stanfield, the
heirs at law of Joshua G. Hix. Joshua G. Hix had 100 acres
in District No. 25 of Bedford County. D. D. Hix was the father
of Joshua G. Hix. On 5 September 1861, Hoshua G. Hix, deceased,
land sold to James F. Arnold. James D. Reagor and Lucinda C.
Stanfield are nephew and niece.

Page 277 - No. 35 - William S. Jett & others]   O. Bill,
                    vs   ] 25 January 1865.
              Meredith P. Gentry   ]
William S. Jett of Bedford County and Mary A. Johnson of Marshall County, Tennessee and Thomas Eakin of New York filed against Meredith P. Gentry. Orator said that on __ day of ___,
18--, sold to Meredith P. Gentry a tract of land in Bedford
County, known as the "Cummings Place", bounded by Flat Creek
and Smith grant. Jett owns judgement, the 2nd now owned by
Thomas Eakin, 3rd owned by Mary A. Johnson, 4th note and held

by R. P. Stephenson.

Page 278 - No. 36 - White & Jordan]
               vs   ]Inj. Bill, October 25, 1859.
          Jett & Hall   ]
R. C. White and T. W. Jordan stated that William H. Walls(Hall)
is indebted to them in their right for sum $27.05 and cost.
W. H. Hall is a non-resident of Tennessee and resides in Arkansas. White & Jordan are residents of Bedford County.

Page 282 - No. 40 - Benjamin Mosely]
              vs   ]Inj. Bill, 22 June 1858.
          Jno. W. Wiggins]
Benjamin Mosely of Bedford COunty filed against John W. Wiggins
who is a resident of texas and Jas. Wortham of Bedford County.
Orator states that in November 1856 in transaction between
orator and Jno. W. Wiggins, he sold to Wiggins a claim he had
against Isham Mosely as admr of Jonathan Mosely who died in
Texas some years since. Claim $800.00. Debt not paid. Isham
Mosely at time of transaction a resident of Texas.

Page 286 - No. 41 - Newcomb Thompson, 2nd]
          guardian & others   ] O. Bill, filed
               vs   ] February 28, 1865.
          Richard Sims, Exr.   ]
George W. Buchanan guardian of Thomas B. Owen a minor of Berry
C. Owen, deceased, Newcomb Thompson, 2nd, guardian of Fannie M.
Owen and Woody Owen minor children of said Owen, filed against
Richard Sims, executor of said Owen, all of Bedford County.
Complts stated that B. C. Owen departed this life in Bedford
County in the 1861, after making and publishing his Last Will
and Testament by which he appointed Richard Sims his executor.
Newcomb Thompson, 2nd, is guardian of Fanny M. Owen and Robert
Owen, the first Owen being about 17 or 18 years old and latter
about 13 years. George W. Buchanan appointed guardian of
Thomas B. Owen, minor about 16 or 17 years of age. B. C. Owen
died seized of large number of lands situated in Bedford
County and a large number of slaves. Sometime before his
death, B. C. Owen filed for a divorce from his wife _____ Owen.
She and her children are in New York and children are in
school there.

Page 291 - No. 43 - Jacob F. Thompson   ]Att. & Inj.Bill
              vs   ]24 June 1858.
        Joseph H. Thompson & others]
Jacob F. Thompson filed against Joseph H. Thompson, Newcomb
Thompson, 3rd, Mary A. Thompson, W. T. Myers and B. M. Tillman,
all of Bedford County. Note for $1000.00. Joseph H. Thompson
executed to Barclay M. Tillman as Trustee for his wife Mary A.
Thompson, a Deed of Gift, the "Home Place" on which he resides.
Borders James L. Scudder, J. G. Johnson and others in the sub-
urbs of Town of Shelbyville, ___ acres and one negro man
Malcolm. Mary A. Thompson married Joseph H. Thompson. Joseph
H. Thompson a brother in law to W. T. Myers.

Page 303 - No. 44 - William Brown   ] O. Bill, filed
              vs   ] 23 November 1864.
        William B. Sutton]
William Brown states that on 7 October 1862, he sold to William
B. Sutton a tract of land in Bedford County, 89½ acres. Land
is situated in the 3rd and 4th Civil District of Bedford
County, on Shelbyville and Fairfield Turnpike, seven miles
from Town of Shelbyville, joins lands of Mrs. Graham and Allen

Wallace and the home place of Maj. John Sutton, deceased. Deed registered in Bedford County, Book "DDD", page 201. William B. Sutton is at this date a non-resident of Tennessee.

Page 304 - No. 45 - Thomas H. Coldwell, Trustee &c] O. Bill,
                        vs   ]20 Jan 1865.
                 F. T. Burrow & others   ]
Thomas H. Coldwell filed against F. T. Burrow, Chesly Arnold and W. G. Knight, all non-residents of Tennessee. Orator states that Samuel P. Phillips on the 12 November 1860 conveyed to him in trust for benefit of certain creditors, among other things a tract of land in Bedford County, Civil District No. 25. Containing 291+ acres, bounded by J. L. Rosborough and Z. Weaver, Chesly Arnold, A. J. Green, Gabriel Maupin and J. H. Scott. Your orator was authorized to sell said land 22 November 1861 and F. T. Burrow purchased the land.

Page 307 - No. 46 - Brown & Wallace, Admrs]Petition to sell
                        vs   ]   slaves.
                 Elizabeth Gaunt & others]October 29, 1863.
John S. Brown and Jackson Wallace of Bedford County states that at October Term 1863, they were appointed admrs of A. J. Gaunt, deceased. Andrew J. Gaunt was unmarried but lived with his mother Elizabeth who was advanced in age also a widow. Andrew J. Gaunt had a brother James A. Gaunt. They lived together in the same house on her dower. Andrew J. Gaunt left the following distributees, Elizabeth Gaunt his mother who claims the property aforesaid, Elizabeth Shearin wife of Matthew Shearin of Bedford County, James K. P. Carlisle a minor and has James Carlisle for his guardian, the said James K. P. being a son of Malinda Carlisle, deceased, formerly Malinda Gaunt. Said Carlisle and guardian residing in Bedford County, Jane Harlen wife of Elisha Harlen residing in Hardin County, Tennessee, Mary McNatt wife of Carr L. McNatt residing in State of Missouri and James Gaunt, Mary Childress wife of Price Childress and ElizabethJane Gaunt residing in Hardin County, Tennessee. The said James, Mary and Elizabeth Jane being children of John Gaunt, deceased, was a brother of said Andrew J. Gaunt. The said Elizabeth Shearin, Mary McNatt and Jane Harlen are sisters of said Andrew J. Gaunt, and said James K. P. Carlisle, James Gaunt, Mary Childress and Elizabeth Jane Gaunt (minor over 14 years old) are nephews and neice of Andrew J. Gaunt. John S. Brown and Jackson Wallace appointed admrs of Andrew J. Gaunt's. deceased, estate at October Term 1863. Andrew J. Gaunt's land bounded by Matthew Shearin, William's tract, Blakemore and Jackson Wallace and Dyer tract, about 166 acres.

Page 318 - No. 47 - W. J. Loyd   ] Att. Bill, filed
                        vs   ] 2 February 1864.
                 Henry H. Manly]
William J. Loyd of Bedford County filed against Henry H. Manly a non-resident of Bedford County. Orator states that on 13 December 1861, he sold by deed to Henry H. Manly a tract of land in Bedford County in Civil District No. 3, bounded by Wartrace Creek, J. F. McCowan (who sold to David Frizzell in Chaffin's line), and W. Pearson. About 43+ acres.

Page 320 - No. 48 - William Gosling]   O. Bill, filed
                        vs   ] January 19, 1865.
                 J. B. T. Smith &]
                 Theo. L. Huiler]
William Gosling of Bedford County states that on or about the

29 May 1860, he sold to J. B. T. Smith, non-resident of Tennessee and then a citizen, a certain house and lot in Bedford County in the Town of Shelbyville on the north side of Skull Camp Road nearly opposite to where your orator now lives. Bounded by Steele & Hammond's Mill, Robert Cannon and Skull Camp Road.

Page 323 - No. 49 - William C. Blanton]
                    vs   ]Att. Bill, filed
            Robert J. Patton &]25 January 1861.
            others   ]
William C. Blanton of Bedford County states that Robert J. Patton who resides in Mississippi, is indebted to him for sum of $145.00 and another for $100.00 and another for $45.00. Robert J. Patton owns land in Bedford County, 130 acres and bounded by Thomas Allison, A. Wilson and Mary King on which land he formerly resided. That Mary E. Patton his wife has filed for divorce and alimony and has attached said land. She resides in bedford County. Orator states that Thomas Allison and Kimbro T. Allison, executors of Thomas Allison, deceased, who reside in Bedford County. A money legacy of $500.00 coming to R. J. Patton under the will of Thomas Allison, deceased.

Page 326 - No. 50 - Stephen Hart]
                    vs   ]O. Bill, February 16, 1865.
            A. S. Lowrance]
Stephen Hart of Davidson County, Tennessee filed against A. S. Lowrance of Bedford County. Orator states some years ago he sold to A. S. Lowrance a tract of land in District No. 25 of Bedford County adjoining lands of Nicholas Troxler, George Cotner and John H. Scott and about 160 acres, the place where your orator formerly resided and where A. S. Lowrance and family now lives. Lowrance has failed to pay.

Page 328 - No. 51 - William Barton &]O. & Att. Bill,
            Samuel McRamsey   ]January 16, 1865.
                 vs   ]
           Edwin H. Ewing, Jr.]
William Barton and Samuel McRamsey of Tennessee filed against Edwin H. Ewing, Jr., non-resident of Tennessee. Orators state on 1st January 1862, they sold to Edwin H. Ewing, Jr. a tract of land in Bedford County in District No. 4. Situated on both sides of the Nashville & Chattanooga Railroad, adjoining lands of C. F. Sutton, K. P. Ransom, Martin Hancock and others, known as the Ramsey part of the McGrew tract of land, about 281 acres. J. C. McCrory as security.

Page 332 - No. 52 - Jos. D. Wilhoite]
                    vs   ]Bill, July 28, 1864.
            Thomas P. Wilhoite]
Joseph D. Wilhoite of Bedford County states that under the firm name of "Wilhoite & Bros.", he and Young Wilhoite and Thomas P. Wilhoite did business as retail merchants in Town of Shelbyville for 2 or 3 years or more. After they had been in business for some time, they bought the interest of Young Wilhoite. Decree in March 1865, that Clement Cannon, Sr. departed this life some years ago, having made and published his Last Will and Testament which was proven and recorded in Bedford County, and that his sons Thomas B. and Charles L. being appointed executors. In the will, he devised that his real estate be sold and also where he now lives at the time of his death, lying immediately south of the Town of Shelbyville, about 463 acres at $50.00 per acre. Complt and Deft

purchased said property.

Page 338 - No. 53 - Blackman Koonce & others] O. Bill, filed
                              vs   ] August 27, 1860.
                    Benjamin Reaves & others]
Blackman Koonce, Polly Morgan and her husband James D. Morgan,
Mary J. Troxler and her husband William S. Troxler, Thomas
Wilhoite admr of W. H. Koonce, deceased, Martha Reed and her
husband William C. Reed, Sarah Sabrina who being a minor sues
by her guardian Young Wilhoite, Virginia T. Koonce who being
a minor sues by her guardian William S. Troxler, John P. Koonce
and James A. Koonce who being minors sue by their guardian
A. L. Landis, ElizabethReaves and her husband William Reaves,
Jane Voorhies and her husband James Voorhies, William P. Koonce,
Robert Hastings admr of Margaret L. Hastings, John P. Koonce
in his own right as admr of Blackman A. Koonce and Elizabeth
Koonce, John H. Shaw, Samuel G. Shaw and William G(?). Shaw,
Margaret Pinckard(Pickard) and her husband Alexander Pinckard
(Pickard), shows that on 21st July 1856, bill was filed which
all the complainants except Thomas Wilhoite were parties and
which Margaret Koonce and Margaret L. Koonce and Blackman A.
Koonce and Elizabeth Koonce and William H. Koonce are also
parties stated that John Koonce, Sr., departed this life intestate in Bedford County some 9 months, seized and possessed
of tract of land in District No. 23 in Bedford County. Land
bounded by William Galbreath's tract, and James Grant tract,
about 212 acres. Polly Morgan, Margaret Pickard, Blackman
Koonce, Elizabeth Reeves, Jane Voorhies and William W. Koonce,
are children of John Koonce, Sr., deceased. Mary J. Troxler,
William H. Koonce, Martha Reed, Margaret Koonce, Sarah Sabrina
Koonce, Virginia T. Koonce, Eliza Ellenor Koonce, John F.
Koonce and James A. Koonce are children of John Koonce, Jr.
who was a son of John Koonce, Sr. William H. and Margaret
Koonce died after sale of land, with Thomas Wilhoite your
orator, admr of their estate. Margaret L. Hastings, John J.
Koonce, Blackman A. Koonce and Elizabeth Koonce are children
of Jesse Koonce who was a son of John Koonce, Sr. and who died
intestate many years ago. Since sale of land, Elizabeth
Koonce died and after her, Margaret Hastings died, and after
her, Blackman A. Koonce died, all of them intestate and John J.
Koonce is admr of the first and last of them and Robert Hast-
ings is admr of Margaret Hastings. John H. and Samuel G. and
William Shaw are children of a daughter of John Koonce, Sr.,
namely Sally and who died long before her father. Benjamin
Reeves and Jesse Rogers are of Bedford County and William
Rogers is of Illinois. Decree, March 1865, stated that John
Koonce, Sr. departed this life in Bedford County intestate,
about 10 years ago (1855) in District No. 23.

Page 345 - No. 54 - William H. Wisener,   ] O. Bill,
                    Surviving executor   ]28 Jan 1865.
                    of Flower Swift's will   ]
                              vs   ]
                    John Cotner & wife & others]
William H. Wisener states that Flower Swift departed this life
at his domicil many years ago in Bedford County, having made
and published his Last Will and Testament and appointed your
orator as executor of his estate. Flower Swift left a widow
Catherine Swift and she was an executrix. Will was proven
and recorded in Bedford County. After two years, a settlement
of the estate according to the will and the estate was handed
over to his widow Catherine Swift, or to her during her natural
lifetime and at her death to be sold, and proceeds be divided

between his daughters to use during their lifetime and at their
deaths respectively to their children, charging Mrs. Jane
O'Neal with a negro as advancement, and Mrs. Mary Kimmons with
what he had to pay as security for William D. Warner her former
husband, and he gave to his grandson Thomas W. Warner, upon
age of 21 years, a horse worth $75.00 and a saddle, bridle
and blanket. That Catherine Swift his widow departed this
life lately and time has arrived to (settle) when the will
is to be executed, finally. On 10 September last, your orator
sold all except the slaves. The widow was quite an old lady
and her children had all long since married and left her. They
all were married before the death of Flower Swift. Her grandson Thomas W. Swift stayed some with his grandmother Catherine
Swift. Flower Swift's daughters, to wit, Margaret Cotner wife
of John Cotner, Mary Kimmons wife of Thomas Kimmons of Bedford
County, also Mary's son Thomas W. Warner of Bedford County.
Also a son Jacob W. Swift who had several children but only
Samuel is known at this time. They reside in Arkansas.
Margaret Cotner has twice married and the mother of two children, John V(U). Hall and William H. W. Hall, the former having
reached 21 years but the latter a minor of 17 years old, both
of Bedford County. His daughter Mrs. Jane O'Neal wife of
Warren O'Neal of Marshall County, Tennessee, they have three
children, Jacob O'Neal who has reached 21 years, a daughter
_____ over 14 years of Marshall County, Tennessee, another
daughter Martha C. Story wife of Francis M. Story of Bedford
County.

Page 349 - Will of Flower Swift, unattached copy.
I, Flower Swift of Bedford County, Tennessee being of sound
mind and disposing memory and knowing the uncertainty of life,
do make this my Last Will and Testament. First - I give my
soul to God who gave it. Secondly - I desire that all my debts
and funeral expenses be paid out of the money that may be on
hand at my death, and debts due me and such perishable property
as my wife can spare and if this be not sufficient, then by
the sale of such slaves as she can spare. All sales for the
payment of debts to be on such terms as my executors may deem
advisable under the circumstances of my estate. Thirdly -
I bequeath and devise all the balance of my estate, real and
personal to my beloved wife (should she survive me) during
her natural life or widowhood. Fourth - It is my will that
my son Jacob W. Swift have none of my estate, and I exclude
him from there from (except the sum of five dollars, which
sum of five dollars I direct my executors to pay to him
immediately after my debts are paid). Fifth - At the death
of my wife (or at my death if I survive her) it is my will
that all my property herein bequeathed and devised to her be
equally divided among my three daughters to their sole and
separate use, free from the contracts, control or debts of
their present or future husbands, and at their deaths to their
children, respectively. That is the share of each daughter
is to go to her own children. In making the division the money
I paid for William D. Warner is to be counted as so much advancement to Mrs. Kimmons, but without interest. And Mrs.
O'Neal is to be charged with a negro boy at one hundred dollars.
And these are the only advancements to her charged in the
division of my property between my daughters. Sixth - If my
wife should survive me and marry again, then the division of
my property is to take place, and to be equally divided between
my wife and three daughters, to their separate use as aforesaid.
One fourth counting advancements between them as aforesaid.
And for the purpose of division under this or proceeding item,

the property is to be sold by my executors or the survivors
of them on 12 months time with good personal security and also
a lien on the real estate for the purpose money. Seventh -
I bequeath to my grandson Thomas W. Warner a horse worth $75.00
to be paid him at the age of 21 years and also a good saddle,
bridle and blanket. Eighth - If my wife cannot manage any
of the negroes, she may hire out such as she cannot manage
and have the hire absolutely. I nominate and appoint my friend
William H. Wisener executor and my wife Catherine Swift as
executrix of this my Last Will and Testament. And hereby revoke all former wills by me heretofore made. In witness where
I hereunto set my hand ans seal this 21st(31st) day of March
1850.   Signed: Flower Swift (Seal)
Acknowledged in our presence and we became witness to it at
the request of the Testator and subscribed our names as such
in his presence.
Test: C. McCuistion
       J. P. McCuistion
Catherine Swift died in August 1864.

Page 351 - No. 55 - Coble & Stamps] O. Bill, filed
                           vs   ] 6 November 1863.
                    Pyron & Johnson]
Benjamin K. Coble and A. L. Stamps of Bedford County states
that they and James M. Johnson sold to C. L. Pyron 40 acres
of land and mill in Bedford County, known as "The Three Fork
Mill Tract". Located on Barren Fork of Duck River below where
the Nashville Railroad crosses the same. Note due 25 December
1861. Pyron and Johnson have both left the state. The government took possession of the mills as abandoned property and
rented them for the year 1864, said Pyron being in the South
and a Rebel. The government are still at the Mills and are
committing injuries to the property and especially the machinery.

Page 354 - No. 56 - George M. Hooser &   ] Att. Bill,
                     Harriet V. Hooser   ] August 2, 1864.
                           vs   ]
                    Elias C. Holt & others]
George M. Hooser and Harriet V. Hooser of Bedford County filed
against Elias C. Holt and Gabriel Maupin formerly of Bedford
County but now beyond the limits of the state, having abandoned
their homes in the state and now residing in parts unknown
and James M. Isom, admr of the estate of J. L. Ayres who reside in Bedford County. They also states that Elias Holt was
guardian of your oratrix Harriet V. Hooser and as such is
chargeable with the sum of $2455.66 on the 15 day of March
1857 plus interest. George M. Hooser and Harriet V. Hooser
have married and they have legal right to collect of Elias
Holt, guardian of Harriet V. Hooser. Elias C. Holt gave as
securities J. L. Ayres and Gabriel Maupin, that J. L. Ayres
is dead and James M. Isom is admr. Holt and Maupin abandoned
their homes in bedford County and gone to parts unknown.
Elias C. Holt own a tract of land in District No. 2, adjoining
lands of Zach Cully, R. B. Maupin and Samuel Yates, about 175
acres. Gabriel Maupin owns land in District No. 25 of Bedford
County and joins Josiah Maupin, A. L. Lowrance and John Evans,
about 125 acres, on which Dr. Whitson now resides. James M.
Isom states that he is owner or part owner in land he purchased
at the sale of his father's property. His three sisters named,
Mrs. Frances Blackburn, M. A. Culley and E. M. Holt. Elias C.
Holt's brother is Joseph Holt. Elias C. Holt was guardian
of Harriet V. Hooser, who was James M. Isom's sister.

Page 359 - No. 57 - William G. Cowan & others]   Att. Bill,
                         vs   ]22 December 1859
                    T. A. Bell & M. C. Moulton]
William G. Cowan and Sarah Cowan his wife, Samuel A. Strickler,
Christina Strickler, Henry Cooper and wife Ann E. formerly
Ann E. Strickler, all of Bedford County and Adam G. Adams and
wife Mary Jane formerly Mary Jane Strickler of Davidson County,
Tennessee filed against M. C. Moulton and T. A. Bell non-residents of Tennessee and reside in the State of Texas. Orators
states that about 2 years ago, they sold by deed, reserving
a lien for the purchase money, to M. C. Moulton and T. A. Bell,
for a Town Lot in Shelbyville, which descended to them under
the will of Benjamin Strickler, deceased, situated on the
northwest corner of the Public Square of Shelbyville, bordered
by Bank of Tennessee, Main Street, Main Street west to an
alley, south with said alley to southwest corner of said lot
and southeast corner of the bank lot. Bell and Moulton were
engaged in Manufacture of Tobacco.

Page 362 - No. 58 - Peter Berron   ]   Att. Bill,
                         vs   ] February 18, 1861.
                    Bernhard Holthoff]
                    & others   ]
Peter Berron of Bedford County filed against Bernhard Holthoff
and wife Lizetta Holthoff, last heard from as residents of
Davidson County, Tennessee and B. F. Duggan and George Moore,
both of Bedford County. Peter Berron stated that on 5 July
1859, he sold to Bernhard Holthoff, a house and lot in the
Town of Unionville, Bedford County, bounded by W. C. Blanton,
W. P. McConnell. Took note. Orator states that B. Holfhoff
left the County of Bedford and after he left, his wife Lizetta
Holthoff filed for divorce. Orator stated that Lizetta Holthoff had abandoned her bill for divorce, that she left Unionville and went to Nashville and joined her husband.

Page 366 - No. 59 - Newcomb Thompson, Sr.]   Att. Bill,
                         vs   ] 20 January 1864.
                    Jacob F. Thompson   ]
Newcomb Thompson, Sr., resident of Tennessee, states that
Jacob F. Thompson, resident unknown and beyond the limits of
Tennessee, is indebted to him by notes and accounts for sum
of $1001.23 including interest. Jacob F. Thompson had real
estate in District No. 6 of Bedford County, being valuable
mills on Duck River known as "Wilhoite's Old Mills", about
50 acres of mill tract, purchased of Dick (Richard) Wilhoite.
J. F. Thompson also has interest in tract of land on north
side of Duck River purchased of John and Jacob Wilhoite and
adjoining Alexander Sanders and others, about 100 acres.

Page 370 - No. 60 - Sanford Sewell & wife] Att. Bill,
                         vs   ] January 28, 1865.
                    G. M. Ray   ]
Sanford Sewell and wife Margaret Sewell of Kentucky, states
that George M. Ray is indebted to them by note dated 10 September 1859. G. M. Ray formerly resided in Bedford County where
he owned property. That he has removed himself from the limits
and has taken some of his property with him.

Page 371 - William McGowan & wife]   Att. Bill,
                         vs   ] 28 January 1865.
              G. M. Ray   ]
William McGowan and wife Lucindy stated that G. M. (George M.)
Ray is indebted to them by note dated 10 September 1859.

Page 372 - Sanford Sewell & wife]
                          vs   ]
           George M. Ray   ]
                   and   ] Decree March 1865.
           William McGowan & wife]
                          vs   ]
           George M. Ray   ]
Court attached property of G. M. Ray. Land in Bedford County
in Civil District No. 24, bounded by Widow Lyons, Widow Bobo,
Peter Wells and Mathew T. Cunningham, Joel Shofner and Bennett
Stephens land on which G. M. Ray lived before he left State
of Tennessee. Another tract of land owned by Ray, bordered
T. P. Wells and Thomas Boyers, M. H. Watson and Mrs. Bobo's
dower, the Martin or Old Shook Place (Mortgage), Boston Philpot tract.

Page 375 - No. 61 - Alexander Hodge &   ]
                          Joseph Ramsey   ]
                                   vs   ] Att. Bill, filed
                          D. L. Reeves & others] August 10, 1864.
Att. Bill filed by Alex. Hodge and Joseph Ramsey of Bedford
County against D. L. Reeves and Lewis Garner resident unknown,
and T. W. Jordan of Bedford County. Orators says that Daniel
L. Reeves and Lewis Garner are indebted to them for $1843.00
on a note executed by them to William Eoff, due 1 day of October 1861. Orators states that Daniel L. Reeves and Lewis
Garner have both left the State of Tennessee. Said Reeves
had land in District No. 1, Bedford County, described as the
"Sharp Tract' and the "Shaw Tract", two tracts and joining
Edmund Cooper, William F. Robertson, McMichael and Bowling
and others, about 800 acres. Lewis Garner is owner of a tract
of land in District No. __ of Rutherford County, Tennessee,
adjoining Robert Woods, Ridley Doblins(?) and the heirs of
William Pinkerson, Jno. F. Howland, James S---es, B. G. White,
Pearson, McNeal and Robert Miller's heirs, about 750 acres.

Page 378 - No. 62 - L. P. Fields   ] O. & Att. Bill,
                                   vs   ] 12 August 1864.
                          Daniel L. Reeves &]
                          T. W. Jordan   ]
Lilburn P. Fields of Bedford County filed against Daniel L.
Reeves non-resident of Tennessee and T. W. Jordan of Bedford
County. Orator stated that sometime in Fall of 1861, he was
engaged in partnership with D. L. Reeves, in purchasing and
selling of horses, mules &c. They also bought of James Porter,
166 acres in District No. 1 in Bedford County, adjoining
Stephenson, McMahan and Caufman. The tract known as "The Woods
Place". Reeves also had land in District No. 1, bounded by
heirs of Shaw, W. F. Robertson, Thomas and Samuel Farrar,
L. P. Fields, Edmund Cooper, Ben Moore, John R. Baily and
McMichael, about 950 acres, on which the family of James Johnson, lately deceased, and John R. Butler are living.

Page 383 - No. 63 - Thomas B. & C. L. Cannon, Exrs]O. & Att.Bill
                                   vs   ]3 Feb. 1864.
                          R. S. Dwiggins & others   ]
Thomas B. and Charles L. Cannon are executors of the Last Will
and Testament of Clement Cannon, deceased, both of Bedford
County filed against R. S. Dwiggins now held as a Political
Prisoner at Nashville, Leroy W. Barrett a non-resident of Tennessee, and James S. Newton, J. E. Jenkins and James Carlisle,
all of Bedford County. Orators states that they are the holders and legal owners of a Bill of Exchange drawn by R. S.

Dwiggins on W. J. Sedyane of Mobile, Alabama, acceptance
waived. Date June 25, 1860 and due in 6 months for sum of
$3000.00, endorsed by L. W. Barrett and James S. Newton.
Orators states that Leroy W. Barrett has left his home in
Tennessee and gone to reside in Alabama, he left owning a tract
of land in District No. 20 of Bedford County, joining lands
of James Carlisle, James S. Newton, R. S. Dwiggins and A. H.
Evans, on which he formerly lived, about 600 acres.

```
Page 386 - No. 64 - R. D. Blair &        ] O. & Att. Bill,
                    A. D. Fugitt         ] August 10, 1864.
                        vs               ]
                  David Vaughn & others]
```
R. D. Blair and Alfred D. Fugitt of Bedford County filed
against David Vaughn of Bedford County and R. S. Thomas,
Thompson B. Ivie and R. P. Ransom of Georgia. Robert D. Blair
states that on 16 March 1859, he sold to Thompson B. Ivie a
tract of land in District No. __ of Bedford County. Bounded
by Railroad, Lot No. 3, Center of Wartrace, Anderson's Creek
about 161 acres.

```
Page 389 - R. D. Blair &       ]
           A. D. Fugitt        ]
               vs              ] Decree March 1865.
         David Vaughn & others]
```
R. D. Blair sold, years ago, to Thompson B. Ivie, land and
took part payment. Afterwards Ivie sold same land to R. P.
Ransom, Vaughn bought land. All above three are non-residents
of Tennessee.

```
Page 390 - No. 66 - Peter Word         ]
                       vs              ]Att. & Inj. Bill,
               William Stewart &]2 February 1860.
               John C. Hix      ]
```
Peter Word of Bedford County filed against John C. Hix of Bed-
ford County and William Stewart a resident of Missouri.
Orator states that William Stewart is indebted to him for about
$200.00 for money collected by Stewart belonging to your orator
and the debt is still unpaid. Orator states that William
Stewart of Missouri is an heir in the estate of Margaret Stewart, who lately departed this life intestate in Bedford County
and John C. Hix had been appointed her admr in May Term 1859.
Mrs. Margaret Stewart had ten (10) children, four of whom had
died before their mother, two of them left children and two
of whom, to wit, Joshua Stewart and Samuel Stewart had died
before their mother, neither of whom left any children who
survived their grandmother, but they both left grandchildren.
Should the great grand children of Margaret Stewart, come and
claim part of her estate, there may not be enough after paying
the debt, and a debt of William Stewart, who is an heir of
Margaret Stewart (he is to get one slave of her estate).

```
Page 394 - No. 68 - O. P. Arnold        ] Inj. Bill,
                       vs               ] April 4, 1861.
               James Mullins & others]
```
O. P. Arnold filed against James Mullins, B. D. Holt as Trust-
ees of W. C. Holt and W. C. Holt of Bedford County. Alexander
Suter and James Suter of parts unknown and the Nashville &
Chattanooga Railroad Co., having V. K.(U. K.) Stephenson as
President. O. P. Arnold states that on 12 October 1858, he
bought of James Mullins and B. D. Holt as Trustees of W. C.
Holt and W. C. Holt, a tract of land in Bedford County, about
201 acres, bounded by Mrs. Caruthers. Orator wants clear title.

Orator states that 48 acre deed is defective and bad. The
48 acres include the place where the Water Tank is situated
and two valuable springs and some of the best ground on entire
tract. He also states that he talked to Robert Maupin, John M.
Stokes, J. M. Townsend, and others, who are old settlers in
the neighborhood and they said the land was known as "Suter's
Land" and the Suter children had not parted with the title.
The 48 acre land title appears at one time to have been in
a family of Stallard, and then in Isaac West and Wiley Riggins
and then W. C. Holt (of which order your orator does not know).
The said land has the N & C Railroad run along over said land
from one side to the other, the Railroad has 100 feet on each
side of roadbed.

Page 398 - No. 69 - Phileman Gosling   ] O. & Inj. Bill,
                         vs   ] August 9, 1860.
                    Gardner & Co. & others]
Phileman Gosling states that years ago, he and John F. Neil
became securities for John Gormly on a note given by Gormly
to C. C. Grizzard for about $179.00, also he stated at the
time the note was signed by him, he was a resident of this
state. Shortly after he sold out and removed from this county
but before he went away, your orator was advised that he placed
in the hands of his co-security John F. Neil a note on Tomapeny
and John G. Fulgum for $175.00 or $180.00, to satisfy the debt
which he was owning to Grizzard.

Page 403 - No. 70 - Baskett & Stamps]
                         vs   ]O. Bill, 28 April 1860.
                    Moses B. Wadley]
G. P. Baskett and Asa L. Stamps of Bedford County, partners
&c filed against Moses B. Wadley of Bedford County. Orators
states that some years ago W. S. Wadley formerly of Bedford
County departed this life intestate, unmarried and without
issue. That at the time of his death, he was owner of some
property, a horse, &c and crop. W. S. Wadley was son of
Moses B. Wadley.

Page 408 - No. 72 - William Jackson]
                         vs   ]Att. Bill, 4 March 1865.
                    Samuel M. Brown]
William Jackson of Bedford County states that he is owner of
two notes on Samuel M. Brown a non-resident of Tennessee, dated
October 2, 1860, signed by Brown and Jos. P. Taylor for $100.00,
other by Brown and W. C. Taylor and M. R. Taylor, dated 18
September 1861 for $50.85. P. and C. P. Taylor are executors
of Vincent Taylor, deceased, and assigned 22 February 1865
by them to your orator. Samuel M. Brown is owner of a tract
of land in Civil District No. 10 in Bedford County, about 300
acres, bounded by John Jackson, William Taylor, John T. Harris
and T. D. Tarpley.

Page 410 - No. 73 - James Carlisle]
                         vs   ]Att. Bill, 22 January 1864.
                    Leroy W. Barrett]
                    & J. E. Jenkins]
James Carlisle of Bedford County states that Leroy W. Barrett
of Alabama is justly indebted to him for one note dated 24
November 1862, sum of $1155.00. Leroy W. Barrett is owner
of a tract of land in District No. 20 of Bedford County, adjoining lands of James Carlisle, James S. Newton and R. S.
Dwiggins and others, about 500 acres. J. F. Jenkins levied
an attachment on same land.

Page 411 - No. 76 - Thomas Hart   ]
                   vs   ]O. Bill, 29 July 1859.
                A. Erwin, Admr &]
                J. H. Alderman   ]
Thomas Hart of Bedford County filed against Andrew Erwin and
Henry Alderman, all of Bedford County. Thomas Hart stated
some years ago he entered into partnership with Archibald
Murphy, for the purpose of selling goods at Wartrace Depot
in Bedford County. Business continued until verbally discon-
tinued also written contract made by Patrick Murphy, a brother
of Archibald Murphy. Archibald Murphy is dead and Andrew
Erwin is executor of his Last Will and Testament. Archibald
Murphy had a son Alonzo Murphy.

Page 414 - No. 77 - Thomas Hart et al   ] Inj. Bill,
                   vs   ] May 23, 1860.
                Strickler Ellis & Co.]
Thomas Hart, Stephen Hart and John Hart states that the late
firm of Hart & Cannon, composed of Thomas Hart and Clement
Cannon, Jr., had dealings with the firm of Strickler Ellis
& Co. of Nashville, Tennessee, from 9 January 1857 to 22 May
1857 for amount of $429.35 by note. That firm dissolved in
1857 and your orator Thomas Hart took the assets and was to
pay the debts. A number of notes, dated when paid April 20,
1858. Signed by Strickler & Ellis & Co. by J. D. Eakin. Wartrace, April 20, 1858.

Page 420 - No. 78 - R. F. Evans   ]
                   vs   ]O. Bill,
                The Bedford County]July 15, 1865.
                Agriculture &   ]
                Mechanical Society]
R. F. Evans of Bedford County filed against The Bedford County
Agriculture and Mechanical Society, a corporate body in Bedford
County and had for its President H. L. Davidson and for its
Secretary James H. Neil of Bedford County. Orator stated that
about 1 April 1859, Joel J. Blackwell sold to B. C. Agriculture
& Mechanical Society, a certain lot of land in the corporate
limits of the Town of Shelbyville near the west boundary of
town and bounded by Lot No. 8 sold to William H. Wisener,
Robert Denniston, and W. A. Griffis and a street.

Page 422 - No. 79 - Samuel Parker   ] Att. Bill,
                   vs   ]25 May 1865.
                Daniel L. Reeves & others]
Samuel Parker of Rutherford County, Tennessee filed against
Daniel L. Reeves a non-resident of Tennessee, T. W. Jordan
and L. P. Fields of Bedford County. Orator states that Daniel
L. Reeves is indebted to him by bill, dated November 19, 1860
for sum of $800.00. Daniel L. Reeves removed from Tennessee
about 2 years ago. He was owner of a tract of land of about
950 acres in District No. 1 of Bedford County, on the Garrison
Fork of Duck River adjoining lands of Edmund Cooper, W. F.
Robertson, L. P. Fields, Thomas and Samuel Farrar, Benjamin
Moore, John R. Baily and McMichaels, which land has been sold
upon a judgement of Circuit Court in favor of Jordan vs Reeves
and bought by Reeves.

Page 425 - No. 80 - C. C. Brown   ]
                   vs   ]Bill, January 20, 1860.
                Thomas Stevens]
This case has already been enrolled by W. J. Whitthorne in
the year 186_.

Page 425 - No. 81 - J. W. Muse   ]
                        vs   ]Bill, August 4, 1865.
                Susan W. Muse]
J. W. Muse states that he married Susan W, Yatt in Bedford
County in January 1859. They had been married about three
years. In 1862, she moved to Town of Shelbyville and at work
there, without any notice, she left by cars (train) to Nashville and then to Paducah, Kentucky. He said she returned
to Nashville and stayed there for sometime and living with
some officer of the Federal Army as his wife, whom she has
married and she has gone off with him our of this state, to
somewhere across the Ohio River. Asked for a divorce because
of adultry and desertion.

Page 426 - No. 82 - John Huffman   ]
                        vs   ]O. Bill, July 5, 1860.
                Thomas Stevens]
John Huffman states that on 25 November 1857, he sold to Thomas
Stevens, a Saw & Grist Mill, situated on the South or Barren
Fork of Duck River in Bedford County and about 33 acres of
land attached to it, known for many years as "Troxler's Mills",
$3000.00. Part of which has been paid. A joint answer of
Ann Eliza, Samuel G., Charles A., Thomas Forrest McFadden by
their guardian Thomas H. Coldwell, heirs of William R. McFadden,
deceased. William R. McFadden departed this life in Rutherford
County, Tennessee about 2 years ago (1863) of which he was
a citizen. They stated that William R. McFadden purchased
the land and mills 7 January 1861. William R. McFadden's widow
still living in September 1865. Heirs of William R. McFadden
are Clementine A., the widow, and William H. McFadden.

Page 430 - No. 83 - Solomon L. Brown]
                        vs   ]O. Bill, March 6, 1865.
                Thomas L. Sharp]
                & others   ]
Solomon L. Brown states that on the day of ___ 185_, John H.
Oneal sold to Thomas L. Sharp for $800.00, a house and lot
in the Town of Shelbyville and Sharp paid in cash and executed
his note. House and lot on Cedar Street and bounded by U. E.
Peacock, Calvin Trollinger and _____ McFerren & Co.

Page 432 - No. 85 & 86 - M. T. Cunningham   ] O. Bill,
                        vs   ]12 September 1857.
                J. J. Crunk & others]
Matthew T. Cunningham of Bedford County states that some years
ago, he and James J. Crunk bought of W. W. Coldwell, several
parcels of small tracts of land, being a part of a tract of
about 68 acres, purchased by W. W. Coldwell at the sale of
the "School Lands". Crunk and orator for the entire tract
and they conveyed all but three lots or parcels to Sam Bobo
to whom Coldwell had sold it, retaining only as above, the
title to the lots as aforesaid (School Lands). One about 1
acre where D. H. Rogers now lives. Another loccupied by said
Crunk as a stable lot. Another 1 occupied by a Store House
and Blacksmith Shop. Another i occupied by a Factory and known
as Factory Lot. All in Bedford County in Flat Creek Village.

Page 436 - No. 87 - Jackson Wallace   ] O. Bill,
                        vs   ]5 November 1864.
                G. W. Cunningham & others]
Jackson Wallace of Bedford County filed against G. W. Cunningham of Bedford County, Chesly Williams and William P. Cannon,
executors of Robert Cannon, deceased, both of Williamson

County, Tennessee. Orator states that 14 January 1862, he
recovered a judgement against G. W. Cunningham and Robert
Cannon for sum of $389.18 and cost. Cunningham being Principal
and Cannon Security, which was stayed by P. Fay (Patrick Fay)
for Gen. Cannon, that P. Fay has removed from the state and
has no property that he knows of. That on 16 October 1862,
an execution was issued upon said judgement, which came into
hands of James C. Snell (a constable of Bedford County) and
before the return day of the same, (said Cannon, said Cunningham in the meantime having become incolvent and being yet so)
forced said Snell under a Military threat to receive in payment
of said execution Confederate Treasury Notes. Having received
said funds under these circumstances said Snell on the ___ day
of ___ 1862 returned said execution satisfied. Afterwards
said Snell offered said funds to complt which he refused to
receive, not being able to pay his debts therewith. Sometime
later, Snell saw Gen. Cannon, deft, and told him that complt
would not receive said Confederate Money from him in payment
of judgement and execution, that he, Cannon, had forced it
upon him, Snell and he must take it back, or words to this
effect. Cannon replied that it was passed or forced upon him
and he would force it upon him (Snell). Thereupon Snell having
in his hands the funds tossed the same down at Cannon's feet,
who walked off, refusing to take the same. And Snell took
up the money and has it yet. Geberal Robert Cannon departed
this life in January 1864, after making his Last Will and Testament, Williams and William P. Cannon, in ___ Term 1864, named
executors.

Page 439 - No. 88 - William Crowell & others] Bill, filed
                              vs   ]August 4, 1865.
                 Joseph McKinley Crowell]
                 & others   ]
William Crowell and John Crowell, admrs of Samuel Crowell,
deceased, and in their own right as heirs at law of Samuel
Crowell, Joshua Crowell, Michael Crowell, John D. Clark and
wife Sarah Clark, Phillip Parsons and wife Catharine, B. F.
Parsons and wife Jennie, E. H. McGowen and wife Nancy, J. H.
Potts and wife Isabella W., Mary Capley, Mary Ann Crowell wife
and widow of Samuel Crowell, all of Bedford County. Jacob B.
Delk and wife Annie of Maury County, Tennessee, Rosena Goar(?)
of State of Illinois, filed against Joseph McKinley Crowell
a minor who has no guardian, Mary Crowell and John Crowell,
minors who have Joshua Crowell for their guardian, Zilphia
Cartwright wife of Phillip Cartwright (Zilphia still a minor
and has no guardian), Jennie Parsons a minor and no guardian,
all of Bedford County. Samuel Crowell departed this life intestate in Bedford County on 24 June 1865, leaving his heirs,
to wit, William; John; Joshua; Michael and Samuel Crowell;
Sarah Clark a daughter Cynthia who married Jacob M. Parsons;
Zilphia Cartwright and Jennie Parsons daughters of deceased
daughter Cynthia Parsons; Jennie Parsons; Nancy McGowen, Isabella H. Potts daughters of deceased son Benjamin Crowell;
Mary Capley; Annie Delk; Rosena Goar; Joseph McKinley Crowell
a son of Benjamin Crowell; Mary and John Crowell, children
of Jacob Crowell; Zilphia Cartwright and Jennie Parsons children of Cynthia Parsons; widow Mary Ann Crowell. William and
John Crowell named admrs July Term 1865. Samuel Crowell was
the owner, at his death, of 3 small tracts of land in Bedford
County. First, Known as the Crowell's Mill tract, bounded
by Duck River, Felix Turrentine, heirs of Jacob Crowell and
others. Shearin purchased of George Smith, about 62½ acres.
Second - Bounded by Felix Turrentine, Michael Crowell, Jacob M.

Parsons' heirs, about 32 acres. Third - Bounded by heirs of
Jacob Crowell, Michael Crowell, Edward Wortham, about 32 acres.
In all about 126½ acres in Bedford County in District No. 11.
Mary Ann Crowell, the widow, has not received the dower tract.
Samuel and Mary Ann Crowell had eleven children.

Page 443 - No. 89 - John Jordan   ]   Att. Bill,
                         vs   ] December 28, 1860.
                W. G. Hight & others]
John Jordan of Coffee County, Tennessee filed against T. N.
McCord of Bedford County and Richard Nance of Rutherford County,
Tennessee and W. G. Hight of Bedford County. John Jordan stat-
ed that on 14 October 1859, he sold to W. G. Hight a tract
of land in Bedford County, bounded by J. W. Simpson, Turnpike
Road (a rock marked J. J.), Old Shelbyville Road, Clems Creek,
and Versailes Road.

Page 448 - No. 90 - J. P. Taylor   ] Att. Bill.
                         vs   ]1 August 1863.
                R. S. Dwiggins & others]
J. P. Taylor states that R. S. Dwiggins is indebted to him
for $1000.00 by note, due 28 February 1863. Orator states
that Dwiggins has absconded and left the State of Tennessee.
The Government of The United States has seized such of his
property as has not been already attached by his creditors.
Orator says Dwiggins is owner by transfer of a claim in suit
in Chancery Court of Shelbyville in name of John Jordan against
Richard Nance and T. N. McCord, Trustees of William G. Hight.

Page 451 - No. 91 - N. Thompson &]   O. Bill, filed
                J. F. Thompson]   17 August 1865.
                         vs   ]
                C. W. Cummings]
Jacob F. Thompson and Newcomb Thomas(Thompson), Sr. filed
against C. W. Cummings of Bedford County. Orators states that
he, Jacob F. Thompson on 27 February 1860 sold to William S.
Spear as Trustee of Susan Spear for $3000.00, the tract of
land lying in District No. 7 of Bedford County, adjoining lands
of Thomas Pettis, Newcomb Thompson, Sr., and Jason T. Cannon
and land on which C. W. Cummings now reside, about 50 acres.

Page 453 - No. 92 - G. B. Morgan] O. & Inj. Bill,
                         vs   ] 4 March 1863.
                R. S. Dwiggins]
Germain B. Morgan of Bedford County filed against Robert S.
Dwiggins late of Bedford County but now a absconding debtor.
Orator states that R. S. Dwiggins is indebted to him by note
to sum over $700.00. After Dwiggins left, the Government of
the United States has seized most of the personal property
of Dwiggins. Orator states that Dwiggins owns land in District
No. 10 of Bedford County, adjoining lands of Bellefont, Manier,
minor heirs of Martin, and Thomas Bullock, about 200 acres.

Page 454 - No. 94 - Abram G. Winsett & others]
                         vs   ] 1 August 1865.
                John Tune & wife & others]
Mary Winsett, Abram G. Winsett, John W. Wood and wife Martha
Jane, William J. Winsett, Alex Green and wife Sarah Ann,
Thomas M. Winsett, and Daniel H. Winsett, states that Jason
Winsett departed this life 1854 in Bedford County, the place
of domicile, having first made his Last Will and Testament,
proven and recorded. In March 1863, all County Records were
destroyed (which is in error, hcm). Your orators, the

287

Winsett's, are sons of Jason Winsett and your oratrixes are his daughters and sonsare his only surviving children. That at the time of his death, he had a son Eli D. Winsett who was appointed one of his executors, who has since died and leaving no children but a widow _____ Winsett since married to John Tune of Bedford County. He also left a daughter Lucinda Burge wife of John H. Burge, since dead leaving the following children, Mary Ann Burge who married Thomas Davis, since dead and leaving one child Lucinda Davis a minor who has no guardian, Rebecca Burge who married to Nathan Ray, James C. Burge, Martha Burge since dead and was unmarried and a minor and no personal representative, William D. Burge, Sarah Burge, Susan Burge and Nancy Burge, the last four being minors with no guardian.

Will of Jason Winsett:
In the name of God Amen. I, Jason Winsett of the County of Bedford and State of Tennessee, knowing the uncertainty of human life, and the certainty of death, being weak of body, but of a sound and perfect mind and recollection do make this my Last Will and Testament, revoking all others heretofore made by me. That is to say then---Item 1st - First of all, I waould commit my soul to God confidently hoping for a better state than remains in this and all my funeral expenses paid out of my estate. Item 2nd - I desire that all my just debts be paid as soon as the nature of the case will admit. Item 3rd - I give and bequeath to my wife Ann all of my household and kitchen furniture together with the farming utensils, all the provisions on hand, all of stock of hogs, horses, cattle, sheep, and all of my farm or land on which I live during her widowhood, but so soon as that shall cease either by marriage or death, then all the said property herein bequeathed to her shall be sold on such terms as my executors shall deem proper and the proceeds equally divided among my children and to have each a horse and cow and calf, feather bed and more than the others to make them equal with what my older children received when they came of age or married. He appointed Eli D. Winsett and Abram G. Winsett executors. Dated in 1854.
Test: Nathaniel O. Burton   Signed: Jason Winsett (Seal)
      Peyton S. Vincent
Proven in the County Court at Term 1854.

Page 457 - Abram G. Winsett, Exr & others] Answer,
                  vs   ]September 12, 1865.
             John Tune & wife & others   ]
Answer of Lucinda Davis, William S. Burge, Sarah Burge, Susan Burge and Nancy Burge by their guardian R. B. Davidson to the bill filed against them by Abram G. Winsett and others. They admit the death of their ancestor but do not know the time of death. They also admit the death of the widow of Jason Winsett.

Page 459 - No. 96 - Thomas C. Coldwell filed against Thomas Holland, Thomas G. Holland and Henry Sipsey, all of Bedford County. Orator states that the firm of Coldwell & Cummings of which he and James F. Cummings, were the firm. They recovered a judgement on 3 November 1859 for $335.77 and cost by James F. Calhoun paid and delivered on 23 August 1860 and levied on the same day upon a house and lot in Town of Shelbyville, District No. 7. Bounded by W. B. M. Brame, Spafford, Tilleton & Co., Main Street and Thomas Holland.

Page 461 - No. 97 - William H. Wisener]   Att. Bill, filed
                          vs   ]   6 November 1863.
                  Barksdale & Brown]
William H. Wisener, Sr. of Bedford County states that James G.
Barksdale formerly of Bedford County is indebted to him for
said sum of $100.00 for professional services in defending
a case in Circuit Court of Bedford County against him as a
security of one _____ Long, guardian of the heirs of _____
Gorr, deceased, which is due 1860 August, about $118.00 or
$120.00. He rendered services for Barksdale in August 1862,
in getting his horses and slaves released from the Federal
Authorities, taken by _____ Illinois, then under command of
Lt. Col. Van Horne. Barksdale had a service against your
orator so they "set off" the account. Barksdale left the state
and your orator rented his farm. Orator states that Henry
Brown of Bedford County has attached all of Barksdale real
estate in Bedford County where Barksdale resided, including
his farm of about 400 acres and a fine residence. He also
owns about 10 acres unattached that bordered his property,
bordered by Wisener, Nathan Ivy and Sarah T. Holland.

Page 463 - No. 97 - William H. Wisener, Sr.]
                          vs   ]
                  James G. Barksdale &   ]
                  Henry Brown   ]
Wisener and Barksdale having settled the debt mentioned in
the bill, it is therefore ordered that James G. Barksdale pay
the costs of this cause for which execution may issue.

Page 463 - No. 98 - James P. Rogers]
                          vs   ]Bill, 29 October 1863.
                  Knott & Lytle]
James P. Rogers of Bedford County states that he purchased
of Amanda F. Lytle on 5 November 1862, a tract of land, about
18 acres, in Civil District No. 10. Bounded by A. F. Knott
and A. Ransom. Shortly after, he had to leave Bedford County
because of his political sentiments and also to keep from going
into Confederate Army and while he was absent, Albert F. Knott
and others told her that the lands would be confiscated to
the Southern Confederacy and she would loose it because your
orator was adhering to the Government of the United States
and within the lines of the Armies, which induced her to sell
to Knott. Knott knew that she had already sold to your orator.
Your orator has deed but no registered. Knott was in possession of land and was cultivating it for the last year. Knott
and Lytle resides in Bedford County.

Page 464 - No. 98 - James P. Rogers]
                          vs   ]
                  Knott & Lytle]
Defts having settled the complts claim since the filing of
this bill, he dismisses his bill and the court orders the defts
to pay the cost and that executions issue for the same.

Page 464 - No. 105 - J. W. Crunk & Co.   ] Att. Bill,
                          vs   ] May 4, 1860
                  Thomas Gaddis & others]
John W. Crunk & Co. of Marshall County filed against John M.
Kimbro of Mississippi and Thomas Gaddis, admr &c of Bedford
County. Orators states that John Kimbro is indebted to them
by account for sum of $41.67 and cost and interest &c, 20 August
1856, by transfer of a judgement in favor of J. A. Blanton
against Jno. Kimbro. Kimbro has no property in this state.

John Kimbro, deceased, the grandfather of the deft. Jno. M.
Kimbro died in the year 185_ in Bedford County, leaving property, and John M. Kimbro thought and in right of his father ____
Kimbro, deceased, is entitled to a share. Thomas Gaddis, admr
of Jno. Kimbro, deceased, estate.

Page 465 - No. 105 - John W. Crunk & Co.]
                     vs   ]Answer, Oct. 5, 1860.
            Thomas A. Gaddis &]
            John M. Kimbro   ]
Thomas A. Gaddis, admr of Jno. Kimbro's estate, states at
Kimbro's death, he owned slaves and small amount of other per-
sonal property. John M. Kimbro is son of Eli Kimbro, deceased,
who left six children. Gaddis was appointed admr in January
Term 1860.
Page 467 - No. 105 - Amended answer, March 6, 1865.

Page 468 - No. 106 - John H. Burns]
                     vs   ]Att. Bill, 29 Dec 1863.
            F. P. McElwrath]
John H. Burns of Arkansas states that F. P. McElwrath, late
of Bedford County is indebted to your orator by note of
$1900.00 and due 25 December 1862. McElwrath has land in
District No. 8, on Fall Creek, adjoining the lands of John
Claxton, P. C. Steele, A. Goodrum, and others, known as the
"Wilson Steele Old Place". McElwrath owns another tract in
Bedford County in District No. 5 and joins lands of G. D.
Hutton and others, Thomas B. Marks, William Houston and others,
known as the "Nash Place". About 125 acres. McElwrath has
left and has been gone about 6 months.

Page 471 - No. 108 - Isaiah Parker   ] O. Bill,
                     vs   ]June 2, 1865.
            Sarah Campbell, admr]
            & others   ]
Isaiah Parker filed against Sarah Campbell widow and admr of
Alfred Campbell, W. W. Stanfield and wife Mary Stanfield, H. H.
Landers and wife Caroline Landers, James Baker and wife Fanny,
Martha Reagor and Catharine, all of Bedford County. Orator
states that about 29 December 1859, he purchased of Alfred
Campbell a tract of land in Bedford County in District No. 22
on waters of Flat Creek and bounded by lands of W. W. Stanfield
and wife, and by Parker, about 62 acres. A bond or note was
issued. The last payment was paid to John C. Hix from whom
Campbell had bought the land. John C. Hix died in Bedford
County and both of the witnesses (G. A. Reagor and J. Y. Moorman) have died since said Campbell. All his papers were destroyed in Bedford County in July 1863 by some soldiers of the
5th Tennessee Cavalry (his house). Alfred Campbell left his
widow Mrs. Sarah Campbell who is his admrx and the following
children, Mary who married W. W. Stanfield, Caroline who
married H. H. Landers, Fanny who married James Baker, Martha
Reagor who is a widow, and Catharine Campbell, all of Bedford
County.

Page 474 - No. 109 - Brown & Smith, Admrs   ] O. Bill,
                     vs   ]28 Aug 1865.
            A. J. Brown & wife & others,]
            Heirs of William R. Smith]
John S. Brown and John R. Smith states that they are admrs
of William R. Smith, deceased, appointed by Bedford County
Court, the place of his domicile. Owns land in Bedford County
and Marshall County, Tennessee. Land to be sold. William R.

Smith, deceased, left the following children, to wit, Basha
Ann Smith who married A. J. Brown, Roena Smith, and John R.
Smith, the last two are minors, with no guardian.

Page 475 - No. 109 - Brown & Smith, Admrs &c   ]
                           vs   ]
                     A. J. Brown and wife Basha Ann,]
                     Roena Smith, John R. Smith,   ]
                     Rezin Smith, James Smith and   ]
                     Haggard Smith   ]
Court says that defts, Roena Smith, John R. Smith, Rezin Smith,
James Smith and Haggard Smith are minors with no guardian.
It is ordered that James L. Scudder be appointed guardian.
A. J. Brown and wife Basha Ann formerly Basha Ann (Smith) more
that 5 days before the present Term of this Court is taken
for confessed because they did not appear.

Page 478 - No. 110 - J. C. Snell and wife & others] O. Bill,
                           vs   ] Aug 10,
                     J. L. Hilton, Admr & others   ] 1864.
J. C. Snell and wife Sarah H. Snell, A. M. Smith and wife Adeline Smith, Jackson Wallace and wife Elizabeth Wallace, George
W. Brown, James Harrison Dyer, Josephine Dyer, Emily Dyer,
Daniel Dyer, Eugene Dyer, the last six being minors and who
petition by their father and guardian W. H. Dyer filed against
J. L. Hilton, admr, D. D. Hilton, deceased, Mrs. Mary E. Hilton
wife of D. D. Hilton, deceased, William N., Peter Alexander,
Mary Jane, Benjamin Newsom, Hannah Catharine, Daniel Davis,
and John Wilson Hilton, all of whom are the children and heirs
of Mrs. Mary E. and D. D. Hilton and all under age of 14 years
old. J. C. Snell and wife and others states that they are
the heirs of William L. Brown, deceased, who departed this
life intestate on or about 8th day of March 1862. In October
Term 1863, J. C. Snell was appointed admr of the estate.
Orators states that sometime in the year 184_, D. D. Hilton
bought of William L. Brown land, about 160 or 180 acres in
District No. __ of Bedford County. Land bordered W. W. Gant,
Tempsey Bledsoe and Benjamin Delk.
Page 480 - Answer of Malinda E. Hilton, March 16, 1865.
Malinda E. states that her husband D. D. Hilton is dead, in-
teste.

Page 483 - No. 115 - B. F. Wiggins]
                           vs   ]Att. Bill, March 7, 1865.
                     Herod G. Holt]
Benjamin F. Wiggins of Bedford County filed against Herod G.
Holt of Alabama. B. F. Wiggins states that Herod G. Holt is
indebted to him for sum of $622.00 on many claims and is due.
Herod G. Holt is a citizen of Alabama, but the death of Jackson
J. Greer, he says he is entitled to one fourth of fifth of
100 acres of land in District No. 21 of Bedford County and
bounded by lands of M. L. Dismukes, K. L. Pybas, the heirs
of John T. Neil and Robert Dixon's heirs. Jackson J. Greer
died intestate and your orator was appointed admr of estate.
Jackson J. Greer left four sisters living and four children
of one deceased sister, the mother of Herod G. Holt.

Page 485 - No. 116 - William Taylor   ]   O. Bill,
                           vs   ] July 20, 1861.
                     George Smith & others]
William Taylor of Bedford County filed against D. G. Deason
of Arkansas, George Smith of Marshall County, Tennessee, and
Robert Mathews of Bedford County. William Taylor states that

he sold to David G. Deason a certain lot in the Town of Shelbyville, on west side of Martin Street, bounded by the alley
leading from Martin Street between said lot and the Methodist
Church Lot, by lot Patrick Fay sold to D. G. Deason which is
now in possession of Frances V. Story. Orator stated that
D. G. Deason was the Post Master at Shelbyville, appointed
by James Buchanan as President of the United States, and as
Post Master, he became a defaulter.

Page 487 - No. 117 - F. P. McElwrath & others] Att-Inj Bill,
                            vs   ]June 15, 1861.
                   W. P. F. Thompson & others]
F. P. McElwrath and wife Mary Elizabeth McElwrath, W. P. Thompson, Judy Thompson, Lavinia F. Thompson, and Thomas Bates,
the last two being minors whose guardian Elizabeth Thompson
and John R. Thompson filed against W. P. F. Thompson and P. H.
Thompson who resides in Arkansas and Richardson Clardy and
W. J. Whitthorne of Bedford County. Orators states that John
Thompson departed this life testate in Bedford County some
years ago, having real and personal property. He appointed
his two sons, W. P. F. Thompson and P. H. Thompson, executors.

Page 492 - No. 118 - C. McGuire   ]   Bill,
                          vs   ] 24 June 1865.
                   Lucy Smith, Admr & others]
C. McGuire filed against Lucy Smith, admrix of S. F. Smith,
deceased, William C. Blanton and Joseph Smith, all of Bedford
County except Joseph Smith of Davidson County, Tennessee.
Orator stated that William C. Blanton sold to S. F. Smith sometime in ____ 185_, a house and lot in Unionville, Bedford
County, District No. 11, bounded bystreet running east and
west through the Village of Unionville, lot of James Moore,
lands of Dr. Jennings Moore, about 1½ acres. Orator states
that S. F. Smith died intestate and Mrs. Lucy Smith, his widow,
is his admrix and is living upon said lot. He only left one
child Joseph Smith who is of age or nearly so.

Page 494 - No. 119 - Mary E. Patton] Bill for divorce,
                          vs   ] December 8, 1865.
                   Robert J. Patton]
Mary E. Patton states that she married Robert J. Patton in
Bedford County in 1859, both of Bedford County. Robert J.
Patton deserted her and left the state six months ago (to
filing bill), she said he was a gambler. He told her he was
going to California. She had to go to her father's to live.
They had two children, William and Thomas now about 14 months
old. She has heard that State of Missouri is where he is at
this time, when Robert J. Patton had land in District No. 11
on west side of the Village of Unionville and bounded by T.
Allison, Thomas Allison, A. Wilson and Mary King, about 130
acres. Mary E. Patton's father was William Wilson.

Page 497 - No. 120 - D. H. Skeen   ] Att. Bill,
                          vs   ]Sept 12, 1864.
                   William B. Sutton & others]
D. H. Skeen filed against William B. Sutton, George W. Chambers
and others. Orator states that in the Fall of 1860, he sold
a tract of land in bedford County, District No. 4, bounded
by Mrs. Snelling, Dr. C. F. Sutton, James Caruthers and Wm. B.
Sutton, about 75 acres. William B. Sutton has since left the
State of Tennessee and gone south. Chambers said he bought
same land from Sutton.

Page 501 - No. 121 - George W. Chambers   ]   Att. Bill,
                        vs   ]August 10, 1864.
                W. B. Sutton & others]
George W. Chambers filed against William B. Sutton of parts
unknown, D. H. Skeen and William Sharp of Bedford County.
Orator states that he purchased of W. B. Sutton on 7 October
1862, land in Bedford County, known as "Skeen Tract". W. B.
Sutton owns land bordered by W. W. Payne and Daniel Gilchrist,
and James Caruthers, land where William Brown now owns, and
the land allotted as Dower to Mrs. Sutton, the same land
assigned to William B. Sutton as one of the heirs of John
Sutton, deceased. Dower tract has about 400 acres belonging
to Mrs. Sutton now Mrs. G. G. Osborne.

Page 507 - No. 122 - Thomas Hart   ]
                        vs   ] Filed 1 January 1862.
                D. S. Bates &]
                J. H. Neil   ]
Thomas Hart of Bedford County filed against David S. Bates
and James H. Neil, both of Bedford County. Orator states that
on 11 January 1861, he recovered two judgements against David
S. Bates. Orator states that John B. Bates departed this life
sometime since leaving a widow and eight children, two of the
children have since died, having never married and without
a will. Among the number of children of John B. Bates is
David S. Bates. At the time of John B. Bates' death, he was
the owner of about five slaves, descended to his widow and
children. Sale of slaves to be on 6th January 1862.

Page 510 - No. 123 - Margaret Ann Whitthorne   ]Petition,
                        vs   ]23 Oct 1865.
                Samuel H. Whitthorne & others]
Margaret Ann Whitthorne filed against Samuel H. Whitthorne,
Lula E., Martha Harding and William J. Whitthorne, 3rd., the
last three being minors, all of Bedford County. Margaret Ann
Whitthorne who is a married woman and wife of Samuel H.
Whitthorne, states that on 13 February 1860, your petitioner's
father Matthew Johnston purchased from William J. Whitthorne,
Sr., a house and lot in Town of Shelbyville, being Lot No.___
in the plan of town known as "Mrs. Newton's Lot" and on which
Mrs. Newton lived prior to her death. Fronting on Pike Street.
Petitioner said that Matthew Johnston, her father, paid the
purchase money for said land and on 10 October 1865, William J.
Whitthorne, Sr. executed to her and children and to her sole
and separate use, a deed to the lot.

Page 514 - No. 128 - W. P. Green   ]   Bill,
                        vs   ] November 12, 1860.
                W. H. Bates & others]
William P. Green of Bedford County filed against William H.
Bates, Ann Bates and L. W. Barrett, admrs of John B. Bates,
deceased, all of Bedford County.Orator says on 4 June 1859,
he recovered three judgements against William H. Bates. Also,
on 19 May 1860, recovered a judgement against William H. Bates.
John B. Bates, the father of William H. Bates, departed this
life in __ of 1860, leaving Ann Bates his widow and William H.
Bates and several other children (named not remembered).
L. W. Barrett appointed admr of estate. Orator states that
since the death of his father John B. Bates, deft William H.
Bates has made a pretended sale and conveyance of his interest
as an heir in his father's estate to his step-mother and co-
deft Ann Bates for about $1000.00.

Page 516 - No. 128 - J. J. Phillips, Admr]
                     of W. P. Green, dec'd]
                          vs   ] Decree,
                     William H. Bates,] 6 March 1866.
                     Ann Bates &   ]
                     L. W. Barrett, admr]
                     of John B. Bates   ]
J. J. Phillips, admr of W. P. Green, deceased.

Page 517 - No. 129 - William Armstrong]
                          vs   ]Bill, 5 Sept 1857.
                     W. J. W. Wakefield]
                     & W. J. Dobson   ]
William Armstrong of Bedford County filed against W. J. W.
Wakefield (Exr of Griffin Randal) and W. J. Dobson, both of
Bedford County. Orator states that Griffin Randal departed
this life in Bedford County sometime in July 1856, having
made and published his Last Will and Testament in which
W. J. W. Wakefield was appointed executor of his estate. In
December last, Wakefield removed against him three judgements
for about $340.00 and cost. Dobson had as security your orator.
Dobson was never sued as he lived in another county and is
now living in Marshall County, Tennessee. Orator states that
Randal was sometime before his death, partner in a Smith Shop
and a Family Grocery.

Page 521 - No. 130 - John Armstrong]
                          vs   ]Bill, December 29, 1860.
                     Trice & Moseley]
John Armstrong of Bedford County states that some 18 months
ago or 2 years, his son, William Armstrong was indebted to
W. W. Gaunt for about $320.00 by note on which Joseph Armstrong
and your orator were securities. 30 acres was out for said
debt. The land was School Land that was purchased by your
orator and two sons William and Joseph. Orator then bought
Joseph's share of the land. Land in Bedford County and joins
"Wilson's Place" on the south and Curtiss' land and others.
Benjamin Moseley and Joseph Trice had owned said property at
one time.

Page 524 - No. 131 - N. D. W. Watson   ] Bill for Divorce,
                          vs   ] 13 November 1865.
                     Amelia Caroline Watson]
N. D. W. Watson of Bedford County filed against Amelia Caroline
Watson a non-resident of the state. He has been a resident
about 2 years before filing this bill, states that in 1861,
he married Amelia Caroline Boswell and lived with her until
she deserted him. In November 1862, your orator joined the
Confederate Army (under effects of Conscript Law) and was in
the army until the failure of the Confederacy. Upon his return
home on 23rd June 1865, he learned to his great sorrow that
his wife had deserted him and left the state under the patron-
age of another man. A friend of your orator met his wife in
Atlanta, Georgia during this last Spring or Summer and she
told him that she had found a man she loved better and would
remain with him. Orator believes she is now in Selma, Alabama.
Final decree for divorce, March 8, 1866.

Page 526 - No. 133 - A. L. Stamps &   ] O. Bill,
                     W. B. M. Brame   ]April 1, 1861.
                          vs   ]
                     Allison, Anderson et al]
A. L. Stamps and W. B. M. Brame filed against Dixon Allison,

Thompson Anderson and Company and Matthew McClung, citizens
of Davidson County, Tennessee. A. L. Stamps of Bedford County
states that sometime in 1859, Mesrs. Allison, Anderson & Co.
recovered a judgement against him for $3025.86. Issue levied
on slaves of your orator, Stamps.

Page 533 - No. 134 - Samuel L. Davidson]
                    vs   ]Bill, January 30, 1861.
              R. B. Blackwell   ]
Samuel L. Davidson, H. L. Davidson, Jr., Mary Rebecca Davidson
and Jane Vance Davidson, the last three being minors, sues
by next friend S. L. Davidson and John I. Davidson. They state
that on 30 April 1847 Thomas B. Moseley executed and delivered
to your orators a Deed of Conveyance, a negro woman Mariah
and several other negroes, in trust for the sole use of his
daughter Mary C. R. Davidson (then the wife of your orator
S. L. Davidson), for and during her lifetime and at her death
to hold for her children. Deed registered in Bedford County,
Book "PP", page 248. Mary C. R. Davidson died in 1849 and
left three children, Hugh L., Mary Rebecca, and Jane Vance
Davidson.

Page 534 - No. 135 - C. T. Philpott]
                  vs   ]Filed 22 January 1864.
             J. W. Brown &]
             Jno. H. Oneal]
Charles T. Philpott of Bedford County filed against J. W. Brown
who resides in Bedford County and John H. Oneal residence un-
known and out of Tennessee. Orator states about 2nd December
1860, he sold to Oneal for $1500.00 for a tract of land in
District No. 3 of Bedford County, adjoining lands of Terry,
John Lane and Jones, about 57 acres. Orator states that J. W.
Brown is now in possession of said land that he bought from
Oneal. The property known as the "Bucket Factory".

Page 541 - No. 136 - Jesse W. Chockley] Bill for Divorce,
                  vs   ] 18 November 1865.
             Mary Chockley   ]
Jesse W. Chockley of Bedford County filed for divorce from
Mary Chockley a non-resident of Tennessee. Orator states that
sometime in the year 1861, he married Mary Edwards then of
Bedford County and lived with her until August 1865. He said
that on 7 August last (1865) his wife deserted him with another
man and gone to parts unknown. He has learned that his wife
went to Illinois.

Page 542 - No. 137 - Woods & Yeatman] Bill,
                  vs   ] 19 December 1860.
             J. F. Cummings]
             & others   ]
James Woods and Henry C. Yeatman stated that on 24 August 1860,
they recovered a judgement against John L. Burt and James F.
Cummings for $815.50 and cost.

Page 543 - No. 139 - Viana C. Grouster] Bill,
                  vs   ]January 23, 1866.
             Martin Grouster]
Viana C. Grouster of Bedford County filed against Martin
Grouster of parts unknown. Oratrix stated that on 4 September
1865, she and Martin Grouster who resided or pretended to reside in Shelbyville, were married. They lived together for
two weeks, her husband abandoned her and she has not seen or
heard from him since. She said when she married him, he was

already married and had abandoned his wife and children who
were in State of Kentucky.

Page 545 - No. 140 - Jesse W. Chockley]
                     vs   ]Bill, July 11, 1865.
             G. B. Harris &   ]
             S. B. Heard   ]
Jesse W. Chockley said that on 16 February 1863, he purchased
of S. B. Harris, land. Registered in Bedford County, Deed
Book "DDD", page 264-265, land in District No. 3 in the Village
of Wartrace, bounded by John Chilton, Railroad and Square of
Wartrace, Mrs. A. Pruitt, Coffey heirs. G. B. Harris is a
non-resident of Tennessee.

Page 547 - No. 141 - David Lane]
                     vs   ]Filed 30 January 1866.
             Milly Lane]
David Lane, a colored man, filed against Milly Lane, also a
colored person, both of Bedford County. Orator stated that
he married Milly Walker in Summer of 1865 in Bedford County
and that Hugh Montgomery, a J. P., married them by license,
issued in Bedford County. Orator states that 27 January, his
wife in the night of said day, committed adultry with Bill
Streater. Orator said they had two children, one aged 3 years
and named Rosanah, other 16 months named Jane. He wants the
children stating their mother is not a suitable person.

Page 549 - No. 143 - Penny S. Melton   ]
                     vs   ] Bill, September 20,
             W. J. W. Wakefield]   1865.
             & others   ]
Penny S. Melton of Bedford County state that Griffin Randal
departed this life in 1856. He had made and published his
Last Will and Testament and after his death said will was
proven in August Term 1856. In his will, he devised and bequeathed his whole estate, except a small legacy or two, to
William J. W. Wakefield, in trust to hold for the descent of
and support of Elizabeth Randal, his wife during her natural
life and at her death, whatever left, was to be vested in real
estate for your oratrix. Elizabeth Randal departed this life
some six years ago. Penny S. Melton's husband is Richard W.
Melton. He has been dead some 4 years. Joseph Trice of
Williamson County, Tennessee was appointed executor of Randal's
estate in the place of William J. W. Wakefield who wanted to
move to Arkansas. Along with Trice, J. H. C. Scales and
George W. Cunningham were appointed executors, in Bedford
County.

Page 552 - No. 144 - Mary E. Wheeler]
                     vs   ]Bill, 1 July 1864.
             W. K. Ransom &]
             others   ]
Mary E. Wheeler of Bedford County stated that her late husband
David J. Wheeler departed this life intestate in Bedford
County in March 1864, leaving children, Martha H. Wheeler,
Newton T. Wheeler, John R. Wheeler, Edney C. Wheeler, Alice
Wheeler, and Thomas R. Wheeler who have Abel Rushing for their
guardian who resides in Cannon Cannon, Tennessee. David J.
Wheeler was owner of about 280 acres of land, at the time of
his death in Civil District No. 5, bounded by Rushing and
William Murphy, Murphree, Horatio Coop and R. B. Rucker. He
also owned a tract that he bought of Abel Rushing and M. R.
Rushing (of parts unknown), executors of the Last Will and

Testament of John Rushing, deceased. David J. Wheeler's admr
is William K. Ransom of Bedford County.

Page 558 - No. 145 - Robert Daniel   ]
                            vs   ]Filed March 5, 1860.
                     Thomas Gattis   ]
                     & Ellis Williams]
Robert Daniel of Bedford County filed against Thomas Gattis,
admr of William Williams, deceased, and Ellis William who is
a non-resident of Tennessee and resides in parts unknown.
Your orator stated that William Williams departed this life
intestate in September 1858 (1859), having as one of his heirs
Ellis Williams and a large family. Orator says that he is
holder of a note by transfer to him, on Ellis Williams, one
of the heirs, for $40.00 and due 25 December 1831. Orator
states that Ellis Williams left state or county before due
date. William Williams, deceased, left a large fmaily of
children and grandchildren (11 distributees), not including
the widow (which makes 12). Ellis Williams when he left, none
of his family had heard from him in over 30 years and may be
dead by now. Jemima Williams, only child of Ellis Williams
and she resides in Williamson County, Illinois, who states
that her father Ellis Williams died many years ago before the
father, William Williams, and has no interest in the estate.

Page 561 - No. 146 - J. H. White   ]
                            vs   ]Bill, 9 February 1866
                     Isaac Larue & others]
John H. White of Marshall County, Tennessee filed against Isaac
Larue of State of Texas, Jas. H. Harrison and William Woods,
admrs of John Larue, deceased, and Jos. H. Thompson. Orator
states that Isaac Larue is indebted to him in sum $310.00 by
note, given 1 June 1859 and due 25 December 1859. Isaac Larue
is a son in law of John Larue, deceased, who died intestate
and that James H. Harrison and Williams Woods were appointed
his admrs at Term 1863. Orator states that they have sold
said property and now have money in their hands belonging to
Isaac Larue. Isaac Larue was married at this time.

Page 563 - No. 147 - A. J. Greer]
                            vs   ]Bill, 16 August 1858.
                     S. H. Gurnee]
A. J. Greer of Bedford County filed against S. H. Gurnee of
Bedford County. Orator states that on 13 November 1856,
Joseph H. Thompson and your orator as equal partners or owners
of a lot or land, near the Town of Shelbyville, sold the same
to S. H. Gurnee for sum $1500.00.

Page 563 - No. 148 - B. K. Coble   ] Bill,
                            vs   ] May 4, 1860.
                     Arch Armstrong & others]
Benjamin K. Coble of Bedford County filed against Arch Armstrong, John Armstrong of parts unknown, Robert Armstrong and
Edmund Cooper of Bedford County. Orator states that some years
ago John Armstrong, Robert Armstrong and Arch Armstrong were
engaged in the Retail Dry Goods Business in Shelbyville, known
as "Armstrong & Co.". The firm had handled all business,
assets &c over to Edmund Cooper. The said property is said
to be more in value that the debts they owe.

Page 568 - No. 149 - R. P. Sutliff   ] Bill,
                            vs   ] 1 February 1858.
                     W. T. Miles & others]

297

R. P. Sutliff of Bedford County states that about 7 April 1856,
he recovered a judgement against Levi Turner, a J.P. for Bedford County, about for $75.68. Debt is still due. Miles is
now a non-resident of Tennessee, that he owns an undivided
interest in a tract of land in Bedford County, adjoining
Absalom L. Landis, heirs of John Koonce and others, formerly
owned by his father_____ Miles.

Page 569 - No. 150 - J. W. Crunk & others] Bill,
                          vs   ] 1 November 1860.
                     Silas Pratt & wife   ]
J. W. Crunk & Co., composed of J. W. Crunk and W. C. Crunk,
states that they are the owners of various judgements against
Silas Pratt. In 1857, James Hastings sold a tract of land
to Silas Pratt and wife Patience of Bedford County, containing
about 112 acres. He took 35 acres back.

Page 573 - No. 151 - M. M. Wilson]
                          vs   ]Bill, February 25, 1861.
                     Trice & Moseley]
M. M. Wilson of Bedford County states that he sold a small
tract of land about 10 acres to Benjamin Moseley on about 12
October 1859, situated in Bedford County in Civil District
No. 19, taking his note. Part still due. Moseley sold to
Joseph Trice said land. Joseph Trice of Bedford County and
Moseley in Alabama or Mississippi.

Page 576 - No. 152 - Barrett & Holt]
                          vs   ]Bill, 25 February 1861.
                     Moseley, Trice]
                     & Wilson   ]
Hiram Holt and Leroy W. Barrett states that W. W. Wilson sold
a small tract of land in bedford County to Benjamin Moseley.
Moseley did not pay his note and your orator has had to pay.

Page 578 - No. 153 - James H. Neil]
                          vs   ]Att. Bill, January 30, 1865.
                     W. G. Knight]
James H. Neil of Bedford County states that he was appointed
receiver for the assets, or a portion of the assets of the
Bank of Tennessee, held by its Branch at Shelbyville, one of
the assets is a Bill of Exchange drawn by Willis Blanton of
Coffee County, Tennessee due to D. D. Holt and by him and
William G. Knight and Middleton Holland endorsed 90 days after
date, and payable at Augusta, Georgia Bank. Knight has removed
from Tennessee over 12 months or 18 months. He formerly of
Bedford County. He left a valuable tract of land in District
No. 2 of Bedford County and on Duck River, where on he resided
before leaving Tennessee.

Page 583 - No. 154 - John R. Jones] Att. Bill,
                          vs   ]June 17, 1865.
                     James F. Cummings]
John R. Jones of Bedford County states that James F. Cummings,
a non-resident of Tennessee, is indebted to him for $318.75
and cost. Orator states that Cummings is the owner of one
undivided, major portion, of a tract of land of 4 acres, near
Town of Shelbyville on south side of Duck River, bounded by
Mill Pond, Robert Cannon's estate and Clement Cannon Mill Lot,
and on which are erected on the Pork Packing Buildings of the
late firm of English Waterhouse & Co., the other being owned
by Morris Burney and Peter S. English.

Page 585 - No. 155 - James H. Harrison & others]Att & Inj.Bill,
                         vs   ]6 October 1865.
                    R. B. Blackwell & others]
James H. Harrison, John Courtner, William Wood, and James Dillard, all of Bedford County filed against Robert B. Blackwell,
Robert Mathews, the former a non-resident of Tennessee and
latter of Bedford County, also against Henry Davis, S. A.
CUnningham, B. Delk, and G. F. Blakemore, all of Bedford
County. Orators states that they became bound as the securities of Robert B. Blackwell on his official bond as Constable,
elected for the 19th Civil District of Bedford County for 2
years, from March 1860 to March 1862. Blackwell has removed
himself and property from Tennessee. Robert Mathews answers
to the bill. He stated that in the Fall of 1864 while in the
State of Alabama, near Montecella (mid October) he did sell
R. B. Blackwell a lot of ground with houses on them (east of
place known as "----ed House Place" sold to Mrs. Mary Blackwell in 1863), about 6 acres. Land in District No. 18.

Page 592 - No. 156 - Sarah A. Hicks & others] Petition,
                         vs   ] Dec 20, 1865.
                    Jno. E. Dromgoole & others]
Sarah A. Hicks and Walter W. Sutton and wife Bettie filed
against James Hicks and Henry Hicks, minor children of Isaac M.
Hicks, deceased. John E. Dromgoole their guardian, all of
Rutherford County, Tennessee. Sarah A. Hicks, widow of J. M.
Hicks of Rutherford County, Tennessee and Walter W. Sutton
and wife Bettie of Bedford County, stated that Isaac M. Hicks
died sometime in the year 186_, he owned a house and lot in
Wartrace, Bedford County, about 2 acres and also 100 acres
of land in Franklin County, Tennessee, Civil District No. 7
and bounded by Shelbyville & Manchester Road and William Gwinn.
Jno. E. Dromgoole guardian of James and Henry Hicks.

Page 595 - No. 157 - Williams & Cannon, Exrs &c] Bill,
                         vs   ] 1 Feb 1866.
                    John F. Neil & others   ]
Chesly Williams and William P. Cannon, executors of Robert
Cannon, deceased, stated that Robert Cannon departed this life
lately, after making and publishing his Last Will and Testament.
Robert Cannon stayed a judgement for Joshua Holt. Note was
executed by Joshua Holt to E. W. Carney for a lot and house
inside the limits of Shelbyville. Bound by Dillon, an alley,
Buchanan and others.
Answer of S. H. Whitthorne, guardian of John and Emma Holt,
children of Joshua Holt, 4th. Joshua Holt died intestate and
John and Emma Holt are his only heirs at law.

Page 597 - No. 158 - W. D. McClure   ] Filed
                         vs   ]23 Dec 1865.
                    Elizabeth Nance & others]
William D. McClure states that he sold to Thomas J. Nance,
then a citizen of Shelbyville, a lot of land in said Town and
houses thereon. Bounded by Brittain Street, lot formerly owned by A. L. Stamps, an alley, the Catholic Church property.
Thomas J. Nance departed this life testate. His Will and
Testament was proven and recorded in Bedford County, the place
of his domicil of which he nominated Milton McClure and Elizabeth Nance, his wife, as executors. Children of Thomas J.
Nance and Elizabeth his wife are, Malinda B. and Jennie Nance,
who are minors with no guardian. The executors and the children aforesaid and Dr. R. W. Pillow reside now in Giles County,
Tennessee, McCullough resides in Marshall County, Tennessee.

Page 603 - No. 127 - J. H. McGrew]
                    vs   ]Petition, 2 May 1859.
                G. W. McGrew]
J. H. McGrew of Bedford County states that at August Term 1856,
a decree was rendered against him as executor of William McGrew
in favor of George W. McGrew as guardian and his own right
of William L. McGrew's children for $1898.88. Your petitioner
was charged with nearly $7000.00.in notes of sale of estate
of William McGrew, deceased. Legatees: Curry McGrew, Mrs.
Keeling, Mrs. Goodwin's children, R. Newsom's children, Mrs.
Eliza J. Newsom, W. P. Goodwin's children, W. L. McGrew's
children.

Page 607 - T. C. McCrory   ]
                    vs   ]Bill, August 20, 1860.
                J. F. Vannoy & others]
T. C. McCrory of Bedford County states that he and Smith Bowlin
are partners of a negro woman Lethe and her two children, Lucy
Ann and Mary Jane.

Page 608 - Robert Mathews   ]
                    vs   ] 15 September 1859.
                Joseph Taylor & others]
Robert Mathews filed against Joseph Taylor, William J. Whitthorne, R. S. McConnell, and Thomas Ragsdale, all of Bedford
County. Orator states that in September 1859, he recovered
a judgement against the deft Joseph Taylor for $337.25 and
cost.

Page 610 - Stanton J. Green]
                    vs   ]June 8, 1865.
                Ray, Watson & Co.]
                & others   ]
Stanton J. Green of Lincoln County, Tennessee filed in Bedford
County against Micajah T. Cooper, George M. Ray, Daniel Parker,
Matthew W. Watson, W. E. and Charles Pearson and W. W. Gill,
all of Bedford County and Henry Hill a non-resident of Tenn-
essee. Orator states that at April Term 1865, he recovered
a judgement against Micajah T. Cooper and George M. Ray for
$520.00 and cost. He also states that George M. Ray, Daniel
Parker, Matthew W. Watson were partners in a Steam Grist Mill
& Distillery in Bedford County, firm under name of Ray, Watson
& Co. They are owners of three bills executed by A. G. Gill,
deceased, of Lincoln County, Tennessee and W. W. Gill his
security to William E. and Charles Pearson. Land in District
No. 24 of Bedford County, about 117 acres, adjoining the Shook
tract, by Mrs. Bobo's dower, T. P. Wells, Thomas Boyers and
Barton Philpot.

Page 612 - M. B. Moorman]
                    vs   ]Bill, 7 August 1863.
                R. S. Dwiggins]
M. B. Moorman of Bedford County states that R. S. Dwiggins
lately residing in Bedford County, is indebted to him for
Book Keeper for Tobacco, sold to him for sum of $615.28 and
cost. Dwiggins has left the state and U. S. by Army, has
seized his property (apart). Some 2 or 3 years ago, W. G.
Hight of Bedford County purchased a tract of land on which
he still lives, adjoining lands of William Knott and others.
About 300 acres from John Jordan who now resides in Coffee
County, Tennessee. Hight sold to Richard Nance.

Page 618 - Rachel Harrison]
                    vs   ]Final Decree, May 28, 1866.
              William Harrison]
On 28 May 1866, William Harrison deserted his wife and child.
(25th District).

Page 618 - Alexander Kimbro, Exr]
           of George Kimbro   ]   O. Bill,
                    vs   ] December 28, 1865.
              Franky Hooser & others]
Alexander Kimbro, executor of George Kimbro, deceased, states
that George Kimbro died in bedford County in August 1860,
having made his Last Will and Testament and in which your
orator was nominated executor at September Term 1860. George
Kimbro owned a valuable tract of land on Duck River in Bedford
County. Your orator sold tract of land to Daniel Hooser for
$6740.25 and took note. Business was standing when Civil War
broke our and while the Town of Shelbyville was occupied by
the Confederate States. The Court House was burned along with
nearly all the public records (which is in error,hcm).
Rev. William Jenkins who wrote the original will, believed
to be the substance of the original and is herewith filed as
Exhibit A. The widow, children and grandchildren, heirs at
law of George Kimbro and Elizabeth Kimbro his widow who resides
in Bedford County, Franky Hooser and Mary Williams, daughter
of the Testator who lives in Gibson County, Tennessee, Thomas
Kimbro who lives in Arkansas, Margaret Holland who lives with
her husband William B. Holland in Bedford County. The said
Thomas and Margaret being children of Benjamin Kimbro who was
a son of George Kimbro, deceased. Berry Kimbro who lives in
Indiana, Rachel Kimbro, Wiley Kimbro, and William Kimbro who
lives in Texas. The last four named being children of James
Kimbro who is a son of George Kimbro, deceased. George Kimbro
had another son named William Kimbro who died many years ago
in Texas and left a widow and a son and a daughter. The daughter Martha died before the Testator, George Kimbro, without
issue, and the son Benjamin died after the Testator without
issue, leaving as his next of kin Saidie Kimbro his mother
who resides in Texas. The Testator's sons, Benjamin and James
died in the lifetime of their father as did also another son
named Allen Kimbro. Allen Kimbro left a widow Mary Kimbro
and five sons, Alexander, Thomas, Benjamin, George and Richard
Kimbro, all of Bedford County except Thomas who died intestate
and without issue since the death of his father.
Defendants to Bill: Elizabeth Kimbro, Franky Hooser, Mary
Williams, Sally Culley, Thomas J. Culley, Neely Kimbro, Thomas
Kimbro, Margaret Holland, William B. Holland, Mary Kimbro,
Alexander Kimbro, Benjamin Kimbro, George Kimbro, and Richard
Kimbro, Sadie Kimbro, Berry Kimbro, Rachel Kimbro, Wiley Kimbro
and William Kimbro.
Substance of George Kimbro's Last Will and Testament:
1 - To the widow (Rachel) all the house hold stuff which she
brought when she married, and also a child's part of the estate
of which he died possessed of.
2 - To Benjamin Coble, a negro biy to be paid for at the valua-
tion price placed upon him by disinterested persons chosen
for said purpose.
3 - To Mary Williams, a family of negroes consisting of the
mother and her two children upon the same terms as the one
above to B. Coble.
4 - To Mary Williams, $100.00, above that of a child's part
for extra services in ministering to the wants of her mother
during her illness, and for attention to him during his de-

clining years.
5 - To Alexander Kimbro, $100.00 extra from a child's part
for services rendered in removing his slaves to Texas. To
Alexander Kimbro, amount which he had to pay for Benjamin
Kimbro as security (the amount is thought to be $140.00), which
sum is to be deducted from the part that the heirs of Benjamin
Kimbro will be entitled to in the general division, and to
be paid to Alexander Kimbro.
6 - All of his property whether personal or real to be sold
to the highest bidder at public sale except the negroes above,
to be divided, share and share alike between each of his children and widow, having respect to the gift to Mary Williams
and Alexander Kimbro as his executors.
The above is the substantial copy of the will of George Kimbro,
deceased, as I now can recollect it.
                              Signed: William Jenkins

Page 622 - R. N. Jones & others] O. & Att. Bill,
                vs   ] December 4, 1858.
          William Brown & others]
R. N. Jones, Thomas G. Holland, and Thomas Holland filed against William Brown, William C. Holt, and Henry Holt. Orators
of Bedford County states that on 9th August 1858, William
Brown recovered a judgement against W. C. Holt, R. N. Jones,
Thomas G. Holland and Thomas Holland for sum of $736.27 and
cost. Henry Holt is father of W. C. Holt.

Page 627 - Alexander Myers   ]
                vs   ]O. Bill, 27 February 1866
           Ailsey Cobb   ]
           (Alias Ailsey Myers)]
Alexander Myers, a free man of color, of Bedford County, filed
against Ailsey Cobb (alias Ailsey Myers) and Charity Moorman,
both of Bedford County and a free woman of color. Orator
states up to 22 February 1865, he was a slave of Andrew Myers
of Bedford County. He was born a slave. He said Charity
Moorman was also a slave (born a slave). She was born 20
years ago. At that time there was no recognizing of marriages
between slaves. At that time your orator became the husband
of Charity. He lived happily for years with her, up to the
year 186_, since the war began. Charity was a slave of M. B.
Moorman of Bedford County. In Autumn of 186_, Moorman went
to Kentucky and took Charity with him. Thus orator has become
separated from her. He became a "Runaway Slave" and suffered
punishment. He therefore remained at home. In 1865, Mr.
Moorman returned to Shelbyville bringing her with him. It
was 3 years since he had seen her. He had heard that she died
in Kentucky. In 1864, your orator, "took up" with Ailsey Cobb
as his wife (also a slave) and remained with her up to June
1865. He and Charity married according to law. He told Ailsey
that if Charity came back from Kentucky he would have to go
to her. In October 1865, Charity returned to Shelbyville and
your orator considered her his only wife and wished to live
with her so much and their children.

Page 630 - William Brown   ]
                vs   ]O. Bill, January 31, 1865.
          Margaret Rogers & others]
William Brown of Bedford County filed against Margaret Rogers
of Bedford County, James Patterson and wife Lavinia of Ark-
ansas, William Rogers, James Rogers, Henry C. Rogers, and
Polly Rogers of Illinois and are minors, Julia Rogers, Ford
Williams and wife Elizabeth formerly Elizabeth Rogers of

Lawrence County, Tennessee, Benjamin Reeves and wife Rhoda
formerly Rhoda Rogers, David Woosley and wife Caroline formerly
Caroline Rogers, Jesse Nelson and wife Sallie formerly Sallie
Rogers, James Rogers, Stephen Rogers, James Pratt and Celia
formerly Celia Rogers, Martin V. B. Rogers, Mary Rogers, John
Hime and wife Martha formerly Martha Rogers, Campbell Rogers,
Almeda Rogers, Elijah Rogers, all of Bedford County, the last
three of whom are minors and have no guardian. Orator states
that 27 November 1858, Jesse Rogers executed to L. B. Knott
for $250.00 due 1 May 1860 for a small tract of land and mills.
The land and mills are situated on Thompson's Ford, Bedford
County, bounded by L. B. Tune (Lane), Hornaday Branch, Anderton
Branch, about 8 acres. Knott sold land to Jesse Rogers. R. B.
Davidson guardian of Campbell Rogers, Almeda Rogers and Elijah
Rogers are children of Jesse Rogers.

Page 633 - W. N. Hailey, Admr]
                 vs   ]O. Bill, May 16, 1865.
         R. S. Dwiggins   ]
W. N. Haley of Williamson County, Tennessee filed against
R. S. Dwiggins of Bedford County, that orator was appointed
in Williamson County, Tennessee, Admr of will annexed of the
estate of Thomas K. Morton, deceased, formerly of Williamson
County, Tennessee. Thomas K. Morton died intestate. He had
land in District No. 10 of Bedford County, bounded by Bellefont,
Warren, Martin's heirs, and Bullock. About 200 acres. R. S.
Dwiggins, Nancy Morton and Lula Thomas Morton an infant, defts.
Lula Thomas Morton's guardian is Dwiggins.

Page 638 - No. 185 - John L. Cooper, Exr]
                 vs   ]Bill, 3 August 1864.
                 Jesse Wood & others]
John L. Cooper, executor of John C. Wood, deceased, and oratrix
Harriet Pate of Bedford County, states that about December
1861 or January 1862, John C. Wood departed this life in Bedford County, having made his Last Will and Testament, proven
and recorded. He owned land in District No. 8, on north side
of Falling Creek and joined lands of F. P. McElwrath, James
Purvis, and others and about 100 acres. The testator was never
married. He left surviving him in his mother Elizabeth Wood,
Sina Phillips wife of William Phillips and a sister. Sina
Phillips who has since died leaving her husband and children,
Martha J., Nancy E., John W., Robert C., and Mary E. Brown
who are minors, no guardian. Jesse Wood, a brother, who resides in Missouri, William Wood, a brother, and Minos C. Wood
who has since died leaving one child Albert who is a minor,
no guardian and lives in Missouri, James Wood who lives in
Marshall County, Tennessee, and Lewis Wood who lives in Illinois. All heirs of John C. Wood, deceased, except your
oratrix and her children (all minors), all of Bedford County.

SUMMARY OF VITAL RECORDS AS ABSTRACTED FROM THIS PUBLICATION

Died - David Norville died December 1835 Bedford County, left
    widow Elizabeth W. Norville.
Died - Daniel Low died in 1824 or 1825 Bedford County.
Died - Martha Low, widow of Daniel Low, died 1836 Bedford
    County.
Died - Michael Meddows died in 1819 Bedford County.
Died - James Meddows, son of Michael Meddows, died short time
    after his father, in Bedford County.
Died - Jesse Putman died 1833 Bedford County.
Died - William R. Wynne died 1814 Brunswick County, Virginia,
    left widow Polly Wynne.
Married - Polly Wynne, widow of William R. Wynne, married
       George R. Scott in 1821 or 1822 in Virginia and moved
       to Bedford County in 1825.
Died - Peter Wynne died 1815 (father of Polly Wynne).
Died - Lemuel Wheeler died 22 September 1835 in Bedford County,
    left widow Sally Wheeler.
Died - Joel Riggs died 13 December 1835 Bedford County, left
    widow Elizabeth Riggs.
Died - Lebanon Nix died before 1834 Bedford County, leaving
    widow Rebecca Nix.
Died - Rebecca Nix died 1834, widow of Lebanon Nix of Bedford
    County.
Married - Edmund S. Daugherty married Ann Nix, daughter of
       Lebanon and Rebecca Nix, after 1834.
Died - Isaac Rainey died 18 June 1836 Bedford County (now
    Marshall County, Tennessee).
Died - Jeremiah Cheek died 1823 Bedford County (now Marshall
    County, Tennessee), left widow Tabitha Cheek.
Died - Tabitha Cheek, widow of Jeremiah Cheek, died 1834 Bed-
    ford County (now Marshall County, Tennessee).
Died - William Craig died 1835 Bedford County.
Died - T. C. Green died before 1837, left widow Mary Green.
Died - William Stuart (Stewart) died October 1834 Bedford
    County, left widow Peggy Stewart.
Died - William B. Sutton died 1833 Bedford County.
Died - William Blanton died before August 1839 Bedford County,
    left widow Sarah Blanton.
Died - James Ray died 5 August 1835 Bedford County, left widow
    Jane Ray.
Died - William Curtis and wife and two or three of his child-
    ren died in their house fire 2 January 1837.
Died - John Bowers died in Summer 1836 Bedford County, left
    widow Mary Bowers (one place her name was Mary).
Died - Elizabeth J. Roberson died 1 April 1813 in Sussex
    County, Virginia.
Married - Martha Ann Cooper married 1834 in Bedford County
       to Abram B. Cooper. Divorced 12 August 1839.
Died - Samuel Escue died in December 1835 Bedford County (one
    year says 1837), left widow Rachel Escue.
Died - William Vannerson died 1802 or 1803 in Hawkins County,
    Tennessee or Sullivan County, Tennessee, left widow
    Elizabeth Vannerson who came to Bedford County.
Married - Dicey Thomas married D. Thomas ca 1825 Bedford
       County. Divorced 1839.
Died - Norvill Meghee died April or May 1836, unmarried and
    no children, leaving his father Henry Meghee of Wake
    County, North Carolina.
Died - Jeremiah Baxter died 1833 in Maury County, Tennessee,
    left widow Catharine Baxter.
Married - Quals T. Mayfield of Bedford County married Elizabeth

F. Sutton, daughter of John Sutton, on 27 December
1832.

Died - Frances Greer died 8 April 1839 Bedford County.

Died - Duke (Green D.) House died 1821 Bedford County, left
widow Susan McIntosh House.

Died - James Brittain died June or July 1833 Bedford County,
left a son Jason T. Brittain.

Died - James Hooper died before April 1837 Bedford County,
left widow Judah Hooper.

Died - William Word died August or September 1838 Bedford
County, left widow Sophia Word.

Died - John Stephens died before August 1831 Bedford County.

Married - James M. Jones married Polly Wilhoite of Bedford
County, before 1839.

Died - _____ McNealy died 1820 or 1821 Bedford County, left
widow Margaret McNealy.

Died - Keziah Galbreath died in Spring of 1839 Bedford County.

Age - Freeman Burrow, aged about 70 years old on 12 November
1838.

Died - Elizabeth Temple died January 1836 Bedford County.

Died - John Guant (Gant) died ca 1840, son of Lewis Guant(Gant).

Died - Richard S. Clardy died 1834.

Died - William Craig died March 1834, left widow.

Died - John Craig died January 1838, son of William Craig,
deceased.

Died - Willis H. Moore died 1822 or 1823.

Died - Benjamin Cox died in Fall of 1824 Dickson County, Tennessee, left widow Winford Cox.

Died - Thomas C. Moore died 1833 Bedford County. His deceased
wife was Nancy Moore, daughter of Benjamin King Cox.

Married - Mrs. Winford Cox, widow of Benjamin Cox, married
Martin Walton.

Died - Dennis S. Springer died July 1840 or 1841 Bedford County.

Married - Edmond Tipton married Mrs. Rachel Escue, widow of
William (Samuel) Escue. Lived in Hickman County,
Tennessee.

Died - Joseph Greer died 1831 Lincoln County, Tennessee, left
widow Mary Ann Greer.

Died - Willis Moore died 1833, no marriage nor issue.

Died - Nancy Moore died shortly after her husband Thomas C.
Moore in 1833 Bedford County.

Married - Mary Dobson married Minos Cannon on 14 June 1810.

Died - Minos Cannon died 7 April 1823 Bedford County.

Married - Mary Dobson Cannon married Thomas F. Ashburn on
8 July 1825.

Died - Thomas F. Ashburn died 8 July 1833.

Married - Mary Dobson Cannon Ashburn married Archibald Dobson
on 16 February 1834.

Died - Archibald Dobson died January 11, 1841.

Died - William Carter died January 1837.

Married - Abram B. Cooper married Martha A. Cooper in 1834
Bedford County. Seeks divorce.

Died - Peter Hays died in Winter of 1834 or 1835 Bedford
County, left widow Keziah Hays.

Married - Mrs. Susan House, widow of Duke House, married John
McIntosh (from case 30 December 1840).

Died - James Houston died ca 1840 or 1841.

Divorce - Elizabeth Short filed for divorce from William Short,
who is now dead (from case in 1843).

Died - Eli Bearden died ca 1831 Bedford County, leaving widow
Nancy Bearden.

Died - Rachel Rainey died April (1843), widow of Isaac Rainey,
deceased.

Married - Emily, wife of Harris Austin, about the time of the
          death of Wiley Wilhoite, was the wife of John Brewton
          and that he deserted her, she afterwards in 1841
          married Harris Austin (John Brewton never gave her
          a divorce).
Married - Delila Ray married James Ray in early part of the
          year 1840. Seeks divorce.
Died - Travis C. Nash died 7 April 1844 Bedford County, left
       widow Johanna Nash.
Died - Peter Lee died about 1844.
Died - John Davis, father of John Davis, died 1827 in Pittsy-
       lvania County, Virginia, left widow Winford Stratton
       whom she married later.
Died - Hugh Snelling died April 1841 Bedford County.
Divorce - Willis and Letsy Cannon divorced on February 13,
          1833.
Married - Kavenaugh Yancy married Elizabeth Watts in Virginia
          about 35 years ago (ca 1805). Elizabeth daughter
          of Frederick Watts, deceased.
Divorce - Delila Ray who married James Ray 14 December 1840.
          Seeks divorce.
Died - Johnathan Wood died ca 1842 or 1843 Bedford County.
Divorce - Mary B. Atkins of Bedford County married about 1830
          to Henderson W. Atkins of Virginia. Seeks divorce.
Died - John Sims died in 1841.
Died - Enoch Head died January 1841 or 1842 Bedford County,
       left widow Charlotte Head.
Died - Mary Head died after her father Enoch Head, about 1842
       Bedford County.
Married - Joel Whorley married Cynthia Brown, some years ago,
          daughter of Jesse Brown, Sr. (no date)
Died - Jesse E. Williams died about 1830 or 1832.
Died - Samuel K. Gibson died February 1841 Bedford County,
       formerly of Coffee County, Tennessee.
Died - William M. Russell died January 1842 Bedford County.
Died - Joseph Johnson died September 1842 of Coffee County,
       Tennessee.
Died - Coleman R. White died years ago, of Greenville, North
       Carolina.
Married - Mary E. Powell married Robert Powell (in Virginia)
          (probably in Sussex County, Virginia).
Died - Robert Powell died in Bedford County after 25 March
       1836.
Died - Seymore Robinson of Parish of Albermarle, Sussex County,
       Virginia, died after 6 November 1780, left widow Eliza-
       beth Robinson.
Died - John Cunningham died 18 December 1842 in Warren County,
       Tennessee.
Died - Tarlton J. Reeves died (Dec) 1846 Bedford County, died
       at Benjamin S. Reeves in Alabama.
Died - Robert P. Harrison died 1 August 1843 Bedford County,
left widow Eliza W. Harrison.
Divorce - Jane Griggs of Bedford County about 1835 married
          Robert W. Griggs. Divorce granted 1 March 1848.
Died - James Reynolds, son of Jane Reynolds, died in Arkansas,
       leaving widow Sally Reynolds.
Died - William Reynolds died many years ago, leaving widow
       Jane Reynolds.
Married - Mrs. Adaline Wilhoite, widow of William Wilhoite,
          deceased, married James Robinson before 1848.
Died - Henry Mooring died about 1826 in Wake County, North
       Carolina, leaving a daughter Mary Ann Haley.
Died - William Warren died 20 March 1845.

Died - James H. Cobb died in 1840's Bedford County, left widow
       Sarah Elkins Cobb.
Died - Archibald Reeves died 1839 Bedford County.
Died - Bushrod Webb died May 1847 Bedford County.
Died - James P. Craig died about 1849, left widow Mary Craig.
Married - Mrs. Martha Looney, widow of William R. Looney,
       married James C. Russell.
Died - John Mayfield died many years ago (long before 1850).
Died - Joseph Palmore died many years ago in Virginia (long
       before 1850).
Died - Frederick Shofner died some years ago (before 1850)
       in Bedford County.
Divorce - William M. Shofner married Jane Koonce on 22 February
       1844 Bedford County. Seeks divorce.
Died - William O. Whitney died about 1826 Bedford County.
Died - Knight Dalby died October 1827 Bedford County, left
       widow Nancy Dalby.
Died - Nancy Dalby, widow of Knight Dalby, died December 1848.
Died - William Gabbert died 26 January 1852 Bedford County,
       left widow Mary Ann Gabbert.
Divorce - Jackson C. Kilingsworth married Elizabeth C., 23
       August 1848. Seeks divorce.
Married - Sarah H. A. Martin married John C. Coldwell, Jr.
       (no date).
Died - Isaac West died some years ago, left widow Sarah West.
Died - James Slaton died many years ago, left widow Martha
       Slaton (before March 1847).
Died - Martha Slaton, widow of James Slaton, died March 1847.
Married - Sarah Ann Hanes married John McGowan in 1811.
Died - William McGrew died 1851 Bedford County.
Died - James H. Myers died some years ago, widow Henrietta W.
       Miles Myers.
Died - Robert Allison died 24 May 1842.
Divorce - Mary G. Kendle (Kendall) and John Kendle (Kendall)
       married 4 March 1821 Bedford County. Mary G. is a
       daughter of Rice Coffey.
Died - Rice Coffey died 29 July 1853.
Divorce - Martha A. Knott and William M. Knott married 9 March
       1851.
Divorce - Elizabeth Smith married Frank Smith, divorced 5
       September 1854.
Married - Amanda J. J. Martin (Norton) married Philaman Gosling.
Died - John Whitesell died 1842, left widow Milly Whitesell.
Died - Daniel L. Barringer died 1852, Bedford County.
Died - Mariah Gambill died about 1852.
Died - George W. Whitesell died about 1852.
Died - Isabel Thomas died since 1852.
Died - John Whitesell died before 1852.
Divorce - Francis C. Thomas married Elizabeth on 21 July 1853,
       seeks divorce.
Divorce - Emily C. Lamb and David Lamb. Divorced 6 March 1855,
       she was daughter of _____ Carrell.
Died - Hayden Trigg died 1845.
Married - Nancy C. Hix married John P. Dean (instrument 6 March
       1855).
Married - Mary Ann Gabbert, widow of William Gabbert, married
       _____ Hastings. (no date)
Died - Samuel Vance died March 1849 Bedford County, left widow
       Christina Vance.
Died - Robert B. Vance died (no date), son of Samuel Vance.
Died - Joseph Kincaid died Spring of 1844 Bedford County, left
       widow Airy Kincaid.
Died - George Pratt died May 1855 Bedford County.

Died - James Green died 1853 Coffee County, Tennessee, left
widow Mary Green.
Died - Jordan C.(Cane) Holt died 1853 Bedford County, left
widow Margaret Wilhoite Holt.
Divorce - Malinda Nichols married Malcom Nichols in Bedford
County. 3 August 1857, now together.
Divorce - Elizabeth H. Quimby married H. B. Quimby. 4 Sept.
1857, now together.
Divorce - Ann Shofner married William M. Shofner. 3 September
1857, married 184_ in Bedford County. Seeks divorce.
Married - Elizabeth Maupin, widow of Blan Maupin, married
Buford Bennett last Winter or Spring (1857).
Married - Susannah Hall married Robert P. Hall on 20 September
1857.
Divorce - Mary J. (Wells) Christopher and D. J. Christopher
seeks divorce. 31 August 1858.
Divorce - Mary E. (Haskins) Wynn married F. J. F. Wynn several
years ago, seeks divorce. 31 August 1838.
Died - John Jacobs died after 6 July 1854.
Died - Andrew Pratt died since last Term of Court. (November
Term 1858)
Died - Peter Singleton born in Virginia died 1839, left widow
Sally Brooks Singleton.
Died - Sally Singleton, widow of Peter Singleton, died February
1848.
Died - Matt Martin died __ October 1846.
Died - William Martin died years before 1846 and before his
father Matt Martin.
Divorce - Harriet P. Scudder divorced Philip J. Scudder. (No
date).
Died - Philip J. Scudder died about 1830.
Married - Harriet P. Scudder married Henry Harrell (after 1830).
Divorce - Harriet P. Scudder Harrell divorced Henry Harrell
about 1849.
Married - Harriet P. Scudder Harrell married William J. Wisener,
Esq., after 1849.
Died - William Wilhoite died June 1839.
Died - Charles Brandon died April 1838 Bedford County, aged
80 years.
Married - Hetty Sweeney, daughter of Charles Brandon and his
2nd wife, married Amos Sweeney 25 to 30 years ago.
(Original Instrument 1850-1851)
Died - Joseph Johnson of Coffee County, Tennessee, died Sept-
ember 1842, left widow Susannah Johnson.
Died - William Bearden died August 1849 Bedford County.
Died - Franklin Holland died 8 January 1850, left widow Julia
Ann Holland.
Died - Philip J. Scudder died 1830.
Died - John Ewell died 1826 Bedford COunty, left widow Mary
Ewell.
Died - Mary Ewell, widow of John Ewell, died 1861.
Married - Anna, daughter of John and Mary Ewell both deceased,
married Asa M. Elkins and living in Texas. Anna
died in Texas about 1851.
Died - Leighton Ewell, son of John and Mary Ewell both deceased,
died 1831.
Died - John Eakin died 19 September 1849 Bedford County, left
widow Lucretia Eakin.
Died - James B. Craig died 184_, left widow Mary H. Craig.
Died - Robert C. Thompson died in Williamson County, Tennessee
in early part of 1832, left widow Martha A. R. Thompson.
Married - Martha R. Thompson, widow of Robert C. Thompson,
married Herbert Owens. Martha died in 1844.

Died - James Ewing died many years ago in Adair County,
        Kentucky. (1849-1850)
Married - Flora L. Ewing, daughter of James Ewing, deceased,
        married 10 November 1849 to Nicholas P. Cheatham.
        They separated.
Died - Robert Lane died 29 April 1849 Marshall County, Tenn-
        essee.
Married - Daniel McLaughlin and Nancy A. Burgess married 7
        September 1848.
Died - Richard N. Elliott died in Fall of 1852 Bedford County.
Married - Widow Elliott, widow of Richard N. Elliott, married
        William Lowe. She died soon after in Bedford County.
Died - William B. Jones died July 1847 or 1848 Bedford County,
        left widow Mahala H. Jones.
Divorce - Nancy A. Cobb married 1843 to Charles Cobb in Bed-
        ford County. Divorced 1848. Nancy A. was daughter
        of Frances W. Daniel.
Died - James P. Craig died 1849 Bedford County, left widow
        Mary A. Craig.
Died - Joshua Yates died 1849 Bedford County.
Age - In March 1846, Andrew Davidson, aged upwards of 80 years
        and very infirm.
Died - Ephraim Burrow died 1833 Bedford County, left widow
        Eve Burrow.
Died - William Houston died 28 March 1853, left widow Elizabeth
        Houston of Bedford County.
Died - (1849) - Joseph Palmer died many years ago in Virginia.
Died - Benjamin C. Ransom died before 1846.
Died - Elizabeth Norville died 1847 Bedford County.
Died - Thomas Summerhill died in Memphis, Tennessee before
        1853, left widow Catherine Summerhill.
Died - Wife of R. J. Greer died between 15 June and 1 July
        1851. She was daughter of John Williams, Sr.
Died - James Morrow died June 1839 Bedford County, left widow
        Margaret Morrow.
Died - Margaret Morrow, widow of James Morrow, died soon after
        her husband in Bedford County.
Died - Charles R. Moore died September 1848 Bedford County,
        left widow Susan Moore.
Married - Mrs. Susan Moore, widow of Charles R. Moore, married
        18__ (after September 1848) to Andrew Venable.
Died - Jane Reynolds, widow of Benjamin Reynolds who died
        many years ago in 1831, died in 1839 Bedford County.
        She was grandmother of Moses Reynolds.
Died - John Gambell died Rutherford County, Tennessee, years
        ago. Instrument made 1852.
Died - Hardy Pope, husband of Jane Pope, is now dead in April
        1852.
Died - William Craig died 1834 Bedford County, left widow Polly
        Craig.
Died - Polly Craig, widow of William Craig, died by 1841.
Died - Nancy Justice, formerly Nancy Craig, died about 1839.
Died - William R. Looney died about 1847, left widow Martha E.
        Looney.
Married - Martha E. Looney, widow of William R. Looney, married
        James K. Russell.
Died - Tarlton J. Reeves died in September 1846.
Died - William Haszlett died by 1848 Bedford County.
Died - John Chandler died 1852.
Died - William Roane died 1842 Bedford County.
Died - William Blakely, Sr. died by 1851 in Bedford County.
Died - William Burgess died 1835 Bedford County.
Died - Jesse Brown died 1843 Bedford County, left widow

Elizabeth Brown.
Information on Jesse Brown: Jesse Brown was born about
1780 Virginia, died 1843 Bedford County and buried in
Word Cemetery, Bedford County. Wife Elizabeth Brown
died 1849 and is buried in Word Cemetery, Bedford
County. Children: Pascal Brown, Cynthia, Jesse W.,
Thomas, John F., Robert A., Daniel, William, Henry,
and Elizabeth Brown.
Died - Jacob Cobb(Coble) died 20 December 1830 Bedford County,
left widow Mary Cobb(Coble).
Married - Mary Cobb (Coble), widow of Jacob Cobb (Coble),
married Richard J. Williams.
Married - Mary Shofner formerly widow of Frederick Shofner,
married Ambrose (Abraham) Evans since 1848.
Died - Frederick Shofner died 1848 Bedford County, left widow
Mary Shofner. Frederick Shofner married twice. Mary
was his second wife.
Died - Melchesdic Brame died 184_ Bedford County, left Sarah
Brame.
Died - Andrew J. Eaton died on 22 or 23 October 1846 Bedford
County, left widow Frances Eaton.
Married - Frances Eaton, widow of Andrew J. Eaton, married
George J. Black since 1846.
Died - William Wilhite died many years ago, widow Adeline A.
Wilhite, Bedford COunty. Instrument made 1851.
Died - John Blackwell, Sr. died Spring of 1849 Marshall County,
Tennessee.
Died - Eli H. Hopkins died 184_, (before August 1850) Bedford
County, widow Mary Jane Hopkins.
Died - James McCarver died May 1841 Bedford County.
Died - James McCarver, only child of James McCarver, deceased,
died after his father in Bedford County. He was under
the age of 21 years.
Died - William Eakin of Davidson County, Tennessee, died Aug-
ust 1849, left widow Felicia Eakin.
Died - John Wray died August 1849 Bedford County, father of
James E. Wray and John M. Wray.
Divorce - Louisa H. Arnold and James H. Arnold married February
1832 Bedford County. Seeks divorce. Louisa H. is
a granddaughter of Hugh Snelling.
Died - Simms Boyd died Bedford County before August 1849.
Died - Elizabeth Allison died 21 June 1851, left widow of
Robert Allison, deceased.
Married - Sarah Ann Holmes married John McGowan (no date).
Died - Permelia M. Campbell died before October 29, 1851.
Died - Hugh M. Gault died before September 1852, left widow
Martha A. Gault.
Divorce - George Usselton and Susan E. Anglin married 14 Nov-
ember 1852 Bedford County. Seeks divorce.
Age - James Hastings arrived at age 21 years in 1847.
Died - Anna Elkins died before September 1853.
Died - Frederick Shofner died September 1848.
Divorce - James M. Culverson and Rebecca Jane Tucker, age 16
years, married 26 August 1850. Seeks divorce.
Died - James Bigger died April 1851, left widow Mariah Bigger.
Married - Jane C. Bigger married William H. Adams January 1843,
Jane was daughter of James and Mariah Bigger.
Died - Travis C. Nash died April 7, 1844, left widow Joanna
Nash.
Divorce - Rebecca C. Townsend married John M. Townsend weeks
before October 1853.
Died - Jonathan Parker died 1837 Bedford County, left widow
Frances Parker.

Divorce - Charlotte Shockley married Jesse Shockley on 8 February 1838. Seeks divorce.
Divorce - Charles L. Capps married Rushamy E. Capps years ago in Bedford County. Seeks divorce.
Died - Keble Terry died 1837 Bedford County, left widow Sarah Terry, no children.
Died - Bushrod Webb died May 1847 Bedford County.
Divorce - William Shofner married Jane Koonce 22 February 1844 Bedford County. Seeks divorce.
Died - Valentine Kyser died shortly after 24 July 1826, left widow Nancy Kyser, Bedford County.
Died - Nancy Kyser, widow of Valentine Kyser, died 1 July 1844 Bedford County.
Died - (Instrument of June 1849) John Mayfield died many years ago in North Carolina.
Married - Thomas Thompson married Tranquilla Ann (under 21 years) on February 1850.
Died - Hiram Holt died 1846 or 1847 Bedford County.
Died - Benjamin Gamble died April 1846 Bedford County, left widow Rachel Gamble.
Died - John Whitsell died early in 1842 Bedford County.
Died - Robert Powell died in Summer of 1842 Bedford County.
Divorce - Rebecca Ann Murphree married William Doke Murphree in Bedford COunty years ago. Seeks divorce.
Died - John H. Lane died shortly after 25 December 1847 Bedford County.
Died - Peter R. Proby died before April 1846 Bedford County.
Died - Mead Hail died September 1850 Bedford County.
Died - Daniel L. Mallard died October 1841 Bedford County, left Elizabeth Mallard.
Divorce - Jane Robinson and Joseph Robinson married 18 February 1836. Seeks divorce.
Died - Levin Wood died in North Carolina before (June) 1843.
Died - Jacob Albright died before March 1845 Bedford County, left widow Sally Albright.
Died - William S. Wade died Spring of 1849 in New Orleans, Louisiana. (Native of Bedford COunty)
Died - Asashel Cross died 1832 Bedford County, left widow Saloma Cross.
Died - Ambrose B. Covington died a few months before August 1847 Bedford County, no wife or children.
Died - Henry Mooring formerly of Wake County, North Carolina, died about 1822 in Wake County, North Carolina.
Died - Nicholas Woodfin died a short time after 1831, left widow.
Died - Robert Wallace died about 1824 Bedford County, left widow Elizabeth Wallace.
Died - Elizabeth Wallace, widow of Robert Wallace, died 4 or 5 years after 1824 Bedford County.
Died - William Warren died April 1846 Bedford County, left widow Sarah Warren.
Died - Edward Kimmons died June 1845.
Died - Milton Powell died January 1844, left widow Eliza Kimmons Powell.
Divorce - Sophia A. M. Snales (Scales) married John Snales (Scales) years ago. Seeks divorce.
Divorce - Malinda Goodwin and Washington P. Goodwin married 26 February 1846 Bedford County. Seeks divorce.
Died - Hugh Allen died in Bedford County 18 years ago (before 1846), left widow Martha Allen.
Died - James G. Whitney died 1840 Bedford County.
Died - Thomas Greer died in Bedford County.
Died - William Nash died 10 December 1847 at San Juan, Mexico.

Died - Charles B. James died December 1846, left widow Rowena
       James.
Died - Frederick F. Bradford died 1 April 1840.
Died - Abel W. Slayton died 7 August 1828 Bedford County, left
       widow Permelia Slayton.
Married - Permelia Slayton, widow of Abel W. Slayton, married
         William P. Campbell (after 1828).
Died - Permelia Slayton Campbell, widow of William P. Campbell,
       has died. (no date)
Died - Mark Manning died before 1844 Bedford County.
Died - Margaret Stewart died March 1858 Bedford County (after
       May 1853).
Divorce - Mary J. Norville married James Norville on 10 Nov-
         ember 1854. Seeks divorce.
Died - Daniel Criscoe died August 1852, left widow Sophia
       Criscoe.
Married - Sophia Criscoe, widow of Daniel Criscoe, married
         John Peck after 1852.
Married - Margaret Ann Criscoe married Joel E. Criscoe in
         1848 or 1849. Lived together until 1857.
Married - Martha F. Smith of Missouri married John L. Rainey
         before August 1857.
Married - L. H. Turner married Eliza R. Smith on 4 July 1847
         Bedford County. Lived together until 1852.
Died - John Warner died 17 April or May 1834 Bedford County,
       left widow Eunice Warner.
Died - Joseph Keller died after August 1840 Bedford County,
       left widow Ann Keller.
Died - Thomas A. Keller died before August 1840.
Died - Ann Keller died before August 1840.
Died - Francis Keller died before August 1840.
Divorce - James Jordan Tolbert and Susan Weaver married 16
         April 1856. Seeks divorce.
Divorce - Rose C. Powell and Henry Powell married 7 December
         1854 Bedford County. Seeks divorce.
Age - 28 September 1857 - Jesse Phillips is now upwards of
      83 years old and very feeble in body and mind. Wife
      still living.
Divorce - Mary E. Hutson married Gabriel Hutson in 185_. Asks
         for divorce.
Died - John Robinson died August 1850 Bedford County, left
       widow Mary Robinson.
Died - Martha C. Norvill died April 1855, wife of Felix B.
       Norvill.
Died - Thomas Cheatham died October 1857 Bedford County, left
       widow Mary Cheatham.
Died - George W. Fogleman died 1853 Bedford County, left widow
       Mary V. Fogleman.
Died - Claiborn McCuistian died May 1859, left widow Frances
       McCuistian.
Divorce - John Cotter married Martha E. Watkins in Bedford
         County in June 1854. Seeks divorce.
Divorce - Mary Wynn, wife of F. L. P. Wynn married 16 June
         1855. Seeks divorce.
Died - Mary Davis formerly Mary Hurley, born about 1776 in
       North Carolina, and wife of Absalom Davis, died 1852
       in Lincoln County, Tennessee.
Died - Absalom Davis died 1854 Lincoln County, Tennessee. He
       was born about 1787 in North Carolina.
       From Lincoln County Records lists child, Amos Davis
       born about 1793 North Carolina and wife Mary.
Died - Mary Cunningham, wife of George M. Cunningham, daughter
       of John Blackwell, Sr., who died Marshall County, Tenn-

312

essee in Spring of 1849.
Died - Haiden Trigg died June 1857 Bedford County.
Divorce - John Hood married Elizabeth Hood about 28 years ago
(1830), filed for divorce October 14, 1858. Asks
for divorce.
Died - Jordan C(Cane) Holt, Sr. died September 11, 1853.
Died - Margaret Wilhoite Holt, wife of Jordan C. Holt, Sr.,
died July 1853.
Died - Jordan C. Holt, Jr. died since September 11, 1853, left
widow Jane Holt.
Died - Peter Huffman died 1821 Bedford County, left widow
Elizabeth Huffman.
Married - Nancy R. Curtiss, about 20 years, married John L.
Curtiss. (Instrument made December 1856)
Divorce - Elizabeth Tune married John Tune 12 June 1853. Asks
for divorce.
Died - Joshua Holt, Sr. died before 1853.
Died - William Woosley died 13 April 1856, left widow Jo
Harriet Woosley.
Died - Eliza Jane Frazier, formerly wife of John S. Frazier
died June 20, 1850 Bedford County. Eliza Jane wife of
Friar Trail married some 12 or 18 months before 1852.
Died - David Orr died prior to July Term Court 1854 Bedford
County.
Died - John Orr died June 1854.
Died - James Green died 1853 Coffee County, Tennessee, left
widow Mary Green.
Died - Johnathan Mosely died in Texas (no date), father of
Theresa Curtiss of Bedford County.
Died - William Eoff, Sr. died January or February 1854 Bedford
County.
Died - William Eoff, Sr.'s wife died before 1854, about 6
months before January or February.
Died - John Whitsell died 1842 Bedford County, left widow Milly
Whitsell.
Died - Richard C. Ogilvie died August 1852.
Divorce - John Cotter married Martha E. Watkins in Summer 1855.
Seeks divorce.
Divorce - Elizabeth Cannon asked for a divorce from Willis
Cannon prior to August 1855.
Died - John K. Lawell died July 1853 Bedford County.
Died - John G. Smotherman died 1847 Bedford County, left widow
Mary Smotherman who has since died.
Divorce - Minerva J. Bartlette married William L. Bartlette
on 5 March 1856. Seeks divorce.
Married - Sally Ann Brantley age 19 years, married William C.
Brantley on November 1852.
Divorce - Ruthy Luellen married Joseph White 2 April 1851 of
Bedford County.
Died - Theoderick F. Bradford, Sr. died on Saturday 4 April
1840 Bedford County.
Died - Roena Bradford married Charles B. Jones, died December
1846 in Missouri.
Died - Erwin J. Frierson died Bedford County (no date), left
widow Mrs. Ann P. Frierson.
Died - Archibald Caruthers died some years ago (no date) in
Bedford County, left widow Juliet Caruthers.
Died - Charles B. Jones died December 1846 Bedford County.
Died - Joseph Kincaid died Spring of 1844, left widow Airy E.
Kincaid.
Died - Thomas Holland, Sr. died August 1853 Bedford County,
left widow Sarah T. Holland. They married when he was
of advanced age. She was his third wife.

Died - Joseph Hickerson died 1849 or 1850 in Coffee County,
    Tennessee.
Died - George Pratt died May 1855 Bedford County.
Died - William Hooser died before February 1855.
Died - Samuel Vance died before April 1849 Bedford County.
Died - Valentine Chadwell died about 1850 Williamson County,
    Tennessee, left widow Elizabeth Chadwell.
Died - R. S. Clardy died before August 1860 Bedford County,
    unmarried.
Married - Emeline Daniel married Rufus T. Daniel (no date).
Died - Benjamin Brown died before June 1857 Bedford County.
Died - Samuel E. Gilliland died before October Term 1860.
Died - Mickey F. Atkinson died January 1861 Bedford County.
Divorce - Martha A. McDougall married W. R. McDougall. (In-
    strument made June 1864)
Died - Eli Griffith died before December 1857, left widow
    Salina A. Griffith.
Divorce - T. A. Usselton (Theresa Ann) married George Usselton
    February 1860. Seeks divorce.
Died - David R. Vance died July 1861 Bedford County, widow
    is deceased.
Died - Mary Norman died before February 1861.
Died - Joshua G. Hix died early part of year 1861, left widow
    Ann Eliza Hix.
Died - Berry C. Owen died 1861 Bedford County, he was divorced
    from his wife _____ Owens.
Divorce - Mary E. Patton files for divorce from Robert J.
    Patton before 1861.
Died - John Koonce, Sr. died before 1860 (about 1855) Bedford
    County.
Died - Flower Swift died prior to 1865, left widow Catherine
    Swift.
Died - Catherine Swift, widow of Flower Swift, lately died
    about 1864, after her husband.
Divorce - Lizetta Holthoff asks for divorce from Bernhard
    Holthoff. She abandoned her bill for divorce and
    joined her husband in Nashville, Tennessee.
Died - Margaret Stewart died before May 1859 Bedford County.
    She was widow of William Stewart, deceased.
Divorce - J. W. Muse married Susan W. Yatt(?) January 1859
    Bedford County. Seeks divorce.
Died - William R. McFadden died about 1863 Rutherford County,
    Tennessee, left widow.
Died - Gen. Robert Cannon died January 1864 Bedford County.
Died - Samuel Crowell died 24 June 1865 Bedford County, left
    widow Mary Ann Crowell.
Died - Jason Winsett died 1854 Bedford County, left widow Ann
    Winsett.
Married - Mrs. Ann Winsett, widow of Jason Winsett, married
    John Tune Bedford County.
Died - John M. Kimbro died 185_ in Bedford County.
Died - William L. Brown died 8 March 1862.
Died - S. F. Smith died before June 1865, left widow Lucy Smith.
Divorce - Mary E. Patton married Robert J. Patton in 1859 in
    Bedford County. Seeks divorce.
Died - John B. Bates died before 1860 Bedford County, left
    widow Ann Bates.
Died - Griffin Randal died July 1856 Bedford County, left
    widow Elizabeth Randal.
Divorce - N. D. W. Watson of Bedford County married Amelia
    Caroline Boswell in 1861. Final Decree March 8,
    1866.
Died - Mary C. R. Davidson died 1849.

Divorce - Jesse W. Chockley married Mary Edwards in 1861. Asks
           for divorce.
Divorce - Viana C. Grouster married Martin Grouster on 4 September
           1865. Asks for divorce.
Divorce - David Lane, colored man, married Milly Walker, color-
           ed woman, in Summer 1865 in Bedford County. Seeks
           divorce.
Died - David J. Wheeler died March 1864 Bedford County.
Died - William Williams died September 1858 or 1859.
Died - Ellis Williams, son of William Williams, deceased, died
        before his father who died 1858 or 1859.
Died - Isaac M. Hicks died 186_ Bedford County (Wartrace).
Died - Robert Cannon died shortly before 1866 Bedford County.
Divorce - Rachel Harrison married William Harrison. He de-
           serted 28 May 1866. Seeks divorce.
Died - George Kimbro died August 1860 Bedford County, left
        widow Elizabeth Kimbro (one place said Rachel).
Died - John C. Wood died about December 1861 Bedford County,
        unmarried.

www.ingramcontent.com/pod-product-compliance
Lightning Source LLC
Chambersburg PA
CBHW021850020426
42334CB00013B/271